MW01603028

Serious fraud: investigation and trial

Serious fraud: investigation and trial

David N Kirk
Partner, Stephenson Harwood

Anthony JJ Woodcock
Solicitor, Stephenson Harwood

Consulting editor
Dr ATH Smith, Reader in Law, Gonville and Caius College, Cambridge

Butterworths
London, Dublin, Edinburgh
1992

United Kingdom	Butterworth & Co (Publishers) Ltd, 88 Kingsway, LONDON WC2B 6AB and 4 Hill Street, EDINBURGH EH2 3JZ
Australia	Butterworths, SYDNEY, MELBOURNE, BRISBANE, ADE-LAIDE, PERTH, CANBERRA and HOBART
Belgium	Butterworth & Co (Publishers) Ltd, Brussels
Canada	Butterworths Canada Ltd, TORONTO and VANCOUVER
Ireland	Butterworth (Ireland) Ltd, DUBLIN
Malaysia	Malayan Law Journal Sdn Bhd, KUALA LUMPUR
New Zealand	Butterworths of New Zealand Ltd, WELLINGTON and AUCKLAND
Puerto Rico	Equity de Puerto Rico, Inc, HATO REY
Singapore	Butterworths Asia, SINGAPORE
USA	Butterworth Legal Publishers, AUSTIN, Texas; BOSTON, Massachusetts; CLEARWATER, Florida (D & S Publishers); ORFORD, New Hampshire (Equity Publishing); ST PAUL, Minnesota; and SEATTLE, Washington

A CIP Catalogue record for this book is available from the British Library.

ISBN 0 406 00366 1

Layout by Doublestruck Limited, London
Printed by Mackays of Chatham plc, Chatham, Kent

Foreword by the Honourable Mr Justice Henry

The indications are that serious fraud is on the increase. We have to be able to deal with it: to deter it, to detect it, and to punish it. Our criminal justice system must play its proper part in this. It must be fair but inevitable. It must be more powerful than the most powerful. It must be effective in convicting the guilty and acquitting both the innocent and those not proved to be guilty. The trials leading to these verdicts must be manageable (for if not manageable, fairness is threatened), and must not be wasteful either of time or of money. That specification is what we require of the system.

The complexities (real and simulated) of serious fraud make that a testing specification for an adversarial criminal justice system which evolved in an oral tradition, memory-based, with short trials and no documents, and in which protections designed for the vulnerable, the weak and the suggestible (into which categories those accused of serious fraud tend not to fall) were extended to all accused. So it is not surprising that serious fraud is today near the limit of criminal jurisprudence, where there is the risk that a system designed for very different trials may be tested to destruction.

Against that background, I welcome this work as a timely book on an important subject by authors with considerable practical experience in the field. It is the more valuable for being a book written by practitioners for practitioners, and the busy reader will find material there not otherwise as easily or as conveniently accessible.

The book usefully examines the history of the legislative changes that have led to the trial of serious fraud being treated in many respects as 'a free-standing system, separate from but within the criminal justice system'. It emphasises the fact that Parliament, faced with the problem of successfully dealing with serious fraud, has introduced an important inquisitorial element into the investigation and proof of fraud.

As to further reform (which I believe to be necessary) the authors rightly ask the rhetorical question as to whether it is right that what they describe (but do not define) as the 'fundamental articles of faith' of the criminal justice system should not apply in a small number of important cases. But it should not be assumed that the old tenets are fixed and immutable. It is anticipated that Lord Runciman's Royal Commission will examine them both in the general criminal justice context, and in the particular serious fraud context. It is said that most British battles were fought on the join of two maps. With the Runciman Commission report and any legislative changes that follow it, it may be that both the criminal justice system and that part of it dealing with serious fraud will see significant changes requiring the redrawing of the maps on which this book is based. I look forward to seeing those changes, and to seeing them set out and commented on in the second edition of this book.

Preface

The genesis of this book was an internal office exercise to gather together in one place all the relevant statutory and other materials relating to fraud. Although much of this material was relatively easily available, the sources were widely scattered. The exercise prompted us to think that what was useful to us may be useful to a wide range of practitioners and advisers in the field of serious fraud, and that in addition to the primary and secondary legislation, Practice Directions and other published material, a commentary on this new and distinct area of criminal law practice would be appreciated.

The main purpose of the book, therefore, was originally to provide ready access to materials. In the course of preparing the book for publication, however, the commentary has assumed a greater significance than we had originally envisaged. In the event, we hope that the balance between the two parts of the book will prove useful to practitioners and advisers, as well as those who are confronted by the ever-increasing menace of fraud in business throughout the UK.

One difficulty we have encountered has been to decide what subject matter falls within our remit. Since the book is about serious fraud, and particularly those frauds to which the Criminal Justice Act 1987 relates, we have not thought it appropriate to deal in any detail with the full range of fraud investigations. We have nevertheless included a chapter on 'Other fraud inquiries' (Chapter 5) where the powers of the police, the Inland Revenue and Customs and Excise are outlined. We considered examining the powers of investigation of Self-Regulatory Organisations, but rejected the idea on the ground that they do not, directly, lead to criminal trials. Investigations by the European Commission and the question of EC fraud in general have also been omitted, although this is a rapidly expanding area of practice. However, there is a chapter dealing with 'Cross-border issues' (Chapter 9) which extensively examines jurisdictional problems.

Another area we have not tackled is that of 'fraud offences'. We considered that the large number of well established works on the Theft Acts obviated the need for such an exercise. A chapter on 'Conspiracy to defraud' (Chapter 6) has been included though, because of its direct relevance to serious fraud cases.

The law is stated as at 1 May 1992. Two important decisions have been reported since then. First the decision of the House of Lords in *R v Director of Serious Fraud Office, ex p Smith* (1992) 3 WLR 66, which we have managed to incorporate into the text. Second, that of the Court of Appeal in *R v Cohen and Others* (1992) Times, 29 July ('The *Blue Arrow* Case') and the subsequent discontinuance of *Blue Arrow II* by Brooke J on 3 August 1992, could not be incorporated in the text. The Court of Appeal judgment was mainly concerned with the issue of long trials, and in quashing the convictions of the four defendants in the *Blue Arrow* trial who had been convicted, Mann LJ referred to the year-long trial as a 'costly disaster'. The Court of Appeal emphasised again the need to avoid overloading indictments, and they recommended the early use of a judge's powers of severance so as to create two or more short and manageable trials in place of one long trial. The encouragement by the Court of Appeal to judges to enter the arena in a more robust manner than some have felt able to do is welcome, as is the encouragement to the Serious Fraud Office, and other prosecutors, to restrict indictments to the core issues. George Staple, the Director of the Serious Fraud Office, has stated that he is alive to these problems, and that his office has to try to make cases simple and comprehensible to a jury (*Sunday Times*, 23 August 1992). Warnings of this nature, however, have frequently been given by the Court of Appeal in the past (see page 90 below), and they do not seem to be heeded for long. It remains to be seen whether the drastic step of quashing the convictions of four defendants largely on the grounds of length and complexity of trial will serve as a more salutary lesson to those who have to deal with these very difficult cases in the future.

In writing this book we have had assistance from a variety of sources. We would particularly like to thank our consultant editor, Dr Tony Smith, for his enthusiastic and helpful assessment of our progress, and for his encouragement. Jeraine Olsen, formerly an Assistant Director of the Serious Fraud Office, read parts of the manuscript and made valuable comments. Her contribution is very greatly appreciated. Even though much of the material in this book covers new ground, some of the subject matter has inevitably been considered in other works. We hope we have acknowledged in the appropriate places any assistance we have derived from them.

Finally, of course, the writing of a book on top of conducting a busy practice creates extra work for others. We are especially grateful to our secretaries, Serena Nathan and Christine Winyard, for so accurately and uncomplainingly typing (and re-typing) the manuscript. To our families, also, who have been deprived of our company for long periods, we owe the greatest debt of all.

DN Kirk
AJJ Woodcock

Contents

CHAPTER 8
DTI investigations   206

CHAPTER 9
Cross-border issues   229

Table of statutes

References in this Table to *Statutes* are to Halsbury's Statutes of England (Fourth Edition) showing the volume and page at which the annotated text of the Act may be found.

Table of statutory instruments

Table of cases

CHAPTER 1
Serious fraud

1 INTRODUCTION

There is no offence known to English law – either common or statutory – as 'fraud'. Fraud, in criminal law terms is a generic term for a type of offence, of which the ingredients are infinitely variable, but probably comprise the following: the dishonest non-violent obtaining of some financial advantage or causing of some financial loss.[1]

Serious fraud is no more nor less than it sounds. It is fraud on a large and complex scale, usually involving the loss of substantial sums of money. There will often be jurisdictional complications. The matter may also be difficult legally.[2]

This book aims to be a manual for professional advisers working on cases of serious fraud. It draws together the strands of what has effectively become a new and distinct area of criminal law practice, which impinges increasingly on modern business life, both in the form of inquiries by the Serious Fraud Office and the Crown Prosecution Service, and as a result of the activities of other fraud investigators such as the DTI, the SIB, The Stock Exchange and the tax authorities (this is by no means an exhaustive list). The book will primarily examine the new procedures brought into force by the Criminal Justice Act 1987 ('the 1987 Act') and Department of Trade inquiries into fraud, covering the investigatory phases of an inquiry, the pre-trial and trial processes.

The new system for bringing serious fraud cases to trial is radically different from existing criminal procedure in two ways: first, the rules relating to investigations are both different and less intricate than for ordinary police investigations; and second, the trial process has in many respects become quasi-civil.

These changes have encouraged prosecutors, as was intended, to venture into territory once considered unsuitable for the criminal law. Where at one time

1 For a definition of fraud see: Roskill paragraph 3.14, which refers to Archbold 42nd edn 17.26, Buckley J in *Re London & Globe Finance Corpn* (1903) 1 Ch D 728 at 732 and 733 and *Scott v Metropolitan Police Comr* [1975] AC 819, [1974] 3 All ER 1032, HL. Roskill also considered, but rejected, a recommendation for the creation of an offence of fraud. For a definition of serious fraud in connection with Revenue offences, see Taxes Management Act 1970, section 20C(1A) (Chapter 5, section 3.5).

2 In the Serious Fraud Office 1st Annual Report the Director stated that he would accept cases where: (a) the facts and/or the law are of great complexity; or (b) sums of money in excess of £1 million are at risk; or (c) there is great public interest and concern for some other reason, eg the identity of the suspect or the employment of a novel method of fraud. See Chapter 2, section 1.3. The 'money at risk' figure was soon to be raised to £2 million, and there is a suggestion (Serious Fraud Office Press Notice: 21 February 1991) that it should be raised to £3 million. The increase is presumably to reduce the number of cases taken on by the Office.

fraud cases could be rejected for prosecution on the single ground that they were far too complicated to be presented satisfactorily to a criminal court, there is no longer any prosecutorial inhibition. The result has been a stream of prosecutions (of which the *Guinness* and *County NatWest* cases are the prime examples) in which the prosecutor has audaciously challenged the complex and secretive practices of the City.

The reasons for the encroachment of the criminal law into areas which once it left well alone are many and various. They are to be found partly in the perception, most neatly coined in Edward Heath's phrase, that there was 'an unpleasant and unacceptable face of capitalism'.[3] Since the Conservative party is intricately linked both to the philosophy and to the captains of capitalism, it was clearly necessary for that party to ensure that the face was more acceptable. In order to do that, ways had to be found to deal with what has come to be called 'serious fraud'.

There was nothing new about serious fraud in 1973. It had not suddenly sprung up. It existed in 1720 when the South Sea Bubble burst, it existed before that date, and it has carried on since. Anthony Trollope wrote about large-scale financial fraud in his novel *The Way We Live Now*, in which the financier Melmotte built a financial empire on paper which collapsed in a way which is not unfamiliar to modern experience. Serjeant Ballantine, writing in 1882, remarked that 'some crimes have assumed larger proportions and the present has been an age of daring and gigantic fraud'.[4] In his memoirs, GD ('Khaki') Roberts QC[5] refers to:

'. . . the share pushers, who in the twenties and thirties dragged the good name of the City of London in the mud with appalling scandals.'[6]

He complained that:

'. . . too seldom were share pushers brought to trial and when they were the prosecution seemed fated . . . As the thirties advanced the bucket shop business in the City of London increased and prospered in direct ratio to the unavailing efforts of the local police to stop it.'[7]

Roberts describes how in December 1936 the Board of Trade set up a Committee under the chairmanship of Sir Archibald Bodkin, to 'consider the operations known as share pushing and share hawking, and to report what, if any, action is desirable.' The Prevention of Frauds (Investments) Act 1939 was passed as a result of the committee's deliberations.

Such was the concern at that time about the evils of share pushing that the Metropolitan and City Police formed a fraud squad in 1946, described by Roberts as the 'most effective step of all to stop share pushing'. An Assistant Commissioner at the Metropolitan Police said:

'It is quite true that share pushing is almost extinct, and the formation of the fraud squad is very largely responsible. Its officers have established close co-operation with the Stock Exchange authorities and the banks, and with police officers in Canada and the USA, from which so many of these 'bucket shop' gentry come. The unpublicised preventative work of this branch [the CID] is a

---

3   Edward Heath's comments related to the affairs of Lonrho in 1973, and to unethical practices rather than fraud.

4   *Some Experiences of a Barrister's Life* by Mr Serjeant Ballantine (1884) Richard Bentley & Son.

5   *Law and Life: the Legal Memoirs of GD Roberts QC* (1964) WH Allen.

6   Ibid, page 100.

7   Ibid, page 102.

strong factor. The wrong sort of visitor soon discovers that his plans for the future are not a secret. In most cases he decides against staying in so unrewarding a country, and, on his return, no doubt passes the information around to his friends.[8]

Fraud comes in all shapes and sizes, large and complex, small and simple, and anything in between. There are fashions in fraud, which last only as long as the public is gullible enough to fall for them and the authorities do not catch up with them.[9] Many such fashions start from business schemes which are conceived in innocence (more or less) but which by their very nature require an element of deception before they can succeed. Pyramid selling is an example. This type of activity flourished during the 1970s, and some people, those at the top of the pyramid, made money. Many others did not, and could never have done given the structure of the scheme. Carbon paper frauds are, at one level, only an extension of the hard sell. Under current conditions, when hard sell is outlawed in so many spheres of activity, it seems obvious that duping someone into buying more than they actually want is a criminal offence. In other climates, at other times, the maxim of caveat emptor would apply.

Spanish villa frauds, advance fee frauds and many others have elements of perfectly honest endeavour, but they have the capacity (which some would say was inherent in their nature) to become criminal endeavour. The reason for this is either because they are conceived as such, or, more likely, that conditions force them to be so. An enterprise, which may be intensely ambitious or of marginally dubious ethical standards, can, with a fair wind, become successful, popularly acclaimed and the recipient of a Queen's Award. With ill-fortune, most obviously a collapse in the economy, but also for a variety of other reasons, the fragility of the original structure may be exposed and either lead to the commission of criminal offences, or to the perception that the whole basis of the business was fraudulently conceived. In other cases, perfectly properly constituted businesses which run into difficulty because of forces beyond their control may resort to deception in order to overcome their problems.[10]

At the time when Mr Heath spoke of the unacceptable face of capitalism, the economy was about to enter the serious crisis which hit the secondary and tertiary banks. The authorities took the first steps towards putting more resources into the detection and prosecution of fraud. The beginnings were small and needed no statutory intervention. Police forces began increasingly to have dedicated fraud squads (some, including as stated above the Metropolitan and City Police, had had such fraud squads for many years), and the prosecution, in the form of the DPP, formed a separate division to deal with company fraud cases. These, however, were piecemeal and minor adaptations of the existing system.

By the recession of the early 1980s it became clear that further and more concerted measures were needed, and the concept of the integrated or unified fraud prosecution began to emerge. Instead of investigators (DTI inspectors, Police or other authorities) and the prosecutor (the DPP and counsel) all proceeding in Indian file, it was recognised that they should advance together with a consequential saving in time and effort. It was also seen that there was an increasing need for other disciplines, notably accountants, to join the team.

8 Quoted by Roberts, op cit, page 106.
9 Roskill gives a list and description of types of fraud: Appendix F.
10 This phenomenon is documented in *The Phantom Capitalist* by Michael Levi (1981) Aldershot, Gower.

This led to the setting up of the Fraud Investigation Group ('FIG') within the DPP.

Ironically, in 1981, when FIG was formed, there was considerable difficulty in finding a suitable case for it to tackle (a situation which the Serious Fraud Office would now find it hard to believe), and when it finally located one,[11] FIG suffered the embarrassment of seeing their prosecution dismissed by the judge on a submission of no case to answer at the close of the prosecution case. Despite this early set-back, FIG flourished and continues to be a major plank in the fight against fraud.[12] It was FIG which grappled throughout most of the eighties with the very problematical *Lloyd's* cases, which were a major factor in the impetus towards the changes wrought by the 1987 Act.

It has been said that fraud was the growth industry of the 1980s.[13] Figures for the cost to the nation are frequently given. They run into billions of pounds.[14] They are usually said to represent only the tip of the iceberg. In February 1991 the Director of the Serious Fraud Office said that fraud investigations by the SFO involved 'money at risk' of £2 billion. The Director stated:

> 'No one knows the extent of commercial fraud. We cannot measure it because it depends upon how many frauds are reported. All we can tell is that the reported incidents of fraud show an ever-increasing trend in number and size.'[15]

By April 1992, the figure had risen to £5 billion.[16] Not only the amount of money at risk had sharply increased, according to the statistics; there was also a significant increase in the number of lawyers employed by the government to deal with the prosecution of fraud cases. In 1981, when FIG was formed, there were six lawyers specifically assigned to fraud cases in the DPP's office. They dealt with all serious company fraud in England and Wales.[17] By 1988 that figure had grown to approximately 40, with 24 lawyers in the newly formed SFO, and 16 at FIG. It is difficult to believe that fraud had increased six-fold during the 1980s, but the increase in the number of the lawyers needed to deal with fraud cases might be seen as an indication of such an increase.

The cost of fraud is widespread and insidious, and its effects are felt in many different ways. Companies are forced into liquidation, employees lose their jobs, savings are reduced in value, and ultimately we all have to pay more for the goods and services we purchase. A recent survey by a consultancy group, Access Parliamentary Public Affairs, for example, claimed that mortgage frauds alone were costing the public purse more than £3 billion. This sum was made up of:

11 Miller Carnegie, a commodities case.
12 See Chapter 5.
13 See eg Bose and Gunn: *Fraud: the Growth Industry of the 80s* (1989) Unwin/Hyman.
14 Ernst and Young, in a pamphlet entitled 'Fraud 1989: the extent of fraud against large companies and executive views on what should be done about it' found that in 1988 the two London fraud squads alone dealt with frauds which placed at risk sums totalling £4,170 million. KPMG Peat Marwick has recently reported that losses resulting from fraud more than doubled between 1987 and 1991: *The Forensic Accountant* (1992) Hilary.
15 Press Notice: 21 February 1991.
16 Barbara Mills QC: 'Let no one profit by fraud', Law Society Gazette, 15 April 1992.
17 Other lawyers in the prosecution system also dealt with more minor fraud offences including lawyers at the DTI dealing with Companies Act offences.

(i)   police investigations (£1.4 billion);
(ii) failure to declare capital gains made on properties (£1.2 billion); and
(iii) fraudulent MIRAS claims (£500 million).

The survey claimed that one in twenty mortgage applications was fraudulent.[18]

These figures are so huge that it is difficult to put them into any realistic proportion, still more to assess what the real loss is, but they give an idea of the extent of the area of endeavour covered by 'fraud', and the importance of the task of providing a legal framework for dealing with it.

The concern felt by the authorities at the rising tide of the problem, particularly in the light of the government's policy on creating a share owning democracy whose interests would need greater protection than the hitherto limited share owning public, was expressed by the setting up on 8 November 1983 of the Roskill Committee.[19] The Committee's terms of reference were 'to consider in what ways the conduct of criminal proceedings in England and Wales arising from fraud can be improved and to consider what changes in existing law and procedure would be desirable to secure the just, expeditious and economical disposal of such proceedings'.[20]

When the Roskill Report was published in early 1986, its opening words were:

> 'The public no longer believes that the legal system in England and Wales is capable of bringing the perpetrators of serious frauds expeditiously and effectively to book. The overwhelming weight of the evidence laid before us suggests that the public is right. In relation to such crimes, and to the skilful and determined criminals who commit them, the present legal system is archaic, cumbersome and unreliable. At every stage, during investigation, preparation, committal, pre-trial review and trial the present arrangements offer an open invitation to blatant delay and abuse.'[1]

The FIG initiative had pointed the way towards a unified organisation for the investigation and prosecution of serious fraud cases. Roskill's solution to the problems he found was to adopt and adapt the success of FIG, and to recommend the setting up of a unified organisation to investigate and prosecute serious fraud cases. He also dealt crucially with powers of investigation and trial procedures, and it is with the results of these recommendations that this book largely deals. The recommendations, in so far as they were followed, were implemented in the 1987 Act which received Royal Assent shortly before the general election in June of that year. The Bill which became the 1987 Act (originally part of a much larger Bill that became the Criminal Justice Act 1988) was saved from falling at the general election in June 1987 by agreement between parliamentary business managers, and its consideration by the legislature was therefore truncated. This may be viewed as a matter of some regret both because the changes that were being introduced

---

18 These claims were made in the *Independent on Sunday*, 24 February 1991. Such claims, it must be said, have more than an element of guess-work. In the figures cited by APPA, £1.4 billion for police investigations suggests that 500,000 police officers are assigned to such cases, which cannot be true. The number of police officers assigned to deal with mortgage frauds in the whole of the UK is unlikely to exceed 300, and the resources they use will add little to the cost of manpower. A figure of £10 million would seem to be nearer the mark.

19 The Fraud Trials Committee Report (Chairman: the Right Honourable The Lord Roskill, PC) (1986) HMSO.

20 Ibid, page 5.

1 Ibid, page 1.

were radical and merited close scrutiny in Committee,[2] and because the Act contained a number of technical flaws which have, in spite of amendments in the Criminal Justice Act 1988, caused unnecessary problems.

The Roskill Committee appears to have spent relatively little time considering the powers of investigation of the new unified department. It concluded that the Police officers who conducted investigations on behalf of the new authority should have powers of investigation similar to those available to Inspectors appointed by the Secretary of State for the Department of Trade and Industry under section 447 of the Companies Act 1985.[3] It is to be noted that this power was to be conferred on the police and not on other members of the office. However, the government decided that the correct way to proceed was to give the lawyers and accountants in the SFO powers of investigation similar to those available to inspectors appointed by the Secretary of State under section 432 of the 1985 Act. There was, however, to be one crucial difference: whereas answers given to inspectors can be used in subsequent criminal proceedings against the witness (section 434(5) of the 1985 Act), answers given in response to questions asked by officers of the SFO cannot be used in criminal proceedings except in special circumstances (s 2(8) of the 1987 Act). This difference between the powers available to DTI inspectors and those of SFO officers has caused some dissatisfaction both to prosecutors and defenders and has given rise to a close examination of the privilege against self-incrimination. The fact that a man can be required by DTI inspectors to answer questions, in the knowledge that his answers will be used against him in subsequent criminal proceedings (if any), thus depriving him of his privilege against self-incrimination, sits oddly with the position of a man who is being directly questioned by the SFO about criminal offences but who still has the protection of the privilege, albeit in a qualified form.[4] In the latter part of 1991 there were a number of cases before the Court of Appeal on this point. With few exceptions the court decided that there was sufficient inference to be drawn from the legislation that the privilege against self-incrimination had impliedly been removed by Parliament, and there could be no objection to individuals being questioned by DTI inspectors (or others, including office holders under the Insolvency Act 1986) without the protection of the privilege, even if the results of interviews would find their way, in an admissible form, to prosecutors.

It may be argued that while all other defendants enjoy the protection of the right of silence (and indeed other protection), there is no reason why those accused of serious fraud should be treated any differently, *unless* there is something in the nature of the crime of fraud that sets it apart from other criminal acts. To what extent, though, does fraud differ from other offences? Many assert that it is different from other offences, but without saying why. It may be that it is simply a matter of scale and difficulty, but if that is the only difference, is there really any justification for putting in place a free-standing system separate from but within the criminal justice system? It is only a matter of expediency, and expediency, it may be argued, should have no place in the law. At this point, however, one returns to the argument outlined in the very first sentences of the Roskill Report. The system does *not* cope with serious

---

2   There was, nevertheless, keen debate on the setting up and powers of the SFO in Committee, reference to which is made in Chapter 2.
3   Roskill Report: paragraph 2.62 and recommendation 5.
4   See Chapter 2, section 2.2.3 and Chapter 8, section 3.8.3.

frauds, and since they are serious crimes by any standards, effective ways must be found to bring offenders to court.

Some believe that the real reason for the failure of the system to cope is that whereas in almost every other type of criminal offence the jury will easily be able to comprehend the circumstances of the offence and apply their own standards of judgment, propriety and common sense to the facts with which they are presented, in fraud cases they are required to understand activities of which they are likely to have had no experience whatsoever. While it can be said that simple honesty is the question at the root of all fraud trials, it is usually honesty in the context of a particular area of business practice.[5] Herein lies the fundamental difficulty which affects all serious fraud cases: they must be made understandable to the kind of individual who is able to give up six months of his life to sit on a jury, whose knowledge of financial affairs may well be elementary and who may not even have a bank account. If it were not for the necessity of proving a case to a jury many of the difficulties which bedeviled the old system would disappear, and the complexities of the new structure would be unnecessary. The Roskill Committee recommended that juries be abolished in serious fraud trials, to be replaced by a fraud trials tribunal. The government did not agree, arguing that improved pre-trial procedures would ease the jury's task in these difficult cases.

The debate about the suitability of juries to try serious and complex fraud will continue to rumble on, given fresh impetus by the results of recent cases. *Guinness I* was hailed by defenders of the jury system as a triumphant vindication of their stance. Doubters may have worried whether a unanimous guilty verdict against all four defendants in reality sent any clearer signals about the system than four acquittals would have done. The complacency of the jury's supporters was dealt a serious blow by the results of three cases within the space of one week in which, for differing reasons, the suitability of juries was called into question. In the second week of February 1992 the jury in *Guinness II*, having been sitting since September 1991, and with only a fraction of the prosecution case completed, was discharged, mainly on the grounds that one of the defendants, Roger Seelig, was too ill to continue defending himself. Mr Justice Henry's remarks when discharging the jury suggested that he thought that more radical reforms were required than those introduced by the 1987 Act which the judge implied were 'just tinkering'.[6]

The *Barlow Clowes* trial ended in acquittals of two out of four defendants, and a failure to secure convictions on conspiracy charges against any defendant. In the *Blue Arrow* trial four defendants were convicted by a jury who, it appears, had been clearly advised to acquit in the judge's summing up. One defendant was acquitted by the jury, five others having been previously acquitted on the direction of the judge. The trial of the *Barlow Clowes* case had lasted seven months; the *Blue Arrow* case just over a year. In the latter case the jury had been absent from the trial for two-and-a-half months at the end of the prosecution case while everyone had a holiday, followed by submissions of no

---

5 But see *R v Lockwood* [1986] Crim LR 244 where the court did not accept that there was one standard of dishonesty for criminal cases in general and a separate and more restricted standard of dishonesty for cases involving commercial fraud. The definition of dishonesty in *R v Ghosh* [1982] QB 1053, [1982] 2 All ER 689, CA is of general application.

6 In an unusual development, however, the foreman of the jury trying this case wrote to the *Financial Times* forcefully stating that the jury had fully understood all the issues in the case, and were only frustrated by the speed with which the defence conducted its cross-examination of witnesses (*Financial Times* 2 March 1992).

case to answer. A further six-week break occurred over Christmas. The jury were shown photographs of some witnesses, to remind them of what they had looked like, their evidence having been given many months earlier. The jury had to consider the verdict on one of the defendants who had not been mentioned in evidence for more than ten-and-a-half months. The dispassionate observer may be excused for wondering how a jury who had listened to evidence, on and off, for a year without having any sophisticated means of note-taking or analysis could possibly have properly considered all the issues relevant to the case. The Court of Appeal will no doubt have to consider, yet again, the impact on juries of such arduous cases.[7]

The results of these cases, taken together with the dropping of charges in *Guinness III* several years after they were preferred, caused a storm of protest and renewed the debate about the viability of fraud trials. Should juries be replaced, as recommended by Roskill, by a fraud trials tribunal? Should fraud trials be heard by a single judge? Should juries be retained at all cost, with pre-trial and trial procedures being tightened up? Should the SFO indulge in formal plea bargaining, or even take a leaf out of the books of the Inland Revenue and the Customs and Excise and settle or compound cases without a trial? Would the creation of an offence of fraud assist? Should the right of silence be abolished altogether?

Most of these solutions carry with them problems which are as great as the problems they are intended to solve, and they come down in the final analysis to the question of whether the criminal justice system is prepared to ditch many of its fundamental articles of faith for the purpose of dealing with a tiny minority of cases.

If it is considered essential to keep cases like *Guinness* and *Blue Arrow* within the criminal justice system, prosecutors may need to learn to be much more selective, and judges must be permitted (or encouraged) to exercise a much higher degree of control over the cases they are asked to try. The delicate balance which exists between, on the one hand, the Crown in being able to require a court to try the indictment which it has lodged, and, on the other, the judge in being allowed to curb prosecutorial zeal, may need to be tipped more in favour of the judge.

The continued determination of the government to fight fraud on all fronts is evident from, for example, the White Paper on Company Investigations published in August 1990,[8] which stated:

> 'One of the primary objectives of the Department of Trade and Industry is to increase confidence in the working of markets by achieving a fair level of protection for the individual consumer and investor. To this end, the government remain determined to uncover and act against fraud and other

7   See Chapter 4, section 2.4.1. Mr Justice McKinnon said, on sentencing those convicted in the *Blue Arrow* trial: 'What is beyond doubt is that all involved in this case have had to endure what no one in our courts should be called upon to cope with. That includes the defendants, their families and the jury and me. I can certainly speak for myself. No jury should be asked to cope with what this jury have had to endure. No defendant or his family should have to suffer through month after month after month after month all that these defendants have had to suffer. There must be some other way.' George Staple the new Director of the SFO has commented on cases involving alleged violations of the 'integrity of the markets' that 'those cases are better dealt with by the disciplinary procedures provided to several bodies under the Financial Services Act. You don't necessarily have to charge those people with fraud and bring them before a jury.' Law Society Gazette, 11 March 1992, page 5.

8   Cm 1149 'Company Investigations: Government's Response to the Third Report of the House of Commons Trade and Industry Committee: 1989–80 Session'.

malpractices in the conduct of commerce. This determination is reflected in the large number of steps which have been taken in recent years to improve the regulatory environment and to enable effective action to be taken. These steps include notably: the Financial Services Act 1986 and the new regulatory framework which it introduced; the setting up of the Serious Fraud Office in 1988 with its special powers under the Criminal Justice Act 1987; the reorganisation of the Department of Trade and Industry investigatory and prosecution functions with the setting up of its Investigation Division in 1988; improved international co-operation with the establishment of Memoranda of Understanding with the United States and Japan in the securities area and the new powers to assist overseas regulators in the Companies Act 1989; the agreement in 1989 on the European Community Directive on insider dealing which will be implemented as soon as the parliamentary timetable allows;[9] and the increased level of activity by the Department itself as well as by other prosecutors and regulators. This is the background against which the Department of Trade and Industry's investigation system now operates.'[10]

Whether the increased level of activity has been brought about by the creation of the SFO, the more assertive behaviour of the DTI, and the whole new regulatory structure by encouraging people to believe that fraud could be satisfactorily dealt with, or whether there has been a sudden upsurge in major fraud caused by the combination of boom and bust in the late 1980s, will probably never be known, but the SFO has never been short of customers since it set up shop, and the DTI inspectorate has never been so busy.

9 As at 1 May 1992 the timetable had not allowed any progress in this direction.
10 Op cit, page 1.

CHAPTER 2
The Serious Fraud Office

1.1 THE STRUCTURE OF THE SFO

The SFO came into existence on 1 April 1988. It was created by the Criminal Justice Act 1987, some parts of which (sections 1 and 12) had come into force on 1 July 1987[1] in order to enable the appointment of a Director and Deputy Director of the new office and to revive at the earliest opportunity the offence of conspiracy to defraud.[2]

At 1 April 1988 the SFO officially took over the conduct of 39 cases of serious and complex fraud (the *Guinness* case being one example) which had up to that point been handled by the Crown Prosecution Service Fraud Investigation Group. From that date it had the duty to investigate and prosecute 'any suspected offence which appears (to the Director) on reasonable grounds to involve serious or complex fraud' (section 1(3)).

The SFO has jurisdiction over cases arising in England, Wales and Northern Ireland (Criminal Justice Act 1987 section 1(1)), and thus has a wider territorial remit than the Crown Prosecution Service. At no stage does there appear to have been a suggestion that it should exercise its authority over Scottish frauds, which are investigated by the Crown Office Fraud and Special Services Unit under the direction of the Lord Advocate. He has powers to investigate serious or complex fraud similar to those of the SFO.[3] It should be noted, however, that section 2 of the Act applies in Scotland to enable the Director to question individuals in that jurisdiction.[4]

The Director of the SFO is appointed by the Attorney General (section 1(2)), and he discharges his functions under the superintendence of the Attorney General. He is accountable to the House of Commons through the Attorney General. He occupies, therefore, a position directly analogous to the Director of Public Prosecutions in terms of appointment and accountability,[5] although whereas the DPP must be legally qualified, the Director of the SFO can be any 'person'.[6]

The Department is staffed by a permanent complement of lawyers and accountants, and a detachment of police officers, sufficient, it is estimated, to handle 60 cases a year, or, assuming a two-year life of each case, 120 at any one

---

1 SI 1989/1061.
2 See Chapter 8 below.
3 Criminal Justice (Scotland) Act 1987 sections 51–54.
4 Criminal Justice Act 1987 section 17.
5 See Prosecution of Offences Act 1985 sections 2 and 3.
6 Advertisements for applications for the post of Director of the Serious Fraud Office in February 1992, however, invited lawyers only to apply.

time. In addition there are clerical support staff. All the lawyers are Grade 6 (Senior Principal Legal Assistants) – a civil service senior career grade – or above. This singles it out from other government legal service departments (the Treasury Solicitor or the CPS) and government departments with legal sections as being staffed solely by 'senior' legal civil servants. All the legal staff are expected to be of high quality, some seniority and relevant experience. They are mainly drawn from the ranks of the CPS, the DTI, Customs and Excise and the Inland Revenue, although lawyers from private practice are encouraged to apply for posts in the SFO.

Although the SFO is primarily a legal department, with lawyers undertaking the tasks of investigating, advising on prosecutions and bringing cases to trial, the accountants and the police play a vital role at the investigation stage. It is important to recognise that the SFO is as much an *investigative* organisation as a prosecuting authority. It is in this function that it differs fundamentally from the CPS.[7] It was a controversial aspect of its formation that it was given an investigative as well as prosecutorial role at a time when it had just been decided, when creating the CPS, that the two functions should be kept firmly separate. The Minister of State at the Home Office said in Committee:

> 'Mr Bermingham was right when he asked whether having laboured mightily in the vineyards to separate investigation from prosecution, we were being asked to eat our words. I was persuaded ultimately that the greater good would be served by combining those powers in the limited number of cases involved. Of 75,000 cases tried on indictment in the Crown Court, only 50 to 100 involve complicated investigations.
>
> The House often commends the work of the Customs & Excise, which combines investigation and prosecution responsibilities perfectly fairly, as does the Department of Trade & Industry, which exercises Companies Act powers with the assistance of many fraud squad personnel, who will be involved in the Serious Fraud Office. We must also bear in mind the fact that investigators will carry out investigations. The lawyers in the SFO will not generally be involved in investigations but will take the decision of whether to prosecute.'[8]

One member of the Committee suggested a partial solution to the problem:

> 'Perhaps some thought should be given to including in Clauses 1 and 2, the concept that in an investigation the Director of the SFO should appoint an officer "who shall be the officer of the potential prosecution and who may, in turn, seek the assistance or employment of" – I put it in general terms at this stage – "other officers, who may become the persons who investigate and who may become witnesses." By delineating a chain of responsibility we would escape the dilemma and continue the tradition envisaged in the creation of the Crown Prosecution Service.'[9]

The government responded:

> 'It seemed that without embarrassment we could suggest the creation of an office in which lawyers, accountants and the various investigators from all the bodies concerned with fraud could work together using all the resources needed to come to grips with especially serious cases. However, we hope that the decision to prosecute will be taken invariably by a legal officer of the Serious Fraud Office who would not have been involved, for the most part, in

---

7 The SFO is like the DTI, Customs and Excise and the Inland Revenue in combining investigating and prosecuting functions under one roof, but it is, unlike those departments, solely a prosecuting authority.
8 *Hansard* 11 December 1986, SC F, col 26.
9 Ibid, col 21.

the day-to-day investigations of the offence. The SFO will not operate differently from the way in which Customs operates when the decision to prosecute lies with the investigator, as it does with the Inland Revenue.'[10]

The SFO adopted this suggestion and its policy is to appoint a case officer who effectively guides the investigation and takes the decisions, while others investigate.[11]

Accountants and lawyers, therefore, investigate suspected offences of serious or complex fraud. Their power to do so is derived from sections 1(3) and (4) which permits the Director to investigate (section 1(3)), joined by 'the police or . . . any other person who is, in the opinion of the Director, a proper person to be joined in it' (section 1(4)). These two subsections do not appear to delegate authority to the Director's own staff, although it is possible (but unlikely) that the 'any other person' referred to includes SFO officers.

Section 1(5) permits the Director to '(a) institute and have the conduct of any criminal proceedings which appear to him to relate to such fraud; and (b) take over the conduct of any such proceedings at any stage'. These powers are delegated to SFO lawyers by section 1(7) and (8), in the same way as powers are delegated to Crown Prosecutors.[12]

Section 1(3) and (4) relates, therefore, to investigations; section 1(5) and (7) to the institution of proceedings. Since the uniqueness of the SFO lies in its investigative powers,[13] it is unlikely that the SFO will take over a case once the investigation is complete.[14] There may be cases which are arguably serious or complex frauds where the need for the use of compulsory powers of questioning becomes apparent late in the day; but the requirement to use the powers cannot justify, in itself, the designation of a fraud as serious or complex. There may be cases which, after the institution of proceedings, become more serious or complex than originally thought. However, the circumstances in which section 1(5)(b) will come into play are necessarily very limited.[15]

The distinction between section 1(3) and (4) and section 1(5) and (7) suggests that, so far as investigation is concerned, the use of the word 'Director' cannot be assumed to mean 'the Director and his staff'. This cannot have been intended, and may simply be the unfortunate result of a combination of plundering other legislation (in the case of section 1(5) and (7)) and original drafting (in the case of section 1(3) and (4)).

In instituting or taking over criminal proceedings the Director of the SFO is put in the same position as the Director of Public Prosecutions[16] as to being

---

10 *Hansard* 16 December 1986, col 35.
11 See [1989] Crim LR 175 at 177 where John Wood confirmed this policy, and defended the integration of powers. In the first annual report of the SFO the Director described the composition of an SFO team: the case controller, who has 'overall responsibility for effective and expeditious investigation and any ensuing prosecution'; police officers; accountants where appropriate; and 'sometimes an investigating lawyer is appointed' (para 16). He went on to say: 'A lawyer who has been actively involved in an investigation under section 2 of the Criminal Justice Act does not decide whether a prosecution is justified' (para 19). Roskill recommended that 'A case controller should be responsible for the control of a serious fraud case from the time of discovery until the verdict' (Fraud Trials Committee Report, paras 2.65 and 2.66).
12 Cf Prosecution of Offences Act 1985 sections 1–3.
13 Other 'designated authorities' – listed in section 4(2) of the Act – being able to make use of the transfer provisions, and the preparatory hearing provisions being available in any case at the discretion of the judge – section 7(l) of the Act.
14 An investigation by the SFO after a DTI inquiry (see sections 1.4 and 2.23 below) is an exception.
15 In theory a prosecution might be taken over from a private prosecutor, but this is unlikely.
16 Schedule 1, paragraph 4 and section 1(16).

entitled to bring proceedings, the need for consents and discontinuing proceedings.[17]

Section 1(9)–(14) makes provision for rights of audience for SFO lawyers, again following the example of the CPS.[18] Such rights are currently restricted to appearing before magistrates' courts, no significant direction having been given by the Lord Chancellor under section 83 of the Supreme Court Act 1981.[19] The Director has said[20] that the Office fully supports 'the application for extending the rights of audience equally to solicitors and barristers in government service'.

1.2   THE ROLE OF THE POLICE

The role of the police in the SFO was the subject of much deliberation by the legislators. The Minister of State said in Committee that:

> 'At first, we discussed whether the Police could be made a full, integral part of the Serious Fraud Office. We concluded that that was inappropriate, because it would make a policeman something other than a policeman if he were part of the pooling of powers arrangements which is inherent in our concept of the SFO. It would blur his line of command, and we know how carefully the responsibilities of a Constable are set out. Furthermore, it would blur the careful arrangements laid down for his accountability to a charge that he has misused his powers. That is why the Police will be put on secondment to work with the office when necessary. Again, that is one of those practical problems which, after consideration, we had to arrive at conclusions which were not necessarily as simple as our initial concept. That is why Clause 1 (3) is so drafted.'[1]

The police are, therefore, seconded to the SFO (in some instances, on a case by case basis; at other times on temporary secondment), but are not part of the SFO, and remain under the operational command of their chief officer. They are paid out of the funds made available for the police force. They are subject to the normal rules that apply to police officers: in other words they are subject to the provisions of the Police and Criminal Evidence Act 1984 ('PACE').[2] Of necessity, however, they work very closely with the SFO, with whom they even share accommodation, and while they investigate under the command of their chief officers, in practice they act as part of a team structure within the SFO.[3] Because an SFO investigation is not led by the police (in the way that a normal criminal investigation is) the part the police play is in some cases

---

17 Cf Prosecution of Offences Act 1985 section 23.
18 Prosecution of Offences Act 1985 section 4.
19 See: Practice Direction (Solicitors: Audience in Crown Court) [1988] 3 All ER 717, [1988] 1 WLR 1427.
20 SFO Annual Report 1990–1991, paragraph 19.7.
1 *Hansard* 16 December 1986: SC F, col 35.
2 See section 2.4 below.
3 See the annual reports of the SFO (1988–89, paragraphs 7–8; 1990–1991, paragraphs 4.1–4.4). In 1991, paragraph 4.1, the Director stated: 'The constitutional independence of the Police, their accountability, and their command structure remain unchanged by the establishment of the SFO or by the attachment of the Police to it. Responsibility for investigating serious or complex cases of fraud is shared between the Director of the SFO and the Police, and their respective powers are designed to complement each other.'

effectively confined to carrying out certain tasks at the request of the SFO. These tasks are limited to:

(a) taking witness statements;
(b) seizing documents (section 2(4)–(7));
(c) interviewing suspects under caution;
(d) arresting and charging suspects.

In other cases their investigative skills are used to a significantly greater extent.

The police are not permitted to take part in interviews under section 2(2); they do not have the power to requisition documents under section 2(3); they do not have overall charge of the investigation and, generally speaking, do not direct it; and they do not make the decision to institute proceedings (section 1(5)(a)).

1.3   SERIOUS OR COMPLEX FRAUD

Serious or complex fraud is not defined. Since there is no such offence as 'fraud', there can clearly be no offence of 'serious or complex fraud'.[4] It therefore does not need definition for the purpose of creating an offence. The only purpose of the phrase is to limit the type of case to be undertaken, by virtue of sub-s 1(3), by the Director of the SFO.

The Minister of State said in Committee:

> 'It has already been established that there is no offence such as serious fraud. With respect to Mr Bermingham, I do not believe that the same considerations apply as they did when we discussed serious arrestable offences. Such matters had a concrete effect in law if a decision were made one way or another. Under these provisions we are discussing the creation of an organisation to facilitate the investigation of certain difficult cases. We are not saying that this is an offence and that that is not. There is no definition of an offence that turns on the use of the words "serious" or "fraud"; nor are we saying that a case will not be investigated if the definition of either word is wrong or if there is no definition, because we know that any complaint of a criminal act will be investigated by the Police in the normal way.'[5]

Nevertheless, the concept of 'serious or complex fraud' was recognised to be of critical significance, and an important addition was made to sub-s 1(3) in Committee by the insertion of the words 'on reasonable grounds'. The Home Secretary acknowledged that a challenge to the reasonableness of the Director's actions was possible:

> 'Any activities undertaken by Police Officers working alongside the SFO would come under the Police Complaints Authority in accordance with PACE. The Director and his staff would not come under the Parliamentary Commissioner, therefore, their accountability would take two traditional forms. One of them is accountability through Parliament. The Director has to make an annual report to Parliament, but in addition, like the DPP, he is responsible to Parliament through the AG. That is no empty form of accountability and can be used by members of Parliament for constituents who wish to complain or bring a point to the Government's attention and, if need be, have it corrected.

4   See Chapter 1.
5   *Hansard* 16 December 1986: SC F, col 36.

The second form of accountability is judicial review. The exercise by the Director of his powers would be reviewable by the High Court on a decision to prosecute if it were thought that that was in bad faith, or in the exercise of investigative powers if it were thought that he was acting unreasonably. Those are the two traditional pieces of machinery. Let us not neglect or despise them simply because they are there and have been there for some time. Both are forceful, as anyone who has had experience of these matters at the receiving end knows. Another factor should also be considered. Bad publicity would undermine the SFO – cases would be lost and so on. Taken together with the atmosphere in which the SFO will have to operate, they are adequate safeguards.'[6]

There have been indications from Directors of the SFO of what is considered to be serious or complex fraud.[7] In the first report of the Serious Fraud Office John Wood, its first Director, said:

'When the decision to establish the Serious Fraud Office was made, it was assumed that the Office would carry a caseload of about 60. The Criminal Justice Act 1987 speaks only of the Office investigating and prosecuting cases of "serious or complex fraud". I have indicated to bodies likely to refer cases to the Office for investigation that we shall normally think it right to accept cases where:
(a) the facts and/or the law are of great complexity; or
(b) sums of money in excess of £1 million are at risk; or
(c) there is a great public interest and concern for some other reason, eg the identity of the suspect or the employment of a novel method of fraud.'[8]

In evidence to the Trade and Industry Committee Mr Wood said:

'It is extraordinarily difficult to define a serious and complex fraud; the 1987 Criminal Justice Act did not do so. I think to some extent it is instinctive. What we describe as the block-buster cases, that is *Barlow Clowes, Guinness,* the *Lloyd's* cases, of course we shall always take. We do look at the amount of money involved and we say we will not look at anything under £1 million. I caught myself saying the other day, "We won't take this case because it's only £1 million", and I wonder whether we shall have to up the limit. Generally speaking we will take cases where the public has been defrauded rather than perhaps an institution or a company, where there are a number of defendants involved, where there is an overseas element and particularly where we think that the powers granted to us by Parliament under section 2 of the Criminal Justice Act (which is power to demand documents and to demand evidence from witnesses) would be of value in the case. It is a very subjective judgment, I am afraid, it is a judgment I make personally and I do also have to consider what our resources are at that particular time, because there really is no point in taking a case if the resources are inadequate to deal with it.'[9]

---

6 *Hansard* 13 January 1987, col 68.
7 It is perhaps important to note the use of 'or' in section 1(3) contrasted, for example, with serious *and* complex in section 4(1) although it is difficult to see why any distinction should exist. The SFO, in submissions to the Runciman Committee, has suggested that 'the distinction between serious fraud cases under section 1(3) and those which are suitable for transfer under section 4(1)(b)(ii) should be abolished, ie it should be possible to transfer either serious or complex fraud'. The submission suggests a level of concern about the limits of seriousness and complexity which is greater than might have been expected in the light of the lack of a statutory definition.
8 The Serious Fraud Office, First Annual Report, paragraph 11.
9 House of Commons: Session 1989–90. Trade and Industry Committee; Third Report: Company Investigations Question 520.

In 1990 the financial guideline was raised from £1 million to £2 million, and comments by the Director in 1991 suggested that it would soon go higher.[10] The cases which the Director of the SFO takes on regularly involve a 'money at risk' figure much greater than £2 million, and an obvious public interest or other qualification.

While, therefore, the possibility seems to exist of challenging the decision of the Director under section 1(3) to investigate a case by way of application for judicial review, such challenges will be rare and probably unsuccessful. The courts will, in any event, be most reluctant to interfere with the SFO's decision-making process even in the special circumstances of an investigation by the SFO.[11] Apart, however, from the inevitable difficulties of persuading a court that it has the power to interfere with the exercise of such a discretion, it is almost certainly the case that an applicant will need to prove bad faith, or at the very least a serious degree of recklessness, before he will be able to prove that the decision of the Director was unreasonable. In addition, it is most unlikely that a situation will arise where a challenge can be mounted on the basis that a case is not serious or complex. The current workload of the SFO makes it almost inconceivable that a case will be taken on which, by any criteria, is neither serious nor complex. Nevertheless, the reasonableness of the decision is vitally important because the act of designating a fraud 'serious or complex' has the extensive and significant consequences of enabling the Director to use the powers granted in section 2 of the 1987 Act. Were a decision to be taken by the Director of the SFO to investigate a case simply because he thought 'that the powers granted to us by Parliament under section 2 of the Criminal Justice Act would be of value to us in the case' where the allegations otherwise consisted of simple and straightforward fraud of less than the current money limit, the decision-making process might be open to challenge.

1.4   THE SFO AND THE DTI

The SFO's cases come to it either directly, when a fraud is uncovered and it is immediately decided to engage the SFO, or after another agency, frequently the DTI,[12] has conducted an investigation. A case may therefore come to the SFO following a DTI inquiry. If there has already been a DTI inquiry, the immediate role of the SFO is to decide whether to prosecute. Their investigative function will have been substantially usurped by the inspectors: further questioning of suspects under section 2 may well be unnecessary,[13] as will the compulsory questioning of witnesses who have already been questioned

10 For example, in a speech on 21 February 1991 to the Irish Centre for Commercial Law Studies; and in an interview published in *The Times* on 11 July 1991. An article in the Gazette on 15 April 1992 confirmed that as at that date the level remains at £2 million: Barbara Mills QC: 'Let no one profit by fraud.'

11 The challenge to discretion in making a prosecution decision was considered in *Chief Constable of the North Wales Police v Evans* [1982] 3 All ER 141, [1982] 1 WLR 1155 and recently in *R v Inland Revenue Comrs, ex p Mead and Cook* [1992] STC 482, DC.

12 25% of cases referred to the SFO came from the DTI, 41% from police forces: SFO Annual Report 1990–1991, paragraph 2.3.

13 Further questioning where a decision has been made to charge would be a breach of the PACE Codes (C.11.2), although it is difficult to envisage that a breach would prima facie be established where the SFO was considering whether to prosecute on the basis of evidence revealed by a DTI inquiry. See also section 2.2.5 below and *R v Director of Serious Fraud Office, ex p Wallace Duncan Smith* [1992] 1 All ER 730.

by inspectors. Much work will no doubt remain to be done including possibly reducing some of the transcripts of DTI interviews into convenient form for trial as witness statements, but it will mainly be of the nature of tying up loose ends and practically preparing the case for trial.

It has become apparent that in some cases there has been co-operation between DTI inspectors and the prosecuting authorities during the course of a DTI inquiry. The nature of the co-operation between the SFO and DTI in circumstances where a prosecution was in prospect was described by John Wood, then the Director of the SFO, in evidence to the Trade and Industry Committee:

> 'In the *Guinness* case the DTI announced the appointment of inspectors on 1 December 1986. On 12 January 1987 the DTI consulted me – and I mean by that me personally – by telephone when I was in the Director of Public Prosecutions Office. We talked about the issues and we decided what was the appropriate manner of taking the case forward. We decided that the proper thing to do was to let the inspectors carry on with their inquiry and pass the transcripts of evidence over to me. That was done and on 5 February 1987 I instructed a team of counsel to advise me as to the criminal aspects. Having received those transcripts over a period of a few months, on 5 May 1987 I formally instructed or asked the Police to carry out a Police investigation. I say 'formally' because up to that time I had been in informal contact with the Police officers. Thereafter the DTI inquiry and the Police inquiry ran, not so much in parallel but I think the Police inquiry one could describe as one step behind because we were getting the transcripts and we were able then to structure the way in which we carried out our investigation. Over the next few months a number of people were arrested. The inquiry continued and by the middle of 1988 – I think probably it is nearer September 1988 – we felt that we were in possession of sufficient evidence to transfer the case under the new powers in the Criminal Justice Act 1987 to the Crown Court. We could not do it at that particular time because the transfer machinery was not in place and we had to wait until it did come into place, which was in November 1988. The transfer provisions came into operation on 30 October 1988 and we transferred the case on 21 November 1988. So there was a very considerable overlap, as you say, between the investigation of the Department of Trade, using their inspectors and the Police, with the Crown Prosecution Service at that time. When the Serious Fraud Office became operational on 6 April 1988 we took over the case and it was only at that time that we were able to use the statutory powers that we have under section 2 of the 1987 Act. I think that it is a good example, if I may say so, of how these things work best because the DTI are carrying out their inquiry, we are being given the information and we can use it in the course of our investigation.'[14]

This begs a serious question which will need to be examined when section 2 is looked at in detail: to what extent can and should the DTI be used as an 'investigator' for the SFO? The question has, to some extent, been answered by section 437(1B) of the Companies Act 1985 as amended by the 1989 Act which allows the Secretary of State to call a halt to a section 432 inspection, if it appears that a criminal offence has been committed and the matter has been referred to the appropriate authority. It raises other questions too: for example, are inspectors appointed by the DTI investigating offences within the meaning of PACE 1984?[15]

---

14 Op cit: Question 557.
15 These points are discussed in section 2.2.3 below.

Whatever the scope of the DTI's powers in relation to the SFO, it is clear that the relationship between the two authorities is, as indeed one would expect, close.[16] There will often be consultation between the two departments when serious fraud allegations arise. Since the Director of the SFO can use his powers under section 1(3) of the Act if it appears appropriate within the section, and there is an equal power for the Secretary of State to appoint inspectors (Companies Act 1985 section 432(2)), neither authority technically has precedence. The consequences for individuals caught up in fraud inquiries of the decisions made by the Director of the SFO and the Secretary of State can be far-reaching, and as stated above the reasonableness of a decision to investigate by the Director of the SFO might be open to challenge: was the case more suitable for the DTI to handle? It is, however, difficult to envisage circumstances in which such a challenge may be mounted.

2.1   INVESTIGATIONS: CRIMINAL JUSTICE ACT 1987 SECTION 2

Section 2 of the Criminal Justice Act 1987 contains provisions relating to the powers available to the Director of the SFO[17] when investigations are carried out under section 1(3) and section 1(4). The Committee considering the Criminal Justice Bill was in no doubt that the Clause 2 provisions would have far-reaching consequences.[18]

The provisions may be divided into three parts:

(a) the power to question individuals (sub-s 2(2));
(b) the power to requisition documents (sub-s 2(3));
(c) powers of search and seizure (sub-s 2(4)–(7)).

(a) and (b) are exercisable by the lawyers and accountants in the SFO, and by no-one else except under the provisions of sub-s 2(11) which permits the Director to appoint 'any competent investigator (other than a constable) who is not a member of that office' to exercise the powers. In practice, this provision has been used to bring in firms of accountants on a sub-contract basis to meet peak demands.[19]

The Roskill Fraud Trials Committee recognised that enhanced powers of investigation were required to enable serious frauds to be properly investigated. The Committee recommended[20] that powers based on the powers available to inspectors appointed by the Department of Trade & Industry under section 447 of the Companies Act 1985 should be given to the Police. The choice of section 447 may have been of some significance since it gives much more restricted

16   It may be expected that in future the SFO will investigate many cases from the outset which formerly might have been the subject of inquiries by inspectors. The number of recent investigations (eg Polly Peck, BCCI, Brent Walker and Maxwell) in which the SFO has taken precedence where formerly a DTI inquiry might have been set up indicates the extent to which the SFO has taken over large fraud investigations from the DTI. It will be interesting to see if the numbers of DTI inquiries decreases significantly in the immediate future.

17   Not to any other authority.

18   See, eg *Hansard* 13 January 1987, SC F, cols 58 and 77. There was extended debate in Committee on the civil liberties' aspects of clause 2 on 13, 15 and 17 January 1987, but very little debate in either House.

19   SFO 1st Annual Report, paragraph 6. But it is curiously used to support the delegation of power to issue section 2 notices to members of the SFO staff (see below).

20   Roskill Report, paragraph 2.62.

powers to inspectors than the powers conferred by section 434,[1] on which section 2 of the 1987 Act was more closely modelled. The main attraction to the Committee of the section 447 powers was that they tended to be exercised much more expeditiously by the DTI than did the powers used pursuant to an inquiry under section 432.

In respect of investigations, Roskill added this footnote:

> 'For the sake of completeness, we should add that if the idea of giving one organisation overall responsibility for the investigation and prosecution of serious frauds were in due course to be accepted, it would, of course, be essential to ensure that the organisation was vested with powers of investigation fully comparable with those at present available separately to the Police, DTI and also the Revenue departments, if the last mentioned were included.'[2]

The issue of comparable powers of investigation assumes some importance in the context of section 2 of the Act, as it relates to requirements to answer questions.

2.2 POWERS OF QUESTIONING

Before the powers given by sub-s 2(2) of the Act can be used:

(a) the Director must have decided that he will investigate a case which he reasonably believes to involve a serious or complex fraud;

(b) he must decide that there is good reason to use the section 2 powers for the purposes of investigating 'the affairs, or any aspect of the affairs of any person'; and

(c) he must then give written notice to 'the person under investigation' or to any person 'whom he has reason to believe has relevant information, that they must answer questions about the investigation either at a specified time and place, or forthwith'.

A notice under section 2 of the Act will be headed 'Notice requiring attendance to answer questions, furnish information, and produce documents'. It will then state who are the persons under investigation, who might be individuals or companies or both. The notice will recite the power of the Director of the SFO under sub-s 1(3) and the delegation to an officer to exercise the powers under section 2 on behalf of the Director. The notice will then assert that for the purposes of the investigation there appear to be good reasons to exercise the powers conferred in section 2.

Finally, the notice will state that the SFO officer has reason to believe that the individual to whom the notice is directed has relevant information about the affairs of the persons under investigation, and a requirement will be made that the individual should answer questions or otherwise furnish information at a specified time and place, or immediately.

The notice will end with the words: 'failure without reasonable excuse to comply with these requirements is a criminal offence'.

---

1 For example, questions may only be asked of officers of the company under investigation and those questions may only be directed towards an explanation of documents seized from the company.

2 Roskill Report, paragraph 2.64.

2.2.1   Section 2 notices and potential witnesses

A notice under section 2 of the Act can be directed either at a potential or actual defendant (who may be named as 'the person under investigation'), or at a person who is likely to be a witness. Most notices issued under section 2 of the Act are directed at potential witnesses, in particular those who are either likely to be reluctant to answer questions or those who owe a duty of confidentiality to the persons under investigation.

Since in fraud cases many witnesses are lawyers, accountants or bankers the extensive use, often the subject of complaint, of notices under section 2, is not surprising.[3] A solicitor, for example, who is asked to give evidence in respect of a client must consider his duty of confidentiality. He may either ask his client to waive confidentiality, or he may consider that exceptional circumstances exist which override the duty.

Among those circumstances the Guide to the Professional Conduct of Solicitors cites the following:

> 'A solicitor should reveal matters which are otherwise subject to the duty to preserve confidentiality where a court orders that such matters are to be disclosed or where a warrant permits a Police officer or other authority to seize confidential documents. If a solicitor is of the opinion that the documents are subject to legal privilege or that for some other reason the order or warrant ought not to have been made or issued, he should either make an application to have the order or warrant set aside without unlawfully obstructing its execution, or he may seek the advice of the legal advisors' branch.
>
> Occasionally, a solicitor is asked by the Police to give information or to show them documents which the solicitor has obtained when acting for a client. Unless the client is prepared to waive confidentiality, the solicitor should insist upon receiving a witness summons or subpoena so that he may, where appropriate, claim privilege and leave the court to decide the issue. If the request is made by the Police under the terms of the Police and Criminal Evidence Act 1984 then, again, the solicitor should where appropriate leave the question of privilege to the court to decide on the particular circumstances.'[4]

He will therefore be in breach of a contractual duty to his client if he co-operates with the police without the coercion of a notice under section 2.[5]

In drafting the Bill, legislators considered restricting the scope of section 2 to the 'connected persons' concept which applies in some financial legislation. In the event this was thought inappropriate. The Home Secretary said in Committee:

> 'It was thought that it might not be sufficient to bring within its scope the great complexity of modern fraud and that the SFO, if confined in that way, might

3   In the first year of the SFO's operations, 233 notices under section 2 were issued (SFO 1st Annual Report, paragraph 21). By 1990–1991 the number had risen to 765 (SFO Report 1990–1991, paragraph 6.1), 590 of which required both answers to questions and the production of documents. In the *Sunday Telegraph* 24 March 1991 an article on the SFO stated: 'But not all of [the Director's] clippings files has been favourable. She has been attacked for the probes under section 2 of the Criminal Justice Act, dubbed Police 'fishing trips' by critics.' According to the article, the Director firmly dismissed such criticism. The powers 'allow investigators – not necessarily the Police – to get on with the job, and are welcomed in a great many cases. People are obliged to co-operate under section 2, and it is not an uncommon reaction for people to say "I would rather you served a section 2 notice." It makes it clear to employers and clients, for instance, that the interviewee had no choice but to co-operate.'

4   The Guide to Professional Conduct of Solicitors, 1990, paragraph 12.4.

5   Legal professional privilege and bankers' confidentiality are dealt with below at section 2.3.5.

find itself brought up against the limits of its powers just when it was reaching a relevant point in the investigation.'[6]

The net can therefore be spread extremely wide when issuing a notice under section 2(2) with only a reason to believe that an individual has relevant information as a criterion for deciding to issue a notice.

2.2.2 Section 2 notices and defendants: the section 2(8) safeguard

Where the notice is directed at a person under investigation or, indeed, a person who has been charged with an offence of fraud in the investigation, an answer given to SFO investigators using the section 2 powers may not be given in evidence against him at subsequent criminal proceedings except:

(a) where proceedings are brought under section 2(14) for giving false information either deliberately or recklessly; or
(b) where the individual 'makes a statement inconsistent with it'.[7]

While this provision protects a defendant from self-incrimination in the strict sense, use of the material provided pursuant to a section 2 notice provides a basis for investigators to pursue their inquiries. The defendant is forced to make available to the investigators the materials with which they will seek to convict him. Moreover, if he fails to answer their questions he makes himself liable for prosecution, and if during the interview he gives answers which he subsequently, in evidence before a court, contradicts, then his earlier statements can be used against him.

The protection offered by sub-s 2(8) of the Act is, therefore, limited in its extent, and sub-s 2(2) does represent a considerable erosion[8] of the right of silence.

2.2.3 Inconsistency of approach: the Criminal Justice Act and other compulsory powers of questioning

In including section 2(8) in the Act, the legislators recognised that they were creating a substantial inconsistency between the powers available to the SFO and certain other provisions, including section 434 of the Companies Act 1985 and section 236 of the Insolvency Act 1986, contrary to the recommendations of the Roskill Committee. Evidence given to inspectors in the course of a DTI inquiry, or to office holders under the insolvency legislation 'may be used in evidence against' the person giving evidence, and in practice is. The situation therefore arises that where a person gives evidence to DTI inspectors or office holders, not knowing whether a criminal investigation will subsequently take place, nor whether he is a potential witness or defendant in that investigation, he is nevertheless required to answer questions, and his answers may subsequently be used as evidence against him. Where, however, a criminal investigation is taking place, a person who knows he is a potential defendant is given the protection of section 2(8).

---

6 *Hansard* 13 January 1989, SC F, column 67.
7 Section 2(8).
8 The precedents for this erosion are said to be the Customs and Excise Management Act 1979, the Companies Act 1985 and the Financial Services Act 1986. However, the extent of the powers of investigation in those statutes is more restricted than that available to the SFO.

This inconsistency was extensively canvassed before Henry J in the preparatory hearings in the *Guinness* case in both the first and second trials. Henry J ruled that confessions obtained by DTI inspectors under compulsory questioning were fairly obtained and could be introduced in evidence at the criminal trial. The Court of Appeal, in *R v Seelig and Spens*[9] (the second *Guinness* trial), upheld Henry J, and also approved his earlier ruling in respect of the first trial.

The Court of Appeal considered four main points. First, whether under section 434(5) of the Companies Act 1985 evidence given by a defendant is admissible in a subsequent criminal trial. The answer to that question was that the trial judge had a discretion to exclude confessions which were unfairly obtained under the general provisions of section 78 of PACE. There was nothing, however, in the statute to restrict their use.

Second, do inspectors appointed by the DTI fall within section 67(9) of PACE, that is, are they charged with the duty of investigating offences within the meaning of that section? Henry J had ruled that 'they are plainly not'. He stated:

> 'When one looks at the obligation on them under the Companies Act, their obligation is to investigate the affairs of the company and to report. In the course of such investigation criminal offences will often emerge, but the fact that they do so does not alter the duty of the inspectors. Their duty is to investigate the affairs of the company and to ascertain the facts. They are not conducting a trial of those investigated. It is for others to investigate any criminal offences that may be uncovered by the inspectors. The inspectors may be required by the Secretary of State to provide under section 437(1)(a) material which might point to the commission of crime, but it is not for them to investigate whether the material constitutes offences as such. Parliament, when setting out the duties of inspectors in the 1985 Act, which was after PACE in my judgment chose their words carefully, and therefore the codes do not apply. If the code did apply it would be extremely difficult to apply them. That difficulty is shown by the form of the caution which the defence submit to me, the inspectors are bound to deliver, and that would be in the form: "you do not have to say anything unless you wish to do so, anything you may say may be given in evidence against you. If you refuse to say anything we may certify your refusal to the High Court who may punish you for contempt".'[10]

The Court of Appeal held that Henry J was correct, Watkins LJ stating:

> 'Our view is, however, that whether a body or a person conducting some kind of inquiry is subject to section 67(9) is a question of fact in each case. It is, in our view, quite impossible to give a generalised answer to the question arising out of sub-section (9). We take Henry J to have found as a fact that the inspectors in the present case were not investigating offences. Upon all the evidence before him it was a conclusion at which we think he could justifiably arrive. We do not therefore agree that his finding in this respect was wrong.'[11]

The language of the court appears to be somewhat less than fulsome in its support for the judge's finding, however, and the fact that each case – presumably each DTI inquiry therefore – must be judged on its own facts reduces the applicability of the judgment. It may be wondered whether the Judges were referred to the Director's comments on the *Guinness* inquiry to the

9 [1991] 4 All ER 429, [1992] 1 WLR 148.
10 [1991] 4 All ER 429.
11 Ibid at 430.

Select Committee,[12] and if not, whether they would have gone so far as they did in agreeing with Henry J. If the inspectors are providing evidence to the SFO for the purposes of their investigation, they are carrying out a duty of investigating offences even if they may not have been charged with that duty.

The Court of Appeal does not seem to have been referred to the decision of Woolf J in *R v Secretary of State for Trade, ex p Perestrello and Another*[13] in which, on a judicial review of the powers of the Secretary of State in relation to an inquiry under section 109 of the Companies Act 1948 (now section 447 of the 1985 Act), consideration was given to the terms in which a notice requiring production of documents could be drawn.[14] In considering the submission that the inspectors acted with bias, Woolf J made the following remarks:

> 'When one considers the functions of those Officers, it really is wholly inappropriate to talk about them not being regarded as biased if they are performing functions properly. Take this very case – it is in my view almost inevitable that before the powers under section 109 are exercised, the Officers concerned, and through his Officers, the Secretary of State, must regard the situation as one where there are matters to be investigated. They are acting in a policing role. Their function is to see whether their suspicions are justified by what they find, and that being so it is wholly inappropriate for the case to be judged in the same way as one would approach a normal judicial role or quasi judicial role; a situation where the person is making a determination.'[15]

Woolf J's remarks purport to be of general application, and do not contain the limitation imposed by the Court of Appeal in *R v Seelig and Spens*, namely that each case must be judged on its own merits. Since the Court of Appeal has not ruled out the possibility that inspectors are 'investigating offences' within the meaning of section 67(9) of PACE, it would appear that there remains good reason to believe that the argument put forward, but rejected, in *R v Seelig and Spens* might succeed on another occasion.

Third, was there oppression, within section 76 of the PACE, in the very fact that witnesses before inspectors are required to answer questions? The answer given by Henry J was that, so far as section 76(2)(a) is concerned, since Lord Spens and Mr Seelig were intelligent and sophisticated, they did not need the inspectors to explain the import of Part XIV of the Companies Act 1985: they could read it themselves and/or take legal advice. With regard to section 76(2)(b), the lack of a caution or warning did not render the confessions unreliable. Henry J stated:

> 'It is not too cynical to assume that the likely consequence of the warning suggested as being appropriate would be either that the witness would be more guarded, more evasive and less frank, or that he would refuse to answer the question altogether and risk punishment for contempt. However wrong that is, I do not see how the failure to give such a warning is likely to render answers freely given unreliable. Therefore, the application under section 76(2)(b) fails.'[16]

Fourth, how much discretion does the judge have? Henry J asked himself the following question:

12 See section 1.4 above; although a passage in the judgment of the Court of Appeal in *R v Seelig* [1991] 4 All ER 429 at 433 suggests that they were made aware of the position by defence submissions.
13 [1981] QB 19, [1980] 3 All ER 28.
14 See Chapter 8 below.
15 [1981] QB 19 at 35.
16 Cited by the Court of Appeal, op cit, page 440.

'Is the fairness of these proceedings threatened by the admission of questions put under a statutory regime designed to discover the facts in a company fraud to the company's merchant banker, before it was considered appropriate to charge him in a case when neither the decision to charge him nor his actual charging had been wrongly delayed?'[17]

The Court of Appeal referred to the case of *Lam Chi-ming v R*[18] a recent Privy Council case which dealt, inter alia, with the question of self-incrimination, and after stating that:

'The privilege against self-incrimination must, of course, unless there is good reason to the contrary, be upheld',

they cited in full, and approved, Henry J's reasons for refusing to use his discretion under sections 78(1) and 82(3) of PACE:

'I have no difficulty in accepting that in the investigation of the role of Guinness plc, its servants and agents in the Distillers' takeover Mr Seelig, as Guinness' leading banker was, because he was subject to the inquisitorial process that I have outlined, worse placed than the average man questioned as to crime, because, of course, that individual can simply refuse to assist the Police with their inquiries and Mr Seelig could not have refused to assist the inspectors without running the risks that I have already indicated.

That, however, is only the starting point for the investigation into the question of fairness. It is not a conclusive answer to that question. It is not for four reasons.

First, because of the public importance which Parliament attaches to the investigation and punishment of company fraud, and the importance that it attaches to getting the truth in such matters.

Second, because those likely to be questioned under that statutory regime are those whose responsibilities under the Companies Act, and at company law in relation to shareholders funds and the integrity of the market are reflected in the privileged position they have. It is not asking too much, in my judgment to impose limits on their civil rights, as Parliament has done by an obligation to answer questions in circumstances where those answers may be used in criminal proceedings against them.

Third, the general protection is designed to be wide enough to protect the weak, the inarticulate and the suggestible from having to answer in the strange and hostile environment of a Police station and less obviously needed to protect those likely to be major witnesses in a section 432 investigation who will usually be intelligent, sophisticated, self-confident and articulate, usually accompanied by lawyers, giving evidence by prior appointment in an environment not so foreign to them.

Fourth, and fundamentally, the fact that they are treated less favourably than the average man accused of crime is because the legislature has decided that they should, and as I have said, a review of the history of the legislation and the authorities concerning it show that that is no accident, no unintended legislative muddle.

Bearing all those matters in mind it seems to me that in the cases on these facts that the admission in the evidence of material obtained under the inquisitorial process before a defendant is charged does not have such adverse effect on the fairness of the proceedings that the Court should exclude it. It will usually be different once the defendant is charged, for a charge usually marks the end of the investigative process and the beginning of the accusatorial process.'[19]

---

17 Ibid, p 440.
18 [1991] 2 AC 212, [1991] 3 All ER 172.
19 Op cit, page 441.

In conclusion, Watkins LJ stated:

'The present case is, as we have said, concerned with extremely astute, professional men, who have been advised at one time or another by very experienced City solicitors. There was, in our judgment, sound reason for admitting the so-called confessions having regard to the relevant legislation which Parliament has deliberately enacted, albeit that that may appear to tend towards unfairness especially when set against the relevant proceedings in the 1984 Act.

However that may be, having carefully considered the submissions of Mr Seelig and Mr Hood, we feel compelled to regard Henry J as having decided the various points in issue correctly and exercised his discretion in a manner which is not open to valid criticism.'[20]

Again, the language used by Watkins LJ does not suggest a whole-hearted approval of the ruling of Henry J and the reference to *Lam Chi-ming* is suggestive of a warning shot about the integrity of the criminal law as it should apply in all criminal cases.

The use of evidence obtained by office holders under section 236 of the Insolvency Act 1986 was considered, in *Re Arrows Ltd*,[1] where counsel for the SFO submitted that in permitting a direction to be given by the court that the written record of an examination by liquidators, pursuant to section 236 of the Insolvency Act 1986, was not to be disclosed to the SFO, its investigators would be deprived of a valuable source of information. Counsel conceded that questions put to the defendant under section 236 could equally well be put to him by the SFO under section 2 of the 1987 Act. He admitted that the disadvantage of using the 1987 Act was that the evidence would not be admissible under section 2(8), whereas any answers given to the liquidators under section 236 of the Insolvency Act 1986 would be admissible.[2] Hoffmann J ruled that it seemed wrong that the SFO should be able to circumvent the protection given to an accused by section 2(8) by obtaining his answers to compulsory questions put under section 236 of the Insolvency Act 1986. The judge adopted a public policy argument to the effect that it was more important that the liquidators obtained the information they wanted under their powers than that the SFO make use of the information.

The argument that a witness before DTI inspectors, or indeed a person giving information to liquidators, might be inhibited by the fact that his answers could be used against him in subsequent criminal proceedings, to the disadvantage of those who are the primary recipients of the information, is one which the authorities might be unwise to ignore. Hoffmann J expressed the view in the *Re Arrows Ltd* case that unless the direction was given as requested by the liquidators, it was likely that the examination of the owner of the company would provide no useful information either for the liquidators or for the SFO.[3] However, the subsequent decisions of the Court of Appeal in *Re London United Investments plc*,[4] and *Re Bishopsgate Investment Management Ltd*,[5] led the parties in the *Re Arrows Ltd* case to allow an appeal by the

---

20 Op cit, page 442.
1 [1992] 2 WLR 923, [1992] BCLC 126.
2 Insolvency Act 1986 section 433.
3 See also *AT & T Istel Ltd v Tully* [1992] 1 QB 315, [1992] 2 All ER 28 and *Marcel v Metropolitan Police* [1992] 1 All ER 72, [1992] 2 WLR 50.
4 [1992] 2 All ER 842, [1992] BCLC 91.
5 [1992] 2 All ER 856, [1992] 2 WLR 991.

Director of the SFO by consent against the prohibition of disclosure to the SFO.[6]

In relation to DTI inquiries, it may be the case that if, for example, the Guinness investigation had arisen after the creation of the SFO, it would have been investigated by that Department and not by the DTI (the list of recent investigations by the SFO demonstrates how far it has penetrated Department of Trade territory). The defendants would therefore have had the protection of section 2(8) in respect of any interviews carried out under section 2(2). In practical terms they would have been at a considerable advantage at their trial.

It has been decided, however, that it is not possible to argue the corollary of this point: that a witness before inspectors can refuse to answer written or oral questions because the SFO should investigate, or might be about to investigate; nor that this fact affects the admissibility of interviews with DTI inspectors.[7] Inspectors appointed under section 432 of the 1985 Act to investigate the affairs of London United Investments Ltd had sought to question Mr Wilson, who had refused to answer on the grounds that his answers might tend to incriminate him. It was submitted on his behalf that his refusal was justified, and that as a matter of law it was improper for the Secretary of State to appoint inspectors to investigate matters which were the subject of allegations of fraud, because it was more appropriate that suspected crime should be investigated by the SFO or the police.

This submission, however, was rejected by the Court of Appeal, Dillon LJ ruling that the wording of Part XIV of the 1985 Act made it an 'impossible contention'. He also took into account that the Secretary of State has a discretion, and not a requirement, under section 437(1B) of the 1985 Act to direct inspectors to take no further steps where matters have been referred to a prosecuting authority. The judge appears to have inferred from this that it was contemplated that inspectors could continue to investigate, and therefore ask questions, after a prosecuting authority had become involved in the matters under consideration. There was also, stated the judge, the power in the Secretary of State to disclose information to prosecuting authorities under sections 449 and 451(A) of the 1985 Act, and from this it could be inferred that inspectors would be asked to act where fraud was being investigated. The judge finally took into account the fact that it was likely that in many cases where inspectors were appointed an investigation by the Police or SFO could also be appropriate.

Dillon LJ recognised that the SFO 'is undoubtably aware of the general situation over LUI' but that no one had been charged with any offence connected with the DTI inquiry, nor had Mr Wilson been questioned by the SFO. 'In these circumstances, it does not surprise me in the least that the inspectors should have wanted to question Mr Wilson.'

Although, therefore, the SFO is now more likely to investigate the type of fraud once dealt with by the DTI, this fact cannot be used to argue that an unfairness is created.

The situation outlined by Dillon LJ will not ease the anxiety of potential defendants in serious fraud cases, namely that the SFO will allow interviews by DTI inspectors to proceed before using their powers under the 1987 Act, so as to enable them to use the answers given to the inspectors in a subsequent trial

---

6   (1992) Times, 1 May. See Chapter 8, section 3.8.3 for further discussion on the privilege against self-incrimination.

7   *Re London United Investments Ltd* [1992] 2 All ER 842, [1992] BCLC 91.

under sections 434(5), 448(8) of the 1985 Act. It is probably cynical to suggest that this is indeed the case, although much the same was admitted by Counsel for the SFO in the *Re Arrows* case.[8]

Another point which it may be appropriate to consider is that even if an investigation begins as a DTI inquiry, the disclosure of matters meriting a criminal investigation might lead to a referral of the matter to 'the appropriate authority' within section 437(1B) of the Companies Act 1985 (as amended by the Companies Act 1989) and the consequent cessation of the DTI inquiry. The Crown would no doubt argue that any interviews conducted up to the moment of the abandonment of the DTI inquiry could be used in evidence, but questions would inevitably be asked about any interviews that were carried out after it had become apparent that a criminal offence had been committed (the wrongful delay point made by Henry J).[9] A fortiori any DTI inquiry which ends up before the criminal courts reaches a point where section 437(1B) applies, and an inference to be drawn from the sub-section (not one of the inferences drawn by Dillon LJ in the *London United Investments* case), is that DTI inspectors should not begin an investigation where there is strong suspicion of fraud, and that they should not become investigators of criminal offences (as Henry J, indeed, ruled that they were not).

Because the powers of the SFO are modelled on those of DTI inspectors, there can in practice be no reason to appoint inspectors in a case where the commission of a serious or complex fraud is believed to have taken place and it is contemplated that criminal proceedings may result. Any decision to appoint inspectors may therefore be viewed with the suspicion that the intention was to be able to use the evidence of interviews conducted by the inspectors in a subsequent trial, and thus circumvent the limitation imposed by section 2(8). There are, of course, other consequences of a DTI inquiry, including the compulsory winding up of a company, directors' disqualification proceedings and the bringing of civil proceedings in the company's name. These consequences, however, did not flow from the Guinness or the County NatWest inquiries and in the House of Fraser Holdings inquiry there were no disqualification proceedings.

2.2.4   Compliance with section 2(2)

A person to whom a notice under sub-s 2(2) is directed must comply. Failure to comply, or purported, but false, compliance with the section is a criminal offence punishable by a maximum of two years' imprisonment.[10] By sub-s 2(8), the answers given to investigators using sub-s 2(2) powers may be used in evidence to prove an offence under sub-s 2(14).

2.2.5   Use of section 2(2) after charge

The House of Lords in *R v The Director of Serious Fraud Office, ex p Smith*[11] considered whether a defendant could be questioned under section 2(2) after he

---

8   [1992] BCLC 126 at 132.
9   *R v Seelig and Spens* [1991] 4 All ER 429 at 440.
10 Section 2(14)–(15) of the Act. During 1991 there was one prosecution under section 2(14) which resulted in a sentence of three months' imprisonment (consecutive to a sentence of three years for fraud).
11 [1992] 3 All ER 456, [1992] 3 WLR 66.

had been charged. In that case Smith was arrested and charged before there was any substantial opportunity to investigate the matters alleged against him. Subsequent to his being charged, the SFO purported to serve a section 2 notice on Smith requiring him to answer questions on certain topics which were identified in the notice. *Smith*'s case relied on the applicability of the Codes of Practice established under PACE. He argued that if he were to be questioned he should be cautioned in accordance with the Codes of Practice, and therefore the requirement to answer questions disappeared.

Smith's arguments had succeeded in the Divisional Court,[12] and the Director of the SFO appealed against that decision. In the Divisional Court the argument on behalf of the Director was stated by Nolan LJ to be in these terms:

'There is no suggestion that the Director is seeking to obtain admissions improperly, or to make use of admissions improperly obtained. Her case is simply that in this instance, and not for the first time, Parliament has overridden the right of silence. Faced with the myriad opportunities for the concealment of fraudulent activities which companies and trusts provide, Parliament has given the Serious Fraud Office the power to call upon a suspected person to come into the open, and to disclose information which may incriminate them.'[13]

The judge went on:

'The only question in the present case is how far Parliament has gone down that road. How far does the 1987 Act remove the protection afforded by the 1984 Act and the Codes of Practice issued pursuant to it.'

Nolan LJ considered the case of *A and B v HM Treasury*[14] which arose under powers given to the Commissioners of Customs and Excise, and stated that he would be minded to adopt a similar approach to that adopted by the judge in that case to the language of the 1987 Act, namely that he would not be persuaded that:

'. . . a proper construction of this statute (the Exchange Control Act 1947) requires me to hold that the rights of a person charged and cautioned – rights which are enshrined in the common law and emphasised in the Judge's Rules – are removed by the provision contained in paragraph 1 of schedule 5 to the Act.'

He stated:

'We accept, of course, that the investigation of a serious and complex fraud will not necessarily or even normally stop with the charging of the accused person, but it is going a crucial step further to suggest that the 1987 Act permits potentially incriminating information to be demanded from the accused person himself after that stage has been reached. Only the very clearest statutory language could produce such a result, and we do not find such language in sections 1 and 2 of the Act. Section 2(1) provides that the powers of the Director under the section are to be exercisable only for the purposes of an investigation under section 1 . . . Section 2(2) and (3) authorise the exercise of the power against, inter alios, "the person whose affairs are to be investigated". This language does not suggest to our minds that Parliament contemplated the exercise of the power against a person whose affairs had already been investigated to the extent of a charge being laid against him, in

12 [1992] 1 All ER 730.
13 Ibid at page 736.
14 [1979] 2 All ER 586, [1979] 1 WLR 1056.

respect of an offence which was no longer merely suspected, but about which there was considered to be sufficient evidence for a prosecution to succeed.'[15]

An argument by the prosecution that the restriction imposed by section 2(8) on the use of evidence acquired under section 2 enabled the case to be distinguished from *A and B v HM Treasury* was rejected by the court on the basis that there is no restriction upon the use by the prosecution of incriminating information or evidence obtained as a result of such a statement:

'The whole purpose of imposing a section 2 requirement upon a suspected or accused person must be to obtain from him information and evidence which in an appropriate case and subject only to the sub-section (8) restriction on the use of statements made by him can be deployed against him.'[16]

The Director of the SFO conceded that there was a direct conflict between paragraph 16.5 and 10.4 of the Codes of Practice and section 2(2) and (13) of the 1987 Act. The Court concluded that the two requirements could not be reconciled, and while the Director was given clear authority by Parliament to override the caution procedure in interviews conducted under section 2 prior to charge, no such relaxation could be read into the situation after charge. Nolan LJ stated:

'The practice which she describes in her affidavit appears to cater admirably for the case of a suspected person who has not yet been charged. For the reasons indicated, we do not think that it caters adequately or at all for the case of a person who has been charged, let alone one who is undergoing trial and who, if the Director is right, may be subjected outside court hours throughout the trial to a parallel process of interrogation about the offence charged against him, subject to penalty for refusal to answer questions.'[17]

When invited by counsel for the Director to accept that section 78 of PACE provided a safeguard in that the judge had a discretion to exclude any prosecution evidence which had been unfairly obtained, Nolan LJ said that he did not consider that the trial judge's discretion constituted an adequate safeguard.

'If Parliament has indeed provided that the power of interrogation should remain exercisable by the Serious Fraud Office throughout the trial it is by no means clear by what criteria the Trial Judge could distinguish between a fair and an unfair exercise of the power. Secondly, even if the Trial Judge did take the view that evidence had been unfairly obtained as a result of information which the accused was required to give, the accused would remain subject to a penalty under section 2(13) if he thereupon refused to give further information.'[18]

The same problem was considered obiter and without hearing argument in *R v Director of Serious Fraud, ex p Saunders*[19] by McNeill J. After asserting that officers of the SFO, in conducting investigations, must have regard to the PACE Codes of Practice, he stated:

'Accordingly, inter alia, they are required to have regard to the Code of Practice as to questioning: the conduct of interviews including the requirement

---

15 Op cit at page 738.
16 Ibid at page 738.
17 Ibid at page 739.
18 Ibid at page 740.
19 [1988] Crim LR 837.

to caution. It is to be noted in passing that consistently with the view we have formed on the construction of section 2(3) of the Criminal Justice Act 1987 – and we are of the same mind in relation to section 2(2), even the code permits for limited purposes the questioning of suspects after arrest: C:17:5 (now C:16:5).

Thus if it were desired to question the applicant after he was charged under section 2(2) of the Criminal Justice Act 1987, there is no reason why the notice should not be issued and the applicant required to respond but he would have first to be cautioned and the questions could only be put for the C:17:5 purposes.'

The same point was made by Henry J in the course of his ruling concerning the admissibility of transcripts in the *Seelig & Spens* preparatory hearing:

'. . . it will usually be different once the defendant is charged, for a charge usually marks the end of the investigative process and the beginning of the accusatorial process.'[20]

These observations were considered by Nolan LJ in the *Smith* case. The judge stated:

'The question remains how the Divisional Court's acceptance of the Director's right to serve a section 2(2) notice for the purpose of questioning a person who has been charged, on pain of penalty under section 2(13) if he refuses to answer, can be reconciled with his right to invoke the protection of the caution. The answer, as it seems to us, must be that the Court regards the enhanced right of silence which common law and statute have traditionally conferred upon a person once he has been charged as providing him, in the language of section 2(13), with a 'reasonable excuse' for failing to comply with the requirements.'[21]

The court therefore held that the applicant succeeded on the third limb of his argument, namely, that he could not be compelled to answer questions relating to the offence with which he had been charged, but must be cautioned in accordance with Code C.16.5, but he could be questioned about other suspected offences under section 2, without the requirement of the caution.

The House of Lords, however, robustly overturned this decision.[1] In a unanimous decision they held that the right to ask questions and demand answers did not come to an end after charge and that section 2(2) could not be interpreted as imposing any limit on the timing of requirements made under the section. Although a police officer was required by the PACE Codes of Practice[2] to charge a suspect as soon as there was sufficient evidence for a prosecution to succeed, nobody expected the police to stop work at that stage. In addition, the 'right of silence' could be interfered with by clear statutory intervention, as it had been on numerous occasions. Lord Mustill described the right of silence as arousing strong but unfocused feelings. However, he said, it did not denote any single right but rather referred to a disparate group of immunities, which differed in nature, origin, incidence and importance and also as to the extent to which they had already been encroached on by statute.

While allowing that section 2(2) went further in this respect than other statutes, Lord Mustill held that the arguments on the right of silence turned on questions of admissibility of confessions. In *Smith*'s case there was no question

20 Cited in *R v Seelig and Spens* [1991] 4 All ER 429 at 442, CA.
21 Op cit at page 742.
1   (1992) Times, 16 June.
2   PACE Codes: C.11.4.

of admissibility since, by section 2(8), anything said by him in response to compulsory questioning could only be used against him at trial in the limited circumstances outlined in the subsection.

Smith's 'logical conclusion' argument, that this interpretation permitted the Director to issue notices under section 2(2) throughout the investigation and trial process, was dismissed. Their Lordships regarded it as impossible to believe that the Director would seek to question a defendant during a trial, or that if he did, the trial judge would regard it as anything other than improper conduct.

Lord Mustill concluded that the Director's powers under section 2(2) did not cease at charge stage, and that the clear and specific words of the section ousted, and were intended by Parliament to oust, the general provisions of Code C.

The effect of this decision will clearly be helpful to the SFO. Where other prosecutors are bound to give careful consideration to the timing of the charging of an individual where they believe that interrogation will produce useful admissible evidence, the SFO can operate without such restraint. This is particularly important in the relatively rare type of circumstances which arose in the *Smith* case, where an alleged fraud suddenly comes to light and the immediate imposition of charges is considered essential.[3] How far the SFO will use the decision remains to be seen. Will they consider questioning a defendant after committal or transfer, for example? Would a trial judge become concerned if a defendant was questioned during a preparatory hearing (which is, after all, part of the trial)? The House of Lords decision does not rule out the possibility of a defendant being questioned about his defence statement, made pursuant to an order under section 9(5).

2.2.6   Disclosure by SFO of the nature of its inquiries

Is the SFO under any obligation to disclose to a person to whom a notice is addressed, particularly 'a person under investigation', the nature of the inquiry that is being conducted, and if so to what extent?

The terms of section 2(2) do not include any explicit requirement on the SFO to divulge any details of their investigation. The notice must state that there is an investigation in being, and it follows therefore that it must sufficiently identify the existence of that investigation by naming the 'persons under investigation'. It is not necessary that the notice gives any further details or recites the reasons why the Director has decided to conduct an inquiry, or the precise areas of inquiry that are being undertaken. In practice, with the majority of notices under section 2(2) served on witnesses, the SFO will usually willingly give details of the areas of interest to their inquiries, in advance of an interview. In respect of a person under investigation, however, is it possible to state precisely what his rights – as opposed to his duties – are? Does he, for example, at any stage before he is arrested, have any right to be told why he is a person under investigation?

3 In paragraph 1.51 of the SFO submissions to the Royal Commission on Criminal Justice, drafted before the House of Lords decision, the SFO said: 'More cases are anticipated where quick and decisive action needs to be taken and persons charged to prevent their absconding, and it is unacceptable for time to run out on the use of such an important weapon long before the conclusion of an inquiry.'

An analogy may be drawn with the position of a suspect who has been arrested, and who must, under the terms of the PACE Codes of Practice, be informed of 'the grounds for his arrest, as soon as practicable and in any case before [he] is then questioned about any offence'.[4] A person on whom a notice has been served is, after all, not a willing participant in an interview, which he is under some form of compulsion to attend. If he does not attend, or if he leaves during the interview, he can be charged with an offence under sub-s 2(13). However, he cannot be prevented, by arrest for that offence (which is not an arrestable offence), from leaving, nor can he be compelled to attend in the first place. Therefore, although there is an element of restriction of movement which is similar to the fact of arrest, the comparison cannot be taken as far as to assert that a person being interviewed under section 2(2) is under arrest.

The precise position, of course, depends on circumstances. If a notice requires co-operation 'forthwith', and the person under investigation is prevented from leaving the premises where the notice is served, he will be de facto detained. He will be in the same position as a person attending voluntarily at a police station who is then not allowed to leave, and therefore 'he must be informed at once that he is under arrest and brought before the custody officer'.[5] He must then be informed of the grounds of his arrest. It is, nevertheless, highly unlikely that such a situation would arise. Even if it did arise, and it was considered that a person had been technically or actually arrested, the duty under PACE to inform a person of the grounds of his arrest can be very restrictively construed. A person may be told that he is under arrest on suspicion of committing offences of fraud, and as long as the language used sufficiently describes the grounds of the arrest, the requirements of the 1984 Act will be met.[6] There is no duty to explain the precise areas which are under investigation, or the reason why such investigations are being carried out.

There is therefore no statutory support for the contention that a person under investigation is entitled to know what aspect of his affairs is being investigated. Can any other comparisons be made which might support a natural justice argument that a person is entitled, at any stage, but in particular in advance of an interview, to be told the grounds on which a notice has been issued? The powers under section 2 are modelled on those available to inspectors appointed by the Secretary of State for the Department of Trade and Industry under section 432 of the Companies Act 1985. No statutory requirement exists for giving notice of the areas to be covered in an interview with DTI inspectors, but the Department's Investigation Handbook provides this guidance:

> 'While it is not always easy to anticipate the line which an inquiry will take, and inspectors may on occasion want the reaction of a witness to unexpected questions, they may find their inquiries will be facilitated if a witness is given advance notice in general terms of the matters on which he is to be examined together with particulars of any documents which the inspectors require him to produce or propose to refer to him while examining him.'[7]

---

4   PACE Codes: C.3.4.
5   PACE Codes: C.3.15.
6   In *Abbassy v Metropolitan Police Comr* [1990] 1 All ER 193, Woolf LJ concluded that the formula used by Lord Simon in *Christie v Leachinsky* [1947] AC 573, [1947] 1 All ER 567 remained correct: there is no need for technical or precise language, provided that the accused knew why he had been arrested.
7   Appendix B paragraph 17.

It would nevertheless be difficult to argue from this that there is entitlement to advance notice of the areas the SFO is investigating.

It is, in theory, possible to challenge the validity of a notice issued under section 2(2). It might, for example, be defectively drafted, but if so it can easily be reissued in proper form. A more fundamental challenge to the propriety of issuing a notice requiring a person to answer questions is unlikely to succeed.[8] The fact that the section encompasses inquiries of anyone whom the Director 'has reason to believe has relevant information' provides an extremely wide discretion. Reference has already been made to the discretion of the Director to institute an inquiry in the first place, and the possibility of challenging that decision on grounds of reasonableness, but once a decision to investigate has been established as reasonable, use of the powers vested in the SFO by section 2 will, a priori, be reasonable so long as the person to whom the notice is addressed is either a person under investigation or has relevant information.

2.3 POWERS TO REQUISITION DOCUMENTS

2.3.1 Criminal Justice Act 1987 section 2(3)

Before he can exercise the powers under section 2(3), the Director must:

(a) have decided that he will investigate a case which he reasonably believes to involve a serious or complex fraud; and

(b) consider that there is good reason to use the section 2 powers for the purposes of investigating 'the affairs or any aspect of the affairs of any person'.

If those conditions are satisfied, he may use the provisions of sub-s 2(3). A written notice must be served on either the 'person under investigation' or on any other person:

> '. . . to produce at such place as may be specified in the notice and either forthwith or at such time as may be so specified any specified documents which appear to the Director to relate to any matter relevant to the investigation, or any documents of a specified description which appear to him so to relate.'

The notice will be in the same form as a notice under sub-s 2(2) (and may often be combined with it), but in respect of the description of the documents to be supplied, the notice will often contain a formula of words corresponding to the following:

> 'I also require you to produce to me the following documents which appear to me to relate to matters relevant to the investigation: all files, papers, documents relating to the persons under investigation.'

It may be questioned whether the use of such a formula is sufficiently specific to bring the notice within the ambit of sub-s 2(3).

2.3.2 Requirements of specificity

A comparison may be made with sub-s 434(1) of the Companies Act 1985, on which sub-s 2(3) is based, by virtue of which all past and present officers and

---

8 But see *R v Secretary of State for Trade, ex p Perestrello* [1981] QB 19 and Chapter 8.

agents of the company which is being investigated are under a duty 'to produce to the inspectors all documents of or relating to the company'. The Companies Act does not, therefore, impose any degree of specificity on the documents to be produced, other than that they are documents of or relating to the company. By contrast, the 1987 Act imposes a requirement of specificity, either in relation to specific documents or documents of a specified description.

In Committee, the Home Secretary was at pains to emphasise that the information demanded under the provisions of section 2 should be relevant:

> 'I use the word relevant advisedly because the Bill provides in clause 2(2) that the information has to be relevant and in clause 2(3) the matter has to be relevant. It is not a matter of "fishing expeditions" – of casting around in the hope that something might come up. The doctrine of relevance is clearly stated.'[9]

The relevance of a document and its identification as a specific document requiring production are clearly linked. A vague request for any document in the possession of a recipient of a notice, which relates to the affairs of a person or company under investigation, would not appear to meet the demands of sub-s 2(3).

In this context, a comparison with section 8 of PACE may be relevant, and in particular section 8(1)(b) which refers to 'material specified in the application which is likely to be of substantial value (whether by itself or together with other material) to the investigation of the offence'.[10]

2.3.3   The validity of a notice under section 2(3) after charge

In *R v Director of Serious Fraud, ex p Saunders*,[11] Saunders, former Chairman and Chief Executive of Guinness plc, argued that notices under section 2(3) served on Guinness were invalid because at the time of service Saunders had been charged with 40 offences arising out of or connected with the documents required by the notices to be produced, and therefore the Director could no longer as a matter of construction of section 1(3) of the 1987 Act be said to be investigating suspected offences by the applicant. The matter was complicated by the fact that in parallel civil proceedings in the Chancery Division by Guinness plc against Saunders and Thomas Ward, an undertaking had been given by Guinness that no disclosure would be made to any person of any information or documents disclosed or served by Saunders or his solicitors in the course of conducting the action, without leave of the court. Guinness had sought leave of the Court to be released from this undertaking, for the purpose of complying with the SFO's notice, but the court had refused.

The court did not accept that an investigation, within the meaning of section 1(3), came to an end when a suspect was charged, and on that main ground of relief the application failed. The court did not have to decide the second point, both because the notice had lapsed and because so long as the undertaking given to the Vice-Chancellor remained in force, Guinness had a reasonable excuse for failing to comply with any such notice. The court then went on to make a number of obiter observations. First, McNeill J referred to the

9 *Hansard* 13 January 1987, SC F col 67.
10 See also Chapter 8, section 3.4.
11 [1988] Crim LR 837.

relationship between PACE and the 1987 Act, and the requirement that SFO officers are bound by the PACE Codes of Practice as referred to above.[12]

Second, the judge stated that nothing in sections 8 or 9 of PACE prevented access to incriminating material, whether in the hands of the accused or a third party, and whether before or after charge.

The judge went on to point out that there were substantial and significant safeguards for a person under investigation, including section 31 of the Theft Act, the reasonable excuse provision under section 2(13) of the 1987 Act, and also section 2(8) of the Act.

Finally, the judge said:

'There is nothing in the wording of section 2 of the Criminal Justice Act 1987 which persuades us that the course taken in *A and B v HM Treasury* [1979] 1 WLR 1056 should be followed. Nothing excludes material obtained in the course of civil proceedings, even if disclosed under an order of the court. At this stage we merely express reservations. If the Vice-Chancellor releases Guinness from the undertaking, the point will have to be fully argued. It is clearly arguable that a person under investigation should not be compelled for purposes which might lead, or have led to criminal proceedings against him to disclose that which under civil process he has been obliged to disclose and which is, or may be, self-incriminatory. At this stage we are not prepared to say, as Mr Chadwick contended, that the safeguards alone are sufficient to permit a breach of the subject's constitutional rights. With this reservation, much of the material specified in the notice – and particularly that not in the hands of Guinness as a result of a court order – would be subject to production. The first decision, however, is left with the Vice-Chancellor. If he releases Guinness, then this court may have to decide the point on which we have expressed reservations. If he does not, the point does not arise in this case.'[13]

The point did not arise.

The judgment of McNeill J was referred to in *R v Director of the Serious Fraud Office, ex p Smith*,[14] where Nolan LJ said:

'Thus it is plain from these dicta, as well as from the ratio decidendi of the case, that the Divisional Court regarded the Director's powers under section 2 to obtain information and documents from third persons as remaining unimpaired after the person under investigation has been charged. Mr Collins reserves the right to challenge that proposition elsewhere (on behalf of Mr Smith). For our part we would regard it as unassailable. It would be astonishing if the Director's powers to require relevant information about suspected offences from third parties were brought to an end by the bringing of a charge against the person under investigation.'

2.3.4 Requirements to explain documents etc

By section 2(3)(a) of the Act, provision is made for the SFO to take copies, or extracts from, documents produced. Circumstances will dictate whether the SFO demands wholesale removal of all documents covered by the notice, and subsequent retention, or whether they indicate to the recipient of the notice the

---

12 Section 2.2.5
13 *R v Director of Serious Fraud, ex p Saunders* [1988] Crim LR 837 (no full report of this case has been published).
14 [1992] 1 All ER 730.

documents which they are interested in. It will be a matter of negotiation (taking into account, for example, the balance of convenience), who carries out the copying, but it is at the expense of the SFO. The SFO is entitled to retain all the originals of documents removed, and there is no obligation in the Act requiring them to return documents, or to provide copies.[15] Originals of documents will normally be retained until the conclusion of criminal proceedings.

Section 2(3) also contains provisions permitting the SFO to 'require the person producing [documents] to provide an explanation of them'; or 'if any such documents are not produced, the Director may require the person who was required to produce them to state, to the best of his knowledge and belief, where they are'.

These requirements derive from section 447(5) of the Companies Act 1985, and perhaps suggest a recognition of the Roskill Committee recommendation concerning police powers.[16] The exercise of the requirement to provide an explanation of a document would presumably occur at the time of seizure, since any later questioning on the subject could be conducted under section 2(2); the nature of the explanation is not restricted by the words of the statute, but in practice it seems unlikely that, during a search, much detailed questioning will take place.

2.3.5   Restrictions on the exercise of section 2 powers

There are two restrictions on the powers provided in section 2(2) and (3).

2.3.5(a)   Legal professional privilege

Section 2(9) provides that:

> '. . . a person shall not under this section be required to disclose any information or produce any document which he would be entitled to refuse to disclose or produce on grounds of legal professional privilege in proceedings in the High Court, except that a lawyer may be required to furnish the name and address of his Client.'

In practicable terms, claiming legal professional privilege can pose problems. Where the SFO is proposing to remove a mass of material, in which it is believed that there are documents which would be protected by section 2(9) of the Act, it should be possible to insist that all the material taken should be sealed, pending an examination of it by lawyers representing the person claiming privilege, and the removal of privileged documents.

In addition, there is no easy way to arbitrate a claim for privilege, at least until the preparatory hearings. The SFO, in submissions to the Runciman Committee, has suggested:

> 'The doctrine of legal professional privilege should be redefined with a view to preventing its use in dubious/artificial situations to prevent the investigation of crime; some practical mechanism is required whereby the person claiming privilege can substantiate it before a court or arbiter.'

---

15 Compare, for example, section 21 of PACE. In section 20CC of the Taxes Management Act 1970 the provision of copies of documents seized by the Inland Revenue in raids carried out under section 70 of the Act is also allowed for.

16 Roskill Report, paragraph 2.62.

The extent to which claims of privilege are dubiously claimed is not apparent, but the very possibility of making a claim in relation to unspecified documents among filing cabinets full of documents creates a serious impediment to the SFO and can cause delay.

The question of whether to claim or waive privilege is a matter which has to be assessed in each individual case. It may only be observed that in a situation where the authorities have considerable and intrusive powers which, as have frequently been stated, infringe the normal rules relating to civil liberties, an individual cannot be criticised for taking advantage of protection which is offered him by statute. It should also be noted, as discussed below, that if privilege is at any stage waived, it cannot subsequently be maintained. Therefore, decisions made about privilege at an early stage of an investigation are of significance.

The general principle of legal professional privilege is that in civil and criminal cases, confidential communications passing between a client and his legal adviser need not be given in evidence by the client, and without the client's consent may not be given in evidence by the legal adviser in judicial proceedings if made either:

(a) to enable the client to obtain, or the adviser to give legal advice;
(b) with reference to litigation that is actively taking place, or was in the contemplation of the client.

Paragraph (b) extends to protecting communications passing between the legal adviser or the client and third parties, if made for the purpose of pending or contemplated litigation. Communications relating to the preparation of a written statement are privileged.

The privilege extends to all communications relating to the normal legal business of a solicitor. There are a number of exceptions to the general principle as stated above, which permit evidence to be given of communications between client and solicitor in evidence notwithstanding that in cases (a) and (c) below the client wishes to assert privilege.

(a) Where legal professional privilege has been waived by the client.
(b) Where the communication has been made in order to facilitate crime or fraud. Accordingly, if a client seeks advice intended to guide him in commission of a crime or fraud, the communication between the client and the legal adviser is not privileged and the adviser may be compelled to disclose the contents of the communication. This principle is also reflected in section 10(2) of the Police and Criminal Evidence Act 1984 which provides that, in relation to the Act's powers of entry, search and seizure, items held with the intention of furthering a criminal purpose are not deemed to be items subject to privilege and are therefore vulnerable to seizure and use as evidence, though in the case of legal material, this would only be on the authority of a circuit judge. This exception applies even where the items are held innocently by the legal advisor.[17]

It should be emphasised that section 10 of PACE is freestanding in relation to police inquiries.[18] Where the SFO investigates, it must rely on section 2(9) which incorporates the common law position (of which the *Cox and Railton* decision is a part).

17 *R v Cox and Railton* (1884) 14 QBD 153 and *Banque Keyser Ullmann SA v Skandia (UK) Insurance Co Ltd* [1986] 1 Lloyd's Rep 336, CA.
18 See Chapter 5, section 2.4.3.

(c) Where information tends to establish the innocence of the defendant in criminal proceedings (see *R v Barton*[19] and *R v Ataou*[20]).

The question of waiver of privilege was raised in *R v NatWest Investment Bank & Others*[1] as a preliminary issue, in the context of whether documents which had been released to inspectors appointed by the Secretary of State for the Department of Trade and Industry under a limited waiver of privilege could subsequently be the subject of a claim for privilege in criminal proceedings. The trial judge, McKinnon J, ruled that the waiver of privilege to the inspectors could not be limited to the immediate purposes of the inspection carried out under section 432 of Companies Act 1985. He said that disclosure of the four documents about which argument was addressed, 'carried with it a waiver of legal professional privilege for all purposes of the inspectors' investigations, including the provision of the documents to the relevant prosecuting authority via the Secretary of State'. He accepted the argument that the scheme of Part XIV of the Companies Act 1985 meant that inspectors were entirely free to pass documents to the Secretary of State and the Secretary of State could pass them on to the relevant prosecuting authority. He found that that was not a purpose collateral to the purposes of the DTI inspectors' investigation. This applied even though it was argued that the waiver to the inspectors was made for the purposes of assisting the inspectors in their investigation and that such a waiver was not a waiver for all purposes.

The decision is important in the context of criminal proceedings following on from a DTI inspection, but may not have a wider application bearing in mind that the judge's ruling was founded on connected purposes. In addition, it was pointed out in the course of argument that, following a refusal to waive privilege, one of the inspectors expressed his concern that documents had been withheld, and he indicated that that was regarded by him as a most serious matter, which was not consistent with the co-operation being provided generally to the inspectors. Arguments that it was in the public interest that documents should be made available to inspectors without the threat that they would be passed on to other authorities did not succeed. The judge ruled:

> 'I reject the notion that there is any public interest in DTI inspectors having access to privileged documents (otherwise relevant and admissible in criminal proceedings) of which no effective use could be made in those criminal proceedings. There is no public policy consideration which warrants or would protect disclosure of documents to DTI inspectors carrying with it a purported waiver of legal professional privilege limited to certain unspecified purposes or powers of the inspectors in carrying out their investigation. If I am wrong about that then any such public policy consideration is clearly overridden by the public interest in the apprehension and prosecution of those who practise fraud upon the public. I would doubt, although the point does not arise for decision, that it would be practicable to draft, or that the law would give effect to, some form of waiver of legal professional privilege expressly limited to specified purposes or powers of the DTI inspectors in carrying out their investigations, so as to prevent the use of the 'disclosed' documents in criminal proceedings. Nor I suspect would DTI inspectors agree to 'disclosure' of privileged documents on any such footing (see section 437(1A).)'[2]

19 [1972] 2 All ER 1192, [1973] 1 WLR 115.
20 [1988] QB 798, [1988] 2 All ER 321, CA.
1   23 January 1991, unreported. Day 44 of Preparatory Hearings.
2   Ibid, pages 23–24.

The judge considered whether the fact that a party might be criticised for refusing to co-operate with inspectors by maintaining a claim to legal professional privilege, had any effect upon the matter, in particular, in connection with section 78 of PACE. He ruled that there was no unfairness in the admission into evidence of the documents, and implicitly, that there was no unfairness in the way they had been obtained.

2.3.5(b) Banking confidentiality

Section 2(10) provides that:

'. . . a person shall not under this section be required to disclose information or produce a document in respect of which he owes an obligation of confidence by virtue of carrying on any banking business unless:
(a) the person to whom the obligation of confidence is owed consents to the disclosure or production; or
(b) the Director has authorised the making of the requirement, or if it is impracticable for him to act personally, a member of the Serious Fraud Office designated by him for the purposes of this subsection has done so.'

A notice under section 2 to a bank must therefore be signed by the Director or his delegate. This discretion in the Director's hands can be compared with the provisions relating to access to special procedure material in PACE under which an application to a circuit judge must be made, under certain stringent conditions, before access to banking records is permitted.[3] The exercise of a judicial power is granted to the executive, and, in addition, to an official who has a direct interest in the matter. It is a responsibility which the Director of the SFO exercises with care, according to the third annual report of the SFO:

'All notices issued to banks under section 2(10) are signed by me personally . . . Before they are signed, the person requesting such a notice has to justify his request in writing.'[4]

2.3.6 Compliance with section 2(3)

Section 2(13)–(17) provides that refusal to comply with any requirements imposed by section 2, false compliance with such requirements, or the falsification, concealment, destruction or other disposal of documents relevant to an investigation are offences for which the maximum sentence is two years' imprisonment.

2.4 POWERS OF SEARCH AND SEIZURE

Section 2(4)–(7) contains provisions relating to the issue of a warrant by a justice of the peace for the search of any premises. These provisions are included to enable the SFO to back up with force, if necessary, the requirement to provide documents in section 2(3), where either that requirement is not being complied with or is not likely to be complied with. A member of the SFO makes the application, but a police officer, accompanied by an appropriate

---

3 See Chapter 5, section 2.4.2. In the Serious Fraud Office Annual Report 1990–91 it is revealed that 45% of section 2 notices are directed at banks.
4 Ibid, paragraph 6.6.

person, executes the warrant. This is the only power granted to a police officer by the Act.

In Committee the Home Office minister explained the position:

> 'Warrants to search for and seize documents will be applied for by the SFO but will, if granted, be executed by the Police . . . in executing such warrants the Police will be subject to the provisions of PACE but especially to section 16 which governs how search warrants will be executed. It stipulates that warrants must be used at a reasonable hour and that the Police must show the proper authority before entering premises . . . we want to make it clear beyond peradventure that that is not intended to provide a loophole whereby the Police can be invested with Department of Trade and Industry inspectors' powers that they could exercise outside the provisions of PACE. I state that clearly now because I hope to provide the reassurance that opposition members seek. We are not providing a way for the Police to escape either the obligations of PACE or the requirements sought by the new clauses. Rather we recognise that the work of DTI inspectors will be an essential element in the SFO.'[5]

A warrant may be applied for in respect of any documents, and no restrictions are provided for in respect of excluded material, personal records, journalistic material, or special procedure material, as defined in PACE, except in respect of banking documents within the terms of section 2(10). The Home Office minister explained in Committee that the restrictions provided by PACE were not resiled from:

> 'However, we are now considering a specialised group of highly qualified investigators and prosecutors. They will be confined by clause 1(3) which will be embellished by the amended clause 2, to serious or complex fraud and will work in a way which is much more akin to Department of Trade and Industry inspectors than to the Police. That is important because, if the aim of the Serious Fraud Office is to facilitate the investigation of serious fraud by Department of Trade and Industry inspectors, it would not make sense to shackle them any further as they regulate the Companies Act provisions to which we all attach much importance.'[6]

3   DISCLOSURE OF INFORMATION

The SFO has a wide power, under section 3 of the 1987 Act, to receive and divulge information obtained from a variety of sources.

In relation to information passed by the Inland Revenue to the SFO, which is covered by an obligation of secrecy under section 6 and Sch 1 of the Taxes Management Act 1970, there are certain restrictions, the effect of which is that such information may only be used for the purposes of prosecuting Revenue offences. Information may also be passed on by the SFO to the Crown Prosecution Service or the Director of Public Prosecutions for Northern Ireland, for these purposes.

The situation is complicated by section 3(2), by which information originally obtained in connection with a Revenue offence, but where subsequently no such offence is charged, can be used by the SFO. The precise boundaries of this facility for exchanging information will remain obscure, because it will no

5   *Hansard* 15 January 1987, SC F, col 99.
6   Ibid, col 98.

doubt be possible for the Inland Revenue to maintain that, at the time of the exchange of information, it was investigating Revenue offences. As was pointed out in Committee, most unlawful acquisitions of money will involve a failure to make proper disclosure to the Inland Revenue.

By section 3(3), information which is subject to an obligation of secrecy imposed by any legislation other than the Taxes Management Act 1970 may be disclosed to a member of the SFO. The section is permissive rather than mandatory. Information thus obtained by the SFO may be recycled for the purposes of any prosecution in England and Wales, but only by a member of the office who is designated by the Director 'for the purposes of this subsection'.

This provision was considered in *Re Arrows*.[7] Hoffmann J held that the SFO could be restricted in its demand for information for a fraud investigation to the extent that its right is outweighed by an overriding public interest in secrecy. The case involved an inquiry by the SFO into the affairs of Arrows Ltd and a Mr Naviede. At the same time as the SFO were investigating, liquidators were appointed. They used their powers under section 236 of the Insolvency Act 1986 to apply to the court for an order that Mr Naviede be examined on the company's affairs. Their application which was made ex parte requested the court to insert a direction that the written record of Mr Naviede's examination was not to be disclosed to the SFO. Their reason for seeking this direction was that they did not wish Mr Naviede to be inhibited in the answers he gave to them by the prospect that his evidence would be used against him in subsequent criminal proceedings.

The SFO argued that section 3(3) of the Act overrode every obligation of secrecy imposed under any enactment, and therefore r 9.5 of the Insolvency Rules 1986, which provided that the written record of an examination should not be open to inspection by anyone other than the applicant for the section 236 order, or any person who could have applied for such an order, was ineffective. Hoffmann J ruled that section 3(3) dealt with statutory obligations of secrecy, but not with heads of public policy which might justify non-disclosure. On considering the various heads of public policy, such as national security and administration of central government, which had been held to justify non-disclosure even for the purposes of justice, he decided that it was impossible that the only public interest Parliament thought capable of taking precedence over fraud investigation was the collection of revenue. Therefore a reasonable excuse under section 2(13) of the 1987 Act for refusing to answer questions could include the heads of public policy, and the doctrine of public policy permitted a balance to be struck between the public interest in preserving secrecy and the public interest in the investigation of fraud.

Section 3(5) and (6) permits the disclosure of information in certain specified circumstances to a variety of authorities.

---

7 [1992] 2 WLR 923, [1992] BCLC 126.

CHAPTER 3
Transfer of cases to the Crown Court

1.1 INTRODUCTION: THE ROSKILL APPROACH

The Roskill Committee[1] recommended that a designated prosecuting authority should be permitted to dispense with committal proceedings by the issue of a 'transfer certificate'. It viewed this proposal as an interim measure for fraud cases pending the government's decision on the proposals of the Royal Commission on Criminal Procedure[2] to abolish committal proceedings generally in criminal cases.[3] To date, the Royal Commission's proposals have not been acted upon. The Roskill Committee's proposals, however, have been implemented in sections 4 to 6 of the Criminal Justice Act 1987 for serious fraud cases but with some significant changes.

Roskill had concluded, after a brief historical survey, that the original purpose of committal proceedings – to protect a defendant against charges initiated by the police which might be capricious or oppressive – had been superseded by the establishment of the Crown Prosecution Service. The Committee thought that:

> 'There are serious deficiencies in a procedure which allows abuse by defendants to go largely unchecked; which is the cause of unacceptable delays and expense; which involves unnecessary duplication of effort; and which produces little by way of compensating advantages for the administration of justice.'[4]

Lay magistrates were not the appropriate tribunal to determine whether a prima facie case of serious fraud existed. If fraud cases were to be brought to trial quickly and efficiently, an alternative means had to be devised to enable the defendant to be brought before the Crown Court, but which at the same time preserved a defendant's right to submit that the evidence was insufficient to put him on his trial.

It was proposed, therefore, that certain prosecuting authorities should have power, before the start of committal proceedings, to issue a 'transfer certificate' removing the case to the Crown Court. The transfer certificate could not be issued after committal proceedings had begun, and it should not be subject to any form of appeal.[5] After transfer, the defendant would have the right to apply to the Crown Court for dismissal of the case on the ground that there

---

1 Fraud Trials Committee Report, para 4. 33.
2 Report of the Royal Commission on Criminal Procedure (1981) Cmd 8092, paras 8.24-31.
3 Ibid, para 4.19 and 4.33–4.36.
4 Ibid, para 4.31.
5 Fraud Trials Committee Report: para 4.39.

was insufficient evidence against him. This right would enable a defendant, in an appropriate case, to obtain his discharge without the trauma and expense of waiting until the close of the prosecution case at trial. However, the legislation would have to ensure that the difficulties previously encountered in committal proceedings before magistrates were not shipped wholesale to the Crown Court. It would defeat the object of the exercise if the defendant were to be allowed to insist on calling the witnesses and 'embark on a prolonged hearing of issues which should properly be examined at the trial stage'.[6] Roskill accepted, however, the legitimate defence need, in some cases, to cross-examine witnesses at the hearing of an application to discharge.

The application to discharge was, therefore, to be in the nature of a compromise. There would not be unlimited scope for the defendant to cross-examine each witness; oral evidence should only be heard with the leave of the judge. Such leave should be refused where the defence were pursuing a fishing expedition or were merely seeking a 'dress rehearsal' of the evidence. The defendant would have to state in advance his grounds for wanting to cross-examine a prosecution witness and, if appropriate, would have to produce an affidavit spelling out the evidence leading him to believe that the witness was either unreliable or untruthful. Applications for discharge would only succeed if the judge, applying the *Galbraith*[7] test, was satisfied that there was no case to answer. Discharge should amount to an acquittal.[8]

The procedure by which a defendant found himself before the Crown Court was, therefore, to be subject to radical change under which a defendant would be brought before the Crown Court as the result of an executive act, which would be difficult to challenge and made without representation, in contradistinction to a judicial decision reached in committal proceedings after the hearing of evidence and representations[9] as to whether there was a prima facie case and challengeable, in certain circumstances, by a judicial review. In order to dispel some of the concern this proposal was likely to arouse, Roskill added that counsel should be involved at an early stage in the preparation of the case. Counsel would participate in the decision as to transfer and his signature should be added to the transfer certificate.

The transfer provisions are now found in sections 4 to 6 of the Criminal Justice Act 1987 (as amended by section 144 of the Criminal Justice Act 1988) and are supplemented by the:

(a) Criminal Justice Act 1987 (Notice of Transfer) Regulations 1988, SI 1988/1691;
(b) Criminal Justice Act 1987 (Dismissal of Transferred Charges) Rules, SI 1987/1695;
(c) Magistrates' Courts (Notices of Transfer) Rules 1988 SI 1988/1701.

The legislative provisions excited little dispute in principle in the Committee debates, government and opposition each endeavouring to out-do the other in showing their concern for the need to combat fraud and ensure that its perpetrators were brought to justice swiftly and effectively.

---

6 Fraud Trials Committee Report, para 4.47.
7 *R v Galbraith* [1981] 2 All ER 1060, [1981] 1 WLR 1039, CA.
8 The prosecution could not, therefore reinstitute proceedings against that defendant for that offence either by recharging him or by preferring a Voluntary Bill of Indictment. Any attempt to do so would be met with a plea of autrefois acquit.
9 Depending on whether the committal was pursuant to section 6(1) or section 6(2) of the Magistrates' Courts Act 1980.

The virtual abolition of committal proceedings in serious fraud cases is, without doubt, a welcome development. The transfer provisions provide a quicker and potentially more effective system of bringing a case to the Crown Court than committal proceedings. The hearing before magistrates of a serious or complex fraud is rarely, if ever, satisfactory and is time-consuming for already heavily-burdened courts. In so far as the abolition of committal proceedings involved any loss of rights by defendants, the Act sought to include new compensating rights before the Crown Court.

1.2   THE POWER TO SERVE A NOTICE OF TRANSFER

The power to serve a Notice of Transfer is given to the authorities 'designated' in section 4(2) of the Criminal Justice Act 1987. These are:

(a) the Director of Public Prosecutions;
(b) the Director of the Serious Fraud Office;
(c) the Commissioners of Inland Revenue;
(d) the Commissioners of Customs and Excise; and
(e) the Secretary of State.

The provisions accordingly extend to a wider range of investigations and offences than those which are the subject of investigation by the Serious Fraud Office. A suggestion in Committee that transfer should be limited to cases 'following investigation by the Serious Fraud Office' was rejected on the ground that the procedure was appropriate for any offence meeting the criteria in section 4(1) of the Act, even if prosecuted by other authorities. In particular, it was felt that the procedure should be available to HM Customs and Excise when prosecuting complex VAT frauds and to the Inland Revenue.

The inclusion of the 'Secretary of State' led to some concern that, as no particular Secretary of State had been specified, any member of the Executive would have power to take a decision which hitherto had rested with the judiciary and that either the Secretary of State or one designated authority could overrule the decision of another. The concern was enhanced by the provisions of section 5 of, and Schedule 1 to, the Interpretation Act 1978 which defines Secretary of State as any one of Her Majesty's Principal Secretaries of State. The context of the inquiry will, in practice, indicate which of the Secretaries of State, in cases not handled by the usual prosecuting authorities, is the most appropriate and the legislation's sponsors gave assurances that it was intended to mean only that Secretary of State whose Department was conducting the relevant prosecution.[10] Experience showed that this would, in most cases, be the Department of Trade and Industry. It was accepted that other departments likely to take responsibility for the conduct of investigation and prosecution of fraud would be the Department of Social Security and the Department of Employment. Only the designated authority responsible for the conduct of the investigation would take the decision, and that decision would not be overruled by any other designated authority.

The decision would be taken by the 'authority or by one of such authority's officers acting on the authority's behalf.' Although in practice experienced counsel will be retained to advise at an early stage of the prosecution, the

10 *Hansard* SC F (20 January 1987), col 194.

proposal in the Fraud Trials Committee Report[11] that the transfer notice should bear counsel's signature has not been implemented. In theory the case could be handled by the designated authority's representative entirely. No definition is provided as to the qualification or experience that such an officer should hold before he may be permitted to exercise the power.

The government anticipated that decisions to prosecute would, following the practice adopted in customs and revenue cases, be taken by lawyers who would not have been involved, for the most part, in the day-to-day investigation of the offence.[12] The SFO has adopted the 'Case Controller'[13] system under which a lawyer of at least Grade 6 rank advises the investigators. The Case Controller, who does not take part in practice in the investigation process nor conducts interviews under section 2, will take the decision to transfer usually after taking counsel's advice.

2 THE CRITERIA FOR TRANSFER

2.1 General

The criteria for the exercise of the power are contained in section 4(1) of the Criminal Justice Act 1987 and are that:

(a) a person has been charged with an indictable offence;
(b) the authority or its officer must be of the opinion that the evidence of the offence charged would be sufficient for the person charged to be committed for trial;
(c) the authority or its officer must be of the opinion that the evidence reveals a case of fraud of such seriousness and complexity that it is appropriate that the management of the case should, without delay, be taken over by the Crown Court.

When the authority or its officer gives the magistrates' court a notice certifying its opinion as to (b) and (c) above, the functions of the magistrates' court cease except as regards bail, making witness orders and granting legal aid. The notice must be given before the magistrates begin to inquire into the case as examining justices. This follows a recommendation of the Roskill Committee and means that the prosecutor may not simply abandon live committal proceedings, which have become difficult or protracted, by the issue of a transfer notice. In such situations an application for a Voluntary Bill of Indictment will remain an option open to him. If the inquiry has not yet begun and the prosecution assure the magistrates in open court that it intends to issue a notice of transfer, the court may lawfully adjourn the mode of trial proceedings although all parties are ready to proceed.[14]

2.2 Sufficient evidence for committal

Section 4(1) gives much operational discretion to the authority in deciding whether to issue a Notice of Transfer. The opinion must, of course, be formed

11 Fraud Trials Committee Report: ibid at para 4.40.
12 *Hansard* SC F (16 December 1986), col 35.
13 See Chapter 2 para 1.1.
14 *R v Stevenage Justices, ex p Johl* (1989) Times, 1 December.

in good faith and upon reasonable grounds,[15] though there is no requirement that reasons for the decision be disclosed. No guidance is given as to the test to be applied in deciding, for the purposes of section 4(1)(b)(i), whether the evidence would be sufficient for the person charged to be committed for trial. The reference to 'committal' is intended to lead the authority to apply the same test as an examining magistrate if the case had proceeded by way of committal proceedings, which requires the authority to be of the opinion that the evidence is sufficient to put the accused on trial by jury.[16] Section 4(1)(b)(i) affords an opportunity, indeed a requirement, for the prosecutor to step back from the investigation and take a quasi-judicial decision that the evidence reaches the appropriate standard. It is open to debate whether this is a realistic expectation. The point was made in Committee that the exercise of setting up the SFO was retrograde in respect of the principle of separation of powers which had led to the establishment of the CPS. The aim of section 4(1)(b)(i) was clearly to satisfy the concern that cases should not, despite the safeguard provided in section 6, find their way to the Crown Court without at least some elementary filtering and review exercise aimed at determining whether there is a sufficient case.[17] Given that it is usually the authority that has decided to charge the accused, on the basis that there is evidence sufficient to warrant a trial and that the authority will, in practice, have regard to the criteria in section 6, the criteria in section 4(1)(b)(i) might be thought otiose.

2.3   Case management considerations

Section 4(1)(b)(ii) defines the type of case appropriate for transfer. The Act does not provide a definition of 'serious or complex' fraud and it is left to the discretion of the designated authority as to whether any given case falls within this category.[18] Cases handled by the Serious Fraud Office will, a fortiori, fall within the definition, but what is the significance of the expression 'fraud of *such* seriousness *and* complexity'? Is every fraud investigated by the Serious Fraud Office automatically a candidate for transfer?[19] Or are there cases which, though 'serious or complex' and rightly within the bailiwick of the SFO, are none the less not appropriate for the transfer procedure? Section 4(1)(b)(ii) requires not just that the case be serious or complex, but that, by reason of its seriousness *and* complexity, it is appropriate that its *management* should, *without delay*, be taken over by the Crown Court. The reason leading to the view that the case should be taken over by the Crown Court must relate to the seriousness and complexity of the case, and not to any external factor. Statistics contained in the Serious Fraud Office Annual Report 1990–91[20] show that the SFO does not assume that all of its cases are suitable for the transfer procedure. Of the 25 SFO cases sent to the Crown Court in that year, 14 were

---

15 *Padfield v Minister of Agriculture, Fisheries and Food* [1968] AC 997, HL. As to the principles of administrative law generally governing the exercise of executive discretion, see Wade *Administrative Law* (6th edn) Part IV.

16 Magistrates' Courts Act 1980 section 6(1).

17 See *Hansard* SC F (20 January 1987), col 194.

18 See Chapter 2 section 1.3.

19 In its evidence to the Royal Commission on criminal justice, the SFO has stated that the procedure should be available in all cases of serious or complex fraud and has drawn attention to the inconsistency between sections 1(3) and 4(3)(b)(ii).

20 Serious Fraud Office Annual Report 1990–91, para 8.1.

committed for trial under section 6 of the Magistrates' Courts Act 1980. What, then, are the factors which would justify the conclusion that the case is of such seriousness and complexity that the Crown Court should, without delay, take over the management of the case? The designated authority must look, in particular, at what it is about the management of a particular case which requires its move to the Crown Court without delay rather than awaiting committal followed by an early pre-trial review in the Crown Court. The intricacy of the facts; the number of defendants; the number of charges, witnesses and documents; the recognition that the case will involve difficult questions of law which, in the interest of all, require an urgent and authoritative answer – all are among the considerations appropriate to be taken into account. Concerns relating to listing delays, length of hearing and the ability of a magistrates' court to handle the case will also influence the decision, and were the concerns at the forefront of the minds of the Roskill Committee in recommending the transfer procedure. The 'burden of proof', if such it is, presumably rests with showing that the case falls within the 'transfer' provisions; if the designated authority is in any doubt, the case should remain to be dealt with in the usual way. The defence may wish the proceedings to be made the subject of transfer whereas the designated authority might have formed the view that the statutory criteria for transfer have not been met. Presumably section 4(3)[1] extends to a decision *not* to give Notice of Transfer and will bar an attempt to compel an attempt by mandamus to force the prosecutor into the transfer procedure rather than committal proceedings.

The legislation does at least try to preserve more fraud cases for committal proceedings than the Roskill Committee appear to have intended. Commenting on which cases would be appropriate for the new procedure, the Committee stated:

> '. . . the new procedure should be made available for use at the option of the prosecution alone as an alternative to committal proceedings in any fraud case where they are of the opinion that it is appropriate to proceed. We do not think it is necessary or desirable to define the class of fraud case to which it should apply nor to specify the criteria by which its suitability is to be determined in any particular case. Cases where the new procedure would be particularly appropriate are likely to be serious or complex fraud cases and especially those where delay is threatened by the prospect of protracted committal proceedings, but it need not be restricted to such cases. It should be available in respect of offences triable only on indictment and offences triable either way.'

The tests in section 4 purport to restrict the designated authority's discretion to an extent not advocated by Roskill.

3 CHALLENGING TRANSFER

Section 4(3) of the Criminal Justice Act 1987 provides that the designated authority's decision[2] to give notice of transfer shall not be subject to appeal or liable to be questioned in any court. The Roskill Committee[3] had considered

---

1 See section 3 below.
2 It has been argued that section 4(3) does not exclude appeal as regards the contents of such a notice: see the commentary on the Criminal Justice Act 1987 in Current Law Statutes.
3 Fraud Trials Committee Report, para 4.39.

whether some form of appeal or judicial review should be available to enable a defendant to argue that the ordinary committal procedure should be followed. It reached the firm conclusion that rights of appeal would provide an opportunity for delay in the proceedings, and undermine the main benefit of the transfer procedure.

Ouster clauses in the nature of section 4(3) are not a new feature of statutes giving executive power, and there is a welter of case law reflecting a cat-and-mouse struggle between a determined executive anxious to ensure that its decisions are not open to review, and a judiciary equally determined not to be ousted.[4] Set in the context of a responsible prosecuting authority taking decisions according to the criteria in section 4, the mischief at which the new procedure is aimed, the need for finality and the right to apply to the court to dismiss a charge under section 6, the ouster clause is arguably more defensible in the Criminal Justice Act 1987 than in other areas and it may well be that the courts will show themselves more ready to accept section 4(3) than they have been to accept similar clauses in other legislation. Clauses, for example, restricting the right to bring civil proceedings for anything done in the absence of bad faith or negligence have been held not to exclude the right to bring an action for judicial review.[5] Similarly, a statutory provision that a decision 'shall be final' has been held to prevent an appeal, but not to bar an application for judicial review,[6] thus allowing the court to examine the legality and vires of an administrative act even though an appeal on the merits is barred. Even a clause forbidding certiorari has been held only to bar applications brought on the basis of error on the record and has not excluded challenge on the basis of error of jurisdiction. The first limb of section 4(3) would not, therefore, bar an application for judicial review in any form. A 'decision' within section 4(3) must be a decision properly reached, both procedurally and on correct grounds. This raises the question as to what is the procedure appropriate to making a decision under section 4. Is there any entitlement, for example, for the defendant to make representations and, if so, what information is he entitled to before these representations are made? The Act does not provide a right to make representations before a transfer decision is made, though that fact has not prevented the courts imposing certain minimum procedural safeguards where executive decisions under other legislation affect the rights or legitimate expectation of those whom the decision affects. It seems unlikely that the courts, given the rights available to a defendant following on from a section 4 decision, will exhibit much interest in imposing any additional procedural hurdles.

The second limb of section 4(3) – 'shall not be . . . liable to be questioned in any court', – though appearing to exclude review completely will not oust the power of the courts to review acts done in excess of jurisdiction or where the decision is otherwise a nullity. In *Anisminic v Foreign Compensation Commission*[7] the House of Lords had to construe section 4(4) of the Foreign Compensation Act 1950 which provided that a determination of the Commission 'shall not be called in question in any court of law'. The House held that such a clause did not bar intervention by the court where the

---

4   For a discussion of ouster clauses see: HWR Wade: *Administrative Law* (6th edn) at p 727; de Smith: *Judicial Review of Administrative Action* (4th edn) at p 199.
5   See for example *R v Medical Appeal Tribunal, ex p Gilmore* [1957] 1 QB 574, [1957] 2 WLR 498.
6   Ibid at 585.
7   [1969] 2 AC 147, [1969] 1 All ER 208.

purported determination was made in excess of jurisdiction or a nullity. If, Lord Reid stated, you seek to show that a determination is a nullity, you are not questioning the purported determination – you are maintaining that it does not exist as a determination. There is nothing, in effect, to be questioned. Lord Reid continued:

'Statutory provisions which seek to limit the ordinary jurisdiction of the court have a long history. No case has been cited in which any other form of words limiting the jurisdiction of the court has been held to protect a nullity. If the draftsman or Parliament had intended to introduce a new kind of ouster clause so as to prevent any inquiry even as to whether the document relied on was a forgery, I would have expected to find something much more specific than the bald statement that a determination shall not be called in question in any court of law. Undoubtedly such a provision protects every determination which is not a nullity. But I do not think that it is necessary or even reasonable to construe the word 'determination' as including everything which purports to be a determination but which is in fact no determination at all. And there are no degrees of nullity. There are a number of reasons why the law will hold a purported decision to be a nullity. I do not see how it could be said that such a provision protects some kind of nullity but not others: if that were intended it would be easy to say so.'

Having concluded that a 'shall not be questioned' clause will not bar intervention in cases of excess of jurisdiction, the House examined what would render a determination null.

'It has sometimes been said that it is only where a tribunal acts without jurisdiction that its decision is a nullity. But in such cases the word 'jurisdiction' has been used in a very wide sense, and I have come to the conclusion that it is better not to use the term except in the narrow and original sense of the tribunal being entitled to enter on the inquiry in question. But there are many cases where, although the tribunal had jurisdiction to enter on the inquiry, it has done or failed to do something in the course of the inquiry which is of such a nature that its decision is a nullity. It may have given its decision in bad faith. It may have made a decision which it had no power to make. It may have failed in the course of the inquiry to comply with the requirements of natural justice. It may in perfect good faith have misconstrued the provisions giving it power to act so that it failed to deal with the question remitted to it. It may have refused to take into account something which it was required to take into account. Or it may have based its decision on some matter which, under the provisions setting it up, it had no right to take into account. I do not intend this list to be exhaustive. But if it decides a question remitted to it for decision without committing any of these errors it is as much entitled to decide that question wrongly as it is to decide it rightly.'

The majority of the House held that misconstruction of the Order in Council relevant to the Commission's determination amounted to an error of jurisdiction in which the court could intervene to put right. As Lord Wilberforce said:

'What would be the purpose of defining by statute the limit of a tribunal's powers if, by means of a clause inserted in the instrument of definition, those limits could be safely passed?'

The only effect of sections such as section 4(3), in the light of *Anisminic*, is to prevent an application for judicial review for errors falling within jurisdiction. A decision taken in bad faith or in misconstruing its powers, or in breach of the rules of natural justice (if they apply), would not count as a decision for the purpose of section 4(3). The *Anisminic* decision has been reaffirmed[8] and has led to the comment that such clauses, in the context of decisions of tribunals, are now totally ineffective: every error of law becomes one jurisdiction; every error of fact, if not jurisdictional, is unreviewable anyway.[9]

'No appeal' clauses are not new to criminal statutes and the same approach has been adopted. In considering section 40(1) of the Powers of Criminal Court Act 1973, which provides that no appeal lies from the making of a criminal bankruptcy order, Lord Scarman held that the prohibition only applied to an appeal 'on the merits' and did not bar an appeal from a sentence which the court had no power to pass.[10]

Similarly, section 41(3) of the Criminal Justice Act 1988 provides that a magistrate's decision to commit certain offences for trial shall not be subject to appeal or liable to be questioned in any court. The Court of Appeal in *R v Miall*[11] held that appeal would not be barred where the magistrates' court reached a decision for which there was no legal basis and which had therefore been made in excess of jurisdiction.

Section 4(3) wraps up a 'no appeal' and 'shall not be questioned' clause in one subsection.[12] There seems no logical reason why the limitations in each clause individually should not also apply when they are found together within the same subsection,[13] nor why Parliament, in re-enacting clauses which have been subjected to exhaustive judicial scrutiny and decision, should not be taken to have accepted the judicial interpretation placed upon them. In the aftermath of the *Anisminic* case, the government proposed a broader ouster clause enabling the Foreign Compensation Commission to interpret the Orders in Council authoritatively for itself. The proposal was dropped in the face of heavy opposition both in and out of Parliament and was replaced with a right of appeal on any question of law to the Court of Appeal. Section 3(10) of the Foreign Compensation Act 1969 permits challenge to a Commission decision on the ground that it is contrary to natural justice. Subject to that, sections 3(3) and 3(9) of the Act bar question in any court of law of 'anything which purports to be a determination' of the Commission. In the light of this history, it is perhaps difficult to regard the parliamentary intention behind section 4(3) as anything other than that the *Anisminic* principle should apply to it. One would envisage, also, substantial opposition in the context of a criminal statute, to a section 4(3) drafted in the terms of 'anything which purports to be a decision of the SFO'.

4   THE ROLE OF THE MAGISTRATES PENDING TRANSFER

The effect of the issue of a Notice of Transfer is to take from the magistrates the task of deciding whether there is sufficient evidence to put the defendant on

---

8   See *Re a Company* [1981] AC 374; *Pearlman v Harrow School Governors* [1979] QB 56, [1979] 1 All ER 365, CA. The decision does not apply, however, where the statute sets up its own appeal scheme. Quaere whether a right to make an application under section 6 is an 'appeal' from a decision to transfer. See *R v Cornwall County Council, ex p Huntington* [1992] 3 All ER 566.

9   HWR Wade *Administrative Law* (6th edn) at p 727.

10 *R v Cain* [1985] AC 46, [1984] 2 All ER 737; see also *R v Wehner* [1977] 3 All ER 553, [1977] 1 WLR 1143; *R v Haggis* (9 March 1990, unreported).

11 [1992] 3 All ER 153, [1992] 2 WLR 883.

12 See also: Interception of Communications Act 1985 section 7(8).

13 See, however, the argument advanced by HWR Wade in *Administrative Law* (6th edn) at p 728.

trial.[14] All other functions up to the issue of the Notice, and some functions after its issue, will remain with the magistrates. A defendant will be arrested and charged, or summoned to come before the court, in the usual way. It may be that, at first appearance, the prosecutor will have decided that the case is one in which he intends to use the transfer provisions (assuming, of course, he has sufficient information to enable him to be satisfied that the criteria in section 4(1) have been met), or that it is suitable for committal proceedings. Alternatively, where the suspect has been charged, the investigation may be far from complete and no decision yet taken as to which procedure is appropriate. While the case is prepared for committal or transfer, the magistrates retain jurisdiction. They will decide in the first instance whether the defendant should be allowed bail and, if so, upon what conditions. They will consider any application for legal aid or extensions of a current legal aid certificate. Roskill also envisaged that the magistrates would continue to exercise control over the proceedings to ensure that there was no undue delay by the prosecution in issuing the Notice of Transfer.[15] Section 4(1) confirms this by specifying that the functions of the magistrates are to cease only upon the giving of the certificate to the court, which may only be done in accordance with section 5 and the regulations made thereunder. Until the Notice is served, the defendant's rights to object to delay, or to apply to dismiss the case on the ground that the prosecution amounts to an abuse of process because of unconscionable conduct or delay in commencing it, remain. If the court were wrongfully to decline to hear such an application or wrongfully to reject it, the right to apply for a judicial review pending transfer or committal would also remain.[16]

There is no time limit specified for the issue of a transfer notice; the only criteria appear to be that the prosecution should have sufficient information to decide whether the criteria in section 4(1) apply and the rules generally relating to delay. Pending the issue of a notice, the magistrates will technically be 'examining justices' and will be looking to embark on mode of trial procedure. The court is, however, entitled to adjourn mode of trial procedure once the prosecution has indicated in open court that it intends the case to proceed by way of transfer.[17]

After transfer, section 4(1) specifically preserves the magistrates' functions as regards bail, the making of witness orders and granting legal aid.[18] Once these functions have been completed, the role of the magistrates ceases. There are no further appearances in the magistrates' court and the matter will await the allocation of a judge, a listing for an application to dismiss, if notice within the requisite period is given, and a preparatory hearing.

5 PROCEDURE

5.1 General

Transfer is effected when the prosecutor serves a Notice of Transfer upon the magistrates' court. The Notice must be in, or be to like effect as, Form 1 of the

---

14 Section 4(2).
15 Fraud Trial Committee Report, para 4.37.
16 See Chapter 4 section 2.1.
17 *R v Stevenage Justices, ex p Johl* (1989) Times, 1 December.
18 See further section 5.4.

Schedule to the Criminal Justice 1987 (Notice of Transfer) Regulations 1988[19] and a copy must be served on the person to whom the Notice relates or his solicitor, on the appropriate officer of the Crown Court and, where the person to whom the Notice relates is in custody, on the Prison Governor.[20] The prosecutor must also serve a Notice in Form 2 of the Schedule,[21] or a notice to like effect, on the defendant which informs him of his right to challenge the proposed place of trial, to apply for bail and to apply for all or any of the charges to be dismissed on the ground that the evidence which has been disclosed is not sufficient for a jury to convict.[22] The Notice also specifies the witnesses and the witness orders to be made in respect of them and warns the defendant that other charges may be included in the indictment. These may be either in substitution for or additional to those specified in the Notice of Transfer, provided that they are founded on the evidence set out in the material accompanying the Notice and that they may lawfully be joined in the same indictment.

5.2   Material to be served

What material has to be served with the Notice of Transfer? Regulation 4 demonstrates the legal importance of the question because the final form of the indictment is dependent upon the 'evidence' available at transfer. In conventional committal proceedings the practice is to serve all, or most of, the statements in the form prescribed by section 102 of the Magistrates' Courts Act 1980, together with copies of all the documentary exhibits and a list of all the exhibits. Such service is necessary before committal proceedings under section 6(2) of the Magistrates' Courts Act 1980 can take place. Even where committal is pursuant to section 6(1), such service will have been effected because the prosecutor at the time of service will have anticipated a section 6(2) committal or will want to minimise the number of witnesses he will have to call to give oral evidence to raise a prima facie case. The evidence produced to the court at committal, whether in deposition or witness statement form, is the source from which the offences included in the indictment are drawn.[1] The prosecution may only include in the indictment those offences for which the defendant was committed for trial, or counts founded on facts or evidence disclosed in any examination or deposition taken before a justice in his presence, or disclosed in a witness statement served for the purposes of section 6(2) of the Magistrates' Courts Act 1980.[2] Although additional evidence in support of existing charges may be served, offences not founded on the committal papers may not be included in the indictment. Whether an offence is so founded will depend on the precise terms of the statements and depositions, and the state of the evidence at the point of committal, accordingly, marks the blueprint for the future development of the proceedings.

19 SI 1988/1691.
20 Ibid, regulations 4, 5 and 6.
21 Ibid, regulation 4.
22 Ibid, regulation 7.
1 See s 2(2) of the Administration of Justice (Miscellaneous Provisions) Act 1933 and s 102(8) of the Magistrates' Courts Act 1980 (as amended by section 40 of the Criminal Justice Act 1988). A change to section 2(2) effected by the Criminal Justice Act 1988 substituted the word 'material' in subsection (2)(iA) for 'statement of evidence'. In its original form, the Criminal Justice Act 1987 had enabled prosecutors to include counts founded on the statement of evidence.
2 See *R v William* [1972] Crim LR 436.

The transfer procedure is treated no differently. Section 2(2) of the Administration of Justice (Miscellaneous Provisions) Act 1933 has been amended to provide that:

> '. . . no bill of indictment charging any person with an indictable offence shall be preferred unless . . .
> (aa) the offence is specified in a Notice of Transfer under section 4 of the Criminal Justice Act 1987.
> Provided that: . . .
> (iA) in a case to which (aa) above applies, the bill of indictment may include, either in substitution for or in addition to any count charging an offence specified in the Notice of Transfer, any counts founded on *material* that accompanied the copy of that notice which, in pursuance of regulations under section 5(9) of the Criminal Justice Act 1987, was given to the person charged, being counts which may be lawfully joined in the same indictment.'[3]

The indictment must, therefore, contain the offences found in the Notice of Transfer or founded on material accompanying the Notice. The word 'material' lacks the clarity of the terms 'examination', 'deposition' or 'witness statement' used in section 2(2) of the 1933 Act for committal cases and the question arises as to whether it is merely shorthand for examination, deposition and witness statement, or whether it conceals a discretion as to what the prosecutor is required to serve. Section 5(2) provides that the Notice shall specify the charge or charges to which it relates and include or be accompanied by such additional matter as regulations under section 5(9) may require. Section 5(9) enables the Attorney General to make regulations requiring the giving of a copy of the Notice of Transfer, together with a Statement of the Evidence on which any charge to which it relates is based on the defendant and the Crown Court, and making such further provision in relation to Notices of Transfer, including provision as to the duties of a designated authority in relation to such notices, as appear to him to be appropriate. Roskill assumed that:

> 'Accompanying the transfer certificate sent to the Crown Court should be a copy of the relevant papers, that is to say, the information, the witness statements and accompanying documentary exhibits. The Magistrates' Court would be responsible for forwarding to the Crown Court any relevant documents held by them, in particular the recognisance of any surety, if bail has been granted.'[4]

Pursuant to section 5(9) the Attorney General made the Criminal Justice Act 1987 (Notice of Transfer) Regulations, regulation 4 of which requires a copy of the Notice of Transfer to be served on any person to whom it relates together with a notice in Form 2 of the Schedule to the regulations and, in accordance with section 5(9), a statement of the evidence.

The Act and its subordinate legislation do not – and perhaps do not need to – contain a definition of 'Statement of Evidence'. It must be a statement of admissible, available evidence; it should not contain anticipated evidence or material which is not probative. It is not intended to be a 'case statement' of the type envisaged in section 9, though it may explain how the prosecution puts its case. In *R v Saunders*,[5] Henry J ruled that it is permissible and desirable that

---

3   Prior to the Criminal Justice Act 1988, proviso (iA) referred to Statement of Evidence rather than material.
4   Fraud Trials Committee Report, para 4.38, note 35.
5   [1989] Crim LR 726.

inferences which the prosecutor sought to draw from the direct evidence should be included in the Statement of Evidence. This would enable the defendant to make a fully-informed decision whether to apply for dismissal of the charges and enable him to deal with his application without having to foresee the inferences which the prosecution was seeking to draw. A Statement of Evidence did not cease to be such because it included inferences to be drawn from the evidence.

The requirement to prepare a Statement of Evidence has been described as burdensome by the SFO in its evidence to the Royal Commission on Criminal Justice, particularly when set against the SFO practice of serving all its witness statements and documents. It is certainly helpful, both to the defence and to the court, in cases of the scale of most serious frauds, to have a summary of the prosecution evidence in one document at an early stage after transfer.

The regulations do not, in terms, require the prosecutor to serve witness statements or documentary exhibits as is required for committal proceedings by section 6(2) of the Magistrates' Courts Act 1980 or rule 6(1) of the Magistrates' Courts Rules 1981.

The specimen Form 2, however, includes the following paragraph:

> '5. I enclose a list of witnesses:
> (a) indicating those whom the Crown proposes to call to give oral evidence at your trial (and in whose case the Magistrates' Court will be invited to make a witness order under section 1(1) of the Criminal Procedure (Attendance of Witnesses) Act 1965), and
> (b) indicating those whose attendance at your trial the Crown considers unnecessary on the ground that their evidence is unlikely to be required or unlikely to be disputed (and in whose case the Magistrates' Court will be invited to make a conditional witness order under section 1(2) of that Act),
> together with in each case copies of the statements or other documents outlining the evidence of those witnesses.
> 6. I also enclose a list of the exhibits in your case together with copies of those exhibits which are in documentary form.'

Although regulation 4 permits some flexibility in the way in which Form 2 is actually drafted,[6] presumably a notice which does not comply with paragraphs 5 and 6, regarding the provision of witness statements or documents, will not be 'to the like effect' of Form 2.

The reference to 'or other documents' is a clear retreat from the rigidity of the requirements of section 6(2) of the Magistrates' Courts Act 1980 and will enable the prosecuting authority to serve, for example, transcripts of evidence before DTI inspectors, unsigned witness statements and any other written information disclosing the evidence that a witness is likely to give. Amendments to the legislation since 1987 confirm this retreat. In its original form, section 5(8) of the Criminal Justice Act 1987 provided that:

> 'For the purposes of the Criminal Procedure (Attendance of Witness) Act 1965
> . . .
> (b) a person whose written statement is tendered in evidence for the purposes of a notice of transfer shall be treated as a person who has been examined by the court.'

This must have presupposed the existence of a signed witness statement. Section 5(8)(b) was amended, however, as follows:

6   Reg 4 (a) . . . 'or in a form to the like effect'.

'a person indicated in the notice of transfer as a proposed witness shall be treated as a person who has been examined by the court.'[7]

Similarly, the reference in section 2(2) of the Administration of Justice (Miscellaneous Provisions) Act 1933 to 'material'[8] was substituted for a reference to 'statement of evidence'.

The strict requirements of section 6(2) of the Magistrates' Courts Act 1980 do not, therefore, apply and the prosecution has some flexibility in the form in which it serves its evidence, though in practice the SFO serves signed written statements, usually well in advance of transfer as part of its duty to give advance disclosure.

5.3   Venue of trial

The Notice of Transfer must specify the proposed place of trial.[9] The decision as to place of trial is taken away from the magistrates and given to the prosecutor, who is enjoined to have regard to the same considerations specified in section 7 of the Magistrates' Courts Act 1980 as would a committing court.[10] These include the convenience of the defence, the prosecution and the witnesses. Roskill summarised and recommended:[11]

'At present the Magistrates' Court which commits the accused for trial is responsible for selecting the place of trial by the Crown Court. The Court must have regard to the convenience of the defence, prosecution and witnesses, the expediting of the trial, and the location or locations of the Crown Court designated by a presiding judge as the location or locations to which cases should normally be committed from their petty sessions area.[12] The Crown Court has power itself to direct that the defendant be tried at a different place from the place selected by the Magistrates' Court or from a place previously directed by the Crown Court.[13] Moreover if the defence are dissatisfied with the place of trial selected by the Magistrates' Court or the Crown Court they may apply in open court to a High Court Judge for a direction varying the place of trial.[14]

For cases transferred to the Crown Court under the new procedure it will be necessary to make some alternative provision for selecting the appropriate place of trial. In our view, selection of the place of trial in these cases should be a matter for the prosecuting authority. They should be required to specify the court of trial on the transfer certificate. If the defence wish to object to, or the Crown Court itself wishes to alter, the place of trial, the existing provisions could, with appropriate modification, be made to apply.'

It is not clear why it was felt necessary to alter the current arrangements and turn a judicial decision affording the parties an opportunity to make representations about venue into an executive function. The prosecutor must apply the same criteria as the magistrates' courts who would, in any event, commit to their local and usual Crown Court, being one which has been designated by the Lord Chief Justice for serious fraud trials.[15] One assumes

7   Section 40 of the Criminal Justice Act 1988.
8   Op cit.
9   Para 5 of Form 1.
10 Section 5(1).
11 Fraud Trials Committee Report, para 4.42–4.43.
12 Section 7 of the Magistrates' Courts Act 1980 and section 75(1) of the Supreme Court Act 1981.
13 Section 76(1) and (2) of the Supreme Court Act 1981.
14 Section 76(3) of the Supreme Court Act 1981.
15 Practice Direction (Crown Court: Fraud Trials) (No 2) [1990] 1 WLR 1310, CA.

that the prosecutor will be receptive to representations about venue before the Notice of Transfer is served and that the withdrawal of the right to make representations to the magistrates (ie one less bite of the cherry than currently exists) will not be missed.

5.4   Bail; witness orders; legal aid

The magistrates' court will remain responsible after transfer for determining whether the defendant is granted bail or is remanded in custody pending trial. The handling of bail following issue of a Notice of Transfer occupied much attention at Committee Stage.[16] Clive Soley MP expressed his concern that section 5, particularly in cases where a remanded defendant elected not to be brought before the court, might tempt a court not to review the defendant's bail position at the transfer stage. The concern was an important one. Committal for trial has long been regarded as a watershed in the case, at which the defendant must be present and at which the court will entertain a fresh bail application. The fact of committal amounts to a 'new consideration' as envisaged in *R v Nottingham Justices, ex p Davies*.[17] The difficulty arises in transfer cases because, unlike committal, transfer does not take place at a court appearance. The notice which actually effects transfer may be given at any time before the magistrates begin to inquire into the case as examining magistrates, and may be issued in-between appearances. The notice is effective immediately, leaving the court seised only of the matters specified in section 5. What, then, if the hearing immediately after the transfer was one at which, pursuant to section 128 of the Magistrates' Court Act 1980 the defendant, believing that nothing further would happen at the hearing, had consented not to appear? The Minister of State offered assurances in the following terms:[18]

> 'The provision that exists can operate only with consent, so the defendant is absent with his consent. However, perhaps the Hon. Gentleman is criticising Clause 5(5) because it could be said that a procedure that is intended to cover remands only in cases where nothing significant has happened is now being used to cover cases where something substantial has happened.
>
> To meet the Hon Gentleman's point we could clarify Clause 5(5) to ensure that the defendant's consent not to appear was made in the full knowledge that the case had been, or was about to be, transferred, and not merely in expectation of a further remand. Before deciding not to appear, the defendant would have to know that, at a particular hearing, the matter would be dealt with in accordance with Clause 5.'

He continued:

> 'Taken with subsection (4) it means that a Notice of Transfer will be served. Subsection (4) provides for unfinished business in a Magistrates' Court to be finished – that is the part of the committal proceedings that involves the decision on whether the defendant should go to the Crown Court on bail or in custody. So even though the magistrates lose control over the issue of the notice of any other aspects of the case, subsection (4) enables them to see the defendant for the purpose of determining bail.'

Where, therefore, the defendant in custody has decided not to appear at a remand hearing and, in the interim, transfer had taken place, he is to be given

16 *Hansard*, SC F (22 January 1987), col 204.
17 [1981] QB 38, [1980] 2 All ER 775.
18 *Hansard*, SC F (22 January 1987), col 204.

an opportunity to 'retake' his decision in the light of the fact that transfer had now taken place and that the hearing was likely to be the last before the magistrates. Form 2 in the Criminal Justice Act 1987 (Notice of Transfer) Regulations 1988[19] so informs the defendant and enables him to notify the court that he consents to the remaining matters being dealt with in his absence. Section 5(3) to (5) purport to effect this objective so that where the defendant gives his written consent, knowing that the Notice of Transfer *has* been issued, the court may deal with the question of bail in his absence. Without such consent, the defendant must be brought back to court for these matters to be dealt with in his presence. Only decisions relating to bail are covered by sections 5(3) and 5(4). However, the attendance of the defendant's representative at the making of witness orders and the granting of legal aid would be deemed to be the attendance of the defendant.[20]

Where the defendant is remanded on bail to attend the magistrates' court at a later date and, in the interim, a Notice of Transfer is issued, section 5(6) operates to discontinue his obligation to attend court on the specified date unless the notice states that it is to continue. This is of particular value where there has been a long remand and the Notice of Transfer has been issued well before the date upon which the case is next listed for hearing. Rule 6 of the Magistrates' Court (Notice of Transfer) Rules 1988 provides that the court shall, where the person charged is no longer required to appear before the court, fix a date on which it will exercise its functions under section 5(8) of the Act relating to the making of witness orders, and notify both the defendant and the designated authority. The Act seems to assume that the bail position will not be reviewed in these circumstances, though it is always open to the prosecution or the defendant to apply for a variation in bail conditions and if the prosecution wishes to object to bail or impose conditions, the defendant will doubtless be required to attend.[1] The usual practice on committal proceedings, even where all parties are content for bail to be continued on the existing terms, is for sureties to be retaken. In a case in which the prosecutor – for the decision is with him – decides that no appearance is required, the retaking of a surety would not now appear to be necessary. For cases where the requirement to appear is continued, section 5(7A) specifically enables the court to enlarge the recognisance in the surety's absence, though, oddly, no similar provision applies where the requirement to attend is discontinued.

None of the provisions in section 5 dealing with bail addresses the question whether transfer, like committal, marks a watershed in the proceedings at which the court is bound to review the bail position. The opposition's pressure for a legislative review of the *Nottingham Justices* decision was resisted[2] but it was at least conceded that magistrates should reconsider bail at this stage. In dealing with Clause 5(5), the Minister said:

'The subsection deals only with the question of whether the defendant is there to witness the proceedings.

Whether the court should receive an application for bail will depend on its judgment of the merits of the case. However, I think I am right in saying that, notwithstanding the *Nottingham Justices* case, when the Court is considering a case for the last time, it might look more liberally at the question of whether

19 SI 1988/1691.
20 Section 122 of the Magistrates' Courts Act 1980.
1 Section 3(8) and (8A) of the Bail Act 1976.
2 *Hansard*, SC F (22 January 1987), col 205.

there were fresh considerations than if it was one of a series of several remands in a Magistrates' Court',

and later:[3]

'The defendant's position is made no worse by the provisions but is perhaps made a little better, because he would have the opportunity of a final hearing. Under subsection (4), magistrates are required to re-determine the basis on which the case should be transferred to the Crown Court. It is unlikely that a defendant would not have the opportunity to be heard on that issue.'

The viewpoint that committal justifies a bail review stemmed from the fact that the committal proceeding would be the last hearing before the magistrates. The weekly remands would come to an end and the court was under a duty to ensure that the objections to bail, perhaps advanced weeks earlier and not reviewed – particularly following the *Nottingham Justices* decision – since, still applied and could justify a further lengthy remand in custody pending the hearing at the Crown Court. Objections, based on the belief, for example, that the defendant would interfere with potential witnesses, might have evaporated once the witness statements had been taken and served. Further, the position would have been reached that the parties had accepted, or the court had decided, that a prima facie case had been made out. The court would now be in a better position to assess the strength or weakness of the prosecutor's case. Largely the same considerations apply on transfer: previous objections might now be unsustainable; the investigation is advanced, perhaps complete, and a decision has been reached – albeit not by the court – that there is sufficient evidence to send a defendant for trial. It seems appropriate that transfer should, equally, entitle the defendant to a full review of bail and this seems to have been the intention of the legislators.

6   DISMISSAL OF TRANSFERRED CHARGES

6.1   Introduction

Any proposal to abolish committal proceedings had to meet the objection that defendants would thereby lose the opportunity to submit at an early stage after charge that there was no case to answer.[4] The right to make such an application was regarded as a safeguard necessary to ensure that a defendant, in an appropriate case, could do so before the close of the prosecution case at trial, which – in the context of a fraud case – may be many months away.[5] The Roskill Committee spoke in terms of its being:

'. . . a necessary concomitant to the new procedure for dispensing with committal proceedings . . . that the defendant should be given an opportunity to make an application for his discharge to the nominated judge at a preparatory hearing on the ground that prima facie the evidence in the witness statements does not support the charges laid in the indictment.'

The difficulty lay, not in the acceptance in principle that the power to make such a submission should exist, but in the precise form that it should take. The

---

3   Op cit, col 208.
4   See generally Roskill Fraud Trial Committee Report, para 4.47.
5   Eg in *R v NatWest Investment Bank* the arrests took place on 9 November 1989; the prosecution case closed in July 1991.

Committee was anxious not to afford defendants the opportunity of embarking on a prolonged hearing, causing unacceptable delays and thus depriving the new procedure of one of its principal advantages. In conventional committal proceedings, it is open to the defence to request the attendance of all prosecution witnesses whose statements had been served[6] and it was in the exercise of this right that Roskill perceived the prime risk of delay.[7]

The Committee recommended that the application to dismiss would take place before the judge nominated to try the case. The usual method of considering an application to dismiss would be by way of examination of the prosecution papers. Oral evidence was to be discouraged and the defendants would no longer have the absolute right to insist on the attendance of prosecution witnesses, nor would they have the right to call evidence on their own account. Roskill accepted, however, that there were some cases where there would 'be an advantage in allowing a limited amount of cross-examination':

> 'We have in mind, for example, the case of a defendant who is one of several defendants indicted together, who might not be able to show, otherwise than by cross-examination of perhaps one or two prosecution witnesses, that there is in fact insufficient evidence that he played any part at all in the alleged fraud.'[8]

Roskill proposed that the defendant would have to satisfy the judge that hearing oral evidence was reasonable and to back the request with 'cogent evidence', in appropriate cases, supported by affidavit that the witness he wished to cross-examine was either unreliable or untruthful. Such an order should be made only in special circumstances.

6.2 Form of application

The concept of an application to dismiss was accepted by the legislators and found its way into section 6 of the Criminal Justice Act 1987 (as amended in the Criminal Justice Act 1988), which provides that where a notice of transfer has been given, any person to whom it relates, at any time before he is arraigned (and whether or not an indictment has been preferred against him) may apply orally or in writing for the charge or any of the charges to be dismissed. The charge or charges will be dismissed if it appears to the judge that the evidence against the applicant would not be sufficient for a jury properly to convict him.

The application is not part of a preparatory hearing and should be made before there is an arraignment.[9] Where the application is to be made orally, the applicant must, not later than 28 days after the day on which Notice of Transfer was given, give notice in the form specified in the Criminal Justice Act 1987 (Dismissal of Transferred Charges) Rules 1988 of his intention to make the application.[10] The 28-day period may be extended either before or after it

---

6 Notwithstanding that the prosecution had served certain statements, it is always open to it not to call all the witnesses whose statements have been served at committal provided that there is a prima facie case. The witness statement could not, however, be adduced in the committal proceeding without defence consent.

7 Op cit, para 4.48.

8 Op cit, para 4.49.

9 See section 6(1) and section 8(2) of the Criminal Justice Act 1987. A power to hear an application under section 6 as part of a preparatory hearing under section 9 was repealed by the Criminal Justice Act 1988.

10 SI 1988/1695.

expires.[11] It would seem that notice of an oral application need not contain the specific grounds upon which it is made. Neither section 6(2) of the Act nor rule 2(1) or (2) require the applicant to give the grounds of his application, in contradistinction to rule 2(4) which requires the grounds to be specified where an application to extend the 28-day period is made. The Form in the Schedule to the rules contains a section entitled 'Grounds for applying' followed by the preprinted statement that 'the evidence which has been disclosed would not be sufficient for a jury properly to convict', with no obligation expressed nor space provided for elaboration. It would appear, therefore, that the draftsmen did not contemplate that applicants need elaborate, though it is becoming the practice for them to do so. The notice must, however, be accompanied by a copy of any 'material' on which the applicant relies, must specify the charge or charges to which it relates and must state:

> '. . . whether the leave of the judge is sought under section 6(3) of the Act to adduce oral evidence on the application, indicating what witnesses it is proposed to call at the hearing.'

The word 'material' is undefined. It clearly extends to documentary exhibits upon which the defence seek to rely as part of the application and which have not already been served by the prosecution. Does it require disclosure, however, of a defence proof of evidence? If it does, it would be requiring disclosure of the defence case and afford the prosecution an opportunity to respond. Such a radical step is unlikely to have been effected in, and would be arguably beyond the vires of, a statutory instrument.[12]

Again, details of the evidence which it is proposed to call need not, subject to existing rules, be provided either with the notice or thereafter.[13] This, of course, is less stringent than the Roskill proposals which, in the context of a defence application to cross-examine witnesses, would have required the defendant to state in advance his grounds and, if appropriate, to swear an affidavit setting out the evidence leading him to believe that the witness is either unreliable or untruthful.

There is, perhaps oddly, little substantive difference between rule 2 for oral applications and rule 3 for written applications. There is no requirement that the grounds of the application be elaborated in the notice beyond the statement that the evidence is not sufficient for a jury properly to convict. In practice, one anticipates that written applications, especially, will include statements of grounds. Notice of the application must, again, be given to the Crown Court within 28 days of the date of transfer. The 28-day period may be extended, either before or after it expires, by the Crown Court. Notice of the application to extend should, again, be supported by grounds.

6.3   The prosecution response

Following the service of the notice of an intention to apply for dismissal, the prosecution may serve a notice under rule 4. The time limit for service of such a notice is seven days from the date of receipt of the defendant's notice, though the Crown Court has power, upon application by the prosecutor, to extend the

---

11 Rule 2(3).
12 See further Chapter 4, section 3.
13 Eg the Crown Court (Advance Notice of Expert Evidence) Rules 1987, SI 1987/716, though quaere whether these strictly apply because the obligation to disclose only arises after committal.

time limit.[14] Rule 4 does not require the prosecutor to state the grounds for the extension of time, though the form specified in the Schedule to the rules requires them.

Where the defence has served notice of intention to apply orally for the dismissal of the charges, the prosecution may apply for leave under section 6(3) to adduce oral evidence at the hearing of the application and must indicate the witnesses it proposes to call.[15]

Where the defence has served notice of intention to apply in writing for the dismissal of the charges, the prosecution may respond by applying for an oral hearing.[16] Further, the prosecution may apply for leave to call oral evidence and must indicate which witnesses it proposes to call.[17]

It is important to note that, in each case, the service by the defence unlocks the prosecutor's right to apply for an oral hearing and to call evidence and is a significant gloss on the Roskill Committee's report which did not contemplate that the prosecution might call evidence. Unlike the provision in rule 4(5) enabling the prosecution to serve materials *in reply* to the materials served by the defence, the prosecution may seek leave to adduce oral evidence from any of its witnesses and is not confined only to calling those which answer or relate to the material raised by the defence.

The application is made on the appropriate form specifying the grounds of the application (unlike the analogous rule for defence applications) and stating whether leave is sought under section 6(3) and, if so, indicating witnesses it is proposed to call.

6.4 Obtaining leave to adduce oral evidence

6.4.1 *Procedure*

The regulations contemplate that the application for leave to adduce oral evidence, whether made by the defence or by the prosecution, will be dealt with by the judge in the absence of oral representations. Rules 2(7) and 4(4) speak of the judge's decision being communicated to the parties by the appropriate officer of the Crown Court. Doubtless the judge has an inherent jurisdiction to hear oral representation on the issue of leave of his own motion or at the request of the parties and it may be difficult properly to reach a decision without representations, but there is no express provision allowing them. In most of the major fraud trials which have taken place under the transfer procedure, such applications have been made orally.

6.4.2 *Grounds*

Section 6(3) provides that the judge should only give leave or make an order if it appears to him, having regard to any matters stated in the application for leave, that the interests of justice require him to do so. The Roskill Committee had envisaged that a defence application for leave would be supported by an affidavit. The Act casts pressure on the defence to specify grounds for its

---

14 Rule 4(6) of the Criminal Justice Act 1987 (Dismissal of Transferred Charges) Rules 1988, SI 1988/1695.
15 Rule 4(1).
16 Rule 4(2).
17 Rule 4(3).

application, though the regulations do not specifically require them.[18] The defence practice is to provide grounds in full because of the importance attached to the dismissal hearing. The terms 'having regard to any matters stated in the application for leave' are not exclusive: the judge must have regard to the interests of justice which may include matters not stated in the application. In the case of an application by the defence, he will have regard to the representation of the prosecutor and vice versa.

By contrast, where the prosecution wishes, in response to an application for dismissal, to adduce oral evidence, rule 4(3) requires the grounds to be specified.

6.4.3   Can the judge order a witness to attend?

In the Bill before Committee, the clause stood thus:

> 'Oral evidence may be given on the hearing of such an application only with the leave of the Judge.'

The Minister of State commented:[19]

> 'That subsection would be improved if it were clear that when a judge decides to allow a witness to give oral evidence, he will have the power to require that witness to be produced. In other words, where a judge has determined that it is appropriate to call somebody, he himself can order that person to come before the court to give evidence and be cross-examined. Clause 6(2) as it stands is not entirely clear on that.'

The Minister elaborated:

> 'We propose that instead of the lawyers being able to call oral evidence, as in the magistrates' court, because that is what he wants to do, he will have to persuade the judge. The lawyer could not say simply, "The case against my client lies only in fact, although there is a vast bundle of depositions from these three witnesses." What they say does not amount to conclusive evidence of dishonesty. It is vague in this particular.
>
> Instead the judge would have to decide whether justice could be done by simply relying on the police statements or whether he agreed with the lawyer that he would be better able to deal with the case if the witness came before the Court and was cross-examined. The witness might be asked to embellish upon three sentences. After listening to Counsel, the judge would have to decide what the impact of the embellishment was and whether it would add to or detract from the case.
>
> We contend that the judge should take the decision. It is a discretionary decision that judges are perfectly able to make. We propose to add to the clause a provision whereby, if the judge thinks that it would be helpful for a witness to appear, he can order the witness to do so.'

In its amended form,[20] section 6(3) states that:

18 Rule 2(b).
19 *Hansard*, SC F (22 January 1987) col 213.
20 Section 6(3) and (4) of the Criminal Justice Act 1987 was amended by the Criminal Justice Act 1988. In its original form section 6(4) read: 'The Judge may order a person who has made a written statement which it is proposed to adduce in evidence to supplement that statement by oral evidence.' The amended version perhaps gives further support to the view that service of statements is no longer a prerequisite to transfer. What is alarming about the amendment, if this analysis is correct, is that there may be some suggestion the statements need not be made available for a section 6 application.

'Oral evidence may be given on such an application only with the leave of the judge or by his order.'

The legislative intent may have been limited to enabling the judge, having decided that leave should be granted, to order the attendance of the witness.[1] It is the judge's, not the parties', decision. The clause appears to go further, however, and would allow a judge to order the attendance of a witness of his own motion, where the parties had not sought leave.

Neither the statute nor the rules limit the witnesses who may be called pursuant to an application under section 6(3). It plainly embraces a witness whose statement has been served by the prosecutor with the Notice of Transfer. It would, equally, include any defence witnesses, if the defence considered it appropriate to adduce any evidence at that stage. This equates with committal proceedings where the defence have the right to adduce evidence prior to the court's decision as to whether the evidence is sufficient to put the defendant on trial. Further, and in what is a departure from committal proceedings, rule 4(5) enables the prosecutor to respond to any point raised by the defence in its notice of application to apply:

'Where, having received the material specified in rule 2(6) or, as the case may be, rule 3(2) above, the authority by or on behalf of whom notice of transfer was given proposes to adduce in reply thereto any written comments or any further evidence, the authority shall serve any such comments, copies of the statements or other documents outlining the evidence of any proposed witnesses and copies of any further documents on the appropriate officer of the Crown Court not later than fourteen days from the date of receiving the said material, and shall at the same time serve copies thereof on all parties to whom the notice of transfer relates.'

The element of surprise is, therefore, taken away in any case (and in the context of fraud cases, probably every case) where the defence submit material upon which they base their own application. Rules 2(6) and 3(2) require that the notice of intention to make an application to adduce evidence 'shall be accompanied by a copy of any material on which the applicant relies'. Again, 'material' is undefined and the clause is potentially of immense width. It plainly includes documents not already part of the prosecution case.

The judge has an overall discretion to grant leave for a witness to give oral evidence notwithstanding that the rules requiring notice of intention have not been complied with.[2] Notice of the judge's decision on an application for leave is given in accordance with rule 2(7).

6.5 Applying to dismiss: evidence

The application to dismiss must succeed if it appears to the judge that the evidence against the applicant would not be sufficient for a jury properly to convict him.[3] The question arises as to what evidence the judge may have regard to. Are the prosecution to be limited to the evidence which was served with the notice of transfer or may they, in the period intervening between the date of transfer and the date of the hearing of the application (indeed, the date

---

1 Though the provisions of the Criminal Procedure (Attendance of Witness) Act 1965 would clearly apply to a dismissal hearing.
2 Rule 5(1).
3 Section 6(1).

of the judge's decision), serve further evidence in support of their case which the judge is entitled to take into account in reaching his decision? In committal proceedings, the prosecution may serve additional evidence up to the time of adjudication.[4] This may take the form of statements and documents served under section 102 of the Magistrates' Courts Act 1980 or, if the defence decline to accept such statements, the witness may be called to provide a deposition.

The Act does not place any restriction on the prosecutor adducing evidence after transfer and relying upon it at the section 6 hearing and it has been the practice of the SFO to do so. Section 6 contemplates a decision taken by the Judge as to the sufficiency of the evidence at the time of the dismissal hearing rather than a review of the transfer decision at the time it was made. The Act permits the judge to hear and rely upon oral evidence from witnesses called either by the defence or the prosecution which will, a fortiori, be evidence adduced post-transfer.

The complication arises as a result of rule 4(5). In conventional committal proceedings, if the defendant introduces evidence or material of his own, the prosecutor has no right to adduce further evidence dealing with the defence material. In this regard, rule 4(5) marks a significant change permitting the prosecutor to respond to defence evidence. If the prosecutor already has free rein to serve whatever fresh evidence he wishes in order to support his transfer decision, what is the purpose of rule 4(5)? The answer may be that it is simply intended to ensure that all documents necessary to deal with the application under consideration are before the court. It would be inherently unsatisfactory for the judge, in deciding whether a jury at some future date could convict the defendant, to be obliged to ignore evidence which, though not available at transfer, would be available to a jury if it was subsequently served by the prosecution as additional evidence.

6.6   The test to be applied

Section 6(1) establishes that the judge, in considering the application to dismiss, must look at 'the evidence against the applicant' and must dismiss the charge or charges to which the application relates if it 'would not be sufficient for a jury properly to convict'. The phraseology used is curious: the burden of proof remains, doubtless, with the prosecution, but the application is made and initiated in court by the defendant. In committal proceedings, of course, the prosecution opens the evidence and sets its evidence forth. Section 6(1) of the Magistrates' Courts Act 1980, which sets the test for examining magistrates, is expressed more consistently with the burden of proof.[5] By contrast, in transfer cases the judge must be satisfied, it would seem, that the evidence is insufficient and the presumption appears to be that the evidence will be sufficient. The application to dismiss is treated, therefore, like an application at trial by the defence at the close of the prosecution case that there is no case to answer.

---

4 There appears to be no provision enabling the prosecutor in committal proceedings to call evidence in rebuttal if the defendant calls evidence at the committal stage, cf rules 13 and 14 of the Magistrates' Courts Rules 1981 as regards summary trial.

5 Section 6(1) of the Magistrates' Courts Act 1980 provides that: '. . . if a Magistrates' Court inquiring into an offence as examining justices is of opinion, on consideration of the evidence and of any statement of the accused, that there is sufficient evidence to put the accused on trial by jury for any indictable offence, the court shall commit him for trial, and, if it is not of that opinion, it shall, if he is in custody for no other course than the offence under inquiry, discharge him.'

How, then, does the judge approach his function under section 6(1)? The expression 'evidence against the applicant' means all the evidence available to the judge at the time he takes his decision, including not only the prosecution witness statements and the oral evidence of any of its witnesses adduced under section 6(3), but also any submissions and evidence advanced by the defence in support of the application, which might more properly be described as 'evidence for the applicant' and by the prosecution in response. There may be conflict between the evidence advanced by the defendant and the prosecution. The evidence that he receives will be far less than will actually be heard by a jury if the matter proceeds to trial. He will not, for instance, have heard many (if any) of the prosecution witnesses 'live' or subjected to cross-examination; equally, he is unlikely to have heard the defendant and the defence are likely to have disclosed only that evidence which assists in showing that the prosecution evidence is insufficient rather than in raising a defence. With this incomplete picture (even by the standards of the usual application to dismiss at the close of the prosecution case), he is required to project forward and assess whether a jury could regard the evidence as sufficient to convict.

The Roskill Committee addressed this problem and concluded[6] that the judge should apply the test which is applicable on a submission of 'no case to answer' at the close of the prosecution case at the trial as laid down by the Court of Appeal in *R v Galbraith*.[7] The approach of the judge to a submission of 'no case' was described in that case by Lord Lane CJ as follows:

'(1) If there is no evidence that the crime alleged, has been committed by the defendant, there is no difficulty. The judge will, of course, stop the case.

(2) The difficulty arises where there is some evidence but it is of a tenuous character, for example because of an inherent weakness or vagueness or because it is inconsistent with other evidence.

(a) Where the judge comes to the view that the Crown's evidence, taken at its highest, is such that a jury properly directed could not properly convict on it, it is his duty, on a submission being made, to stop the case.

(b) Where, however, the Crown's evidence is such that its strength or weakness depends on the view to be taken of a witness's reliability, or other matters which are generally speaking within the province of the jury and whereon one possible view of the facts there *is* evidence on which a jury could properly come to the conclusion that the defendant is guilty, then the judge should allow the matter to be tried by the jury . . . There will, of course, as always in this branch of the law, be borderline cases.'[8]

Trial judges in serious fraud cases have followed Roskill's recommendation and have accepted that *Galbraith* is the appropriate test on an application under section 6(1).[9] In the *R v NatWest Investment Bank* case, a prosecution concerning a rights issue to finance the take-over by Blue Arrow of Manpower, McKinnon J gave the following account of the judicial approach to section 6:

'No one should think that the dismissal of any charge is in the court's gift. It is not. The court cannot dismiss a charge because a defendant is likely to be acquitted or because the prosecution case against him is not a strong one or is unlikely to result in conviction . . .

I agree with Mr Justice Henry's view, expressed in the *Guinness* case, his Lordship's ruling on an application by the defendant Mayhew on 29 April

6 Fraud Trials Committee Report, paras 4.52 and 4.53.
7 [1981] 2 All ER 1060.
8 Ibid at 1062e–g.
9 See *R v Saunders* [1989] Crim LR 726 per Henry J.

1989, that the section 6 test: "is undoubtably that test laid down in *R v Galbraith*" reported in 1981, 73, page 124.

What the test comes to is this. The court has to ask itself, looking at the admissible evidence against a defendant whether a properly directed and reasonable jury could properly convict that defendant. Could a reasonable jury properly say "we are sure of guilt". That test, of course favours the Prosecution. It is not a test which any defendant – and of course I am speaking generally – would seek.

I have no doubt that where the admissible evidence, whether at this stage, or at the close of the Prosecution case, is as consistent with guilt as with innocence, it could not appear to me, within section 6(1), that the evidence would be sufficient for a jury properly to convict.

I say that very much subject to what follows. The Court is not permitted to usurp the jury's function: it is not permitted to embark upon any kind of fact finding exercise. If the admissible evidence discloses a proper inference of guilt, a proper inference which is available to a reasonable jury properly to draw, then it is not for this Court, on an application for dismissal to weigh up and put into a balance competing inferences which are presented as not being consistent with guilt. That is the function of the jury. The guiding principle is whether the admissible evidence, including proper inferences available to be drawn from it, could lead to a properly directed and reasonable jury properly to convict.

There may be cases where the evidence is such that the inferences to be drawn from it are as consistent with guilt as with innocence, so that, on proper analysis, there is simply not available for the jury a proper inference pointing clearly, or sufficiently clearly, to guilt. In other words, as Mr Purnell said, in effect, and I agree with him, it would be a case in which there was no factual foundation for the jury to be in a position to choose between an inference of guilt and an inference inconsistent with guilt.

This is not, in my judgment, such a case. The ordinary procedure, whereby defendants are committed for trial by justices if there is a case to answer, is by-passed by the transfer charge procedure. A transfer charge procedure in such a case as this places a great burden of responsibility upon the court; responsibility to the prosecution to ensure that a defendant who is properly charged and against whom there is sufficient evidence within section 6(1) should stand his trial; and responsibility to a defendant to ensure that he should not be put to the ordeal and expense of a long trial, spread over many months, if there is not sufficient evidence against him within section 6(1).'

Galbraith contemplates that the judge will approach the case having heard oral evidence from the major, if not all of, the prosecution witnesses, allowing him to assess whether the case falls within approach (1) or (2). In section 6 applications, however, the judge will frequently be approaching the application with regard only to what appears in the prosecution witness statements, which will not have been probed. The chance that the prosecution witness statements, for the purposes of approach (1), will disclose '*no* evidence that the crime alleged has been committed by the defendant', will be remote, notwithstanding that, under cross-examination, that same evidence may prove to be worthless. Approach (2) is even more difficult to apply relying, as it does, on forming a view as to the tenuous or vague nature of the evidence, or of inconsistencies with it, or of the unreliability of witnesses. Take the case, for example, of a witness alleged to be an accomplice with an acknowledged and obvious motive for not telling the truth. Is it conceivable under *Galbraith* that the judge could, when given the witnesses statement and when informed of his status, reach any view other than that there was evidence, no matter how tenuous, which a jury might believe and, therefore, properly accept? How can the defence seriously raise an application without testing such evidence orally? Presumably this is the sort of case when the judge would, without too much persuasion, grant leave under section 6(3).

The difficulty with the *Galbraith* test in any case (a difficulty increased in a case where the judge is reaching his decision on the basis of his reading of the documents rather than hearing witnesses), is that it allows no room for the exercise of judicial discretion in cases where, though an inference may properly be drawn, it would be a weak inference and potentially dangerous for a jury to rely upon. In rejecting the school of thought that a judge should allow an application where he thought it would be 'unsafe or unsatisfactory' for a jury to convict, and thereby limiting the exercise of judicial discretion in such application, Lord Lane CJ enlarged the opportunity for unsafe and unsatisfactory inferences to be drawn. The hurdle to be crossed was, in *Galbraith*, set very low:

> 'Where however, the Crown's evidence is such that its strength or weakness depends on the view to be taken of a witness's reliability, or other matters which are, generally speaking, within the province of the jury and where, on the possible view of the facts there *is* evidence on which a jury could properly come to the conclusion that the defendant is guilty, then the judge should allow the matter to be tried by the jury.'

How fanciful can the possibility referred to be? At what point does it evaporate so that it is, in fact, no evidence at all? Assuming such a point can be reached, is it ever likely to do so when consideration of the evidence is limited to the papers alone?

The position appears to be that once the possibility arises, the matter must be left with the jury. It may be reading too much into McKinnon J's ruling to interpret the reference to 'a proper inference which is available to a reasonable jury properly to draw' as a subtle move away from the baldness of the test expressed in *Galbraith*. 'Proper' does not mean 'possible'; it carries with it more the connotation of 'credible', 'likely' or 'correct'. The ruling may, therefore, represent a move towards the exercise by the judge of a more rigorous filtering process at the transfer stage. Arguably, the test at present is too easy for the prosecution to meet and too difficult, in the context of what is essentially a paper exercise, for the defence to challenge consistently with the objectives sought by Roskill; and too close to the test which, one assumes, is applied by the designated authority's officer in deciding whether there is sufficient evidence to commit for trial.

6.7   Appeal

The Act does not provide a right of appeal from a judge's decision on application under section 6.[10] In its unamended version, section 9(3) enabled the judge to consider an application under section 6 at the preparatory hearing stage. The right of appeal to the Court of Appeal accorded to other functions of the judge under section 9(3) carefully excluded a right of appeal as regards a section 6 application. The amended version of section 9(3) took away the power to consider a section 6 application at the preparatory hearing stage and separated beyond doubt the right to make a dismissal application and the preparatory hearing. The separation is also evident from the provision in

10 Cf section 9(11) of the Criminal Justice Act 1987.

section 6(1) requiring the application under section 6 to be made at any time before the defendant is arraigned and the requirement of section 8(2) that arraignment shall take place at the start of the preparatory hearing. Accordingly, although the right of appeal contained in section 9(11) extends to decisions relating to the admissibility of evidence or any other question of law relating to the case, the right is limited to such decisions (1) taken in the course of a preparatory hearing and (2) referable to the purposes specified in section 7(1) of the Act,[11] and, by analogy with the decision in the *Gunawardena* case, an application under section 6 is unlikely to be regarded as referable to a purpose specified in section 7.

There is, however, no provision akin to section 4(3) which would prevent the decision of a judge being the subject of an appeal or questioned in any court.[12] Is judicial review, therefore, available? Section 29(3) of the Supreme Court Act 1981 provides that the Divisional Court has jurisdiction to make orders of mandamus, prohibition or certiorari in relation to a decision of the Crown Court, other than a decision relating to trial on indictment. In *R v Central Criminal Court, ex p Randle and Pottle*,[13] the Divisional Court accepted jurisdiction to hear an appeal from a Crown Court judge's decision to reject an application to dismiss a prosecution as an abuse of process. Watkins LJ, rejecting an argument that such an appeal was barred by section 29(3), held that the application did not so much affect the conduct of a trial on indictment as determine whether there should ever be a trial at all. It is difficult to see why this reasoning should not apply equally to an application made under section 6. The objection may, of course, be advanced that '*Galbraith*' applications are not in practice, and ought not, to be susceptible to challenge by judicial review, and that they are, plainly, part of the trial process. The crucial difference in transfer cases is that the application under section 6 (as opposed to an application of 'no case' at the close of the prosecution evidence) is not part of the trial, which is deemed, by section 8(1), only to start with the preparatory hearing.

It seems clear, therefore, that judicial review of a dismissal hearing would be available in principle, but it is likely that the Divisional Court would exercise its right to intervene sparingly. There has been adverse comment on the delay caused to serious fraud trials by the right of appeal in section 9(11),[14] and such concerns will apply with equal justification to the right to apply for judicial review. In the context of committal proceedings, the court has consistently shown itself reluctant to intervene save in cases where the procedure was at fault or a decision was reached in bad faith,[15] and it will not, in particular, control the magistrate in his conduct of a case or prescribe, in the course of committal proceedings, the evidence which the magistrate should accept or reject.[16] The areas most likely to provide opportunity for challenge are procedural issues such as a decision under section 6(3) to deny leave to adduce oral evidence, or decisions circumscribing the evidence, and it can only be left

---

11 See *Re Gunawardena, Harbutt and Banks* [1990] 2 All ER 477, [1990] 1 WLR 703 in which the Court of Appeal held that section 9(11) did not extend to an appeal from a decision rejecting an application to dismiss as an abuse of process.

12 See section 3 above.

13 [1992] 1 All ER 370, [1991] 1 WLR 1087.

14 Serious Fraud Office Annual Report 1990–91, para 8.5.

15 *R v Ipswich Justices, ex p Edwards* (1979) 143 JP 699; *R v Oxford City Justices, ex p Berry* [1988] QB 507, [1987] 1 All ER 1244; *R v Carden* (1879) 5 QBD 1; *R v Marsham* [1892] 1 QB 371, CA.

16 *R v Wells Street Magistrates' Court, ex p Seillon* [1978] 3 All ER 257, [1978] 1 WLR 1002; *Gleaves v Deakin* [1980] AC 477, [1979] 2 All ER 497, HL.

to speculate whether the restrictive attitude indicated in the approach to the review of committal proceedings will be continued, or whether the court will err, in order to ensure that *Galbraith* can be properly applied, on the side of allowing evidence to be called.

If the application under section 6 is rejected, nothing in the Act prevents the defence from applying at the conclusion of the prosecution evidence that there is no case to answer.

6.8 Effect of dismissal

The Roskill Committee envisaged that a successful application for a discharge should amount in law to an acquittal, entitling the defendant to raise a plea of autrefois acquit to any subsequent charge on the same facts.[17] It continued:

'The dismissal of a charge by magistrates at committal proceedings does not amount to an acquittal and the prosecution may bring a fresh charge or apply to a judge for consent to prefer a Voluntary Bill of indictment. To this extent, therefore, defendants would be in a better position under the new procedure than those who are subject to the ordinary committal procedure.'

The clear intention was that no proceedings would follow, whether by re-charge or by preferring a Voluntary Bill of Indictment.

The Act did not, however, implement this recommendation, though a cursory glance at section 6(5) may leave the non-lawyer with an impression that it did. Section 6(5) provides:

'Dismissal of the charge, or all the charges, against the applicant shall have the same effect as a refusal by examining magistrates to commit for trial, except that no further proceedings may be brought on a dismissed charge except by means of the preferment of a Voluntary Bill of Indictment.'

It is well established that the refusal by examining magistrates to commit for trial does not operate as an acquittal and the prosecution may thereafter prefer fresh charges either for the same offence or other offences and on the basis of the same evidence.[18] In the case of a 'dismissed charge', section 6(5) clearly operates to direct the prosecution to seek a Voluntary Bill if it wishes to resurrect that charge. What, however, if the prosecutor prefers a different charge in respect of the same evidence? In cases of the size and complexity of those covered by the transfer provisions it will rarely be difficult to conceive of another charge founded on the same events. On a strict interpretation of section 6(5), it would also be open to him in such cases to employ either the transfer procedure or conventional committal proceedings. If this interpretation is correct, the prosecution possesses the same power following a failed committal, save for the limited change that any further proceedings in respect of the dismissed *charge* must, rather than may, be commenced by Voluntary Bill. In a case where the prosecution wanted to resurrect the charge it is difficult to believe that they would want to do so in any way other than by applying for a Voluntary Bill. They would not (unless they had reached the view that the case against the defendant, without other defendants and the evidence associated with them, was no longer one of such seriousness and complexity that the transfer provisions were not appropriate) seek to bring the

17 Fraud Trials Committee Report, para 4.53.
18 *R v Manchester City Stipendiary Magistrate, ex p Snelson* [1978] 2 All ER 62, [1977] 1 WLR 911.

defendant before the Crown Court by means of committal proceedings. If it was a case, for example, where other defendants had already been transferred to the Crown Court and were awaiting trial, the prosecution is unlikely to want to commence by transfer and afford the defendant a further opportunity of making a section 6 application. It would seem, therefore, that section 6(5) does no more, in this context, than enact good and familiar prosecution practice.

The Roskill Committee did not give its reasons for concluding that the dismissal of the charge should count as an acquittal. The usual result of a successful *Galbraith* application is that an acquittal is entered and there are no instances of a Voluntary Bill of Indictment being either granted or sought where a case has been dismissed at the close of the prosecution evidence. The Act does not specify the circumstances in which a Voluntary Bill may be applied for following a successful application under section 6 and the general law, accordingly, applies. The general principle is set out in the *Practice Direction (Crime: Voluntary Bills)*[19] which provides:

> '1. The usual means of bringing a defendant to trial on indictment is by committal for trial in the Magistrates' Court. A voluntary bill should only be granted where good reason to depart from the normal procedure is clearly shown and only where the interests of justice, rather than considerations of administrative convenience, require it.'

There seems no reason why this broad statement of principle should not apply equally in transfer cases. The cases show that the procedure is appropriate in a number of instances, many of which are unlikely to be of relevance to the situation where a judge has dismissed a case pursuant to section 6. The familiar situations are where, for example, the committal has foundered on a technicality; or where the defendant or his advisers have abused the committal process and made it unmanageable; or where a suspect has been arrested shortly before the trial of his co-defendant and it is deemed necessary to join them both in the same indictment. It is also accepted that an application for a voluntary bill may be appropriate where examining justices have, contrary to the weight of the evidence, refused to commit the defendant for trial. The granting of an application is by no means a formality and the judge must exercise his discretion judicially, though it has been held that there is no right to judicial review of a judge's decision to grant an application to prepare a Voluntary Bill.[20] There is no guidance as to how such an application, following a successful section 6 application, should be handled. Is it, for example – and assuming that the section 6 application was heard by a High Court judge – appropriate for the Voluntary Bill application to be listed before the same judge; would it be improper for the application to be placed before a different High Court judge? In what circumstances could a High Court judge who has dismissed a prosecution pursuant to section 6 properly thereafter grant an application to prefer a Voluntary Bill? Presumably if cogent and fresh evidence becomes available the interests of justice may require that a bill be preferred. Equally, it may be inappropriate to grant such an application where the evidence was available at the time of the transfer hearing and was not presented because of some failing on the part of the prosecution. Further, it may be that an application to prefer a Voluntary Bill should be granted where the transfer has been successful as a result of some technicality. It must be remembered of

---

19 [1991] 1 All ER 288, [1991] 1 WLR 1633.
20 See *R v Manchester Crown Court, ex p Williams and Simpson* [1990] Crim LR 654.

course that the reinstitution of criminal proceedings in this manner would be subject to the general jurisdiction of the court to dismiss the further prosecution as an abuse of process of the court.[1]

1   See chapter on Preparatory Hearings relating to abuse of process principles generally.

CHAPTER 4
Preparatory hearings

The Roskill Fraud Trials Committee placed considerable emphasis on the need for a substantial pre-trial procedure with a view to simplifying, expediting, and shortening fraud trials.[1] The Committee recommended that, so important was such a procedure, that it 'should be treated as a formal preparatory part of the trial'.[2]

The legislators had little quarrel with the Committee on their proposals for what became known as preparatory hearings and most of the recommendations put forward by the Committee were implemented in ss 7–10 of the Act.[3]

Preparatory hearings have assumed, in some cases, a very significant stature in terms of length of hearing. For example, in *Guinness* parts 1 and 2 the preparatory hearings lasted a total of nearly 100 days spread over 22 months. In the *County NatWest* case the hearings occupied 30 days over two months. In *Barlow Clowes*, the hearings lasted 10 days, spread over ten months.[4]

1 PRELIMINARY[5]

Following the committal or transfer of a serious and complex fraud case to the Crown Court, one of the first practical matters to be considered will be the appointment of a trial judge. The Roskill Committee recommended that 'the judge presiding at the preparatory hearings must be the judge who, save in exceptional circumstances, is to conduct the trial'.[6] This is not a precept which is enshrined in the legislation, save for the practical consequences of the fact that the preparatory hearing marks the beginning of the trial.

1.1 Ordering a preparatory hearing

The judge's first job will be to decide whether there should be a preparatory hearing. He may make this decision either at his own discretion, or it may be

1 Roskill Report, paragraph 6.1.
2 Ibid, Recommendation 31; paragraph 6.25.
3 There was, however, disquiet in many quarters about the provisions relating to disclosure of the defence case, and section 9(5) was a compromise version of the original clause, worked out at committee stage in the House of Lords: see section 1.4 below.
4 SFO evidence submitted to the Royal Commission: para 4.21.
5 For an account of preparatory hearings, which describes them as 'the most important of the new provisions' in the 1987 Act, see Archbold News, Issue 13, 27 March 1992: 'Preparatory Hearings and the Criminal Justice Act 1987' by Barbara Mills QC.
6 Recommendation 34, paragraph 6.32.

ordered at the application of either the prosecution or the defence,[7] because 'the evidence on an indictment reveals a case of fraud of such seriousness and complexity that substantial benefits are likely to accrue from a preparatory hearing'.[8]

A judge may order a preparatory hearing under section 7(1) in any case where the 'evidence on an indictment reveals a case of fraud of such seriousness and complexity that substantial benefits are likely to accrue from a hearing before the jury are sworn'. Preparatory hearings, therefore, under the scheme of the Act are not limited to cases brought by the SFO. The substantial benefits are defined as:

'(a) identifying issues which are likely to be material to the verdict of the jury;
(b) assisting their comprehension of any such issues;
(c) expediting the proceedings before the jury; or
(d) assisting the judge's management of the trial.'[9]

It is likely that a preparatory hearing will be ordered in most fraud cases, replacing the informal 'pre-trial reviews' which have been in existence in one form or another since 1974.[10]

1.2 The timetable

In outline, the procedure for regulating the holding of a preparatory hearing is as follows.

1. An application for a hearing may be made by either the prosecution or the defence within 28 days of committal or transfer (subject to any extension of time granted by the court).
2. An indictment must be lodged, so that the judge can consider whether it discloses the requisite features set out in section 7(1).
3. The judge must order, either on his own initiative, or following an application by the prosecution or defence, that a preparatory hearing should be held.
4. A date for a preparatory hearing should be fixed.
5. The judge may order the prosecution and defence to 'prepare and serve any documents' which could be ordered to be served under section 9(4) and (5) in advance of the preparatory hearing.
6. Any applications to dismiss should be heard.
7. The beginning of the preparatory hearing marks the commencement of trial, and the defendants are therefore arraigned.[11]
8. The preparatory hearing takes place, and orders pursuant to section 9(4) and (5) can be made (if not previously made under point 5 above).
9. The jury is sworn.
10. The prosecution opens its case.

This timetable may be subject to a number of variations depending on the exigencies of each case. The following paragraphs deal with elements of the timetable, and consider some of the variables.

7 Criminal Justice Act 1987 section 7(2).
8 Criminal Justice Act 1987 section 7(1).
9 Criminal Justice Act 1987 section 7(1).
10 Pre-trial reviews were introduced at the Central Criminal Court, and are now governed by Practice Rules dated 21 November 1977. Similar rules have been provided for other courts.
11 Section 8 of the Act.

Since it is the 'evidence on an indictment' which is the deciding factor in a judge's discretion as to the ordering of a preparatory hearing, section 7(1) means that the judge cannot make any decision until an indictment is lodged. The Roskill Committee stated:

> 'In our view the first preparatory hearing should take place as soon as possible after committal or the issue of a transfer certificate. We consider that it should be the duty of both prosecution and the court, in practice, the listing officer, to ensure that not later than a specified period after committal or transfer certificate, or such longer period as the court may allow, a date for the first preparatory hearing is fixed.'[12]

The period suggested was 28 days, which coincidentally is the period within which an indictment should be lodged. Under the Criminal Justice Act 1987 (Preparatory Hearings) Rules 1988, rule 4(1):

> 'An application for a preparatory hearing shall be made not later than 28 days after the day on which the case was committed for trial or, as the case may be, a notice of transfer or consent to the preferral of the bill of indictment was given in relation to the case.'

In most fraud trials an application will be made by the prosecution for a preparatory hearing under section 7(2) of the Criminal Justice Act 1987 as soon as practicable after committal or transfer. The timing, however, results in certain consequences which can cause practical difficulties. First, two events need to happen before a preparatory hearing can be ordered: an indictment must be lodged, and a judge must be appointed to consider the application. In many cases, particularly where there has been a committal, neither event will take place within 28 days. Nevertheless, an application for a preparatory hearing should be made within 28 days. Although an application can be made before an indictment is lodged and before a judge is appointed, and although there is provision for extending the time limit for making the application,[13] there is a logical consistency. Given that the impetus behind the legislation is to ensure that fraud trials proceed as quickly as possible, it is clearly desirable that the time limits are adhered to.

So far as lodging an indictment is concerned, there would appear to be no excuse for counsel, who in an SFO case will have been involved in the proceedings for a considerable period of time, not to lodge an indictment which is essentially the same form as the transfer or committal charge, within the time limit of 28 days specified by the Indictments Rules.[14] Other prosecutors, however, do not necessarily follow the example of the SFO in engaging counsel at an early stage, and committal or transfer charges may differ radically from the indictment. Considerable delay may occur between committal or transfer and the lodging of an indictment since extensions to the time for doing so are regularly granted up to 56 days and beyond.

While the intention of the legislation, therefore, is to ensure that the case does not 'go to sleep' after committal or transfer and that it is placed in the hands of a judge who will seek to ensure that the trial takes place at the earliest possible opportunity, there may be delays.

Second, by rule 4(2) of the Criminal Justice Act 1987 (Preparatory Hearings) Rules 1988, where there is an application to dismiss a transferred charge and

---

12 Roskill Report, paragraph 6.49.
13 Criminal Justice Act 1987 (Preparatory Hearings) Rules 1988 rule 4(3).
14 Indictments (Procedure) Rules 1971 rule 5(1)(a).

that application fails, 'an application for a preparatory hearing in relation to that charge shall be made not later than seven days after the day on which the application for its dismissal was determined'. In cases where there is more than one defendant, a decision on whether there should be a preparatory hearing will normally be made in advance of the hearing of applications to dismiss under section 6 of the 1987 Act. Where notice has been given under section 6, however, it may be seen as inappropriate to make orders under section 7(4) in relation to the preparatory hearing until the challenge to the transfer has been determined. The preparatory hearing itself cannot, of course, begin until an application to dismiss has been heard.

In practice this may not be of significant concern, since a defendant is likely to have disclosed to the court all matters which he may have been required to prepare and serve under section 7(4) in the course of an application to dismiss. An application in writing will, of necessity, have set out any matters which could have been contained in a document prepared and served under section 7(4); and on an oral application, the defence will have made clear 'in general terms the nature of his defence and . . . the principal matters on which he takes issue with the prosecution' and all the other matters specified in section 9(5)(b)(i)–(iv).

Such matters, although technical in nature, will create difficulties in the making and drafting of coherent orders under the provisions of section 7.[15] It is nevertheless important that these orders should be clear, and that the timetables provided in them are adhered to, and the tasks to be undertaken are performed.

1.3 Prior to the preparatory hearing

It is normal practice for the judge, once allocated to the case, to have the case listed 'for mention' (ie for an informal hearing, specifically outside the preparatory hearing) at an early stage so that a timetable can be established for the running of the case. The matters to be considered at such a hearing are likely to include the following:

1. if there are to be applications under section 6 for dismissal of a transferred charge, the date on which such applications will be heard, and the dates by which the defence and prosecution should serve their applications and responses respectively;
2. the date for commencement of the preparatory hearing;
3. what orders should be made under section 7(3) and (4), and what time limits should be attached to those orders;
4. the probable length of the preparatory hearing;
5. a date for the commencement of the trial.

1.4 Pleadings

At this preliminary stage, if there has been a transfer, there will already be in existence the statement of the evidence served by the prosecution at the time of transfer pursuant to rule 4(b) of the Criminal Justice Act 1987 (Notice of Transfer Regulations) 1988. Other 'pleadings' will probably follow, and

15 See also Criminal Justice Act 1987 (Preparatory Hearings) Rules 1988, SI 1988/1699, section 1, rule 8(1).

depending on the orders made by the judge under section 7 (if any) these pleadings may come into existence before the preparatory hearing starts. It will often make good sense for exchanges of documents, pursuant to sections 7 and 9, to be completed before the preparatory hearings start, although it is equally possible for the hearing to be formally 'opened' at a very early stage after transfer, with orders being made under section 9 to be complied with under fixed time limits with a view to embarking on a substantive hearing at a later date.

The pleadings, which will include a case statement, and other materials, prepared pursuant to section 9(4) of the 1987 Act, may be ordered to be produced under section 7(4). They must set out:

> '(a) . . .
>> (i)   the principal facts of the prosecution case;
>> (ii) the witnesses who will speak to those facts;
>> (iii) any exhibits relevant to those facts;
>> (iv) any proposition of law on which the prosecution proposes to rely; and
>> (v)   the consequences in relation to any of the counts in the indictment that appear to the prosecution to flow from the matters stated in pursuance of sub-paragraphs (i)–(iv) above.'

The Crown may also be ordered by the judge:

> '(b) to prepare their evidence and other explanatory material in such a form as appears to him to be likely to aid comprehension by the jury and to supply it in that form to the court and to the defendant, or if there is more than one, to each of them.
> (c) to give the court and the defendant or, if there is more than one, each of them notice of documents the truth of the contents of which ought in the prosecution's view to be admitted and of any other matters which in their view ought to be agreed;
> (d) to make any amendments of any case statement supplied in pursuance of an order under paragraph (a) above that appear to the court to be appropriate, having regard to objections made by the defendant, or, if there is more than one, by any of them.'

If the prosecution has been ordered to produce the matters listed above, in advance of the preparatory hearing, pursuant to section 7(4), the defendant may be ordered:

> '(i)   to give the court and the prosecution a statement in writing setting out in general terms the nature of his defence and indicating the principal matters on which he takes issue with the prosecution;
> (ii) to give the court and the prosecution notice of any objections that he has to the case statement;
> (iii) to inform the court, and the prosecution of any point of law (including a point as to the admissibility of evidence) which he wishes to take, and any authority on which he intends to rely for that purpose;
> (iv) to give the court and the prosecution notice stating the extent to which he agrees with the prosecution as to documents and other matters to which a notice under subsection (4)(c) above relates and the reason for any disagreement.'[16]

The exchange of pleadings, imposed on both prosecution and defence by the 1987 Act, introduces a novel concept into criminal law. The intention is to

---

16 Section 9(5).

clarify and simplify the issues being tried by the court, but the imposition of the rule requires the defence to disclose its case. Certain consequences flow from this requirement.

As the Roskill Committee recognised, the normal practice of criminal procedure imposes no obligation on a defendant to give any information to the Crown in advance of, or even during, a trial. 'The fundamental principles at play here are the burden of proof, the right of silence, the protection against self-incrimination and the free choice of giving or tendering evidence on behalf of the defence.'[17] The Committee was, however, persuaded that these rules should be departed from for serious fraud cases, and they agreed with submissions made to them 'that a system of pleadings should be introduced along the lines of the procedures which are a feature of civil proceedings whereby during the early stages of litigation the parties define the matters which are at issue between them'.[18] The main advantages of advance disclosure by the defence were anticipated to be that:

(a) trials would be shorter and more efficient;
(b) they would be clearer for the jury, because at the outset the jury would be told in outline what part of the prosecution's case the defence intended to challenge; and
(c) there would be less scope for fabricated defences because the prosecution would be able to investigate them in advance.[19]

However, it was accepted during the passage of the Bill, particularly in the House of Lords,[20] that there were dangers in this approach. It infringed civil rights in the sense of eroding the right of silence and shifting the burden of proof. The system would move away from the adversarial towards the inquisitorial because a defendant would be required to 'put up' a case, and the prosecution, rather than establishing and proving its own case, would spend its time discrediting the defence case. The providing of a detailed defence statement was therefore abandoned in favour of 'a statement in writing setting out in general terms the nature of his defence'.

The section as amended, nevertheless, creates a number of problems, some of which stem from the explicit attempt to link civil and criminal procedures; for example, in the fact that the burden of proving a case remains on the prosecution, and, also, that there is no realistic sanction against a defendant for complying inadequately with orders made under section 9(5) of the Act.[1] While in civil proceedings, a defendant who enters an inadequate defence risks having judgment entered against him in default, or requests can be made for further and better particulars of the defence, there is no such sanction in a serious fraud trial. A defendant can effectively enter 'pleadings' in response to an order which amount to no more than a not guilty plea and taking issue with each allegation made by the prosecution.

The only specific mention of a judicial power to compel a defendant to comply with an order under section 9(5) comes in section 9(8) which states:

17 Roskill Report, paragraph 6.69.
18 Ibid, paragraph 6.71.
19 Ibid, paragraph 6.72.
20 See eg Lord Hutchinson: *Hansard* HL 12 May 1987, col 586.
1   The SFO, in submissions to the Royal Commission of Criminal Justice, has recommended that 'there should be a stringent legal requirement on the defence to produce detailed and comprehensive case statements'. It is conceded (paragraph 4.25) that 'there is no real sanction against a defendant for refusal to submit a case statement'. See section 9(7) below.

'If it appears to a judge that reasons given in pursuance of sub-section (5)(iv) above are inadequate, he shall so inform the person giving them, and may require him to give further or better particulars.'

Subsection (5)(iv) relates to 'documents the truth of the contents of which ought in the prosecution's view to be admitted and of any other matters which in their view ought to be agreed'.[2]

This is an important power of intervention on the part of the judge, since it goes to the heart of one of the main causes of lengthy trials, the requirement to prove the contents of documents. Nevertheless, a defendant can perfectly properly insist on strict proof of a document, and of its contents, and must, of course, do so if there is any point to be made by the prosecution on the evidence relating to the document.

A general sanction for non-compliance is contained in section 10 of the Act which permits the judge, or with his leave, any other party, to 'make such comment as appears to him to be appropriate and the jury may draw such inference as appears proper' where there is, at trial, a departure from the case disclosed at the preparatory hearing, or where there has been a 'failure to comply with a requirement imposed at the hearing'.[3]

By section 9(7) the judge must warn defendants of the possibility that section 10 will be invoked in respect of non-compliance with orders made pursuant to section 9(5).

This provision in section 10 nevertheless adds further difficulty to the 'pleadings' procedures. The threat of comment being made will discourage a defendant from committing himself to a defence at an early stage of the proceedings. He may quite properly argue that it is inappropriate to do so before he has heard the prosecution evidence, which might easily be radically different from the Statement of Case and Case Statement produced by the prosecution. Such considerations might provide adequate excuses for failing to comply in anything other than a token manner with orders made under section 9(5) of the Act, particularly if courts adhere to the general principle of the privilege against self-incrimination.

It is important to note that the Act makes no provision for cross-service of defence 'statements' made pursuant to section 9 (or any other defence document) on other defendants.[4]

Such documents are often, as a matter of practice, exchanged by consent, and the SFO seeks to encourage this practice by writing to defence solicitors with a view to cross-service unless objections are raised.

2 Section 9(4)(c).
3 This provision overrides the decision in *R v Hutchinson* [1985] Crim LR 730 in which the Court of Appeal held that admissions made at pre-trial review could not become evidence at the subsequent trial unless the person making them consented to their introduction. It nevertheless preserves the position that, save in the circumstances set out in section 10, the pleadings produced as a result of orders under section 9 are not evidence. In Archbold (para 2.21, 44th edn) it is submitted that, because of section 9(7), the sanction in section 10 only applies to the defence. Comment cannot be made about changes in the prosecution case; but see *R v Saunders* (6 November 1989, unreported) per Henry J; and since section 9(7) only applies to non-compliance (as opposed to departure from case statements etc) this view does not appear to be correct.
4 See *Re Tariq* [1991] 1 All ER 744, [1991] 1 WLR 101, CA.

2 THE PREPARATORY HEARING: I

At the preparatory hearing the judge 'may determine: . . . (b) any question as to the admissibility of evidence; and (c) any other question of law relating to the case'.[5] Taken at its face value this provision permits the judge to range very widely over issues which may affect the trial. A 'question of law relating to the case' must include any legal argument arising out of the bringing of the prosecution which could include arguments about the indictment (motions to quash, severance and amendment), abuse of process, and a number of other related matters.

There are, however, a number of factors which complicate this simple proposition. First, since the preparatory hearing begins with arraignment, it may be argued that it is not appropriate to ask defendants to plead to an indictment which is subsequently to be the subject of argument. Therefore motions to quash, submissions on severance and amendment, should probably be argued before the preparatory hearing starts.

Second, in *Re Gunawardena, Harbutt and Banks*[6] the Court of Appeal decided that the purposes of a preparatory hearing are limited to the matters outlined in section 7(1)(a)–(b) of the Act. Since the matters referred to in section 7(1) relate exclusively to the manageability of the trial as it affects the jury, this decision represents a very considerable restriction on the matters capable of being considered at a preparatory hearing, and seems to be inconsistent with the express provisions of section 9(1) and (3).

In *Gunawardena*, a CPS Fraud Investigation Group case, the appellant applied to the trial judge to stay the indictment on the ground of abuse of process. The judge rejected the application, and the appellants thereupon applied to him for leave to appeal against his decision. The trial judge ruled that 'the application made to him as to abuse of process was not a matter which came within the relevant provisions as to a preparatory hearing in the Act of 1987'.

It is not clear from the judgment of Watkins LJ whether there was in fact a properly constituted preparatory hearing in this case. He stated that counsel for one of the defendants argued, in effect, 'that the court purported to carry out a preparatory hearing . . .' Nevertheless the Court of Appeal treated the appeal as if a preparatory hearing had been formally constituted under section 7 of the Act.

Watkins LJ decided:

> 'In our judgment the words of section 7, 8 and 9 themselves plainly demonstrate the object of Parliament in creating the preparatory hearing. It must have been, according to the language used, we think, the intention of Parliament, in introducing this novel procedure – novel in that it has not been introduced in respect of any other kind of criminal trial – to ensure that it be used for a specific purpose or purposes. It deliberately so enacted, in our view, the provisions of subsection (1) of section 7 in order to make it clear that it was creating this new and very valuable procedure for the specified purposes and no other. We cannot bring ourselves to believe that Parliament can possibly, by using the clear words which it has used in sections 7 and 9, have intended to allow a preparatory hearing to commence for a sudden specified purpose and then permit, once a preparatory hearing for that purpose is in being, argument

---

5   Section 9(3) of the Act. Section 9(3)(a), which was repealed by the 1988 Act, referred to hearing applications to dismiss. The obvious muddle that this provision entailed is one of many instances of the lack of care given to procedural matters in the 1987 Act.

6   [1990] 2 All ER 477, [1990] 1 WLR 703.

to range around all manner of issues which cannot be said to relate to any of the specified purposes.'[7]

The judge went on:

'Finally we look at the words which are bracketed in section 7(1) in this Act referred to as a "preparatory hearing" and then at the words which begin section 9(1) "at the preparatory hearing". That is another indication we think that the material legislation means that the set purposes and no other may be served throughout the existence of the preparatory hearing and in respect of every application which is made to the judge during the hearing. Care must be taken to avoid confusion between the preparatory hearing under the Act and the informal pre-trial review.'[8]

The importance of the argument, of course, related to the question of whether the applicants had a right of appeal from the judge's ruling on the abuse of process argument. If it could be said that the ruling came within section 9(3)(c) then, by section 9(11): 'an appeal shall lie to the Court of Appeal from any order or ruling of a judge under subsection (3)(b) or (c) above, but only with the leave of the judge or of the Court of Appeal'. An appeal from decisions made by a judge outside the preparatory hearings provisions does not lie until the conclusion of the proceedings, save in relation to abuse of process applications.[9]

The court in *Gunawardena* made it plain that it was within the discretion of the judge to decide whether any ruling made by him fell within or without the confines of the preparatory hearing. That case may be viewed as an unreliable precedent for the future, both because of the uncertainty as to whether there was, de facto, a preparatory hearing in being at the time when the decision was being made, and second, because of the way in which the judge exercised his discretion. It is anticipated that most judges, having ordered a preparatory hearing under section 7(1) of the Act, will accede to an argument that their rulings on almost all matters raised in the hearing will come within the definition of 'any other question of law relating to the case'.[10]

The range of issues which can be raised at a preparatory hearing is, *pace Gunawardena*, very wide indeed. First, there are the tasks which a judge may order the prosecution and defence to carry out, including prosecution and defence statements, as discussed above, and the preparation by the prosecution of their evidence in such a way as to facilitate comprehension by the jury. This latter point covers the non-traditional means of presenting evidence, as recommended by the Roskill Committee[11] including the use of glossaries, flow charts and computer graphics on in-court visual display units.

Second, the judge will have to decide questions of admissibility, and apart from the normal questions of admissibility, and a consideration of sections 24 and 25 of the Criminal Justice Act 1988,[12] subsidiary issues such as legal professional privilege[13] and public interest immunity.[14]

---

7 Ibid at 706.
8 Ibid at 707.
9 See section 2.1 below.
10 But see section 4, this chapter, below. Concerns about delay caused by interlocutory appeals may encourage judges to be selective as to the matters heard within the preparatory hearing.
11 Roskill Report, paragraph 6.63–6.66.
12 See below at section 3.1.
13 See below at section 2.3.5(a).
14 See below at section 3.7.

Third, the court will need to consider practical matters such as the length of the trial,[15] and the questions which may need to be asked of the panel of jurors so as to eliminate those who may have difficulties in being available for a long trial, or those who have an 'interest' in the case.[16] If the trial has been severed, consideration will need to be given to reporting restrictions on the first trial.[17]

Last, but not least, the judge will need to rule on any questions of law, in so far as they are not encompassed within the matters set out above. Although it may be argued, following *Gunarwardena*, that issues such as abuse of process, motions to quash the indictment, amendments to the indictment and severance cannot properly be considered part of a preparatory hearing, they are dealt with here because even if they are not argued within the preparatory hearing, they will be considered either immediately prior to the commencement of the preparatory hearing or, indeed, at subsequent stages of the trial.

2.1 Abuse of process

That the criminal courts have an inherent power to stay proceedings which amount to an abuse of their process is now well beyond doubt,[18] though the scope of the power is still in a state of rapid growth and has not, save as regards abuse in the context of extradition proceedings, been the subject of scrutiny by the House of Lords.[19] The power is of especial significance in fraud cases. Frauds usually take time to come to light. The perpetrators – at least the sophisticated ones – will have taken steps to conceal their wrongdoing. Once discovered, the first investigative steps may not be directed towards proving a criminal offence: the defrauded party may first consider and embark upon civil proceedings for the recovery of stolen proceeds; in the context of frauds upon a company, the criminal investigation and proceedings may have been preceded by a DTI investigation under section 432 of the Companies Act 1985 which, though empowered to obtain evidence and make recommendations, will not take the decision whether or not to commence criminal proceedings;[20] an insider dealing investigation will frequently have been preceded by an investigation by the Stock Exchange, an investigation by the DTI under section 177 of the Financial Services Act 1986 and only then, if so recommended, will criminal proceedings be considered and commenced. On the other hand, frauds generate paper, much of it contemporaneous with the offences; frauds involve systems of deceit, sometimes practised over many months.

The prosecutor is less likely, therefore, to be relying upon a witness's recollection of a single incident or conversation, and the argument that delay will prejudice the preparation of the defence because of the fading memory of witnesses may ring hollow where the defendant has left a paper-trail.[1] Each

---

15 See below at section 2.4.1.
16 See below at section 3.5.
17 See below at section 3.6.
18 See later, however, the remarks of Lord Dilhorne in *DPP v Humphrys* [1977] AC 1, [1976] 2 All ER 497; *Connelly v DPP* [1964] AC 1254, [1964] 2 All ER 401, HL.
19 *R v Governor of Pentonville Prison, ex p Sinclair* [1991] 2 AC 64, [1991] 2 WLR 1028, HL.
20 See however the comments of John Wood, Director of the Serious Fraud Office in evidence given to the Trade and Industry Committee relating to the passing of transcripts of evidence in the Guinness Inquiry from the DTI to the SFO: Chapter 2, section 1.4.
1 See *R v Buzalek and Schiffer* [1991] Crim LR 115, CA.

case will, of course, depend on its own circumstances, though in all cases – and particularly in fraud cases where the courts recognise that some delay is inevitable in order to conduct a thorough investigation – the power to stay proceedings should only be exercised in exceptional circumstances.[2] In any event, the power to stop proceedings on the ground of abuse is not to be regarded by judges or magistrates as a means by which they may vet and reject those prosecutions which they feel should not have been brought.[3]

The power is vested in all courts of criminal jurisdiction, notwithstanding some early expressions of doubt as to whether magistrates possessed the power. In *DPP v Humphrys*,[4] Viscount Dilhorne commented, obiter dicta:

> 'In *Mills v Cooper* [1967] 2 QB 459 where magistrates had dismissed a summons on the ground that it was oppressive and an abuse of process of the Court Lord Parker CJ while holding that it was not, said, at page 467:
> > ". . . every court has undoubtably a right in its discretion to decline to hear proceedings on the ground that they are oppressive and an abuse of process of the court."
> I must confess to some doubt whether this is a correct statement of the law in relation to magistrates' courts. If it is, it appears to me to be fraught with considerable dangers. One bench thinking a prosecution should not have been brought will dismiss it as oppressive and vexatious. Other benches on precisely the same facts may take a considerably different view, with the result that there is a lack of conformity in the administration of justice.'

Lord Salmon would express no concluded view on whether courts of inferior jurisdiction possessed such power but accepted that the statement of Lord Selbourne LC in *Metropolitan Bank Ltd v Pooley*[5] that 'the power seemed to be inherent in the jurisdiction of every court of justice to protect itself from the abuse of its own procedure' was as applicable to criminal proceedings as to civil proceedings. In *R v Horsham Justices, ex p Reeves*,[6] Skinner J, in deciding to issue an order of prohibition to a magistrates' court directing them not to proceed with summonses on the ground that they were oppressive and vexatious expressly reserved the question whether the magistrates themselves had a discretion to stay the proceedings. Subsequent authorities have, however, confirmed the existence of such a discretion[7] and there is no reason in principle why, for these purposes, the magistrates and the Crown Court should be treated differently.[8] The salient point is that the court is not putting itself into the shoes of the prosecutor or making a reassessment of the merits of the proceedings, but is looking for the existence or otherwise of prejudice to the defendant, having regard to evidence produced to it or to any presumption raised, by reason of manipulation of the court's process or delay in bringing

---

2 See *DPP v Humphrys* [1977] AC 1, [1976] 2 All ER 497, HL; *R v Oxford City Justices, ex p Smith* [1982] 75 Cr App Rep 200.
3 *DPP v Humphrys* [1977] AC 1 at 14 per Viscount Dilhorne and at 35 per Lord Salmon.
4 See also *Atkinson v United States of America Government* [1971] AC 197.
5 [1881–5] All ER Rep 949 at 954.
6 (1980) 75 Cr App Rep 236n.
7 See eg *R v Brentford Justices, ex p Wong* [1981] QB 445 at 450, [1981] 1 All ER 884 at 887F; cf *R v Governor of Pentonville Prison, ex p Sinclair* [1991] 2 AC 64, [1991] 2 WLR 1028, which held that magistrates had no jurisdiction to dismiss proceedings under the Extradition Act 1870 for abuse of process.
8 The jurisdiction seems now to be well established: *R v Brentford Justices, ex p Wong* [1981] QB 445, [1981] 1 All ER 884; *R v Oxford City Justices, ex p Smith* [1982] 75 Cr App Rep 200; *R v Canterbury and St Augustine Justices, ex p Turner* (1983) 147 JP 193; *R v Colwyn Justices, ex p DPP* (1988) 154 JP 989; *R v Sunderland Magistrates' Court, ex p Choudhury* [1988] CO/616/88; *R v Telford Justices, ex p Badhan* [1991] 2 QB 78, [1991] 2 All ER 854.

proceedings. The fears of Viscount Dilhorne are, it is suggested, unwarranted. The power applies to magistrates both when they are trying a case summarily and in their role as examining justices.[9] There seems to be no reason in principle why the transfer provisions of the Criminal Justice Act 1987 should affect the right to make an application to stay proceedings on the grounds of abuse to magistrates in serious fraud cases.

The bases upon which a criminal court may stop a prosecution as an abuse of process are:

(a) if the prosecution has manipulated or misused the process of the court so as to deprive the defendant of a protection provided by the law or to take unfair advantage of a technicality;[10] or

(b) if, on the balance of probability, the defendant has been or will be prejudiced in the preparation or conduct of his defence by delay in the bringing of the proceedings.[11] The existence of substantial delay will raise a presumption in favour of the defendant that he is so prejudiced and it will be for the prosecution to rebut that presumption.[12] The justifiability of the delay will be a factor, though not a conclusive factor in determining whether the application should succeed.[13]

The application will usually be made at an early stage before the magistrates, with a right of appeal by way of judicial review in both summary cases and committal proceedings to the Divisional Court. In cases committed for trial, the application may be renewed at the Crown Court, usually before arraignment, but the prospects of success before a Crown Court judge after an unsuccessful appeal to the Divisional Court cannot be high in the absence of fresh material indicating prejudice.[14] There is now authority that a right to apply for judicial review exists from the decision of a Crown Court Judge refusing an application to dismiss proceedings on indictment as an abuse of process, and the prosecution have a similar right where the application has been successful.[15] In *R v Central Criminal Court, ex p Randle and Pottle*[16] the Divisional Court held that the defendants, who published a book in 1989 describing their part in the escape of master-spy George Blake from prison in 1967 and who were charged in 1990 with aiding and abetting the escape, could apply for an order of certiorari to quash the refusal of the trial judge to stay the proceedings against them. Section 29(3) of the Supreme Court Act 1981[17] did not obstruct

9 *R v Canterbury and St Augustine Justices, ex p Klisiak* [1982] QB 398, [1981] 2 All ER 129; *R v Canterbury and St Augustine Justices, ex p Turner* (1983) 147 JP 193.

10 *R v Derby Crown Court, ex p Brooks* (1984) 80 Cr App Rep 164 at 168 per Sir Roger Ormrod.

11 *R v Derby Crown Court, ex p Brooks* (1984) 80 Cr App Rep 164.

12 *R v Bow Street Stipendiary Magistrate, ex p DPP* (1989) 91 Cr App Rep 283 at 297 per Watkins LJ.

13 Op cit at p 297.

14 See *R v Grob and Hart* (15 January 1990, unreported) – Southwark Crown Court where Judge Denison QC was prepared to stop a prosecution despite the rejection of a similar motion a year earlier by McNeil J.

15 The Court of Appeal has recently indicated, however, that the appropriate course where an application to stay is unsuccessful is for the trial to proceed and, if necessary, for the point to be reargued on appeal. This view may be sound for short trials; it may, however, be more appropriate for short, strong abuse points to be taken to the Divisional Court before a lengthy and complex trial is undergone: *A-G Reference (No 1 of 1990)* (1992) Times, 16 April.

16 [1992] 1 All ER 370, [1991] 1 WLR 1087.

17 Section 29(3) provides: 'In relation to the jurisdiction of the Crown Court *other than its jurisdiction in matters relating to trial on indictment*, the High Court shall have all such jurisdiction to make orders of mandamus, prohibition or certiorari as the High Court possesses in relation to the jurisdiction of an inferior court.'

such an application because it did not, said Watkins LJ, so much affect the conduct of a trial on indictment as determine whether there should ever be a trial at all. The decision in *R v Central Criminal Court, ex p Raymond*,[18] prohibiting judicial review of an Order that an indictment should lie on the file, was distinguished on the ground that abuse of process contemplated that there never would be a trial whereas an Order that the indictment lie on the file marked 'not to be proceeded without leave' contemplated that there might be.[19] In the event of conviction before the Crown Court, the rejection by the trial judge of an application to stay is a matter which could provide a ground of appeal to the Court of Appeal (Criminal Division).[20] It remains to be seen whether the decision in *Randle and Pottle* has any affect on this, although it is unlikely to do so.

On a pre-trial application to stay criminal proceedings as an abuse of process, the judge has no power to order discovery of evidential material and must act on the evidence before him. The witness summons procedure under the Criminal Procedure (Attendance of Witnesses) Act 1965 relates to the trial on indictment and is not applicable outside the confines of the trial itself.[1] Each of the bases will now be considered.

2.1.1   *Manipulation or misuse by the prosecution of the process of the court*

Examples of this head of abuse are not, fortunately, often found. In *R v Brentford Justices, ex p Wong*[2] the Divisional Court held that magistrates were entitled to conclude that it was an abuse of the process of the court for a prosecutor to lay an information against a defendant when he had not yet decided to prosecute in order to gain further time to make that decision. The purpose of section 104 of the Magistrates' Courts Act 1952,[3] which imposed a six-month time limit on commencing the prosecution of summary offences, would, said Donaldson LJ, be wholly frustrated if a prosecutor could obtain a summons and then, in his own good time and at his convenience, serve it.

In *R v Horsham Justices, ex p Reeves*,[4] the Divisional Court stayed summonses which had been served on the defendant in respect of offences of theft, the particulars and evidence of which were identical to offences upon which the magistrates had earlier refused to commit the defendant for trial. In a judgment which has other lessons for fraud prosecutors Ackner LJ said:

> 'It seems to me that the reason for not adopting the ordinary course of applying to the High Court for a voluntary bill was quite simply this. Because there was in the material that was before the magistrates so much that was either irrelevant or of little probative value it would have been difficult on the basis of that material to pinpoint the real foundation of the prosecution charges. Whether or not the prosecution so anticipated, I would have no difficulty in anticipating that a judge reading such a volume of material, a high

18 [1986] 2 All ER 379, [1986] 1 WLR 710.
19 See also *R v Norwich Crown Court, ex p Belsham* [1992] 1 All ER 394, [1992] 1 WLR 54 where the decision in *Randle and Pottle* was explained and followed.
20 See for example *R v Buzalek and Schiffer* [1991] Crim LR 115, CA; see also *A-G's Reference (No 1 of 1990)* (1992) Times, 16 April in which the Court of Appeal held that this was the appropriate course.
1   *R v Manchester Crown Court, ex p Brokenbrow* (1991) Times, 31 October.
2   [1981] QB 445, [1981] 1 All ER 884.
3   Now section 127 of the Magistrates' Courts Act 1980.
4   (1980) 75 Cr App Rep 236n.

proportion of which was either irrelevant or of no probative value, would have shown little sympathy for such an application and that the probabilities are that a dusty answer would have been given and the application dismissed. It seems to me that the course adopted of applying to the justices was looked upon as one whose outcome was likely to be more successful.

Should the prosecution be entitled, as they seek, to treat the first committal proceedings, for all practical purposes as a dummy run, and, having concluded that they over-complicated them, bring virtually the same proceedings but in a form in which they should have been brought if proper thought had been given by the prosecution to them, in the first place?

In my judgment, to allow such a course in the particular circumstances of this case would be vexatious to the applicant, and for that reason it would in my judgment, be an abuse of the process of the Court. There has been considerable anxiety no doubt experienced by the applicant in having to deal with the three-day trial. There has been the passage of time since his arrest in May 1977 and January 1979 when the second run of the prosecution was to take place. There has been considerable expense incurred by him which he will be unable to recover. The suggestion now of course is that he should face a second batch of proceedings.

To grant such an indulgence would, in my judgment, encourage poor preparation with resultant waste of time and money. To allow prohibition in this case should bring home to the prosecution the desirability of following the advice which Appellate Courts have given again and again. The prosecution must direct its energies to the simplification of cases they desire to present. All too often juries, and to a lesser extent magistrates, are treated like computers into whom superfluous and ill-digested material is fed in the over-optimistic hope that somehow or other they will produce the right result. For these reasons I would grant the application.'[5]

The principle here is that *the court* will not allow *its own process* to be manipulated so as to deprive the defendant of a protection. It is open to argument whether a decision by the regulatory authorities to investigate fraud in a company with a view to prosecution by means of the powers contained in section 432 of the Companies Act 1985 rather than by using the more appropriate powers in section 2 of the Criminal Justice Act 1987[6] could result in a decision by the court to stay proceedings commenced as a result of such an investigation (though there may be an argument that this evidence should simply be excluded under section 78 of the Police and Criminal Evidence Act 1984).[7]

In *R v Rotherham Magistrates' Court, ex p Brough*,[8] the defendant allegedly committed an offence ten weeks before his seventeenth birthday. The CPS papers were ready five weeks before his birthday but the police were instructed to secure his attendance in court one day after his seventeenth birthday. The CPS denied that there was any particular reason for this conduct and the court, while holding that the CPS had acted improperly, dismissed an application for judicial review because the CPS had not, it seemed, acted in bad faith or misused or manipulated the process of the court. Doubtless the application would have succeeded if it had been shown that the CPS had delayed commencing proceedings in order to deprive the defendant of juvenile court proceedings and to cause his appearance before a Crown Court.

5 By contrast see *R v Grays Justices, ex p Graham* [1982] QB 1239, [1982] Crim LR 595.
6 Ie because answers given to DTI inspectors are compulsory and admissible in criminal proceedings whereas answers to the SFO, though compulsory are not, save in very limited circumstances, admissible in criminal proceedings.
7 See further Chapter 2, section 2.2.3.
8 [1991] Crim LR 522.

2.1.2   *Delay*

> 'We see no warrant for not following ample precedent, now well set, for the proposition that mere delay which gives rise to prejudice and unfairness may by itself amount to an abuse of the process.'

So concluded Watkins LJ in *R v Bow Street Stipendiary Magistrate, ex p DPP*; *R v Bow Street Stipendiary Magistrate, ex p Cherry*,[9] better known as the '*Wapping* case' because of its origin in the disturbances arising outside printing premises at Wapping in January 1987. The Court of Appeal has, more recently, indicated that stays imposed on the ground of delay (or for any other reason) should only be granted in exceptional circumstances.[10]

Delay as a ground for staying proceedings is long established. In *R v Robins*,[11] Baron Alderson directed a jury to acquit a defendant, charged with an offence of bestiality occurring nearly two years before the case was heard, stating:

> 'It is monstrous to put this man on his trial after such a lapse of time. How can he account for his conduct so far back? If you accuse a man of a crime the next day, he may be enabled to bring forward his servants and family to say where he was and what he was about at the time; but if the charge be not preferred for a year or more, how can he clear himself? No man's life would be safe if such a prosecution were permitted. It would be very unjust to put him on his trial.'

This statement of the common law position, quoted for more than historical curiosity, reflects the present state of the law that the court is concerned with the effect of delay on the ability of the defendant to prepare his defence and its effect on the fairness of the proceedings.

In *Jago v District Court of New South Wales*,[12] a decision of the Supreme Court of Australia, Deane J identified five factors to be considered in deciding whether proceedings should be stayed because of delay. These were:

(i)   the length of the delay;
(ii) the reasons given by the prosecution to justify the delay;
(iii) the defendant's responsibility for, and past attitude to, the delay;
(iv) the proven or likely prejudice to the defendant,
(v)   the public interest in the disposition of charges and serious offences and in the conviction of those guilty of crime.

Deane J observed:

> 'Those five heads provide convenient reference points for answering the question whether the effect of a delay in a particular case is such as to bring about a situation where any trial will necessarily be an unfair one from the accused's point of view. Or, a situation where the continuation of proceedings would be so unfairly oppressive that it would constitute an abuse of process. They should not, however, be treated as a code or permitted to divert attention from the fact that what will ordinarily be involved in answering that question is the formation of a value-judgment in the context of the nature and seriousness of the alleged offence; and having regard to all other relevant circumstances.'

---

9   (1990) 91 Cr App Rep 283.
10 (1992) Times, 16 April.
11 (1844) 1 Cox CC 114.
12 [1989] 87 ALR 577. See also *Bell v DPP* [1985] AC 937, *Barker v Wingo* 407 US 514 (1972).

In the *Wapping* case the Divisional Court held that the burden of showing that the delay complained of had produced genuine prejudice and unfairness rests with the defendant,[13] but conceded that in cases of substantial delay, prejudice will be presumed and it will be for the prosecution, if it can, to rebut the presumption. Watkins LJ expressed reservations as to whether the prosecution should, in every case where delay occurred, justify it before the trial could proceed.[14] In *A-G's Reference (No 1 of 1990)*,[15] in what was an attempt to curb the frequency with which applications were being made, the Court of Appeal stressed that it is for a defendant to show, on a balance of probabilities, that owing to the delay he would suffer serious prejudice to the extent that no fair trial could be held. In assessing the likelihood of prejudice, the trial court should bear in mind the judge's power at common law and under the Police and Criminal Evidence Act 1984 to regulate the admissibility of evidence and the fact that all issues arising from the delay would be placed before the jury as paort of their consideration of the case.

None of the factors described by Deane J will, per se, lead to a stay of proceedings. They are indicators only as to whether, either alone or cumulatively, they have produced prejudice. Mere passage of time, therefore, from offence to trial will not automatically result in a stay of proceedings. The 20-year gap between the alleged offence and trial in *Randle and Pottle*,[16] which the Divisional Court found as a fact, not a result of any fault or inefficiency of the prosecution, was insufficient to stay the proceedings, Mann LJ commenting that it was 'in no sense inappropriate to observe that, in the light of the contents of the book the plea of fading memory could simply not be advanced'. The effect of the length of the delay will, it seems, vary with the circumstances of the case.[17] Courts are prepared to accept that fraud cases, particularly those with an international element requiring cross-frontier inquiries and translation of documents will take longer to bring to trial and that 'the delay that can be tolerated for an ordinary street crime is considerably less than for a serious, complex conspiracy charge'.[18] In every case, however, the longer the delay, the less likely it is that the trial will be fair, even if the accused cannot point to any specific prejudice. When the delay can be justified, such justification is now one factor, and not the conclusive factor, which may be taken into account. Prior to the decision in the *Wapping* case there was some authority that if the delay could be justified, the application for a stay should fail. In *R v Derby Justices, ex p Brooks*,[19] Sir Roger Ormrod's statement of the law disregarded any delay which had been justifiable, such as, for example, 'delay not due to the complexity of the inquiry and preparation of the prosecution case, or to the action of the defendant or his co-accused, or to genuine difficulty in effecting service'.[20]

13 On a balance of probabilities: *R v Telford Justices, ex p Badhan* [1991] 2 QB 78, [1991] 2 All ER 854.
14 Op cit at page 300; see also *Bell v DPP* [1985] AC 937 at 950D.
15 (1992) Times, 16 April 1992.
16 Op cit.
17 *Bell v DPP* [1985] 1 AC 937 per Lord Templeman; see also: *Barker v Wingo* 407 US 514 [1972]; *R v Buzalek* [1991] Crim LR 115 per Taylor LJ; *R v Derby Justices, ex p Brooks* (1985) 80 Cr App Rep 164; *R v Bow Street Magistrates' Court, ex p DPP* (1992) Independent, 31 January.
18 *Bell v DPP* [1985] AC 937 at 951E; see also per Lord Lane CJ in *A-G's Reference (No 1 of 1990)* (1992) Times, 16 April.
19 (1985) 80 Cr App Rep 164.
20 Op cit at 169.

In *R v Colwyn Justices, ex p DPP*,[1] where the Divisional Court upheld the decision of magistrates to stay proceedings against two police officers for assault, Watkins LJ stated:

> 'It is quite impossible for any other decision to be reached than that there was here, regardless of excuse, inordinate delay which would profoundly affect the capacity of the respondents personally to defend themselves.'

In *Bell v DPP*[2] and *Jago*[3] again, justification was regarded as one factor among many to be considered in deciding whether the proceedings should be stayed. In *R v Oxford City Justices, ex p Smith*[4] a two-year delay due to the inefficiency of the prosecution in hearing proceedings for an offence against section 6(1) of the Road Traffic Act 1972 was stayed because, whilst the accused might be able to recall driving the car and being drunk, he could not explore the availability of any other defences open to him.[5] In *R v Grob and Hart*[6] the application to stay succeeded notwithstanding the acknowledged difficulties encountered by the DPP in investigating a complex international insurance fraud. In the *Wapping* case, the proceedings were stayed notwithstanding a policy decision by the CPS not to commence proceedings until all investigations into allegations of police misconduct had been completed. In the context of fraud and insider dealing, therefore, where prosecutions are frequently preceded by some form of statutory inquiry, the court may accede to an application based on delay even though the decision to hold such an inquiry was justifiable.

The decision in *A-G's Reference (No 1 of 1990)*[7] confirms that justification is a factor to be taken into account even where there has been no fault on the part of the prosecutor. The court indicated, however, that where the delay was unjustifiable, a stay should be the exception rather than the rule; where the delay was justifiable, a stay would only be rarely granted.

In determining whether delay has caused prejudice to the defendants, the court is concerned to safeguard three interests of the defendant in facing a prompt trial:

(i)   preventing oppressive pre-trial incarceration;
(ii) minimising the anxiety and concern of the defendant;
(iii) limiting the possibility that delay will impair preparation of the defence.[8]

Item (iii) has been described as the most serious[9] and ability to demonstrate, or raise a presumption of, impairment is likely to determine the success of the application. In *R v Derby Justices, ex p Brooks*,[10] the Divisional Court held that the five to six year delay in commencing proceedings had not prejudiced the defendant because he had always admitted his guilt and would, the court believed, inevitably plead guilty at his trial. This peculiar approach was reiterated, though perhaps less enthusiastically, in *Randle and Pottle*[11] by Watkins LJ who said:

1   (1988) 154 JP 989.
2   Op cit.
3   Op cit.
4   (1982) 75 Cr App Rep 200.
5   See also: *R v Watford Justices, ex p Outrim* [1982] Crim LR 593.
6   (15 January 1990, unreported) Southwark Crown Court.
7   (1992) Times, 16 April, CA.
8   *Bell v DPP* [1985] AC 937.
9   Op cit at p 951E.
10 (1984) 80 Cr App Rep 164.
11 Op cit.

'It is maintained that it is irrelevant that courts may suspect that the applicants have no good defence. We disagree. There is a significant difference, in our judgment, between a case where guilt is squarely in issue and one in which it is suspected that it is not, or may not be. The value to be attached to that in the judgment of the court depends entirely upon the circumstances. It cannot, in our view, be left entirely out of account in this case but we regard it as being far from the most influential of the factors which should govern the decision. The judge appears to have paid little or no attention to it.'

A distinction is also drawn between those cases which rely entirely upon a witness's memory and those which rely heavily upon documents.

In *R v Buzalek and Schiffer*,[12] in rejecting a submission that prosecution for offences of unlawful trading six-and-a-half years after the offences had been committed, Taylor LJ, said:

'So far as [impairment] is concerned, the learned Judge, sensibly in our view, bore in mind that this was a case which turned largely on documents and that it would be possible by reference to those documents for memories and recollections to be charged.

It is important to distinguish between the sort of case in which what is going to be in issue at the trial is the recollection of witnesses about some event unsupported by documents and a case which largely (like this one) turns upon the documents. If after 6 years a case is going to have to turn on what witnesses saw in an affray, or in the course of an assault, or in the course of some road accident, then clearly the passage of time is going to be much more prejudicial than it is if there are documents indicating what was sent from one party to the other and what one party was saying to the other at the time.'

Similarly, in *R v Bow Street Magistrates' Court, ex p DPP*,[13] a delay of 18 years was insufficient to stay proceedings in a case where the issues to be decided depended on documents which were still in existence. In *R v Bow Street Magistrates' Court, ex p Watts Langstone and Parlane*,[14] the existence of a video film of the disorder likely to be at issue in the trial led to the rejection of an application to stay.

Conversely, in *R v Telford Justices, ex p Badhan*,[15] the Divisional Court stayed committal proceedings commenced in May 1989 for an offence of rape allegedly committed on a date unknown between 15 February 1973 and 14 February 1974. The complaint had not been made until mid-September 1988, by which time it had become impossible to conduct an investigation for the purpose of preparing a defence. The court described the exercise of investigating, for example, an alibi for an unknown Saturday evening in a year commencing 16 years previously as a 'doomed enterprise'. The court also appears to have had regard to the strength of the evidence and one is left wondering whether the same result would have been reached had the complaints been corroborated and an admission made to the police.

Other factors to which the court will have regard are the availability of witnesses and the health of the defendants[16] and, where a potential defendant has died or become ill, the inability of other defendants to cross-examine him. The court also has regard to the seriousness of the offence. In one sense, such a consideration should not only be irrelevant, but should operate more

12 [1991] Crim LR 115, CA.
13 (1992) Independent, 31 January.
14 (19 October 1990, unreported) Divisional Court.
15 [1991] 2 QB 78, [1991] 2 All ER 854.
16 See, for example, the chronicle of disasters that beset the case of *R v Grob and Hart* op cit.

stringently in favour of a defendant where the offence with which he is charged is more serious. But authority clearly points to a readier acceptance of the existence of prejudice in less serious cases.[17]

2.2   Motions to quash the indictment

Arguments about motions to quash the indictment in serious fraud cases are no different from those advanced in all other criminal cases. Arguments about the form of the indictment, however, are in some cases more problematical because of the prevalence of the use of the charge of conspiracy to defraud. The possibility of bringing a motion to quash the indictment is also increased by the mechanics of the transfer provisions. As stated in Chapter 3, the material which must be produced on transfer may be restricted to a 'statement of the evidence on which any charge to which the notice of transfer relates is based',[18] and there is no specific provision for the supply to the defence of the statements and documents supporting the 'statement of evidence'. Even if statements and documents are supplied, (as, in fact, they invariably will be) there may well be elements of the statement of evidence which are not supported by those documents. A transfer notice issued pursuant to the regulations will state that:

> 'The bill of indictment against the defendant may include either in substitution for or in addition to any count charging an offence specified in the notice of transfer, any counts founded upon evidence set out in the material that accompanies this notice, being counts which may lawfully be joined in the same indictment.'

Section 2(2)(iA) of the Administration of Justice (Miscellaneous Provisions) Act 1933[19] states:

> 'Subject as hereinafter provided no bill of indictment charging any person with an indictable offence shall be preferred unless either –
>
> (a) the person charged has been committed for trial for the offence; or
> (aa) the offence is specified in a notice of transfer under section 4 of the Criminal Justice Act 1987 . . .
>   Provided that –
>   (i)   where the person charged has been committed for trial the bill of indictment may include either in substitution for or in addition to counts charging the offence for which he was committed, any fact founded on facts or evidence disclosed in any examination or deposition taken before a justice . . .
>   (iA) in a case to which paragraph (aa) applies the bill of indictment may include either in substitution for or in addition to any count charging an offence specified in the notice of transfer, any counts founded on material that accompanied the copy of that notice which, in pursuance of regulations under section 5(9) of the Criminal Justice Act 1987, was given to the person charged, being counts which may lawfully be joined in the same indictment.'

There is no definition of 'material' in proviso (iA), but it was clearly intended to include matter set out in the statement of the evidence.[20] There is very little authority on the question of the extent to which facts or evidence as set out in

17 See eg *R v Oxford City Justice, ex p Smith* (1982) 75 Cr App Rep 200.
18 The Criminal Justice Act 1987 (Notice of Transfer) Regulations 1988, regulation 4(B).
19 As amended by the 1987 Act, Sch 2, para 1(1) and by the 1988 Act, Sch 15, para 10.
20 See Chapter 3, section 2.2.

proviso (i) includes anything other than evidence founded on statements and documents produced by the Crown at committal. In *R v Thomas*[1] it was held that for an offence to be disclosed, some evidence, facts or material showing that the offence had been committed was needed, even if it was the case that the prosecution might need further evidence to consolidate their case.[2]

A motion to quash cannot be used, in normal criminal cases, as a second pre-trial opportunity to challenge the prosecution case on the ground that there is no case to answer.[3] Where the case has been transferred, however, particularly where the statement of the evidence is not fully supported by evidence in proper form, a motion to quash might be seen as a convenient way of challenging a transfer, as opposed to making an application under section 6 of the Act. On such a motion, it would be necessary for the prosecution to set out the evidence which purportedly supports the material contained in the statement of evidence, and also to prove that that evidence was available at the time of transfer.

Where there is documentary evidence, which has not been produced by a statement at the time of transfer, there should be no difficulty in showing that there was material on which the transfer was properly based. Nevertheless the prosecution will wish to consider whether an early transfer of a case to the Crown Court, before all essential evidence has been assembled in proper form, may not lead to difficulties at a later stage on a motion to quash.

A successful motion to quash leads to a discharge and not an acquittal, and therefore it is possible for the prosecution to reinstate the proceedings. However, a quashed indictment nullifies the proceedings ab initio, and therefore the prosecution will in practice need to apply for a voluntary bill of indictment to reinstate them.

2.3 Amendments to the indictment

Applications to amend the indictment should probably, as stated above, be made in advance of the preparatory hearing, although an indictment can be amended at any stage of a trial which, in the case of a serious and complex fraud, would include the preparatory hearing.

The procedure for amending an indictment is no different in serious fraud cases than it is in any other criminal cases, and follows the provisions of section 5 of the Indictments Act 1915. Once again, however, difficulties with the form of a count alleging conspiracy to defraud may provide more fertile ground for applications to amend than counts founded on statutory provisions. The difficulties posed by various judicial pronouncements in conspiracy to defraud cases[4] can still lead to extensive argument about the proper form in which to plead this offence.

2.4 Severance

The power to sever an indictment and to order separate trials derives from section 5(3) of the Indictments Act 1915:

---

1 (1947) 32 Cr App Rep 50, CCA.
2 Ibid at page 53.
3 See *R v Chairman County of London Quarter Sessions, ex p Downes* [1954] 1 QB 1, [1953] 2 All ER 750.
4 See Chapter 6 below.

'Where, before trial, or at any stage of a trial, the Court is of opinion that a person accused may be prejudiced or embarrassed in his defence by reason of being charged with more than one offence in the same indictment, or that for any other reason it is desirable to direct that the person should be tried separately for any one or more offences charged in an indictment, the Court may order a separate trial of any count or counts of such indictment.'

It is clear from this provision that an application for severance can be made before the preparatory hearing, or as part of it. Such an application may, indeed, be made 'at any stage of the trial', and a decision made by a judge before the preparatory hearing can be reviewed and altered during the preparatory hearing or the trial.[5]

2.4.1 Length and manageability of trial

Among the main problems confronting a court which is trying a serious and complex fraud will be length of trial, manageability and fairness. The court will wish to ensure that the indictment lodged by the Crown is capable of being understood by a jury, does not impose too great a burden on them by reason of probable length of trial, and at the same time gives the Crown the opportunity to present its case fully against the defendants. Where the indictment contains a count of conspiracy to defraud, the Crown will wish to try all defendants together on all the particulars of the conspiracy alleged in the indictment, and it is clear that although there is no rule of law which requires that co-conspirators should be tried together in one trial, a joint trial is to be preferred.[6]

Arguments in serious fraud cases on severance will often encompass both severance by defendant and severance by count. In the *Guinness* case, severance by subject matter resulted in orders for three separate trials which, had they run to their conclusion, would probably have spanned more than two-and-a-half years.[7] In severing defendants, and thereby ordering second or third trials, judges will inevitably bear in mind the fairness and feasibility of a subsequent trial, in the light of a number of important factors:

(a) Will a defendant be so prejudiced by the reporting and result of a first trial that his second trial will be unfair?[8]
(b) Is it inherently unfair on a defendant to have to wait weeks or months for his trial?
(c) If defendants are acquitted in one trial but convicted in another trial, will the acquittals cast doubt on the safety of the convictions?
(d) Will the same witnesses have to give evidence in the separate trials, and will any differences in their evidence cause doubt to be cast on their integrity?
(e) Will the sheer length of time taken to complete the cycle of trials result in a sense of surfeit in the judge and prosecuting counsel, and a feeling in the jury that the case has been over-prosecuted?

These considerations, and others like them, will lead to submissions that second and subsequent trials are an abuse of process. In all the circumstances,

---

5 See *R v Wright* (1989) 90 Cr App Rep 325, CA.
6 See eg *R v Moghal* (1977) 65 Cr App Rep 56, CA.
7 The first trial started on 5 February 1990, but if the preparatory hearings are included as part of the trial, a further year needs to be added to the time span. In February 1992, when Henry J stopped the second *Guinness* case, only 10 out of 80 witnesses had been called to give evidence in a period of five months.
8 See this chapter below, section 3.6.

therefore, severance by defendant is an innately unattractive option, particularly in cases where the evidence which will be adduced in the second trial is essentially the same as that adduced at the first trial. Severance by count, or by allegation within a count of, for example, conspiracy to defraud also has its difficulties. The result of such severance may well be two or more trials for individual defendants. The Crown will be very unwilling to countenance such a procedure when it must be clear that, in the event of an acquittal in the first trial, it will be unattractive to proceed with a second trial; and, conversely, a conviction in the first trial will have the effect of making a second, or even third, trial oppressive.

The problems of severance for reasons of good management of potentially long trials have been the subject of trenchant judicial comment in a number of cases. In these cases, judges have united in condemning long trials. At the same time, they have shown a distinct unwillingness to allow appeals based on submissions that the trial was unfair by reason of its length.

In *R v Thorne*[9] a number of defendants were charged with a series of conspiracies to rob. The trial lasted 111 working days. At the appeal it was contended that the trial was so long and so complicated that it was impossible for the appellants to have a fair trial. Lord Justice Lawton said:[10]

'Like Topsy, this case just grew and grew. In the end it became a mammoth of a case. Until a few weeks ago it was the longest criminal trial ever in our Courts. Others of the same breed are around, their extinction is desirable ... The Court has noticed a tendency recently for prosecuting counsel to overload indictments. There must be an end to this. Indictments must be kept short. No more accused should be indicted together than is necessary for the proper presentation of the prosecution case against the principal accused. Necessity, not convenience, should be the guiding factor.'

In *R v Simonds*,[11] a case concerning conspiracies to cheat and defraud the Inland Revenue, the defendants appealed on the ground, inter alia, that the length and complexity of the trial had been such that justice could not be done to the individual defendants, whatever care the judge took. The case lasted 81 days, and the Court of Appeal clearly expressed concern about the 'inordinate burden' which such a trial imposed on all concerned, thereby greatly increasing the risks of injustice. Fenton Atkinson J said:

'If upon examination of material before him the Judge considers that the presentation of the case in the way proposed by the prosecution involves undue burdens on the Court in general and jurors in particular, and is for this or other reasons contrary to the interests of justice, he has a right and, indeed, a duty to ask that the prosecution recast their approach in those interests, even if a considerable adjournment is entailed.'[12]

The judge also considered the position of the jury, but while expressing concern for their ability to handle such a case, he said:

'As regards the jury, everyone must sympathise with them on the ordeal to which they were put. It is, however, right to mention that the calibre of juries today can be high, and that their capacity to follow weeks of evidence should not be underestimated. It is, for instance, far from unknown nowadays for

---

9   (1977) 66 Cr App Rep 6.
10 Ibid at page 12.
11 [1969] 1 QB 685, [1967] 3 All ER 399n.
12 Ibid at page 692.

several members of the jury to correct counsel or the Court in the course of such a trial should a wrong exhibit number or date be quoted. The summing up commences with a reference to tributes paid to this particular jury by Counsel for the prosecution and the defence and goes on:

> "Those of us who have spent our working lives in the Courts and who have been present in this Court have not failed to notice with admiration the attention and concentration which you have paid hour after hour, day after day, week after week, and month after month."

Moreover, an examination of the transcript shows how keenly and accurately the foreman in particular followed the case and that the above tributes were no mere formality.'[13]

In *R v Novac*[14] the Court of Appeal expressed the conviction that nothing short of the criterion of absolute necessity could justify the imposition of the burdens of a very long trial on the court. Brevity and simplicity, the court held, are the handmaidens of justice, length and complexities its enemies.[15]

In *R v Landy, White and Kay*[16] the Court of Appeal pointed out that:

> 'Robust pre-trial review might have avoided many of the troubles that were to follow thereafter . . . Prosecuting counsel who have become immersed in the details of a case for months sometimes do not appreciate the difficulty which a judge and jury may have in assimilating the evidence. At the pre-trial review the Judge who should normally be the one who is going to try the case should be ready and willing to take the initiative to ensure that all unnecessary detail is omitted.'

These injunctions to judges and prosecutors have not always been found easy to follow. It is argued that it would be unsatisfactory if, simply because the case was so complicated as to make a trial unmanageable, the alleged perpetrators of the fraud went unpunished. The Serious Fraud Office maintains that it has a mandate to investigate and to bring to trial complex frauds, and this will inevitably mean that from time to time cases are tried which run the risk of being unmanageable. They seek to minimise this risk by the use of computer graphics, glossaries, admissions and intensive weeding out of irrelevant documents, but the extent to which they succeed in achieving manageability will always be a subject of debate.

The Roskill Committee expressed concerns about length of trial, particularly as it impacted on juries.[17] The Committee's conclusion was that for a very few of the most serious and complex fraud trials, the jury was not an appropriate tribunal. In a comment which, arguably, should cause concern to those who maintain that a randomly selected jury can comprehend serious and complex fraud trials, the report states:

> 'Research findings strongly support the view of experienced observers and the promptings of common sense, that the most complex of fraud cases will exceed the limits of comprehension of members of the jury. We have no doubt that most ordinary jurors experience great difficulties in following the arguments and retaining in their minds the essential points at issue, particularly in a long hearing of a complex character. This creates the serious risk either that the jury will acquit a defendant because they have not understood the evidence or will

---

13 Ibid at page 694.
14 (1976) 65 Cr App Rep 107.
15 Ibid at page 119.
16 [1981] 1 WLR 355, 72 Cr App Rep 237.
17 Roskill Report, paragraphs 8.31ff.

convict him if they mistakenly *think* that they have understood it when they have in fact done little more than applied the maxim "there's no smoke without fire".'[18]

However, since no research can be carried out into the way in which juries deal with long and complex trials,[19] any views expressed about the way they reach their conclusions must remain speculation, even if supported by 'the promptings of common sense'.[20]

3   THE PREPARATORY HEARING: II

Once the form of the indictment has been agreed, the defendant or defendants may be asked to plead to it. With arraignment, the preparatory hearing and the trial technically begin.

While any number of matters may be raised within the preparatory hearing, consideration is given below to issues which are most likely to be raised.

3.1   Admissibility of documentary evidence

3.1.1   Selection of documents

It has increasingly become the practice of fraud prosecutors to be very selective in compiling bundles of documentary exhibits for the jury at trial. In any serious and complex fraud case there will be a mass of documents from which to make this selection, some emanating from previous investigations (including inspections under the Companies Act 1985), some from the immediate investigation.

Prosecutors have rightly understood the virtue of brevity, and recognised the evil of photocopying every available document, and in so doing have gone a long way towards the goal of simplifying trials for the jury's comprehension.[1]

Selection, however, poses its own problems. An attempt to over-simplify can result in the presentation of a case which fails to comprehend the true complexities of the issues involved. A selection can appear to be biased if it omits prosecution documents which provide support for the defence case. Documents may be taken from a variety of sources, and different copies of the same document might exist. Where these copies have manuscript markings or other additions subsequent to their creation selecting a single version may be prejudicial to the defence or prosecution. At the other end of the scale, a selection which is simply a vague pruning of large numbers of documents will serve little useful purpose.

At the preparatory hearing, the Crown will produce a schedule of the documents to go into the jury bundle. The defence will be entitled to make

---

18 Ibid, paragraph 8.34.
19 Contempt of Court Act 1981 section 8.
20 The Royal Commission on Criminal Justice has indicated that it will carry out research into jury behaviour. The SFO, in its submissions to the Royal Commission, firmly supported the retention of juries in fraud trials (paragraphs 5.31–5.44).
1 In the 3rd SFO Annual Report (1990–1991) the Director noted that 'in one case the pages copied for the jury have been reduced to a few hundred pages out of approximately 65,000 pages of exhibits' (para 10.4).

submissions about the inclusion (or even exclusion) of documents on the ground of admissibility, and it is these submissions which will frequently occupy the majority of the time taken up by the preparatory hearing.

Arguments about inclusion will be complicated, in a multi-defendant case, by the competing wishes of the defendants, since one defendant wishing to include prosecution documents which others wish to exclude will prevail, and the document will be allowed to remain in the jury bundle. The situation will arise where a document is admissible as regards one defendant and is inadmissible as regards others. In an extreme case, an argument on admissibility in these circumstances could lead to separate trials if the judge concludes that the prejudice to one or more defendants outweighs other considerations.

The problems of selection of documents for jury bundles do not end with arguments over admissibility. The fact remains that in any case where, say, 65,000 documents available to the prosecution are whittled down to a few hundred, many of the 65,000 pages will still constitute available admissible evidence, some of which, at some stage of the trial, could be added to the jury bundle or shown to the jury on a VDU. While the technical production or presentation of documents will pose few problems, there may well be arguments over admissibility which will interrupt the trial. In other words, the points raised in a preparatory hearing will not exhaust the capacity for legal argument in the case as a whole.[2]

3.1.2   Criminal Justice Act 1988 Part II

The law relating to documentary hearsay has an important application in fraud cases where proving a case will depend to a much greater extent on documentary evidence than most other criminal cases.

The perception of the importance of this subject in fraud cases was reflected in the attention which it received from the Roskill Committee. Their report provided a summary of the history of the admissibility provisions relating to documentary hearsay, reviewed the evidential problems in fraud cases, and concluded:

> 'We believe that the basic rule should be that in criminal proceedings arising from fraud, documents should be allowed to speak for themselves and thus become admissible without further proof. Whether or not a particular document which is currently inadmissible should be permitted to be given in evidence should be a matter for the Judge to decide by the exercise of a discretion in advance of the trial. In other words, the Judge should be given an "inclusory" discretion.'[3]

The common law rule on admissibility of statements contained in documents for the purpose of proving the truth of the statement is that to be admissible they must come within the exceptions to the hearsay rule.[4]

The common law rule was altered by statute, the Criminal Evidence Act 1965, so as to make certain trade or business records admissible where those records had been compiled from information provided by a person who had a personal knowledge of the matters recorded, provided that that person was

---

2   In *R v Natwest Investment Bank*, there were ten days of legal argument during the prosecution case (which lasted a total of 103 days).
3   Roskill Report, paragraph 5.35.
4   *Myers v DPP* [1965] AC 1001.

unable to testify or could not reasonably be expected to have any recollection of the information provided.

The 1965 Act was repealed, and its provisions relating to admissibility of documentary evidence were replaced, by section 68 of PACE. Although this provision made it simpler to introduce such evidence, its admissibility continued to be governed by the dual requirements of compilation pursuant to a duty and lack of availability, or inability, to testify of the witness. One major consideration behind the enactment of this provision was to extend the scope of the hearsay rule exception, which had been provided by the 1965 Act, to public records.

The impetus for further change, partly prompted by the Roskill Report, resulted in the provisions contained in Part II of the 1988 Act, which repealed section 68 of PACE.[5] The intention of the legislation is:

(a) to make first-hand hearsay in a document admissible in certain circumstances (section 23);
(b) to make statements in business documents admissible in certain circumstances (section 24);
(c) to give a discretion to the court to exclude material which otherwise comes within (a) and (b) (section 25).

Much has been written about Part II of the Act[6] and interpretation of its provisions has caused some problems. It addresses the requirement to allow certain documents to 'speak for themselves' rather than having to be strictly proved by oral evidence from witnesses. Roskill gave the example of a cheque. In itself, a cheque could not prove the transaction which it purported to carry out. 'The drawer of the cheque, the Bank Clerk and the payee, should come for they alone can speak of the transaction.' As a result, documents '. . . merely support the oral evidence of live witnesses. It is they who must both identify the document and tell of the truth or otherwise of its contents.'[7]

Section 23   In order to avoid this problem, section 23 of the 1988 Act allows statements made in documents to be admitted in evidence, where oral evidence of the same would be admissible, if the person who made the statement is unavailable because they are either dead, ill, out of the jurisdiction and 'it is not reasonably practical to secure his attendance', or they cannot, in spite of reasonable steps having been taken, be found.[8] A witness statement recorded by a police officer 'or some other person charged with the duty of investigating offences or charging of offenders' can be admissible if the maker of the statement is too frightened to give evidence or is 'kept out of the way'.[9]

In order to procure admission of such evidence under the section, the Crown will need to prove, to the satisfaction of the court,[10] the various conditions precedent for admissibility. Death or medical certificates should cause no problems. However, proving that all reasonable efforts have been made to

---

5   Criminal Justice Act 1988 Sch 16.
6   See eg Di Birch [1989] Criminal Law Review 15–31; Mark Ockelton [1992] Criminal Law Review 15–21; and there are sections in *Cross on Evidence* (7th edn pp 628–634 and Zander *Police and Criminal Evidence Act 1984* (2nd edn) pp 176–180.
7   Roskill Report, paragraphs 5.10–5.11.
8   Section 23(2).
9   Section 23(3).
10 See *R v Case* [1991] Crim LR 192, CA where it was held that the burden of proof is on the prosecution and it is the criminal burden; *R v De Orango* [1992] Crim LR 180, CA; and *R v Bray* (1988) 88 Cr App Rep 354.

secure the attendance of a witness who is overseas, for example, may cause more difficulty. There is no method by which the attendance of a witness who is out of the jurisdiction can be secured[11] but the Crown must, presumably, at least request attendance. A witness summons can be served under section 2 of the Criminal Justice (International Cooperation) Act 1990, and proof of service of process may assist the argument. A letter from the potential witness refusing to attend, and giving reasons, may also assist, and should probably be considered conclusive in the absence of special considerations. The reasonable practicality of securing attendance must be looked at 'against the background of the whole case'.[12]

Proving that sufficient or reasonable efforts have been made to trace a witness who is thought to be within the jurisdiction could rely on a letter sent to a last known address being returned by the Post Office with an assertion that there is no forwarding address. Courts, however, might require more cogent evidence of inquiries where it is considered that the evidence is of particular importance, and section 25(2)(d) might have to be carefully considered by the court.

Where proof of 'fear' or 'being kept out of the way' is required, for the purposes of section 23(3)(b) it has been held that the prosecution must prove the matter beyond reasonable doubt by admissible evidence.[13] Although it is unlikely that the Crown will need to rely on section 23(3) in fraud cases, it is nonetheless to be noted that the identity of the 'other person charged with the duty of investigating offences' could include a Department of Trade inspector who could, in some circumstances, be described as having a duty to investigate offences.[14] Statements made to inspectors in documentary form, for example as a preliminary statement or in a submission subsequent to an interview, might be admissible. This would require, however, a concession from the Crown that inspectors appointed by the Secretary of State for Trade and Industry are investigating offences, a concession which would not otherwise be in their interests.

Section 23(4) preserves the integrity of section 76 of PACE as it applies to confessions, and therefore makes clear that the section has no relevance to confession evidence.[15]

Section 24   Documents 'created or received by a person in the course of' a business etc are admissible in evidence if the information in the document 'was supplied by a person (whether or not the maker of the statement) who had, or may reasonably be supposed to have had, personal knowledge of the matters dealt with'. The section relaxes the previous conditions for admissibility, under Section 68 of PACE, by avoiding the concepts of 'duty' and 'records' which were imported into the law on admissibility because they were thought to guarantee reliability. These requirements, however, restricted availability to what the Roskill Committee regarded as an unnecessary extent,[16] and section

---

11 See this chapter, section 3.4.5. below.
12 *R v Bray*, supra.
13 *R v O'Loughlin and McLoughlin* [1988] 3 All ER 431, 85 Cr App Rep 157 (a decision under the similar Criminal Justice Act 1925 section 13(3)); *R v Acton Justices, ex p McMullen*; *R v Tower Bridge Justices, ex p Lawlor*, (1990) 92 Cr App Rep 98.
14 See Chapter 2, section 2.2.3.
15 See Birch, op cit at page 24 for an argument that the subsection is in any event unnecessary.
16 Roskill Report, paragraph 5.16.

24 releases the court from such a restriction by the formula of 'creation in the course of trade'.

The section also goes further in an important respect than its predecessor by rendering admissible a document which is not only 'created', but also 'received', in the course of business, so long as the person supplying the information had, or 'may reasonably be supposed to have had, personal knowledge of the matters dealt with'. If the information is supplied indirectly, each person through whom the information passes must have received it in the course of business etc or as the holder of a paid or unpaid office. The information need not pass in documentary form, so that the index number of a car, for example, can be passed on from police officer to police officer orally before being committed to a statement in a document (although the chain would presumably be broken if a passer-by became one of the links in it).

In addition, the section contains no pre-condition (as in section 68(2) of PACE) that in order for the records to be admissible the Crown has to prove that it was not reasonably practicable to secure the attendance of the maker of the document.

Taken on its own, section 24 has some elastic consequences,[17] but it may be assumed that the judicial discretion contained in section 25 will limit the admissibility of business documents within reasonable bounds. In other words, the relaxation provided by section 24 constitutes only a procedure of provisional admissibility, and it may be seen as more satisfactory that limits have been pushed back at the same time as imposing a judicial discretion.

The problem, however, of pushing back the limits lies in defining where the absolute limit, beyond which a document is clearly inadmissible, exists. For example, does section 24 affect the rules which apply to memory-refreshing documents? Does it render an aide memoire admissible where it is intended to call a witness to give evidence? This question may have considerable significance in a fraud case where reliance is placed by the Crown on memoranda which serve the purpose of assisting witnesses to give evidence, to the extent of wanting the memoranda to be placed before the jury in a jury bundle.

It may be argued that the importance of live witnesses is the oral evidence that they give in court, not the production to the court of a note they made on a previous occasion. The witness may refresh his memory from the note, but it does not go before the jury unless it is judged appropriate for the jury to see it for the purpose of following the cross-examination upon it.[18] The document, it is argued, should not become evidence itself and assume greater importance than oral testimony, particularly in the sense of being seen as a previous consistent statement such as to enhance the testimony in the eyes of the jury.

This argument depends on acceptance of the submission that the section does not envisage that the maker of the statement in the document is called. Indeed, it may be asked what purpose can possibly be served by producing both witness and document. The argument is given added emphasis by Schedule 2 para 2 to the Act:

> 'A statement which is given in evidence by virtue of Part 2 of this Act shall not be capable of corroborating evidence given by the person making it.'

---

17 See, eg Birch, op cit, page 25.
18 *R v Sekhon* (1986) 85 Cr App Rep 19.

This suggests that a memory-refreshing purpose should not justify the admission into evidence of an aide memoire. Further reinforcement for the argument is, it may be argued, provided by section 25(2)(b) of the Act.

Section 25   Any statement in a document which is admissible by virtue of sections 23 or 24 may nevertheless be excluded if the court 'is of the opinion that in the interests of justice' the statement ought not to be admitted. In considering whether to admit a document, the court has a *duty* to have regard to the following considerations:[19]

> '(a) the nature and source of the document containing the statement and whether or not, having regard to its nature and source, to any other circumstances that appear to the court to be relevant, it is likely that the document is authentic;
> (b) the extent to which the statement appears to supply evidence which would otherwise not be readily available;
> (c) the relevance of the evidence that it appears to supply to any issue which is likely to have to be determined in the proceedings; and
> (d) any risk, having regard in particular to whether it is likely to be possible to controvert the statement if the person making it does not attend to give oral evidence in the proceedings, that its admission or exclusion will result in unfairness to the accused or, if there is more than one, to any of them.'

As stated above, the section provides a form of conditional admissibility for documentary evidence, and effectively turns the question of admissibility upside down. The balance of arguments on admissibility has now shifted away from the concept that statements in documents are 'inadmissible unless . . .', towards the concept that such evidence is 'admissible unless', as recommended by the Roskill Report.

Sections 26–28   Section 26 concerns statements which have been prepared for the purposes of criminal proceedings or investigations. The court must grant leave before such a document can be adduced in evidence without calling the witness and, in deciding whether to give leave, the court must consider whether it is in the interests of justice, particularly bearing in mind

> '. . . any risk, having regard in particular to whether it is likely to be possible to controvert the statement if the person making it does not attend to give oral evidence in the proceedings, that its admission or exclusion will result in unfairness to the accused or, if there is more than one, to any of them.'

The purpose of the section is to clarify the point that witness statements and depositions are admissible – a point which was not clear from section 68 of PACE.

Section 27 states that a statement in a document may be proved either by the production of the original document, or

> '. . . (whether or not that document is still in existence) by the production of a copy of that document, or of the material part of it, authenticated in such manner as the court may approve; and it is immaterial for the purposes of this subsection how many removes there are between a copy and the original.'

Section 28 confirms that: 'A statement not made by a person while giving oral evidence in court which is admissible otherwise than by virtue of this part of

19 Section 25(2).

this Act' is still admissible; and that the court retains powers to exclude at its discretion a statement admissible by virtue of Part II of the Act.

Schedule 2   Where a statement has been admitted without the witness being called, Schedule 2 preserves the right of the accused to call evidence as to:

(a) the credibility of the person making the statement;
(b) the witness's credibility in so far as it might have been tested in cross-examination by matters which could not have been adduced in evidence; and
(c) as to previous inconsistent statements.[20]

A statement in a document is not capable of corroborating other evidence given by the person making it.[1] The court is also directed to consider the weight to be attached to a statement in a document, by having regard to 'all the circumstances from which any inference can reasonably be drawn as to its accuracy or otherwise'.[2]

3.1.3   Computer evidence: PACE section 69

The admissibility of evidence deriving from computer records has created significant problems ever since computer records became common place. Section 69 of PACE governs the current position on the admissibility of computer records, permitting the admission into evidence of such records, subject to conditions.[3]

Some of the problems have stemmed from the fact that computers have differing functions. A computer can be seen as simply an elaborate calculator, on the one hand, and on the other hand it is a storer, retriever and analyser of information.

As a calculator, any printout it produces does not offend against the rules of hearsay; it is, rather, a primary source of fact which constitutes real evidence. As such, it does not have to be brought within the provisions of sections 23 and 24 of the Criminal Justice Act 1988 or section 69 of PACE.

Many cases relating to this type of computer evidence have arisen out of the intoximeter used to test the level of intoxication of drivers and radar speedometers used to test car speeds. In such instances 'information is recorded by mechanical means without the intervention of a human mind' and it is reasonable to accept the validity of such evidence provided that the machine is reliable. Questions relating to the reliability of the machine go to weight rather than admissibility and have nothing to do with the hearsay rule.[4] In *R v Spiby*[5] the Court of Appeal held that a computer installed to record by purely mechanical means and without human intervention the telephone calls made by hotel guests for accounts purposes, produced printouts which were admissible as real evidence and were not subject to section 69 of PACE.

20 Paragraph 1 (a)–(c).
1   Paragraph 2.
2   Paragraph 3.
3   Section 69 was based on proposals contained in the Criminal Law Revision Committee, 11th Report, and it closely follows the Civil Evidence Act 1968 section 5.
4   See 'The Admissibility of Statements by Computer' by Professor JC Smith [1981] Crim LR 387 and a note by the same author at [1983] Crim LR 472, cited with approval by Steyn J in *R v Minors* [1989] 2 All ER 208 at 211.
5   (1990) 91 Cr App Rep 186.

Section 69 of PACE, supplemented by Parts II and III of Schedule 3 to the Act, provides, in a negative way, for the admissibility of evidence stored in and retrieved from computer records. Such records are not admissible unless:

(a) there are no reasonable grounds for believing that the statement is inaccurate because of improper use of the computer;
(b) at all material times the computer was operating properly in relation to the relevant document; and
(c) that any relevant rules are satisfied.[6]

The Schedule adds a further hurdle to the admission of such evidence by requiring the production of a certificate stating, to the best of the knowledge and belief of the maker of the certificate, the way in which the document was produced, identifying the fact that the document was produced by a computer, ruling out the possibility of improper use of the computer; and the certificate must be signed by a person 'occupying a responsible position in relation to the operation of the computer'.[7] Such information may be required to be given by oral evidence in court[8] and any person knowingly making a false statement may be guilty of an offence.[9]

By paragraph 11, the court may consider the weight to be attached to evidence derived from a computer record, taking into account whether (a) the information was recorded contemporaneously, and (b) whether the operator had 'any incentive to conceal or misrepresent the facts'.

Finally, the Schedule[10] invites the court to draw 'any reasonable inference' in deciding whether a statement is admissible from the circumstances surrounding the production of the 'statement' or the form and contents of the document.

In *R v Minors*,[11] Steyn J commented on the way in which a court should treat the question of computer failure:

'The only comment we would make is that the failure of a computer, or a software program may occasionally result in a total failure to supply the required information, or in the supply of unintelligible or obviously wrong information. It will be a comparatively rare case where the computer supplies wrong and intelligible information, which pertinently answers the questions posed. Nevertheless, such cases could occur. In the light of these considerations trial judges, who are called upon to decide whether the foundation requirements of section 69 have been fulfilled ought perhaps to examine critically the suggestion that any prior malfunction of the computer, or software, has any relevance to the reliability of the particular computer record tendered in evidence.'

3.2   Visual aids for the trial

By section 9(4)(b), the prosecution may be ordered by the judge:

'To prepare their evidence and other explanatory material in such a form as appears to him to be likely to aid comprehension by the jury and to supply it in that form to the court and the defendant, and, if more than one, to each of them.'

6 No rules, under section 69(2), have been made.
7 PACE, Sch 3, Part II, paragraph 8.
8 Ibid, paragraph 9.
9 Ibid, paragraph 10.
10 Paragraph 14.
11 Op cit, page 448.

In the Roskill Report it was recommended that, in a case of any substance or complexity, each juror should be provided with:

'(a) The Prosecution's Case Statement;
(b) A Case Statement by the Defence in reply;
(c) One or more simple charts prepared by the Prosecution for each of the charges, summarising essential figures in an intelligible form and explaining how the alleged fraud was carried out;
(d) Such charts as the Defence wish to submit;
(e) The written statements of expert witnesses;
(f) The Prosecution and Defence should be able, if they so wish, to set down in writing a short statement of what each regards the principal issues in the case, to be handed to the jury at the conclusion of the evidence.'[12]

The Committee went on to recommend the use of visual aids, such as overhead projectors, slide projectors and computer terminals.

Section 9(4)(b) gives the judge a wide discretion, but the format suggested by the Roskill Committee has not been carried through into legislation. In particular, any defence 'pleadings' are specifically excluded from disclosure to the jury by section 10(3), by which:

'Except as provided in this section no part –

(a) of a statement supplied under section 9(5) above; or
(b) of any other information relating to the case for the defendant or, if there is more than one, the case for any of them which was given at the preparatory hearing,

may be disclosed at a stage in the trial after the jury has been sworn without the consent of the person who supplied or gave it.'

The Prosecution Case Statement is not in practice provided to the jury. There are a number of practical reasons for this: first, an opportunity is given to defendants, by section 9(5) to make any amendments, and 'to give the court and the Prosecution notice of any objections that he has to the Case Statement'. The difficulty of producing a definitive Case Statement, agreed by all parties, for production to the jury will usually be considerable. Second, it is quite likely that by the date of the trial the Case Statement will have been overtaken by events. Prosecuting counsel will prefer to rely on an opening note drafted immediately prior to the beginning of the trial, which may incorporate those matters set out in section 9(4)(a) in so far as they are relevant to an opening speech to the jury, but which may be in a significantly different form. The extent to which such a note will be provided to the jury will depend on the preference of the prosecutor and any order the judge may make. Third, the evidence given in a case may differ markedly from assertions made in the Case Statement, and it is not unlikely that the document will be, to a significant extent, out of date by the time the jury retires to consider its verdict.

Other documents which might be prepared for the jury include a glossary of terms used in the area of business practice which the allegations involve; a directory of defendants and witnesses; and a chronology.

The Director of the SFO[13] has described the use of graphics as falling into three categories: concept graphics, which can illustrate unfamiliar concepts,

---

12 Roskill Report, page 158, paragraph 9.13.
13 1st Annual Lecture of Society for Computers and Laws; and see article by David Cornwall, The Lawyer, 17 September 1991.

such as the futures market or the Stock Exchange; fact graphics, which can set out admitted facts such as company structures or passing of invoices; and case graphics, which can set out the Crown case in graphic form.

A member of the SFO explained[14] that lessons learned in two cases in the late 1980s (*Relton* – the Brinks Matt laundering case – and *Aspin*) were applied in the *Alexander Howden* case.[15] This case involved not only the arcane world of the Lloyd's reinsurance market, but also a multitude of transactions and a network of companies. More than forty graphics were used, which could be grouped under the headings identified by the Director:

(a) the information graphics 'explained the relationship between the various trusts, anstalts and companies involved in the case and were designed to be read in tandem with the glossaries which contained more detailed information';

(b) the factual graphics 'showed how it was alleged that the money had been removed from the Alexander Howden Group of companies by the defendants, ie the 'facts' that formed the substance of the case. They were harder to design than the information graphics as the basic data was not necessarily admitted and the overall structure amounted only to an allegation – not to fact';

(c) concept graphics which were 'the hardest of all. It was central to the prosecution that the jury understood how reinsurance companies function . . . Could an analogy be used? A plumbing system seemed to be particularly apposite and so stills were produced showing how money comes into a fund from policies, is "laid off" through reinsurance companies and is then retrieved at a later date to meet claims.'

Increasing use is made of visual display units in serious and complex fraud trials. They are used to show explanatory graphs, as well as to provide easy and quick access to documents.

While the prosecution is entitled to open and display its case in any way it considers appropriate, the normal practice is for the defence to have an opportunity to comment on material placed before the jury for the purpose of aiding their comprehension of the case. The extent to which the defence will be able to 'compete' with the prosecution in the production of visual aids is problematical. It is unlikely that the legal aid fund will agree to bear the cost of such an undertaking, and only private clients with long pockets will wish to use the computer technology which is available.

3.3   Admissions

By section 9(4)(c), the prosecution may be ordered:

> 'To give the court and the defendant, or if there is more than one, each of them, notice of documents the truth of the contents of which ought, in the prosecution's view to be admitted, and of any matters which in their view ought to be agreed.'

By section 9(5)(b)(iv) the judge may order a defendant:

> 'To give the court and the prosecution a notice stating the extent to which he agrees with the prosecution as to documents and other matters to which a

14 Mark Tantam 'Explaining Serious Fraud' The Lawyer, 30 January 1990.
15 *R v Posgate and Grob* (17 August 1989, unreported).

notice under subsection (4)(c) above relates, and the reason for any disagreement.'

By section 9(8):

'If it appears to a judge that reasons given in pursuance of subsection (5)(iv) above are inadequate, he shall so inform the person giving them, and may require him to give her further or better reasons.'

The discretion of the judge in ordering further or better particulars is wide, but, as discussed above, in the context of 'pleadings', it is doubtful whether a defendant can be forced to disclose his hand in circumstances where he genuinely asserts that facts or documents should be strictly proved.

3.4   Witnesses

3.4.1   *Disclosure of identity of defence witnesses*

By section 9(6) of the 1987 Act:

'Crown Court rules may provide that except to the extent that disclosure is required –

(a)   by section 11 of the Criminal Justice Act 1967 (alibi); or
(b)   by rules under section 81 of the Police and Criminal Evidence Act 1984 (expert evidence),[16]

a summary required by virtue of subsection (5) above need not disclose who will give evidence.'

This marks an important reservation on the general scheme of the preparatory hearings, in that it expressly permits the defence to withhold information about the way in which it will conduct its case.

3.4.2   *Experts*

The calling of expert evidence is frequently considered in serious fraud trials.[17] The purpose of an expert giving evidence:

'is to furnish the judge or jury with the necessary scientific criteria for testing the accuracy of their conclusions, so as to enable the judge or jury to form their own independent judgment by the application of these criteria to the facts proved in evidence.'[18]

It is a question for the trial judge to decide whether a witness is competent to give evidence about the subject in which he claims expertise,[19] and he may take into account a wide variety of factors in exercising this discretion, applying the test of whether a witness has sufficient skill to give expert evidence, or has the necessary means of knowledge to make his opinion material. It is not necessary

---

16 Crown Court (Advance Notice of Expert Evidence) Rules 1987 (SI 1987/716). These rules, in short, allow the admission of expert evidence in a wide variety of circumstances, although they are clearly intended to ensure that advance notification is given.

17 The importance of expert evidence in fraud trials may possibly be gauged from the fact that one chapter of the SFO submissions to the Royal Commission of Criminal Justice (out of five chapters in total) is devoted to this subject.

18 *Davie v Edinburgh Magistrates* 1953 SC 34 at 40.

19 *R v Silverlock* [1894] 2 QB 766.

that the witness has acquired his knowledge professionally. He may have made a special study of it, or have acquired relevant experience of it.[20]

In *R v County NatWest Ltd* the principles governing the admission of expert evidence in criminal trials were expressed by McKinnon J to be as follows:

'1. Expert witnesses must be independent.
2. Their evidence should not encroach on the ultimate issues.
3. Their evidence must be necessary.
4. Expert evidence should be directed, so far as it is necessary, to explain technical terminology, market practice and professional rules, relevant to an issue in the trial.
5. What experts should not be permitted to do is to give opinion evidence as to the wrongfulness of the defendants' conduct.
6. Experts are only permitted to give expert evidence in their areas of expertise.'[1]

Expert evidence must be 'necessary' in the sense that it must 'furnish the court with . . . information that was likely to be outside the experience and knowledge of the judge or jury.'[2]

The extent to which a witness in a serious fraud case can hold himself out as an expert on, for example, market practice in the Stock Exchange or Lloyd's, is very much open to question. Experts in criminal cases are usually confined to scientific matters (pathologists, fingerprint experts, handwriting experts etc). A witness who claims expertise in a particular area of commercial practice will rarely have a certified qualification to do so. He may claim to have practised in a particular field for many years, and that may, in itself, be accepted as a qualification to speak with authority. But where his evidence amounts simply to saying that he would not have done what a defendant is alleged to have done in the circumstances in which the action was taken, the witness will usually suffer the difficulty of having to express an opinion on imperfectly established facts in a very complex situation. That opinion is almost bound to be hedged about with doubts which spring from the fact that the opinion has no precise scientific basis.

An additional problem is that an expert may, in these circumstances, be seen to usurp the position of the jury in expressing an opinion about honesty or dishonesty. Where a pathologist simply gives evidence as to the cause of death, an expert on commercial practice who is asked to comment on whether certain actions are proper or improper will inevitably be seen to be drawing inferences as to the guilt or innocence of the defendant.

The admissibility of expert evidence is a matter which should be given careful consideration at a preparatory hearing. A trial which proceeds on the assumption that a witness will give expert evidence at the conclusion of the prosecution case, when, in fact, that evidence is later ruled as being inadmissible, may suffer from crucial gaps in the Crown case which, if anticipated at the preparatory hearing, could be filled in.

By section 30 of the Criminal Justice Act 1988, expert reports:

'shall be admissible as evidence in criminal proceedings whether or not the person making it attends to give oral evidence in those proceedings.'

20 There are a number of nineteenth century authorities which relate to expertise in matters of trade, but no recent cases. As an example of an expert who lacked professional qualifications, the case of *R v Chatwood* [1980] 1 All ER 467 is of interest: the expert witness was a drug addict who was considered sufficiently knowledgeable to give evidence about the nature of a drug.
1 Day 92, page 4.
2 *R v Turner* [1975] QB 834 at 841, [1975] 1 All ER 70 at 74.

Under this section expert evidence is only admissible with the leave of the court, and in deciding whether to grant leave the court:

'shall have regard –

(a) to the contents of the report;
(b) to the reasons why it is proposed that the person making the report shall not give oral evidence;
(c) to any risk, having regard in particular to whether it is likely to be possible to controvert statements in the report if the person making it does not attend to give oral evidence in the proceedings, that its admission or exclusion will result in unfairness to the accused or, if there is more than one, to any of them; and
(d) to any other circumstances that appear to the Court to be relevant.'

The object of the section is to give a discretion to the court to admit a written statement rather than leaving it entirely to the defendant to choose whether the witness will be subject to a full or conditional witness order. In section 30(5) an 'expert report' is defined as 'a written report by a person dealing wholly or mainly with matters on which he is (or would if living be) qualified to give expert evidence.' From the words in brackets can be inferred a reason behind the section, although it must be seen as a reason with limited usefulness.[3]

Although not expressly stated, it must be the case that if a defendant maintains that he wishes to cross-examine the witness, the court would be most reluctant to admit the evidence under the section.

3.4.3   Witness statements

In serious fraud cases witness statements may take a number of forms. Where there has been an inquiry by inspectors appointed by the Secretary of State for the Department of Trade and Industry, for example, many of the witnesses in a subsequent criminal trial will have given evidence to the inspectors, and there will be a transcript of that evidence. The Crown is not obliged to take a witness statement under section 9 of the Magistrates' Courts Act 1980 dealing with all the matters raised in the transcript, and if the evidence is to be relied on at committal or trial the transcript may be produced by a witness statement made by the witness, who will simply testify as to its truthfulness. Where there is a transfer, a transcript of evidence can be relied on as material supporting the opinion that the evidence would be sufficient for the person charged to be committed for trial.[4] The Crown will wish to convert any transcript evidence upon which they intend to rely into witness statements at the earliest stage possible, since they will wish to make clear to the court and the defence the extent to which they rely on the evidence of a witness. In addition, evidence in a transcript will often be prolix, and it may also not follow a chronological sequence, and there will be benefits from converting the transcript into the form of a witness statement.

The transcript evidence, where not relied upon by the Crown in its original form, will constitute unused material in the case, and will be disclosed to the defence. In addition, any addenda, preliminary statements and submissions will constitute disclosable unused material.

---

3   The section would appear to overrule the decision in *R v McGuire* (1985) 81 Cr App Rep 323.
4   Section 4(1) of the 1987 Act.

The same principles apply to evidence given to other inquiries conducted, for example, by the Securities and Investments Board or the Stock Exchange.

The process of making a witness statement in a serious fraud case is often tortuous. One Director of the SFO has complained that statements take too long to be put in final form for signature, causing delays to the investigation. The reason for the delays is that witnesses seek legal advice about making statements, and as a result a draft, or several drafts, of a witness statement may be produced. Those preparing and commenting on drafts should bear in mind that drafts may in some circumstances constitute disclosable unused material. In *R v Saunders & Others* Henry J ruled that drafts prepared by the police, and altered by lawyers, were disclosable.[5] However, he also commented that:

> 'Inevitably, there will be summoned to attend before Inspectors, and to answer inspectors' questions men powerful and sophisticated who will take legal advice. It is clearly extremely desirable that they should take legal advice because having regard to the nature and extent of the Department of Trade and Industry's powers, and the consequences that may follow from evidence given, the best evidence is likely to be that honesty is the best policy for those summoned before such inspectors.
>
> Any legal advisor advising his client in those circumstances is likely to be advising in strong terms his client to tear up any fanciful statement that the client came to him with as a means of attempting to escape from the full rigours of the inquisitorial process. That being so, there is clearly a strong public interest in such communications between the witness and his solicitor not being disclosed in court because if the solicitor is to give the best advice to his client, he must be able to speak fully and candidly.'[6]

Drafts passing between the solicitor and client, therefore, need not be disclosed, but all drafts produced in concert with the police and the SFO will be subject to disclosure. The former will, in any event, be subject to the protection of legal professional privilege.

A previous Director of the SFO threatened to solve this problem by using her office's powers under section 2 of the Act to obtain testimony from witnesses who appear to be taking too long to finalise their witness statements.[7] This solution is attractive neither for the SFO nor the witness; for the SFO, because a long tape-recorded interview under section 2 will suffer from many of the problems associated with transcripts of interviews with DTI inspectors; and for the witness, because he will have to answer any questions put to him, which will give him less opportunity to give considered replies to those questions.

The alternative procedure for bringing a witness before a court to give evidence where he is taking too long to produce a statement will be to issue a

5   29 September 1989: the Attorney General's Guidelines on disclosure of unused material may apply therefore, to material which is 'preparatory', eg 'preliminary thoughts and expressions of those preliminary thoughts'. The judge decided that such material 'may, in certain circumstances, have an evidential value . . . relating to inconsistency, but . . . the question does not begin and end with inconsistency. Also it seems to me that the Defendants are right in their submission that this is a matter for them to judge.'

6   28 November 1989.

7   In a speech to the Law Society Conference on 19 October 1990, the Director said: 'Solicitors may know that we have powers under section 2 of the Criminal Justice Act 1987 to ask witnesses to come before us and to bring relevant documents with them . . . I have to warn you that if there are serious delays caused in a case because it is going backwards and forwards for drafting and more redrafting I shall have to use them.' And see the SFO submissions to the Royal Commission on Criminal Justice, paragraphs 1.74 and 1.75 in which a determination on the part of the SFO to circumvent any tactics used by solicitors to pin the SFO down on the subjects to be raised at interview is apparent.

witness summons. This will, in particular, be feasible where the witness has been examined by DTI inspectors, and it is therefore known what he will say. The disadvantage is, however, that the questions put by the inspectors may have been directed at one point of view, and the witness's true alignment may not be apparent from the transcript.

3.4.4 Refreshing memory

Witnesses may seek legal advice before giving evidence. In particular, they may wish to see a copy of the statement which they have made before going to court. That statement may have been made many months, or even years, previously, and their memory of the events covered by the statement will often be hazy. If a witness is to be in a position to give useful evidence in court, he should be able to refresh his memory from his statement. There is clear authority that there can be no objection to his statement being made available for this purpose.[8] It is arguable that he should also be encouraged to look at documents so that the events in question are more clearly recalled. However, care has to be exercised in advising witnesses in these circumstances, so as to avoid any suggestion that the witness has been 'primed'. In particular, it may be argued that a witness should not be asked to study documents which he has not seen before, partly because his recall of events which happened some time before he is asked to make a statement and appear in court may be uncertain. It is therefore important that that recall should be contemporaneous, and not subject to later knowledge, hindsight and speculation. For the witness giving evidence in a serious fraud trial, the task of bringing to mind the relevant facts, without the overlay of later knowledge, can be extremely difficult.

3.4.5 Accomplices

At the preparatory hearing the Crown may indicate whether any of the witnesses to be called by the Crown are to be treated as accomplices. In cases involving allegations of, or similar to, conspiracy to defraud, there may often be a number of witnesses who participated in the events which make up the allegation, but whom, in the view of the Crown, it would not be appropriate to charge. This view will either have been formed because the Crown does not believe that the witness knowingly played any part in the conspiracy, or because the Crown has limited its case to those individuals who were at the centre of the alleged offences. An example of this will be the situation of a solicitor who has acted for clients in property transactions where false applications for loans have been made. The question often arises as to whether the solicitor knew that offences had been committed, and in continuing to act for his clients assisted them in their endeavours. Where the Crown takes the view that the solicitor has not acted dishonestly, it may nevertheless be an issue for the jury to decide whether he was criminally involved with the defendants. If it is the case that they decide, having heard all the evidence, that the solicitor was an accomplice of the defendant, the judge must direct the jury that it would

---

8 See Home Office Circular No 82/1969 ('Supply of Copies of Witness Statements') and *Lau Pak Ngam v R* [1966] Crim LR 443; *Worley v Bentley* [1976] 2 All ER 449, 62 Cr App Rep 239; *R v Westwell* [1976] 2 All ER 812, 62 Cr App Rep 251.

be dangerous for them to convict on his evidence unless it is corroborated.[9] In this instance, the witness is termed an accomplice 'vel non', and the position of the witness must be explained to the jury in the judge's summing up.

It is arguable that directions should be given to the jury at an earlier stage, for example, before the witness gives evidence. However, there is no authority for such a proposition, and it will be in the discretion of the judge in each case to decide when it is appropriate to issue a warning.

Similar considerations apply in cases where it can be said that a witness has 'some purpose of his own to serve', and in such circumstances the judge should give a warning against uncorroborated evidence.[10] This caution was given in the *Prater* case where one defendant gave evidence against a co-defendant, but it has been held to have a wider significance, in including witnesses who may have some purpose of their own to serve.[11] The judge's discretion in such cases has been expressed in this way:

> 'While we in no way wish to detract from the obligation upon a judge to advise a jury to proceed with caution where there is material to suggest that a witness's evidence may be tainted by an improper motive, and the strength of that advice must vary according to the facts of the case, we cannot accept that there is any obligation to give this warning with all that entails, when it is common ground that there is no basis for suggesting that the witness is a participant or in any way involved in the crime the subject matter of the trial.'[12]

3.4.6   Witness orders and service of witness summons

The making of witness orders in serious fraud cases will be considered in Chapter 3, and apart from the arrangements which have to be made as a result of transfer, there is no distinction between cases to which the 1987 Act applies, and all other criminal cases. At the preparatory hearing, however, the final list of witnesses to be called, and the order of calling them, will often be canvassed.

The attendance of witnesses at the Crown Court may be secured in the usual way under the provisions of the Criminal Procedure (Attendance of Witnesses) Act 1965 where the witness is within the jurisdiction. Witnesses outside the jurisdiction cannot effectively be made to attend court. By section 2 of the Criminal Justice (International Co-operation) Act 1990 service of process requiring attendance before a court for the purpose of giving evidence in criminal proceedings can be effected out of the jurisdiction 'in accordance with arrangements made by the Secretary of State'. However, by section 2(3):

> '. . . service of any process outside the United Kingdom by virtue of this section shall not impose any obligation under the law of any part of the United Kingdom to comply with it and accordingly failure to do so shall not constitute contempt of any court, or be a ground for issuing a warrant to secure the attendance of the person in question or, in Scotland, for imposing any penalty.'

9   *Davies v DPP* [1954] AC 378, [1954] 1 All ER 507, HL.
10 *R v Prater* [1960] 2 QB 464, [1960] 1 All ER 298, CCA; *R v Stannard* [1965] 2 QB 1, [1964] 1 All ER 34, CCA; *R v Beck* [1982] 1 All ER 807, [1982] 1 WLR 461, CA.
11 *R v Beck*, op cit.
12 *Beck* op cit; see also *R v Spencer* [1987] AC 128, [1986] 2 All ER 928, HL.

Arrangements can be made, under section 6 of the 1990 Act, for serving prisoners in other jurisdictions to be brought to the United Kingdom to give evidence.

3.5 Questions for potential jurors

In any fraud case which is likely to last more than a few weeks, the panel of jurors will need to be asked about their availability to sit through a long trial. It is now a not uncommon practice for potential jurors in a very large scale trial to be handed a list of questions which will include:

(a) whether they have any specific reasons for not sitting on the jury in a long trial, such as illness, pregnancy, holidays, running their own business or employment problems generally, which would cause personal hardship;
(b) whether they or any close friend or relative know any of the defendants or witnesses;
(c) whether they have had any dealings with any of the companies or commercial entities with which the trial is concerned;
(d) whether they have any special knowledge of the particular type of commercial activity with which the trial is concerned.[13]

The form of the questions to be put before the jury panel will need to be agreed between the parties at the preparatory hearing.

3.6 Reporting restrictions

No reports of preparatory hearings may be published, except with the leave of the Crown Court.[14] The only reporting of preparatory hearings is that permitted by section 11(8) and (9).

These restrictions on reporting are lifted in a case involving only one defendant where that defendant applies to the court under section 11(2). In multi-defendant cases, the court has a discretion to lift the restrictions if one or more, but not all, of the defendants applies under section 11(2) 'if, and only if, it is satisfied, after hearing the representations of the accused, that it is in the interests of justice to do so.'[15] There may be a report of the outcome of any application made under section 11(2).[16]

By section 11(7) reports of a preparatory hearing may be made at the conclusion of the trial. The SFO has commented[17] that there is an unfortunate side effect to this subsection in that 'some rulings of general importance are being made in preparatory hearings which cannot be reported until the conclusion of the trial which may be many months later.'

It should be noted that the restrictions relating to preparatory hearings do not apply to interlocutory matters raised outside the preparatory hearings.

---

13 The danger addressed by this question is that a juror with such knowledge might unduly influence the rest of the jury. Whether this type of question is appropriate will depend on circumstances.
14 Section 11(1) and (2) of the Act as amended.
15 Section 9(3).
16 Section 11(4).
17 See the SFO submissions to the Royal Commission on Criminal Justice paragraph 4.19.

Therefore, if an argument on, for example, abuse of process is heard before the preparatory hearing begins, reporting of that application can only be restricted by the use of an Order under section 4(2) of the Contempt of Court Act 1981.

By section 11(12) editors and publishers, rather than reporters, are made liable for any breaches of the section. Any proceedings brought under the section must have the consent of the Attorney General.[18]

By section 11(14):

> 'subsection (i) above shall be in addition to, and not in derogation from, the provisions of any other enactment with respect to the publication of reports of court proceedings.'

This refers in particular to section 4(2) of the Contempt of Court Act 1981, and it may particularly be noted that the use of the Contempt of Court Act may be considered in a case where there will be two or more trials arising out of the same facts. The judge will have to give consideration to the reporting of the first trial as it is likely to impinge on any question of prejudice to a subsequent trial or trials. The problem arose in both the *Guinness* and *County NatWest* cases and was resolved by the respective judges in favour of allowing reporting, without restriction, of the proceedings in the first trials. The judges, however, stressed that they would pay close attention to the contents of such reporting, with particular reference to the cases of the defendants in the subsequent trials. They considered that the public interest in seeing reports of the proceedings in these high-profile cases outweighed the risk of prejudice to defendants.

3.7   Legal professional privilege and public interest immunity

Legal professional privilege[19] and public interest immunity may also be raised at a preparatory hearing as being within the definition of 'questions of admissibility' or of 'questions of law relating to the case' under section 9(3)(b) and (c) of the Act.

Disclosure of documents and claims of public interest immunity by public authorities may arise in the course of serious fraud trials. For example, where there has been an inquiry by inspectors appointed by the Department of Trade and Industry most of the documents relied on by the inspectors, or created during the course of the inquiry, will be disclosed to the defence, either as evidence or as unused material within the Attorney General's Guidelines.[20] It is likely, however, that there will be classes of documents which will be in the possession of the Department which it considers should be subject to immunity from disclosure on the grounds of public interest.

The application will be made by a defendant, and it will be for the relevant department or authority, rather than the prosecution, to argue that documents should not be disclosed on this ground.

The circumstances in which an application can be made that immunity should be granted, and the cases relevant to a consideration of the matter, were set out by Wood J in *Evans v Chief Constable of Surrey*.[1] This case involved an application by the plaintiff for the disclosure of a police report sent to the

---

18 Section 11(13).
19 See Chapter 2, section 2.3.5.
20 The Guidelines for the disclosure of unused material to the defence in cases to be tried on indictment: (1982) 74 Cr App Rep 302.
1 [1988] QB 588.

Director of Public Prosecutions concerning the investigation of a murder. The plaintiff was the main suspect and was arrested and held in custody for questioning on two occasions.

Wood J summarised the law as follows. First, the issue of whether material is subject to public interest immunity is interlocutory, and a decision is within the discretion of a judge at first instance. Second, public interest immunity is not a privilege that can be waived; it must be considered by the court. Third, once public interest immunity is properly raised, the burden is upon the party seeking disclosure to show why the document should be produced for inspection by the court privately.[2]

Fourth, there are two stages to discovery, disclosure of the existence of a document and production of the document for inspection. The document should only be inspected after a production order (which may be subject to an appeal), unless the court has 'definite grounds for expecting to find material of real importance to the party seeking disclosure'[3] or where the court feels it necessary to inspect the document to verify the fact that a class claim is validly made.

Fifth, any document for which disclosure is requested must be disclosable within the rules of discovery normally applicable in litigation. Wood J. quoted remarks of Lord Scarman in *Burmah Oil Co Ltd v Bank of England*:[4]

> 'Foster J based his decision on the view which he had formed that production of the documents for which immunity is claimed would not materially assist the plaintiffs' case at trial. He was, I think, right, when faced with the public interest immunity objection to disclosure, to ask himself whether production could be said to be necessary for fairly disposing of the case.
>
> For, if it be shown that production was not necessary, it becomes unnecessary to balance the interests of justice against the interests of the public service to which the Minister refers in his certificate.'

Sixth, before the court can be persuaded to take the step of inspecting the document for which public interest immunity is claimed the plaintiff must at least satisfy the court that the documents are very likely to contain material which would lend support to a substantial degree to his argument on an issue, or issues, which are raised in the case, and he must be able to show that he would be deprived of the means of presenting his case properly without production of the documents. If he can demonstrate this, the court will then proceed to undertake a balancing exercise.

In balancing the interests in a criminal case the judge has a wide discretion. The exercise of that discretion was summarised by Mann LJ in a Divisional Court decision in *Re Lorraine Esme Osman*:[5]

> 'The seminal cases in regard to public interest immunity do not refer to criminal proceedings at all. The principles are expressed in quite general terms. Asking myself why those general expositions should not apply to criminal proceedings, I can see no answer but that they do. It seems correct in principle that they should apply. The reason for the development of the doctrines seem equally applicable to civil proceedings. I acknowledge that the application to the public immunity doctrine in criminal proceedings will involve a different balancing exercise to that in civil proceedings. I shall come in one moment to

---

2 See *Air Canada v Secretary of State for Trade (No 2)* [1983] 2 AC 394 at 433.
3 Op cit at p 436.
4 [1980] AC 1090 at 1141.
5 [1991] 1 WLR 281 at 288.

the concept of the balancing exercise. Suffice it to say for the moment that a judge is balancing on the one hand the desirability of preserving the public interest in the absence of disclosure against, on the other hand, the interests of justice. Where the interests of justice arise in a criminal case touching and concerning liberty or conceivably on occasions, life, the weight to be attached to the interests of justice is plainly very great indeed.'

In carrying out a balancing exercise, therefore, in a criminal case, the court will lean in favour of disclosure. However, there is usually a serious obstacle for the plaintiff (ie in the criminal case the defendant) to overcome, namely that although he can identify a class of document which exists he would be unable to satisfy the court that he knows sufficient about its contents to show that his request for disclosure is anything other than 'a fishing expedition'. In a situation where the nature of the documents suggests that, within the definition in section 2(2) of the Criminal Procedure (Attendance of Witnesses) Act 1965, it is unlikely that the disputed documents will constitute material evidence, or evidence that would lead to 'foreseeable, proper cross-examination', the court may not have to consider the issue even to the extent of inspecting the documents.

Where, however, in the *Evans* type of case, it is clear that the material contained in the disputed document is relevant to the issues of the case (namely, the basis upon which a prosecution decision was taken) the court would have to proceed to balance the interests of justice against the public interest. *Evans* was not a criminal case, and therefore the special considerations urged by Mann LJ in the *Osman* case did not apply. There were, in addition, other reasons why disclosure was inappropriate (a form of legal professional privilege being one).

The disputed material may consist, for example, of communications and documents arising out of a Department of Trade inquiry, in particular, internal reports, communications between the Department and regulators and requests for advice from the inspectors to the Department. It is likely that there will be a number of reasons for considering that such documents are covered by public interest immunity or that a claim for their production will be defeated on the grounds of relevance within the terms of section 2(2) of the Criminal Procedure (Attendance of Witnesses) Act 1965.

4   APPEALS

By section 9(10):

'An order or ruling made at or for the purposes of the preparatory hearing shall have effect during the trial, unless it appears to the judge on application made to him during the trial that the interests of justice require him to vary or discharge it.'

There is, therefore, a process for varying orders made at preparatory hearings, although inevitably the circumstances in which the order was originally made must have changed in order to justify a variation or discharge.

An immediate appeal from an order at a preparatory hearing is provided for in section 9(11):

'An appeal shall lie to the Court of Appeal from any order or ruling of a judge under subsection (3)(b) or (c) above, but only with the leave of the judge or of the Court of Appeal.'

The rules governing such appeals are the Criminal Justice Act 1987 (Preparatory Hearings) Interlocutory Appeals Rules 1988.[6] Under the rules an application to the judge for leave to appeal must be made orally within two days of the date of the order.[7] Where leave is granted by the judge, the appellant must serve, within seven days of the date of the order or ruling, notice of appeal on:

(a) the registrar;
(b) the appropriate officer of the Crown Court; and
(c) all parties to the preparatory hearing directly affected by the said order or ruling.[8]

The time limit for service of notice can be extended by the Court of Appeal, but since speed will usually be of the essence at this stage of the proceedings, and the court will not wish to have its timetable upset by appeals pending before the Court of Appeal, it may be anticipated that leave will be granted sparingly to make application out of time.[9]

Where the application is not made orally in open court on the occasion of the making of an order or ruling, the appellant shall serve notice in writing, with grounds, on the appropriate officer of the Crown Court and on all parties to the hearing directly affected by the order or ruling.[10] It is not clear from the rules how this provision fits in with Rule 3(1), although it appears to relate solely to applications for leave to appeal to the Crown Court judge which are not made orally. The confusion arises from the difference between the two days specified in Rule 3(1) and the requirement to apply orally on the occasion of the making of the order or ruling in Rule 3(2).

If the judge refuses leave to appeal, an application for leave may be made to the Court of Appeal under Rule 3(3), by serving an application on the same persons as specified above.

By Rule 3(8):

'Where the judge of the Crown Court has given leave to appeal the notice of appeal shall state that fact and specify the grounds on which leave is given.'

The notice of appeal or the application for leave to appeal must: (a) specify the questions of law which are raised, giving details of such facts as are necessary to consider the matter properly; (b) provide a skeleton argument; and (c) give a list of authorities.[11]

The respondent must reply within seven days of receiving notice of appeal or application for leave, by serving a notice on the registrar, providing a skeleton argument and giving a list of authorities.[12]

The rules also make provision for the hearing of any applications for leave, or substantive appeals, following the normal pattern for appeals.

By section 9(13):

'The judge may continue a preparatory hearing notwithstanding that leave to appeal has been granted under subsection (11) above, but no jury shall be sworn until after the appeal has been determined or abandoned.'

---

6 SI 1988/1700 (L22).
7 Rule 3(1).
8 Rule 3(3).
9 Rule 3(4).
10 Rule 3(2).
11 Rule 3(7).
12 Rule 4(1).

The SFO has expressed concern that the system for interlocutory appeals is slowing down the progress of serious fraud cases. In submissions to the Royal Commission on Criminal Justice[13] the SFO stated:

> 'Interlocutory appeals have a huge potential for causing great delay and expense. They are an anomaly at a pre-trial stage in a criminal case, and were not presaged by Roskill.'

They suggested that the system should be reviewed so as to limit the delay, and pointed out, in addition, that an interlocutory appeal is not definitive, nor does it have any advantage over an appeal at the end of a trial.

5   THE BEGINNING OF THE TRIAL

As soon as all matters to be considered at the preparatory hearing have been resolved and all interlocutory appeals have been heard, the trial before the jury may begin. Because the preparatory hearing is part of the trial, in reality there should be no gap between the end of the preparatory hearing and the empanelling of the jury. Indeed, there is no reason why the jury should not be empanelled at the beginning of the preparatory hearings, although this will present some practical difficulties in any case where it is expected that there will be a significant delay between that date and the opening of the prosecution case.

It is certainly desirable in most cases, bearing in mind the importance of maintaining the momentum of the proceedings and avoiding unnecessary delay, for the opening of the prosecution case to follow very quickly from the conclusion of the preparatory hearing. The timetable fixed by the judge at an early stage[14] should, it may be argued, set an ambitious and tight target for the trial to begin.

The SFO has consistently urged that proper use should be made of preparatory hearings. For useful results to emerge from these hearings, all parties, prosecution, defence and judge, must play their part. It is idle to believe, however, that these results can be achieved easily, if only because the combination of an efficient prosecution, a compliant defence and a strong judge will rarely come together in the same trial. It is also unlikely that all the problems which will be encountered in a long fraud trial will be evident at preparatory hearing stage, and therefore substantial amounts of time will usually be lost during the trial for the hearing of legal argument.

13 Paragraph 4.39.
14 See this chapter, section 1.3 above.

CHAPTER 5
Other fraud inquiries

1 INTRODUCTION

Most serious and complex frauds are investigated and tried by the traditional means available to investigators and prosecutors prior to the implementation of the Criminal Justice Act 1987. Since the SFO only has the capacity to deal with approximately 120 cases at any one time, those frauds which are not referred to it, or which it refuses to take on, are investigated by the police and prosecuted by the Crown Prosecution Service. With the SFO becoming increasingly overburdened, and therefore more choosy about the cases it investigates, the size, seriousness and complexity of the cases left to the CPS will inevitably increase.

Serious and complex fraud is also investigated and prosecuted by other authorities, including the Inland Revenue, Customs and Excise and, to a lesser extent, the Department of Trade and Industry. Other government departments prosecute fraud, including, for example, the Ministry of Agriculture Fisheries and Food and the Department of Social Security.[1]

The decision by the Director of the SFO to adopt a case for investigation and trial by that organisation has significant consequences for an accused person.[2] Most of the consequences flow from the powers of investigation given by section 2 of the 1987 Act, in particular the abrogation, albeit limited, of the right of silence. A person accused of fraud, therefore, is probably better off being investigated by the CPS (or some of the authorities listed above) because they are bound by the traditional rules of evidence gathering. There are, however, disadvantages. The investigation and prosecution of fraud requires a level of expertise which is not acquired in the prosecution of most other types of criminal offence. A lack of expertise in this area can lead to deficiencies in the prosecution which can in turn lead to unsatisfactory results.

The CPS deals with fraud cases on two fronts: they are either referred to the Fraud Investigation Group ('FIG') or they are dealt with locally. The arrangements which govern the allocation of cases are ad hoc, but are partly governed by the capacity of FIG to take on cases. In the same way as the SFO has to limit the number of cases it takes on, so does FIG. There are other considerations: the CPS has a deliberate policy of devolved power. Chief Crown Prosecutors in all the CPS areas of the country can decide for themselves whether they wish to conduct the prosecution of large fraud cases

---

1 See the discussion in Chapter 3, section 2.1 on the meaning of 'Secretary of State' in section 4(3)(e): the list in section 4(3) suggests that all the authorities there listed are likely to investigate and prosecute serious fraud.
2 Chapter 2 section 1.3.

but whether they choose to do so will depend on a variety of factors, one of which will be the relations between CPS lawyers and the local police. It may also be more convenient for all concerned for a case to be handled locally and without reference having to be made at frequent intervals to a relatively remote headquarters division. Another factor will be the capacity of individual CPS areas to handle large cases in terms of being able to provide lawyers with sufficient expertise and time, and support staff.

It may be argued that this provides an unevenness of approach which is not altogether satisfactory. With increasing calls for special skills to be applied to fraud cases it makes some sense to gather such expertise under one roof and to ensure that all those involved in the process, prosecutors, judges and court staff, are fully prepared for the demands such cases make.

FIG has a number of advantages over local CPS offices: first it employs accountants full time, in the same way as the SFO does, and it can call on their experience on a regular, rather than an ad hoc, basis. Second, it has a concentrated pool of experience of handling large fraud cases.

While the CPS and the other prosecuting authorities do not have to concern themselves about definitions of serious and/or complex fraud in order to exercise such powers as they have, they must give consideration to the definition if they wish to make use of the transfer and preparatory hearing provisions of the Act. Cases prosecuted by these authorities can make use of the transfer provisions, but there are no figures currently available for the number of occasions on which transfer has been used. Extensive use of section 4 is not thought to have been made. It is also not known how often the courts have considered making orders under section 7 of the 1987 Act for preparatory hearings in non-SFO cases but again it is thought that the use of the provisions has been limited. This may be because of a perception that it is only cases handled by the SFO which can be considered serious and complex, but it may be argued that the courts should listen sympathetically to any applications, whether from prosecution or defence, for preparatory hearings to take place. The Roskill Committee found that use of pre-trial reviews was patchy and inefficient, and there will be a significant number of fraud cases which can benefit from the preparatory hearings provisions.

2   POLICE INVESTIGATIONS

The main difference between SFO cases and non-SFO cases is that in the latter all investigations are undertaken by traditional investigators. In CPS cases, the police investigate. For the Revenue, Customs and Excise, the DTI and other government departments, specialist investigators acting separately from the prosecuting lawyers conduct inquiries. Frequently these inquiries are completed before the prosecuting lawyers see the results, although it has increasingly become the norm, particularly since the setting up of FIG in the early 1980s, for lawyers to advise on the course of an investigation as it progresses. Nevertheless, there is generally a separation of powers which is much more distinct than in SFO investigations.

While it is not within the scope of this book to review police powers, or the powers available to other prosecuting authorities, in any detail,[3] it is proposed

---

3   See eg Michael Zander *The Police and Criminal Evidence Act 1984* (2nd edition).

in this chapter to provide an outline of the main aspects of investigation powers of the police, the Inland Revenue, and Customs and Excise, as they affect fraud cases. These powers may be broken down into the following headings:

(a) Questioning of suspects;
(b) Questioning of witnesses;
(c) Production of documents;
(d) Search and seizure.

2.1 Questioning of suspects

The questioning of suspects is now governed by the provisions of PACE, and in particular the Codes of Practice issued under section 66 of the Act. The Codes of Practice[4] cover a number of aspects of the detention and questioning of suspects, including the length of time a suspect may be held without charge, the number and duration of interviews, the provision of refreshments, the length of rest periods and access to legal advice.

Most fraud cases will involve charges which constitute arrestable offences.[5] Once arrested, a suspect must be taken to a police station as soon as practicable,[6] and he must be brought before the 'custody officer' as soon as practicable so that that officer may determine 'whether he has before him sufficient evidence to charge that person with the offence for which he was arrested and may detain him at the police station for as long as is necessary to enable him to do so'.[7] The arrested person may thereafter be held in custody and interviewed for so long as the Custody Officer, or in a case where no charge has yet been preferred, an officer of the rank of inspector or above who has not been directly involved in the investigation,[8] determines after periodic reviews.

A person may attend voluntarily at the police station, without having been arrested, and a person who is in this position is not subject to the Custody Officer's regime under the Act. He may also leave the police station at any time he wishes to do so.[9] However, there are disadvantages. A person attending voluntarily does not have to be informed of his right to legal representation, nor does he have to be informed specifically that he is not under arrest and that he is free to leave the police station. Furthermore, the police do not have to caution him, but such questioning as takes place before caution cannot form evidence against him at a subsequent trial.

Once there are grounds to suspect that an offence has been committed the suspect must be cautioned 'before any questions about it (or further questions if it is his answers to previous questions that provide grounds for suspicion) are put to him for the purpose of obtaining evidence which may be given to a court

---

4 PACE 1984: Codes of Practice (HMSO): revised edition. Effective from 1 April 1991.
5 Arrestable offences are defined by section 24 of PACE, and include (section 24(1)(b)) offences for which a person of 21 or over may be sentenced to imprisonment for a term of five years or more. The section also includes in its definition 'offences for which a person may be arrested under the Customs and Excise Acts as defined in section 1(1) of the Customs and Excise Management Act 1979.
6 PACE section 30(1).
7 PACE section 37(1).
8 PACE section 40(1)(b).
9 PACE section 29. Codes of Practice: C.3.15.

in a prosecution'.[10] The caution must be in terms similar to: 'You do not have to say anything unless you wish to do so, but what you say may be given in evidence.'[11] Thereafter, the suspect need not answer any questions.

If the subject chooses to exercise his right of silence, and answers no questions put to him in a police interview, the fact that he has remained silent cannot be the subject, as things stand at present, of adverse comment. The question of adverse comment at trial is currently under review, and a report of a Home Office working group on the right of silence, published in July 1989, approved in general terms a recommendation contained in the Criminal Law Revision Committee 11th Report published in 1972, that where a suspect failed to bring a fact to the attention of the interviewing officers on which at his subsequent trial he sought to rely, his initial failure to draw the officers' attention to that fact could become the subject of adverse comment by the prosecution and the judge. An inference could be drawn from silence that a line of defence used at trial was untrue. Furthermore, the fact of remaining silent could go to the issue of a defendant's general credibility.

These changes have not been brought in, and there are at present no specific proposals for legislation.

Almost all interviews conducted in police stations are now tape recorded, and some are recorded on video.

As things presently stand, a defendant is not obliged to answer any questions or to provide the prosecuting authority with any assistance in prosecuting the case against him. Since most interviews with suspects will be tape recorded, there will be little or no scope for argument about what took place during interviews. Fraud cases have rarely turned, in any event, on the disputed contents of interviews.

2.2   Interviewing witnesses

Where the SFO may use its powers under section 2 to compel witnesses to give evidence, no such assistance is given to other prosecuting authorities.[12] There is therefore no power to compel reluctant witnesses, or witnesses such as solicitors, accountants and bankers who are under a duty of confidentiality, to make witness statements. Should a witness be reluctant to make a statement, he can be subpoenaed to appear before the court, and a prosecutor who needs the evidence of a particular witness to prove his case may subpoena him to appear at committal proceedings so as to get his evidence in deposition form. Such a method is rarely if ever used because a prosecutor will not usually wish to call a witness without knowing precisely what he will say.

2.3   Production of documents

The production of a range of documentary evidence during the investigation and prosecution stage of criminal proceedings may be obtained pursuant to

---

10 PACE Codes: C:10.1.
11 PACE Codes C:10.4.
12 In the context of an inquiry under section 432 of the Companies Act 1985, the inspectors are not a prosecuting authority.

orders made by the courts. In fraud cases there will be a variety of types of documents which are required for production, including, in particular, company records, documents from professional advisers and documents obtained from defendants. Different rules apply to the obtaining of such documentary evidence, and these rules are mainly provided in statutory form in Part II of PACE. Banking evidence is, however, an exception.

2.3.1 Banking evidence

The admission of evidence derived from the ledgers and account books of banks is governed by the Bankers' Books Evidence Act 1879[13] which, by section 3, provides that:

> 'A copy of any entry in a banker's book shall in all legal proceedings be received as prima facie evidence of such entry, and of the matters, transactions, and accounts therein recorded.'

By sections 4 and 5 a statement must be made by a partner or officer of the bank to the effect that:

(a) the relevant book was 'one of the ordinary books of the bank', and
(b) the entry 'was made in the usual and ordinary course of business', and
(c) 'the book is in the custody or control of the bank'; and further, that the copy has been compared with the original and is correct.

By section 6, a banker may not be called to produce his books or give evidence about them 'unless by order of a judge made for a special cause'.
  By section 7:

> 'On the application of any party to a legal proceeding a court or Judge may order that such party be at liberty to inspect and take copies of any entries in a banker's book for any of the purposes of such proceedings. An Order under this section may be made either with or without summoning the bank or any other party, and shall be served on the bank three clear days before the same is to be obeyed, unless the court or Judge otherwise directs.'

An application under section 7 cannot, therefore, be made until charges have been laid, and such an application may be made ex parte. However, 'there is much to be said for notice to be given. There is much to be said for a frank attitude in all criminal proceedings'.[14]
  Applications are usually made to magistrates' courts, which may be faced with difficult decisions. It has been held that applications must not constitute 'fishing expeditions', and before an application can succeed the justices should be satisfied that the Crown has other evidence against the defendant apart from evidence which they may hope to acquire from bank accounts. Magistrates should also ensure that there is a proper limit on the period of disclosure which relates closely to the charge faced by the defendant. Where magistrates are in doubt, they are encouraged to refer the application to the High Court.[15] In section 10 of the Act 'legal proceeding' is given a wide definition: 'Any civil or

---

13 As amended by the Banking Act 1987.
14 *R v Marlborough Street Magistrates' Court Metropolitan Stipendiary Magistrate, ex p Simpson* (1980) 70 Cr App Rep 291.
15 *William v Summerfield* [1972] 2 QB 512, [1972] 2 All ER 1334 and *R v Nottingham Justices, ex p Lynn* (1984) 79 Cr App Rep 238.

criminal proceedings or inquiry in which evidence is or may be given', including solicitors' disciplinary tribunals.

By section 9(2) 'bankers' books' are defined to include 'ledgers, day books, cashbooks, account books and other records used in the ordinary business of the bank, whether those records are in written form or are kept on microfilm, magnetic tape or any other form of mechanical or electronic data retrieval mechanism'.

Whether 'bankers' books' include the daily record sheets, or notes written by bank employees in the course of doing business with their customer, is open to question. Banks sometimes supply such details, but arguably they should not. If they are so included, they must, it may be argued, be produced by the person making them and even then it may be thought that they would constitute only a memory refreshing document which they may use to assist them in recollecting the details of transactions. It is to be noted that bank correspondence files were held not to constitute bankers' books in *R v Dadson*, although this case was decided before the definition was amended by the Banking Act 1987 Schedule 6, but which added the words 'other records' to the section. The view has been expressed that the change will not affect the decision in *R v Dadson*.[16]

The definition of 'bankers' books' in section 9(2) does not include cheques and paying-in slips, and documents of this nature.

2.3.2   *Special procedure material: PACE sections 9, 14 and Schedule 1*

Access to material held subject to a duty of confidentiality (for example, bank records, including all the material available under the 1879 Act, and in addition correspondence, daily record sheets and cheques and paying-in slips) may be obtained before or after charges are laid by the making of an application under section 9 and Schedule 1 of PACE. Such material constitutes 'special procedure material' which is defined, by section 14(2) of the Act, as:

> '. . . material, other than items subject to legal privilege and excluded material, in the possession of a person who –
>
> (a) acquired or created it in the course of any trade, business, professional or other occupation or for the purpose of any paid or unpaid office; and
> (b) holds it subject to an express or implied undertaking to hold it in confidence; . . .'

An application for special procedure material must be made pursuant to Schedule 1 of PACE by a constable to a circuit judge. The constable must satisfy the judge that one of two sets of access conditions is fulfilled. Applications for such orders are made inter partes.[17]

The access conditions are set out in the Schedule, the most relevant part of which relates to the 'first set of access conditions', the second set of conditions having rarely been used. The conditions will be fulfilled, according to the Schedule, if there are reasonable grounds for believing that a serious arrestable offence has been committed, that special procedure material exists, that the material is likely to be of substantial value to the investigation, and that it is likely to be relevant evidence; that other methods of obtaining the material

16 See *Archbold* (44th edn) paragraph 9-128.
17 Schedule 1 para 7.

have been tried without success or would be bound to fail; and that it is in the public interest to obtain the material.

The second set of access conditions is that there is a reasonable belief that excluded or special procedure material is on the premises, a warrant to search could have been issued prior to the enactment of PACE (section 9(2)), and it would have been appropriate to issue a warrant under that provision.

If the judge is satisfied that the constable has given information which fulfils the first or second set of access conditions, he may make an order requiring the person who appears to have been in possession of the material to produce it to the constable for removal, or to give him access to it within a specified period, not to exceed 7 days from the date of the order.

Those to whom notices relating to the making of orders under section 9 are addressed should ensure that the notice is valid and that the order made by the court is correctly obtained. For example, the documents requested must relate to the investigation, and no material must be included in the order which falls outside the scope of the investigation. The recipient of the order may consider that it is appropriate to contest it if, in his view, there is any defect in the application.[18] In *R v Central Criminal Court, ex p AJD Holdings Ltd*,[19] the Divisional Court made a number of observations about applications made under section 9, including that it was important, before any search warrant was applied for, that careful consideration was given to what material it was hoped a search would reveal, so as to be clear to anyone subsequently considering the lawfulness of the warrant, and readily understood by the officers executing the warrant. Further, the application should make clear that the material sought related to the crime under investigation. The court recommended that officers conducting a search should be carefully briefed both about the nature of the material which was the subject of the Order, but also how the material might relate to the crime under investigation. The search team should clearly understand the limits of the search and seizure operation. Further, in order to be clear about the nature of the Order made, a note should be taken of anything said in support of the application beyond what was set out in writing.[20]

Finally, the court emphasised the importance of the 'safeguards' in sections 15 and 16. These sections may be thought to state the obvious (for example, section 16(8): 'A search under a warrant may only be a search to the extent required for the purpose for which the warrant was issued'), but for those conducting searches and for recipients of orders they serve as a checklist for ensuring proper compliance with the Act.[1]

Where a bank, accountant or solicitor receives a notice under section 9 he may choose whether or not to inform the client to whom the notice obviously relates. It has been established that the person (if any) who is the subject of the investigation has no right to be given notice of the application.

---

18 In *Barclays Bank plc v Taylor: Trustee Savings Bank of Wales and Border Counties v Taylor* [1989] 3 All ER 563, [1989] 1 WLR 1066 the Court of Appeal held that no implied contractual obligation arose, by virtue of its confidential relationship with its customer, to oppose an application.
19 (1992) Times, 24 February.
20 By section 16(4) a constable will be under oath when responding to questions put by the judge; although in many cases counsel or an officer of the prosecutor makes an application under section 9 of the Act.
1 See also *R v Chief Constable of Lancashire, ex p Parker and McGrath* (1992) Independent, 1 April.

By the same token a bank is not under any duty to inform its customer of the existence of an application, the confidentiality with its customer giving rise to no implied contractual obligation that it should do so.[2] The court (Lord Donaldson MR) expressed the view that a bank was under no inhibition from informing its customer if it so chose, even if the police requested the bank to keep the information from its customer. The judge went on to suggest that he would be surprised if a bank took such action in the face of a specific request not to do so.

Since the application is made inter partes, information must be passed to the respondent (who may not necessarily be the defendant) about the nature of the application. The courts have held, albeit to a limited extent, that respondents are entitled to see the material placed before the judge in support of the applications. They should also be given details, as fully as possible, of the documentary material which is being sought.

In *R v Manchester Crown Court, ex p Taylor*,[3] Lord Justice Glidewell said that 'the party against whom the order is made should know before the order is made what it is he has to produce or allow access to, and in my judgment, he should know the nature of the offence that is being investigated'. This information could be given orally, although it was preferable that it should be written down.[4]

In *R v Inner London Sessions Crown Court, ex p Baines & Baines*,[5] the Divisional Court ruled that the respondent to an application must be provided with the evidence which the police intended to rely on at the hearing, although this evidence did not have to be provided until the day of the hearing. In this context 'evidence' does not need to comply with the strict rules of evidence, but it must exclude 'statements which have no substance to the prejudice of the party who is subject to the order sought'.

In *R v Central Criminal Court, ex p Adegbesan*,[6] Lord Justice Watkins held that the respondent was entitled to be supplied with some information as to what material the police wished to obtain – otherwise they would not be in a position to comply with the order – but the police were not under a duty to produce a schedule which they had compiled prior to the hearing. This information would be made available at the hearing, but the police were behaving reasonably in not disclosing full details prior to the hearing. The court took account of the risk that the document to be taken under the provisions of the order might be shredded if too much advance notice was given, but stated, nevertheless, that some information should be given.

The position, therefore, appears to be that a notice must give sufficient details of the application to enable the person on whom the notice is served to prepare for the hearing of the application, but full details, both of the evidence supporting the application and of the material sought, need only be given by the police in court.

2   *Barclays Bank plc v Taylor: Trustee Savings Bank of Wales and Border Counties v Taylor* [1989] 3 All ER 563, [1989] 1 WLR 1066, CA.
3   [1988] 2 All ER 769, [1988] 1 WLR 705.
4   Cf the position regarding a notice served under section 2 of the 1987 Act: see Chapter 2 section 2.2.6.
5   [1988] QB 579, [1987] 3 All ER 1025.
6   [1986] 3 All ER 113, [1986] 1 WLR 1292.

2.3.3 Legal privilege

Section 10 of PACE defines 'items subject to legal privilege' as:

'(a) communications between a professional legal adviser and his client or any person representing his client made in connection with the giving of legal advice to the client;

(b) communications between a professional legal adviser and his client or any person representing his client or between such an adviser or his client or any such representative and any other person made in connection with or in contemplation of legal proceedings and for the purposes of such proceedings; and

(c) items enclosed with or referred to in such communications and made

  (i) in connection with the giving of legal advice; or

  (ii) in connection with or in contemplation of legal proceedings and for the purposes of such proceedings, when they are in the possession of a person who is entitled to possession of them.'

By section 10(2): 'Items held with the intention of furthering a criminal purpose are not items subject to legal privilege.'

It is important to note that section 10 does not provide the same protection as is provided by section 2(9) of the 1987 Act.[7]

The courts have held that only communications made in connection with the giving of advice are protected by section 10, and the provision of legal services, such as conveyancing, did not constitute the giving of advice.[8] However, if a communication about a conveyancing transaction contained legal advice rather than simply passing on information the document would be privileged. It is clear that documents which happen to be in the possession of a legal adviser, even if provided for the purpose of obtaining legal advice, are not privileged unless it can be said that they were created in connection with the seeking or giving of legal advice.[9]

Section 10(2) has been very widely construed by the courts. In *R v Central Criminal Court, ex p Francis and Francis*[10] the House of Lords decided that where documents are otherwise protected by privilege and are held without any criminal intent by the solicitor on behalf of his client, they can nevertheless lose the protection of privilege if a third party intended that the documents should be used for furthering a criminal purpose. In *Francis and Francis* the documents which were the subject of the application were to be used for the purpose of laundering the proceeds of drugs trafficking. Neither the solicitor nor his client knew this fact, but the court decided that it was appropriate that the documents should be produced because they had been intended by a third party to perform a criminal function. That party was using the client and the solicitor as tools for his unlawful actions.

The document will only lose the protection of privilege if the criminal intent existed at the time when the document came into the solicitor's possession.[11]

7 See Chapter 2: section 2.3.5(a).
8 See *R v Inner London Sessions Crown Court, ex p Baines and Baines* [1988] QB 579, [1987] 3 All ER 1025.
9 *R v Guildhall Magistrates' Court, ex p Primlaks Holdings Co (Panama) Inc* [1990] 1 QB 261, [1989] 2 WLR 841.
10 [1989] AC 346, [1988] 1 All ER 677.
11 For further argument on this subject see Eric Hiley 'Production Orders under PACE; two important cases', Law Society Gazette, 28 October 1987, page 3088; Peter Stevenson 'Privilege; *Francis and Francis* and other recent cases', Law Society Gazette, 1 February 1989, page 26; and Michael Zander *The Police and Criminal Evidence Act 1984* (2nd edition, 1990) pages 30 to 33.

2.4   Search and seizure: general provisions

A search warrant may be obtained by a constable, on application to a Justice of the Peace, under section 8 of PACE. Such a warrant may not be obtained for the purposes of seizing excluded material or special procedural material or material subject to legal privilege. The application is made ex parte, and the constable must satisfy the justice of the peace that a serious arrestable offence has been committed; that there is material on the premises to be searched which is likely to be of substantial value to the investigation of the serious arrestable offence; and that it is likely to be relevant evidence. In addition, the constable must satisfy the magistrate that one of four conditions set out in section 8(3) apply, all of which relate to the practicality of entering the premises which it is desired to search without a warrant.

The reference to special procedure material and material subject to legal privilege shows that any approach for documents which are subject to a duty of confidentiality or for which legal professional privilege may be claimed must be made under section 9 and Schedule 1 of PACE. This was the conclusion reached in the case of *R v Guildhall Magistrates' Court, ex p Primlaks Holdings Co (Panama) Inc*[12] where, on application under section 8, magistrates had granted search warrants in relation to documents in the possession and control of two firms of solicitors. In the material placed before the magistrates on the application for the warrant, the police stated that the protection of legal professional privilege could not apply because the documents were held in furtherance of a criminal enterprise. The recipients of the search warrants applied for judicial review, which was granted because the material placed before the magistrates could not have satisfied them that there were no grounds for considering that the documents specified in the application were not covered by the provisions of section 10 of PACE relating to legal professional privilege. It was clearly much more appropriate for an application for the production of such material to be made under the provisions specifically provided for such circumstances in section 9 and Schedule 1. The *Primlaks* case makes it clear that the courts regard the provisions of Pt II of PACE as being subject to very strict construction, and that magistrates and judges should consider applications made to them very carefully and not regard themselves as mere functionaries in an executive process.

This sentiment was also expressed in the case of a search warrant applied for under Schedule 1, paragraphs 12 to 15, where the Divisional Court said that judges should always consider carefully whether all the access conditions were fulfilled, and should never treat an application as if it were a matter of routine. The case, *R v Maidstone Crown Court, ex p Waitt*[13] concerned a solicitor, who sought judicial review on the grounds that most of the documents seized by the police were subject to legal privilege. The warrant had apparently been granted on the basis that it was not practicable to communicate with the person entitled to grant entry to the premises, but the court found that in the case of a firm of solicitors there would be no practical difficulty in seeking the assistance of the senior partner. The court commented that it would always be preferable to avoid the issue of a search warrant in such cases, and to have applications for the production of special procedure material heard inter partes.

---

12 [1990] 1 QB 261, [1989] 2 WLR 841.
13 [1988] Crim LR 384.

One point which arose for discussion in the case concerned the question of whether a solicitor, faced with a request to produce a file relating to a client, would automatically refuse to do so unless under the compulsion of an order. Macpherson J thought that such an assumption should not be made. However, under the confidentiality rules relating to the conduct of solicitors, a solicitor may not breach confidentiality save in limited circumstances, including the making of an order under section 9 of PACE. A solicitor will normally feel safer relying on this exception to the rule, rather than relying on information provided by a police officer to the effect that his duty of confidentiality has been overridden by the fact that communications between the client and his solicitor were for the purpose of being guided or helped in the commission of a crime.[14]

2.5 Schedule 1 warrants for special procedure material

A search warrant under Schedule 1 of PACE, for the entry and search of premises in order to see special procedure material may be granted on an application by a constable to a circuit judge. The access provisions set out in paragraph 2 or 3 must be fulfilled and either (in the case of the second set of access conditions) an order has not been complied with, or (in relation to either set of conditions) any one of four further conditions is fulfilled. The further conditions relate to practicality of communication (as in the *Waitt* case) or 'that service of notice of an application for an Order under paragraph 4 above may seriously prejudice the investigation'.

It may be assumed, following the judicial pronouncements in the *Waitt* case, that a circuit judge will need strong persuasion by significant evidence (even if not evidence which complies strictly with the rules of evidence) that serious prejudice to an investigation will result from notice being given.

2.6 Provisions relating to arrest, entry to premises and search after arrest

Sections 17–23 of PACE govern the circumstances in which a police officer may enter and search premises without a search warrant. By section 17 a police officer may enter premises for the purpose of executing an arrest warrant, or to arrest a person for an arrestable offence, or for other purposes which are not relevant to fraud cases. It will be rare for the provisions of section 17 to be used in a fraud case.

By section 18:

> 'A constable may enter and search any premises occupied or controlled by a person who is under arrest for an arrestable offence, if he has reasonable grounds for suspecting that there is on the premises evidence other than items subject to legal privilege, that relates:
>
> (a) to that offence; or
> (b) to some other arrestable offence which is connected with or similar to that offence.'

---

14 See generally chapter 12 of the *Guide to the Professional Conduct of Solicitors* and Chapter 2 section 2.2.1 above.

Items found during such a search may be seized and retained.

By section 19 a police officer is given a general power of seizure in circumstances where he is lawfully on any premises. First, he may seize anything which he reasonably believes to have been obtained 'in consequence of the commission of an offence'. In order to justify such seizure he must also have reasonable grounds for believing that it may be concealed, lost, damaged, altered or destroyed if he does not secure it. Second, a police officer may seize anything which is on the premises 'if he has reasonable grounds for believing that it is evidence in relation to an offence which he is investigating or any other offence'. He must also believe that the evidence might otherwise be concealed, lost, etc. Finally, the police officer

> '. . . may require any information which is contained in a computer and is accessible from the premises to be produced in a form in which it can be taken away and in which it is visible and legible if he has reasonable grounds for believing:
>
> (a) that
>   (i)   it is evidence in relation to an offence which he is investigating or any other offence; or
>   (ii) it has been obtained in consequence of the commission of an offence; and
> (b) that it is necessary to do so in order to prevent it being concealed, lost, tampered with or destroyed.'

By section 21(1) the occupier of the premises on which the material was seized, or the person having custody control of it immediately before the seizure, may request a record of all items seized; such a person may also subsequently have access to the seized material under the supervision of a police officer.[15] Photocopies of the material may also be requested, and should be provided within a reasonable time from the making of the request.[16] These provisions as to access and copying do not apply if the officer in charge of the investigation has reasonable grounds for believing that to grant access would prejudice an investigation.[17]

Section 22 of PACE provides for the retention of material seized under the Act for 'so long as is necessary in all the circumstances'.[18]

3   CRIMINAL INVESTIGATIONS BY THE INLAND REVENUE

Criminal inquiries with a view to the institution of criminal proceedings must be differentiated from inquiries made by the Inland Revenue for the purposes of assessing the amount of tax payable by a taxpayer. The Inland Revenue inevitably possesses a range of powers designed to obtain information for the purpose of making assessments. In the majority of cases, even where the Inland Revenue believes that there may have been fraud or dishonesty, its purpose is

---

15 Section 21(3).
16 Section 21(4) and (7).
17 Section 21(8).
18 See also PACE Codes of Practice B.6.

to recover tax, not to prosecute wrongdoers. This philosophy was reported by the Keith Report[19] as follows:

'In the main the department deals with the tax evader not by prosecution but by money penalties graded according to the gravity of the offence . . . Criminal prosecution for tax offences is undertaken only in a small minority of cases . . . a selection of the most serious cases of fraud.'

In evidence submitted by the Board of Inland Revenue to the Commission on Criminal Procedure the Inland Revenue described the policy behind their decision to prosecute as being that they regard it as essential:

'To prosecute in some examples of all classes of tax fraud. This policy is essential because it is the possibility of prosecution which prevents the spread of tax fraud to unacceptable limits.'

The Inland Revenue policy is also set out, most famously, in the answer given by the Chancellor of the Exchequer to a question in the House of Commons on 5 October 1944 (the *Hansard* statement), in which the Chancellor, referring to section 34 of the Finance Act 1942, said:

'The Commissioners have a general power under which they can accept pecuniary settlements instead of instituting criminal proceedings in respect of fraud or wilful default alleged to have been committed by a tax payer. They can, however, give no undertaking to a tax payer in any such case that they will accept such a settlement and refrain from instituting criminal proceedings even if the case is one in which the tax payer has made full confession and has given full facilities for investigation of the facts. They reserve to themselves complete discretion in all cases as to the course which they will pursue, but it is their practice to be influenced by the fact that the tax payer has made a full confession and has given full facilities for investigation into his affairs and for examination of such books, papers, documents or information as the Commissioners may consider necessary.'

Whether an investigation by the Inland Revenue, therefore, will lead to criminal proceedings may not be clear until well on into the inquiry. A number of investigative steps might have been taken by the time that decision is made, mainly under the powers provided in section 20 of the Taxes Management Act 1970 (TMA). In addition, interviews might have been conducted, of which notes will have been made.

Any subsequent actions leading to a criminal trial will be subject to the normal rules of the criminal justice procedure, including all matters relating to interviewing under caution and charging (which must take place in a police station); appearance before a magistrates' court and granting of bail; committal (or, in the case of a serious and complex fraud, transfer under the provisions of section 4 of the 1987 Act); pre-trial reviews or preparatory hearings; trial and sentence.

3.1 Questioning of suspects

At any stage of an Inland Revenue inquiry the taxpayer may be invited to an interview with Inland Revenue officers. There are no powers available to

19 The Committee on Enforcement Powers of the Revenue Departments, Cmnd 8822 (published March 1983), paragraph 9.10.

compel attendance at such interviews or to require answers to be given to questions. Where an interview takes place it is likely that a record will be kept. Such record will not be a verbatim transcript, but attempts will normally be made to obtain agreement that the record is accurate. If such agreement is made by the taxpayer the record can become evidence in any criminal proceedings against him.

When the practice of giving *Hansard* to taxpayers was first used in the 1920s and through its development into the early 1940s (that is, giving them the opportunity to make full disclosure in return for a promise to consider not to institute criminal proceedings) any statement made in response to a promise of immunity from prosecution was ruled as inadmissible on the grounds that it had been induced by the *Hansard* statement. In *R v Barker*[20] the Court of Criminal Appeal held that, given the wording of the *Hansard* announcement, books and records produced under this inducement were no different from a confession made under it, and were equally inadmissible. This decision was seen as being so unsatisfactory that it was remedied by legislation, and now, by section 105 of the Taxes Management Act 1970 any statements made or documents produced after a *Hansard* statement has been made to a taxpayer are admissible.

Where a taxpayer has been arrested in connection with an Inland Revenue inquiry into tax matters, and it is desired to question him, that questioning must be conducted under caution in accordance with PACE and the Codes of Practice.

3.2   Production of documents

Section 20 of the TMA provides a variety of powers under which the Inland Revenue can demand production of documents. Taxpayers may also be required to 'furnish particulars'. By section 20(1) of the TMA an inspector of taxes, with the consent of a general or special commissioner, may request a tax payer to produce documents and furnish particulars, but only if he has previously been given a chance to provide the information voluntarily.[1] The documents required to be produced must be in the power or possession of the taxpayer, and the inspector must reasonably be of the opinion that they are relevant to his tax affairs, either in the UK or (by section 125 of the Finance Act 1990) other EC member states.

By section 20(2) similar requests can be made by the Board of the Inland Revenue, who must have reasonable grounds for believing that the tax payer has committed or will commit a serious breach of the tax rules.[2]

The requirement in both these subsections to 'furnish particulars' relates to answering questions, but does not compel the tax payer to attend an interview. The questions will be set out in the Notice and will be answered in writing.

By section 20(3) a Notice may be served on a third party, for example, the professional advisers of the taxpayer or his bank. The Notice is issued by an inspector of taxes with the consent of a general or special Commissioner, and it must specify the name of the taxpayer.

---

20 [1941] 2 KB 381, [1941] 3 All ER 33.
1   TMA section 20B(1).
2   TMA section 20A(7).

The Notice may only relate to 'such documents as are in his (the third party's) possession or power and as (in the inspector's reasonable opinion) contain, or may contain, information relevant to any tax liability to which the taxpayer is or may be, or may have been, subject, or to the amount of any such liability'.

This subsection , therefore, differs from the previous subsections in that it does not relate to the furnishing of particulars.

When served on a bank or professional adviser any duty of confidentiality to a client is overridden by the duty to comply with the Notice. Legal professional privilege may, however, apply.[3]

A Notice issued under section 20(3) must also be provided to the taxpayer to whom it relates,[4] unless the inspector applying for the Notice satisfies the general or Special Commissioner that a copy should not be given to the taxpayer because he has reasonable grounds for suspecting the taxpayer of fraud.[5]

The reasonableness of an inspector's opinion in relation to the matters set out in section 20(3)[6] was considered in *R v IRC, ex p TC Coombs & Co*[7] where it was decided that unless strong evidence could be adduced that documents sought to be produced under the Notice had no relevance to the tax affairs of the taxpayer, the courts will find that the opinion was reasonable.

Further powers to obtain information from third parties are contained in sections 745 and 788 of the Income and Corporation Taxes Act 1988. Section 745 concerns the transfer of assets abroad, including the setting up of offshore trusts and companies, and section 778 concerns UK land transactions. These sections provide wide-ranging powers to the Inland Revenue to obtain documents from third parties, and can be drafted in wide terms. For example, a firm of solicitors or accountants may be required to furnish particulars of all their files relating to the setting up of offshore trusts between certain dates. Whether such a Notice would be too wide will have to be judged according to the circumstances of each case. However, in *Royal Bank of Canada v Inland Revenue Commissioners*[8] Megarry J said, per curiam, that it seemed to him:

> 'The wider the powers that Parliament confides to the commissioners, the more important it is that the commissioners should not exercise those powers in an unduly burdensome or oppressive way. A question asked in September 1969 which requires the bank to ascertain whether any of its officers, employees or agents, wherever they may be in the world, knows or believes that any person had on June 1st 1964, or subsequently any beneficial interest in Poinsettia is of an amplitude which, if repeated, may hereafter attract to itself robust judicial criticism.'[9]

In relation to the powers under TMA section 20 and Income and Corporation Taxes Act 1988 sections 745 and 778 there are sanctions for failure to comply. These sanctions may be imposed by the commissioners in proceedings brought under TMA section 98; the maximum penalty for failure to comply in relation to each Notice is £300, with a further £60 per day for any failure to comply

---

3 See section 3.4 below.
4 Section 20B(1A).
5 Section 20B(1B).
6 But applicable to other parts of the section.
7 [1991] 2 AC 283, [1991] 2 WLR 682, HL.
8 [1972] Ch 665, [1972] 1 All ER 225.
9 See also *Clinch v IRC* [1974] QB 76, [1973] 1 All ER 977.

after the commissioners have imposed a penalty. In addition, a maximum penalty of £3,000 may be imposed for furnishing incorrect information either fraudulently or negligently.

If a recipient of a Notice wishes to contest its validity, an application may be made for judicial review. Alternatively, the recipient can simply refuse to produce the information and contest the penalty proceedings brought under section 98 of the TMA.

By section 20BB anyone who 'falsifies, conceals, destroys or otherwise disposes of a document which is the subject of a Notice under section 20, or permits someone else to do the same, may be sentenced to two years' imprisonment or a fine or both on conviction on indictment. The matter may also be tried summarily.

It should be noted that an offence under section 20BB can be committed before a Notice under section 20 has been issued. By section 20BB(1)(b) an offence lies if papers are falsified etc after a person has been given a reasonable opportunity, by the provisions of section 20B(1), to deliver documents without compulsion.

3.3   Powers of search

Powers of search are granted by section 20C of the TMA:

'If the appropriate judicial authority is satisfied on information on oath given by an Officer of the Board that –

(a) there is reasonable ground for suspecting that an offence involving serious fraud in connection with or in relation to tax is being, has been or is about to be committed and that evidence of it is to be found on premises specified in the information; and

(b) in applying under this section the officer acts with the approval of the Board given in relation to the particular case,

the authority may issue a warrant in writing authorising an officer of the Board to enter the premises, if necessary by force, at any time within fourteen days from the time of issue of the warrant and search them.'

The 'appropriate judicial authority' is a circuit judge.

The application is made ex parte, and notice is not given to the taxpayer of the existence of the Notice. There is no right to be heard. Following the issue of a warrant the Revenue will normally conduct a 'dawn raid'. The warrant will specify the maximum number of Inland Revenue officers who may exercise the powers conferred by the warrant and the times of day between which the warrant must be executed. A police constable in uniform will be present, unless the judicial authority decides otherwise.

A warrant under section 20 cannot be applied for unless there are reasonable grounds for suspecting that an offence involving serious fraud is involved, and 'serious fraud' is defined in section 20C(1A):

'Without prejudice to the generality of the concept of serious fraud –

(a) any offence which involves fraud is for the purposes of this section an offence involving serious fraud if its commission has led, was intended or likely to lead, either to substantial financial gain to any person or to serious prejudice to the proper assessment or collection of tax; and

(b) an offence which, if considered alone, would not be regarded as involving serious fraud may nevertheless be so regarded if there is reasonable

> ground for suspecting that it forms part of a course of conduct which is, or but for its detection would be, likely to result in serious prejudice to the proper assessment or collection of tax.'

By section 20(C)(3) the officer who enters the premises may 'seize and remove any things whatsoever found there which he has reasonable cause to believe may be required as evidence for the purposes of proceedings in respect of such an offence as is mentioned in subsection (1) above' and he may also conduct searches of 'any person found on the premises whom he has reasonable cause to believe to be in possession of any such things'.

The issue of warrants under this section was extensively examined in *IRC v Rossminster Ltd*,[10] in which the House of Lords held that a warrant was valid in spite of the fact that it did not particularise the alleged offences. The warrant obtained by the Inland Revenue to search premises connected with Rossminster Limited had recited that an information on oath had been laid before the court 'stating that there is reasonable ground for suspecting that an offence involving fraud in connection with or in relation to tax had been committed'. The House of Lords held that this was a sufficient description of the suspected offences and that the occupier of the searched premises had no right to be told the precise nature of the alleged offences, nor did he have the right to be informed of the 'reasonable grounds' which satisfied the judge that offences had been committed.[11]

A record of the documents seized pursuant to a raid under TMA section 20C must be provided to a person who requests it provided he is either the occupier of the premises from which it was removed or can show that he had custody or control of the material immediately before its removal.[12] In addition, material should be returned to its owner if a photocopy of it is sufficient for the purposes of the Inland Revenue, or alternatively a photocopy of the material shall be provided to the owner on request, provided that the officer in charge has no reasonable grounds for believing that prejudice to his investigation would be caused.[13]

3.4 Professional privilege

By TMA section 20B(8) any Notice issued under section 20(3): 'does not oblige a barrister, advocate or a solicitor to deliver or make available, without his client's consent, any document with respect to which a claim to professional privilege could be maintained'. It is to be noted that this protection only applies to material in the hands of a lawyer, and not to material which may in other circumstances be considered to be subject to the protection of legal professional privilege which is found in the possession of the taxpayer.

By TMA section 20C(4) a warrant issued under section 20C to search the premises of a lawyer does not permit the removal of documents in the lawyer's possession 'with respect to which a claim to professional privilege could be maintained'.

Once again, the protection of privilege does not extend to documents in the possession of the taxpayer.

---

10 [1980] AC 952, [1980] 1 All ER 80.
11 Per Lord Wilberforce at page 999.
12 Section 20CC(1).
13 Section 20CC(3), (5) and (8).

In the context of a tax case, privilege extends to legal advice generally, whether or not given in contemplation of legal proceedings. It therefore includes instructions to counsel, counsel's advice and notes of conferences with counsel, correspondence between a client and his solicitor in which legal advice is given, and documents created for the purpose of instructing a barrister or solicitor, for example, copies of original documents, even if those originals are not themselves privileged.

By section 20B(9)–(13) a form of professional privilege is created for auditors and tax advisers. By section 20B(11) the protection of professional privilege does not extend to: 'any document which contains information explaining any information, return, accounts, or other document which the person to whom the Notice is given has, as tax accountant, assisted any client of his in preparing for, or delivering to, the Inspector or the Board'. Otherwise, protection is given to documents which are an auditor's 'property and were created by him or on his behalf for or in connection with the performance of his functions' as an auditor; and to communications between a tax adviser and his clie it for the purpose of giving tax advice.

4   POWERS OF INVESTIGATION OF THE CUSTOMS AND EXCISE

4.1   Applicability of PACE

It is the responsibility of Customs and Excise to collect not only certain domestic taxes, but also certain taxes levied by the European Community. The responsibility extends to controlling the import of certain classes of goods into the United Kingdom and collecting import duties.[14] Where frauds occur relating to these taxes, it is the responsibility of HM Customs and Excise, not the police, to investigate offences and to take steps to enforce the tax, including, where appropriate, by prosecuting tax evaders. The core of Customs' powers to require information and investigate offences is found in the Customs and Excise Management Act 1979. These powers are, however, supplemented by the various statutes which impose the duty on Customs to collect the tax. The prime example is the Value Added Tax Act 1983, which provides its own regime for the administration, collection and enforcement of VAT, including detailed provisions enabling customs officers to enter and search premises and to take away documents[15] and its own offences relating to fraudulent evasion of VAT.[16] In the absence of penal provisions under Community law, Customs have responsibility for investigating frauds within the United Kingdom on community funds, for investigating breaches of EC

---

14 Which may be United Kingdom import duties or EC import duties: see section 5 of the European Communities Act 1972.
15 See Schedule 7 – section 4.2.1 below.
16 See section 39 of the Value Added Tax Act 1983. Other examples include the Customs Duties (Dumping and Subsidies) Act 1969 section 14 which enables the commissioners to demand information from importers relating to goods in respect of which a dumping charge under the Act has been imposed. Powers similar to those held by Customs are given to the Secretary of State and his officers in respect of enforcement of the Vehicles (Excise) Licence Act 1971, see sections 3 and 27; Hydrocarbon Oil Duties Act 1979 section 27(2); Tobacco Products Duty Act 1979; Finance Act 1982 section 11.

customs law,[17] collecting certain duties on behalf of other states[18] and for collecting and exchanging information in the field of customs and agricultural matters.[19]

Unlike the SFO and CPS, HM Customs and Excise is not only a prosecuting authority. Its main hat is that of a collector of revenue and many of its powers are directed towards acquiring information for the purpose of that function. Where, however, Customs are investigating offences relating to 'assigned matters',[20] the same rules of investigation apply to officers of HM Customs and Excise as apply to investigations carried out by the police to the extent to which 'the Treasury may by order direct'.[1] Customs officers investigating offences must have regard to any relevant provision of Codes of Practice issued under section 67 of the Police and Criminal Evidence Act 1984.[2]

The Police and Criminal Evidence Act 1984 (Application to Customs and Excise) Order 1985[3] applies many of the investigative and procedural provisions of PACE to customs officers.[4] It does not, however, permit a customs officer to charge a person with an offence, or to release a person on bail or to detain a person for an offence after he has been charged with that offence.[5] The usual practice, therefore, on conclusion of an interview (which may be held at a designated customs office rather than a police station[6]), is to take the defendant to a police station, report the offence to the custody officer, who will decide whether there is sufficient evidence to charge. The Order applies, in particular, the provisions of section 8, 9 and Schedule 1 of PACE to Customs investigations, so that applications for excluded or special material must be made to a circuit judge. The provisions relating to custody officers, limits on detention, the right to have someone notified of arrest and access to legal advice also apply.[7]

4.2   Special provisions under the Customs and Excise Management Act 1979

A power of arrest is attached to many of the offences contained both in the Customs and Excise Management Act 1979 and the Value Added Tax Act 1983, even though many would already be arrestable offences as defined in section 24 of the Police and Criminal Evidence Act 1984.[8] The powers of arrest

---

17 *Re Casati: 203/80* [1981] ECR 2595, [1982] 1 CMLR 365, ECJ.

18 Section 11(1) of the Finance Act 1977 under which Customs may enforce in a United Kingdom court duty claimed by an authority in a member state pursuant to Directive of the Council of the European Communities 15 March 1976 No 76/308/EEC. This now covers, for example, VAT due in another member state: EEC Council Directive 79/1071.

19 Council Regulation 1468/81 OJ 1981, L144/1 as extended by Council Regulation 945/87 OJ 1987, L90/3.

20 'Any matter in relation to which the Commissioners are for the time being required in pursuance of any enactment to perform any duties': section 1 of the Customs and Excise Management Act 1979.

1   Section 114 of the Police and Criminal Evidence Act 1984.

2   Because, under section 69(9) they are 'persons other than police officers who are charged with the duty of investigating offences or charging offenders'.

3   SI 1985/1800 as amended by SI 1987/439.

4. Article 3 and Schedule 1.

5   Article 4.

6   Article 3 Schedule 2.

7   Schedule 1 to the Order.

8   See, for example, section 167 (making untrue declarations); section 170 (fraudulent evasion of duty); section 39 of the Value Added Tax Act 1983 (fraudulent evasion of VAT).

carry with them the investigative rights attendant on arrest such as the right to search an arrested person,[9] and to enter and search premises for the purpose of arresting a person, and searching premises after arrest.[10]

The Customs and Excise Management Act also provides wide powers of seizure in respect of goods liable to forfeiture. These include, for example, not only items such as drugs and obscene literature, but also goods imported without payment of duty,[11] vehicles and containers used for the purposes of the commission of the offence,[12] and goods zero-rated for export for VAT purposes but which have not been exported.[13] In support of the right of forfeiture, Customs have power to search premises and seize any goods liable to forfeiture,[14] and vehicles.[15]

Several provisions of the Act require traders to provide information. Importers and exporters are required to keep and procure records[16] and to furnish any information relating to imported and exported goods as Customs may require.[17] The requirement to provide information has recently been extended to every person who is concerned (in whatever capacity) in the importation or exportation of goods and any person in possession of the information.[18]

Similarly, in relation to the grant and enforcement of excise licences, revenue traders are required to keep and preserve records and to furnish information to Customs.[19] Powers of entry, search and seizure are given.[20]

4.3   Value added tax

VAT is subject to the regime of administration, collection and enforcement contained in Schedule 7 to the Value Added Tax Act 1983.

4.3.1   Disclosure of documents

Paragraph 7 of Schedule 7 requires every taxable person to keep and preserve records of their business.[1] The records may be preserved on computer or by such other means as the Commissioners approve and are admissible in civil or

---

9   Section 32 of PACE as modified by Article 5 of the Police and Criminal Evidence Act 1984 (Application to Customs and Excise) Order 1985 (op cit) which allows customs officers on such a search to seize evidence of any offences not just customs offences.
10 Section 17(1)(b), (2) and sections 18 and 19(4) are applied to Customs by the PACE Order.
11 CEMA 1979 section 49.
12 CEMA 1979 section 141; this includes aircraft, liability is strict and it is not necessary to prove intent: *Customs and Excise Comrs v Air Canada* [1991] 2 QB 446, [1991] 1 All ER 570, CA; *Customs and Excise Comrs v Jack Bradley (Accrington) Ltd* [1959] 1 QB 219, [1958] 3 All ER 487.
13 VAT Act 1983 section 16(9).
14 CEMA 1979 section 161: either by Writ of Assistance or by a magistrate's warrant.
15 CEMA 1979 section 163.
16 CEMA 1979 Parts IV and V; section 75A.
17 CEMA 1979 section 77.
18 Section 77A(1) and (2), which were inserted by section 10 of the Finance Act 1987.
19 Sections 118A and 118B of CEMA 1979.
20 Sections 118C, 118D and 118E.
1   The precise form of the records is set out in the VAT (Accounting and Records) Regulations 1989, SI 1989/2248.

criminal proceedings pursuant to para 7(3).[2] By paragraph 8 of Schedule 7, Customs may require a person to give information or supply documents relating to goods or services supplied or imported. Paragraph 8(2) provides:

> 'Every person who is concerned (in whatever capacity) in the supply of goods or services in the course or furtherance of a business or to whom such a supply is made and every person who is concerned (in whatever capacity) in the importation of goods in the course or furtherance of a business shall:
>
> (a) furnish to the Commissioners, within such time and in such form as they may reasonably require, such information relating to the goods or services or to the supply or importation as the Commissioners may reasonably specify; and
> (b) upon demand made by an authorised person, produce or cause to be produced for inspection by that person
>   (i)   at the principal place of business of the person upon whom the demand is made or at such other place as the authorised person may reasonably require, and
>   (ii) at such time as the authorised person may reasonably require,
>   any documents relating to the goods or services or to the supply or importation.'

The information or documents are not limited to the records maintained under paragraph 7, the recipient of a request does not have to be a taxable person, and it seems that the power is wide enough to enable Customs to obtain information from third parties as part of an investigation against another. The customs officer may take copies of the documents or may, if it appears to him necessary to do so, remove them at a reasonable time and for a reasonable period.

Powers in broadly the same form were considered by the House of Lords in *Customs and Excise Comrs v Harz*.[3] Customs, in the course of investigating a purchase tax fraud, subjected the appellant to three hours of interrogation, during which he made incriminating admissions. They purported to derive their authority from a provision similar to para 8(2) and had threatened both the appellant and his solicitor that the appellant would be prosecuted if he did not answer the questions. The admissions were ruled inadmissible and the conviction was quashed. Lord Reid observed:

> 'There is here a clear distinction between the right of an officer to demand production of documents and the right of the commissioners to require information to be furnished at such time and in such manner as they may require. The right of the officer is to require immediate production of documents, and, if the trader fails to produce documents in his possession of the kind demanded, he can be prosecuted. No doubt the officer can ask questions relating to documents of the kinds which he has demanded, and the trader's answer or refusal to answer may be admissible in evidence; but the prosecution will not be for refusal to answer questions, it will be for refusal to produce documents, and I can see nothing to require the trader to give answers which may incriminate him.
>
> The right of the commissioners to require information is quite different. If a demand for information is made in the proper manner the trader is bound to answer the demand within the time and in the form required whether or not the answer may tend to incriminate him, and if he fails to comply with the

2 Subject to para 7(5), which applies the provisions of sections 68–70 of the Police and Criminal Evidence Act 1984 to records held on computer.
3 [1967] 1 AC 760, [1967] 1 All ER 177.

demand he can be prosecuted. If he answers falsely he can be prosecuted for that, and, if he answers in such a manner as to incriminate himself, I can see no reason why his answer should not be used against him. Some statutes expressly provide that incriminating answers may be used against the person who gives them and some statutes expressly provide that they may not. Where, as here, there is no such express provision the question whether such answers are admissible evidence must depend on the proper construction of the particular statute. Although I need not decide the point, it seems to me to be reasonably clear that incriminating answers to a proper demand under this section must be admissible if the statutory provision is to achieve its obvious purpose.

If the admissions with which the appeal is concerned had been obtained by a proper exercise of this power of the commissioners, they might well have been admissible in evidence in this prosecution . . . The trader is only bound to furnish information within such time and in such form as the commissioners require. The information will often be complicated, and the commissioners can be relied on to fix a reasonable time. If the information required is simple and easily provided, the time required may be short. I do not think, however, that this entitles the commissioners to send a representative to confront the trader, put questions to him orally and demand oral answers on the spot; and I am certainly of opinion that it does not entitle them to send their representative to subject the trader to a prolonged interrogation in the nature of a cross-examination. This provision is in sharp contrast with provisions which expressly entitle officers to question persons with regard to particular matters, eg, to question passengers entering the country with regard to their luggage. When it is intended that officers shall obtain information by asking oral questions that is made plain in the statute.'

Paragraph 8(2) should not, accordingly, be used to justify detailed questioning of a suspect. Where Customs wish to obtain information or otherwise question a person whom they suspect has committed an offence, the appropriate course is to question under the provisions of PACE.[4] Customs do not need to obtain any judicial consent for making such requirements, and the only curb on their authority is that they should act reasonably.

4.3.2   Entry and search of premises

Paragraph 10(1) of Schedule 7 gives Customs a right, for the purpose of exercising any powers under the VAT Act, at any reasonable time, to enter premises used in connection with the carrying on of a business. This is a right of entry at large, not specifically for the purposes of investigation of a crime, and permits Customs to enter premises for the purposes of, for example, a control visit or spot checks.[5] Where, however, there is reasonable ground for suspecting that a serious VAT fraud is being,[6] has been or is about to be committed on any premises, or that evidence of the commission of such an offence is to be found there, a magistrate may issue a warrant in writing authorising customs officers to enter and search the premises. Once on the

4   Section 67(9): see also Royal Commission on Criminal Procedure (Cmnd 8092) paragraph 4.135.
5   See also para 10(2) which permits Customs to enter premises used in connection with the supply of goods under taxable supplies and to inspect the goods.
6   The power is exercisable in respect of 'a fraud offence which appears to be of a serious nature'. 'Fraud offence' is defined as one offence under any provision of section 39(1) to (3) of the VAT Act 1983: paragraph 10(4).

premises, which may if necessary be entered by force, the authorised person may seize and remove any documents or other things whatsoever found on the premises which he has reasonable cause to believe may be required as evidence for the purposes of proceedings and may search any person found on the premises whom he has reasonable cause to believe to be in possession of such documents or things.[7]

4.3.3   Orders for access to information

Paragraph 10A provides a less traumatic mechanism for obtaining evidence than search and seizure. Where a magistrate is satisfied, on application by an authorised person, that there are reasonable grounds for believing:

(a) that an offence in connection with VAT[8] is being or has been or is about to be committed; and
(b) that any recorded information (including any document of any nature whatsoever), which may be required as evidence for the purpose of any proceedings in respect of such an offence is in the possession of any person,

he may make an order that the person in possession of the recorded information shall, within seven days of the order (or such longer period as the order may specify):

(a) give an authorised person access to it; and
(b) permit an authorised person to remove and take away any of it which he reasonably considers necessary.

This applies to any VAT offence and is not limited to taxable persons.

4.3.4   Procedure on removal of documents

Where documents or any other things are removed under paragraph 10 or 10A, the authorised person must provide the occupier of the premises from which they are removed or the person who had custody of them before removal, on request, with a record of what he removed.[9] The request must be complied with within a reasonable time[10] and, if Customs fail to comply with a request for a record, they may be ordered by magistrates to provide one.[11]

Persons having custody or control of items removed are entitled to have access to the removed material and to photographs or copies of it, unless there are reasonable grounds for believing that granting access to, or supplying a copy of, anything would prejudice the investigating of any offence or any criminal proceedings.[12] If Customs fail to provide access or copies, they may be ordered by a magistrates' court to do so.[13]

---

7 Paragraph 10(3).
8 Paragraph 10A(1)(a) refers to 'the tax'; this is limited, in section 48(1), to Value Added Tax.
9 Paragraph 10B(1).
10 Paragraph 10B(2).
11 Paragraph 10C(2)(a).
12 Paragraph 10B(3).
13 Paragraph 10C(2)(b).

4.3.5   *Professional privilege*

None of the powers in Schedule 7 of the Value Added Tax Act 1983 contains a saving for legal professional privilege.[14] The Keith Committee[15] recommended that legal advice given to a taxpayer and materials coming into existence as part of the preparation for proceedings should be protected from disclosure, and that all claims to privilege advanced in the course of any search of premises should be adjudicated upon and determined by the judge who issued the warrant. In a press notice dated 6th August 1985, Customs stated:

> 'The Keith Committee made a number of specific recommendations about protecting certain communications entitled to the benefit of legal professional privilege from disclosure under the wider VAT information powers. These recommendations are being discussed with interested parties and will be the subject of further legislation probably in 1986. Until legislation is enacted, ministers have given an assurance that Customs & Excise will respect any reasonable claim to legal professional privilege in connection with the new VAT information power.'[16]

No legislation has ever been enacted in relation to professional privilege in VAT investigations and reliance must still be placed on the assurance contained in this press notice.[17]

5   PRE-TRIAL HEARINGS

Once a case has been committed for trial or transferred under the provisions of section 4 of the 1987 Act, there may be an application for a preparatory hearing under section 7 of the 1987 Act, or the case may be listed for a pre-trial review under any practice rules promulgated by the courts.

The Roskill Report expressed some dissatisfaction with the pre-trial review process in complex fraud cases[18] including:

(i) that the judge dealing with the pre-trial review was not always the trial judge;

(ii) that counsel, both prosecution and defence, were ill prepared;

(iii) that pre-trial reviews tended to be held either too far in advance of a trial or too close to it; and

(iv) that no sanctions existed for failure to comply with orders made at the hearing.

---

14 Nor does the Customs and Excise Management Act 1979. Compare the detailed provisions of sections 20B and 20C of the Taxes Management Act. See also the VAT Tribunal Rules which do contain a saving for legal professional privilege.

15 Report of the Committee on Enforcement Powers of the Revenue Departments (Cmnd 8822) Chapter 26.

16 Press Notice number 1029. The reference to 'new information power' relates to the expansion of information that Customs may, under the 1983 Act, require. In the previous legislation, the request was limited to taxable supplies of services, to information and documents relating to the consideration for such supplies and to the name and address of the person to whom the supply was made: section 35 of the Finance Act 1972. The basis for the limitation appears to have been the anxiety to preserve the position of lawyers, who might otherwise be permitted to disclose privileged information: Keith Committee Report, op cit at para 4.9.11.

17 For other Customs inquiries, however, such as into importation of drugs, frauds in relation to other taxes etc, the PACE Scheme will afford protection to legally professionally privileged material.

18 Roskill Report, paras 6.9–6.22.

Nevertheless, inspection of the practice rules, drawn up on 21 November 1979, for use in the Central Criminal Court (and adopted in more or less the same form by most Crown Court Centres) shows that they are intended, at least, and have the capacity, to deal with most matters relevant to a complicated fraud trial.[19] In particular, a pre-trial review can deal with all matters of law which might arise during the trial and with the admissibility of evidence. The judge may hear in open court and rule upon any application by any party relating to the severance of any count or any defendant, and hear any amendments to the indictment. By rule 7 of the Central Criminal Court Practice Rules: 'the judge may make such order or orders as lie within his powers as appear to him to be necessary to secure the proper and efficient trial of the case'.

The courts have encouraged use of pre-trial reviews, particularly when there are a large number of defendants and the case is otherwise complex.[20] The courts have also emphasised the need for preparation for pre-trial reviews, including time for the trial judge to form his own judgement on severance. In *R v Simonds*,[1] the Court of Appeal recommended that the judge should be given a transcript of the Crown's opening speech at the committal and of any submissions by the defence. Transcripts of such speeches and submissions are not normally available, but any summary of the case provided by the Crown, together with notes of the defence submissions, should suffice.

In *R v Hutchinson*,[2] the Court of Appeal decided that admissions made at a pre-trial review could not be used in evidence at the trial without the consent of the defendant on whose behalf they were made. A pre-trial review, therefore, does not have the same bite in this respect as a preparatory hearing, where admissions made under section 9(5) can be placed before the jury without consent.

Both prosecution and defence may consider, however, that there are significant advantages to holding a pre-trial review rather than a preparatory hearing. For the prosecution, there is not the requirement to produce a formal case statement, which in most cases will be a more formidable undertaking than a summary of the evidence. For the defence there is the advantage that the defendant does not have to reveal, under section 9(5)(b)(i) of the 1987 Act 'in general terms the nature of his defence', nor does he have to indicate 'the principal matters on which he takes issue with the prosecution'.

---

19 These rules are, of course, of general application for all types of criminal cases.
20 See, eg, *R v Thorne* (1977) 66 Cr App Rep 6, CA.
1 [1969] 1 QB 685, [1967] 3 All ER 399n.
2 [1985] Crim LR 730.

CHAPTER 6

Conspiracy to defraud

1 BACKGROUND TO SECTION 12 OF THE CRIMINAL JUSTICE ACT 1987

Conspiracy to defraud remains one of the most versatile and effective weapons in the armoury of the fraud prosecutor. Indeed it is displaying signs of remarkable vigour for a patient which has, in recent years, come close to demise on several occasions and over which a death sentence has hung since 1976. In 1961 it survived an attempt in *Welham v DPP*[1] to deny its existence as a common law offence. Later, in *Scott v Metropolitan Police Commissioner*,[2] the House of Lords rejected a submission that conspiracy to defraud, along with the offence of cheating, had been abolished by section 32(1) of the Theft Act 1968. Further doubt over its survival as an offence was cast by the Law Commission in 1976[3] in its general review of the law of conspiracy. The Commission recommended that:

'. . . the object of a conspiracy should be limited to the commission of a substantive offence . . . An agreement should not be criminal where that which it was agreed should be done would not amount to a criminal offence if committed by one person.'

This posed a particular problem for conspiracy to defraud, which, as Viscount Dilhorne had acknowledged in *Scott*, could embrace dishonest conduct which would not be criminal when committed by one person, but which none the less deserved punishment when committed by two or more persons acting jointly. The Commission recognised that the abolition of conspiracy to defraud as a common law offence might leave unacceptable gaps in the law and that it should be retained pending consideration as to specific statutory offences to replace it. The Commission concluded:

'We hope that eventually implementation of our recommendations on fraud will lead to the abolition of the common law offence of conspiracy to defraud (and also of cheating the revenue). In the meantime, however we believe that the common law offence of conspiracy to defraud should be specifically retained.'

This provisional lease of life for the offence found its way into section 5(2) of the Criminal Law Act 1977, which both preserved the common law offence and sheltered it entirely from the changes made to the general law of conspiracy in section 1 of the Criminal Law Act 1977, most notably perhaps the reform

---

1 [1961] AC 103, [1960] 1 All ER 805.
2 [1975] AC 819, [1974] 3 All ER 1032.
3 Law Com No 76: Conspiracy and Criminal Law Reform, para 1.9.

outlawing only those agreements which necessarily amounted to or involved the commission of a criminal offence.

The interpretation of section 5(2) did not, however, in the words of the Criminal Law Revision Committee,[4] prove straightforward. There emerged a conflict of judicial opinion as to whether conspiracy to defraud could be properly charged where the facts also revealed a conspiracy to commit a substantive offence. In *R v Quinn*[5] Drake J, recognising that his decision might have the effect of greatly limiting the scope of the Act, held that a conspiracy to steal could also properly be charged as a common law conspiracy to defraud. In *R v Walters, R v Tovey* and *R v Padfield*,[6] the Court of Appeal in a case in which the defendants, though convicted of conspiracy to defraud, had clearly been guilty of conspiracy to steal cars and obtain money by deception in selling them, rejected an argument that they could only have been convicted properly of a statutory conspiracy. The offence of conspiracy to defraud had been preserved, observed the court, and its elements had been proved. Lord Widgery CJ tentatively supported Drake J's ruling in Quinn and added:

'In many ways it must be preferable that conspiracy to defraud should be regarded as the greater container, as it were, and able to mop up conspiracy to steal if and when that is convenient, having regard to the nature of the case.'

This was the forerunner of one of the arguments later put forward by the Criminal Law Revision Committee[7] and the Law Commission[8] for the retention of conspiracy to defraud.

In 1979, however, the Court of Appeal in *R v Duncalf*[9] reached a different conclusion, feeling at liberty to do so because of the tentative way the Court in *Walters* had accepted the ruling in *Quinn*. The appellants, who had been convicted of conspiracy to steal contrary to section 1 of the 1977 Act, argued that they could only have been convicted properly of conspiracy to defraud. The argument failed. Roskill LJ said:

'It was said that Parliament must have intended to use the phrase "conspiracy to defraud" in section 5(2) in the sense in which Viscount Dilhorne had then defined it, and therefore section 5(2) must be given a meaning wide enough to embrace every conspiracy, the objective of which was dishonestly to injure some proprietary or other right of the victim. If section 5(2) is to be literally construed, this argument has obvious force. But we do not think it right to give so strict or literal a construction to the sub-section when the effect of so doing would be so largely to destroy the obvious purpose of this Act, and a sensible construction can, as we think, be given to both section 5(2) and section 5(3) as preserving the old law to, but only to, such extent as is necessary to ensure that a lacuna was not left in the law by section 1(1). There may well be cases where it is still proper to charge a conspiracy to defraud at common law, as was done in *R v Walters*, rather than a conspiracy to commit one or more specific offences contrary to section 1 of the 1977 Act. But where, as in the instant case, the obvious purpose of the conspiracy was to steal, we think that the Act requires a conspiracy to be charged as such contrary to section 1.'

4 Criminal Law Revision Committee, Eighteenth Report: Conspiracy to Defraud (1986).
5 [1978] Crim LR 750.
6 (1979) 69 Cr App Rep 115, CA.
7 Op cit – see note 3.
8 Working Paper No 104 – *Conspiracy to Defraud* (1987).
9 [1979] 2 All ER 1116, [1979] 1 WLR 918, CA.

The court was unable to agree with Drake J's ruling in *Quinn* or with Lord Widgery's approval of the ruling in *Walters*. The convictions were, accordingly, upheld.

The House of Lords considered the point in *R v Ayres*.[10] The certified question was:

> 'Whether a conspiracy to defraud at common law can only be charged when the evidence does not support any statutory substantive conspiracy, having regard to section 1 and 5 of the Criminal Law Act as amended?'

The appellant had been convicted of conspiracy to defraud an insurance company by falsely claiming that a lorry and its contents had been stolen in transit. At trial and before the Court of Appeal the appellant argued that the offence was a conspiracy to obtain money by deception and should have been charged under section 1(1) of the Criminal Law Act 1977. Conspiracy to defraud should only be charged, the submission continued, when the evidence did not support any statutory, substantive conspiracy. The House accepted that argument, disapproving *Quinn* and, by implication, *Walters*. The House looked to the purpose of the Criminal Law Act 1977 and had regard to the Law Commission Report on Conspiracy and Criminal Law Reform.[11] In the main judgment, Lord Bridge stated:

> 'It is legitimate to look at that report to ascertain the mischief which the statute was intended to remedy. To attempt briefly to paraphrase and summarise, without quoting, I read the report as identifying the defect in the previous law of criminal conspiracy as arising from the uncertainty as to what might constitute the subject matter of an agreement amounting to a criminal conspiracy, which, in general terms, could only be eliminated by restricting criminal conspiracies to agreements to commit substantive criminal offences. But as a gloss on this main theme, the report recognised that an unqualified restriction of criminal conspiracies to such agreements might leave gaps in the law in certain areas, including fraud, which only the retention of the common law conspiracy offence could cover. This reading of the Law Commission's report seems to me to lend powerful support to the construction adopted in *R v Duncalf* of sections 1(1) and 5(2) of the 1977 Act.
>
> Further considerations point to the same conclusion. Adopting a purposive approach of construction, it is difficult indeed to suppose that Parliament, whilst limiting the punishment of conspirators generally to the maximum appropriate to the substantive offences they had conspired to commit and giving them the added protection of requiring approval from the DPP to their prosecution if the substantive offences were summary offences, should have intended to deny both these advantages to any person agreeing to commit a substantive offence involving an element of fraud, however trivial that offence might be.'

Lord Bridge, approving the decision in *Duncalf*, concluded that the phrase 'conspiracy to defraud' in section 5(2) of the 1977 Act should be construed as limited to an agreement which, if carried into effect, would not necessarily involve the commission of any substantive criminal offence by the conspirators.

In a comment which he subsequently described as an optimistic prognosis,[12] Lord Bridge suggested that the ruling would not create undue difficulty for

---

10 [1984] AC 447, [1984] 1 All ER 619, HL.
11 Law Com No 76.
12 In *R v Cooke* [1986] AC 909, [1986] 2 All ER 985, HL.

prosecutors. In fact, prosecutors did encounter difficulties and, given that the Law Commission review was likely to take longer than prosecutors could bear, the Criminal Law Revision Committee[13] was asked 'to review the restrictions on the use of a charge of conspiracy to defraud in the light of the decision in *Ayres* and subsequent cases, and to consider whether these restrictions could be removed without causing injustice to defendants'. The Committee found that the Court of Appeal had had to quash convictions in unmeritorious appeals, permitting large-scale frauds to go unpunished or inadequately punished. The appeals had been brought, the Committee reported, not on the basis that a charge of conspiracy to defraud was unfair or had produced a wrong verdict, but on technical grounds aimed at evading conviction or achieving a lesser sentence.

The Committee described the problems caused by *Ayres* with reference to several cases which had reached, though not necessarily foundered in, the Court of Appeal.[14] One area of difficulty had been where the commission of the substantive offence was merely incidental to a larger fraud,[15] or did not, in the court's view, truly reflect the gravity of the defendant's conduct.[16] Another difficulty was the need for prosecutors to scour the statute book and closely examine the details of the case to ensure that there was no substantive offence disclosed, the existence of which would exclude the possibility, since *Ayres*, of charging a conspiracy to defraud. If the prosecutor discovered a minor Companies Act offence or offences, which were embraced in the fraud, he would be obliged to charge those offences, rather than conspiracy to defraud. Such offences, and more importantly their penalties, would not reflect the true evil perpetrated by the fraudster. In *R v Lloyd*,[17] the appellants' convictions for conspiracy to steal were quashed because their activity of borrowing and copying films did not amount to theft. The Court of Appeal would not substitute a conviction for the count of conspiracy to defraud which had been left on the file because the prosecution conceded that the agreement between the parties amounted to a conspiracy to contravene section 1 of the Copyright Act 1956, thus excluding the possibility of a conviction for conspiracy to defraud. The maximum penalty would have been two years' imprisonment. This problem faced the prosecutor not only when considering the witness statements at the time of drafting the indictment, but remained with him as the evidence was unfolding in court. If a substantive offence was disclosed relating to the 'fraud', a change would have to be sought in the indictment.

A further difficulty arose in respect of presentation of the case to a jury. The task of the judge in summing up, and the task of the jury in understanding, perhaps complicated and allegedly fraudulent transactions would be eased considerably if the case could be presented under one charge relating to the general scheme of conduct rather than a multitude of lesser charges, each requiring separate legal and factual analysis.

---

13 Op cit.
14 *R v Tonner* [1985] 1 All ER 807, [1985] 1 WLR 344; *R v Cox and Mead* (1984) Times, 6 December, CA; *R v Lloyd* [1985] QB 829, [1985] 2 All ER 661, CA; *R v Grant* [1986] Crim LR 127, CA; *R v Pain, Jory and Hawkins* [1986] Crim LR 168, CA; *R v Hollinshead* [1985] AC 975, [1985] 2 All ER 769, HL.
15 See *R v Tonner*. The Court of Appeal was able to substitute convictions on some of the lesser charges left on the file, in respect of which sentences were passed consecutively.
16 See *R v Cox and Mead* (1984) Times, 6 December.
17 [1985] QB 829, [1985] 2 All ER 661.

Recognising the difficulties produced by its decision in *Ayres*, the House of Lords engaged in a limited and inelegant 'patching' exercise in *R v Cooke*.[18] Lord Bridge said:[19]

'It seems to me that where an agreement to pursue a course of conduct is to be the subject of a conspiracy charge and every element in that course of conduct of which the prosecution can properly make complaint amounts to or involves the commission of a specific criminal offence, the only proper course is to charge a statutory conspiracy to commit that offence or those offences. It may, of course, be appropriate to charge more than one such conspiracy. At the other end of the spectrum, if persons agree to pursue a course of fraudulent conduct which does not involve the commission of any specific offence, the appropriate charge will be conspiracy to defraud at common law. The difficulty arises in the many cases, to which I regret I did not apply my mind in *Ayres*, where a course of conduct is agreed to be pursued which involves the commission of one or more specific criminal offences, but over and above such specific criminal conduct the agreement, if carried out, will involve a substantial element of fraudulent conduct of a kind which, on the part of an individual, would not be criminal at all. In this situation I decline to allow the shortcomings of the language I used in *Ayres* to prevent me from reaching the sensible conclusion that it is perfectly proper for the prosecution to charge one or other or both of two conspiracies: (a) a statutory conspiracy in respect of that part of the agreed course of conduct which amounts to or necessarily involves the commission of one or more specific criminal offences; (b) a common law conspiracy in respect of that part of the course of conduct agreed upon which is fraudulent but would not be criminal on the part of an individual acting alone. It may be that there is only one agreement, but it is an agreement to pursue courses of conduct which can and should be distinguished because they involve different categories of behaviour which the criminal law classifies in different ways. A single agreement to pursue a course of conduct which involves the commission of two different specific offences could perfectly properly be charged in two counts alleging two different conspiracies, eg a conspiracy to steal a car and a conspiracy to obtain money by deception by selling the car with false registration plates and documents. By the same token, if, in addition to any specific offences which conspirators have agreed to commit, they have agreed to pursue a further course of conduct which defrauds a victim in a manner which does not amount to, or, involve the commission of any specific offence, I can see no reason why that should not also be charged and proved as a separate conspiracy.'

Lord Mackay of Clashfern added:[20]

'. . . the principal difficulty which he has highlighted of not being able to use a single count indictment of conspiracy to defraud to comprehend all the dishonesty in a case where the agreement involves the commission of statutory or other offences, is an inescapable consequence of the Criminal Law Act 1977 . . . While I greatly regret any unnecessary difficulty in the way of successful prosecution of complicated frauds, I consider that this difficulty is not one which this House, in its judicial capacity, can remove.'

The Criminal Law Revision Committee report, and the Lords' expressed inability to remedy a problem essentially of Parliament's making, paved the way for section 12 of the Criminal Justice Act 1987 and the guidance given to Crown Prosecutors on the charging of conspiracy to defraud. The Committee

18 [1986] AC 909, [1986] 2 All ER 985.
19 Ibid at 919–920.
20 Ibid at 935–936.

had concluded that the 'simplest solution' was to restore the full ambit of conspiracy to defraud. It doubted that there was any serious risk of misuse of such a charge by the prosecuting authorities, but recommended that the guidelines issued by the Director of Public Prosecutions to Crown Prosecutors under section 10 of the Prosecution of Offences Act 1985 include guidance on the circumstances in which it is, and is not, appropriate to charge conspiracy to defraud. Section 12(1) and (2) provides:

'(1) If –
  (a) a person agrees with any other person or persons that a course of conduct shall be pursued; and
  (b) that course of conduct will necessarily amount to or involve the commission of any offence or offences by one or more of the parties to the agreement if the agreement is carried out in accordance with their intentions,
the fact that it will do so shall not preclude a charge of conspiracy to defraud being brought against any of them in respect of the agreement.
(2) In section 5(2) of the Criminal Law Act 1977, the words from "and" to the end are hereby repealed.'

The Committee did not get all its own way. Its suggestion that the sentence for the offence remain at large was rejected and a maximum sentence of ten years' imprisonment for conspiracy to defraud is now in place.[1]

2 THE ELEMENTS OF THE OFFENCE

2.1 Definition

A challenge to the existence of the offence of conspiracy to defraud in *Scott v Metropolitan Police Comr*[2] gave the House of Lords its first opportunity, since *Welham v DPP*[3] and the passing of the Theft Act 1968, to reaffirm its existence and to define it. Viscount Dilhorne, delivering the main judgment of the Appellate Committee, said:

'In my opinion, it is clearly the law that an agreement by two or more by dishonesty to deprive a person of something which is his or to which he is, or, would be, or, might be entitled and an agreement by two or more by dishonesty to injure the proprietary right of his, suffices to constitute the offence of conspiracy to defraud.'

Lord Diplock summarised:

'(1) Although at common law no clear distinction was originally drawn between conspiracies to "cheat" and conspiracies to "defraud", these terms being frequently used in combination, by the early years of the nineteenth century "conspiracy to defraud" had become a distinct species of criminal agreement independent of the old common law substantive offence of "cheating". The abolition of this substantive common law offence by section 32(1)(a) of the Theft Act 1968, except as regards offences relating to the public revenue, thus leaves surviving and intact the common law offence of conspiracy to defraud.

1 Section 12(3) of the Criminal Justice Act 1987.
2 [1975] AC 819, [1974] 3 All ER 1032.
3 [1961] AC 103, [1960] 1 All ER 805.

(2) Where the intended victim of a "conspiracy to defraud" is a private individual the purpose of the conspirators must be to cause the victim economic loss by depriving him of some property or right, corporeal or incorporeal, to which he is, or, would, or, might become entitled. The intended means by which the purpose is to be achieved must be dishonest. They need not involve fraudulent misrepresentation such as is needed to constitute the civil tort of deceit. Dishonesty of any kind is enough.

(3) Where the intended victim of a 'conspiracy to defraud' is a person performing public duties as distinct from a private individual it is sufficient if the purpose is to cause him to act contrary to his public duty, and the intended means of achieving this purpose are dishonest. The purpose need not involve causing economic loss to anyone.'[4]

In its radical overhaul of the law of conspiracy in the Criminal Law Act 1977, Parliament deliberately left conspiracy to defraud unaffected. The purpose of so doing was not to give parliamentary sanction to the offence in its existing form – indeed, it was recognised that conspiracy to defraud suffered the very defects which were about to be put right in the general law of conspiracy – but to enable the Law Commission to suggest alternative offences. Abolition simpliciter of the offence would, it was said, have left unacceptable gaps in the law,[5] particularly in the area of commercial swindles. Sections 5(1) and (2) of the Criminal Law Act 1977 provides:

'(1) Subject to the provisions of this section, the offence of conspiracy at common law is hereby abolished.

(2) Subsection (1) above shall not affect the offence of conspiracy at common law so far as relates to conspiracy to defraud . . . [words repealed by Criminal Justice Act 1987 section 12].'

Conspiracy to defraud remains, therefore, a common law offence and should be charged as such.

2.2   Dishonesty

Mens rea is an essential ingredient in the crime of conspiracy, and:

'. . . this mens rea consists in the intention to execute the illegal elements in the conduct contemplated by the agreements, in the knowledge of those facts which render the conduct illegal.'[6]

In the context of conspiracy to defraud, this will require an intention dishonestly to execute conduct which causes the victim economic loss by depriving him of some property or right, corporeal or incorporeal, to which he is, or would be, or might be, entitled, knowing that its effect will be so to deprive the victim.

In *R v Landy*,[7] Lawton LJ said:

'What the prosecution had to prove was a conspiracy to defraud which is an agreement dishonestly to do something which will or may cause loss or prejudice to another. The offence is one of dishonesty. This is the all-important

---

4   The width of para (2) has been criticised in *Wai Yu-tsang v R* [1992] 1 AC 269, [1991] 4 All ER 664. See this chapter, section 2.3, below.

5   See Law Commission Working Paper No 104 *Criminal Law: Conspiracy to Defraud Part IV* 'Identification of the gaps which would be left by the abolition of conspiracy to defraud'.

6   *Kamara v DPP* [1974] AC 104 at 109 (per Lord Hailsham of St Marylebone LC).

7   [1981] 1 All ER 1172 at 1181, [1981] 1 WLR 355 at 365.

ingredient which must be stressed by the Judge in his directions to the jury and must not be minimised in any way. There is always a danger that a jury may think that proof of an irregularity followed by loss is proof of dishonesty. The dishonesty to be proved must be in the minds and intentions of the defendants.'

Lawton LJ proceeded to expound a purely subjective test of dishonesty which was subsequently disapproved.[8] In *R v Ghosh*,[9] the Court of Appeal concluded that the test for dishonesty for offences under the Theft Acts and for conspiracy to defraud is the same. Lord Lane CJ set out the now classic test of dishonesty for all such offences:[10]

'In determining whether the prosecution has proved that the defendant was acting dishonestly, a jury must first of all decide whether according to the ordinary standards of reasonable and honest people what was done was dishonest. If it was not dishonest by those standards, that is the end of the matter and the prosecution fails. If it was dishonest by those standards, then the jury must consider whether the defendant himself must have realised that what he was doing was by those standards dishonest. In most cases, where the actions are obviously dishonest by ordinary standards, there will be no doubt about it. It will be obvious that the defendant himself knew that he was acting dishonestly. It is dishonest for a defendant to act in a way which he knows ordinary people consider to be dishonest, even if he asserts or genuinely believes that he is morally justified in acting as he did. For example, Robin Hood or those ardent anti-vivisectionists who remove animals from vivisection laboratories are acting dishonestly, even though they may consider themselves to be morally justified in doing what they do, because they know that ordinary people would consider these actions to be dishonest.'

A direction in these terms is required only where the defence is that the defendant believed that he was acting honestly.[11] The prosecution must show deliberate dishonesty and knowledge of the loss or risk of loss likely to follow on from the defendant's conduct. Recklessness is unlikely to suffice.[12]

2.3 The meaning of defraud

Neither deceit, nor an intention to deceive, is required. In *Scott v Metropolitan Police Comr*[13] the appellant admitted that he had agreed with the employees of cinema owners temporarily to abstract films, without the permission of the cinema owners or the copyright owners, in return for making payments to the employees for the purpose of making infringing copies and distributing them on a commercial basis for his own benefit. He was convicted of conspiring 'to defraud such companies and persons as might be caused loss by the unlawful copying and distribution of films the copyright in which and the distribution rights of which belonged to companies and persons other than the said persons conspiring.' There was no evidence of any deceit practised upon any of the alleged losers, nor of any intention to deceive them. Drawing on dicta of Buckley J in *Re London and Globe Finance Ltd*,[14] the appellant argued that a

---

8 See also *R v Sinclair* [1968] 3 All ER 241, [1968] 1 WLR 1246, CA.
9 [1982] QB 1053, [1982] 2 All ER 689 of *R v McIvor* [1982] 1 All ER 491, [1982] 1 WLR 409, CA.
10 At 696.
11 *R v Squire* [1990] Crim LR 341.
12 See section 2.3 below.
13 [1975] AC 819, [1974] 3 All ER 1032, HL.
14 [1903] 1 Ch 728 at 732.

man could not be defrauded unless he was deceived. The House of Lords held that the essence of conspiracy to defraud was dishonestly depriving another of something that was either his, or, to which he was or would be, or, might be, entitled but for the commission of the fraud. The House concluded, having regard to several early authorities,[15] that 'fraudulently' meant 'dishonestly' and, accordingly:

> '. . . to defraud ordinarily means . . . to deprive a person dishonestly of something which is his or of something to which he is or would be or might, but for the perpetration of fraud, be entitled.'

Deceit was not a necessary element, though in many cases deceit is likely to be present.

It would appear from *Welham v DPP*,[16] a case on the meaning of 'intent to defraud' in the Forgery Act 1913, that there need be no intent to gain though this will be the usual concomitant and purpose of causing loss to another. Lord Radcliffe made the following observations:

> 'Now I think there are one or two things that can be said with confidence about the meaning of this word "defraud". It requires a person as its object; that is, defrauding involves doing something to someone. Although in the nature of things it is almost inevitably associated with the obtaining of an advantage for the person who commits the fraud, it is the effect on the person who is the object of the fraud that ultimately determines its meaning.'

He continued:

> 'Secondly, popular speech does not give, and I do not think ever has given, any more guide as to the limits of what is meant by "to defraud". It may mean to cheat someone. It may mean to practise a fraud on someone. It may mean to deprive someone by deceit of something which is regarded as belonging to him or, though not belonging to him, as due to him or his right . . . There is nothing in any of this that suggests that to defraud is, in ordinary speech, confined to the idea of depriving a man by deceit of some economic advantage or inflicting on him some economic loss. Has the law ever so confined it? In my opinion, there is no warrant for saying that it has. What it has looked for in considering the effect of cheating on another person and so in defining the economical intent is the prejudice of that person; what Blackstone's Commentaries, Vol 4 page 245 called "to the prejudice of another man's right".'[17]

Lord Radcliffe then refers to:

> '. . . that special line of cases where the person deceived is a public authority or a person holding a public office, deceit may secure an advantage for the deceiver without causing anything that can fairly be called either a pecuniary or an economic injury to the person deceived. If there could be no intent to defraud in the eyes of the law without an intent to inflict a pecuniary or economic injury, such cases as these could not have been punished as forgeries at common law, in which an intent to defraud is an essential element of the offence, yet I am satisfied that they were regularly so treated.'

15 Their Lordships drew on a large number of old authorities: JF Stephen's *History of the English Criminal Law* (1883) Vol II pages 121–122; *R v Orbell* (1703) 6 Mod Rep 42; *R v Button* (1848) 11 QB 929; *R v Yates* (1853) 6 Cox CC 441; *R v De Kromme* (1892) 66 LT 301; *R v Quinn* (1898) 19 Cox CC 78; *R v Radley* (1973) 58 Cr App Rep 394, CA; *Welham v DPP* [1961] AC 103, [1960] 1 All ER 805, HL.
16 [1961] AC 103, [1960] 1 All ER 805, HL.
17 See also East's *Pleas of the Crown* (1803) Vol 2 pages 852–854.

This has led to the odd, but valid, comment that most conspiracies to pervert the course of justice consist in agreements to deceive a public official so that he acts contrary to his duty and are, therefore, also conspiracies to defraud.[18]

Lord Radcliffe's remarks indicate that an intent to cause economic loss, though usually present, is not a necessary ingredient.[19] Lord Denning took the same view.[20]

> 'To defraud, [these scholars] say, involves the idea of economic loss. I cannot agree with them on this. If a drug addict forges a doctor's prescription so as to enable him to get drugs from a chemist, he has, I should have thought, an intent to defraud, even though he intends to pay the chemist the full price and no one is a penny the worse off.'

In *Scott v Metropolitan Police Comr*, Viscount Dilhorne thought that Lord Radcliffe's remarks on the meaning of 'defraud' were of general application, and applied them accordingly to conspiracy to defraud.[1] He specifically left open the question whether a conspiracy to defraud may exist even though its object is not to secure a financial advantage by inflicting an economic loss on the person at whom the conspiracy was directed.[2] Lord Diplock's statement that the defendant must intend to cause the victim economic loss was disapproved by the Privy Council in *Wai Yu-tsang v R*.[3] Lord Goff concluded from the authorities that:

> '. . . the expression "intent to defraud" is not to be given a narrow meaning, involving an intention to cause economic loss to another. In broad terms, it means simply an intention to practise a fraud on another, or an intention to act to the prejudice of another man's right.'

The distinction between intending to cause economic loss and an intention to practise a fraud on another is clear both from the facts of *Wai Yu-tsang* and *R v Allsop*.[4] In *Allsop* the defendant was a sub-broker who entered false particulars on forms submitted to an insurance company to induce it to accept applications for hire purchase facilities which it might otherwise have rejected. The defendant believed the hire purchase obligations would be met by the clients and that the insurance company would achieve its contemplated profit. The defendant's purpose was to increase the insurance company's business and, thereby, an increase in his own commission. No loss, in fact, occurred on these particular transactions. The trial judge directed the jury that they must be sure that the conspirators knew that they were inducing the company to act in circumstances in which they might cause or create the likelihood of economic loss or prejudice. The Court of Appeal approved:

> 'If the deceit which is employed perils the economic interest of the person deceived, this is sufficient to constitute fraud even though in the event no actual loss is suffered and notwithstanding that the deceiver did not desire to bring about an actual loss.'[5]

---

18 Smith and Hogan *Criminal Law* (6th edn) at page 271.
19 See note 16, supra.
20 Op cit at 814.
1 [1975] AC 819 at 839; see also *Wai Yu-tsang v R* [1992] 1 AC 269, [1991] 4 All ER 664 at 667; per Lord Goff.
2 Op cit at 669–670.
3 Op cit at 669–670.
4 (1976) 64 Cr App Rep 29.
5 (1976) 64 Cr App Rep at 31.

Lord Goff in *Wai Yu-tsang*[6] added:

> 'Their lordships can see no reason why such an agreement should not be a conspiracy to defraud the company, substantially for the reasons given by the Court of Appeal. The defendant was, for his own purposes, dishonestly supplying the company with false information which persuaded it to accept risks which it would or might not have accepted if it had known the true facts.'

So much for cases where the defendant *realises* that his act will or may imperil another's interests. Is there a place for recklessness? Is the defendant liable to be convicted if he did not realise the risk he was creating but, perhaps, should have done so? If the defendant foresaw the consequence, is he taken to have intended it? In its attempt to overcome what is perceived as the difficulties left by Lord Diplock in *Scott*, the Court of Appeal in *Allsop* drew on Lord Diplock's judgment in *Hyam v DPP*[7] where concepts of purpose, intent, foresight and recklessness had been analysed in the context of the mental element in murder. In *Wai Yu-tsang* Lord Goff indicated that the House was:

> '. . . reluctant to allow this part of the law to become enmeshed in a distinction, sometimes artificially drawn, between intention and recklessness. The question whether particular facts reveal a conspiracy to defraud depends upon what the conspirators have dishonestly agreed to do, and in particular whether they have agreed to practise a fraud on somebody. For this purpose it is enough for example that, as in *Allsop* and in the present case, the conspirators have dishonestly agreed to bring about a state of affairs which they realise will or may deceive the victim into so acting, or failing to act, that he will suffer economic loss or his economic interests will be put at risk. It is, however, important in such a case, as the Court of Appeal stressed in *Allsop*'s case, to distinguish a conspirator's intention (or immediate purpose) dishonestly to bring about such a state of affairs from his restive or underlying purpose. The latter may be benign to the extent that he does not wish the victim or potential victim to suffer harm; but the mere fact that it is benign will not, of itself, prevent the agreement from constituting a conspiracy to defraud. Of course, if the conspirators were not acting dishonestly, there will have been no conspiracy to defraud; and in any event their benign purpose (if it be such) is a matter which, if they prove to be guilty, can be taken into account at the stage of sentence.'

There must, therefore, be an actual and dishonest realisation by the defendant of the loss or risk of loss following or likely to follow from his conduct.

In *Sinclair*,[8] the Court of Appeal had to consider the application of conspiracy to defraud in the context of business activities which, inevitably, entailed some degree of risk to the company and its shareholders. The same principles apply, though the difference is that, whereas in *Allsop* and *Wai Yu-tsang*, there seems little basis upon which the defendant could argue that he had any right to do what he did, in some contexts it may be difficult to ascertain what is an acceptable business risk and what is not. The court distinguished between normal business risks honestly taken and the dishonest risk deliberately taken with knowledge that there was no right to take such a risk.

There is some Commonwealth authority that recklessness as to the truth of a representation made to a victim will suffice.[9] The decisions in *Allsop* and *Wai Yu-tsang* indicate that such an approach is unlikely to be followed here.

6 [1992] 1 AC 269 at 279, [1991] 4 All ER 664 at 670.
7 [1975] AC 55, [1974] 2 All ER 41, HL.
8 [1968] 3 All ER 241, [1968] 1 WLR 1246, CA.
9 *Maltingley v Tuckwood* [1989] Australian Crim LR III.

2.4 Agreement

The actus reus of the common law and statutory offence of conspiracy is the act of agreement to execute the unlawful conduct. It is unnecessary to show that the agreed course has been performed, though on a charge of conspiracy, performance of the alleged agreement ('overt acts') may be adduced in evidence to show the existence of the agreement. The offence is committed as soon as the agreement is made, and continues until the combination is brought to an end by performance, abandonment or frustration of the agreement.[10] The agreement may be express or implied; or in part express and in part implied. There is no conspiracy at common law, and therefore no conspiracy to defraud, where the only parties to the agreement are husband and wife,[11] though a husband and wife can be convicted as co-conspirators where others are involved[12] or in respect of a conspiracy entered into before their marriage.[13] Equally, a director of a company who is solely responsible for the conduct of the company's business cannot be convicted of conspiracy with the company, since the director's mind and that of the company are inseparable, even though the company is a separate legal entity.[14] The company may be convicted of conspiracy with the director and other parties. A company may be convicted of conspiracy to defraud.[15]

There must be a concluded agreement. Negotiation or 'talking around' an offence is insufficient. Criminal conspiracies will rarely bear the sophistication of commercial agreements and it may be difficult to discern at what point exactly negotiations are transformed into agreement. There will frequently be little difficulty in showing that the agreement was concluded as the evidence is likely to include overt acts in pursuance of the conspiracy. In *R v Walker*[16] the appellant's conviction for conspiracy to rob was quashed because it had not been shown that the defendants had concluded the agreement by the time the appellant withdrew from the venture. In *R v Barnard*,[17] the defendant's conviction for conspiracy to steal was quashed when he withdrew from an incomplete plan to steal from a jeweller's shop.[18]

Once the agreement is reached, the offence is complete and withdrawal by a conspirator provides grounds for mitigation only. Establishing that the agreement is complete may be direct evidence[19] but will more usually be proved by indirect evidence such as inferring a pre-existing agreement from the conduct of the parties. Though it is unnecessary to show that each of the conspirators has met one another, it is necessary to show that each was party to the same agreement.[20]

---

10 *DPP v Doot* [1973] AC 807, [1973] 1 All ER 940, HL.
11 *Kowbel v R* [1954] 4 DLR 337; *Mawji v R* [1957] AC 126, [1957] 1 All ER 385.
12 See eg *R v Whitehouse* (1852) 6 Cox CC 38 – conspiracy involving husband, wife and daughter, though a conviction should not, presumably, follow where the child is under the age of criminal responsibility – conspiracy involving husband, wife and daughter. The rule has been applied to polygamous marriages: *Mawji v R* [1957] AC 126, [1957] 1 All ER 385; see also *R v Chrastny* [1992] 1 All ER 189, [1991] 1 WLR 1381, CA.
13 *R v Robinson* (1746) 1 Leach 37.
14 *R v McDonnell* [1966] 1 QB 233, [1966] 1 All ER 193.
15 *R v ICR Haulage* [1944] KB 551, [1944] 1 All ER 691, CCA.
16 [1962] Crim LR 458.
17 (1979) 70 Cr App Rep 28, CA; see also *R v El Ghazal* [1985] Crim LR 52, CA.
18 See GF Orchard 'Agreement in Criminal Conspiracy' [1974] Crim LR 297.
19 Eg using a conspirator as a prosecution witness; secret tape-recordings; contemporaneous documents.
20 See *R v Griffiths* [1966] 1 QB 589, [1965] 2 All ER 448, CCA.

3   JURISDICTION

The Law Commission, in its 1989 Report on Jurisdiction over Offences of Fraud and Dishonesty with a Foreign Element,[1] did not mince its words about the common law rules of jurisdiction: they were, it said, unduly narrow, technical and insular in character; they were antiquated, having evolved before the introduction of modern methods of communication and transfer of money across national boundaries; and were in urgent need of reform if this country was adequately to meet the new situation created by wide-ranging international fraud. To date, the Law Commission's recommendations have not been acted upon and the common law largely still applies.[2] The issue of jurisdiction in fraud generally is addressed in Chapter 9. This section describes the common law as it applies to conspiracy to defraud.

The same principles apply both to 'statutory conspiracies' and to common law conspiracies, including conspiracy to defraud. Section 1(4) of the Criminal Law Act 1977 provides that 'offence' for the purposes of Part I of the Act means:

> '. . . an offence triable in England and Wales, except that it includes murder notwithstanding that the murder in question would not be so triable if committed in accordance with the intentions of the parties to the agreement.'

In other words, statutory conspiracies apply only to offences that are to be committed within the jurisdiction. Section 1(4) follows the common law rule. In *Board of Trade v Owen*[3] the defendants were charged on count 3 of the indictment with conspiracy in London to defraud the West German export control department by fraudulently representing to the department, in order to induce it to grant licences to export certain metals from Germany, that the metals would be supplied to and consumed by Irish manufacturers, knowing that the metals were in fact to be exported to Czechoslovakia, Poland, Romania and the USSR. Count 5 of the indictment charged conspiracy in London to utter forged documents purporting to be end-user certificates of the Irish Department of Industry and Commerce. The German government would not grant licences to export strategic metals to Eastern European countries. The appellants bought the metals in Germany and put false documents before the department in Germany showing that the metal would only be used in Ireland. The end-user certificates were forged in Dublin and were sent to London where they were posted to Germany. The defendants were convicted on both counts. The Court of Criminal Appeal allowed the appeal on count 3 on the ground that the contemplated crime was not within the jurisdiction. The conviction on count 5 was upheld on the basis that the uttering of the documents had taken place in London.

On the prosecutor's appeal, the House of Lords upheld the decision. Lord Tucker giving the main judgment said:[4]

> 'I have reached the conclusion that the decision of the Court of Criminal Appeal that a conspiracy to commit a crime abroad is not indictable in this country unless the contemplated crime is one for which an indictment would lie here is correct, and from what I have already said it necessarily follows that a conspiracy of the nature of that charged in count 3 as proved in evidence –

---

1   Law Com No 180 (27 April 1989).
2   Cf Offences Against the Person Act 1861 section 4; Criminal Law Act 1977 section 1(1).
3   [1957] AC 602, [1957] 1 All ER 411, HL.
4   At p 634.

which, in my view, was a conspiracy to attain a lawful object by unlawful means, rather than to commit a crime – is not triable in this country, since the unlawful means and the ultimate object were both outside the jurisdiction. In so deciding I would, however, reserve for future consideration the question whether conspiracy in this country which is wholly to be carried out abroad may not be indictable here on proof that its performance would produce a public mischief in this country or injure a person here by causing him damage abroad.'

Would the result have been different if the uttering of the forged end-user certificates had been alleged as one of the particulars of the conspiracy to defraud? The report is not clear as to whether the prosecution presented the uttering of the forgeries as part of the conspiracy to defraud, as it clearly was.[5]

The easiest factual situation to contemplate is that found in count 3 of the *Owen* indictment: the only connecting factor with the jurisdiction was the agreement – the making of the fraudulent misrepresentations, the obtaining of the advantage and the locus of the victim were all in West Germany. It is not difficult to imagine more complicated situations: suppose the fraudulent misrepresentation is made from England; or the advantage is obtained in England pursuant to an English conspiracy as a result of fraudulent misrepresentations made abroad.

The Court of Appeal confronted some of these problems in *R v Hornett*[6] and examined the width of Lord Tucker's remarks. The court concluded that a conspiracy is indictable in England when conspirators in England agree to do an unlawful act in England with intent to defraud persons abroad.

The appellants were charged with conspiracy to forge road haulage permits issued by the Department of the Environment with intent to defraud, conspiracy to utter the same documents with intent to defraud, and conspiracy to utter the same documents with intent to deceive. The permits had been forged in London and some had been handed in England to drivers taking vehicles used in haulage business on continental journeys. The intention was to use the permits on the Continent in order to defraud or deceive the authorities there. It was argued, citing *Board of Trade v Owen*, that the crimes contemplated by the conspiracies charged in *Hornett* were not crimes which themselves would have been indictable in this country. The Court of Appeal alluded to the distinction drawn in *Owen* by Lord Tucker between count 3 on the indictment, which charged conspiracy to defraud, and count 5 on the indictment, which charged conspiracy to utter forged documents:

'The distinction drawn appears in Lord Tucker's speech. In relation to count 3, Lord Tucker said this: "Although the count does not expressly state the locality where the fraudulent representations were to be made or the licence was to be obtained, the evidence showed not only that the representations were in fact made in Germany and the licence was issued there but that the

5 This led to the comment by Lord Goddard CJ that: 'It is not altogether easy to appreciate what offence it was intended to allege in count 3, as distinct from that alleged in count 5. The evidence would seem to be identical on both counts. Presumably, count 3 was intended to refer to the fraudulent representations as to the destination of the goods and to the false shipping documents used in support, whilst count 5 is confined to the forged end-user certificates subsequently produced in support of the earlier representations.' It may, alternatively, have been that the prosecution used count 5 of the indictment as a safety net because of the jurisdictional problems, but adduced the evidence of the forged certificates on count 3 as well. If so, why should the uttering of the letters not also found jurisdiction for the conspiracy to defraud charge?

6 [1975] RTR 256.

circumstances were such that the conspiracy must have been one in which the representations were designed to be made in Germany and that the licence obtained there." Lord Tucker then goes on: "*It is, accordingly, to be distinguished from count 5 where the crime designed to be committed was the uttering of a forged document in this country with intent to defraud,* it being immaterial whether the person or persons to be defrauded were in Germany or elsewhere. Such a count is admittedly triable here."

So the distinction is clear. In count 3 the crime contemplated by the conspiracy was not a crime unless and until certain acts were carried out in Germany: that is the making of the false representations. As the crime contemplated would not become a crime unless and until certain acts, constituting the very essence of the crime, were done outside the jurisdiction, the conspiracy was not indictable in this country. In count 5, on the other hand, the crime designed to be committed involved uttering a forged document in this country, and the intent to defraud was in the minds of the conspirators in this country, the contemplated crime would be completed in this country, without any essential part or element of the crime being done abroad. It was therefore indictable here. It did not matter, said Lord Tucker, that the persons whom it was intended to defraud were outside this country. The crime was completed with the intent to defraud, even though the defrauding had not taken place . . .'

The essence of the distinction is that in one case there was no conspiracy to do an unlawful act within the jurisdiction, whereas in the other the conspiracy included the performing of an unlawful act in England. In count 3 the making and uttering of the forged document took place, as had been contemplated in the conspiracy, in England, as did the intent to deceive. The object of the deceit, and its actual practice, were abroad.

The court went on to apply the dicta in *Owen* to the facts in *Hornett*:[7]

'Now let us look at the facts relevant to the counts of conspiracy in the present case. When they are examined, it is clear that they are, to use the count numbers in *Board of Trade v Owen*, of the count 5 class and not of the count 3 class, because the offences contemplated by the conspiracies on the admitted facts would be completed in this country. Count 1 is a conspiracy to forge the road haulage permits. The whole of the contemplated crime was carried out in this country. It was in London that the false documents were intended to be made, and were in fact made in order that they might be used as genuine, with the intention to defraud. The only question that could arise in respect of that count therefore is whether the contemplated crime would not be indictable in this country because the intention might have been to defraud persons outside England, and not persons in England. To that question we shall return in a moment . . . Therefore both in respect of the conspiracy to forge (count 1) and the conspiracy to utter forged documents (counts 2 and 7, the latter bringing in Gartside as a conspirator and alleging an intent to deceive) on the admitted facts the only possible argument for contending that the conspiracies are not indictable in this country is that the intent to deceive or defraud someone might have been an intent to defraud or deceive someone not within the jurisdiction. That is the point dealt with in Lord Tucker's speech already quoted, relating to count 5 in *Board of Trade v Owen*: "it being immaterial whether the person or persons to be defrauded were in Germany or elsewhere". In that context we would refer to a further passage from the judgment of the Court of Criminal Appeal in the same case, delivered by Lord Goddard CJ: "The only other point in regard to this count of the indictment relates to the alleged intent to defraud. The same argument was put forward as

7   At 259.

was relied on in regard to count 3, but it is to be noted that in regard to count 5 the intent to defraud is alleged in general terms and is not directly related to ZAK. Even if it were right that no intention to defraud ZAK was or could be established, it is clear that German suppliers were to be defrauded by means of the conspiracy alleged in count 5, and in these circumstances it was open to the jury to take the view that an intent to defraud was proved." That is part of the ratio decidendi of the Court of Criminal Appeal in that case. Since the question of count 5 was not submitted on appeal to the House of Lords, therefore, as has been said, Lord Tucker's reference is strictly obiter. It follows equally that that passage from Lord Goddard CJ's speech is a part of the ratio decidendi of the case in relation to that matter which was indeed binding on the trial judge in the court below. Again, it is not strictly binding on this court.

That passage in Lord Goddard CJ's judgment involves by the clearest implication, as a part of the ratio decidendi, the rejection of any suggestion that, where there is a forgery or uttering of a forged document in England with intent to defraud, the offence is not indictable in England merely because the persons intended to be defrauded (that is persons to whom the document is to be represented as genuine), are or may be outside the jurisdiction. That which is clearly implied in Lord Goddard CJ's words is made express in Lord Tucker's speech. While we are not bound by the decision of the Court of Criminal Appeal nor by the unanimous opinion of the House of Lords, we respectfully agree with both. We have had no reason offered to persuade us that they are wrong.'

These were, of course, conspiracies to utter forged documents with intent to defraud. Again, would (or should) it make any difference if the charge had been one charge of conspiracy to defraud with the evidence of the uttering of the forged documents being adduced as part of the conspiracy?

Owen was followed in *R v Cox*.[8] The defendant agreed in England with another man, who ha.' acquired a cheque book containing unused cheques, to use them in France by falsely representing that they or one of them had an account at the bank on which the cheques were drawn. The defendant intended to return to England to sell the goods. The court quashed the conviction on the basis that there was no evidence of any criminal conduct within the scope of the alleged agreement that was agreed to be or was committed in England.[9]

The question left open by Lord Tucker in *Owen* as to whether a conspiracy in this country which is wholly to be carried out abroad is indictable here if the performance could produce a public mischief in this country or injure a person here by causing him damage abroad was raised for decision in *Attorney-General's Reference (No 1 of 1982)*.[10] The defendants were charged with conspiracy to defraud by conspiring in England together and with others to defraud such companies and persons, and in particular X Co, as might be caused loss by the unlawful labelling, sale, supply or marketing of whisky purporting to be that of X label products, X Co being the proprietors of the labelled products and owning the copyright of the labels. It had been alleged that the defendants had arranged for labels, purporting to be those of X Co, to be printed and brought to London. The labels were to be transmitted to Frankfurt where they were to be affixed to bottles of whisky (not produced) by X Co for onward transmission to the Lebanon where they were to be sold as X Co's product. The German authorities seized the whisky before the plan could be completed. X Co, whose registered office was in England, had reasonably

8   [1968] 1 All ER 410, [1968] 1 WLR 88, CA.
9   See also *R v Governor of Brixton Prison, ex p Rush* [1969] 1 All ER 316, [1969] 1 WLR 165.
10 [1983] QB 751, [1983] 2 All ER 721, CA.

substantial sales of its product in the Lebanon and evidence was given that X's interests would suffer if a counterfeit product was sold there because their own sales could be less, because their trademarks, one of their most valuable assets would be infringed, and because their reputation might suffer. The trial judge, following *Board of Trade v Owen*, ruled that the court had no jurisdiction to try the indictment since a conspiracy in England to commit a crime abroad is not indictable in England unless the crime contemplated is one for which an indictment would lie in England. Two points of law were referred to the Court of Appeal:

'(i)   Whether, on a charge of conspiracy to defraud where the conspiracy is to be carried out abroad, it is indictable if its performance will cause economic loss and damage to the proprietary interests of a company within the jurisdiction;

(ii)   Whether on a charge of conspiracy to defraud where the conspiracy is to be carried out abroad, it is indictable if its performance would injure a person or company here by causing him or it damage abroad.'

It has to be assumed, though the questions do not so state, that the conspiracies are formed in England.

The Court of Appeal's answer in each case was 'No'. Lord Lane CJ rejected the prosecutor's argument that the facts amounted to a conspiracy hatched in England to defraud an English company by infringing its copyright abroad, saying:[11]

'The real question must in each case be what was the true object of the agreement entered into by the conspirators? In our judgment, the object here was to obtain money from prospective purchasers of whisky in the Lebanon by falsely representing that it was the X Company's whisky. It may well be that if the plan had been carried out, some damage could have resulted to the X Company. But that would have been a side effect or incidental consequence of the conspiracy, and not its object. There may be many conspiracies aimed at particular victims which in their execution result in loss or damage to third parties. It would be contrary to principle, as well as being impracticable for the courts to attribute to defendants constructive intentions to defraud their parties based on what the defendants should have foreseen a probable or possible consequences. In each case to determine the object of the conspiracy, the court must see what the defendants actually agreed to do. Had it not been for the jurisdictional problem, we have no doubt the charge against these conspirators would have been conspiracy to defraud potential purchasers of whisky, for that was the true object of the agreement. Accordingly we reject the first argument.'

In other words, the conspiracy should have been framed as a conspiracy to defraud the potential whisky buyers who would be deceived into thinking they were buying X Co's whisky. Such victims were to be found abroad. So drafted, the indictment would clearly have shown that the 'true object' was the defrauding of persons abroad, and therefore outside the court's jurisdiction. Prosecutors must look, accordingly, for the true object of the conspiracy to defraud, and cannot simply cast around for a 'third party' victim in England or Wales to establish jurisdiction. There appears not to have been a sufficient act in furtherance of the conspiracy to found jurisdiction here within the ambit of *R v Doot*. The act of passing the false labels through London was not, it seems, sufficient to found jurisdiction for conspiracy to defraud in this country.

11 At 757.

Presumably the false whisky labels would qualify as 'forgeries' and the question arises as to whether it would have been open on the evidence to charge the perpetrators with a conspiracy to utter a forged document.

The second and wider argument advanced by the appellant, relying specifically on the point left open by Lord Tucker, was that a conspiracy to defraud which, although wholly carried out abroad, would cause injury to an individual or company within the jurisdiction, is indictable in England on the basis that the protection of economic interests in England was a legitimate and proper function of the criminal law. Lord Lane CJ rejected the argument on two bases: because of the technical anomalies that would result, and because of width and uncertainty of such a test:

> 'Whenever a fraudulent conspiracy made abroad and to be carried out abroad sent ripples back to England washing over and damaging some economic interest here, an indictment would lie.'

The Lord Chief Justice relied heavily upon *R v Doot*.[12] As Halsbury states it,[13] where such consequences are merely incidental to, rather than the object of, the conspiracy, no indictment lies in England. Where such consequences are the object of the conspiracy, it is indictable if acts in furtherance of the foreign conspiracy are pursued within the jurisdiction.

The question of law in *Doot* was:

> 'Whether an agreement made outside the jurisdiction of the English courts, to import a dangerous drug into England and carried out by importing it into England is a conspiracy which can be tried in England.'

The case related to a conspiracy to import dangerous drugs, but was decided prior to the Criminal Law Act 1977 on common law principles.

The defendants, having agreed abroad to import cannabis into the United States by way of England, brought vans loaded with cannabis into the jurisdiction and were stopped by Customs officers. They were charged, inter alia, with conspiracy to import dangerous drugs, but contended that the court had no jurisdiction to try them on that count.[14] The Court of Appeal allowed the appeal on the basis that the offence had been completed abroad when the agreement was concluded. The House of Lords restored the conviction. Viscount Dilhorne said:[15]

> '. . . though the offence of conspiracy is complete when the agreement to do the unlawful act is made and it is not necessary for the prosecution to do more than prove the making of such an agreement, a conspiracy does not end with the making of the agreement. It continues so long as the parties to the agreement intend to carry it out. It may be joined by others, some may leave it. Proof of acts done by the accused in this country may suffice to prove that

12 [1973] QB 73, CA
13 Vol 11(i) para 69. *R v Parnell* (1881) 14 Cox CC 508; *R v Meyrick* (1929) 21 Cr App Rep 94, CCA; *R v Hammersley* (1958) 42 Cr App Rep 207, CCA.
14 It is worth noting that this case was tried before the Practice Direction [1977] requiring prosecutors, where the indictment charged conspiracy and substantive offences in relation to the same matters, to elect on which to proceed. Lord Pearson commented: 'On the question of prosecuting policy, whether it was appropriate to include the count of conspiracy in addition to the charges of specific offences, I would say that it was appropriate because it provided for each conspirator being held responsible, as morally and legally he was responsible, for each of the illegal importations in pursuance of the conspiracy.' Presumably, the Practice Direction would not affect a case such as this.
15 [1973] AC 807 at 825.

there was at the time of those acts of conspiracy in existence in this country to which they were parties and, if that is proved, then the charge of conspiracy is within the jurisdiction of the English courts, even though the initial agreement was made outside the jurisdiction.'

Doot is authority for the proposition, therefore, that a conspiracy concluded out of the jurisdiction to commit a crime is indictable in England if acts in furtherance of that agreement are committed in England.[16] What, however, if the conspirators come to England and do nothing, or if they come to England and carry out an act which is lawful in pursuance of the conspiracy. Lord Dilhorne (above) does not draw a distinction between lawful and unlawful acts carried out in pursuance of the conspiracy. Lord Salmon contemplated that the offence of conspiracy would be committed:

'Suppose the conspirators came to England for the purpose of carrying out the crime and were detected by the police reconnoitring the place where they proposed to commit it, but doing nothing which by itself would be illegal, it would surely be absurd if the police could not arrest them then and there but had to take the risk of waiting and hoping to be able to catch them as they were actually committing or attempting to commit the crime.'

This, of course, is the position where an act (albeit an act lawful in itself) is done in furtherance of the conspiracy. Lord Salmon left open what the position might be if the conspirators came to England for an entirely innocent purpose unconnected with the conspiracy. One wonders why the act of bringing to London the printed and false whisky labels in *A-G's Reference No 1 of 1982* was not a sufficient act done in furtherance of the conspiracy. That case, of course, involved a conspiracy hatched in England, whereas *Doot* was a conspiracy hatched abroad. The distinction would appear unwarranted.

There appears to be a divergence – which may indicate a difference in the jurisprudential basis for holding that a conspiracy formed abroad is indictable here – in respect of the situation where a single conspirator enters England and does an act in furtherance of a conspiracy formed abroad. Lord Salmon thought it unrealistic to regard the single conspirator as agreeing with himself, whilst here, on behalf of all the other conspirators. Lord Pearson, on the other hand, commented:

'It is not necessary that they should all be present in England. One of them, acting on his own behalf and as agent for the others, has been performing their agreement, with their consent and authority in England. In such a case the conspiracy has been committed by all of them in England.'

The Salmon approach belies the view that what really makes the defendants guilty is what they did in England in the sense that it was a new conspiracy born in England under the wing of an old conspiracy hatched abroad. The Pearson approach reflects the assumption within the jurisdiction on an agency basis of the major conspiracy hatched abroad.

The position as regards foreign conspiracies is plainly unsatisfactory for the reasons expressed by Lord Salmon and the Court of Appeal had to confront that very problem in *R v Sansom*.[17] The defendants were found in possession of half a ton of cannabis and arrested on board vessels, one in Plymouth Harbour and the other in the English Channel. Vessel A had sailed with the cannabis

---

16 See also per Lord Salmon.
17 [1991] 2 QB 130, [1991] 2 All ER 145.

from Morocco into the Channel where the cannabis was transferred to Vessel B. Vessel A then sailed into Plymouth Harbour where it, and its crew, were arrested. Vessel B, in the meantime, was stopped in the Channel and the cannabis was seized. There was a dispute as to whether Vessel B was within British territorial waters or not at this time. It was submitted that to constitute a triable offence in England there would have to be proved some unlawful act in pursuance of the conspiracy in England. If, as the defence alleged, Vessel B was arrested outside territorial waters, no such unlawful act could be proved. The submission was rejected by the trial judge on the ground that one of the alleged conspirators had acted in England in pursuance of the alleged conspiracy which was still subsisting by commissioning Vessel B and sailing in her to collect the cannabis from Vessel A – a clear case for applying the principles in *Doot*. The argument was renewed on appeal. In the meantime, the Privy Council, in relation to a conspiracy to import heroin to the United States from Thailand, the proceeds to be collected in Hong Kong, held that it is not necessary to show some overt act within the jurisdiction in order to found jurisdiction to try a conspiracy formed out of the jurisdiction.[18] Lord Griffiths, giving the decision of the Board, said:

'There has as yet, however, been no decision in which it has been held that a conspiracy entered into abroad to commit a crime in England is a common law crime triable in English courts in the absence of any overt act pursuant to the conspiracy taking place in England. There are however a number of dicta in judgments and academic commentaries suggesting that it should be so.'

Lord Griffiths then reviewed the authorities and continued:

'But why should an overt act be necessary to found jurisdiction? In the case of conspiracy in England the crime is complete once the agreement is made and no further overt act need to be proved as an ingredient of the crime. The only purpose of looking for an overt act in England in the case of a conspiracy entered into abroad can be to establish the link between the conspiracy and England or possibly to show the conspiracy is continuing. But if this can be established by other evidence, for example the taping of conversations between the conspirators showing a firm agreement to commit the crime at some future date, it defeats the preventative purpose of the crime of conspiracy to have to wait until some overt act is performed in pursuance of the conspiracy. Unfortunately in this century crime has ceased to be largely local in origin and effect. Crime is now established on an international scale and the common law must face his new reality. Their Lordships can find nothing in precedent, comity or good sense that should inhibit the common law from regarding as justiciable in England inchoate crimes committed abroad which are intended to result in the commission of criminal offences in England. Accordingly, a conspiracy entered into in Thailand with the intention of committing the criminal offence of trafficking in drugs in Hong Kong is justiciable in Hong Kong even if no overt act pursuant to the conspiracy has yet occurred in Hong Kong.'

The Court of Appeal held that, on the facts, the trial judge had ruled correctly within the principles outlined in *Doot*. The conspirator had carried out an unlawful act, ie commissioning Vessel B, and a lawful act, ie sailing out in her, and had acted thereby in furtherance of the conspiracy. These acts had, according to *Doot*, founded jurisdiction in the English courts, permitting prosecution of however many of the co-conspirators the Customs men could

18 *Somchai Liangsiriprasert v US Government* [1991] 1 AC 225, [1990] 2 All ER 866.

lay their hands on. The court went on to hold, however, that the principle expressed by Lord Griffiths should be regarded as the law of England on this point. This is obiter only, but it offers clear guidance to any court faced directly with the issue in the future.

3.1   Proposals for reform of rules relating to jurisdiction in conspiracy

The Law Commission[19] regarded the uncertainty and inconsistencies surrounding the rules of jurisdiction for conspiracies having an international element as regrettable and leading to the situation where the law enforcement agencies, in the absence of an act done here in furtherance of a foreign conspiracy, are prevented from taking action in support of legitimate interests of foreign states. A conspiracy hatched in England to commit an offence was, it said, offensive to the laws of England irrespective of where the offence was to be committed. In the context of fraud, the insularity of the present rules would seriously affect the United Kingdom's important reputation as an international financial centre 'if it came to be perceived as a haven from which international fraud can be directed with impunity.'[20]

The Commission has recommended that:

> 'Every party to (i) a conspiracy to perform abroad what, if performed in England and Wales would constitute a listed offence or (ii) a conspiracy to defraud outside England and Wales should be made here if at least one conspirator (through his own or his agents' acts) became a party to it in England and Wales, or if he (or his agent) did anything here relating to the formation of the conspiracy or in pursuance of its objects.'

There are no plans to implement these proposals.

4   PRACTICE AND PROCEDURE

4.1   Special rules of evidence

It is rarely the case that conspiracy is proved by direct evidence, written or oral, as to the existence of an agreement. Proof of the conspiracy is usually drawn as a

> '. . . matter of inference deduced from certain criminal acts of the parties accused, done in pursuance of an apparent criminal purpose between them.'[1]

It is now well established that the acts and declarations by a conspirator in the furtherance of the conspiracy are admissible against all the conspirators. As the editors of *Phipson*[2] have commented, this is not a rule limited to the offence of conspiracy but applies to any offence where it is alleged that the defendants act in furtherance of a common design. In *R v Blake and Tye*,[3] the accused were charged with conspiring to pass goods through Customs without paying duty. Tye had made entries incriminating Blake as well as himself in two books. One of the entries was a necessary part of the fraud, the other was purely for Tye's

19 Op cit.
20 Op cit at Part I.
1   *R v Brisac* (1803) 4 East 164; *Mulcahy v R* (1868) LR 3 HL 306.
2   *Evidence* (14th edn) para 25-10.
3   (1844) 6 QB 126.

own convenience. It was held that the first entry was admissible against Blake as something tending to the advancement of the common object. In *R v Whitaker*,[4] a letter written by the defendant Ness to the effect that:

'Colonel Whitaker writes me today for his six-monthly cheque stating that as he wishes the matter kept as privately as possible, he would like me to send the cheque as before. This I have done today by cheque no [. . .] He adds "I suppose the contract will require renewal, let me hear soon about this, I have not yet had the pleasure of meeting Mr Minto but hope to see him when I next go to London."'

Minto subsequently paid a cheque into Ness's account to fund the payment to Whitaker. On appeal from his conviction for conspiracy to commit corruption, the Court of Criminal Appeal held that, once it had been proved that the money had been paid to the appellant by Ness, who had been funded by Minto, the letter became admissible both as against Minto and the appellant. In this case, there was a body of evidence to found the conspiracy, without reliance upon the letter, upon which it could then be inferred that the content of the letter was in furtherance of the conspiracy. A problem of circularity arises where the only evidence of the conspiracy against a conspirator is in the statements or acts of an alleged co-conspirator. As it was put in *R v Mayet*:[5]

'Since what A says in B's absence cannot be evidence against B of the truth of what was said unless A was B's agent to say those things, how can one prove that A was B's agent to say them by showing what A said?'

This point was considered in *R v Governor of Pentonville Prison, ex p Osman*.[6] The court concluded that:

'. . . there must always be some evidence other than the hearsay evidence of a fellow conspirator to prove that a particular defendant is a party to a conspiracy. Provided there is some other evidence, it does not matter in what order the evidence is adduced.'[7]

Where there is no other separate evidence, the hearsay evidence is inadmissible. The question may then arise as to whether the evidence is admissible on any other basis. It is, of course, admissible against its maker, though in the absence of independent evidence of a conspiracy, the jury should be directed that it is evidence only against the maker. In *Cross on Evidence*,[8] it is noted that in many cases out-of-court assertions and actions of conspirators may be admissible as circumstantial evidence of a conspiracy quite independently of reliance upon any admission, express or even implied, and so arguably outside the operation of the hearsay rule.

The acts and declarations in pursuance of the conspiracy made by a conspirator who is not charged are admissible in the proceedings against those who are charged.[9] Where a conspirator joins the conspiracy after it began, only those acts and declarations made while he was party to the conspiracy are admissible against him personally, though acts and declarations made before

---

4 [1914] 3 KB 1283, CCA.
5 1957 (1) SA 492 (AD).
6 [1989] 3 All ER 701 at 731.
7 See also *R v Donat* (1985) 82 Cr App Rep 173, CA; *R v Walters* (1979) 69 Crim App Rep 115, CA; *R v Windaes* (1988) 89 Cr App Rep 258, CA.
8 Page 589, n 13.
9 *R v Duguid* (1906) 94 LT 887.

he joined the conspiracy are admissible to prove the conspiracy itself.[10] Acts and declarations after the conspiracy is concluded are not admissible against all co-conspirators, but only against their makers. Acts and declarations not referable to the conspiracy are, of course, inadmissible.[11]

4.2   Particulars of the offence

In *R v Landy*,[12] the Court of Appeal gave guidance on the framing of indictments for conspiracy to defraud. In complicated cases, the prosecutor should ensure that the indictment does not lack particularity:

> 'Junior Counsel for Landy asked for particulars at the beginning of the committal proceedings, the committal charge being the same as Count 1 of the indictment. He was told he would get all the information he needed from the opening speech of leading Counsel for the Crown. Attempts to get particulars at a later stage of the case were met with the same answer. We were told by Counsel that this is the answer almost always given by prosecuting Counsel. In our judgment, particulars should have been given, and for these reasons: first, to enable the defendants and the trial judge to know precisely and on the face of the indictment itself the nature of the Crown's case, and second, to stop the Crown shifting its ground during the course of the case without leave of the trial judge and the making of an amendment. The words "and by divers and other fraudulent devices" are a relic to the past and should never again appear in an indictment. In criticising the form of indictment used in this case, we should not be taken as adjudging that particulars of conspiracies to defraud should be set out in the same kind of detail as would be required in a statement of claim in an action for damages for conspiracy to defraud. What is wanted is conciseness and clarity.'

The court then effectively redrafted the indictment to show how it could fairly have been, specifying the dishonesty acts alleged. The court advised against the use of terms such as 'falsely representing' and 'to the prejudice of', though subsequent commentators have questioned whether this advice is correct.[13] It is unnecessary to specify particular overt acts of the conspiracy so long as the accused knows the case he has to meet.[14]

4.3   Including a conspiracy count with substantive counts in the same indictment

The inclusion of a conspiracy count may be impugned as oppressive if the indictment also contains substantive offences relating to the same matter. In bygone days, the use of a conspiracy charge in itself, carrying the heavier penalties than the substantive offences,[15] would have caused severe concern to a defendant.[16] The matter is now governed broadly by a Practice Direction[17]

---

10 *R v Dwyer* (1890) 24 ILTR 111; see also *R v Blake and Tye* (1844) 6 QB 126; *R v Pepper* [1921] 3 KB 167, CCA; *R v Steward* [1963] Crim LR 697.

11 *R v Blake and Tye* (1844) 6 QB 126.

12 [1981] 1 All ER 1172 at 1178–1179.

13 See *Archbold* para 28-35; *Halsbury's Laws of England* Vol II(i) para 67 note 9.

14 *R v Addis* [1965] 2 All ER 794n; *R v Churchill* [1965] 2 All ER 793, [1965] 1 WLR 1174; *R v Churchill (No 2)* [1967] 1 QB 190, [1966] 2 All ER 215, CCA.

15 See eg *Verrier v DPP* [1967] 2 AC 195, [1966] 3 All ER 568, HL; *R v Field* [1965] 1 QB 402, [1964] 3 All ER 269, CCA.

16 See *R v Jones* (1974) 59 Cr App Rep 120, CA.

17 [1977] 2 All ER 540, [1977] 1 WLR 537.

and guidelines given to Crown Prosecutors, supplemented by a number of decisions as to how the judge should exercise his discretion to allow conspiracy and substantive charges to be tried together.

The Practice Direction requires the prosecution to justify to the judge the joinder of substantive counts with a related conspiracy count. Failing justification, the prosecution must elect whether to proceed in the substantive or the conspiracy counts. Joinder is justified if the judge considers that the interests of justice demand it.

The cases bear out the following principles.

(a) A conspiracy charge should not be included where there is an efficient and effective substantive charge.

In *Verrier v DPP*, the appellant was convicted of conspiracy to defraud and sentenced to seven years' imprisonment. He appealed against sentence on the ground, inter alia, that as the maximum sentence for the completed offence was five years' imprisonment it was improper for a more severe sentence to be imposed for the offence in its inchoate form. The House of Lords rejected the argument. Lord Pearson said:

'I think it is desirable to add some words of caution:

(1) Normally it is not right to pass a higher sentence for conspiracy than could be passed for the substantive offence: it can be justified only in very exceptional cases.
(2) Although it must follow logically from what is said above that it could in a very exceptional case be right to charge conspiracy even when the substantive offence had been committed and was charged, it should undoubtedly remain the general rule that, when there is an effective and sufficient charge of a substantive offence, the addition of a charge for conspiracy is undesirable because it will tend to prolong and complicate the trial: see *R v Dawson* and *R v Davey*.
(3) I cannot imagine any case in which it would be right to give a greater sentence for an attempt than could be given for the substantive offence. It was held to be wrong in *R v Pearce*, and I agree with the reasons given in that case.'

(b) Where charges of substantive offences do not adequately represent the overall criminality it may be appropriate and right to include a charge of conspiracy.

In *Verrier*, Lord Pearson, quoting RS Wright's *Law of Criminal Conspiracies and Agreements*, said:[18]

'There may be cases in which the agreement or concurrence of several persons in the execution of a criminal design is a proper ground for aggravation of their punishment beyond what would be proper in the case of a sole defendant. Such would be cases in which the co-operation of several persons at different places is likely to facilitate the execution or the concealment of a crime, or in which the presence of several persons together is intended to increase the means of force or to create terror, or cases of fraud in which suspicion and ordinary caution are likely to be disarmed by the increased credibility of a representation made by several persons.'

18 (1873), cited with approval in *R v Field* [1965] 1 QB 402, [1964] 3 All ER 269, CCA and *R v Blamires Transport Services Ltd* [1964] 1 QB 278, [1963] 3 All ER 170, CCA.

In *R v Jones*,[19] a prosecution for conspiracy to intimidate arising out of the 1972 miners' strike, the Court of Appeal upheld the trial judge's decision to reject a motion to quash the conspiracy count on the basis that the alleged criminality disclosed by the witness statements could not be adequately presented in the interests of justice by preferring a small number of charges of substantive offences.

(c) A conspiracy may be charged if it helps to simplify the case for a jury.

In *R v Jones*,[20] another ground for rejecting the motion to quash was that:

> '. . . the task of the judge and jury was simplified by proceeding on one count of conspiracy instead of a large number of counts alleging substantive offences.'

The implication here, of course, is that the conspiracy charge will be employed *in place of* separate substantive charges. The indictment ought to include charges only which make for the simplification of the issues and which avoid complexity and the need for a multiplicity of counts. In *R v Simmonds and others*,[1] the Court of Appeal observed:

> 'As a preliminary it is to be noted the ever-mounting intricacy of the legislation imposing taxes has been followed by ever-increasing ingenuity on the part of numbers of persons conspiring together fraudulently to evade the taxation. Such are the complexities of these fraudulent schemes and the devices used in them that only too often the only way that the interests of justice can be served is by presenting to a jury with the aid of schedules an overall picture of the scheme and charging a conspiracy to cheat and defraud. Obviously every effort should be made to present instead to the jury a relatively small series of substantive offences – but they cannot always be done and this case is one of those where only a conspiracy charge can provide for the protection of the interests of the community when once the legislative produces intricate laws.'

The court concluded that the substantive offences should not have been tried with the conspiracies.

(d) A conspiracy charge should be employed where there is clear evidence of conspiracy and only unreliable or 'nebulous' evidence that any of the conspirators has committed a substantive offence.[2]

(e) A conspiracy charge is justifiable and necessary where there is clear evidence of conspiracy but little evidence that any of the conspirators committed any of the criminal overt acts. Similarly, if there is evidence that some of the defendants, but not all, committed a few of the criminal overt acts, a conspiracy charge is justified.[3]

(f) A conspiracy charge should not be included if it will lead to unfairness to the defence.

Examples of such unfairness are primarily drawn from the fact of the differing rules of evidence relating to substantive offences and where it becomes almost impossible to explain to a jury that evidence inadmissible against an accused on the substantive offence may be admissible on the conspiracy count once he is

---

19 (1974) 59 Cr App Rep 120, CA.
20 Op cit.
1   See *R v Simmonds* [1969] 1 QB 685 at 691 for general advice as to the conduct of long fraud trials.
2   *R v Cooper and Crompton* [1947] 2 All ER 701, CCA.
3   *R v Greenfield* [1973] 3 All ER 1050, [1973] 1 WLR 1151, CA. See especially Lord Widgery CJ's remarks on the use and history of conspiracy generally at pages 1157–1158.

shown to be a conspirator. In *R v Griffiths*[4] appeals against conviction for conspiracy to defraud in a case where the prosecution had included a 'rolled-up' conspiracy to defraud charge on the indictment, which also included 24 substantive counts, were allowed. The conspiracy embraced each of the substantive counts and related to the obtaining by G, a supplier of lime to farmers, his servant B and seven farmers to obtain subsidies from the Ministry of Agriculture. Three counts charged G and B with fraudulently obtaining money from the Ministry; the remaining counts charged B and G, and, in turn, one of the farmers who had obtained money. It had been conceded by the prosecution that there was no link between any of the farmers as between themselves or as between any of them and B and G, other than that each separately had entered into contracts with G for time to be supplied by G. There was no evidence that any farmer knew what, if any, contracts other than his own had been entered into by G. At the end of the prosecution case the type of fraud was not alleged to be the same in each case. The Court of Criminal Appeal was extremely critical of the way the case had been handled:[5]

'It is not surprising that at one stage the jury were complaining strongly at their having to try the case with all its details and ramifications. We have no hesitation in saying it was a case where it was almost impossible for any judge to sum up the various issues clearly and at sufficient length without making his summing-up so long as to make it almost certain that the jury would carry no clear picture of all the issues into the jury room.

The practice of adding what may be called a rolled-up conspiracy charge to a number of counts of substantive offences has become common. We express the very strong hope that this practice will now cease and that the courts will never again have to struggle with this type of case, where it becomes almost impossible to explain to a jury that evidence inadmissible against the accused on the substantive count may be admissible against him on the conspiracy count once he is shown to be a conspirator.

We do not believe that most juries can ever really understand the subtleties of the situation. In our judgment, except in simple cases, a conspiracy count (if one is needed at all) should be tried separately to substantive counts. The danger of not doing so becomes startlingly clear in this case where it is now admitted without argument that in two counts upon which the appellant Bishop was convicted, there was literally no receivable evidence at all against him, the evidence being entries in Griffiths' books of account, evidence in the conspiracy count once Bishop is brought into a conspiracy but not evidence upon which he can be brought into the conspiracy.

It would have been simple, as was indicated in Dawson's case to be the proper procedure, to have charged Griffiths and his accountant book-keeper Booth with a conspiracy to defraud and to have had separate prosecutions against each farmer who was alleged to have obtained fraudulently any money from the Ministry of Agriculture by false pretences. In such a case what was evidence against any farmer would have been simple to resolve. Certainly Griffiths' books could not be evidence against any of the farmers, none of whom had any knowledge of them. Yet the whole of Griffiths' method of accounting and whether that method was an honest method or a dishonest method became in the words of the judge: "the central factor in the case for the prosecution", a matter hopelessly prejudicial to each and every farmer.'

The court referred to *R v Dawson*[6] where defendants were charged both with conspiracy to defraud and substantive offences emerging from the conspiracy.

4   [1965] 1 QB 589, [1965] 2 All ER 448, CCA.
5   At 594.
6   [1960] 1 All ER 558, [1960] 1 WLR 163, CCA.

The court warned of the dangers in such a practice which could work injustice in admitting what would otherwise be inadmissible evidence before the jury. Further, it tended to add to the length and complexity of the trial and impose an intolerable strain on both the judge and the jury.

A distinction must, of course, be drawn between the *Griffiths* line of case where there is little or nothing in common between the defendants (or most of them) and the situation in *R v Meyrick and Ribuffi*[7] where each individual, though ignorant of the details of others concerned, knew that there were others involved in the same enterprise (ie a standard 'wheel' conspiracy).

Dawson also confirmed that the rules relating to duplicity applied to conspiracy charges as well as to substantive offences.[8] If, therefore, a count charges more than one conspiracy, it is bad in law. If, however, as the trial progresses, the evidence becomes consistent with the existence of two or more conspiracies, Lawton LJ in *R v Greenfield*[9] indicated how the matter should be handled:

'Duplicity in a count is a matter of form; it is not a matter relating to the evidence called in support of the count. This is shown by contrasting *R v West*[10] and *R v Davey*[11] with *R v Griffiths*. In *R v West* the reference in the conspiracy count to the Defence (General) Regulations 1939 should have alerted the trial court to the fact that during the period of the alleged conspiracy the regulations which the accused were said to have conspired to infringe had changed from time to time. They could not be said to have conspired together to infringe regulations which had not been issued but during the period specified in the count they could have conspired to infringe each regulation after it was issued. It followed that the count embraced not one conspiracy but a number. In *R v Davey* the conspiracy was alleged to have gone on for 11 years and it was manifest from the form of the count and the depositions considered as particulars that the prosecution were alleging that the accused had conspired to defraud companies which either had not been incorporated at the beginning of the conspiracy or had been wound up before some of the accused were alleged to have joined it. The charge against the accused was one of being members of a number of conspiracies.

In *R v Griffiths* the conspiracy count alleged one conspiracy and was not bad for duplicity; but the evidence led to support that count wholly failed to prove the conspiracy charged. Instead of proving that the accused had all conspired together for a common purpose, it proved that many of them had conspired with one of their number for their own purposes. No such common purpose as charged was ever established so, as a matter of proof, there had to be an acquittal.

In our judgment the distinction which exists between form and proof is the clue to the problem provided by this case. The prosecution was alleging that these appellants and the other accused had had a common purpose to cause explosions. All the accused in their different ways challenged this basic allegation of a common purpose; and they did so by submitting that the evidence revealed the possibility that those charged may have had in relation to some of the incidents purposes which were not common at all. What they were doing was challenging the existence of the conspiracy as charged which is but a way of saying that they were denying that the prosecution had proved their case. A charge which is not bad for duplicity when the trial starts does

7   (1929) 21 Cr App Rep 94, CCA.
8   [1960] 1 All ER 558 at 563, [1960] 1 WLR 163 at 172.
9   [1973] 3 All ER 1050 at 1054–1055.
10 [1948] 1 KB 709, [1948] 1 All ER 718, CCA.
11 [1960] 3 All ER 533, [1960] 1 WLR 1287, CCA.

not become bad in law because evidence is led which is consistent with one or more of the accused being a member of a conspiracy other than the one charged. Such evidence may make it impossible for the prosecution to establish the existence of the conspiracy charged. *R v Griffiths* was such a case. At the end of the prosecution's case the evidence may be as consistent with the accused, or some of them, having been members of a conspiracy which was not the one charged as with the one charged. In such a situation the trial judge should rule that there is no case to answer. But if at the end of the prosecution's case there is evidence on which, if uncontradicted, a reasonably minded jury could convict the accused, or two or more of them, of the conspiracy charged despite evidence of the existence of another conspiracy, then the trial judge should let the case go to the jury.'

It is ordinarily unnecessary to look further than the count itself to determine whether the conspiracy count is bad for duplicity. If particulars have been requested, they should be considered; where they have been refused, the judge may have regard to the depositions and witness statements to determine whether the count is bad for duplicity.

5   THE FUTURE – A GENERAL OFFENCE OF FRAUD

In its Working Paper on Conspiracy to Defraud,[12] the Law Commission reviewed a number of options replacing conspiracy to defraud. One of these, which has excited recurring interest, is the option of a general offence of fraud. Scots law has a precedent for such an offence, but the definition[13] has been described as breathtakingly wide,[14] and yet is narrower than the English offence of conspiracy to defraud because of the requirement for deception.[15] The Roskill Committee briefly considered both the suggestion that there should be a general offence of fraud and that the prosecution should be able to allege, in charging a single offence on aggregate loss over a given period of time.[16] It did not, however, make any recommendation because the matter was under consideration by the Law Commission, and there the matter rests.

12 Law Commission Working Paper No 104, op cit.
13 'The bringing about of some definite practical result by false pretences.' See Gordan *The Criminal Law of Scotland* (2nd edn, 1978) para 18.01.
14 It would not, for example, appear to be limited to causing disadvantage of any description, let alone economic disadvantage. See Prof Leonard Leigh 'The Control of Commercial Fraud' (1982) p 82.
15 *Scott v Metropolitan Police Comr* [1975] AC 819, [1974] 3 All ER 1032, HL.
16 Roskill Report paras 3.14–3.16.

CHAPTER 7
Sentencing

1 INTRODUCTION[1]

It needs little spelling out that offenders convicted of dishonesty on a substantial scale deserve, and receive, sentences of imprisonment. That, however, is about as specific as one can be. Within the parameters of fraud, the degrees of moral culpability are many. There must, in fairness, be a distinction drawn between those who set out to defraud the weak and vulnerable and who obtain for themselves lavish lifestyles as a result, and those who have, albeit improperly, yielded to business pressures and have derived no benefit. The defendant in a fraud trial is frequently a man of previous good character; it is usually highly unlikely that the offence will recur; he may be an individual who has, hitherto, been held high in the estimation of his colleagues; his reputation and career will be in ruins, and often his family life as well. Additionally, and more so than in non-property crimes, the court must consider issues such as compensation, restitution and confiscation, and the extent to which they should be combined with custodial sentences. This chapter aims to draw together in short compass the strands of principle these issues raise and to outline, with specific reference to fraud, the measures open to the convicting court.

2 IMPRISONMENT

2.1 Dishonesty in breach of trust

In an effort to achieve consistency in sentencing practice, the Court of Appeal has provided basic guidelines for sentencing in large-scale theft cases. The landmark decision in *R v Barrick*[2] described the factors to be taken into account in cases of theft committed in breach of trust. The case has been treated as a guide for offences under section 15 of the Theft Act 1968 and for conspiracy to defraud, which share the same maximum sentence as theft. It is also useful for other cases of dishonesty in showing the attitude of the court to issues such as whether imprisonment is appropriate for a first offence, or where the offender has brought ruin upon himself and his family and is unlikely to repeat the offence.

---

1 In any consideration of sentencing principle and practice, regard should be had to DA Thomas *Encyclopaedia of Sentencing Practice* (1982) Sweet and Maxwell, which is by far the most comprehensive and clear work on the subject.
2 (1985) 7 Cr App Rep (S) 142.

Barrick was convicted of stealing £9,000 from a small company to which he had acted as accountant for some years. He was 41 years old and was of previous good character. He was sentenced to two years' imprisonment on conviction following a plea of not guilty. The court accepted that it was practically certain that he would not offend again and that he would never again be able to secure similar employment. He and his family would endure disgrace and hardship. While appreciating that it was dangerous to generalise and that cases vary widely, the court concluded that a term of imprisonment in such cases is inevitable, save in very exceptional circumstances or where the amount of money obtained is very small. Despite the great punishment that offenders bring upon themselves, a substantial term of imprisonment should be imposed to mark publicly the gravity of the offence. The Court of Appeal indicated that the amount stolen was a consideration relevant, though not conclusive, to the sentencing court and provided the following broad tariff for such cases:

(1) where the amounts involved were not small but were less than £10,000, a term of imprisonment ranging from the very short up to about 18 months is appropriate;[3]
(2) where the sum involved was between £10,000 and £50,000 a term of two to three years is appropriate;
(3) where greater sums are involved, for example, those over £100,000, then a term of three-and-a-half to four years will be justified;[4]
(4) where a plea of guilty is entered, the court should give the appropriate discount (usually up to one-third of the sentence);
(5) it will not usually be appropriate in cases of serious breach of trust to suspend any part of the sentence.

While the science of sentencing is not exact, *Barrick* was decided in 1985 and appropriate allowance should, it is suggested, be given for changes in the value of money.

The court then considered the factors to which the sentencing court should pay regard when determining the proper level of sentence within that tariff. These include:

(i) the quality and level of trust reposed in the offender, including his rank;
(ii) the period over which the fraud or the thefts have been perpetrated;
(iii) the use to which the money or the property dishonestly taken was put;
(iv) the effect upon the victim;
(v) the impact of the offences upon the public and public confidence;
(vi) the effect on fellow-employees or partners;
(vii) the effect on the offender himself;
(viii) his own history;
(ix) those matters of mitigation special to himself such as illness, being placed under great strain, excessive responsibility or the like, or where there has been a long delay (the court suggested over two years) between being confronted with his dishonesty by his professional body or the police and the start of his trial;
(x) any assistance he has given to the police.

---

3 See, for example, *R v Weston* (1980) 2 Cr App Rep (S) 391, CA.
4 *R v Strubell* (1982) 4 Cr App Rep (S) 300, CA.

Although criticised for being insufficiently specific as to the effect of each of those factors,[5] the decision is helpful in setting the ceiling for such offences and for indicating the approach the court should generally adopt. It has been broadly followed. In *R v Seal*,[6] the sentence of three years' imprisonment on a bank cashier who had stolen £69,403 from his employer was reduced to two years. The Court of Appeal gave credit for the appellant's immediate frankness with the police, his assistance to the bank in reimbursing customers, his plea of guilty and his previous good character. His conduct did not cause the 'shadow of suspicion' to fall upon other employees. In *R v Strubell*,[7] the appellant, who had obtained employment as an accountant by falsely pretending that he was a member of the Institute of Chartered Accountants, stole £166,500 from his employer. His sentence of five years' imprisonment was reduced to three years. He had pleaded guilty and most of the property had been recovered. The court indicated that, had he contested the case and finally been convicted, a sentence of five years would not have been appropriate, although unlikely to be exceeded on a first conviction.

In *R v Offord*[8] the appellant, a solicitor who had defrauded clients of £242,000, had his sentence of five years' imprisonment reduced to three years. Watkins LJ referred to the current sentencing climate in such cases.

> 'More moderate sentences than used to be passed are thought to be sufficient to assuage the sense of public outrage felt because of the kind of conduct which brings about serious abuses of trust.'

Though a decision on theft, *Barrick* has been accepted as applying to offences of dishonestly obtaining property by deception.[9] In *R v Goring*[10] the appellant, who was a company finance director, pleaded guilty to dishonestly obtaining £110,858 from the company by deception. He admitted the offence at a very early stage and all the money was repaid. His sentence of three years' imprisonment was reduced to 12 months. The court commented:

> 'Examination of the cases we have looked at reveals that a sentence of three years in a case where some £100,000 is involved is usually passed upon persons who initially show no contrition and make no reparation whatsoever. All these factors lead us to the belief that the sentences in this case were passed by the judge without consideration of matters which should have affected him but which plainly did not.'[11]

2.2   Mega-fraud

In the context of serious and complex fraud, the courts have to deal with misappropriation of vaster sums of money than were stolen in *Barrick*, sometimes obtained in breach of trust and sometimes not. In principle the factors which were there approved still apply, though account is taken of the higher sum. In *R v Higgs*,[12] the Court of Appeal had to consider the impact of

---

5 Levi *Regulating Fraud* (1988) at p 266.
6 (1989) 11 Cr App Rep (S) 297, CA.
7 (1982) 4 Cr App Rep (S) 300, CA.
8 (1985) 7 Cr App Rep (S) 327, CA.
9 Obtaining a pecuniary advantage by deception carries a lesser maximum penalty and presumably the sentences suggested in *Barrick* would be scaled down.
10 (1986) 8 Cr App Rep (S) 243, CA.
11 See also *R v Mossop* (1985) 7 Cr App Rep (S) 283, CA.
12 (1986) 8 Cr App Rep (S) 440, CA.

Barrick in cases involving theft of sums far in excess of those referred to. Higgs was a management accountant in a company who pleaded guilty to stealing more than £3 million, most of which was gambled away, over a period of five years. He was sentenced to a total of 14 years' imprisonment, comprising seven years on one set of offences and seven years' consecutive on a second set of offences.

Taylor J (as he then was) said:

'In [*Barrick*] the learned Lord Chief Justice said, "The sum involved is obviously not the only factor to be considered, but it may in many cases provide a useful guide." He went on to indicate a sliding scale of appropriate sentences where the amount taken was less than £10,000, between £10,000 and £50,000, or over £100,000. It is of course absolutely right, as Mr Elfer has submitted, that one does not proceed by mathematical progression to add years or months to a sentence in direct proportion to the amount of money taken until one reaches a very large number of years with the figure of £3.5 million. But the amount taken cannot be regarded as irrelevant, nor can it be said that after a certain ceiling of stealing has been reached, any further stealing should make no or little difference to the period of sentence.'

The court reduced his total sentence to eight years' imprisonment. In *R v Penn*[13], the appellant was convicted of conspiracies to steal and to obtain by deception and had stolen thereby in excess of £2 million. His sentence of seven years' imprisonment was upheld. In *R v Wheeler*,[14] the appellant, who was the director and major shareholder in a company which purchased investments and insurance policies on behalf of clients, stole and used for his own benefit a sum in excess of £800,000 from the company's client account over a period of four years. Other funds which were intended by clients to be invested in low risk securities were invested in speculative companies controlled by the appellant. The Court of Appeal would not disturb his sentence of eight years' imprisonment describing the offence as 'a persistent fraud on a huge scale prompted by greed'. In *R v Bingham*,[15] a sentence of six years' imprisonment on a solicitor who stole £730,000 from funds under his administration in what the court described as a persistent and blatant misuse of client money, was upheld. In *R v Peter Clowes*,[16] the defendant ran an off-shore investment company offering services to elderly people preparing for retirement and seeking security, and promising to invest their savings in gilt-edged government bonds. Instead the money was used to finance speculative schemes and the defendant's lavish lifestyle. He was convicted on sample counts of stealing £16.9 million and sentenced to ten years' imprisonment. Phillips J commented that he did not believe a judge in this country had been called on to sentence on a worse case of fraud.

The court may adopt an alternative approach, even in large cases, where there has been no breach of trust or gain by the defendants. In *R v National Westminster Investment Bank*,[17] four defendants had been convicted of conspiracy to defraud by misleading the stock market into believing that what had been described as the largest rights issue ever in the City had been a success. McKinnon J held that conspiracy to rig the market is a serious offence however much it was shown that what was done was not intended either to cause other people loss or to achieve personal gain, and should be visited by a

13 (1989) 11 Cr App Rep (S) 86, CA.
14 (1992) 13 Cr App Rep (S) 73.
15 (1992) 13 Cr App Rep (S) 45, CA.
16 Unreported, 12 February 1992, Central Criminal Court.
17 Unreported. The sentencing remarks were made on 14 February 1992.

custodial sentence. In determining the length of the sentence and whether the sentence could be wholly or partly suspended, the judge said:

> 'I wholly reject the notion that the length, complexity, expense or notoriety of this trial should in some way make it impossible, if it is otherwise right to do so, for this court to suspend those sentences. How can this court reach the conclusion in a case of conspiracy to defraud involving indirectly, at least, very large sums of money that it is right to suspend the sentences?
>
> Conspiracy to defraud covers a very wide range of offences of varying degrees of seriousness. This case is notable for the lack of any planning, for the absence of any intent to gain personally, coupled with the fact that there was no actual personal gain. The agreement, the subject matter of the offence, was reached, as I say, without planning as an unexpected crisis arose. Once the agreement was made, there was no turning back with very little time to withdraw from it. There was no attempt apart from the announcement itself to conceal or disguise what had been done.'

The factors leading the judge to suspend the prison sentences included:

(1) the conspiracy was not planned in advance;
(2) it was not unlawful to carry out a late take-up in a rights issue;
(3) it was a one-off offence, committed under great personal pressure that no one, particularly existing shareholders, should suffer loss;
(4) the defendants had made no attempt to conceal what they had done;
(5) the defendants had not gained personally;
(6) the defendants were all of excellent reputation; their careers, prospects and reputations had been destroyed; and
(7) the defendants' and their families' lives had been focused, almost to the exclusion of all else, on the trial for over 235 days.

2.3   Other cases of dishonesty

There is no significant difference in the principles adopted in frauds not involving a breach of trust. Pleas of guilty and assistance in recovering the stolen proceeds will achieve a significant reduction in sentence. In *R v Silverman*,[18] the appellant, who was described as a 'front man', pleaded guilty to several offences of handling stolen property and of forgery relating to cheques totalling £27,000. He asked for 575 offences to be taken into consideration. His sentence of six years was reduced to four years' imprisonment. The court drew attention to the specific need to impose a deterrent sentence. Sophistication, and the likelihood of repetition are also taken into account. In *R v Ruelle*,[19] the appellant was convicted of attempting to obtain £22,000 from an insurance company after he had deliberately set fire to his restaurant. The court, though reducing the sentence from five years' imprisonment to two years, drew attention to the sophistication of the plan and the fact that it could have endangered life, and that frauds of this nature had to be discouraged. However, the most important factor weighing in the court's mind was that the offence was unlikely to be repeated. For a person like the defendant, the main deterrent was the mere fact of being sent to prison.

There is a tendency to be more lenient in the case of an honest business which hits difficulties than with an enterprise established for the purpose of fraud. In

18 (1983) 5 Cr App Rep (S) 46, CA.
19 (1981) 3 Cr App Rep (S) 74, CA.

R v Pal and Dhorajiwala[20] the appellants' business was conducted honestly for several years. When it ran into serious financial difficulty, it continued to trade. Goods were obtained on credit to meet existing liabilities, leading to a loss of some £225,000. On *Barrick* criteria, this figure would have justified a sentence of four-and-a-half to five-and-a-half years. The appellants pleaded guilty. Their sentences of four years and two years' imprisonment were reduced to 30 months and 12 months. Taylor LJ said:

'This was a fraud which developed from an honest, but unsuccessful business. It was not initially dishonest. It developed by robbing Peter to pay Paul, rather than by a deliberate attempt to amass money fraudulently.'[1]

2.4 Frauds on the public revenue

Convictions for offences of tax evasion will usually be followed by a custodial sentence, even where the amount of the evasion was small. As Glidewell J stated in *R v Thornhill*[2:]

'Defrauding the Inland Revenue is a serious offence because it means defrauding the vast body of innocent taxpayers. It should be generally known that an immediate sentence of imprisonment may well be the result of pleading guilty to or being convicted of such an offence.'

In cases not involving huge amounts, the courts are more prone to accept that it is the fact of imprisonment, rather than its length, which is the deterrent and sentences have tended to be short, though again falling broadly within the *Barrick* tariffs. In *R v Hayes*,[3] a two-and-a-half years' sentence after pleading guilty to defrauding the Inland Revenue of £19,424 was reduced to nine months. In *R v Beale*,[4] in upholding a sentence of two months' imprisonment with a £2,000 fine for a plea of guilty to defrauding the Revenue over a period of four years, McCullough J said:

'. . . there is nothing wrong in principle with a short sentence of immediate imprisonment in a case like this. Indeed where, as here, a deliberate fraud has been carried on over a period of years and concealed by a falsification of documents, such a sentence is virtually inevitable. It is necessary to deter proprietors of other businesses who are tempted to behave like this. Until not very long ago sentences for this kind of offence would have been of the order of 18 months' imprisonment. Nowadays it is thought possible to pass very much shorter sentences, but the need to mark the gravity of such offences by immediate sentences of imprisonment remains.'

The *Hayes* and *Beale* guidelines do not apply where substantial sums are involved or where there is some other extraordinary exacerbating factor. In *R v Sivyer*,[5] the appellants were convicted of conspiracy to cheat and defraud the Revenue by failing to deduct tax from payments to employees. Some £400,000 was lost to the Revenue. The Court of Appeal dismissed appeals against sentences of four years' imprisonment upon the main conspirators who had

---

20 (1981) 3 Cr App Rep (S) 343, CA.
1 See also *R v Kazmi* (1985) 7 Cr App Rep (S) 115, CA; cf *R v Riaz and Rehman* (1989) 11 Cr App Rep (S) 543, CA.
2 (1980) 2 Cr App Rep (S) 320, CA.
3 (1987) 3 Cr App Rep (S) 205, CA.
4 (1981) 3 Cr App Rep (S) 289.
5 (1987) 9 Cr App Rep (S) 428, CA.

pleaded not guilty. The court took into account the sheer scale of the case in money terms, the fact that an element of deterrence was required in an industry in which tax fraud was widespread, and the temptation that had been and would be proffered to otherwise honest citizens encouraged to fall in to live with the conspiracy. In *R v McNamara*,[6] a sentence of four years' imprisonment was imposed where the appellant had received a number of stolen Inland Revenue exemption certificates and vouchers and had dealt with them in such a way as to cause a loss of £116,000 to the Revenue. Drake J held:

> 'We view the evils of the trade and the evil of a person dealing in the way in which this appellant was dealing with vouchers as being that they are ready and willing to tempt honest people in the trade to fall into dishonesty by supplying them with more tax exemption certificates. Accordingly, we do not regard the case of *Hayes* as any guide whatsoever to the appellant's situation.'

The Court of Appeal has recognised that the Revenue must adopt a policy of selectivity in deciding whom to prosecute, bring proceedings against some tax evaders and reaching compounded settlements with others. The court will not probe the reasons why the Revenue has opted for criminal proceedings in any given case, and will not allow a sentence to be influenced by what financial penalty the Revenue could have inflicted if it had kept the matter to itself.[7]

The pattern is similar for VAT frauds, although cases of falsely claiming, for example, reimbursement of VAT and of failing to register have brought a harsher response. In *R v Brown*,[8] a sentence of four years' imprisonment on a defendant who had, over a period of several years, obtained the repayment of Customs and Excise of over £73,000 was upheld, and in *R v Richardson*[9] a sentence of 12 months was imposed for fraudulently reclaiming £7,900 in VAT.

In *R v Tuffey*,[10] a failure to register a business which led to the evasion of £965 in VAT resulted in a committal prison sentence for the manager of the businesses. By any standards, this seems harsh, particularly in contrast with *R v Thornhill*,[11] where a sentence of two months was imposed for VAT fraud of over £3,000. The court distinguished Thornhill on the basis that imprisoning *Thornhill* was going to lead to the collapse of his business and unemployment in a small community.

2.5   Corruption

As with breach of trust cases, sentences for corruption usually include a deterrent element, even though the offender may be unlikely to reoffend. This stems largely from the fact that such offences are difficult to discover and that the most the courts can do is to impose severe sentences when offences are discovered. In *R v Wellburn and Nurdin*,[12] sentences of 12 months suspended for two years and 18 months' immediate imprisonment were passed on the managing director and sales director respectively of a company which had paid bribes of £23,000 to secure arms supply contracts benefiting the company by £4–5 million, were upheld. Lawton LJ said that:

6   (1986) 8 Cr App Rep (S) 438, CA.
7   *R v Milbern Investments Ltd* (1981) 3 Cr App Rep (S) 107, CA.
8   (1979) 1 Cr App Rep (S) 189, CA.
9   (1992) 13 Cr App Rep (S) 51, CA.
10 (1986) 8 Cr App Rep (S) 485, CA.
11 (1980) 2 Cr App Rep (S) 320, CA.
12 (1979) 1 Cr App Rep (S) 64, CA.

'Corruption in all forms has become widespread. The courts must do what they can to stop the spread of corruption in public and commercial life. All they can do is show by the sentences passed that the giving and accepting of bribes will not be tolerated in this realm. This must mean in most cases severe sentences, perhaps larger than some which have been imposed recently. This is particularly so when bribery has involved large sums.'

A suspended sentence is unlikely, even in cases where the sums involved are not large and when the offender is of previous good character.[13] In *R v Wilson*, the appellant, a man of previous good character, was convicted of conspiracy and three offences of corruption. He received gifts worth £2,500 from a company in return for receiving contracts. Watkins LJ said:

'This kind of conduct is damaging to commercial life, and those who indulge in it must expect to be imprisoned immediately, although of good character previously.
    The only question which remains is not whether the appellant should have gone to prison, but whether he was sentenced too harshly. The plain fact is that the appellant, who was enjoying a privileged position for which he had worked hard, is now ruined. He has lost his home, his family has broken up, he is no longer acceptable in commercial and business life and the strain of these convictions will inevitably repel any would-be employer from placing him in positions of trust.'

His sentence of three-and-a-half years' imprisonment was, however, reduced to 18 months. Corruption of a larger scale was considered in *R v Hopwood*[14] where the appellant had earned more than £200,000 for himself by favouring a supplier whose goods were of inferior quality to those of other suppliers who had not tendered bribes paid and in return for failing to disclose a fraud being carried out against his employers by a third party and which cost his employers in excess of £1 million. His appeal against a sentence of three-and-a-half years' imprisonment was dismissed, with an indication from Lawton LJ that he was exceedingly lucky not to have been sentenced more severely.

3   FINES

In the context of a main defendant in a serious fraud, a financial penalty alone will usually be regarded as insufficient. In *R v Sisodia*, for example,[15] the Court of Appeal expressed surprise that an immediate custodial sentence and a criminal bankruptcy order had not been imposed upon the appellant who had pleaded guilty to VAT fraud committed over two years and causing £500,000 loss to Customs and Excise. He had received a suspended sentence of two years' imprisonment, a fine of £25,000 and a costs order of £20,000. Roskill LJ added:

'It is said, and the judge's reasons in sentencing support this, that the judge did not impose an immediate custodial sentence, because he thought and hoped that this man would be able to apply the very substantial sum in gold and jewellery which was then in the hands of the Customs, the value of which has

---

13 *R v Jones* (1981) 3 Cr App Rep (S) 238: sentence of nine weeks on a council worker who had accepted a corrupt gift of £21.
14 (1985) 7 Cr App Rep (S) 402, CA.
15 (1979) 1 Cr App Rep (S) 291, CA.

been variously described as between £50,000 and £100,000, towards the payment of the fines.

What the learned judge does not appear to have had in mind was the possibility, which has now eventuated, that the whole of that which he so carefully planned could be defeated by this man going bankrupt on his own petition and that is what has happened. As a result, this gold and jewellery has been properly released by the Customs to the trustees in bankruptcy, who are also in the course of collecting his other assets.'[16]

The court is discouraged, therefore, from taking into account the ability to pay a fine where the offence merits imprisonment. The converse also applies: a sentence of imprisonment should not be imposed for an offence meriting a fine because the offender has no means to pay the fine.[17]

It is, however, open to the court to impose a fine as well as a custodial sentence or indeed any other measure.[18] In such cases, the usual principles relating to the imposing of fines apply, so that a court must ensure that the fine is within the capacity of the offender to pay[19] and, for that purpose, may draw such inferences, in the absence of information from the offender, as are appropriate.[20] Fines should only be imposed in addition to an immediate custodial sentence where the offender has profited substantially from the offence[1] and has the means to pay.[2] Even if there is no evidence that the offender has the means to pay, the court may impose a fine in addition to a custodial sentence provided that the total of the custodial sentence and the length of any term of imprisonment which would be served in default if the fine is not paid is not excessive in relation to the offence.[3]

4   COMPENSATION ORDERS

4.1   General power

Section 35 of the Powers of Criminal Courts Act 1973 empowers a convicting court to order a defendant to pay such compensation as it considers appropriate for any personal injury, loss or damage resulting from the offence or any offence taken into consideration.[4]

The order may be instead of or additional to any other sentence imposed by the court and, in determining whether to make an order and its amount, the court must have regard to:

(1) the means of the defendant so far as they appear or are not known to the court; and
(2) its duty, where a confiscation order is also made and the defendant's means are insufficient to satisfy both orders, to direct that the compensation

---

16 See also *R v Messana* (1981) 3 Cr App Rep (S) 88, CA.
17 *R v McGowan* (1 November 1974, unreported).
18 Section 30 of the Powers of the Criminal Courts Act 1973; *R v Waterfield* (17 February 1975, unreported).
19 *R v Chelmsford Crown Court, ex p Birchall* (1989) 11 Cr App Rep (S) 510.
20 *R v Higgins* (1988) 10 Cr App Rep (S) 144; *R v Wright* (12 November 1976, unreported).
1 *R v Forsythe* (1980) 2 Cr App Rep (S) 15, CA.
2 *R v Maud* (1980) 2 Cr App Rep (S) 289.
3 *R v Savundranayagan* (1968) 52 Cr App Rep 637, CA; *R v Lott-Carter* (1978) 67 Cr App Rep 404, CA; *R v Benmore* (1983) 5 Cr App Rep (S) 468, CA; *R v Garner* (1985) 7 Cr App Rep (S) 285, CA.
4 Note that the maximum order that a Magistrates' Court may make is £2,000: section 40 of the Magistrates' Courts Act 1980.

order shall be paid out of any sums recovered under the confiscation order.[5]

Similarly, where the court imposes both a fine and a compensation order, the court must give preference to the compensation order.[6]

Before making an order, the court must have regard to any evidence and to any representations made by the accused or the prosecutor,[7] and may then make such order as it considers appropriate. No order should be made unless the sum claimed by way of compensation is either agreed by the defendant or has been strictly proved by evidence.[8] There was some debate as to whether the provisions of section 35(1A) reduced the obligation of the court to require proof of loss before making an order. This was rejected in *R v Horsham Justices, ex p Richards*,[9] Neill LJ said:

'. . . the court has no jurisdiction to make a compensation order without receiving any evidence where there are real issues raised as to whether the claimants have suffered any, and if so what, loss. The new subsection seems to contemplate that the court can make assessments and approximations where the evidence is scanty or incomplete. It can then make an order which is appropriate . . . the defendant should have a proper opportunity to test the grounds upon which the order was to be made against him. In my view it is not enough to say that he could have given evidence himself. In a case such as the present, where there were plain issues as to liability, it was for the prosecution to place evidence before the court.'

The loss claimed must have resulted from the offence in respect of which the order has been made,[10] but it is, and is intended to be, a rough and ready machinery for awarding compensation and the court should not be troubled by strict concepts of causation relevant to the assessment of damages in contract and tort.[11] The procedure should be, accordingly, confined to simple, straightforward cases and where no great amount is at stake.[12] Similarly, while the court may hear evidence as to whether loss resulted from the offence as to the amount of loss, the court should not embark on any complicated investigation of the facts, even at the suit of the defendant.[13] For this reason, the scope for making compensation orders in serious fraud cases may be limited and most of the authorities on compensation relate to comparatively minor cases of dishonesty and offences of violence. The award may include an element by way of interest.[14]

An order should not be made which involves payment by instalment over a long period of time.[15]

If a compensation order is ever to be made in a case involving serious fraud, it is likely to be combined with a custodial sentence. There is no objection in

5 Section 35(4), as amended by the Criminal Justice Act 1988 section 170(1), Schedule 15 paragraphs 38, 40.
6 Section 35(4A).
7 Section 35(1A) of the Powers of the Criminal Courts Act 1973.
8 *R v Vivian* (1978) 68 Cr App Rep 53.
9 (1985) 7 Cr App Rep (S) 158, CA.
10 *R v Boardman* (1987) 9 Cr App Rep (S) 74, CA; *R v Derby* (1990) 12 Cr App Rep (S) 502.
11 *R v Thomson Holiday Ltd* (1973) 58 Cr App Rep 429; *Rowlston v Kenny* (1982) 4 Cr App Rep (S) 85, CA.
12 *R v Kneeshaw* (1974) 58 Cr App Rep 439; *R v Donovan* (1981) 3 Cr App Rep (S) 192, CA; *R v Halliwell* (1991) 12 Cr App Rep (S) 692.
13 *R v Kneeshaw* (1974) 58 Cr App Rep 439 per Lord Widgery CJ.
14 *R v Schofield* (1978) 67 Cr App Rep 282.
15 *R v Daley* [1974] 1 All ER 290, CA.

principle to combining a custodial sentence with a compensation order, but the court should not allow defendants effectively to buy themselves out of prison by their ability and readiness to pay compensation.[16] Where a custodial sentence is imposed, a compensation order should not be of such a nature as to saddle the defendant with such a liability to meet when he emerges from prison that he will be tempted to return to crime to meet it,[17] and should not be imposed where the defendant has no means to pay.[18]

4.2 Appeal

A defendant may appeal against the making of a compensation order in the same way as any other part of the sentence, and the person in whose favour the order is made is not entitled to receive the amount due to him until there is no further possibility of an appeal.[19] The Court of Appeal may annul or vary a compensation order even though the conviction is not quashed[20] and the House of Lords may, if it restores a conviction, make any compensation order that the court of trial could have made.[1]

4.3 Review

The order may be discharged or reduced by a magistrates' order,[2] on the application of the person against whom it was made, if it appears to the court that:

(1) the damage or loss has been held in civil proceedings to be less than it was taken to be for the purposes of the order;
(2) the property has been recovered by the person in whose favour the order was made; or
(3) the means of the person against whom the order is made is insufficient to satisfy both a confiscation order and a compensation order; or
(4) the person against whom the order was made has suffered a substantial and unexpected reduction in his means and they are unlikely to increase for a considerable period.

The magistrates' court has jurisdiction even if the original order was made by Crown Court, though in cases (3) and (4), the consent of the Crown Court must first have been obtained.[3]

---

16 *R v Inwood* (1974) 60 Cr App Rep 70, CA; *R v Dorton* (1987) 9 Cr App Rep (S) 514, CA.
17 *R v Morgan* (1982) 4 Cr App Rep (S) 358, CA; cf where the defendant has realistic prospects of employment on his release from a moderate sentence: *R v Townsend* (1980) 2 Cr App Rep (S) 328, CA.
18 *R v Gill* (1992) 13 Cr App Rep (S) 36, CA.
19 Section 36(1).
20 Section 36(2).
1 Section 36(3); also section 30 of the Criminal Appeal Act 1968 as amended by Schedule 15 paragraphs 20 and 28 of the Criminal Justice Act 1988.
2 Section 37. The application is made by complaint pursuant to rule 104(1) of the Magistrates' Courts Rules 1981. The magistrates must issue a summons to the person in whose favour the order was made, requiring him to show cause why it should not be amended or revoked.
3 Section 37.

4.4 Effect on civil proceedings

Where a compensation order has been made, the damages in civil proceedings in respect of the injury are to be assessed without regard to the order but the plaintiff may only recover any amount by which the damages exceed the compensation order and any portion of the order which he fails to recover.[4]

4.5 Enforcement

Enforcement of the order lies with the magistrates' court and is treated, for the purpose of collection and enforcement, as if it had been imposed on conviction by a magistrates' court.[5] The sum may also be enforced as if the sum were due in pursuance of a judgment or order of such court.[6] The maximum terms of imprisonment that a magistrates' court may impose in default are set out in Schedule 4 of the Magistrates' Court Act 1980 but the Crown Court may, if it makes an order for an amount exceeding £10,000 and considers that a maximum default term is insufficient, fix a longer period, not exceeding the term specified for the equivalent amount in section 31(3A) of the 1973 Act.

5 RESTITUTION ORDERS

Section 28 of the Theft Act 1968 enables a court, where goods have been stolen[7] and a person is convicted of *any offence*[8] with reference to the theft or such an offence is taken into consideration,

(a) to order *anyone* having possession or control of the goods to restore them to any person entitled to recover them;

(b) to order any other goods directly or indirectly representing the stolen goods to be delivered to any applicant entitled to recover them; or

(c) to order a sum not exceeding the value of the stolen goods to be paid, out of any money of the convicted person which was taken out of his possession on his apprehension,[9] to any person who, if the goods were in the possession of the person convicted, would be entitled to recover them.

Where the convicted person has sold the goods to a person acting in good faith, the court may, on restoring the goods to their rightful owner, order the innocent purchaser to be compensated out of money taken from the convicted person on his apprehension.[10]

---

4 Section 38.

5 Section 4 of the Administration of Justice Act 1970. The appropriate court is either the magistrates' court which actually imposed the order or, where imposed by the Crown Court, such magistrates' court as is imposed in the order.

6 Section 4(3) of the Administration of Justice Act 1970.

7 'Stolen' is defined for these purposes in section 24 of the Theft Act 1968 and includes, for example, goods stolen whether in England and Wales or elsewhere.

8 Stealing does not have to be the gist of the offence for which the person has been convicted: section 28(1).

9 Apprehension means arrest. Money seized prior to the defendant's arrest may not be made the subject of a restitution order: *R v Hinde* (1977) 64 Cr App Rep 213. Money seized after arrest may be made the subject of a restitution order: *R v Ferguson* (1970) 54 Cr App Rep 410 (money taken out of the offender's safe deposit two weeks after his arrest).

10 Section 38(3).

A restitution order should only be made in cases where there is no doubt that the person, in whose favour the order would be made, is entitled to recover the goods. In *R v Ferguson*,[11] Salmon LJ said:

'If there is any doubt at all whether the money or goods in question belong to a third party, a criminal court is not the correct forum in which that issue should be decided, it is only in the plainest cases, when there can be no doubt that the money belonged to the convicted man,[12] that the court would be justified in exercising its discretion in making an order for restitution. To do so in any case of doubt might cause the gravest injustice to a third party because the third party to whom the money may belong has no locus standi to appear before a criminal court. Nor is there any appropriate machinery available in the criminal courts for deciding the issue as to who is the true owner. Discovery is sometimes a very important part of the necessary machinery for resolving issues of that sort, and discovery for this purpose can be obtained only in the civil courts. A civil court is the correct forum for deciding matters of that kind.'[13]

It should, further, only be made in respect of property or the proceeds of property which is the subject matter of the conviction.[14]

The wording of section 28(1) indicates that the order should be made on conviction (whether or not the passing of sentence is in other respects deferred). Further, the order may only be made if, in the opinion of the court, the relevant facts appear from evidence given at the trial or available documents. This has been interpreted strictly so that a restitution order was quashed where it had been made a considerable period after sentence had been passed and on the basis of evidence received at hearings long after the conclusion of the trial.[15]

6   RECLAIMING THE BENEFITS OF CRIME

6.1   Introduction

Whatever custodial sentence is imposed upon a person convicted of an offence of fraud, there will be justifiable public concern and cynicism if, upon release, he is permitted to enjoy the fruits of his dishonesty. Until 1986 in cases of drug trafficking and 1988 in cases of other serious offences, no formalised procedure to confiscate the proceeds of wrong-doing existed. The compensation and restitution provisions[16] were limited both as to what, and the circumstances in which, orders could be made, and were, in any event, unsuitable in complex cases. Some crimes, for example, 'victimless' crimes, would generate enormous profits which could not be forfeited on the basis of compensation or restoration to any identifiable loser.

6.2   Mareva relief and its limitations

Attempts were made to adapt the Mareva jurisdiction of the civil courts to deprive offenders of the proceeds of crime, but the path was difficult and

11 (1970) 54 Cr App Rep 410, CA.
12 This would be a paragraph (c) situation.
13 See also *R v Calcutt and Varty* (1985) 7 Cr App Rep (S) 385.
14 *R v Parker* (1970) 54 Cr App Rep 339, CA.
15 *R v Church* (1970) 55 Cr App Rep 65, CA.
16 See sections 4 and 5 above.

unreliable.[17] In *Chief Constable of Kent v V*,[18] the majority of the Court of Appeal granted an application to restrain the defendant from dealing with money in his bank account which had been obtained by stealing blank cheques from the victim and forging his signature. The police did not have a cause of action against the defendant, a fact which in other cases would have precluded the granting of any such relief to an applicant, but Lord Denning MR held that the police had a right or interest, once they knew or had reason to believe that goods had been stolen or unlawfully obtained, to seize and detain the goods pending the trial of the offender.[19] Lord Denning thought the right extended to enable recovery of the proceeds of crime. Donaldson LJ thought the right to an injunction extended to money in bank accounts which could be shown to be or have been obtained from another in breach of the criminal law. He left open whether the police could obtain an injunction in respect of proceeds of the realisation of stolen goods. Mareva relief was refused, however, when the police sought to restrain use of the proceeds of the sale of properties which had been purchased with bank loans redeemed by the profits of the defendant's alleged fraudulent sale of motor cars.[20] Similarly, the police could not detain profits made as a result of obtaining mortgage advances by fraud and investing the money in properties which had increased substantially in value.[1]

Mareva relief was, in any event, restitutive rather than confiscatory in nature. It could be obtained by the police only as a preliminary to the true owners' civil right of recovery of the stolen property or as ancillary to a restitution or compensation order.[2]

6.3 Confiscation orders

6.3.1 Background

In 1984, the Hodgson Committee[3] recommended the abolition of criminal bankruptcy orders and their replacement with a sentence of confiscation designed to catch the major benefits of crime. The Committee also recommended a statutory power to freeze a defendant's assets, modelled on the Mareva relief, to ensure that assets were preserved pending the satisfaction of a confiscation order. Detailed provisions relating to the confiscation of the benefits of an indictable offence and to the freezing of assets are now contained in Part VI of the Criminal Justice Act 1988.

Similar confiscation provisions are found in the Drug Trafficking Offences Act 1986, though the regime under that Act is harsher in that it presumes that all assets held by a defendant at the time of his apprehension are the benefits of drug trafficking[4] and it imposes a duty on the convicting court to make a

---

17 For a full amount of use of the Mareva jurisdiction in a criminal context see: Gee *Mareva Injunctions* Chapter 20; Bean *Injunctions* (4th edn, 1987) Longman.
18 [1983] QB 34, [1982] 3 All ER 36.
19 This reasoning was not followed either by the other members of the court or in subsequent cases. See, for example: per Slade LJ at 45; Chief Constable of Hampshire [1985] QB 139; *Chief Constable of Leicester v M* [1988] 3 All ER 1015, [1987] 1 WLR 20.
20 *Chief Constable of Hampshire v A Ltd* [1985] QB 132, [1984] 2 All ER 385, CA.
1 *Chief Constable of Leicester v M* [1988] 3 All ER 1015, [1989] 1 WLR 20; *Chief Constable of Surrey v A* (1988) Times, 27 October.
2 *Marcel v Metropolitan Police Comr* [1992] 1 All ER 72, [1992] 2 WLR 50, CA.
3 *The Profits of Crime and their Recovery* Heinemann (1984). The Committee was not set up under the auspices of the Howard League for Penal Reform.
4 Section 2 of the Drug Trafficking Offences Act 1986.

confiscation order.[5] Part VI does not make the same assumption and gives the court a discretion as to whether an order should be made.[6] Much of the case law relates to the 1986 Act but, because of the similarity of the provisions of the two Acts, is equally applicable to the 1988 Act.[7]

The basic tasks of the court are:

(i)   to determine whether it has jurisdiction to make a confiscation order and, if so, whether it ought to make one;

(ii)   to assess the benefit the defendant, or if more than one, each of them, has made from the offence;

(iii) to determine in respect of the defendant, or each of them, the amount that may be realised and how much the defendant ought to pay;

(iv) where assets are available, to make an order.

6.3.2   When can an order be made?

A confiscation order may be made by the Crown Court when an offender is found guilty of any indictable offence (other than a drug trafficking offence or an offence under Part III of the Prevention of Terrorism (Temporary Provisions Act 1989)[8] or by a magistrates' court where an offender is convicted of an offence listed in Schedule 4 to the Act.[9] In either case, the court must be satisfied that:

(1)   the offender has benefited from the offence or from the offence when taken together with some other offence of which he is convicted in the same proceedings (which, in the case of a magistrates' court must also be a Schedule 4 offence) or which the court takes into consideration when determining sentence; *and*

(2)   that his benefit is at 'least the minimum amount'.[10] This is currently £10,000 but may be varied by statutory instrument.[11]

A person benefits from an offence if he obtains property as a result of or in connection with its commission. His benefit is the value of the property so obtained,[12] or, where he has obtained a pecuniary advantage, a sum of money equal to the pecuniary advantage.[13]

In the exercise of assessing whether the defendant's benefit is in excess of £10,000, the court may have regard only to convictions *in the same proceedings* and offences taken into consideration. Joinder of counts in the same indictment now assumes, therefore, an additional importance. The sentencing court must only have regard to the defendant's benefit, and cannot make joint orders.[14]

---

5   Section 1(1) of the Drug Trafficking Offences Act 1986.

6   Section 72(2). For a detailed comparison of the confiscation provisions of the Drug Trafficking Offences Act 1986 and Part VI of the Criminal Justice Act 1988 see David Feldman's *Criminal Confiscation Orders – the New Law* (Butterworths, 1988).

7   And vice versa: see per Lord Donaldson MR in *Re O* [1991] 2 QB 520, 1 All ER 330, CA.

8   For which separate and more severe provision is made in other legislation.

9   Offences relating to sex establishments and cinemas.

10 Section 71(2) and (3).

11 Section 71(7) and (8). The instrument is subject to annulment by either House of Parliament.

12 Section 71(4).

13 Section 71(5).

14 *R v Porter* [1990] 3 All ER 784, [1990] 1 WLR 1260, CA – see further section 6.3.3 below. This may have the effect of significantly limiting the use of Part VI.

6.3.3 In what sum can the order be made?

Where an order is made, it must be at least the minimum amount, but must not exceed either the actual benefit to the defendant or the amount appearing to the court to be the 'amount that might be realised' at the time the order is made, whichever is the less.[15]

The order is aimed at the value of the defendant's benefit, and is not limited to chattels stolen or money found on the defendant at the time of the defendant's apprehension.[16] The 'amount that might be realised' is the total at the time of making the order of all the 'realisable property' held by the defendant less amounts payable under certain obligations having priority, and less the total of the values at the time of the order of all 'gifts caught' by the Act. An obligation has priority if it is an obligation of the defendant to pay a fine or other amount pursuant to a court order made on conviction of an offence, where the fine was imposed or order made before the confiscation order, or to pay a preferential debt[17] under section 386 of the Insolvency Act 1986.

In *R v Smith*,[18] the Court of Appeal held that no allowance should be made for business expenses in determining the amount of a confiscation order under the Drug Trafficking Offences Act 1986. The provisions of that Act relate to 'any payments or other rewards received . . . at any time'. The section deals with receipts not profits and was deliberately worded:

'. . . so as to avoid the necessity, which the appellant's construction of the section would involve, of having to carry out an accountancy exercise, which would be quite impossible in the circumstances of this case. It may be that the wording is draconian, and that it produces a draconian result. But it seems to us that, if that is the case, it was a result intended by those who framed the Act.'

It is an open question as to whether use of the term 'benefit' in the 1988 Act would lead to a different approach, though it seems unlikely that it would do so.

Where two or more defendants are convicted arising out of a joint venture, the court must assess the respective shares of any joint benefit of each of them and make separate orders. A joint order may not be made. In *R v Porter*,[19] the two defendants were convicted of drug trafficking and were found to have benefited jointly in the sum of £9,600. They were ordered jointly and severally to pay £9,600. They jointly owned a house, subject to a mortgage, and had an estimated equity of £25–30,000. The defendants were given nine months to pay, which was based on the contemplated sale of the property after their release from custody.

The joint order was quashed and varied to separate orders in the sum of £4,800. Garland J said:

'Where property is jointly owned, particular problems may arise. In this case there was quite fortuitously both a joint enterprise and a joint asset.

However, this court takes the view that the 1986 Act does not contemplate, as the Judge thought, joint penalties even though there has been a joint

---

15 Section 71(6).
16 Compare section 28 of the Theft Act 1968, ie once the benefit is obtained, the court can recover its value from the defendant's existing assets even if the actual proceeds have been disposed of.
17 Section 71(9).
18 [1989] 2 All ER 948, [1989] 1 WLR 765.
19 [1990] 3 All ER 784, [1990] 1 WLR 1260, CA.

venture. There must be certainty in sentencing. A convicted person is entitled to know the extent of his monetary liability; a fortiori when he is liable to lose his liberty if he fails to discharge a monetary penalty.

It appears to us that, in assessing benefit in accordance with the provisions of the 1986 Act, the court must, as between co-defendants, determine their respective shares of any joint benefit that they may have received as a result of drug-trafficking. In the absence of any evidence, whether from the co-defendants or elsewhere, a court is entitled to assume that they were sharing equally. Then, when it comes to arriving at the amount of the confiscation order pursuant to section 4 of the Act, section 4(3) makes it quite clear that, if the means of the co-defendants differ, then the amount of the confiscation order can be tailored to those means.'

Each defendant is, accordingly, treated separately: *his* benefit is assessed and *his* means are considered in order to establish the amount of *his* order. A defendant should not have his order increased because of the inability of another defendant to meet an order. Where, however, only one defendant has been convicted (and the other has, for example, escaped – as in *R v Chrastny (No 2)*,[20] and the convicted defendant has benefited to the same degree from the offence and has sufficient control to realise the property, an order in the total sum may be made.[1]

6.3.4   What is 'realisable property'?

Complex provisions are contained in section 74 for determining what property is 'realisable' for the purposes of determining the amount of an order and of enforcing it. The concept is important for determining the amount that may be realised, how the order may be enforced, and what property may be restrained.

'Realisable property' includes any property held by the defendant[2] and any property held by a person to whom the defendant has directly or indirectly made 'a gift caught by the Act'.[3] For these purposes, a gift is made if the defendant transfers property to another person directly or indirectly for a consideration the value for which is significantly less than the value of the consideration provided by the defendant.[4] The gift is caught by the Act if it was made by the defendant at any time after the commission of the offence or the earliest offence to which the proceedings relate and the court considers it appropriate in all the circumstances to take the gift into account.[5] This contrasts sharply with the analogous provisions of the Drug Trafficking Offences Act 1986 under which all gifts are treated as proceeds, leaving the court with no discretion to determine whether it is appropriate to take the gift into account.[6]

---

20   [1992] 1 All ER 193, [1991] 1 WLR 1385, CA; see also *R v Viner* (25 May 1990, unreported), CA.
1   [1992] 1 All ER at 201.
2   Subject to certain exceptions relating to deprivation and forfeiture orders: see section 74(2). Property is held by the defendant (or any other person) if he holds any interest in it: section 102(7).
3   Section 74(1)(b).
4   Section 74(12)(b).
5   Section 74(10).
6   Section 5(1)(b) of the Drug Trafficking Offences Act 1986.

6.3.5 What is 'value'?

Value, for the purposes of ascertaining the defendant's benefit, means 'market value'.[7] Where any other person holds an interest in the property, the amount that might be realised is the market value of the defendant's (or in the case of a gift caught by the Act, the donee's beneficial interest less the amount required to discharge any incumbrance (other than a charging order) on that interest).[8]

A third party does not have a right to make representations as to the interest held as between him and the defendant. The situation may arise where the Crown Court has to determine the interest a defendant holds in freehold property, the legal ownership of, and part of the equity in which, is shared between him and a non-defendant.[9] The non-defendant will only become involved if, in order to enforce the confiscation order, a receiver is appointed by the High Court under section 80, in which case section 80(8) provides an opportunity for 'persons holding any interest in the property to make representations to the court'.

Similarly, if a defendant owns a house which is subject to a mortgage, the defendant's interest is the equity he holds in it, and value for the purposes of section 5(3) of the Drug Trafficking Act 1986[10] is the market value less the amount required to discharge the mortgage.[11]

6.3.6 When is value determined?

Value is determined at the time the confiscation order is made. For times of rampant inflation or deflation, or of rapid increase or decrease in the value of property, provision is made for adjusting the value of the benefit accordingly. The value of any property obtained by the defendant (or donee) as a result of, or in connection with the commission of an offence may be adjusted to take account of subsequent changes in the value of money. Where the defendant (or donee) holds property (not being cash) which he obtained as a result of or in connection with the offence, or property which in whole or in part directly or indirectly represents in his hands the property which he obtained, the appropriate value is the market value at the time of making the order.[12]

A similar provision applies for the valuation of gifts, so that changes in the value of money or of the property received by the donee will be taken into account.[13]

In determining the value of an asset, the court must act on accurate and up-to-date information. In *R v Lemmon*,[14] the court assessed the defendant's benefit from drug trafficking at £5,535 and made a confiscation order in that sum, having concluded that the defendant's equity in his house was sufficient to enable him to meet the order. A subsequent valuation had shown that the

---

7 Section 74(4)(b).
8 Section 74(4)(a)(ii).
9 See, for example, *R v Robson* [1991] Crim LR 222.
10 Equivalent to section 74(3) of the 1988 Act.
11 *R v MacDonald* (1990) 12 Cr App Rep (S) 457. This is a straightforward application, in effect, of section 74(4).
12 Section 74(5) and (6).
13 Section 74(7) and (8).
14 (1992) 13 Cr App Rep (S) 66, CA.

defendant's equity was no more than £245. The Court of Appeal quashed the confiscation order saying:

> 'It is obvious that a court must be provided with accurate contemporary information if a fair order is to be made. If a confiscation order is based upon an erroneous and over-optimistic valuation, then injustice and hardship are likely to result. A court must also have in mind that estimation of the values of real property is not a wholly precise science and that some safety margin for possible error must be allowed.'

6.3.7   Procedure

(a) *Notice by the prosecutor*   A confiscation order may only be made when the prosecutor has given written notice to the court that it appears to him that, were the court to consider that it ought to make an order, it would be able to make an order requiring the offender to pay at least the minimum amount.[15] There was concern expressed in Parliament over the discretion this provision conferred on the prosecutor in sentencing matters, but the wording makes it clear that the decision to make an order rests entirely with the court and that the prosecution are indicating that – presumably after making inquiries – there are sufficient available assets to give the court jurisdiction to make an order if it considers it appropriate.

(b) *When should the notice be served?*   Confiscation will be considered after conviction, but before sentencing or otherwise dealing with the offender.[16] The Act is silent as to when the prosecution may serve its notice on the court, though it would be tempting fate for the prosecution to serve it before conviction. More importantly, there is no provision entitling defendants to know in advance that a notice will be served on the court or the contents of any such notice, though if a restraint or charging order has been made they will know the prosecutor's intention. Where a defendant is seriously inconvenienced by receiving late notice or where the prosecution are not yet ready to consider benefit, the court may adjourn and frequently does so, though it may not sentence the defendant before determining whether to make such an order.[17] This has, in some cases, led to serious delay between the date of the conviction and the date of sentence and the making of the confiscation order. In a case where the defendant has been remanded in custody, it may operate to delay his entitlement to release on licence.[18]

(c) *The court determines whether it ought to make an order*   In considering whether to make a confiscation order, the court may take into account any information that has been placed before it showing that a victim has instituted or intends to institute civil proceedings in respect of loss, injury or damage sustained in connection with the offence.[19] No provision is made, however, for a case where civil proceedings are commenced after an order has been made

15 Section 72(1) and (2). This distinguishes the procedure immediately from the provisions of the Drug Trafficking Offences Act 1986 under which the court is obliged, where a person appears before it for a drug trafficking offence, to determine the benefits obtained by the defendant from trafficking.
16 Section 72(4).
17 Section 72(3).
18 See Commentary on *R v Robson* [1991] Crim LR 222.
19 Section 72(4).

and satisfied. The clear purpose is to prevent the defendant from having the benefit taken from him twice over. Many offences, however, will not have a victim, though the defendant will have benefited. These include particularly offences against the Obscene Publications Acts 1959–64 and the offences listed in Schedule 4 to the Criminal Justice Act 1988. In other cases, the victim's loss and the defendant's benefit will not necessarily coincide, and it seems implicit that the court considering a confiscation order will take into account not only the fact of civil proceedings but the amount of the claim.[20]

(d) *Section 73 statements*   The Criminal Justice Act 1988 follows the pattern of the Drug Trafficking Offences Act 1986 in providing for the exchange of statements, but stops short of presuming that all the defendant's assets are proceeds. Section 73(1) enables the prosecution to tender to the court a statement as to any matters relevant:

(i)   to determining whether the defendant has benefited from the offence or any other offence to which the confiscation provisions apply of which the defendant is convicted in the same proceedings or which is taken into consideration;
(ii) to an assessment of the value of the defendant's benefit.

If the defendant accepts the statement to any extent, the court may treat his acceptance as conclusive of the matters to the extent to which it relates.

The provisions of section 73(2) and (3) exert pressure on a defendant to make some response to a prosecution statement. Where the prosecution serve a statement and the court is satisfied that a copy has been served on the defendant, it may require the defendant to indicate to what extent he accepts each allegation in the statement and, so far as he does not accept any allegation, to indicate any matters he proposes to rely on. Failure in any respect to comply with such a requirement entitles the court to treat the defendant as accepting every allegation apart from any allegation in the statement and, so far as he does not accept any allegation, to indicate any matters he proposes to rely on. Failure in any respect to comply with such a requirement entitles the court to treat the defendant as accepting every allegation apart from any allegation in respect of which he has complied with the requirement and any allegation that he has benefited or that property was obtained as a result of or in connection with an offence.

A similar procedure enables the defendant to serve a statement as to any matters relevant to determining the amount that might be realised at the time the confiscation order is made. If the prosecution accepts to any extent the allegation in the statement, the court may, for the purposes of determining such amount, treat the acceptance by the prosecution as conclusive of the matters to which it relates.

Rule 25AA of the Crown Court Rules 1982[1] provides that statements served pursuant to section 73 must be served within such time as the court may require and should include:

(a) the name of the defendant and the indictment number;
(b) the name of the person by whom the statement is tendered and, if different, the name of the person by whom it was made;

---

20 See section 6.3.9 below for relationship between confiscation orders and other orders.
1   As amended by the Crown Court (Amendment) Rules 1989, SI 1989/299.

(c) the date on which, and the place where, the conviction for the offence occurred;

(d) the facts relied on in support of any allegation or matter indicated.

(e) *Hearing evidence*   Where there is a dispute between the prosecution and the defendant as to the fact of, or amount of, benefit, the court must hear evidence before it determines whether an order should be made, and if so, its terms. In *R v Dickens*,[2] the Court of Appeal gave guidance on how such hearings should be conducted. Although the case involved the Drug Trafficking Act regime, the principles seem applicable to cases under Part VI of the Criminal Justice Act 1988.[3] Lord Lane CJ said:[4]

'The prosecution have the task of proving both the fact that the defendant has benefited from drug trafficking and the amount of such benefit. In our judgment the context of the Act and the nature of the penalties which are likely to be imposed make it clear that the standard of proof required is the criminal standard, namely proof so that the judge feels sure or proof beyond reasonable doubt.'[5]

Lord Lane indicated that the judge could take into account evidence heard at the trial as well as any evidence presented by the parties after conviction:[6]

'The evidence on which the judgment is based will come in part from the trial, if there has been one, in part from the statements tendered by the parties to the court under section 3 of the Act (which we shall later deal with in this judgment) and in part from evidence adduced before the court.'

This places, as Lord Lane described it, a heavy burden on the prosecution which, in the context of a drug trafficking case, was considerably lightened by the assumptions contained in section 2 of the 1986 Act. Those assumptions are not, however, incorporated into the 1988 Act scheme.[7] He continued:

'We now turn to the hearing. This, in a complicated case is likely to be protracted and difficult. However, section 3 of the 1986 Act[8] goes a little way to simplifying proceedings and crystallising the issues. It provides that the prosecution may tender a statement dealing with any matter relevant to either of the first two issues,[9] and also provides, no doubt by way of clarification, that, if the defendant accepts any of those facts, that acceptance may be treated as conclusive. By section 3(4)[10] a similar provision is made with regard to any statement tendered by the defendant relating to the amount which might be realised at the time the confiscation order is made.

Section 3(2)[11] imposes restrictions on the defendant when he has been served with a copy of the prosecution's section 3(1) notice, because the court may then require him to indicate to what extent he accepts the prosecution allegation and, if he does not, to indicate any matter he proposes to rely on.

2 [1990] 2 QB 102, [1990] 2 All ER 626.
3 There was a delay of over three months between conviction and sentence, and confiscation took up two full days' hearing.
4 Op cit at 629c.
5 See also *R v Enwezor* [1991] Crim LR 483, CA; *R v Redbourne* (1992) Times, 26 June.
6 Op cit at 629d.
7 Under the 1986 scheme, the assumptions can be displaced if they are 'shown to be incorrect in the defendant's case'. The burden of displacing the presumptions rests on the defendant on the balance of probabilities.
8 Equivalent to section 73 of the 1988 Act.
9 Ie whether the defendant has benefited and, if so, by how much.
10 Equivalent to section 73(4) of the 1988 Act.
11 Equivalent to section 73(2) of the 1988 Act.

That will have the effect, one hopes, of containing the ambit of the inquiry. Section 3(3) imposes sanctions on him if he fails to comply with a requirement under section 3(2).

It is clear from these provisions that, where the prosecution statement is not accepted by the defendant, the prosecution, if they wish to rely on any of its contents, must adduce evidence to establish them.'

The statements are, therefore, rather like pleadings in a civil action. They do not form evidence in themselves, but in so far as any part of them is admitted by the other party, they may be treated as conclusive by the court. Where not so admitted, evidence must be called to substantiate them.[12]

That evidence may come from the trial itself, or be adduced when the court is considering confiscation. It would seem right in principle that the strict rules of evidence should apply. In *R v Chrastny (No 2)*,[13] the defendant was convicted of conspiracy to supply controlled drugs. Her husband, the only co-defendant,[14] had escaped before trial. In the confiscation proceedings against the defendant, the prosecution adduced notebook jottings by her husband which the prosecution contended listed sales of drugs with dates and amounts of sale prices. The document was unintelligible by itself but the husband allegedly had, in interview under caution, admitted that it was a record of sales, quantities and prices. The Crown conceded that the statement under caution and the explanation of the jottings was inadmissible against the defendant both at the trial and in the confiscation proceedings. The Crown contended, however, that as the list itself was evidence against the defendant in the conspiracy trial because of the special rules applying to evidence in conspiracies, it was therefore admissible in relation to confiscation, even though it would not have been admissible if the prosecution had been for an offence other than conspiracy. The Court of Appeal did not find it necessary to decide the issue, but expressed doubt as to whether such evidence would be admissible.

In *Dickens*, Lord Lane concluded:

'Where [the court] is satisfied that the amount that might be realised is less than the value of the proceeds of drug trafficking, the court has then to carry out a further exercise to determine what "the amount appearing to the court to be the amount that might be realised" is.[15] If the amount is less than the proceeds of drug trafficking as found, the confiscation order will be for such lower sum.'

In this context it would appear that the burden is on the defendant to show that the amount that might be realised is less than the value of the proceeds.[16] It is unclear whether this is an evidential burden, requiring the prosecution to prove to a criminal standard that the defendant's assets are not less than the benefit or not less than the prosecution's assessment of them, or whether the burden of proving that his assets are less shifts to the defendant on a balance of probabilities.[17]

---

12 Where a defendant pleads guilty but contests confiscation, the court should not reduce the discount on sentence that his plea of guilty has achieved: *R v Nicholson* (1990) 12 Cr App Rep (S) 58.

13 [1992] 1 All ER 193, [1991] 1 WLR 1385, CA.

14 She was, none the less, guilty of conspiracy because there were other parties to the conspiracy: see *R v Chrastny* [1992] 1 All ER 189, [1991] 1 WLR 1381, CA.

15 Section 71(6)(b).

16 *R v Isemann* [1991] Crim LR 141; *R v Comiskey* [1991] Crim LR 484.

17 See commentary to *R v Comiskey* at [1991] Crim LR 485.

6.3.8   *Appeal*

In *R v Johnson*,[18] the Court of Appeal held that a confiscation order made under the Drug Trafficking Offences Act 1986 forms part of the sentence and may be the subject of an appeal against sentence. The court reached this conclusion notwithstanding that section 1(4) of the Act[19] provides that the confiscation order should be considered and made 'before sentencing or otherwise dealing with the defendant' and that section 1(5)(c)[20] provides that the order shall be left out of account 'in determining the appropriate sentence or other manner of dealing with him'. The court reasoned that various provisions of the Act imply that there is a right of appeal,[1] that the Court of Appeal had jurisdiction to make confiscation orders,[2] and that the order fell within the description of sentence in *R v Hayden*.[3] There, Lord Widgery CJ, held that an order to pay costs came within the definition of 'sentence' for the purposes of section 50(1) of the Criminal Appeal Act 1968. He said:

> 'First of all it is an order. It is not a recommendation but an order, and furthermore it is an order which is contingent on there having been a conviction and it is contingent on the person by whom the payment is to be made, having been convicted in that way.'

The reasoning is equally applicable to Part VI confiscation orders though no case has yet so decided.[4]

6.3.9   *Relationship with other orders*

Confiscation orders are additional to any other sentence.[5] The court considers whether it should make an order and, if so, makes the order before sentencing or otherwise dealing with the offender.[6] The court should not take account of the fact that a confiscation order has been made in determining the appropriate sentence except before:

(a) imposing a fine;
(b) making any order involving payment by the defendant (other than a compensation order);
(c) making a forfeiture order under section 27 of the Misuse of Drugs Act 1971 or a deprivation order under section 43 of the Powers of the Criminal Courts Act 1973.[7]

---

18 [1991] 2 QB 249, [1991] 2 All ER 428.
19 Equivalent to section 72(4) of the 1988 Act.
20 Equivalent to section 72(5).
1   Sections 11(1)(b) and 38(13); equivalent to sections 80(1)(b) and 102(13) of the 1988 Act respectively.
2   Section 6(6); equivalent to section 75(6) of the 1988 Act.
3   [1975] 2 All ER 558, [1975] 1 WLR 852.
4   It should be noted that the Crown Court may vary its sentence within 28 days under section 47 of the Supreme Court Act 1981. In *R v Miller* [1991] Crim LR 311 the court determined that the defendant had benefited from drug trafficking but had also determined that the amount that might be realised was nil. However, in a search of the defendant's premises within the 28-day period, £630 was found. The Court of Appeal upheld the Crown Court's decision to vary its order and confiscate the cash under the provisions of the Act.
5   Section 71(1).
6   Section 72(4).
7   Section 72(5).

The court should not take account of the confiscation order before making a compensation order; where both a compensation order and a confiscation order are made and it appears to the court that the defendant will not have sufficient means to satisfy both orders in full, the court must direct that so much of the compensation as will not in its opinion be recoverable because of insufficiency of the defendant's means, shall be paid out of any sums recovered under the confiscation order.[8]

In addition to the statutory direction, the courts have provided guidance as to how confiscation orders should be combined with other, and in particular financial, penalties in the context of the drugs trafficking legislation. The principles are applicable in 1988 Act cases. In *R v Hedley*,[9] the Court of Appeal quashed a fine which had been imposed on a defendant who had been convicted of possession of cannabis with intent to supply and who had also been both imprisoned and made the subject of a confiscation order. The prison sentence had not been reduced to take account of the fine, and the confiscation order deprived the defendant of the benefits. There was no basis upon which a fine could be justified.

In *R v Makarijnola*,[10] the trial judge, having conducted an inquiry under the Drugs Trafficking Act and having concluded that the defendant had not benefited from the offence, imposed a three-year prison sentence and a fine of £1,000. The Court of Appeal quashed the fine.

A defendant should not be ordered to pay the costs of the prosecution unless he has the means to do so after taking account of what is to be paid under the confiscation order.[11]

6.3.10 Enforcement

(a) *Enforcement as a fine*   A confiscation order may be enforced in the same way as a fine.[12] The court, at the time of making the order, should specify a term of imprisonment which the defendant will undergo if the order is not satisfied.[13] Enforcement is the responsibility of the magistrates' court which either made the order or committed the defendant for trial, or which is specified by the Crown Court.[14]

If the enforcing court commits a defendant to imprisonment in default for non-payment of a confiscation order, the term to be served in default does not begin to run until the end of any term of imprisonment imposed in respect of the offence.[15]

Before deciding to issue a warrant of commitment in a case where a confiscation order has been made, the court must have regard to the following factors:[16]

(1) the object of a confiscation order is to divest the defaulter of money or other realisable assets;

---

8   Section 75(7).
9   (1989) 11 Cr App Rep (S) 298.
10   (1991) 12 Cr App Rep (S) 643.
11   *R v Hopes* (1989) 11 Cr App Rep (S) 38, CA.
12   Section 75(1) and (2).
13   Section 31 of the Powers of Criminal Courts Act 1973.
14   Section 32 of the Powers of Criminal Courts Act 1973.
15   Section 75(3).
16   *R v Harrow Justices, ex p DPP* [1991] 3 All ER 873, [1991] 1 WLR 395.

(2) it is not a matter of choice for the defaulter to buy his way out of such an order by serving the term of imprisonment imposed in default of responding to the order of confiscation;[17]

(3) the mere fact of a confiscation order is evidence that at the date it was made there were realisable assets available to meet the requirements of the order;

(4) even if at the date when justices have to consider the question of enforcement the value of realisable assets is less than it was at the date of the confiscation order, it is open to the defaulter to apply for a certificate of inadequacy under section 83 of the Act, which will lead to a reduction in the amount of the original order;

(5) the inter partes nature of the procedure leading to the making of a confiscation order means that the prosecution is likely to have information available which is relevant to the granting of a warrant of commitment; the prosecution has a legitimate interest in being heard before the justices come to any decision.

(b) *Given the purposes of the 1988 Act, it is incumbent on magistrates to consider all methods of enforcement short of issuing a warrant before doing so*[18]   Problems have arisen in the enforcement of order and, to ensure co-ordination between the enforcing authorities, the Home Office has issued guidance in Circulars 98/1986 and 10/1988.

(c) *Special provisions relating to confiscation orders*   In addition to the usual means of enforcing a fine, the Act contains provisions enabling the prosecutor to secure enforcement against property held by the defendant (or a donee). The High Court may make a restraint or charging order[19] at any time before the proceedings are concluded.[20] For these purposes, proceedings are concluded when there is no further possibility of a confiscation order being made in the proceedings or on the satisfaction of a confiscation order,[1] and restraint orders may accordingly be used not only to preserve assets pending the making of a confiscation order, but also to enforce it.

Further, and the usual accompaniment to a restraint order made after sentence, the High Court may appoint a receiver in respect of realisable property.[2] The receiver may be empowered:

(a) to enforce any charge imposed under section 78 on realisable property or on interest and dividends relating to such property;[3] and

(b) to take possession of realisable property which is not subject to a charging order.[4] In this case, the court may also order any person having possession of realisable property to give possession of it to the receiver and may order any person holding an interest in realisable property or the recipient of a gift caught by the Act to make a payment to the receiver in respect of any

---

17 *R v Clacton Justices, ex p Customs and Excise Comrs* (1987) 152 JP 129.
18 These comments were made in the context of a Drug Trafficking Act case, but seem applicable in principle to 1988 Act cases.
19 See further section 7.2 below.
20 Sections 77 and 78.
1 Section 102(12).
2 Section 80(1) and (2).
3 Section 80(3)(a).
4 Section 80(3)(b).

beneficial interest held by the defendant.[5] The court may empower the receiver to realise any property in such manner as the court may direct.[6]

Proceeds from the realisation of realisable property are applied to satisfy the confiscation order and any expenses of the receiver and any other sum as the court may direct.[7]

7 INTERIM RELIEF

7.1 General

The Criminal Justice Act 1988 provides two means of ensuring that property held by the defendant and others is preserved pending the making or satisfaction of a confiscation order. These are the restraint order under section 77, which prohibits any dealing in realisable property, and the charging order under section 78, which secures for the Crown an amount equal to the value of the property charged or, where a confiscation order has been made, an amount not exceeding the amount payable under the confiscation order.

The need for interim relief in criminal cases was advocated in the Hodgson Committee Report[8] and is also found, in very similar form, in the Drug Trafficking Offences Act 1986. It is similar to Mareva relief in concept and in the way it is obtained, though it avoids the difficulties encountered in trying to adapt the Mareva from a civil to a criminal context.[9] The court no longer has to search for a cause of action, or to find a basis upon which a police authority has locus to make an application, and may make an order purely for the purpose of preserving assets pending an order under Part VI.[10]

Applications are made to the High Court, and have been described as civil in character. There is with a right of appeal to the Court of Appeal (Civil Division).[11]

7.2 When may restraint or charging orders be made?

Jurisdiction to make a restraint or charging order arises where:

(a) proceedings have been instituted in England and Wales against the defendant for an indictable offence or an offence listed in Schedule 4 to the Act;
(b) the proceedings have not been concluded as defined in section 102(12); and
(c) either a confiscation order has been made, or it appears to the court that there are reasonable grounds for thinking that a confiscation order may be made.[12]

---

5 Section 80(5).
6 Section 80(4).
7 Section 81(1).
8 Op cit.
9 See section 6.2, 'Mareva relief and its limitations'.
10 In so far as the Mareva jurisdiction is available to confiscate the benefits of a crime.
11 *Re O* [1991] 2 QB 520, [1991] 1 All ER 330 per Lord Donaldson MR. This was an appeal in relation to an order made under Part VI of the Criminal Justice Act 1988, but Lord Donaldson thought the principle was equally applicable to restraint orders made under the Drug Trafficking Offences Act 1986. See also *Re Peters* [1988] QB 871, [1988] 3 All ER 46, CA.
12 Section 76(1).

As with Mareva relief, the powers are also exercisable before the institution of proceedings provided that the court is satisfied that, whether by the laying of an information or otherwise, a person 'is to be charged' with an offence and it appears to the court that a confiscation order may be made in those proceedings.[13] However, in contrast to Mareva relief, the prosecutor does not have to show a substantial risk that assets will be dissipated if the relief is not granted.

The implication of the words 'is to be charged' is that there must be a settled intention to proceed and it would be an abuse of process to apply for the relief to preserve assets pending a decision as to charge.[14] If proceedings are not instituted within such time as the court considers reasonable, the order must be discharged.

The powers may be exercised not only to preserve assets pending the making of a confiscation order, but – as with Mareva relief[15] – also as an aid to the enforcement of confiscation order after it has been made.[16]

7.3   Restraint orders

7.3.1   Who may apply?

The High Court may make a restraint order prohibiting any person from dealing with any realisable property.[17] The order may only be made on the application of a prosecutor,[18] which is defined as the person who the High Court is satisfied is to have the conduct of the proposed proceedings.[19] Applications are not limited to the Crown Prosecution Service or the Serious Fraud Office, and may be made by any prosecutor including a private prosecutor. The order may be made on an ex parte application to a judge in chambers,[20] though there is no objection in appropriate circumstances to an inter partes hearing.[1]

7.3.2   To which property may the order attach?

Any realisable property held by any specified person may be restrained.[2] The Act clearly envisages an order being directed to a third party, perhaps the alleged donee of a gift caught by the Act, or an innocent custodian of the property. However, by section 102(7), property is held by any person if he holds any interest in it. It would appear, therefore, that once a defendant has an interest in the property, both he, and any innocent third party who also holds an interest in the property, can be restrained from dealing with it.[3] The order is not limited to property which is the actual benefit or proceed of the

---

13 Section 76(2).
14 By analogy with *R v Brentwood Justices, ex p Wong* [1981] QB 445, [1981] 1 All ER 884.
15 *Orwell Steel (Erection and Fabrication) Ltd v Asphalt and Tarmac (UK) Ltd* [1985] 3 All ER 747.
16 Section 76(1)(a) and (b).
17 Section 77. In 1991, 241 restraint orders were made.
18 Section 77(5)(a).
19 Section 76(3)(b).
20 Section 77(5)(b).
1   See further section 7.5.2 below per Otton J in *Re R* [1990] 2 QB 307, [1990] 2 All ER 569.
2   Section 77(3)(a).
3   See further section 7.3.5 'Third-party interests'.

crime but extends to any property held by the defendant (or alleged donee) at the time the order is made. The powers under the Act must, however, be exercised with a view to allowing any person other than the defendant or the recipient of a gift to retain or recover the value of any property held by him.[4]

The order may extend to property transferred in the future to the person specified in the order[5] and may be made in respect of property wherever situated.[6]

7.3.3 Effect of the order

The effect of the order will depend on its precise terms. Invariably, dealing with the property will be prohibited. There is no definition of dealing in the Act but it plainly includes disposing of all or any interest in the property and destroying it. Section 77(9) provides, additionally, that dealing with property held by any person includes:

(a) where a debt is owed to that person, making a payment to any person in reduction of the amount of the debt; and
(b) removing the property from Great Britain.

A police officer or Customs officer may, where the High Court has made a restraint order, for the purpose of preventing any realisable property being removed from Great Britain, seize the property.[7]

Where the court has made a restraint order it has power at any time to appoint a receiver to take possession of any realisable property and manage it in accordance with the court's directions.[8]

7.3.4 Disclosure orders

In making a restraint order, the court has an ancillary power to require a defendant to disclose his assets and income, which it frequently exercises, in order to render the restraint order effective. In *Re O*,[9] a restraint order was made against the appellants. Four months later, a further order was made requiring the appellants to swear affidavits disclosing the full value and giving personal particulars of any salary, money, goods or other real and personal assets held by them. Although the Criminal Justice Act 1988 contains no provision expressly allowing the High Court to make such an order, the Court of Appeal held that various features of the legislation dictated that there should be some means of identifying and ascertaining the whereabouts and the value of assets affected by the restraint order.

In so holding, the court had to consider the impact of disclosure orders on the common law rule against self-incrimination. Lord Donaldson MR said:

'I cannot construe section 77, or any other relevant provision of the Criminal Justice Act 1988, as abrogating the common law rule against self-incrimination. It follows that the appellants would be entitled to refuse to

---

4 Section 82(3).
5 Section 77(3)(b).
6 Section 102(3).
7 Sections 77(10) and 102(1).
8 Section 77(8).
9 [1991] 2 QB 520, [1991] 1 All ER 330, CA.

comply with the disclosure order made in this case, if and in so far as to do so might tend to incriminate them. This would or might frustrate the purpose of the order and, if there were no way round the problem, might suggest that Parliament had impliedly varied the common law rule. There is, however, a way round, namely, to impose conditions on the use which may be made of the affidavits sworn in compliance with the order. An appropriate condition, which should be inserted in all orders for disclosure in aid of a restraint order, would read:

> "No disclosure made in compliance with this order shall be used as evidence in the prosecution of an offence alleged to have been committed by the person required to make that disclosure or by any spouse of that person.'"

It should accordingly be the practice to include such a condition in the disclosure order.[10] The court rejected the argument that the discretion of the trial judge to exclude evidence would adequately protect persons who made disclosure.

This position is consistent with that in SFO cases. The SFO can, and frequently does, use its powers under section 2 to trace assets; any disclosure, however, would be subject to the limitation on its use contained in section 2(8).[11]

7.3.5 Third-party interests

Frequently third parties will have an interest in the same property as a defendant. Both the confiscation and restraint provisions leave untouched the interests of third parties (subject to the provisions as to gifts), but the property in which those interests subsist is still capable of being the subject matter of a restraint order.[12] Section 82(4) of the Act, however, requires the powers to be exercised 'with a view to allowing any person other than the defendant or the recipient of any such gift to retain or recover the value of any property held by him.' Section 77(7), also, permits any person affected by a restraint order to apply for its discharge or variation. The court must endeavour to balance the interests of the prosecution in preserving assets for the purpose of meeting confiscation orders and the rights of owners of other interests in the same property. It has, for example, been suggested that it is preferable in cases where several people hold an interest in the same asset, to make a charging order over the defendant's interest in the asset rather than to impose a restraint order over the asset itself.[13]

In *Re K*[14] the court had to consider the right of a bank to set off monies held in an account which was subject to a restraint order against liabilities owed to the bank on accounts held by the same account-holder. Otton J held that to exercise a right, contractual or otherwise, to set off one account against another of the same customer in order to determine the total state of

---

10 The court considered it preferable to impose a condition rather than seek an undertaking; see also *Re Thomas* (1992) Independent, 26 May.

11 See also section 72 of the Supreme Court Act 1981 which protects information disclosed in intellectual property and passing off disputes from being adduced in evidence in criminal proceedings connected with the breach of intellectual property rights. See also *Rank Film Distributors Ltd v Video Information Centre* [1982] AC 380.

12 *Re Peters* [1988] 3 All ER 46 per Lord Donaldson MR at 51a.

13 See D Feldman *Confiscation Orders – the New Law* (Butterworths, 1988).

14 [1990] 2 QB 298, [1990] 2 All ER 562.

indebtedness between customer and bank did not amount to a disposal or diminution of assets – it merely determined what those assets were. Otton J added:[15]

'Finally, if the Crown is right then the rights of the bank would be severely and fundamentally undermined by the 1986 Act. The statute would have the effect of depriving a third party who had acted in good faith and in ignorance of the tainted source of the deposited money of its right to combine or set-off the indebtedness against the credit balance. In other words, the bank's property, be it money or close in action, would become the subject of the restraint order and the vested rights of the bank would be in peril. There is a presumption that a statute does not alter vested rights.'

He continued:

'I can find nothing, even in the most draconian provisions, which provides expressly or by implication that the bank's vested rights are extinguished or diminished.'

Reliance was, again, placed on section 5(4) of the 1986 Act[16] to show that the Act left untouched, both for the purposes of restraint and confiscation orders, the interests of third parties and Otton J said that such interests could be asserted even after a restraint order is made without resort to the court. He suggested however it would, none the less, be prudent to apply to the court for a variation for the avoidance of doubt and when no assurance had been given by the CPS that any point adverse to them would not be taken.

Similarly, a restraint order does not prevent a third-party landlord from exercising a right of forfeiture over a lease held by, nor of distraining on goods held at premises occupied by, an alleged drug trafficker, though the prudent course is to apply to the court in any case of doubt for a variation of the restraint order.[17]

A restraint order will not be varied, however, at the application of a bona fide third-party creditor to allow payment of a judgment debt.[18]

7.3.6 *Living expenses, legal costs and other expenses*

Section 77(2) empowers the court to make such provision as it thinks fit for living expenses and legal expenses. As in the exercise of the Mareva jurisdiction, the court must strike a balance between the need to preserve assets to satisfy a confiscation order, to prevent a convicted person from using the profits of his crime and of recognising the reasonable needs of an unconvicted person who might be acquitted.[19]

In *Re Peters*,[20] this was held to include on-going costs such as for the defendant's maintenance and his legal costs, but it did not extend to the 'anticipatory discharge of liabilities which could be expected to arise only after Mr Peters had either been acquitted or convicted'. It was open to the defendant, accordingly, to continue to pay for the termly costs of his son's

15 [1990] 2 All ER 562 at 568.
16 Equivalent to section 74(4).
17 *Re R* [1990] 2 QB 307, [1990] 2 All ER 569. The same principle will apply to restraint orders under the 1988 Act.
18 *Re W* (1990) Times, 15 November, per Buckley J.
19 *Re Peters* [1988] QB 871, [1988] 3 All ER 46, CA.
20 Op cit.

education, so that the education was not interrupted, but he could not make a capital payment to his son for future school fees.

Legal costs include those needed to enable a defendant to proceed with an appeal against his conviction, and may be met from the restrained funds even though the defendant would otherwise qualify for legal aid.[1]

Once a confiscation order has been made, no exemption for living expenses applies and no account is to be taken of any obligations of the defendant which conflict with the obligation to satisfy the confiscation order.[2]

7.4   Charging orders

A charging order may be made on realisable property for securing the payment to the Crown of an amount not exceeding the amount payable under a confiscation order or, where a confiscation order has not been made, of an amount equal to the value from time to time of the property charged.[3] The charge may only be imposed on:

(a) any beneficial interest held by the defendant, or by a person to whom the defendant has directly or indirectly made a gift caught by the Act, under any trust or in:

   (i) land in England and Wales;
   (ii) securities in:
     – government stock
     – stock of any body (other than a building society) incorporated in England and Wales;
     – stock of any body incorporated outside England and Wales but which is registered in England and Wales;
     – units of any unit trust in respect of which a register of the unit holders is kept within England and Wales;

(b) any interest in realisable property held by a person as trustee of a trust if the interest is in such an asset or is an interest under another trust and a charge may be imposed by virtue of paragraph (a) above by a charging order on the whole beneficial interest under the first mentioned trust.

In principle it seems that disclosure orders should also be available on an application for a charging order so that the property to be charged can be identified.

7.5   Procedure

7.5.1   *Applications must be made to the High Court*

Restraint orders and charging orders are made in the High Court.[4] They are collateral to the confiscation procedure in sections 71–75 of the Act but are

---

1   *Customs and Excise Comrs v Norris* [1991] 2 QB 293, [1991] 2 All ER 395, CA.
2   See per Lord Donaldson MR in *Re Peters* op cit at 51b.
3   Section 78(1).
4   Section 76(1); save for matters relating to the registration of external confiscation orders, proceedings are assigned to a judge of the Queen's Bench Division or the Chancery Division in Chambers.

civil in character[5] and orders cannot be made or varied or subjected to further conditions by the Crown Court.[6]

7.5.2 Ex parte hearing and notice to interested parties

The application for a restraint or charging order may only be made by a prosecutor[7] and may be made ex parte to a judge in chambers.[8] Once made, the order must provide for notice to be given to persons affected by it. This includes innocent third parties. In *Re R*,[9] a case in which landlords had been notified of the existence of a restraint order in a drug trafficking case over the assets of their tenant held at premises leased from the landlords and against which the landlords had sought to distrain for arrears of rent, Otton J said:

> 'It is true that section 8(4)(c) does provide for notice to be given to interested parties. It is unfortunate, and indeed regrettable, that the landlords here were not so informed. I can well understand the need for speed to freeze the assets and to ensure that the proceeds of the drug trafficking offences are not dissipated or enjoyed by the defendants. There is also an understandable desire not to disclose to too many persons either that an order is being sought or that it has been granted.
>
> However, after the order has been obtained, it is, in my view, incumbent on the commissioners, or any other body which is exercising the powers granted under the restraint procedure, to consider carefully who should be informed. There can be no suggestion in this case that the landlords were not proper persons to be informed of the existence of an order. If the Customs and Excise had thought about it they might well have decided to inform the landlords of the intended ex parte application, or preferably to serve him with a copy of the order.'

The prosecutor must, accordingly, consider whether it is appropriate to proceed ex parte, and consider upon whom the order should be served. Where the prosecutor fails to serve notice of the order on a person affected by it, it appears that that person has no remedy for costs incurred or damage sustained by reason of failure to serve the notice,[10] but no notice for contempt could be made.[11]

7.5.3 Applications made by originating motion and affidavit

Applications for a restraint or charging order are made by originating motion and must be supported by an affidavit[12] stating:

(a) the grounds for believing that the defendant has benefited from an offence to which Part VI of the Criminal Justice Act 1988 applies;

---

5 *Re O* [1991] 1 All ER 330 per Lord Donaldson MR at 334d.
6 *Re K* [1991] COD 18 per McCullough J.
7 See section 7.3.1 above.
8 Section 77(5)(a) and (b); section 78(3)(a) and (b).
9 *Re R* [1990] 2 QB 307, [1990] 2 All ER 569.
10 Ibid.
11 An application to commit for contempt for breach of a restraint or charging order relates to civil proceedings and should be made to a single judge and not to the Divisional Court: *Re H* (1988) Times, 1 April.
12 RSC Order 115 r 3(1) and (2).

(b) either that proceedings have been instituted against the defendant for an offence to which Part VI applies *and* that they have not been concluded, or that whether by the laying of an information or otherwise, a person is to be charged with such an offence;

(c) to the best of the deponent's ability, the full particulars of the realisable property in respect of which the order is sought and specify the person or persons holding that property;

(d) where the prosecution has not yet been instituted, that the prosecutor is to have conduct of the proposed prosecution;

(e) where proceedings have not yet been instituted, when it is intended that they should be instituted.

In common with other applications for interim ex parte relief, the affidavit may (unless the court otherwise directs) contain statements of information or belief with the sources and grounds thereof[13] and hearsay evidence is admissible.[14] There must be full and frank disclosure to the court of all material facts.[15] This does not, however, require the making of police witnesses or informers, provided the court is satisfied that the information is reliable.

7.5.4   *Undertakings as to damages*

The restraint order may be made subject to conditions and exceptions, including conditions relating to indemnifying third parties against expenses incurred in complying with the order. The prosecutor may not, however, be required to give an undertaking to abide by any order as to damages sustained by the defendant as a result of the order.[16] Section 89 provides, instead, that where proceedings do not result in a conviction, or where the defendant's conviction is quashed or he is pardoned, any person who held property which was realisable property may apply to the High Court for compensation. The court may only order compensation to be paid if it is satisfied that there has been some serious default on the part of a person concerned in the investigation or prosecution of the offence and the applicant has suffered loss in consequence of anything done in relation to the property by or in pursuance of an order.

There is little comfort, however, for innocent third parties who cannot bring themselves within section 89. In *Re R*[17] it was held that an innocent third party could not obtain redress in respect of damage caused by the making of the order. Landlords of a tenant whose assets were subject to a restraint order sought an indemnity from Customs and Excise in respect of their loss of rent and costs. Otton J held that the court had no jurisdiction either by statute or in its inherent jurisdiction to award damages, and that there was no basis for implying a cross-undertaking. It does appear to have been accepted by the prosecutor that the court has an inherent jurisdiction to compensate anybody who has suffered by the implementation of an order of the court if the order

---

13 RSC Order 115 r 3(4).

14 RSC Order 41 r 5(2) and see *Savings and Investment Bank Ltd v Gaxco Investments (Netherlands) BV* [1984] 1 All ER 296, [1984] 1 WLR 271.

15 *Re a defendant* (1987) Times, 7 April per Webster J, a case under the Drug Trafficking Offences Act 1986, where it was accepted that the duty to make full and frank disclosure did not extend to naming the police officers who had been involved in detailed surveillance of the defendant.

16 RSC Order 115 r 4(1).

17 [1990] 2 QB 307, [1990] 2 All ER 569.

had been improperly obtained.[18] No authority was cited for the proposition, which was not, in any event, commented upon by Otton J, and the only other options are an action for malicious prosecution or a tortious abuse of process.[19]

7.5.5 Discharge or variation

A restraint order or a charging order may be varied or discharged.[20] A restraint order shall be discharged where proceedings for the offence are concluded.[1] A charging order must be discharged if the proceedings are concluded or if the amount, payment of which is secured by the charge, is paid into court.[2]

An application to vary or discharge a restraint or charging order may be made by any person affected by it[3] and is made by a summons.[4] The summons and any affidavit in support must be lodged with the court and served on the prosecutor and the defendant (where he is not the applicant)[5] not less than two clear days before the date fixed for the hearing.[6]

Where the prosecutor wishes to vary or discharge a restraint or charging order or to apply for such an order over other realisable property, or to appoint a receiver, he may do so by summons, or in urgent cases, ex parte. The application must be supported by affidavit, and must be served on the defendant not less than two clear days before the day fixed for the hearing.[7]

Orders may be discharged or varied by consent. A consent order may be drawn up, signed by the parties and sent to the Crown Office. The draft is placed before a judge and, if accepted, neither a summons nor affidavits are required. This procedure is probably suitable only for the most straightforward of cases. Where a variation may have an impact on others having an interest in the property, the prudent course is to place the matter before the court.

7.6 Enforcement of restraint and charging orders

7.6.1 Restraint orders

The High Court may appoint a receiver to take possession of any realisable property and to manage or deal with it in accordance with the courts director.[8] Any person who has possession of the property may be required to give possession of it to the receiver.[9]

---

18 *Re R* op cit at 573h.
19 See Halsbury's Laws of England (4th edn) Volume 45 paragraph 1368; *Metall und Rohstoff v Donaldson Inc* [1990] 1 QB 391, [1989] 3 All ER 14; *Speed Seal Products Ltd v Paddington* [1986] 1 All ER 91, [1985] 1 WLR 1327. See further Gee *Mareva Injunctions* page 253 for a discussion of the limitations of these causes of action.
20 Sections 77(6)(a) and 78(7).
1 Section 77(6)(b) – as defined in section 102(12): RSC Order 115 rule 5(3).
2 Section 78(7); RSC Order 115 rule 5(3).
3 Sections 77(8) and 78(9).
4 RSC Order 115 rule 5(1).
5 Quaere where the defendant is making an application which may have an impact on third parties having an interest in the property.
6 RSC Order 115 rule 5(2).
7 RSC Order 115 rule 6(3).
8 Section 77(8).
9 Section 77(8).

Further, the Land Charges Act 1972 and the Land Registration Act 1925 apply to restraint orders as they apply to orders affecting land made by the court for the purpose of enforcing judgments or recognisances; and an application for a restraint order can be registered as a pending land action.[10]

7.6.2 Charging orders

The Land Charges Act 1972 and the Land Registration Act 1925 apply to charging orders made under the 1988 Act as they apply in relation to orders or writs issued or made for the purpose of enforcing judgments.

8 ENFORCEMENT OF EXTERNAL CONFISCATION ORDERS

The 1988 Act empowers Her Majesty by order in council to direct in relation to another country ('a designated country') that, subject to such modifications as may be specified, Part VI of the Act shall apply to 'external confiscation orders' and to proceedings which have been or are to be instituted in the country.[11] An external confiscation order means an order made by a court in a designated country to recover property or pecuniary advantage obtained as a result of or in connection with conduct corresponding to an offence to which Part VI of the Act applies.[12] The only order in Council so far made is the Criminal Justice Act 1988 (Designated Countries and Territories) Order 1991,[13] which has designated Italy, Nigeria and Sweden. Other foreign countries are expected to follow suit. The order contains various modifications of Part VI and, where such orders are considered, regard must be had to the terms of the Order rather than the enabling Act.[14]

9 DISQUALIFICATION UNDER THE COMPANY DIRECTORS' DISQUALIFICATION ACT 1986

Section 2 of the Company Directors' Disqualification Act 1986 enables the court to make a disqualification order against a person who is convicted of an indictable offence (whether it is tried on indictment or summarily) in connection with the promotion, formation, management or liquidation of a company, or with the receivership or management of a company's property.[15] Such an order will usually be part of the sentence of the convicting court, but the power is also given to any court having jurisdiction to wind up the company in relation to which the offence is committed.[16]

The power is not limited to offences involving the internal management of a company. In *R v Corbin*,[17] the defendant director pleaded guilty to dishonestly

---

10 Section 77(12).
11 Section 96.
12 Section 96(2).
13 SI 1991/2873.
14 There is, for example, no reference to a 'minimum amount' in the provision of this Order.
15 The maximum period of disqualification that the magistrates may impose is five years; in any other case, it is 15 years: section 2(3).
16 Section 2(2)(a).
17 (1984) 6 Cr App Rep (S) 17.

obtaining money by deception from finance companies in the course of his business and was disqualified under section 2. It was argued on appeal that the court had no jurisdiction to make the order because the fraud related to third parties and not to the company's internal management. McCowan J, upholding the order, said that the legislature, if its intention had been to limit the power in the manner argued by the appellant, could have used the expression 'in respect of the management of the company'. In *R v Austen*,[18] Mann J, upholding a ten-year disqualification in respect of a fraud involving £300,000, said:

> '. . . there is no reason in language for differentiating between internal affairs and external affairs. Indeed, as a matter of policy it may be thought appropriate that management should extend to both internal and external affairs. The section should cover activity in relation to the birth, life and death of a company. That, in the judgment of this court, would accord with legislative's intent.'[19]

In *R v Georgiou*, a five-year disqualification was upheld in respect of carrying on an insurance business without authorisation.

Although in most cases of substantial dishonesty it may be implicit that a defendant is not fit to be concerned in the management of a company, a criminal court, unlike the Companies Court exercising its jurisdiction under section 6, is not obliged to make findings that the person in question was unfit to be concerned in the management of a company. In *R v Young*,[20] the convicting court accepted that the defendant, who had pleaded guilty to managing a company as an undischarged bankrupt, had not acted dishonestly or with intent to defraud or to abuse the system of limited liability. Brooke J said that the power to disqualify is a completely general and unfettered power and that Parliament had decided not to give the sentencing court any guidance as to the way in which it ought to exercise its powers. The prohibition by Parliament on undischarged bankrupts taking part in the management of a company was a serious offence usually meriting disqualification. The court quashed the two-year disqualification order, however, because it was inconsistent with the conditional discharge which had been imposed.

The court, where it imposes a compensation order, should be careful not to reduce or inhibit a defendant's means to pay and it is generally wrong in principle to inhibit a defendant from freely engaging in business activities, which must have been contemplated as necessary in order to fulfil his obligations under the compensation order, by disqualifying him from being a director.[1]

---

18 (1985) 7 Cr App Rep 214, CA.
19 (1988) 10 Cr App Rep (S) 137, CA.
20 (1990) 12 Cr App Rep (S) 262, CA.
1 *R v Holmes* (1992) 13 Cr App Rep (S) 29, CA. This was in the context, however, of a compensation order for £25,000. The court will clearly have to balance the size of the order as against the available means of the defendant to meet it at the time of sentence and as against the other ways in which a defendant can earn a living.

CHAPTER 8
DTI investigations

1 GENERAL

Investigations by the Department of Trade and Industry, or by inspectors appointed by the Department, can lead to the institution of criminal proceedings either directly by the Department, which has a prosecuting function, or by another prosecuting authority. This chapter mainly addresses the consequences of an inspection by the DTI as they relate to the institution of criminal proceedings for serious fraud.

In one recent statement the Department has said:

'One of the primary objectives of the Department of Trade and Industry is to increase confidence in the working of markets by achieving a fair level of protection for the individual consumer and investor. To this end, the Government remained determined to uncover and act against fraud and other malpractices in the conduct of commerce. This determination is reflected in the large number of steps which have been taken in recent years to improve the regulatory environment and to enable effective action to be taken. These steps include notably: the Financial Services Act 1986 and the new regulatory framework which it introduced; the setting up of the Serious Fraud Office in 1988 with its special powers under the Criminal Justice Act 1987; the reorganisation of the Department of Trade and Industry investigatory and prosecution functions with the setting up of its investigations division in 1988; improved international cooperation with the establishment of memoranda of understanding with the United States and Japan in the securities area and the new powers to assist overseas regulators in the Companies Act 1989; the agreement in 1989 on the European Community directive on insider dealing which will be implemented as soon as the parliamentary timetable allows; and the increased level of activity by the Department itself as well as by other prosecutors and regulators. This is the background at which the Department of Trade and Industry's investigation system now operates.'[1]

From this statement it can be seen that the role of inspectors appointed by the Secretary of State is increasingly only a part of a regulatory structure where once it was the pre-eminent force. It may be, as suggested in Chapter 2 above, that the days of the DTI inspection into cases of alleged serious fraud are numbered, and DTI inspectors will in future be faced with a much less controversial case load. Nevertheless, capacity exists for inspections to be set up under Part XIV of the Companies Act 1985 for wide-ranging and probing inquiries into alleged malpractice, and there remains the possibility that

1 Company Investigations (Government's response to the Third Report of the House of Commons Trade and Industry Committee: 1989–1990 session, page 3).

an investigation that begins as a DTI inquiry will result in criminal proceedings.

Historically, DTI inquiries have rarely resulted in prosecutions. For example, out of 50 inspections under section 432 (as it now is) between 1970 and 1986, criminal proceedings were instituted in only four cases.[2] Since 1986 there have been several high profile investigations by DTI inspectors, including those into Guinness plc and County NatWest Limited. Both investigations resulted in highly publicised and lengthy criminal trials. Another report, into House of Fraser Holdings plc, in spite of leading to an investigation by the Serious Fraud Office did not precipitate criminal proceedings. The trend, however, has been for more assertive action by prosecutors based on DTI inquiries, and a number of current prosecutions have their roots in inspectors' reports. The results of DTI inquiries are by no means limited to prosecutions (indeed some would argue that such a result is peripheral to the purpose of an inquiry). There are also powers to wind up a company, to disqualify directors, and to apply regulatory sanctions. In addition, there is the not inconsiderable power to criticise which can result in loss of reputation, loss of employment, and may lead to action being taken by other regulatory authorities.

The terms of appointment of inspectors, their powers and their duties are often of critical importance to a fraud investigation, and steps taken at early stages of an inquiry both by the inspectors and by witnesses and those advising them can be of considerable significance at later stages of an inquiry.

Since only inquiries under sections 432 and 447 are likely to lead to prosecution for serious fraud, discussion in this book is confined mainly to those sections and their accompanying sections. Under other sections within Part XIV of the Act there are relatively rarely used powers to appoint inspectors; under section 442 inspectors may be appointed for the purpose of investigating the ownership of shares in a company and under section 446 there are powers to investigate share dealings.[3] Under the Financial Services Act 1986 there are similar provisions for conducting investigations; by section 105 there are powers to appoint inspectors to investigate persons or companies who are carrying out investment business. These powers are normally exercised by the Securities and Investment Board. Under section 94 of the 1986 Act investigations can be made into unit trusts or collective investments schemes. Again, these powers are normally exercised by the SIB.

2 INQUIRIES UNDER SECTION 447

Inquiries instituted under section 447 of the 1985 Act are relatively extensively used by the Secretary of State.[4] Investigations under section 447 are normally carried out by officers employed by the Department and they are frequently

---

2 (i) Following two investigations into Austin EJ Limited Kenneth Howarth was charged with offences relating to fraudulent mining projects. He was sentenced to five years' imprisonment in 1975; (ii) Mr Spilsbury was convicted of fraud offences and sentenced to 18 months in prison in relation to Cornhill Consolidated Group Limited in 1980; (iii) Mr Hearn and Mr Allbright were sentenced to 18 months' imprisonment and nine months' suspended in relation to Kina Holdings Limited in 1981; (iv) Mr Crosby and Mr Williams were fined £250 for theft offences; Mr Hentzchell and Kuehne & Nagel Ltd were found not guilty following an investigation into that company in 1978.

3 Between 1979 and 1990 29 appointments were made under section 442; three under section 446.

4 There were 157 such inquiries in 1989–90, an increase of 15% over the previous year.

used for the purpose of establishing as a preliminary matter whether a more wide-ranging inquiry, including a serious fraud investigation, would be justified.

The Secretary of State has a wide discretion to order an investigation under section 447, and he does so by giving directions to a company to produce specified documents.[5] He may also give authority to a DTI official or other competent person to require a company to produce specified documents 'forthwith'.[6] The power to requisition documents extends to the power to require production of documents from a person who is in possession of them. Therefore, if the company's documents have been removed from the company's premises, anyone who is in possession of them, even if claiming a lien, must produce them.[7]

Where documents are produced, copies or extracts may be taken from them, and the person producing them 'or any other person who is a present or past officer of, or is or was at any time employed by, the company' may be required to provide an explanation of the documents. Where documents are not produced, the person who was required to produce them must state where they are.[8] Failure to comply with any of these requirements is a criminal offence punishable by a fine.[9] It is a defence under this section to prove that the documents 'were not in his possession or under his control and that it was not reasonably practicable for him to comply with the requirement.[10]

Evidence given under section 447(5) may be used in evidence in subsequent criminal proceedings[11] and thus it is directly analogous to evidence taken by inspectors under section 434. Inquiries under section 447 of the Act are never announced, and any report prepared as a result of the inquiries is not published.

The Roskill Fraud Trials Committee recommended that the DTI should use section 447 rather than sections 431 and 432, on grounds of expedition.[12] In other words, the Committee saw the DTI performing a valuable function in carrying out a preliminary inquiry, the results of which (including interviews which can be used in evidence against the person giving them) can be passed on to the SFO.

This is a recommendation which does not seem to have been extensively followed up, but the DTI and the SFO might wish to remedy that deficiency. The propriety of doing so, given the suspicion that the power may be used simply to enable the Crown to use a compulsory interview at trial, and given that the SFO has similar powers in any event, may be open to question.[13]

The search warrant procedure under section 448 of the Act was, until it was amended in the 1989 Act,[14] referable only to inquiries under section 447 of the Act. The change possibly reflects increased assertiveness on the part of the legislators in relation to section 432 inquiries, but it also recognises the value of speedy acquisition of documents.

---

5 Section 447(2).
6 Section 447(3).
7 Production in such circumstances is without prejudice to the lien.
8 Section 447(5).
9 Section 447(6).
10 Section 447(7).
11 Section 447(8).
12 Roskill Report, page 31, paragraph 2.61.
13 See generally, Chapter 2, section 2.2.3.
14 Section 64 of the Companies Act 1989.

The Roskill Fraud Trials Committee recommended that the police should be given powers analogous to those available to the Secretary of State under section 447 of the 1985 Act.[15] As stated above, the reason for this was that inquiries under section 447 tended to be more expeditiously carried out than inquiries under section 432. In the event, the powers granted to the SFO are more akin to the powers granted to inspectors under section 434 of the 1985 Act. However, in many circumstances where the Secretary of State may have thought it appropriate to take action under section 447, it may now be considered more appropriate to invite the SFO to set up an inquiry, particularly where there is a clear indication that criminal offences may have been committed.

Nevertheless, section 447 is used in many cases where the suspicion of the commission of criminal offences is remote and, in any event, the scale of the matters which are to be investigated does not constitute 'serious or complex fraud', so as to bring the matter within the scope of the Serious Fraud Office.

3   INQUIRIES UNDER SECTION 432

3.1   Appointment of inspectors under sections 431 and 432 of the Companies Act 1985

Under section 432(1), inspectors can be appointed on the order of a court, if the court considers that the affairs of a company ought to be investigated. The powers in this section, together with those in section 431 (which are very rarely used[16]) are exercised on an application by a company or by its members.

Where a court makes an order, the Secretary of State has no discretion as to whether to appoint inspectors.

The normal method of initiating an investigation by inspectors appointed by the Secretary of State for DTI is under section 432(2), by which:

> The Secretary of State may make such an appointment if it appears to him that there are circumstances suggesting:
>
> (a) that the company's affairs are being or have been conducted with intent to defraud its creditors or the creditors of any other person, or otherwise for a fraudulent or unlawful purpose or in a manner which is unfairly prejudicial to some part of it members, or
>
> (b) that any actual or proposed act or omission of the company (including an act or omission on its behalf) is or would be so prejudicial, or that the company was formed for any fraudulent or unlawful purpose, or
>
> (c) that persons concerned with the company's formation or the management of its affairs having in connection therewith been guilty of fraud, misfeasance or other misconduct towards it, or towards its members, or
>
> (d) that the company's members have not given all the information with respect to its affairs which they might reasonably expect.'

Where inspectors are appointed under section 432 of the Companies Act a public announcement is always made.[17] The discretion of the Secretary of State to appoint inspectors is thought to be so wide that his decision is most unlikely

---

15 Roskill Report, page 31, paragraph 2.62.
16 There have been no appointments since 1979.
17 In contrast to inquiries under section 447 of the Companies Act 1985 and under section 177 of the Financial Services Act 1986.

to be successfully challenged. In *Norwest Holst Ltd v Secretary of State for Trade and Industry*[18] the Court of Appeal held that only bad faith or an improper purpose on the part of the Secretary of State can provide a valid basis for challenging a decision. The Secretary of State does not have to give any reason for his decision, and it will be for an applicant to prove bad faith or improper motive. In these circumstances the possibility of challenging a decision must be seen as very limited.

An investigation under section 432 can only be directed at companies registered under the Companies Act.[19]

3.2   Purposes of an inquiry

The main aim of inspectors appointed by the Secretary of State for Trade and Industry under section 432 will be to discover whether there have been irregularities in the way in which a company has been managed and to make findings of fact. These matters will be contained in a report which will be submitted to the Secretary of State.

The inspectors' function is inquisitorial and investigative and not judicial.[20]

The purpose of the report compiled by the inspectors will be either to enable a prosecuting authority to consider whether criminal proceedings should be instituted; or to enable consideration to be given to winding the company up; or to bring civil proceedings in the company's name;[1] or to petition the court for an order granting relief against the company where its members have been unfairly prejudiced;[2] or it may form the basis for proceedings to be brought against individual directors under the Company Directors Disqualification Act 1986; or it may act as an impetus for the reform of legislation.[3]

It may be argued that with the introduction of the SFO the function of considering whether company law and regulations need to be reformed is paramount and that inquiries conducted under the Companies Act should be confined to those cases where the public interest in the matter extends beyond a consideration of the possibilities of criminal prosecution.

3.3   Powers of inspectors

It has been said that inspectors are masters of their own procedure. They may therefore conduct their inquiries within a wide range of discretion, but subject always to overriding rules of natural justice. In exercising their powers, which are provided by statute, they act independently of the DTI. Although there may be close liaison between the inspectors and the Department, and inspectors are encouraged to report on progress from time to time, it is expected that they will suffer no interference during the course of their investigations. Challenges to the decisions and conduct of inspectors, up to the

18   [1978] Ch 201, [1978] 3 All ER 280.
19   'Company' is defined in section 735 of the 1985 Act, and includes, in addition to the above, a company formed and registered under the former Companies Acts, viz the Joint Stock Companies Acts, the Companies Act 1862, the Companies (Consolidation) Act 1908, the Companies Act 1929 and the Companies Act 1948–1983.
20   See *Re Pergamon Press Ltd* [1971] Ch 388 at 406 per Buckley LJ.
1   Sections 438 and 440.
2   Section 460.
3   See generally Investigation Handbook Appendix B paragraph 4.

point of delivery of their report, are to the inspectors themselves and not to the DTI.

The powers exercised by inspectors relate to the company which they are appointed to investigate. By section 433, however, inspectors have a discretion to investigate related companies (subsidiaries or holding companies) if they 'think it necessary for the purposes of their investigation'.

Inspectors have the power to require production of documents and the giving of evidence. By subsection 434(1) officers and agents of the company (or companies within the scope of section 433) are under a duty:

'(a) to produce to the inspectors all [documents] of or relating to the company or, as the case may be, the other body corporate which are in their custody or power,
(b) to attend before the inspectors when required to do so, and
(c) otherwise to give the inspectors all assistance in connection with the investigation which they are reasonably able to give.'

By section 434(2):

'If the inspectors consider that an officer or agent of the company or other body corporate, or *any other person* is or may be in possession of information relating to a matter which they believe to be relevant to the investigation they may require him –

(a) to produce to them any documents in his custody or power relating to that matter, and
(b) to attend before them, and
(c) otherwise to give them all assistance in connection with the investigation which they are reasonably able to give;

and it is that person's duty to comply with the requirement.'

The emphasis is clear: those who are officers and agents of a company have a duty to comply with the section; any other person who has relevant information may be required to comply with the section. Nevertheless, it is difficult to see why subsection 434(2) was amended by the 1989 Act from its form in the 1985 Act where the requirement was placed simply on 'a person other than an officer or agent of the company or other body corporate'. If officers and agents of a company are under a duty to comply with the subsection, adding a requirement on them to comply would not seem to add significantly to the powers of the inspectors. With the amendment in the 1989 Act, subsection 434(1) appears to be redundant.

The phrase 'officers or agents' includes bankers, solicitors and auditors of the companies, and it covers past as well as present 'officers or agents'. Section 744 defines 'agent' as not including 'a person's counsel acting as such'.

3.4 Production of documents

Documents are defined[4] as:

'information recorded in any form; and, in relation to information recorded otherwise than in legible form, the power to require its production includes the power to require production of a copy of the information in legible form.'

---

4 Section 434(6). Added by section 56 of the Companies Act 1989.

The only categories of documents which are not automatically subject to production are those protected by legal professional privilege[5] and material to which an obligation of confidence is owed by virtue of the carrying on of the business of banking.[6]

The extent of the legal professional privilege that can be claimed has been discussed above in Chapter 2, and the provisions relating to bankers' confidentiality are also similar to those in section 2 of the 1987 Act. In place of the Director's authorisation, the Secretary of State is empowered to make a requirement to disclose.

Although there is clear statutory protection for documents subject to legal professional privilege, inspectors frequently ask that such privilege should be waived. It is reported that in one case (probably not unique), inspectors indicated that they would criticise a company for maintaining a claim to privilege. Such criticism (had it been made) would have been wholly misplaced, and it is clear that maintenance of a claim to privilege is a proper course to take in view of the possibility that a Department of Trade and Industry inspection may be followed by criminal proceedings. Therefore any consideration given to the question of privilege should be thorough and cautious.

A lawyer must disclose the name and address of his client.

The requirement to produce documents pursuant to section 434(1)(a) and 434(2)(a) may be notified to the person to whom it relates either formally or informally. If compliance with an informal request for documents is refused, formal notice will have to be given, and indeed it is normal for such a notice to be issued. The contents of such a notice were considered by the Divisional Court in *R v Secretary of State for Trade, ex p Perestrello*.[7] Perestrello received a notice under section 109(2) of the Companies Act 1948 (now section 447 of the 1985 Act) requiring him to produce a variety of documents. It was argued as a factual matter in support of an application for judicial review, and an order of prohibition against officers of the Department of Trade and Industry from continuing their inspection into the affairs of Kendall and Dent Silverbank Limited, that the notice served under section 109 was drafted in such wide terms as to require Perestrello to produce every document concerning the affairs of the company, including those out of the jurisdiction. Compliance with the notice, it was said, would bring the company to a complete standstill. It was said that the way in which the notice was drafted indicated a bias in the attitude of the officers of the Department of Trade and Industry towards the applicant.

Woolf J decided that the notice was too widely drawn:

> 'On the material before me and making the allowances that I have indicated, I regard the notices which were served in this case as being unreasonable and excessive in the circumstances. I can see no justification whatsoever for a notice in the terms being put forward in this particular case on the evidence which is put before me. I do not say that that same view would be taken with regard to other cases, I am dealing with this particular case.
> First of all I would draw attention to the fact that the notice does not indicate that it only relates to documents in the possession of Mr Perestrello. If it was meant only to refer to documents in Mr Perestrello's possession then in my view, bearing in mind the nature of the documents, it should have said

---

5 Section 452(1).
6 Section 452(1A) added by section 69(3) of the Companies Act 1989.
7 [1981] QB 19, [1980] 3 All ER 38.

so; and it should not be a notice which is drawn in a manner which relies on Mr Perestrello ascertaining his rights under the Act, and then reading the notice as being subject to the Act in order to understand what the notice requires.

Secondly, in the circumstances of this case, if the notice was only intended to refer to documents in the United Kingdom, as is contended by the Department to be the intention in this case, in my view, it should have said so. It should be borne in mind by the Department that this is a case which under this very provision of the Act, the notice can lead to criminal proceedings. It is true that if the notice is not complied with the person concerned has a defence under the Act, but that, in my view, is no justification for a notice being in unreasonably wide terms as I regard this notice as being.

It was contended on behalf of the applicants that the effect of this notice was, if it was fully complied with, to cause them to give up business and although I am not in a position to form a concluded view as to whether it went as far as that, what I do feel is that the notice goes too far bearing in mind in particular, as I have already stressed, the documents had to be taken to the Department of Trade's premises; the applicants would therefore be without the documents for a time; and that it was not a situation where Mr Perestrello who had been co-operating up till that time, was merely being required to deal with a general request in circumstances where the documents would be produced but remain at his own business premises so that the business could be conducted in the meantime.'[8]

The judge emphasised that each case must be considered on its own merits, but the importance of the decision lies in the recognition that the terms of a notice can be open to challenge. It is not satisfactory for a notice to be drafted in such wide terms as to include all a company's documents, and notices requiring production of documents should be as specific as possible.

3.5   Powers of search and seizure

Apart from the powers that inspectors have to require the production of documents, they have the further power in section 448, to apply for a warrant to a justice of the peace to enter and search premises. The circumstances in which a warrant may be issued are, first, where the Secretary of State or an Inspector gives information on oath that compliance with a requirement has been refused, and that there are documents on the premises which should be produced; or second,

'(a) that there are reasonable grounds for believing that an offence has been committed for which the penalty on conviction on indictment is imprisonment for a term of not less than two years and that there are on any premises documents relating to whether the offence has been committed;

(b) that the Secretary of State, or the person so appointed or authorised, has the power to require the production of the documents under this part; and

(c) that there are reasonable grounds for believing that if production was so required the documents would not be produced but would be removed from the premises, hidden, tampered with, or destroyed.'[9]

8   [1981] QB 19 at 31.
9   Section 448(2).

This subsection was added by the 1989 Act, and the section as a whole now relates to Part XIV of the 1985 Act, and not just to a requirement made under section 447.

There is a logical inconsistency in the section in this respect: that if 'there are reasonable grounds for believing that an offence has been committed for which the penalty on conviction on indictment is imprisonment for a term of not less than two years' it is likely that section 437(1B) will apply. In other words, it must de facto appear 'to the Secretary of State that matters have come to light in the course of the inspectors' investigation which suggest that a criminal offence has been committed'. The case may therefore be referred to 'the appropriate prosecuting authority', with the result that the Secretary of State may direct the inspectors to take no further steps.

Although the Secretary of State's power in this regard is discretionary, it may be argued that in any case where it can be said that the suspicion exists that a serious offence has been committed, the matter should from the beginning have been investigated by another authority, in particular, the Serious Fraud Office.

Nevertheless, the powers exist for inspectors to apply to magistrates for a warrant, and that warrant is exercisable by a constable and other named persons, who may:

'(a) enter the premises specified in the information, using such force as is reasonably necessary for the purpose;
(b) search the premises and take possession of any documents appearing to be such documents as are mentioned in subsection (1) or (2) as the case may be, or to take, in relation to any such documents, any other steps which may appear to be necessary for preserving them or preventing interference with them;
(c) to make copies of any such documents; and
(d) to require any person named in the warrant to provide an explanation of them or to state where they may be found.'[10]

The validity of a warrant expires one month after issue.[11]

3.6   Powers of questioning

A requirement to 'attend before the inspectors' is normally given in writing and should be accompanied by a copy of the inspectors' Minute of Appointment. Reasonable notice of a requirement should be given, although the reasonableness may vary between a day and two weeks.[12]

No notice need be given of the questions which are to be asked, although the Investigation Handbook[13] suggests that the inspectors may find their inquiries will be facilitated if a witness is given advance notice in general terms of the matters on which he is to be examined, together with particulars of any documents which the inspectors require him to produce, or propose to refer to while examining him.

Inspectors also frequently invite a witness to make a statement in writing in advance of an interview. Such a statement is usually incorporated into the interview, by inviting the witness to adopt it, and it therefore becomes evidence which can be used against him.

10 Section 448(3).
11 Section 448(5).
12 Department of Trade Investigation Handbook, Appendix B paragraph 17.
13 Ibid.

In practice, since inspectors are free to carry out their investigations in any way which seems to be appropriate,[14] the way in which they conduct their inquiries will vary considerably, with some inspectors giving little notice that they wish to interview witnesses and not requiring statements, preferring to obtain immediate reaction to questions without a prepared response, while others prefer the prepared route.

Section 434(1)(c) and 434(2)(c) make it plain that wide-ranging cooperation is required, without any conditions being imposed on the inspectors. This does not mean that it is not perfectly proper, for example, to invite the inspectors to give details of the areas which they wish to examine, or to give an explanation of the reason why a witness has been summoned under subsection 434(2) as 'any other person'.

3.7   Informal interviews

Witnesses summoned before inspectors may as a preliminary step be asked to attend for an informal interview.[15] Informal interviews are usually only offered to witnesses who will be able to help the inquiry, and not to those whose integrity the inspectors doubt. The implication of paragraph 10 of Appendix B of the Investigation Handbook is that informal interviews will not be recorded. However, this is by no means always the case. The evidence given may therefore, by virtue of section 434(5), be used in evidence against the witness.

Whether a person summoned for an informal interview is subject to subsections 434(1)(c) and 434(2)(c) in the sense of being required to 'give them all assistance in connection with the investigation which he is reasonably able to give', and thereby subject to the sanctions in section 436, is open to question. The likely result of a refusal to attend an informal interview will simply be a requirement to attend a formal interview, and therefore it may be that the question is unlikely to arise.

3.8   Formal interviews

3.8.1   *Transcripts*

Witnesses attending a formal interview will normally be examined on oath[16] and a transcript must be recorded.[17] The transcript should record who was present, the times at which the interview began and finished, the times when any break in the interview began and finished, and whether any refreshments were served in any such break. The Handbook recommends: 'normally there should be a short break for refreshment at intervals of about two hours'.[18] Complaints are sometimes made that the procedure adopted by inspectors does not follow these recommendations. Since they are only recommendations the scope for rectifying matters may be limited. However, in the context of subsequent criminal proceedings, where the Crown is proposing to use the transcript of an interview conducted by inspectors as evidence against an accused, it may be argued that the failure to follow the recommendations in the Investigation Handbook tends to show that any confessions obtained during

14 Ibid, paragraph 8.
15 Ibid, paragraph 10.
16 Subsection 434(3).
17 Department of Trade Investigation Handbook Appendix B paragraph 23.
18 Ibid.

the course of the interview were obtained by oppression and therefore may possibly be excluded.[19]

3.8.2   *Use of transcripts of evidence in criminal proceedings*

The question of whether evidence given to inspectors in the course of an inquiry under section 432 can be used against the witness in subsequent criminal proceedings has been considered in Chapter 2.[20] In *R v Saunders and Others*, Henry J decided, in the preparatory hearings, that the words of section 434(5) of the Companies Act 1985 made it clear that in the absence of proving oppression within section 76 of PACE or other special circumstances transcripts of the evidence of witnesses were admissible as evidence against a defendant.[1]

3.8.3   *Refusal to answer questions: the privilege against self-incrimination*

Given that a witness before inspectors may be cited for contempt of court if he fails to attend before the inspectors and give them all assistance in connection with the investigation which he is reasonably able to give, and given that the assistance which he gives, in the form of answers to questions, can subsequently be used in evidence against him, the question has been raised as to whether the circumstances of questioning by inspectors can give rise to a plea that the witness wishes to take advantage of the privilege against self-incrimination. The question has acquired a particular prominence in the last year or so because of an apparent desire by prosecutors to take advantage of the possibility of obtaining evidence from a defendant who has been denied the right of silence in high profile cases.[2] The courts have robustly concluded that although there is a privilege against self-incrimination it has been excluded by the legislation.

What happens in practice, however, when a witness at an interview with inspectors, particularly where there is any prospect that the results of the inquiry will be forwarded to a prosecuting authority, refuses to answer questions on the ground that the answer might tend to incriminate him? The short answer is that he is obliged to give assistance to the inspectors by responding to their questions, and that he risks being cited for contempt of court if he does not. The precise position, however, is less clear.

The House of Lords has held[3] that it would be 'a wrongful assumption of power to insist that a witness answer a question'. It was stated that section

19 Police and Criminal Evidence Act 1984 section 76.
20 Section 2.2.3.
1 21 November 1989.
2 The authors of a paper on the right to silence and the privilege against self-incrimination in commercial fraud investigations and prosecutions (Mary Arden QC, Dorian Lovell-Pank and Dr ATH Smith) cited twelve cases in 1991 and 1992 in which the issue was raised: *AT & T Istel Ltd v Tully* [1992] 1 QB 315, [1992] 2 All ER 28, CA; *R v Seelig and Spens* [1991] 4 All ER 429, [1992] 1 WLR 148, CA; in *Re Jeffrey S Levitt Ltd* [1992] 2 All ER 509, [1992] 2 WLR 975; *Re London United Investments plc* [1992] 2 All ER 842, [1992] BCLC 91; *Sociedade Nacional de Combustiveis de Angola UEE v Lundquist* [1991] 2 QB 310, [1990] 3 All ER 280, CA; *Bank of England v Riley* [1992] 1 All ER 769 [1992] 1 WLR 840, CA; *Tate Access Floors Inc v Boswell* [1991] Ch 512, [1990] 3 All ER 303; *R v Director of Serious Fraud Office, ex p Smith* [1992] 1 All ER 730; *Re A E R Farr Ltd* [1992] BCC 150; *Re Arrows Ltd* [1992] 2 WLR 923, [1992] BCLC 126; *Price Waterhouse v BCCI Holdings (Luxembourg) SA* (1991) Times, 30 October; *Bishopsgate Investment Management Ltd v Maxwell* [1992] 2 All ER 856, [1992] 2 WLR 991, CA.
3 *McClelland, Pope & Langley v Howard* [1968] 1 All ER 569n, HL.

436(2) and (3) of the 1985 Act 'makes it plain that a witness may refuse to answer questions and, if he does so, the question whether he did so properly was a matter for the court, if the inspectors so referred the matter, and not for the inspectors.[4]

Where the refusal to answer questions has been claimed as a right against self-incrimination, the courts have not been ready to accept that the right exists in connection with the genus of inquiries of which those set up under section 432 of the 1985 Act are an example. In *R v Saunders & Others*[5] Henry J put it this way:

'If information that might incriminate were to be excluded, it would be in that section that one would find such exclusion (ie section 452). So, it seems to me, that as a matter of construction, this point is clear, namely that inspectors may ask witnesses questions that tend to incriminate them, and the witness is under a duty to give all assistance to the inspectors, which duty extends to answering questions, even if they may incriminate him.'

He went on to state that the statutory construction is reinforced by case law and equivalent statutory formulae.[6] He cited *R v Scott*,[7] in support of the contention that while there is undoubtedly a privilege against self-incrimination, 'Parliament may take away this privilege and enact that a party may be bound to accuse himself'.[8] In *Re O*[9] Lord Donaldson MR stated that:

'It is part of the common law of England that no man shall be subject to an order compliance with which might tend to incriminate him . . . The common law can, of course, be varied or overruled by statute, but it requires clear words, or even clearer implication to achieve this result particularly where so old and fundamental a freedom is involved.'

Henry J, in *R v Saunders*, considered a number of authorities in considering whether clear words were contained in the 1985 Act, including *R v Erdheim*,[10] *Re Atherton*,[11] *Re Paget*,[12] *Customs and Excise v Harz and Power*,[13] *R v Harris*,[14] *London and County Securities Ltd v Nicholson*.[15] He also cited an Australian authority *Mortimer v Brown*.[16] From an analysis of these cases he drew the following conclusions:

'1. That inspectors are under an overall obligation to act fairly.
2. Inspectors may ask any relevant question even if it might tend to incriminate the witness.

---

4   See DTI Investigation Handbook, Appendix B paragraph 21.
5   Unreported 21 November 1989, p 10.
6   Henry J stated: 'One finds equivalent statutory formulae reaching the same end result in the Insolvency Act 1986 and the Financial Services Act 1986, and this statutory formula reflects the position as was reached in bankruptcy through the statute and through the cases.'
7   (1856) Volume 169 ER 909.
8   Ibid at 914.
9   [1991] 2 QB 520 at 527, [1991] 1 All ER 330 at 335.
10 [1896] 2 QB 260.
11 [1912] 2 KB 251.
12 [1927] 2 Ch 85.
13 [1967] AC 760.
14 [1970] 3 All ER 746, [1970] 1 WLR 1252.
15 [1980] 3 All ER 861, [1980] 1 WLR 948.
16 (1970) 122 CLR 493. For a similar analysis of this line of authority see the judgment of Dillon LJ in *Re London United Investments* [1992] 2 All ER 842, [1992] BCLC 91.

3. It is a matter for the inspectors' discretion whether they do ask any such question. The practice is not to ask such a question after the witness has been charged.

4. The witness is under a duty to give all assistance, which duty may extend to answering questions which might tend to incriminate him.

5. The answers he gives to any such questions may be used in Court proceedings, including criminal proceedings, against him.

6. If a refusal on self-incrimination grounds is taken before the inspectors, then under section 436 the Inspector will, if he thinks it right to do so, certify that refusal to the Court as an obstruction of the inquiry.

7. The Court will then have to consider, first, whether the refusal to answer was an obstruction of the inquiry and, second, whether the refusal to answer should be punished. And, as to the matters that the Court may take into account in relation to that, whilst it is beyond the scope of this judgment the good guidance is there to be found in the case of *Mortimer*.'[17]

In referring to *Mortimer*, he approved a substantial public interest argument, to the effect that the honest conduct of the affairs of the company is a matter of great public concern, and 'overcomes some of the common law's traditional consideration for the individual'.[18]

The privilege against self-incrimination in the context of a DTI inquiry was considered again in *Re London United Investments Ltd.*[19] After agreeing that clear words were needed to oust the privilege, and citing as an example of clear words section 171 of the Queensland Companies Act 1961 and section 296 of the Victoria Companies Code, Dillon LJ expressed regret that there is no express provision either in the 1985 Act or in the Insolvency Act 1986. He reviewed the cases considered by Henry J in *R v Seelig and Spens*,[20] and concluded 'without hesitation' that the privilege against self-incrimination is impliedly excluded and is not available to the person being questioned by the inspectors, because:

'(i) inspectors will in very many cases have been appointed where there are circumstances suggesting that there has been fraud in the conduct or management of a company's affairs, and

(ii) persons questioned are bound to answer the inspectors' questions, and

(iii) the inspectors' report may lead the Secretary of State to petition for the winding-up of the company or to bring civil proceedings in the company's name in the public interest.'

The subject was given another extensive, and highly public, airing in *Bishopsgate Investment Management Ltd v Maxwell*,[1] where the Court of

---

17 *R v Saunders* op cit at 18.

18 But see *Re Arrows Ltd* [1992] 2 WLR 923, [1992] BCLC 126, where Hoffmann J recognised the opposite public interest argument, that witnesses (in this instance, individuals called before liquidators appointed under section 236 of the Insolvency Act 1986) should not be discouraged from giving information by the fear that it will subsequently be used against them in criminal proceedings. See also *AT & T Istel Ltd v Tully* [1992] 1 QB 315, [1992] 2 All ER 28, CA, where a right against self-incrimination was recognised in the context of an order for a Mareva injunction. The fear that information given in compliance with the order might incriminate the defendants, who were under investigation by the police, justified non-disclosure. The decision in *Marcel v Metropolitan Police Comr* [1992] Ch 225, [1991] 1 All ER 72, CA also contains some comments about disclosure of documents – in this instance from the police to litigants in civil proceedings – and public interest.

19 [1992] 2 All ER 842, [1992] BCLC 91.

20 Op cit.

1 [1992] 2 All ER 856, [1992] 2 WLR 991.

Appeal considered whether the privilege against self-incrimination had been impliedly abrogated in the case of examinations under section 236 of the Insolvency Act 1986. For this purpose the court looked at the Insolvency Act as a whole and in reaching their decision the judges considered its legislative antecedents. As part of this exercise, the court examined and compared the provisions for both public and private examinations in bankruptcy and corporate insolvency, and their historical development. The court noted that under the Bankruptcy Act 1914 a bankrupt was not entitled to refuse to answer any question on the grounds of the privilege against self-incrimination. The purpose of the Act was to secure a full and complete examination and disclosure of the facts relating to the bankrupt, in the interests of the public and not merely in the interests of the creditors. It was stressed that in matters of bankruptcy it is not merely creditors who have rights: the public themselves have interests which must be safeguarded.

Section 366 of the Insolvency Act 1986 now governs private examinations in bankruptcy, and it has been confirmed, following the authorities (many of them considered by Henry J)[2] that the privilege against self-incrimination is not available to the bankrupt. The court recognised that many of the principles applicable to private examination in bankruptcy apply also to private examination in corporate insolvency, including the principal object, to obtain information. The powers available to examiners have been conferred by the legislature both in winding-up and in bankruptcy because justice requires it.

These investigative powers had been greatly extended by the Insolvency Act, placing a company's officers and certain other individuals under a duty to assist office holders. Recognising that bankrupts could not rely on the privilege against self-incrimination the court held that it would be illogical if directors of a company could rely on the privilege in a private examination under section 236 of the 1986 Act.

The court therefore held that although there were no express words in the Insolvency Act which abrogated the privilege against self-incrimination for the purposes of examination by office holders under section 236, the whole scheme of the Act made it clear that such an abrogation was implied. To decide otherwise would be to frustrate the purpose of the legislation.

3.8.4   *Justification for refusal to answer questions*

The argument that it is for the court to decide whether the refusal to answer questions is reasonable is consistent with the statement that inspectors do not fulfil a judicial function. In deciding whether a refusal has been reasonable, the court has a wide discretion, which can be the subject of appeal to the Court of Appeal. In *Mortimer* Walsh J stated:

> 'I think that in deciding whether a particular line of questioning to which objection is taken, should be allowed, the Court may sometimes take into account the fact, if it be a fact, that the answers might tend to incriminate the witness. But in my opinion it would not be in accordance with the plain language of the section to hold that the possibility of self-incrimination must be regarded by the Court as decisive against allowing a question to be put. This can never be more than one factor, to be considered with others, in deciding as a matter of discretion whether to allow or disallow a question. Indeed, in many cases, the possibility or even the certainty that an answer

2   Supra.

would incriminate the person being examined would not itself provide a sufficient reason for disallowing the question, since questions will normally be directed to the investigation of all the relevant facts in order that it may be ascertained whether or not there has been fraud or concealment of material facts. I think it is the intention disclosed by the section that any questions that will be of real assistance towards the fulfilment of that purpose could be answered. There may, however, be some cases in which it appears to the Court that a particular question or a particular line of questioning has such a remote or doubtful bearing upon the investigation with which the Court is concerned, that the harm that may be done to the individual will outweigh any benefit to be obtained and that, therefore, that question or line of questioning ought to be disallowed. The section gives the Court an unqualified discretion.'[3]

For the witness and his legal adviser considering their position in advance of an interview with inspectors, there is the comfort that a blanket refusal to answer questions, or a refusal to answer questions without advance warning of the areas to be covered, can be certified to the court, and then argued, on the basis that the witness will answer questions if the court decides that a refusal would be unreasonable. One advantage of this approach would be that if, at a later stage, the evidence given to the inspectors by the witness was introduced into a criminal trial as evidence against that witness, he could point to his reluctance to testify to the inspectors as proof of oppression and unfairness. It is, however, clear from recent authority that the chances of persuading the court that a refusal to answer questions is justified is remote in the absence of elements such as mistake or bad faith, which will be rarely encountered.

3.9   Preparation for interview

Where no notice has been given of the questions to be asked, preparation for interview can be a dauntingly wide-ranging prospect. Often the witness will not be in possession of the relevant papers, and even if he has access to some papers it is likely that other material will be put to him in the course of the interview which he has not previously seen. In addition, he may be asked to comment on evidence given to the inspectors by other witnesses.

It is perhaps important to emphasise that a refusal to comment should not be taken as a refusal to answer a question, even though it might be construed by a harsh tribunal as a refusal to give the inspectors all assistance in connection with the investigation which a witness is reasonably able to give. A witness should be entitled to refuse to comment on a document he has not seen before, on speculation, or on comments made by other witnesses. In particular, it is submitted that answers to nypothetical questions can be avoided.

3.10   Position of legal advisers

Legal advisers are firmly told that they may not answer questions on behalf of their client.[4] They may, however, seek to clarify questions, and they may intervene if they consider that questioning has become oppressive, or if an answer is being demanded in circumstances where no answer need be given. Since a transcript of the interview will be produced and consideration may at a

---

3   *Mortimer v Brown* op cit at 502.
4   DTI Investigation Handbook, Appendix B paragraph 19.

later stage be given to whether the interview was being conducted fairly, any suggestion at the time that it was oppressive should be clearly recorded.

At the end of an interview, a legal adviser is usually asked if he wishes to put any questions to his client, and he may also take the opportunity of making submissions to the inspectors.

The DTI Investigation Handbook suggests that inspectors have the power to prevent one legal adviser from representing more than one client.[5] Clearly the normal rules of conflict of interest apply,[6] but further than that the inspectors may suggest that the confidentiality of their inquiries would be prejudiced if one legal adviser were able to inform several clients of the progress of an inquiry and the points in which the inspectors were showing particular interest.

The Department recognises, however, that the representation of more than one client by a legal adviser can have advantages, in that, for example, their knowledge of the documents and of the facts of the case assists in arriving at a summary of the facts.

3.11   Criticisms of witnesses to an inquiry

Inspectors are encouraged to take steps to give a witness an opportunity to answer criticisms which are made of him.[7] This should entail giving a witness the chance during an interview to answer criticisms which have been made by other witnesses.[8] The witness should then have an opportunity to study his transcript and make any alterations or corrections to the transcript that he considers appropriate.[9] At this stage, before any specific criticisms are notified to him, he will be invited to make submissions about the interview in general. If it is considered that the interview was unfairly conducted, and that there are genuine grounds for complaint, it might be appropriate to make such submissions at this stage. However, it may not always be appropriate to anticipate criticisms and a witness may consider it preferable to wait until the inspectors have made clear their intention to criticise before any submissions are made.

Submissions made subsequent to an interview may become evidence in criminal proceedings, and apparent sensitivity on a particular subject may either encourage the inspectors to look more closely at the matter, or, even if they do not criticise in relation to that matter, a prosecutor may subsequently take note of it.

The DTI Investigation Handbook suggests that:

> '. . . once the inspectors have prepared a first draft of their report they may think it appropriate, even though they have put to the witness at interview the substance of the evidence against him, to write to the witness setting out the

5   Appendix B paragraph 31.
6   See *The Guide to Professional Conduct of Solicitors*: Chapter 11.
7   DTI Investigation Handbook, Appendix B paragraphs 37–42.
8   *Maxwell v Department of Trade and Industry* [1974] QB 523 at 541.
9   The Trade and Industry Committee recommended 'that witnesses should be provided with a copy of the transcript of their evidence'. The government accepted this recommendation: 'Inspectors will be advised to supply witnesses with a copy of the transcript of their evidence at an appropriate time during the inquiry unless in a particular case the inspectors have compelling reasons such as fears about confidentiality for withholding it altogether.' Government's Response to the Third Report of the House of Commons Trade and Industry Committee 1989–90 Session, p 12.

intended criticisms with notice of the evidence on which they are based, giving him a fixed period of, for example, twenty one days to respond.'[10]

While any submissions made in relation to criticisms can become evidence in subsequent criminal proceedings, it is vital that any areas of uncertainty or misunderstanding should be clarified at this stage, and that any matters of disagreement are firmly recorded.

The Trade and Industry Committee Third Report on company investigations considered: 'should inspectors just find facts or should they also draw conclusions?'[11] They found that opinions among their witnesses were divided, and that the Secretary of State had a fairly open mind. Such august bodies as the Bank of England and the Securities and Investments Board thought that inspectors should be simply finders of fact. Most witnesses, however, agreed with the advice given in the DTI Investigation Handbook,[12] where it is said that, if a report is to have value, the inspectors must:

'. . . state their findings on the evidence and their opinions on the matters referred to them, with courage and frankness, keeping nothing back.[13] Inspectors should avoid superfluous epithets and the eye-catching phrase that is likely to lead to unbalanced comments, and to limit remarks about conduct to conduct in the company's affairs.'

The Trade and Industry Committee recommended:[14]

'. . . that inspectors should continue to draw conclusions from the evidence they take.'

The government[15] agreed with this recommendation, and their response went on to state:

'This practice has a number of valuable purposes such as 'exculpating' those who the inspectors find to be without blame as well as criticising those who are found to blame; helping regulators and those who have been affected by the conduct uncovered by the inspectors to understand the full import of the matters addressed in the report and helping them to consider what action might appropriately be initiated.'

Once the inspectors have decided on the form of their report it is submitted to the Secretary of State. The question arises as to whether their report is entirely free-standing, or whether it should have appendices and riders which are seen only by the Secretary of State. The Trade and Industry Committee recommended[16] that inspectors should make recommendations about taking further action, and that recommendations for prosecution or disciplinary action should be contained in a separate appendix. The government responded that they did not approve of the idea of an appendix and:

'. . . a preferable alternative which would have the same effect whenever the report was publishable would be to invite the inspectors to inform the Secretary of State (otherwise than in their report) of any matters coming to

10 DTI Investigation Handbook, Appendix B paragraph 41.
11 Trade and Industry Committee Third Report: Company Investigations paragraph 63.
12 Appendix B paragraph 35.
13 Per Denning MR *Maxwell v Department of Trade and Industry* [1974] QB 523 at 533.
14 Op cit, paragraph 73.
15 Government's response to the Third Report to the Third Report of the House of Commons Trade and Industry Committee: 1989–1990 session, p 11.
16 Op cit recommendations 13 and 14.

their knowledge as a result of their investigations which they believed were relevant to further action against individuals.'[17]

3.12 Publication

The inclusion or otherwise of criticism in a report has consequences for its publication.

The normal rule is that reports of inspections conducted under section 432 are published.[18] Publication may be delayed by a number of factors, including in particular the prospect of the institution of criminal proceedings. This consideration delayed publication of the reports into House of Fraser Holdings plc and Guinness plc.[19] The report by Michael Crystal QC and David Spence on County NatWest Limited and County NatWest Securities Limited, which led to the institution of criminal proceedings, was published before those proceedings were begun. No substantial point was taken at the trial that the publication of the report unfairly prejudiced any of the defendants. The discretion of the Secretary of State on publication is, therefore, very wide.

By section 432(2A):[20]

'Inspectors may be appointed under subsection (2) on terms that any report they may make is not for publication; and in such a case, the provisions of section 437(3) (availability and publication of inspectors' reports) do not apply.'

There has yet to be a case in which this provision has been used. In addition, by section 437(1C) a final report need only be made to the Secretary of State where a direction has been made under section 437(1B) if the inspectors' appointment was by the court or they are directed to do so by the Secretary of State.

By section 441 a certified copy of a report:

'. . . is admissible in any legal proceedings as evidence of the opinion of the inspectors in relation to any matter contained in the report and, in proceedings on an application under section 8 of the Company Directors Disqualification Act 1986, as evidence of any fact stated therein.'

This section is intended to enable regulators to rely on the opinions expressed by inspectors and, in particular, to enable the courts, considering disqualifying a person from acting as a director, to reach conclusions.

In criminal trials, evidence of opinion is inadmissible, in general terms, unless it is given by an expert. For the purposes of section 441, it may not be assumed that the inspectors are experts. If they were to express the opinion that a person's conduct was dishonest, the reception of that opinion into evidence would effectively usurp the function of the jury.

17 Op cit p 11.
18 Section 437(3)(c): the Secretary of State 'may, if he thinks fit cause any such report to be printed and published.' The DTI has stated that 'it has always been the policy to publish reports on the affairs of public companies' subject to the overriding discretion of the Secretary of State: Government's Response, op cit: recommendation 16.
19 Since in the case of *Guinness* there were to have been be as many as four separate trials, and at the time of writing the last trial has not begun, it is likely that the delay between completion of the report by the inspectors and its publication will be as much as four years.
    Publication of the House of Fraser Holdings plc. report was delayed by more than a year by the consideration given by the Director of the SFO to the institution of criminal proceedings.
20 Inserted by section 55 of the Companies Act 1989.

Nevertheless, a person who has been subjected to an investigation by inspectors appointed under section 432, and who has been 'cleared' by the inspectors, is placed in an unfortunate position if criminal proceedings are subsequently brought based on the same evidence. Although it can be said that inspectors and prosecutors perform differing functions, and that inspectors perform a fact-finding, not a judicial function, it may be argued that the fact that inspectors reach a certain conclusion based on evidence they have collected should not be contradicted by a different arm of the executive. Where inspectors, on hearing all the evidence, conclude that an individual has not acted dishonestly there must, at the very least, exist a substantial doubt that the individual is guilty of dishonest conduct.

Those considering whether criminal charges should be preferred will wish to rely on findings of fact by inspectors and not on their opinions. They may well wish to argue, with the Bank of England and the Securities and Investments Board (even if for different reasons) that criticisms should be altogether excluded from reports.

The difficulty posed by this ambivalence lends further support to the proposition that it is no longer appropriate, following the creation of the SFO, for inspectors appointed under section 432 to investigate matters which appear to involve serious fraud.

3.13   Expenses of an investigation

By section 439 of the Act the Secretary of State must, in the first instance, pay the expenses of an investigation. However, 'he may recover those expenses from the persons liable in accordance with this section'. The amount of expenses recoverable is defined as 'such reasonable sums as the Secretary of State may determine in respect of general staff costs and overheads.'[1]

Expenses may be recovered, in instances of serious fraud prosecutions, where a person is convicted on a prosecution 'instituted as a result of the investigation'.[2]

The section is mainly aimed at recovering expenses where the inquiry has been instigated at the behest of someone other than the Secretary of State, and the procedure for making an order for costs against a company or individual at the conclusion of a prosecution is not clearly spelt out. Section 439(2) simply says that a person who is convicted 'may in the same proceedings be ordered to pay those expenses to such extent as may be specified in the Order'. It does not appear that this is a provision which has been widely used by the courts.[3]

---

1   Section 439(1).
2   Section 439(2).
3   The House of Commons Trade and Industry Committee Third Report Company Investigations recommended that 'greater steps be taken to recover the costs of investigations from the companies and individuals involved unless inspectors find no evidence of wrongdoing'. (Recommendation 33 – paragraph 187). The government responded that the cost of investigations 'is already largely met by the corporate sector through the fees charged by Companies House rather than by the taxpayer'. After referring to the increased powers conferred by the 1989 Act, the Response continued: 'We will seek actively to recover costs in those cases where the powers enable us to do so. There are a number of reasons against a more general power to recover such costs: for example, the company may be the victim of the fraud rather than the perpetrators; a fear of having to pay the costs of the inquiry might discourage a company from reporting fraud.' The combined cost of the County NatWest Ltd and House of Fraser Holdings plc inquiries was a little over £2.5 million' (DTI Report on Companies in 1989–90, p 12, paragraph 30).

4 INSIDER DEALING INVESTIGATIONS

Following the creation of the offence of insider dealing in the Companies Act 1980, and the further definition of the offence in the Company Securities (Insider Dealing) Act 1985, it was considered necessary to reinforce the powers available to those investigating suspected offences. This resulted in the inclusion in the Financial Services Act 1986 of provisions enabling the Secretary of State to appoint inspectors to investigate allegations of insider dealing. The powers granted to inspectors are similar to those contained in Part XIV of the Companies Act 1985, and the scheme of an inspection under the Financial Services Act is similar in almost all respects to an inspection under section 432(2) of the 1985 Act.

The impetus behind the provisions in the Financial Services Act 1986 stemmed from a belief that people committing offences of insider dealing were either not being investigated at all, or, if investigations were set in train, those investigations were ineffective. The reason for the latter problem was that, because of the secretive nature of most insider dealing activity, normal powers of investigation were insufficient to obtain the evidence required to bring a prosecution.

The person accused of insider dealing, therefore, is subject to a markedly different investigative regime to those accused of almost every other type of criminal offence. In particular, the right of silence in these cases is specifically removed, where in all other cases, including serious fraud, that right is preserved.[4]

Investigations into insider dealing are also carried out by the International Stock Exchange ('ISE'), and prosecutions for insider dealing may be carried out by authorities other than the Department of Trade and Industry, including specifically the ISE.[5]

The number of prosecutions for insider dealing has remained at a very low level since the legislation was first introduced. The number of successful prosecutions, as a proportion of prosecutions instituted, is also low, perhaps reflecting the great difficulties encountered in investigating the offence, and subsequently proving it against the very complex background of the Company Securities (Insider Dealing) Act 1985.[6] Dissatisfaction with the current state of affairs frequently surfaces, and the position was specifically addressed by the Trade and Industry Committee in their Third Report on Company Investigation. They reported that:

> '. . . the DTI has a poor record on insider dealing, but is showing signs of improvement. What is particularly alarming is its speed of response to a new offence. The City of London depends partly for its reputation on innovations. The DTI regulatory record in dealing with new developments is not impressive. If it takes ten years to start to get to grips with one new offence, what can be expected of it as new schemes of commercial malpractice are invented.'[7]

---

4 Except in so far as section 434(5) of the Companies Act 1985 applies.
5 Companies Act 1989 section 209.
6 At the end of 1990, only two prosecutions for insider dealing were pending. In that year nine defendants were acquitted, against four convicted. Several long-running inquiries under section 177 continue.
7 House of Commons Trade and Industry Committee Third Report Company Investigations: paragraph 166.

The Committee suggested a variety of different ways of attacking the problem of insider dealing, including a system of compounding similar to that used by the Inland Revenue, and introducing civil law sanctions against insider dealing.[8]

The Committee recommended that insider dealing inspectors should be expected to report within three months.[9] It does not appear likely that this timetable will ever be achieved save in the most straightforward of cases. The Secretary of State may 'limit the period during which he is to continue his investigation, or confine it to particular matters'.[10] It is not thought that any time limitation, apart from an exhortation to proceed with all possible expedition, has been imposed.

4.1   Powers of inspectors

By the Financial Services Act 1986 section 177(3):

> 'If the inspectors consider that any person is or may be able to give information concerning any such contravention they may require that person –
>
> (a) to produce to them any documents in his possession or under his control relating to the company in relation to whose securities the contravention is suspected to have occurred or to its securities;
> (b) to attend before them; and
> (c) otherwise to give them all assistance in connection with the investigation which he is reasonably able to give;
>
> and it shall be the duty of that person to comply with that requirement.'

There is therefore no restriction on who may be summoned to see the inspectors, with the discretion of the inspectors to summon witnesses being very widely expressed. The powers of compulsion are in exactly the same terms, mutatis mutandis, as those provided in section 434(1) and (2) of the 1985 Act, and other provisions, including the administration of the oath, the use of witnesses' statements in evidence against them, and protection for material subject to legal professional privilege and banking confidentiality, are copied from the 1985 Act.

Failure to comply with the requirements of inspectors is treated in the same way as a failure to comply with requirements under section 434 of the 1985 Act. However, in addition to the power of the court to punish a person for contempt of court, the court may also 'direct that the Secretary of State may exercise his power under this section in respect of him; and the court may give a direction under paragraph (b) above, notwithstanding that the offender is not within the jurisdiction of the court if the court is satisfied that he was notified of his right to appear before the court and of the powers available under this section.'[11] The powers the Secretary of State may exercise relate to authorisation of the conduct of investment business as defined in the Financial Services Act 1986.[12]

The practice of inspectors conducting inquiries under section 177 of the 1986 Act is similar to that adopted by inspectors appointed under the Companies

8   Ibid, paragraphs 163 and 169.
9   Ibid, paragraph 53.
10 Financial Services Act 1986, section 177(2).
11 Financial Services Act 1986, section 178(2)(b).
12 See section 178(3).

Act. Appendix C of the Investigation Handbook repeats many of the requirements set out in Appendix B.

4.2 Confidentiality

Section 179 of the Financial Services Act 1986 contains extensive provisions relating to confidentiality. The section imposes restrictions on the disclosure of information which has been obtained by inspectors for the purposes of carrying out their inquiries. Information obtained by the inspectors for the purposes of, or in the discharge of, their function may become information which is passed on to persons summoned before the inspectors for interview. Therefore, information gathered during the course of an interview is 'restricted information' and it is an offence under section 179(6) to disclose such information to a third party.

It should be noted that under section 179 it is not an offence for a person summoned to appear before the inspectors under section 177 to discuss the fact of his summons, or the information which he is already in possession of, with a third party. Once the information has been given to inspectors it may become 'restricted information', although it would appear that the restriction only applies to someone who 'obtains the information', and not a person who already has it.

Inspectors frequently impose conditions of confidentiality on witnesses whom they summon to appear before them. This confidentiality cannot be imposed as a result of the provisions of section 179, but it may be said to be imposed under the general requirement, in section 177(3)(c): 'Otherwise to give (the inspectors) all assistance in connection with the inspection which he is reasonably able to give'.

4.3 Publication

Reports on insider dealing are never published. They are sent to the Secretary of State for the purpose of deciding whether proceedings under the Company Securities (Insider Dealing) Act 1985 should be instituted.

No announcement is made, either, of the appointment of inspectors,[13] and the result of an inquiry is equally not announced, unless it emerges in the form of the institution of criminal proceedings. The Department's practice if asked whether an inquiry under section 177 is being conducted is neither to confirm nor deny that an inspection is being made.[14]

4.4 Criticisms of individuals

Since the reports of inspectors appointed to inquire into allegations of insider dealing are not published there is no requirement to give an individual the right to respond to criticisms, as is required under the arrangements made pursuant to section 432 of the Companies Act 1985.

---

13 It is sometimes considered to be in the public interest to make an announcement but this is very rarely done.
14 DTI Inspection Handbook, Appendix C paragraph 15.

Nevertheless, the Inspection Handbook states that:

> '. . . if inspectors are minded to conclude that a person has contravened the Act then they should put to him the substance of the evidence against him and give him an opportunity to respond, either at an interview (or further interview) or in writing if he so wishes.'[15]

4.5   Further investigations

Inspectors appointed under section 177 of the Financial Services Act 1986 are stated to be required to 'establish whether or not a contravention [of the Company Securities (Insider Dealing) Act 1985] has occurred and to report the results of their investigations to [the Secretary of State].'[16] In these circumstances, it would appear that such inspectors are charged with the duty of investigating offences within the meaning of section 67(9) of the Police and Criminal Evidence Act 1984. It is their specific duty to consider contraventions of the 1985 Act, and to investigate them. Their report to the Secretary of State will be similar to a police report, supported by statements and documents, and although the inspectors themselves do not have the power to decide whether charges should be brought, they will make recommendations to the Secretary of State.[17]

Once a report has been delivered to the Secretary of State, further inquiries may be made either by officials of the Department or by the police. Evidence which has been obtained in transcript form from witnesses must be converted into witness statements, and documents must be properly produced. It may be necessary to obtain further evidence.

The role of the inspectors, however, is central to the investigation, and the powers they are given are intended, like the powers granted to the Serious Fraud Office, to be an investigative tool used as an essential preliminary to the mounting of a prosecution.

---

15 Ibid, paragraph 42.
16 Financial Services Act 1986 section 177(1).
17 See, for example, DTI Investigation Handbook, paragraph 42 cited above.

CHAPTER 9
Cross-border issues

Fraud is no respecter of national boundaries. The Law Commission[1] observed in its report on jurisdiction in fraud cases that:

> 'Modern crimes of dishonesty often involve complex operations designed to conceal dishonest conduct and to make detection and conviction as difficult as possible, and the planning, preparation and execution of the many operations which are involved in a complicated swindle frequently take place in several different countries.'

Dealing with cross-border crime is not a new exercise for the courts,[2] but the ease with which money, documents and information can now be transferred has increased the frequency with which international problems arise in a criminal context.

Those problems tend to focus on three main areas: do the English criminal courts have jurisdiction over the conduct complained of; if so, in what circumstances can the attendance of a suspect or of a witness abroad be compelled; and what are the obligations of other states to assist in the investigation and the provision of evidence for the purposes of a fraud trial in this jurisdiction. The answers are far from clear. In some respects, the law has been slow to respond to the fast-developing phenomenon of international fraud. In 1987, for example, the Law Commission and the Home Office initiated a review of the law relating to jurisdiction in fraud cases, which led to a Law Commission report in April 1989[3] recommending a radical overhaul of the rules relating to jurisdiction. The report has not, to date, been implemented generally, though some recent statutes have followed the recommendations fairly closely.[4] On the other hand, the Extradition Act 1989 and the Criminal Justice (International Co-operation) Act 1990 were enacted to ease the processes by which suspects could be brought to justice and evidence obtained from abroad.[5]

---

1 Law Commission: Jurisdiction over offences of Fraud and Dishonesty with a Foreign Element (Law Com No 180) 27 April 1989.
2 See, for example, *R v Ellis* [1899] 1 QB 230; *R v Holmes* (1883) 12 QBD 23.
3 Op cit.
4 See, for example, the Computer Misuse Act 1990; Financial Services Act 1986, section 47.
5 See sections 2 and 3 below. Section 68 of the Police and Criminal Evidence Act 1984 and sections 23 and 24 of the Criminal Justice Act 1988 enable documentary evidence from abroad to be admitted more easily.

1   JURISDICTION

1.1   **Introduction**

The rules of criminal jurisdiction are still largely governed by the common law. The intervention of statute has been piecemeal and sporadic. Few of the statutory provisions extending criminal jurisdiction beyond its usual territorial scope have related generally to fraud, though some statutes have widened and clarified the common law rules in respect of certain specific offences.[6] The result has been the development on a case-by-case basis of rules of jurisdiction which have been described as antiquated, narrow, technical and insular,[7] and which have been criticised for their complexity and eccentricity.[8] The rules have produced much jurisprudential analysis concerned with whether offences are subjective or objective, terminatory or initiatory,[9] or are conduct-crimes or result-crimes.[10] Judges have accepted these classifications with varying degrees of enthusiasm, and no uniform approach has been adopted. In a number of instances Lord Diplock has, for example, been ready to classify offences of deception as result-crimes. By contrast, Lord Salmon doubted whether such 'esoteric classifications' were of any practical utility in deciding cases and he did not envy the task of the trial judge in explaining such concepts to a jury who might well regard them as 'pieces of legal jargon beyond their comprehension'. In practice courts have looked for the 'gist' of the offence and, having found it, decided as a matter of fact whether it has, either physically, or constructively, or by some form of agency or other principle of civil law, or by the introduction of the concept of the continuing offence, been committed within the territorial jurisdiction. The approach has not always been consistent, and has been frequently artificial.

It is perhaps unsurprising that most of the authorities on jurisdiction involve offences of fraud and, in particular, obtaining by deception. Crimes of violence rarely cause jurisdictional problems: both the act of the offender and the consequence to the victim usually take place, not only within the same jurisdiction, but also very close to each other. In any event, such crimes tend to be classified as conduct-crimes, ie those in which the elements of the actus reus include only the behaviour of the offender and the circumstances in which it takes place.[11] The actus reus does not include a particular result and the common law looks only to where the conduct has taken place. Obtaining by deception, however, has been described as a result-crime[12] – the offender deceives dishonestly, but the offence is completed only when the property or pecuniary advantage is obtained, usually as the result of an act of the victim, which may be widely separate from the deception both in time and place. The

---

6   See Archbold *Criminal Pleading Evidence and Practice* (44th edn) paras 2-37 to 2-74 for a list of offences. Section 47 of the Financial Services Act 1986 specifies that offences under that section are justiciable if the misleading statement is made, or has effect, in the United Kingdom. See also section 35(2) of the Banking Act 1987.

7   Law Commission: op cit at page (v).

8   Hirst 'Jurisdiction over Cross-Frontier Offences' (1981) LQR 80.

9   Glanville-Williams 'Venue and Ambit of Criminal Law' (1965) LQR 518.

10   Gordon *The Criminal Law of Scotland* (2nd edn, 1978).

11   Murder is treated as an exception because the physical acts of the defendant only amount to murder if the victim dies as a result of the defendant's acts, which might take place at a time and place different from the defendant's act. Blackmail, on the other hand, has been classified as a conduct-crime: *Treacy v DPP* [1971] AC 537.

12   Per Lord Diplock in *DPP v Stonehouse* [1978] AC 55 at 67.

jurisdictional issues arise where, for example, the deception is practised in or from one jurisdiction and the obtaining effected in another.

1.2 General principles

English criminal jurisdiction is territorial; no person can be tried under English law for an offence committed on land abroad, unless there is some clear and specific statutory provision to the contrary.[13] The converse statement of the same principle perhaps focuses more clearly the particular point that the courts have to answer – no person can be tried under English law unless the offence was committed, subject to statutory exception, in England and Wales.[14] The basis of the principle was that the purpose of the criminal law was to 'maintain the Queen's Peace in her realm'[15] and that 'all crime is local' and 'belongs to the country where it is committed'.[16] Rules of international comity were thought to prohibit probing into conduct occurring in other jurisdictions and punishing it under English law.

The principle is buttressed by two presumptions. First, where Parliament creates an offence, it is presumed only to apply to offences committed within the United Kingdom. The principle was expressed uncontroversially by Lord Morris of Borth-y-Gest in *Treacy v DPP*[17] as follows:

> 'In general, therefore, acts committed out of England, even though they are committed by British subjects, are not punishable under the criminal law of this country. But, as Parliament is supreme, it is open to Parliament to pass an enactment in relation to such acts. It is, however, a general rule of construction that unless there is something which points to a contrary intention a statute will be taken to apply only to the United Kingdom. It would be open to Parliament to enact that if a British subject committed anywhere an act designated as blackmail he would commit an offence punishable in England. Such an enactment would, however, have to be in clear and express terms: specific provision would have to be made with regard to acts committed abroad.'

Second, even where the statute creating the offence clearly includes conduct committed outside England and Wales, there is a presumption that, in the absence of a contrary intention, it extends only to British subjects. The principle was stated by Lord Russell of Killowen CJ in *R v Jameson*.[18]

> 'One other general canon of construction is this – that if any construction otherwise be possible, an Act will not be construed as applying to foreigners in respect of acts done by them outside the dominions of the sovereign power enacting.'

The canon of construction applies also to powers delegated to ministers by statute. A minister only has power to make an Order under which acts committed abroad, whether by British subjects or not, are to be triable in the

---

13 *Cox v Army Council* [1963] AC 48, [1962] 1 All ER 880, HL; *Air India v Wiggins* [1980] 2 All ER 593, [1980] 1 WLR 815, HL.
14 Not Scotland, Northern Ireland, the Isle of Man nor the Channel Islands.
15 *Board of Trade v Owen* [1957] AC 602 at 625.
16 *McLeod v A-G for New South Wales* [1891] AC 455 at 458.
17 [1971] AC 537 at 552; see also *Cox v Army Council* [1963] AC 48, [1962] 1 All ER 880, HL; *Air India v Wiggins* [1980] 2 All ER 593, [1980] 1 WLR 815, HL.
18 [1896] 2 QB 425 at 430.

English criminal courts, where such power is confirmed by words in the statute so clear and specific as to be incapable of any other meaning.[19]

It is, of course, clear that foreign subjects committing an offence within the jurisdiction are amenable to the criminal courts.[20]

Lord Diplock opened the way, however, to a more liberal (or 'unorthodox', as described by one commentator)[1] approach to construing statutes which updates notions of international comity and which was adopted by the Law Commission.[2] In *Treacy v DPP* he stated:[3]

> 'The Parliament of the United Kingdom has plenary power, if it chooses to exercise it, to empower any court in the United Kingdom to punish persons present in its territories for having done physical acts wherever the acts were done and wherever their consequences took effect. When Parliament, as in the Theft Act 1968, defines new crimes in words which, as a matter of language, do not contain any geographical limitation either as to where a person's punishable conduct took place or, when the definition requires that the conduct shall be followed by specified consequences, as to where those consequences took effect, what reason have we to suppose that Parliament intended any geographical limitation to be understood?
>
> The only relevant reason, now that the technicalities of venue have long since been abolished, is to be found in the international rules of comity which, in the absence of express provision to the contrary, it is presumed that Parliament did not intend to break. It would be an unjustifiable interference with the sovereignty of other nations over the conduct of persons in their own territories if we were to punish persons for conduct which did not take place in the United Kingdom and had no harmful consequences there. But I see no reason in comity for requiring any wider limitation than that upon the exercise by Parliament of its legislative power in the field of criminal law.
>
> There is no rule of comity to prevent Parliament from prohibiting under pain of punishment persons who are present in the United Kingdom, and so owe local obedience to our law, from doing physical acts in England, notwithstanding that the consequences of those acts take effect outside the United Kingdom. Indeed, where the prohibited acts are of a kind calculated to cause harm to private individuals it would savour of chauvinism rather than comity to treat them as excusable merely on the ground that the victim was not in the United Kingdom itself but in some other state.
>
> Nor, as the converse of this, can I see any reason in comity to prevent Parliament from rendering liable to punishment, if they subsequently come to England, persons who have done outside the United Kingdom physical acts which have had harmful consequences upon victims in England. The state is under a correlative duty to those who owe obedience to its laws to protect their interests and one of the purposes of criminal law is to afford such protection by deterring by threat of punishment conduct by other persons which is calculated to harm those interests. Comity gives no right to a state to insist that any person may with impunity do physical acts in its own territory which have harmful consequences to persons within the territory of another state. It may be under no obligation in comity to punish those acts itself, but it has no ground for complaint in international law if the state in which the harmful consequences had their effect punishes, when they do enter its territories, persons who did such acts.

19 *Air India v Wiggins* [1980] 2 All ER 593, [1980] 1 WLR 815, HL.
20 *R v Keyn* (1876) 2 Ex D 63 at 160, CCR.
1   Hirst – op cit at p 90.
2   Law Comm, op cit at para 1.9.
3   [1971] AC 537 at 561.

The consequence of recognising the jurisdiction of an English court to try persons who do physical acts in England which have harmful consequences abroad as well as persons who do physical acts abroad which have harmful consequences in England is not to expose the accused to double jeopardy. This is avoided by the common law doctrine of autrefois convict and autrefois acquit, a doctrine which has always applied whether the previous conviction or acquittal based on the same facts was by an English court or by a foreign court: see *R v Roche* (1775) 1 Leach 134 and for a modern instance *R v Aughet* (1918) 13 Cr App Rep 101.'

The issue in *Treacy* was whether a demand written and posted in England, but only received by its intended victim in Germany, was 'made' within the jurisdiction for the purposes of section 21 of the Theft Act 1968. Lord Reid and Morris held that it was not: a demand could not be made until it was received – which had occurred outside the jurisdiction.[4] The other law lords considered that a person can 'make' a demand, even though the demand is not received by the victim and, accordingly, the offence had already been committed within the jurisdiction before the letter ever left English shores. The House of Lords defined making a demand in such a way that, on the facts of *Treacy*, the prohibited conduct had taken place squarely within the territorial jurisdiction. However, Lord Diplock's statement of the principles by which the Theft Act should be interpreted ranged well beyond section 21 and has implications for other offences under the Act, and potentially for offences of fraud under other Acts:

'The source of any presumption that Parliament intended that the right created by the Act to punish conduct should be subject to some territorial limitation upon where the conduct takes place or its consequences take effect can, in my view, only be the rules of international comity and the extent of the limitation, where none has been expressed in words, can only be determined by considering what compliance with those rules requires. I can leave aside the question of territorial limitation as between the different jurisdictions (England and Wales, Scotland and Northern Ireland, etc) within the United Kingdom, for this depends on constitutional practice, not on international comity. For reasons which I stated earlier, the rules of international comity, in my view, do not call for more than that each sovereign state should refrain from punishing persons for their conduct within the territory of another sovereign state where that conduct has had no harmful consequences within the territory of the state which imposes the punishment. I see no reason for presuming that Parliament in enacting the Theft Act 1968 intended to make the offences which it thereby created subject to any wider exclusion than this. In my view, where the definition of any such offence contains a requirement that the described conduct of the accused should be followed by described consequences the implied exclusion is limited to cases where *neither* the conduct *nor* its harmful consequences took place in England or Wales.

It follows that, even if the definition of "blackmail" in section 21 of the Act falls into the category of offences in which the physical acts of the accused must be followed by consequences occurring after completion of those acts, it is sufficient to constitute the offence of blackmail if either the physical acts are done or their consequences take effect in England or Wales.'

In the context, therefore, of obtaining property by deception it would, on Lord Diplock's analysis, be within the jurisdiction of the English court to try a

---

4 Because of the wording of section 1(4) of the Criminal Attempts Act 1981 by which attempts may be charged only in respect of offences which, if completed, are triable in England and Wales, Treacy could not have been charged with attempt.

defendant who either obtained property in England by a deception practised abroad, or alternatively who dishonestly deceived a victim in England, leading to the obtaining of property abroad. This does not, however, represent the general view of the law, which only regards the offence as justiciable here if the obtaining takes place here.[5]

1.3   Where is the offence committed?

In respect of each offence, therefore, the question arises as to where, in law and in fact, the prohibited conduct has been committed. There need not be a physical presence of the defendant within the jurisdiction. He may, for example, cause an innocent agent (or an accomplice) to commit the offence on his behalf.[6] In *R v Oliphant*[7] the defendant, a clerk in the Paris branch of a London tailor, was charged with omitting, and concurring in omitting, material particulars from a book belonging to his employers, with intent to defraud. He was required to send to London an account of all sums received by him in Paris in order that the amounts might be entered up in the 'Paris cash book' held in London. He stole payments received in Paris and omitted to send an account with the result that the partner in London omitted to record the payments in the Paris cash book. The charge related to the omission from the book held in London, not the omission in Paris to send an account to London. The court upheld the conviction: an entry made by an innocent agent under the direction of another is an omission by that other:

> 'The defendant did not enter upon the slips all the sums which he received; and as the defendant knew that an omission from a slip would necessarily involve an omission from the book, it seems to me to follow that he has omitted, or concurred in admitting, a material particular from the book. I am unable to draw a distinction between sending information by post or by telephone and giving the same information by direct personal communication in London.'

Two of the judges, referring to *R v Munton*,[8] took the view also that receipt of the fraudulent account slips in London made the offence complete in London. The offence was not charged as such, but the comments are of plain relevance in determining jurisdiction in cases of false accounting under section 17 of the Theft Act 1968.

1.4   Conduct-crimes

In the context of conduct-crimes, the crime is regarded as committed where the last of its constituent elements took place. In *Treacy*, in which Lord Diplock classified blackmail as a conduct-crime, it was held that a demand is 'made' for the purposes of section 21 of the Theft Act 1968 when it is posted and that it is unnecessary to show also that it was received within the jurisdiction, or indeed, anywhere. Presumably, if the defendant had written the letter and, instead of posting it, took it himself to the victim out of the jurisdiction or posted it in Germany, the demand would not have been made within the jurisdiction.

5   *R v Ellis* [1899] 1 QB 230; *R v Harden* [1963] 1 QB 8 which Lord Diplock thought was open to doubt; *R v Tirado* (1974) 59 Cr App Rep 80, CA; and further at para 1.6 below.
6   *R v Butt* (1884) 15 Cox CC 564.
7   [1905] 2 KB 67.
8   (1793) 1 Esp 62.

1.5 Result-crimes generally

In result-crimes, the offence is within the jurisdiction if any part of the proscribed result takes place within England and Wales. In *Secretary of State for Trade v Markus*,[9] the defendant was involved in the management of companies in London which had made false representations to victims in West Germany inducing them to invest in a trust fund. The victims were shown by salesmen in Germany a brochure which, inter alia, bore a conspicuous notice that all correspondence was to be addressed to one of the London companies. The victims' applications for units in the fraud were 'processed' in London and the consideration paid for the units found its way, via London, into the company's own account in Switzerland. The defendant was charged with conniving at a corporation fraudulently inducing the victims to take part in investments arrangements contrary to sections 13(1)(b) and 19 of the Prevention of Frauds (Investment) Act 1958. Lord Diplock stated:[10]

> 'The offences with which the appellant was charged were "result-crimes" of the same general nature as the offence of obtaining goods on credit by false pretences which was the subject of the charge in the case of *R v Ellis*.[11] That case is well-established authority for the proposition that, in the case of what is a result-crime in English law, the offence is committed in England and justiciable by an English court if any part of the proscribed result takes place in England.'

Lord Diplock analysed the proscribed result for the purposes of an offence against section 13(1)(b) and considered how, in a case in which the victims had not entered the jurisdiction, any part of the proscribed result could have taken place within the jurisdiction:

> 'The proscribed result in the instant case is the taking part in the arrangements by the victim of the fraudulent inducement. So if anything the victim did in England amounted to taking part in the arrangements, the offence was committed in England and is justiciable in this country.
>
> To decide whether anything that the victims did in England amounted to taking part in the arrangements involves a further question of construction of the statute, viz, what is meant by "take part in any arrangements". Taking part in arrangements is not confined to a single act which can only be done at a single point in time. Depending upon the nature of the arrangements, it may include a whole variety of acts done over a period. The nature of the arrangements dealt with in section 13(1)(b) is that they should be arrangements with respect to property other than securities and that their pretended purpose or effect should be to enable persons taking part in them to participate in or receive profits or income alleged to arise or to be likely to arise from the acquisition, holding, management, or disposal of such property. Anything that a person does to enable him to participate in or receive such profits or income thus constitutes taking part in the arrangements.'

The evidence had shown that the management of the scheme and the issuing of the share certificates was centred at the London office. The salesmen in Germany had no authority to accept offers from would-be investors, who could only take part in the arrangements once their application forms and cheques had been forwarded on their behalf by the salesman to London and

9 [1976] AC 35.
10 [1976] AC 35 at 61.
11 [1899] 1 QB 230.

accepted in London. Some of the would-be investors were induced to part with shares in another fund as payment for units in the bogus fund, and this was effected by giving powers of attorney to the London office which sent the share certificates and powers of attorney to Switzerland for encashment. Investors' applications were not accepted until the London company was notified that its account had been credited. Monthly payments were sent by the investors to the London office. Correspondence had to be addressed to the London office and delivered there. Lord Diplock said that since such letters from investors would not be acceptances of contractual offers that had been made by post to the London company,[12] the rule of law that the Post Office acts as agent of the addressee in receiving the letter containing an acceptance, at the place where it is posted, did not apply; in delivering correspondence by investors at the London office the Post Office would be acting as agent of the addressor. Lord Diplock concluded that the steps taken to process the applications were undertaken on behalf of the investors, though they had no physical presence within the jurisdiction and amounted to a taking part in the arrangements connived at by him. He rejected the argument that what was done after the investors handed the application to the salesman was done on behalf of the company.

Lord Diplock thus adopted the traditional approach of identifying both the result and an element of it within the jurisdiction. His approach in *Treacy* – assuming the evidence so allowed – would have enabled him to found jurisdiction on the basis of the company's own acts within the jurisdiction rather than upon the approach that the defendant and his company and the salesman acted as agents within the jurisdiction for the investors outside it. As with many of the previous cases on jurisdiction, the case, perhaps unfortunately, involved a detailed analysis of complicated facts and the use of civil principles of agency to establish jurisdiction. It would not be difficult to imagine circumstances in which, with only a slight change in the facts, a different result could have been reached, though with no collateral change in the merits.

1.6   Obtaining by deception

The offences of obtaining property and pecuniary advantage by deception are committed where the property is obtained.

In *R v Ellis*,[13] the defendant obtained credit in Durham by means of false representations made by him in Glasgow. The Court of Crown Cases Reserved held that the 'gist and kernel' of the offence is the obtaining of the property or advantage and there was some support for the view that it was irrelevant where the false representations were made.[14] It was also accepted that the representation, though made in Glasgow, was operative and continuing in Durham. In *R v Holmes*,[15] the defendant's deception was contained in a letter written and posted in England and sent to an address in France. Money was subsequently received from France by the defendant in England and the case

---

12 Cf *R v Harden* [1963] 1 QB 8, [1962] 1 All ER 286, CCA.
13 [1899] 1 QB 230.
14 The rule also applies for obtaining pecuniary advantage by deception: *R v Bevan* (1986) 84 Cr App Rep 143, CA.
15 (1883) 12 QBD 23.

was triable here. Lord Diplock has described obtaining by deception as a result-crime, though other judges have been less ready to adopt this terminology and more ready simply to accept the authority of *Ellis*.[16]

In the converse situation – obtaining property abroad as a result of a dishonest deception in England or Wales – it is clear that the English courts do not have jurisdiction.[17]

Despite the simplicity with which the principle can be expressed, it is frequently difficult to ascertain where the property or advantage has been obtained. In *R v Harden*,[18] the defendant made false representations inducing a company in Jersey to post cheques to the defendant in England. The defendant had indicated that the offer could be accepted by sending a cheque to the defendant. The company duly posted cheques, which were received by the defendant. His conviction was quashed because, having invited the company to send the cheques by post, he was deemed in law to have obtained them when they were posted by the sender in Jersey, because the Post Office would in law be acting as agent of the addressee, the defendant. The court, after considering a number of earlier authorities,[19] held that there was no single and universal rule which decided that a cheque transmitted through the post was to be treated as having been obtained at the moment of posting, but that would be the case where a defendant has agreed that receipt by the Post Office should be equivalent to receipt by himself. Plainly the defendant's moral culpability did not depend upon any agreement he had reached as to the posting and the receipt of the cheques. In *R v Tirado*,[20] the appellant, who ran an employment agency in Oxford, wrote to his victims in Morocco stating that he had work for them and inviting them to post their fees to his agency or arrange transfer through a Moroccan bank. The Court of Appeal held that the trial judge had been right to leave to the jury the 'highly technical' question of whether there had been an obtaining in England of the money remitted here by the Moroccan bank. The fact that the appellant had recommended that the money be posted was not enough for him to be deemed to have received it when it was posted rather than as its actual receipt.

Harden has been criticised on several grounds. In *Treacy v DPP*,[1] Lord Diplock commented that the court had assumed, without giving reasons, that the receipt of cheques in Jersey had deprived the English court of jurisdiction. He saw nothing inconsistent between the decision reached in *Ellis*[2] and the view that an English court would have jurisdiction only where the false pretences took place in England and the obtaining had taken place abroad. The rule also requires detailed investigation of factual issues relating to jurisdiction by the jury[3] and encourages the 'unwelcome'[4] intrusion of concepts of civil law into the criminal courts. Again in *Harden*, the court held that the obtaining relied upon must be an obtaining of the property in the thing charged, and not merely possession or control of it and that, in the context of payment by cheque, the

---

16 *DPP v Stonehouse* [1978] AC 55, [1977] 2 All ER 909, HL.
17 Law Commission, op cit at paras 2.4 and 2.29(a); *R v Harden* (infra). This proposition was also accepted in *Re Naghdi* [1990] 1 WLR 317 per Woolf LJ.
18 [1963] 1 QB 8, [1962] 1 All ER 286, CCA.
19 *R v Stoddart* (1909) 2 Cr App Rep 217; *R v TS Jones* (1850) 4 Cox CC 198, *R v Holmes* (1883) 12 QBD 23; *R v Marston* (1918) 13 Cr App Rep 203, CCA.
20 (1974) 59 Cr App Rep 80, CA.
1 [1971] AC 537 at 562–563.
2 Op cit.
3 See, for example, *R v Tirado* (1974) 59 Cr App Rep 80, CA.
4 See per Sachs LJ in *R v Baxter* [1972] 1 QB 1.

defendant obtains the cheque when the victim actually delivers it to him or constructively delivers it such as by handing it to an agent duly appointed by him. This part of the decision may, however, have been superseded by section 15(2) of the Theft Act 1968 which defines the offence to include obtaining ownership, possession or control.

In *R v Thompson*,[5] a computer operator employed by a bank in Kuwait programmed the bank's computer to debit accounts of other customers and credit his own accounts in Kuwait with corresponding amounts. On his return to England, he wrote to the Kuwaiti bank requesting sums held in his Kuwait accounts to be telexed to accounts he held in England with another bank. He withdrew the money from his English accounts and used it for his own purposes. He was charged with obtaining by deception. The Court of Appeal, in determining whether the English courts had jurisdiction, had to decide where the obtaining had taken place. Was it in Kuwait when the moneys had initially transferred, or was it in England? The indictment alleged that the obtaining had taken place in England when he received into the bank account the sterling equivalent of the credit balance in the Kuwaiti account. The defendant argued that he had obtained possession and control in Kuwait when the money had been transferred from the victims' to his own accounts. He had, at that point, obtained the victims' chose in action as against the Kuwaiti bank and, therefore, had then obtained control over the money in Kuwait. The court rejected the argument and held that the transfer in Kuwait had been vitiated by fraud and had transferred no interest to the defendant. The obtaining took place when the moneys were received in the English banks as a result of the deception practised upon the Kuwaiti bank in the defendant's letter of request.

There is an inconsistency in the decision because the vitiating factor as between the victims' accounts and the defendant's Kuwaiti account ought also to have vitiated the purported transfer between the defendant's Kuwaiti accounts and his English accounts on two bases: first, that the transfer from Kuwait to London was also contaminated by fraud; and second, that – because there had been no effective initial transfer – the defendant's Kuwaiti account contained nothing to be transferred to England.

The Law Commission has criticised *Thompson* because:

> 'It would therefore seem to follow that, if instead of instructing the bank in Kuwait to transfer the amount to his account in England, the accused's message from England had required cash to be withdrawn from his account in Kuwait and posted to his bank here (on the understanding that posting should be equivalent to delivery), the Court would not have had jurisdiction. The distinction between the two situations is highly artificial; in general, indeed, the element of "obtaining" is of little practical significance in relation to electronic and other modern methods of transferring money. Furthermore, the question where the obtaining took place could give rise to difficulty in some circumstances. For example, if by deception a fraudster were to induce his victim to execute abroad a share transfer relating to shares in an English company, it would not be easy to state with confidence whether his shares were "obtained" here or abroad.'[6]

The tangible obtaining in *Thompson* was when the defendant withdrew money from his accounts and there seems no reason why this should have not formed

5   [1984] 3 All ER 565, [1984] 1 WLR 962, CA.
6   Law Commission, op cit, para 2.9.

part of the proscribed result for the purposes of founding jurisdiction.[7] The withdrawal of the money from his own bank follows an implied representation to his own bank that he has good and valid title to money obtained from his account. On the facts of *Thompson* that would have been possible; but it would hardly be desirable for jurisdiction to depend solely on whether such a tangible withdrawal, or appropriation – for example, by paying bills – takes place within this jurisdiction.

The Law Commission has responded to these difficulties by recommending that the English courts should have jurisdiction over such offences if any event that is required to be proved in order to obtain a conviction of that offence takes place in England or Wales. Where, therefore, the definition of the offence forbids conduct producing a certain result the English courts would have jurisdiction if any part of the conduct, or any part of the defined specified result, takes place in England or Wales. It would be insufficient to establish jurisdiction, however, on the basis of a merely preparatory or incidental act or event that happened to form part of the narrative took place here.[8]

1.7   Theft

The offence of theft takes place where the property is appropriated, and the appropriation takes place where the property is situated.[9]

Section 4(1) of the Theft Act defines appropriation as any assumption by a person of the rights of an owner. It is not, however, necessary for the thief to have assumed all of the rights of an owner; assumption of any of the owner's rights will suffice for theft.[10] Accordingly anyone who draws, presents and negotiates a cheque on a particular bank account is assuming the rights of the owner of the credit in the account or of the pre-negotiated right to draw on the account up to the agreed figure.[11] Similarly, the act of sending a telex instructing a bank to debit an account is a sufficient act of appropriation.[12] In either case it matters not that the funds which are the subject of the cheque or telex are not, in the event, transferred.[13] For jurisdiction purposes, the presenting of the cheque, or the sending of the telex, must occur within England and Wales.[14]

1.8   False accounting

In *R v Governor of Pentonville Prison, ex p Osman*, the Divisional Court did not think it possible to lay down any general rules as to the place where the offence

---

7   As in *Tirado*.
8   Law Commission, op cit, para 2.28; and see *Re Naghdi* [1990] 1 WLR 317.
9   *R v Tomsett* [1985] Crim LR 369, CA; *R v Governor of Pentonville Prison, ex p Osman* [1989] 3 All ER 701 at 715.
10   *R v Morris* [1984] AC 320, [1983] 3 All ER 288, HL.
11   *Chan Man-sin v A-G of Hong Kong* [1988] 1 All ER 1, [1988] 1 WLR 196.
12   *R v Governor of Pentonville Prison, ex p Osman* [1989] 3 All ER 701 at 712.
13   *R v Governor of Pentonville Prison, ex p Osman*. The court rejected an argument that, by analogy with the acceptance of contractual offers, the appropriation takes place where the telex is received. The act of sending the telex was the appropriation and the place where that act was performed is the place of the appropriation. The court did not rule out the possibility of dual jurisdiction in the place where the telex was received.
14   See *Osman* op cit.

of false accounting is committed.[15] The defendant in Hong Kong had furnished monthly returns for consideration by its parent bank in Malaysia. It was argued that jurisdiction rested in the place where the returns were required for use, ie Malaysia, not the place where the defendant had made or concurred in making the returns. The court, while accepting that the place of intended use of the documents might in certain circumstances found jurisdiction, held that it would be artificial to regard Malaysia as the place of the offence when the falsified documents were prepared and created in Hong Kong and related to a business carried on there exclusively by the defendant.

1.9   Attempts

A person is guilty of attempting to commit an offence if, with intent to commit the offence, he does an act which is more than merely preparatory to its commission.[16] Section 1(4) of the Criminal Attempts Act provides that the offence must be one which, if completed, would be triable in England and Wales as an indictable offence. In determining whether the offence is triable in England and Wales, the same principles described above will apply. The Law Commission,[17] by way of highlighting the faults in this approach, provided the example of a defendant resident in London devising a scheme in which false representations are made to a bank here inducing it to instruct its New York branch to hand over money to the defendant in New York. If the fraud is detected and the New York bank refuses to give him money when he calls to collect it, the defendant will clearly have done an act which is more than merely preparatory to the commission of the offence, but could not face trial in this country because the obtaining would not, if the offence had been completed, have taken place here. If the New York bank telexed money to its London branch and only then was the fraud discovered, it seems from *Thompson* that, whether or not the defendant actually withdraws money from the London bank, an obtaining (not merely an attempt) within the jurisdiction will have taken place.

The consequences of section 1(4) and the decision in *Harden* were considered by the Divisional Court in *Re Naghdi*[18] in which the applicant sought to avoid his extradition to the United States for offences of deception by arguing that applying English rules of criminal jurisdiction – as the English court must when considering an application extradite a defendant – he would not be triable in the United States courts. Woolf LJ concluded that, on the facts, there was sufficient evidence that the obtaining would have occurred in the United States, but:

> 'Although the language of section 1(4) is not entirely clear, I am satisfied that sub-section (4) in its reference to England and Wales is referring to the jurisdiction to try the completed offence. That means that, because of the decision in *Harden*, where an attempted obtaining is alleged, if the full offence would have been completed outside England and Wales, the attempt is not triable in England and Wales even though all the preparatory steps towards the commission of the full offence took place in England and the defendant had the necessary intent. Thus, taking an example which is relevant to this

---

15 Op cit at 719.
16 Criminal Attempts Act 1981 section 1(1).
17 Law Comm, op cit at para 4.8.
18 [1990] 1 WLR 317.

case, if false pretences are made in this country to obtain a letter of credit but the letter of credit is to be delivered abroad, then, even if the full offence is never completed and all the ingredients of attempt occur in this country, there is no jurisdiction to try the attempt in this country.'

He added his voice to the criticism of *Harden* expressed by Lord Diplock in *Treacy* and continued:

'It creates very real problems, for example, in the case of international transactions where the parties have not agreed where the obtaining is actually to occur. A position could arise where, according to the English approach to jurisdiction to try attempts, no country would have jurisdiction to try the offence, which is hardly a satisfactory result.'

In each of these situations, the acts which are more than merely preparatory have themselves taken place entirely within the jurisdiction and it is the completed offence which is to take place abroad. What if the acts constituting the attempt take place abroad in respect of an offence to be completed within the jurisdiction? The courts have jurisdiction to try a charge of attempt when the acts which are more than merely preparatory to the commission of the offence are intended to, and do, produce an effect in this country. In *R v Baxter*,[19] the defendant posted letters from Northern Ireland and addressed to pools promoters in Liverpool falsely claiming winnings for correctly forecasting the outcome of certain football matches. The pools promoters were suspicious and did not pay the winnings alleged to be due. The defendant was charged with attempting to obtain property by deception. The trial judge ruled that the attempts were of a continuing nature, were intended to be effective here and were accordingly triable here.[20] The Court of Appeal assumed that if the claim had been successful, the obtaining would have been within the jurisdiction.[1] The court concurred that the offence was a continuing one and it mattered not that the attempt commenced out of the jurisdiction provided it continued, through innocent agency or otherwise, within the jurisdiction. Sachs LJ said:

'It matters not whether on any particular set of facts the attempt is best described as a continuing offence (as where a time bomb set to explode at a given hour in this country is being sent by rail) or as a series of offences (as where there are series of blows on a cold chisel to force a door open). If the time bomb is discovered on the train it matters not whether it is known on which side of some border it was placed there. The position is no different if what is being transmitted is a letter and the moment when its contents come to light occurs on the premises where it is meant to produce the intended result, an obtaining by deception of money from someone within the jurisdiction. The attempt has occurred within the jurisdiction. On those principles it is accordingly manifest that there is no reason why the jurisdiction of the courts here should not attach to the offence.

An alternative but no less effective way of expressing the matter is to say that he who dispatches a missile or a missive arranges for its transport and delivery (essential parts of the attempt) and is thus committing part of the crime within the jurisdiction by the means which he has arranged. The physical personal presence of an offender within this country is not, according to our law, an essential element of offences committed here.

---

19 [1972] 1 QB 1, [1971] 2 All ER 359, CA.
20 Op cit at 8.
1   Op cit at 10G. This seems untenable in the light of *R v Ellis* (supra) but there may have been an agreement that posting in England would be deemed to be receipt in England by the defendant.

There is certainly no authority against the above conclusions. Such dicta as can be found strongly favour it. It is sufficient simply to mention one or two of the well-selected passages quoted in the ruling of the recorder. Thus in *R v Rogers* (1877) 3 QBD 28, a venue case where the charge was embezzlement, Field J said at p 34:

> "A letter is intended to act on the mind of the recipient, its action upon his mind takes place when it is received. It is like the case of the firing of a shot, or the throwing of a spear. If a shot is fired, or a spear thrown, from a place outside the boundary of a county into another county with intent to injure a person in that county, the offence is committed in the county within which the blow is given."

Again in *R v Oliphant* [1905] 2 KB 67 at 72 there occurs in the judgment of Lord Alverstone CJ a relevant passage:

> "I am unable to draw any distinction between sending information by post or by telephone and giving the same information by direct personal communication in London."

Finally, in *Halsbury's Laws of England*, 3rd edn, vol 10 (1955), p 318, para 581, it is stated:

> "If a person, being outside England, initiates an offence, part of the essential elements of which take effect in England, he is amenable to English jurisdiction"

– a passage which correctly states the law.'

The effect, of course, was that the claim *did* attempt to persuade the pools promoters in England that winnings were due to the defendant. Quaere if the letter got lost in the post in England – or Northern Ireland? Lord Diplock has asserted that, in either case, the court would have jurisdiction even though no effect was felt in this country.[2] Intention alone that it should do so would suffice.

In *DPP v Stonehouse*,[3] the defendant, a member of Parliament and former government minister, was convicted, inter alia, of attempting by deception to enable his wife to obtain money from a life insurance company by falsely pretending that he had drowned. The defendant had travelled to the United States and faked his death by accidental drowning. His disappearance and supposed death hit the headlines in the media in England, ensuring, as he had intended, that news of his death should be communicated to his wife in England who would claim the policy moneys. The certified question for the House of Lords was whether the offence of attempting to obtain property in England by deception, the final act alleged to constitute the offence of attempt having occurred outside the jurisdiction, was triable in an English court, all the remaining acts necessary to constitute the complete offence being intended to take place in England. The defendant's wife was not party to the plan and had not claimed on the policies. The Crown's submissions[4] were, in essence, accepted by the House of Lords and succinctly reflect the current state of the law.

(1) It is well settled that a person may be indicted in England for a criminal offence committed by his agent in England notwithstanding that he was physically outside the jurisdiction at all material times.

---

2 In *DPP v Stonehouse* [1978] AC 55 at 67. This is, of course, consistent with the view he expressed in *Treacy v DPP* [1971] AC 537 at para 1.2 above.
3 [1978] AC 55, [1977] 2 All ER 909, HL.
4 [1978] AC 55 at 63.

(2) It is immaterial whether the agent is an innocent or a willing participant in the crime. In either case the principal may be indicted as a principal in the crime.

(3) It is immaterial whether the act or acts of attempt are performed within or outside the jurisdiction. They merely evidence the fact that he is trying to commit the crime in England.

(4) If (3) is too widely stated, there is jurisdiction to try in England any attempt to commit a crime in England where (a) any act of preparation takes place in England or (b) the act or acts of attempt abroad may have effect in England, whether through an accident or otherwise.

The Lords confirmed that, in the case of a result-crime, the English courts have jurisdiction to try the offence if the described consequence of the conduct of the defendant were to take place in England.[5] The defendant's acts caused an effect in England which was inevitable and intended, namely, the communication through the media to Mrs Stonehouse and the insurance companies of the false representation that the defendant had actually drowned.

Lord Diplock ventured further than other Law Lords in his analysis of *Baxter*,[6] suggesting that the English courts would have had jurisdiction even if no part of the defendant's intended conduct was carried out in this country:

'It was held that the English Court had jurisdiction on what in the head-note are described as alternative grounds – (i) that the attempt was still in being when the contents of the letters containing the fraudulent claims came to light in Liverpool where they were meant to produce the intended result; or, alternatively, (ii) that when a person despatches a missive and arranges for its transport and delivery, this delivery forms an essential part of the attempt and is committed in the place where it is delivered.

If these are not really expressing a single ground in different words, I have some doubts about ground (i). Both grounds appear, however, to treat as the foundation of territorial jurisdiction in the offences of an attempt that something should actually have happened in England as a result of the physical acts done by the offender abroad. For my part I think there would have been jurisdiction in Baxter's case even if the fraudulent claims had been intercepted in the post while still in Northern Ireland.'

In so saying, Lord Diplock was the only member of the Appellate Committee to accept the Crown submission at (3).

The Law Commission thought the present law of jurisdiction for attempted offences was satisfactory but recommended that jurisdiction should exist whether or not the attempt was made in England and Wales and whether or not it had an effect here.[7]

1.10 Conspiracy

The same principles apply both to statutory conspiracies and conspiracies to defraud and have already been described.[8] Section 1(4) of the Criminal Law Act 1977 provides that the offence, for the purposes of a statutory conspiracy, means an offence triable in England and Wales and would appear to rule out

5 Op cit per Lord Diplock at 67; per Viscount Dilhorne at 75; per Lord Salmon at 78; per Lord Edmund Davies at 83; per Lord Keith at 92.
6 [1972] 1 QB 1.
7 Law Comm, op cit at para 4.11.
8 See Chapter 6.

the possibility of a conviction for statutory conspiracy where the conspirators leave open the question where the offence will take place.[9] The starting point, therefore, will be to look at the offence as if it had been completed, and to determine, according to the rules applicable for substantive offences, whether the offence would, if completed, have been triable here.

So that, for example, a conspiracy in England to make false representations in Glasgow in anticipation of an obtaining in England would, by analogy with *R v Ellis*,[10] be triable in England. Equally, a conspiracy here to obtain abroad would not be triable here.[11]

The question has arisen whether a conspiracy entered into abroad is triable here and has been discussed elsewhere.[12] The current position is that, provided there is evidence to show a link between the conspiracy and England, such a conspiracy is indictable here. There had, hitherto, been some doubt as to whether it was necessary to show some overt act in England pursuant to a conspiracy hatched abroad. In *R v Sansom*,[13] a conspiracy to import drugs prosecution, Lord Griffiths concluded:

> 'The only purpose of looking for an overt act in England in the case of a conspiracy entered into abroad can be to establish the link between the conspiracy and England or possibly to show the conspiracy is continuing. But if this can be established by other evidence, for example, the taping of conversations between the conspirators showing a firm agreement to commit the crime at some future date, it defeats the preventative purpose of the crime of conspiracy to have to wait until some overt act is performed in pursuance of the conspiracy.'

There remains, clearly, an inconsistency between attempt and conspiracy. In attempts, some effect on the jurisdiction must, on the majority view in *Stonehouse*,[14] be shown rather than simply an intended link with England or Wales. There is also considerable vagueness as to what constitutes a 'link' for these purposes.

1.11   Incitement

The Law Commission found no direct authority as to whether the English courts have jurisdiction to try a person for inciting, outside England and Wales, another to commit an offence triable in this country.[15] The Commission further found no direct authority that a person who, in England and Wales, incites another to commit an offence abroad is triable here. By analogy with the rules relating to attempt, the Commission concluded that such an offence would not be triable here.[16]

---

9   *R v Kohn* (1864) 4 F & F 68, 176 ER 470.
10 [1899] 1 QB 230.
11 See *R v Governor of Brixton Prison, ex p Rush* [1969] 1 All ER 316, [1969] 1 WLR 165.
12 See further Chapter 6.
13 [1991] 2 QB 130, [1991] 2 All ER 145, CA.
14 [1978] AC 55 per Lord Diplock.
15 Law Commission, op cit at para 4.12.
16 Law Commission, op cit at para 5.21.

1.12 The Law Commission's recommendations

The Law Commission has recommended a radical reform of the rules relating to jurisdiction in fraud cases. The present rules would be abolished entirely. In respect of substantive 'listed offences',[17] an offence would be triable in England and Wales if any event proof of which is required for a conviction of the offence takes place in England and Wales, irrespective of whether at the time of the event, the accused was present in England and Wales. For these purposes property despatched from outside but received in England and Wales and, conversely, property despatched from England and Wales and received elsewhere would be regarded as appropriated or obtained in England and Wales. Similarly, information communicated from outside but received in England and Wales, or vice versa, would be regarded as communicated in England and Wales.

Conspiracy to commit a listed offence triable here and conspiracy to defraud in England or Wales would be triable here wherever the conspiracy was formed and whether or not any act in furtherance of the conspiracy takes place in England and Wales.

The attempts would be triable here in respect of listed offences triable here whether or not the attempt was made or had an effect here. Incitements to commit a listed offence would be triable here wherever the indictment took place.

Further amendments have been recommended regarding frauds hatched in England and Wales but intended to take place abroad. In the case of a conspiracy to perform abroad what, if performed in England and Wales, would amount to a listed offence or a conspiracy to defraud outside England and Wales, the English courts would have jurisdiction if at least one conspirator (through his own or his agent's acts) became a party to the conspiracy, or advanced it, here. Similarly, the courts would have jurisdiction over an attempt or incitement to perform actions abroad which, if performed in England and Wales, would amount to a listed offence if some or all of the acts constituting the attempt or incitement take place here. In both instances, there would be a 'double criminality' rule requiring that the completed offence conspired at or attempted or incited should be an offence in the place where it is to take place.

The recommendations would rid the present law of many of its complexities and anachronisms. It does, however, extend jurisdiction considerably. It would not be difficult to imagine circumstances in which an isolated act, in furtherance of a conspiracy to commit an offence abroad, is committed here but which, apart from that act, has no substantial link with this country at all. That act might amount to no more than a telephone call in a lounge at Heathrow, or a call from a portable phone on a ship that has left Dover, though is still inside territorial waters. Does international comity require that the English courts assume jurisdiction, particularly against the background of a more effective scheme for international co-operation and provision of evidence for the purpose of proceedings in the state where the substance of the offence has been committed?

17 Theft; obtaining property by deception; obtaining pecuniary advantage by deception; false accounting; false statements by company directors; procuring the execution of a valuable security; blackmail; handling stolen goods; obtaining services by deception; evasion of liability by deception; forgery; copying; using or using a copy of a false instrument; offences relating to money orders, share certificates and passports.

2   EXTRADITION

2.1   Defects in the pre-1988 extradition laws

In its White Paper entitled 'Criminal Justice: Plans for Legislation',[18] the government accepted the need to amend extradition law to enable it effectively to meet the huge expansion in international crime, particularly terrorism, drug trafficking and fraud. The United Kingdom was, it claimed, widely regarded as one of the most difficult countries from which to secure the extradition of fugitives and was failing to meet its responsibilities to combat international crime. It was thought desirable that the United Kingdom should become a party to the European Convention on Extradition.[19]

The principal difficulty in the existing law was the requirement, both for foreign states under the Extradition Acts 1870–1935 and Commonwealth countries under the Fugitive Offenders Act 1967, to produce before an English Court such evidence as would, according to the law of England and Wales, justify the committal for trial of the fugitive if the crime had been committed in England and Wales.[20] This caused particular difficulty to countries with an inquisitorial system because they used arrest as part of the investigation process and led to the denunciation by Spain of its extradition treaty with the United Kingdom in 1978. Doubt was cast, however, on the strength of this as an objection to current procedures in debate.[1] In addition to imposing an evidential burden, requests were exposed to the idiosyncrasies of English law by permitting extradition only in respect of matters which, if they had been committed within UK jurisdiction, would constitute an offence against the law of the United Kingdom. In *R v Governor of Brixton Prison, ex p Rush*,[2] for example, the Divisional Court rejected a Canadian request because the fugitive's alleged dishonest obtaining had occurred in the United States and not in Canada. If this case were tried as a domestic offence, the court would have had no jurisdiction,[3] and that quirk of English law led to rejection of the request even though, under its own law, the Canadian court would have had jurisdiction.

2.2   Which extradition scheme applies?

Part I of the Criminal Justice Act 1988 brought into force a new scheme of extradition for foreign states and made amendments to the existing scheme for Commonwealth countries. Following a report of the Law Commission,[4] the law relating to foreign states and the Commonwealth was consolidated in the Extradition Act 1989.[5] The Extradition Acts 1870–1935 and the Fugitive

---

18 Cmnd 9658, March 1986; preceded by the report of an Inter-departmental Working Party entitled 'A Review of the Law and Practice of Extradition in the UK' (Home Office, 1982) and a Green Paper entitled 'Extradition' (Cmnd 9421). For a more detailed exposition of extradition law see V Hartley-Booth *Extradition Law*.
19 Signed in Paris on 13 December 1957.
20 The Extradition Act 1870 section 10 and the Fugitive Offenders Act 1967 section 7(5).
1   See, for example, per Lord Hutchinson, HL Debates, Vol 490, col 97, 17 November 1987.
2   [1969] 1 All ER 316, [1969] 1 WLR 165; see also *Tarling v Government of the Republic of Singapore* (1978) 70 Cr App Rep 77 at 136; *R v Governor of Pentonville Prison, ex p Osman* [1989] 3 All ER 701, [1990] 1 WLR 277.
3   Because the obtaining had taken place out of the jurisdiction: see previous section.
4   Law Commission (Cm 712) No 182.
5   The Act applies to Northern Ireland and came into force on 27 September 1989.

Offenders Act 1967 have now been repealed.[6] Extradition arrangements with the Republic of Ireland are still governed by the Backing of Warrants (Republic of Ireland) Act 1965.

The Extradition Act 1989 continues to give authority to Orders in Council made under the Extradition Acts 1870–1935 which implement existing extradition treaties.[7] These Orders in Council will continue to govern extradition to and from foreign states, under an amended procedure in Schedule 1 of the 1989 Act, until those treaties are replaced and Orders in Council are made under the 1989 Act. Until all such Orders are replaced, the old scheme and the new scheme will co-exist. Annex A to this section (on p 254) lists the Orders in Council made under section 2 of the 1870 Act and the foreign states to which the provisions of the 1870 Act, as amended and preserved by Schedule 1 of the 1989 Act, still apply.[8] The 1989 Act enables the UK government to enter into extradition arrangements to which the provisions of the Act apply. These may be 'general extradition arrangements' or special ad hoc arrangements under section 15.[9]

Commonwealth countries may, by Order in Council, be designated under section 5(1) and (3) as countries to which the 1989 Act applies. No Orders in Council have yet been made under this section but Orders made under section 2 of the Fugitive Offenders Act 1967 are preserved by section 17(2)(b) of the Interpretation Act 1978 and effectively apply the 1989 Act to all Commonwealth countries which had been designated under the Fugitive Offenders Act 1967. If a Commonwealth country has ratified the European Convention it may be treated as a foreign state for the purposes of the 1989 Act.[10]

2.3 The Extradition Act 1989

The Extradition Act 1989 implements a number of the proposals made in the White Paper and the Green Paper.[11]

The Act does not remove the requirement that requesting states must establish a prima facie case, but it does contain a power to dispense with that requirement where an Order in Council under section 4 of the Act, giving effect to general extradition arrangements with a foreign state, so provides. It will, therefore, be a matter for agreement between the UK and each foreign state as to whether the prima facie case rule should apply and it would appear that such agreement may only be reached in the context of general extradition arrangements and not as part of any ad hoc arrangements reached pursuant to section

---

6 The only provision to survive the Extradition Act 1873 was section 5 of the Extradition Act 1873 relating to the power to take evidence in the UK for foreign criminal matters. This has now been replaced by the Criminal Justice (International Co-operation) Act 1990.
7 Extradition Act 1989 section 1(3) and Schedule 1.
8 Section 3(2); 'foreign state' means any state other than the United Kingdom, Commonwealth countries, a colony or the Republic of Ireland.
9 These may relate to certain individuals or to certain crimes. The United Kingdom is already party to extradition arrangements in respect of specific crime, such as aircraft hijacking and attacks on diplomats, with states with which it has no general extradition arrangements.
10 Cyprus is a party to the Convention. The Convention, which was prepared under the auspices of the Council of Europe, is, however, open only for European signatories and most other Commonwealth countries will not be eligible to ratify it.
11 'Criminal Justice: Plans for Legislation' (Cmnd 9658) and 'Extradition' (Cmnd 9421).

15 of the Act.[12] Commonwealth countries remain subject to the requirement and cannot, by virtue of the terms of section 9(4) and (8), dispense with it.[13]

Only one Order in Council has been made under section 4 of the Act. The European Convention on Extradition Order[14] was made on 24 July 1990 and was effective from 14 May 1991 when the European Convention on Extradition came into force in the UK. The Order applies to Austria, Cyprus, Denmark, Finland, France, Germany, Greece, Iceland, Israel, Italy, Luxembourg, Netherlands, Norway, Portugal, Spain, Sweden, Switzerland and Turkey. It revokes all previous Orders in Council implementing extradition arrangements with these states except (a) as regards requests in respect of which an order under paragraph 4(2) of Schedule 1 to the Act was made before 14 May 1991; or (b) in so far as they relate to extradition between the UK and any territory for whose relations a Convention state is responsible but to which the Convention does not apply.

Article 3 of the Order provides that where an extradition request is made by a Convention state in respect of a person accused of an offence, it is not necessary for that state to furnish the court of committal with, nor for the court to be satisfied that there is, evidence sufficient to warrant the trial of that person if the extradition crime had taken place within the jurisdiction of the court. As regards Convention states, therefore, the prima facie case rule is abolished.

The move away from a prima facie case requirement was heavily criticised in the Bill's passage through Parliament. Even in cases where the fugitive would, without doubt, receive a fair trial in the requesting state, it was argued that it was unacceptable to order return of the fugitive without some judicial consideration of the evidence upon which his return was sought. The decision to uproot an individual (who might be a United Kingdom citizen) ought only to follow on from a judicial act and the function of the magistrate was being relegated to little more than an executive function. An Order in Council which dispenses with the prima facie case requirement is subject to annulment in pursuance of a resolution of either House of Parliament[15] and it remains to be seen whether the issue will be aired further.[16]

For other foreign states and designated Commonwealth countries, the prima facie requirement still applies, though English rules of practice need not apply. Evidence obtained by foreign police officers, for example, is not inadmissible by reason only of the fact that it was not obtained in accordance with the judge's rules.[17]

The procedure under the 1989 Act bears close resemblance to the previous legislation. The extradition request is made to the Secretary of State[18] and must be accompanied by:

(a) particulars of the person whose return is requested;
(b) particulars of the offence of which he is accused or was convicted (including evidence sufficient to justify the issue of a warrant for his arrest);[19]

---

12 Section 9(4) and (8).
13 Section 9(4): except Cyprus, which has ratified the Convention.
14 SI 1990/1507.
15 Section 4(4) and (5).
16 The Order implementing the European Convention attracted little attention.
17 *Beese v Governor of Ashford Remand Centre* [1973] 3 All ER 689, [1973] 1 WLR 1426, HL; and, presumably now, the PACE Codes of Practice.
18 Section 7(1).
19 This requirement applies in all cases, even where the requirement of a prima facie case has been dispensed with.

(c) in the case of a person accused of an offence, a warrant for his arrest issued in the requesting state; and

(d) in the case of a person unlawfully at large after conviction, a certificate of the conviction and sentence.

Copies must be served on the person whose return is requested before he is brought before the court of committal.[20] Unless the Secretary of State considers that an Order for return could not lawfully be made, or would not in fact be made, he will issue an 'authority to proceed', specifying the offence or offences under the law of the United Kingdom which would be constituted by equivalent conduct in the United Kingdom, to the Chief Metropolitan Magistrate or a metropolitan magistrate designated by the Lord Chancellor to hear extradition cases.[1] The Act provides, for the first time, for a Scottish court to have jurisdiction for extradition rather than requiring all applications for extradition from the United Kingdom to be dealt with in England.[2]

On receipt of the authority to proceed, the court may issue a warrant for the fugitive's arrest.[3] When a warrant is issued for an offence of stealing or receiving stolen property, the court may also issue a warrant to search for the property.[4] Following arrest, the fugitive must be brought as soon as practicable before a metropolitan magistrate, who may remand him on bail or in custody[5] and who may, if the arrest is made under a provisional warrant, fix a period after which he will be discharged from custody unless an authority to proceed has been received.[6] A person arrested pursuant to section 8 or to paragraph 5 of Schedule 1 to the 1989 Act may consent at any time to his return without a hearing. Consent is signified by issuing a Notice in the form specified in Form 2 of the Magistrates' Court (Extradition) Rules.[7]

Where the court is satisfied that the offence is an extradition crime and, in the case of a person accused of an offence, that the evidence would be sufficient to commit him for trial in the United Kingdom[8] or that the fugitive has been convicted and appears to be at large, the court must commit him to custody or on bail to await the Secretary of State's decision as to his return and if the Secretary of State so decides, his return.[9] The court may refuse to commit if return would be prohibited by any provision of the Act.[10] In particular, a person's return, or committal for the purposes of return, is prohibited if it appears to the court that any of the grounds in section 6 applies. These include where the offence is of a political character, or is an offence under military law which is not also an offence under the general criminal law;[11] where the purpose of the fugitive's return is to prosecute or punish him, or if returned, he

---

20 Section 7(2).
1 Section 7(4) and (5), section 8(1) and (2).
2 Section 8(1) and 9(1).
3 Section 8(1). The power to issue a provisional warrant on information that the fugitive is or is believed to be in or on his way to the United Kingdom and pending the receipt of an extradition request is preserved.
4 Section 8(6).
5 Section 9(1) and (2).
6 Section 9(5). The court must have regard to any period specified by the Order in Council relating to the requesting state.
7 SI 1989/1597 rule 6.
8 Subject to the provisions of an Order in Council made pursuant to section 9(4).
9 Section 9(8).
10 Section 9(8).
11 Section 6(1)(a) and (b).

will be prejudiced, punished, detained or restricted in his personal liberty, because of his race, religion, nationality or political opinions;[12] where the conviction in respect of which his return is sought was obtained in his absence and it would not be in the interests of justice to return him;[13] and where, if charged with that offence in the United Kingdom, he would be entitled to be discharged under any rule of law relating to a previous conviction or acquittal.[14] Furthermore, if returned, the fugitive may only be prosecuted in respect of the offence for which his extradition was ordered or an offence disclosed by the facts on which his extradition was ordered, or for an extradition crime in respect of which the Secretary of State consents to his being dealt with.[15] He may, subject to anything to the contrary in the extradition arrangements, only be prosecuted for other offences if he has first had an opportunity to leave the requesting state.[16]

2.4   What is an 'extradition crime'?

The Act, and any extradition arrangement (general or special) made thereunder, only applies to an 'extradition crime'. There is no longer a list of offences to which extradition arrangements may apply.[17] Instead, the Act defines 'extradition crime', and the extradition arrangements made with a foreign state may either embrace all offences falling within the definition or may exclude offences from the arrangements. 'Extradition crime' is defined as:

'(1) . . .
    (a) conduct in the territory of a foreign state, a designated Common-wealth country or a colony which, if it occurred in the United Kingdom, would constitute an offence punishable with imprisonment for a term of 12 months, or any greater punishment, and which, however described in the law of the foreign state, Commonwealth country or colony, is so punishable under that law;
    (b) an extra-territorial offence against the law of a foreign state, designated Commonwealth country or colony which is punishable under that law with imprisonment for a term of 12 months, or any greater punishment, and which satisfies –
       (i) the condition specified in subsection (2) below; or
      (ii) all the conditions specified in subsection (3) below.
(2) The condition mentioned in subsection (1)(b)(i) above is that in corresponding circumstances equivalent conduct would constitute an extra-territorial offence against the law of the United Kingdom punishable with imprisonment for a term of 12 months, or any greater punishment.
(3) The conditions mentioned in subsection (1)(b)(ii) above are –
    (a) that the foreign state, Commonwealth country or colony bases its jurisdiction on the nationality of the offender;
    (b) that the conduct constituting the offence occurred outside the United Kingdom; and

12 Section 6(1)(c) and (e).
13 Section 6(2).
14 Section 6(3).
15 Section 6(4).
16 The rule of specialty.
17 See, for example, Extradition Act 1870 Schedule 1.

(c) that, if it occurred in the United Kingdom, it would constitute an offence under the law of the United Kingdom punishable with imprisonment for a term of 12 months, or any greater punishment.'[18]

These provisions considerably extend the previous range of extradition offences and would include, particularly, offences against the Revenue or Customs authorities, conspiracy to defraud, insider dealing[19] and many offences under the Companies Acts. The definition is, however, only an 'enabling' definition and it is open to states to agree a limitation. The Convention, for example, excludes extradition for fiscal offences (offences in connection with tax, duties, Customs and exchange) unless the parties agree to include them.[20] The provision relating to extra-territorial offences means that *R v Governor of Brixton Prison, ex p Rush*[1] would today be decided in the same way.

In the context of serious frauds it may frequently happen that the conduct constituting the offence takes place in several jurisdictions. For extradition purposes, ie in considering whether the conduct would have amounted to an offence in the United Kingdom, cases under the earlier legislation decided that the court may only take into account the acts or omissions which took place in the requesting state.[2]

2.5 Rights of appeal

2.5.1 Case stated

Prior to 1988, a requesting state had no right to challenge a refusal to commit a fugitive for extradition by way of case stated.[3] The Criminal Justice Act 1988 amended the Fugitive Offenders Act 1967 to permit a Commonwealth country or colony, where the court refused to commit the fugitive for return, to question the proceeding on the ground that it was wrong in law by applying to the committing court to state a case for the opinion of the High Court.[4] This right is extended by the 1989 Act to extradition requests by foreign states under Part III of the Act.[5] Pending such an application for, and the hearing of, a case stated the court may remand the fugitive in custody or on bail if the requesting state immediately informs the court that it intends to make such an application.[6] In the event that the requesting state does not immediately inform the court of its intention to make an application, there is no provision allowing a further remand pending the hearing. If the High Court directs the committing court to consider the matter afresh,[7] it seems likely that a further warrant for arrest could be issued, but there is no obvious statutory power to do so.[8]

---

18 Section 2.
19 Insider dealing was, in any event, added to the list of extradition offences in the Extradition Act 1870 by the Criminal Justice Act 1988 Schedule 1.
20 None of the parties has so agreed, save France in one limited instance.
1 [1969] 1 All ER 316, [1969] 1 WLR 165.
2 *Tarling v Government of the Republic of Singapore* (1978) 70 Cr App Rep 77 at 136; *R v Governor of Pentonville Prison, ex p Osman* [1989] 3 All ER 701 at 713.
3 *Atkinson v Government of the United States of America* [1971] AC 197.
4 Section 7A (inserted by Part III of Schedule 1 to Criminal Justice Act 1988).
5 Section 10(1), but not to extraditions under Schedule 1 of the 1989 Act, ie where the 1870 procedure is preserved.
6 Section 10(2).
7 Section 10(5).
8 The terms of section 8(1) would not appear, strictly, to apply.

Rules of court provide the procedure by which such an application should be made. The application to state a case must be made within the period of 21 days following the day on which the court refuses to commit.[9] The High Court has power to remit the case to the court of committal to decide it according to the opinion of the High Court on the question of law or to dismiss the appeal. Where the appeal relating to an offence is dismissed, the High Court must by order declare that the offence is not an offence in respect of which the Secretary of State has power to make an order for return.[10] There is a further right of appeal (with leave) to the House of Lords pursuant to section 1 of the Administration of Justice Act 1960.[11]

2.5.2   Habeas corpus

The well established right of appeal for a person committed for extradition is an application for habeas corpus.[12] This right is preserved as regards both new scheme and Commonwealth extradition by section 9 of the Extradition Act 1989 and, as regards old scheme extradition under preserved Orders in Council, by Schedule 1 paragraph 8 of the Extradition Act 1989. However, the scope for challenge by habeas corpus will be considerably lessened in cases where the prima facie case requirement has been dispensed with. A large number of habeas cases have concerned the magistrates' approach to assessing and admitting evidence. The committing court must inform the fugitive in ordinary language of his right to apply for habeas corpus.[13] The fugitive will not be returned before the expiry of 15 days beginning with the day on which the order is made or before the determination (including any appeal) of the habeas corpus application.[14]

In addition to any other reason for ordering the discharge of the fugitive,[15] section 11(3) requires the High Court to order discharge if it appears to the court that:

(a) by reason of the trivial nature of the offence; or
(b) by reason of the passage of time since he is alleged to have committed the offence or to have become unlawfully at large; or
(c) because the accusation made against him is not made in good faith in the interests of justice,

it would, having regard to all the circumstances, be unjust or oppressive to return him.[16] The High Court may receive fresh evidence relevant to the exercise of its jurisdiction under section 6 or under section 11(3).

---

9   See the Magistrates' Courts (Extradition) Rules 1989, SI 1989/1597.
10 Section 10(6). This may relate to all the offences in the request or only some of them.
11 For the purposes of appeals under section 10, the general requirement that leave may only be granted where a point of law of general public importance is involved which ought to be considered by the House of Lords is abrogated.
12 Section 11 of the Extradition Act 1870; section 8 of the Fugitive Offenders Act 1967.
13 Section 11(1).
14 Section 11(2).
15 Any of the grounds, for example, under section 6.
16 Section 11(3); previously section 8(3) of the Fugitive Offenders Act 1967; there was no similar provision in the Extradition Acts 1870–1935. See *R v Governor of Brixton Prison, ex p McCheyne* [1951] 1 TLR 1155 and *Re Clemetson* [1956] Crim LR 50.

Section 14 enables a fugitive to waive his right under section 11 to apply for habeas corpus and enables a magistrate to order the committal for return of a person with his consent at any time after his arrest. Waiver of rights must be signified in a notice in the form specified in the Magistrates' Courts (Extradition) Rules 1989.[17]

2.5.3 Order for return

The decision whether or not to return the fugitive rests with the Secretary of State.[18] The power to decide arises only where the fugitive has been committed under section 9 of the 1989 Act and has not been discharged.

The Secretary of State may not order the return of the fugitive if the return is prohibited by the Act, for example, on the grounds established in section 6. Further, the Secretary of State must not make an order if it appears to him, in relation to the offence or each of the offences in respect of which the fugitive's return is sought, that:

(i) by reason of its trivial nature; or
(ii) by reason of the passage of time since its commission or the fugitive's escape; or
(iii) because the accusation is not made in good faith in the interests of justice

it would, having regard to all the circumstances, be unjust or oppressive to return him.

These matters may already have been adjudicated upon by a court,[19] but the Secretary of State is under an obligation to consider them and, if it appears that they apply, to refuse to order the fugitive's return. There are, however, further grounds upon which he may refuse to make an order, which will not have been considered by a court. He may decide not to order return if the fugitive could be, or has been, sentenced to death[20] or if another extradition request has been made in respect of that fugitive and it appears, having regard to all the circumstances of the case and in particular:

(a) the relative seriousness of each of the offences;
(b) the date on which each request was made;
(c) the nationality or citizenship of the person concerned and his ordinary residence;

that preference should be given to the other request.[1]

Where the fugitive is serving a sentence or is charged with an offence in the United Kingdom, he must not be returned until any sentence is served or until the charge is disposed of.[2]

The procedure for returning fugitives is dealt with largely in section 13. The Secretary of State must notify the fugitive that he is contemplating making an

---

17 SI 1989/1597 rule 5 and Form I. A fugitive may consent to his return immediately upon arrest by serving a notice in the form specified in Form 2.
18 Section 12(1); for Extradition Act 1970 cases see Schedule 1 para 8(2) to the 1989 Act.
19 Sections 6 and 11.
20 Section 12(2)(b).
1 Section 12(5).
2 Section 12(3).

order for his return[3] and of his right, to be explained in ordinary language,[4] to make representations, within 15 days of such notification, as to why he should not be returned.[5] Unless the fugitive waives the right to make representations, no order shall be made before the expiry of the 15 days.

If the representations, which the Secretary of State is under a duty to consider,[6] are unsuccessful a warrant for the fugitive's return will be issued. He will not, however, unless he waives this right,[7] be returned to the foreign state until the expiration of seven days,[8] during which time he may apply for leave to seek judicial review of the Secretary of State's decision to make the order. The right to judicial review is not new.[9] What is new, however, is the imposition of a rigid seven-day time limit in place of the time limit in most judicial proceedings in RSC Order 53. The fugitive may not be returned until the judicial review proceedings (including any appeal therefrom) are finally determined.[10]

The right to apply for judicial review was described as little more than window dressing in the debates on this clause and it was confidently asserted that few, if any, applications would succeed.[11]

2.5.4   Discharge in cases of delay

Once a committal for return under section 9 is made, the fugitive must be returned promptly. If the fugitive is still in the United Kingdom after the expiration of two months beginning with the first day on which, having regard to section 11(2), he could have been returned, or after the expiration of one month of the issue of a warrant for return under section 12, he may apply to the High Court for his discharge.[12] Where the fugitive applied for judicial review of the Secretary of State's decision to order his return, he may apply for discharge if he has not been returned within one month of the determination of the judicial review proceedings.

Where such an application is made and the court is satisfied that reasonable notice of the proposed application has been given to the Secretary of State, the court may, unless sufficient cause is shown to the contrary, by Order direct the applicant to be discharged and, if a warrant has been issued under Section 12, quash the warrant.

---

3   Section 13(1).
4   Section 13(3) – and presumably in the fugitive's own language.
5   Section 13(2).
6   Section 13(4).
7   Section 13(5).
8   Or within such longer period as section 84 of the Supreme Court Act 1981 may provide.
9   See, for example, *R v Secretary of State for the Home Department, ex p Kirkwood* [1984] 2 All ER 390, [1984] 1 WLR 913.
10 Section 13(8).
11 Per Lord Irvine of Lairg.
12 Section 16(1) and (2).

ANNEX A

Orders in Council under the Extradition Acts 1870–1935 which have been preserved by section 1 and Schedule 1 of the Extradition Act 1989

Foreign state	Statutory Instrument	Description of document
Albania	1927/605	Albania (Extradition) Order in Council 1927
Argentine Republic	1894/76	Order in Council directing that the Extradition Acts shall apply in the case of the Argentine Republic
	1980/185	Argentine Republic (Extradition) (Amendment) Order 1980
Belgium	1902/208	Order in Council directing that the Extradition Acts shall apply in the case of Belgium
	1907/544	Order in Council directing that the Extradition Acts shall apply in the case of Belgium, and of the Supplementary Convention of 5 March 1907
	1911/793	Order in Council directing that the Extradition Acts shall apply in the case of Belgium
	1975/1034	Belgium (Extradition) (Amendment) Order 1975
Bolivia	1898/1065	Order in Council directing that the Extradition Acts shall apply in the case of Bolivia
Cameroon Republic	1928/575	France (Extradition) Order in Council 1928
Chile	1898/597	Order in Council directing that the Extradition Acts shall apply in the case of Chile
Colombia	28 Nov 1889	Order in Council directing that the Extradition Acts shall apply in the case of Colombia
Cuba	1905/558	Order in Council directing that the Extradition Acts shall apply in the case of the Republic of Cuba
Czechoslovakia	1926/1466	Czechoslovakia (Extradition) Order in Council 1926
Ecuador	26 June 1886	Order in Council directing that the Extradition Acts shall apply in the case of the Republic of Ecuador
Guatemala	26 Nov 1886	Order in Council directing that the Extradition Acts shall apply in the case of Guatemala

Foreign state	Statutory Instrument	Description of document
Guatemala *(contd)*	1914/1323	Order in Council directing that the Extradition Acts shall apply in the case of Guatemala in accordance with a treaty of 4 July 1885, as amended by a Protocol of 30 May 1914
Haiti	5 Feb 1876	Order in Council directing that the Extradition Acts shall apply in the case of the Republic of Haiti
Hungary	17 Mar 1874	Order in Council directing that the Extradition Acts shall apply in the case of Austria and Hungary
	1902/737	Order in Council directing that the Extradition Acts shall apply in the case of Austria and Hungary
	1937/719	Hungary (Extradition) Order in Council 1937
Iraq	1933/357	Iraq (Extradition) Order in Council 1933
	1934/925	Iraq (Extradition: Commonwealth of Australia and New Zealand) Order in Council 1934
Liberia	1894/114	Order in Council directing that the Extradition Acts shall apply in the case of the Republic of Liberia
Mexico	6 Apr 1889	Order in Council directing that the Extradition Acts shall apply in the case of the United States of Mexico
Monaco	9 May 1892	Order in Council directing that the Extradition Acts shall apply in the case of Monaco
Nicaragua	1906/382	Order in Council directing that the Extradition Acts shall apply in the case of the Republic of Nicaragua
Panama	1907/648	Order in Council directing that the Extradition Acts shall apply in the case of the Republic of Panama
Paraguay	1911/662	Order in Council directing that the Extradition Acts shall apply in the case of the Republic of Paraguay
Peru	1907/383	Order in Council directing that the Extradition Acts shall apply in the case of the Republic of Peru
Poland	1934/209	Poland (Extradition) Order in Council 1934
	1934/1413*	Poland (Extradition: Commonwealth of Australia and New Zealand) Order in Council 1934

Foreign state	Statutory Instrument	Description of document
Romania	1894/119	Order in Council directing that the Extradition Acts shall apply in the case of Romania
Salvador	16 Dec 1882	Order in Council directing that the Extradition Acts shall apply in the case of Salvador
San Marino	1900/168	Order in Council directing that the Extradition Acts shall apply in the case of San Marino
Siam (now Thailand)	1911/1151	Order in Council directing that the Extradition Acts shall apply in the case of Siam
Thailand. *See* Siam		
Togo Republic	1928/575	France (Extradition) Order in Council 1928
Tunisia	1909/1458	Order in Council directing that the Extradition Acts shall apply in the case of France in accordance with a treaty of 14 August 1876, as supplemented by additional Conventions of 13 February 1896, and 17 October 1908; and in the case of Tunis in accordance with Agreements of 31 December 1889; and 29 July 1909
United States of America	21 Mar 1890*	Order in Council directing that the Extradition Acts shall apply in the case of the United States of America
	1901/544*	Order in Council directing that the Extradition Acts shall apply in the case of the United States of America
	1907/110*	Order in Council directing that the Extradition Acts shall apply in the case of the United States of America, and of the Supplementary Convention of 12 April 1905
	1935/848*	United States of America (Extradition: Commonwealth of Australia) Order in Council 1935
	1976/2144	United States of America (Extradition) Order 1976
Uruguay	5 Mar 1885	Order in Council directing that the Extradition Acts shall apply in the case of Uruguay
	24 Nov 1891	Order in Council directing that the Extradition Acts shall apply in the case of Uruguay

Foreign state	Statutory Instrument	Description of document
Yugoslavia (formerly Serbia)	1901/586	Order in Council directing that the Extradition Acts shall apply in the case of Serbia

* The orders marked with an asterisk in the list above are dependent for any continuing operation they may have upon the law of the territories concerned.

3   MUTUAL ASSISTANCE IN CRIMINAL PROCEEDINGS

3.1   Introduction

On 29 August 1991 the United Kingdom government ratified the European Convention on Mutual Assistance in Criminal Matters and its Additional Protocol relating to fiscal offences.[13] The UK had, for some years, been a party to the Commonwealth Scheme for Mutual Assistance, but mutual assistance had, with one or two isolated exceptions,[14] lacked any legislative structure and was dealt with on an ad hoc and informal basis. There are well-established and important channels for the communication of information and acquisition of evidence on an informal basis between police forces internationally, the DTI, Customs and tax authorities under various bilateral arrangements,[15] and it was the clear intention of the framers of the Convention and of Parliament that the mutual assistance provision should complement, rather than derogate, from these practices.[16] It is envisaged, for example, that requests in cases of urgency will continue to be handled by Interpol, as will police-to-police requests for assistance and for information required during preliminary investigations.[17]

Although the Convention had followed on directly from the European Convention on Extradition, it was decided that mutual assistance in criminal matters should be independent of extradition and should be granted even in cases where extradition would be refused.[18] It would apply, for example, to minor offences and, as a general rule, assistance would not be confined to

---

13 Cm 1577. The Convention was opened for signature on 20th April 1959; the Additional Protocol was opened for signature on 17th March 1978. The Convention has been signed and ratified by Austria, Belgium, Denmark, France, Germany, Greece, Iceland, Italy, Netherlands, Norway, Spain, Sweden, Switzerland, Turkey and the United Kingdom. Portugal has signed the Convention but has not deposited the instrument of ratification. Finland, Israel and Liechtenstein have acceded to the Convention.

The Additional Protocol has been signed and ratified by Austria, Denmark, France, Greece, Iceland, Italy, Netherlands, Norway, Switzerland, Turkey and the United Kingdom. It has been signed by Belgium, Germany, Portugal, Spain and Switzerland. Finland has acceded to it.

14 The Evidence (Proceedings in Other Jurisdictions) Act 1975 and the Extradition Act 1873.

15 See, for example, the Statute of the International Criminal Police Organisation; the Naples and Nairobi Customs' Co-operation Council arrangements; the European Convention on Insider Dealing; and the European Community Mutual Assistance Directive.

16 See Explanatory Report on the European Convention on Mutual Assistance in Criminal Matters (Council of Europe, Strasbourg 1969). The Report is to facilitate the understanding of the Convention rather than an authoritative guide to its interpretation; see also Articles 15.4, 15.5 and 15.6.

17 See United Kingdom Guidelines on International Mutual Assistance in Criminal Matters, para 6.

18 See Explanatory Report, op cit.

offences which were offences under the law of both the requested and requesting country.[19]

Originally, assistance could be refused if the request concerned a fiscal offence.[20] Fiscal offence is not defined because the meaning of the term varies from county to county, but is described as 'offences in connection with taxes, duties, Customs and exchange'. However the Additional Protocol provides that assistance may not be refused on the sole ground that the request relates to a fiscal offence.

In order to enable the United Kingdom to ratify the Convention, Part I of the Criminal Justice (International Co-operation) Act 1990 had been enacted, the main provisions of which:

(a) permit the service on individuals in the UK of summonses and other judicial documents relating to criminal proceedings in other countries;
(b) enable the UK courts and prosecuting authorities to obtain evidence overseas for use in investigations and proceedings here, and to facilitate the provision of evidence from the UK for criminal proceedings overseas;
(c) provide for UK prisoners to be transferred temporarily to give evidence or assist investigations overseas;
(d) permit search and seizure in the UK on behalf of courts and prosecution authorities overseas; and
(e) assist in enforcing overseas forfeiture orders.

The principles behind the Act were described by the Minister of State as:

'First, having recognised the inadequacies of our existing legislation, we have been determined to secure arrangements which will place us in the first rank internationally in our ability to co-operate with other countries in this most important of areas. Secondly, we have sought to ensure that, once the measures which are proposed in the bill are enacted, we will be able to seek assistance from other countries to just the same extent, and in the same ways, as we are able to offer help to them. Thirdly, we have been conscious that, however much we may wish to assist other countries, we cannot allow Parliament to make greater powers available on behalf of overseas authorities than are available to our own police or prosecuting authorities in domestic cases.'[1]

Dissatisfaction with the existing legislation stemmed largely from the lack of any power to effect service of summonses or documents relating to overseas criminal proceedings[2] or power to provide evidence in overseas criminal proceedings unless those proceedings had already been instituted.[3] The latter

---

19 Though contracting parties are free to derogate from this principle in the case of letters rogatory for search and seizure.
20 Article 2. Assistance may also be refused if the request concerns a political offence, an offence connected with a political offence or if the requested party considers that execution of the request would prejudice its sovereignty, security, order public or other essential interests.
1 Earl Ferrers 513 HL Official Report Col 1217, 12 December 1989.
2 Proceedings initiated abroad by arrest would be the subject of an arrest and request pursuant to paragraph 8 of Schedule 1 of the Extradition Act 1989. Compare the long established and sophisticated schemes set up under various international Conventions relating to civil proceedings and the enforcement of judgments.
3 See section 5 of the Extradition Act 1873 and section 5 of the Evidence (Proceedings in Other Jurisdictions) Act 1975, both of which have been repealed by the 1990 Act.

rule had led one commentator to remark that 'the UK can give us evidence in any case in which we already have evidence'.[4] Both deficiencies have now been remedied and the Act, though intended to implement the UK's international obligations under the European Convention, applies to any overseas state which requires assistance of the type permitted by Part I, though in certain instances assistance is more easily available to Convention and Commonwealth states.[5]

All mutual assistance provisions of the Act were in force by 10 June 1991.[6]

3.1.1   The Central Authority

The functions of the Secretary of State under the Act are carried out by the United Kingdom Central Authority, which is part of the Home Office. All requests for mutual assistance (whether relating to UK requests for assistance abroad or to requests for assistance within the UK) are addressed to the Central Authority unless they are more appropriate to the Interpol scheme. Requests relating to Scotland and Northern Ireland are also coordinated by the Central Authority.[7]

3.1.2   When will assistance be refused?

The Secretary of State retains in all cases an overriding discretion whether or not to comply with the request. As regards requests from Convention states, it is assumed that he will comply,[8] but requests may be received from states which are not parties to the Convention. The Central Authority has indicated that the United Kingdom will give maximum assistance and it expects refusals of assistance to be rare.[9] A request may be refused on political, security or national interest grounds.[10] The United Kingdom has also made an express reservation that it reserves the right to refuse assistance if the person who is the subject of a request has been convicted or acquitted in the United Kingdom or in a third state of an offence which arises from the same conduct as that giving rise to proceedings. The United Kingdom has also reserved the right not to obtain evidence where UK law recognises privilege, non-compellability or other exemption from giving evidence.

3.2   Mutual service of process

3.2.1   Service of overseas process in the United Kingdom

The government of, or other authority in, a country or territory outside the United Kingdom may request the Secretary of State to serve on a person in the

4 Cited by Earl Ferrers on second reading.
5 See, for example, section 4(3).
6 See Criminal Justice (International Co-operation) Act 1990 (Commencement No 1) Order 1991, SI 1991/1072; note, however, that the provisions in Part III relating to drug trafficking money were brought into force in September 1991.
7 United Kingdom Guidelines, op cit at para 7.
8 This was accepted by Earl Ferrers at second Reading: 513 HL Official Report 1232.
9 United Kingdom Guidelines para 40. It undertakes to consult requesting states in advance of a refusal and to discuss ways of overcoming any difficulties.
10 As contemplated in Article 2.

United Kingdom (whatever his nationality) a summons or other process requiring that person to appear as a defendant or to attend as a witness in criminal proceedings in that country or territory.[11] The Secretary of State may be requested to serve a document, issued by a court exercising criminal jurisdiction in that country or territory, recording a decision of the court made in the exercise of that jurisdiction.[12] Although there is no specific requirement as regards the 'summons or other process' that it should have been issued by a court, the words clearly imply some judicial process, and a letter, for example, from lawyers requesting the attendance of an individual as a prosecution or defence witness would not suffice. Unlike the provisions relating to extradition and certain of the provisions under the 1990 Act, there is no requirement that the offence in respect of which the process is issued should be an offence under the law of any part of the UK, nor any restriction on the type of offence for which the request may be made.[13]

The request must be made in writing[14] and should contain details of:

(i)   the authority making the request;
(ii) the purposes and reason for the request;
(iii) the person to be served;
(iv) a description of the offences under investigation.[15]

If the request is not in English, it must be accompanied by a translation.[16] Where the document to be served requires the attendance of a witness abroad, it should state what allowances, travelling and subsistence expenses the witnesses will receive and claim. It should also indicate the evidence sought and the procedure for taking the evidence.[17]

On receiving a request the Secretary of State[18] may cause the process or document to be served by post or, if the request is for personal service, he may direct the Chief Officer of Police to serve it personally.[19] Where service is effected by post, it is deemed to be effected by properly addressing, pre-paying and posting a letter containing the document and, unless the contrary is proved, it is deemed to have been effected at the time at which the letter would be delivered by ordinary course of post.[20]

Service of a summons or process requiring attendance as a defendant or witness does not impose any obligation under the law of any part of the UK to comply with it[1] and any person served must, by notice, be so informed.[2] This peculiar provision reflects article 8 of the Convention, which the Explanatory

---

11 Section 1(1)(a).
12 Section 1(1)(b).
13 See para 3.1, 'Introduction'.
14 UK Guidelines, para 14. The Central Authority has indicated that it will not normally be possible to act on oral requests, but advance fax copies of requests will be acted upon if accompanied by an undertaking to forward the original request by air mail or courier within a reasonable period.
15 UK Guidelines, para 16; Article 14 of the Convention.
16 UK Guidelines, para 18; Article 16.2.
17 UK Guidelines, para 16.
18 Where the person to be served is in Scotland, the appropriate officer is the Lord Advocate.
19 Section 1(2); implementing article 7.
20 Section 7 of the Interpretation Act 1978. The UK Guidelines indicate that process will normally be served by post unless the requesting state has requested personal service.
1 Section 1(3).
2 Section 1(4)(a).

Report indicates is derived from an international custom by which witnesses and experts are completely free not to go to the requesting country.[3] The notice must also indicate that the person served may wish to seek advice as to the possible consequences of his failing to comply with the process under the law of the country or territory where it was issued, and that, under the other state's law, he may not, as a witness, be accorded the same rights and privileges as would be accorded to him in criminal proceedings in the UK.[4] He may not, for example, enjoy a privilege against self-incrimination nor the right, in certain circumstances, not to be compelled to give evidence.

Where a witness or suspect does respond to a summons by attending before the judicial authorities of the requesting state, article 12 of the Convention provides that he shall not be prosecuted or detained or subjected to any other restriction of his personal liberty for acts or convictions *anterior* to his departure.[5] The immunity ceases, however, at the expiry of 15 days from the date when his presence is no longer required if he has had an opportunity of leaving the jurisdiction and has remained or, having left it, has voluntarily returned.[6] The immunity has been the subject of an express reservation by the United Kingdom government[7] with the result that the United Kingdom may claim the reciprocal benefit of article 12 only in so far as it has accepted it. It will be necessary, therefore, for the Central Authority, the witness or suspect or his advisers to establish with the requesting state the extent, if any, to which a witness will have immunity and, where appropriate, specifically to request immunity.[8]

Where the police have been directed to serve any process or document, the Secretary of State must be informed after service[9] as to when and how it was served and (if possible) be provided with a receipt signed by the person upon whom it was served. Equally, the Secretary of State must be notified if the process or document has not been served and the reasons why not.[10]

3.2.2   Service of United Kingdom process overseas

Section 2 of the Act provides that a summons or order requiring a person to appear as a defendant or a witness in criminal proceedings in the United Kingdom may be issued notwithstanding that the person in question is outside the United Kingdom.[11] Such summons or order may be served outside the United Kingdom in accordance with arrangements made by the Secretary of State. It is not a power to serve outside the jurisdiction, nor does it widen the rules of criminal jurisdiction. The power also applies to a summons requiring a person charged with a civil offence to appear before a service court or to attend before such a court to give evidence.[12]

---

3 Op cit at page 18.
4 Section 1(4)(b) and (c).
5 Article 12.1 and 12.2.
6 Article 12.2.
7 See Article 23: see further at para 3.2.2.
8 Clearly in the case of a suspect, if the requesting state wants the suspect to stand trial the appropriate course is to seek extradition. This Article effectively prevents extradition 'through the back door', in respect of minor offences.
9 Or, in Scotland, the Lord Advocate.
10 Section 1(5).
11 Section 2(1).
12 Section 11(1).

Whereas failure to comply with such a summons in the United Kingdom could amount to an offence under the statute from which the power to issue the summons or order derives, or to a contempt of court, or would be a ground for issuing an arrest warrant, actual service of process outside the United Kingdom pursuant to section 2 does not impose any obligation under the law of any part of the United Kingdom to comply with it.[13] Nor will it impose any obligation on the individual served in the requesting state to comply with it.[14] However, if the summons or order is subsequently served on the person in the United Kingdom and is not complied with, that person may be guilty of an offence or of contempt of court and be liable to arrest.[15]

Although the Convention provides for immunity for suspects or witnesses in respect of acts or convictions anterior to their departure from the requested state, the United Kingdom government has entered into an express reservation. The UK has indicated that it will only grant immunity under Article 12 where it is specifically requested by the person to whom the immunity would apply or by the authorities of the state from whom assistance is sought. A request for immunity will not be granted where it would be contrary to the public interest.

Rules of Court have been made[16] governing the procedure of magistrates' courts and Crown Courts in relation to summonses or orders issued under section 2. The Magistrates' Courts (Criminal Justice (International Co-operation)) Rules 1991[17] provide that where a summons or order is issued, the Justices' Clerk must send it to the Secretary of State with a view to its being served in accordance with arrangements made by the Secretary of State. Service of the summons or order may be proved in any legal proceedings by a certificate given by or on behalf of the Secretary of State. A statement in any such certificate that a summons has been served, of the manner in which service was effected and of the date of service is admissible as evidence of any facts so stated.[18] The Crown Court Rules 1982[19] have been amended to provide that a witness summons or order issued by the Crown Court in accordance with section 2(1) must be sent to the Secretary of State to be served in accordance with arrangements made by the Secretary of State.[20]

3.3 Mutual provision of evidence

3.3.1 Overseas evidence for use in the United Kingdom

Section 3 of the 1990 Act enables a magistrate or a judge,[1] where it appears that:

(a) an offence has been committed or there are reasonable grounds for suspecting that an offence has been committed, and

---

13 Section 2(3) and para. 3.2.1 above.
14 Article 8.
15 Section 2(4).
16 Pursuant to section 10.
17 SI 1991/1074 rule 3.
18 Rule 4.
19 SI 1982/1109.
20 SI 1991/1288 rule 2.
1 Or, in Scotland, a sheriff or a judge.

(b) proceedings in respect of the offence have been instituted or the offence is being investigated,

to issue, upon application, a letter requesting assistance in obtaining outside the United Kingdom such evidence as is specified in the letter for use in the proceedings or investigation. An application may be made by a prosecuting authority[2] or by a person charged in the proceedings. An application by a person charged may, a fortiori, only be made after proceedings have been instituted.[3] The procedure is not open to a person seeking to obtain evidence to put before the prosecuting authority prior to the commencement of proceedings in an attempt to avoid proceedings ever being instituted. It would also seem to preclude such an application where the defendant was charged with one offence and wished to obtain evidence abroad in an effort to avoid being charged with further offences.

A 'designated prosecuting authority' may itself issue a letter of request without the need for an application to the court if it is satisfied as to the matters set out in (a) above and the offence is being investigated or the authority has instituted proceedings in respect of it. A designation order has been made in respect of:

(a) the Attorney General for England and Wales;
(b) the Director of Public Prosecutions and any Crown Prosecutor;
(c) the Director of the Serious Fraud Office and any person designated under section 1(7) of the Criminal Justice Act 1987;
(d) the Secretary of State for Trade and Industry;
(e) the Commissioners of Customs and Excise;
(f) the Lord Advocate;
(g) any procurator fiscal;
(h) the Attorney General for Northern Ireland;
(i) the Director of Public Prosecutions for Northern Ireland.[4]

Like the decision to transfer under section 4 of the Criminal Justice Act 1987, there is no judicial supervision over the exercise of the power of a designated authority to issue a letter of request and, given that the designation order includes all of the prosecuting authorities likely to want to obtain from evidence from abroad, it is difficult to see that section 3(1) will often be put to use by prosecutors. Although there is not an equivalent to section 4(3) curtailing any right of appeal, it is unlikely, of course, that an individual under investigation will be aware of the issue of a letter of request by the prosecuting authority and the power is, effectively, unchallengeable. It has been suggested[5] that the requirement that the letter of request be channelled through the Secretary of State will act as a safeguard to prevent 'fishing expeditions' by a

---

2 There is no definition of 'prosecuting authority'. It presumably excludes an application by a private prosecutor.
3 Because charging, presumably, counts as an institution of proceedings. Section 3(2), however, makes it clear that requests by a potential defendant cannot be made.
4 The Criminal Justice (International Co-operation) Act 1990 (Designation of Prosecuting Authorities) Order 1991, SI 1991/1224; this implements the third declaration made by the United Kingdom government pursuant to article 23; see also para 43 of the United Kingdom Guidelines.
5 Current Law Statutes Commentary.

designated authority. It will be rare, however, that the Secretary of State will have sufficient information to determine whether an application amounts to a fishing expedition and if so, whether it is possible to prohibit the request. In cases of urgency, the Secretary of State may be bypassed.[6] In any event, where a case is subject to investigation, drawing the line between what is a legitimate investigative path and what is 'fishing' will be difficult.

A defence request must always be made through a court and always, whatever the urgency, be channelled through the Secretary of State. On Second Reading, the power of the defence to request assistance was described thus:

> 'By virtue of Clause 3(2) it will be open to a defendant, in any case in which proceedings have been instituted to apply to a justice of the peace to issue a letter of request. If such a letter is issued it will then be sent to the Central Authority acting in the name of the Secretary of State for onward transmission to the appropriate court or other authority in which the evidence requested is to be subject.'[7]

There is little in this statement which conveys scrutiny by the Secretary of State and one presumes that prosecution and defence requests will be dealt with alike. One assumes also that requests will be treated in confidence and that the substance of defence requests will not be passed on to other government departments which have been designated as prosecuting authorities. Defendants and their advisers will need to have regard to the extent to which their own investigations will be kept confidential by both the authorities responsible for transmitting the requests and the authorities abroad responsible for receiving and responding to them.

Rules of Court make provision for applications under section 3. The Magistrates' Court (Criminal Justice (International Co-operation)) Rules 1991[8] provide that notice of an application in the magistrates' court is given to the justices' clerk and is to be made in writing, stating the particulars of the offence which it is alleged has been committed or the grounds for suspecting that an offence has been committed, whether proceedings have been instituted or the offence is being investigated and the particulars of the assistance requested in the form of a draft letter of request.

Applications may be heard ex parte and the court may, if it thinks it necessary in the interests of justice, direct that the public be excluded from the court. Where a letter of request is sent, in a case of urgency, direct to any court or tribunal, the justices' clerk must forthwith notify the Secretary of State and send to him a copy of the letter of request.[9] The court may, in exceptional circumstances, dispense with the need for notice.

Identical provisions exist for applications made to a judge in the Crown Court.[10]

---

6 Section 3(5). In such cases, the request may only be made of a court or tribunal under section 3(4)(a) and not of another authority under section 3(4)(b). Court Rules provide that requests sent direct by the court to the overseas court or tribunal must be notified forthwith to the Secretary of State. There is no provision requiring designated authorities to notify the Secretary of State when a direct request has been made.

7 513 HL Official Report 1231 (Earl Ferrers).

8 SI 1991/1074 rules 5, 6 and 7.

9 There is no such requirement for designated authorities.

10 Crown Court (Amendment) Rules 1991, SI 1991/1288 which add rule 31 to the Crown Court Rules 1982, SI 1982/1109.

No guidance is given as to which court is the appropriate forum for an application. Clearly the magistrates' court is appropriate where the offence is summary, or the request is straightforward, or the case has not yet been committed, or the committal proceedings are being heard or are pending. Equally, the Crown Court may be the most appropriate where the case has been committed or is being heard when the need for the information arises.

The letter of request is sent by the Secretary of State for transmission either to the court specified in the letter and exercising jurisdiction in the place where the evidence is to be obtained, or to any authority recognised by the overseas government as the appropriate authority for receiving requests for assistance in the provision of evidence.[11] In cases of urgency, the request may be made direct to a court (though not to an authority) without the need to channel it via the Secretary of State.[12]

Section 3(7) provides that evidence obtained by virtue of a letter of request shall not, without the consent of the authority recognised by the overseas country as the appropriate authority for receiving requests for assistance, be used for any purpose other than that specified in the letter. Where any document or article obtained pursuant to a letter of request is no longer required for that purpose or any other purpose for which consent has been obtained, it shall be returned unless the authority indicates that it need not be returned. It would appear, therefore, that even where the letter of request has been directed to, and a response received from, a court or tribunal under section 3(4)(a), the appropriate body for handling any request for consent to enlarge the use of the evidence is made to an authority falling within the description of section 3(4)(b). Evidence obtained pursuant to section 3 may not be used, for example, in civil proceedings for asset recovery arising out of the same subject matter as the criminal proceedings, unless the appropriate consent has been obtained from overseas. There would appear to be no power in the court to sanction use of the evidence in other proceedings.[13]

Where the requested overseas country provides the evidence sought in a letter of request, the question will arise as to how that evidence is to be adduced before an English court. In some instances, the party adducing it will wish to have the maker of a statement present in court to give oral evidence, in which case a summons for service under section 2 of the Act will be issued. However, in the debate in both Houses, much was made of the fact that the Criminal Justice Act 1988 now made the reception of written evidence easier[14] and one may expect therefore statements to be admitted pursuant to sections 23 and 24 of that Act.[15] The 1990 Act does not affect the basic rules of admissibility of first-hand hearsay under section 23. It will still be necessary for the party seeking to adduce overseas evidence under section 23 that the maker of the statement is outside the United Kingdom and that it is not reasonably practicable to secure his attendance.[16] Section 3(8), however, provides that in exercising its discretion to exclude admissible evidence under section 25 in

---

11 Section 3(4).
12 Section 3(5).
13 Compare the analogous position of documents disclosed in discovery and Order 24 Rule 14A RSC and also the position of documents obtained in criminal proceedings in England following *Marcel v Metropolitan Police Comr* [1992] Ch 225, [1992] 1 All ER 72, CA.
14 168 HC Official Report 148; 513 HL Official Report 1232.
15 See Chapter 4, para 3.1.2.
16 Criminal Justice Act 1988 section 23(2)(b).

relation to a statement contained in evidence taken pursuant to a letter of request, the court shall have regard:

(a) to whether it was possible to challenge the statement by questioning the person who made it; and
(b) if proceedings have been instituted, to whether the local law allowed the parties to the proceedings to be legally represented when the evidence was being taken.

These factors are additional to those required to be considered by section 25(2), and the United Kingdom Guidelines request an authority or court executing a request from the United Kingdom[17] to indicate whether such challenge and legal representation were allowed, whether evidence was taken on oath and whether witnesses assert any privilege under United Kingdom law.[18] The Guidelines also indicate that in many cases the United Kingdom will formally request that a United Kingdom police officer or official be permitted to attend the taking of evidence, to participate in the questioning and to bring back to the United Kingdom a copy of the evidence.[19]

There is a greater latitude to admit overseas business documents because section 24(4) specifically excludes from the conditions of admissibility of a business document sought to be admitted under section 24(1) any statement prepared in accordance with section 3 of the Criminal Justice (International Co-operation) Act 1990 for the purposes of pending or contemplated criminal proceedings or of a criminal investigation. Accordingly, where the attendance of the maker of a statement in a business document could be secured, the business document would, nevertheless, be admissible.

3.3.2   Obtaining evidence in the United Kingdom for use overseas

Section 4 enables evidence to be obtained in the United Kingdom for the purposes of criminal proceedings or a criminal investigation overseas. The section proved to be the most controversial of the provisions of Part I of the Act because of its potential use by overseas authorities in proceedings for 'fiscal' offences and the consequent threat to confidentiality under domestic banking law. The government fought off two attempts in the House of Lords to restrict the provision to non-fiscal offences,[20] but a Commons amendment, now found in section 4(3), prohibits assistance relating to fiscal offences where proceedings have not yet been instituted unless:

(a) the request is from a county or territory which is a member of the Commonwealth or is made pursuant to a treaty to which the United Kingdom is a party; or
(b) the Secretary of State is satisfied that the conduct constituting the offence would constitute an offence of the same or a similar nature if it had occurred in the United Kingdom.[1]

17 Even in Scottish cases where section 3(8) does not apply.
18 Op cit at para 48.
19 Op cit at para 47; article 4.
20 514 Official Report HL, cols 879–885.
1 Section 4(3).

Where proceedings for a fiscal offence have been instituted, evidence may be obtained in the United Kingdom for use in those proceedings. As in all cases, the Secretary of State will have a discretion as to whether to meet a request and issues such as the threat to confidentiality under domestic banking law may be taken into account when that discretion is exercised.

The request must be received by the Secretary of State from a court or tribunal exercising criminal jurisdiction, or from a prosecuting authority, in a county or territory outside the United Kingdom, or from any other authority in such a county or territory which appears to him to have the function of making such requests.[2]

The request must satisfy the Secretary of State[3] that an offence under the law of the overseas country has been committed or that there are reasonable grounds for suspecting that such an offence has been committed, *and* that proceedings have been instituted[4] or that an investigation is being carried on in the requested state. The evidence sought must be relevant to the investigation or proceedings in question.[5] For the purpose of satisfying himself on both matters, the Secretary of State shall regard as conclusive any certificate issued by the requesting authority.[6] There is accordingly no scope for scrutiny, either by the Secretary of State or by the court of the basis upon which the application is made. Thereafter, the Secretary of State may, if he thinks fit, by notice in writing nominate a court in England, Wales, or Northern Ireland[7] to receive such of the evidence to which the request relates as may appear to the court to be appropriate for the purpose of giving effect to the request.[8] Again, the Secretary of State retains a discretion whether to comply with the request.[9]

The nominated court may order the attendance of witnesses in the same manner as for domestic criminal proceedings[10] and may administer oaths.[11] The witness may not be compelled to answer questions or produce any document or article which he could not be compelled to give:

(a) in criminal proceedings in the part of the United Kingdom in which the nominated court exercises jurisdiction, or[12]

(b) in criminal proceedings in the requesting state, provided that the claim to be exempt is conceded by the requesting court or authority.[13] Where the claim to be exempt is not conceded, the witness may be required to give evidence, but it shall not be transmitted to the requesting court or authority if a court in the requesting state upholds the claim.[14] The

---

2 Section 4(1). The formal requirements of an arrest such as being in written form, with reasons etc, follows the form described at 3.1 above.
3 Or, in Scotland, the Lord Advocate.
4 Section 4(2).
5 UK Guidelines, para 21.
6 Section 4(4).
7 If the evidence is to be obtained in Scotland, this function is carried out by the Lord Advocate who will nominate a court in Scotland.
8 Section 4(2).
9 See above para 3.1 generally as to refusals to assist.
10 Schedule 1 para 1.
11 Schedule 1 para 3.
12 Schedule 1 para 4(1)(a).
13 Schedule 1 para 4(1)(b) and para 4(2).
14 Schedule 1 para 4(3).

evidence is liable not to be transmitted until the claim to privilege has been determined by the foreign state.[15]

A witness may not be required to give evidence if his doing so would be prejudicial to the security of the United Kingdom or his capacity as an officer of the Crown.[16]

The Act does not specify which court may be nominated, but rules have been made for Magistrates' Courts and Crown Courts.[17] The Rules permit the court, if it thinks it necessary in the interests of justice, to direct that the public be excluded from the court and provide for the keeping of records of the proceedings, in particular, specifying:

(a) which persons with an interest in the proceedings were present;
(b) which of the said persons were represented and by whom;
(c) whether any of the said persons were denied the opportunity of cross-examining a witness as to any part of his evidence and the reasons for any such denial.[18]

The Secretary of State may request the court to provide to him a copy of the record.[19]

Once the evidence[20] has been obtained by the court, it must be furnished to the Secretary of State, or in Scotland to the Lord Advocate, for transmission to the requesting court or authority,[1] together with any certificate, affidavit or other verifying document required by the requesting court or authority.[2] Original documents or articles must be transmitted if so requested.[3]

The court has no jurisdiction to make an order for costs.

3.4 Search and seizure in the United Kingdom for the purposes of investigations and proceedings overseas

Sections 7 and 8[4] of the Criminal Justice (International Co-operation) Act 1990 permit, for the first time, police officers and Customs officers[5] to search for and seize evidence in the United Kingdom for the purposes of proceedings or investigations being carried out abroad. The powers may only be exercised (i) in pursuance of a direction given by the Secretary of State in response to a

---

15 See United Kingdom Guidelines, para 22. The wording of the paragraph leaves one with the uneasy feeling that the Central Authority considers it has a discretion to transmit evidence pending a determination as to whether privilege attaches to it. Although the position is not specifically covered in the Act, the protection offered by para 4(3) is pointless if transmission takes place in those circumstances. It can be inferred, therefore, that Parliament intended no such discretion.
16 Schedule 1 para 4(4) and (5).
17 Magistrates' Courts (Criminal Justice (International Co-operation)) Rules 1991, SI 1991/1074, rule 8; Crown Court (Amendment) Rules 1991 rule 32.
18 Ibid, rules 9(1) and 32(3).
19 Ibid, rules 9(4) and 32(4).
20 Which expression includes not only oral evidence but also any document or article: section 4(5).
1 Schedule 1 para 5(1).
2 Schedule 1 para 5(2).
3 Schedule 1 para 5(7).
4 Section 8 relates exclusively to Scotland.
5 See section 7(7) and the Criminal Justice (International Co-operation) Act 1990 (Exercise of Power) Order 1991, SI 1991/1297.

request received from a court or tribunal exercising criminal jurisdiction, or from a prosecuting authority in an overseas country, or from any other authority in the overseas country which appears to him to have the function of making requests for the purposes of section 7; *and* (ii) with the authority of a court. There is no power of summary arrest under the mutual assistance provisions, even if the overseas offence would, had it been committed in the United Kingdom, have amounted to an arrestable offence, and accordingly there is no power of a summary search upon arrest.[6]

The request, in addition to specifying the matters referred to in article 14,[7] must also give full details of the property to be seized, and must contain a reasonable explanation of how the evidence sought would be materially relevant to the investigation or proceedings in question.[8]

Section 7(1) provides that Part II of the Police and Criminal Evidence Act 1984 (powers of entry, search and seizure) shall have effect as if references to serious arrestable offences in section 8 of, and Schedule 1 to, that Act included conduct which is an offence under the law of the requesting country and would constitute a serious arrestable offence if it had occurred in any part of the United Kingdom. The Central Authority requires information to be provided to enable a court to decide that the criteria in sections 8, 9 and Schedule 1 have been satisfied.[9]

A magistrate or a circuit judge may accordingly grant a search warrant or order in respect of overseas offences on the same bases upon which they could be granted if the conduct had taken place inside the United Kingdom, and the cases decided on the scope and operation of PACE will apply to applications on behalf of a requesting state.[10]

Limited powers of search and seizure are given as regards 'arrestable offences'. Again, they may only be exercised by a court upon an application made pursuant to a direction of the Secretary of State in response to a request. Section 7(2) permits the magistrate, upon application by a police officer or a Customs officer,[11] if satisfied:

(a) that criminal proceedings have been instituted *against a person* in an overseas country or *that a person has been arrested* in the course of a criminal investigation carried on there;
(b) that the conduct constituting the offence which is the subject of the proceedings would constitute an arrestable offence[12] if it had occurred in any part of the United Kingdom; and
(c) that there are reasonable grounds for suspecting that there is on premises in the United Kingdom *occupied or controlled by that person* evidence relating to the offence other than items subject to legal privilege[13]

---

6 If the suspect is arrested pursuant to the provisions of the Extradition Act, or for a domestic offence, then a power of search would exist in the normal way.
7 See para 3.1 above, relating to the general form and contents of a referral.
8 United Kingdom Guidelines, para 28.
9 United Kingdom Guidelines, para 29.
10 This will show some interesting diversity of approach between states, particularly in the areas of privilege and confidentiality.
11 See above extension of the powers to HM Customs and Excise.
12 As defined in section 24 of the Police and Criminal Evidence Act 1984.
13 As defined in section 10 of the Police and Criminal Evidence Act 1984.

to issue a warrant authorising the police officer or Customs officer to enter and search those premises and to seize *any such evidence* found there. It is only a power to search to the extent that is reasonably required for the purpose of searching for evidence relating to the offence for which the power has been granted.[14]

Evidence seized pursuant to a warrant or order under section 7(1) or a warrant under section 7(2) must be furnished by the police officer or customs officer to the Secretary of State for transmission to the requesting court, tribunal or authority,[15] together with any certificate, affidavit or other verifying document specified in the Secretary of State's direction and required in order to comply with the request.[16]

3.5   Transfer of prisoners to give evidence or assist investigations

Article 11 of the Convention requires signatories to make provision allowing prisoners to be transferred to overseas states for the purpose of giving evidence and assisting investigations. Section 5 of the 1990 Act enables the United Kingdom to transfer its prisoners[17] provided that either the prisoner, or in circumstances in which it appears to the Secretary of State inappropriate by reason of the prisoner's physical or neutral condition of his youth for him to act for himself, the appropriate person acting on the prisoner's behalf, gives consent. Having received a request with which he is prepared to comply, the Secretary of State will issue a warrant authorising the transfer of the prisoner to a place of departure from the United Kingdom into the custody of a person representing the appropriate authority of the country to which he is to be transferred and authorising the bringing of the prisoner back to the United Kingdom and his transfer into custody to serve the rest of his sentence.[18] The prisoner is deemed, under the warrant, to be in legal custody at any time when, being in the United Kingdom, he is on board a British ship, aircraft or hovercraft. Although the Act does not make provision, he is presumably in legal custody when held in the overseas country and, for the purposes of computing the time he spends in custody, he will be deemed still to be serving his sentence.

Requests must include information to enable the prisoner's informed consent to be sought and to satisfy the UK prison authorities that arrangements will be made to secure the prisoner's custody. This will include details of collection of the prisoner, his escort, where and in what type of accommodation he will be held, the estimated duration of his presence in the requesting state, the dates of any hearings, privileges to which he will be entitled and whether he will be accorded any immunity in respect of previous offences.[19]

Section 6 makes reciprocal provisions enabling foreign persons to be transferred here for the purposes of giving evidence or assisting an

---

14 Section 7(3).
15 Section 7(4).
16 Section 7(5).
17 The power extends to persons serving a sentence in a prison or other institution to which the Prison Act 1952 or the Prisons (Scotland) Act 1989 apply and to persons held in custody awaiting trial or sentence or committed for default in paying fines: section 5(1) and 5(9).
18 Section 5(3).
19 United Kingdom Guidelines, para 16(n).

investigation here. The Secretary of State may, where a witness summons or Order has been made in respect of a foreign prisoner, or where it appears to the Secretary of State desirable for a prisoner to assist proceedings or an investigation by his presence, and if satisfied that the requested country will make arrangements for him to come to the United Kingdom and that the prisoner has consented, issue a warrant authorising the prisoner's transfer to this country, his detention in custody and his return.

3.6   Enforcement of overseas forfeiture orders

Section 9 of the 1990 Act provides for Orders in Council to be made enabling the United Kingdom courts to enforce forfeiture made by courts of designated countries. The forfeiture order must have been made in respect of an offence corresponding or similar to an offence under the Misuse of Drugs 1971, a drug trafficking offence,[20] an offence to which the Criminal Justice (Scotland) Act 1987 relates, or an offence to which Part VI of the Criminal Justice Act 1987 relates.[1]

A forfeiture order, for these purposes, means an order for the forfeiture and destruction or forfeiture and other disposal of anything in respect of which any such offence has been committed or which was used in connection with the commission of such an offence.[2]

Notwithstanding the width of the enabling powers, the Criminal Justice (International Co-operation) Act 1990 (Enforcement of Overseas Forfeiture Orders) Order 1991,[3] which is the only order yet to have been made under section 9, is limited to drug trafficking offences.[4] The designated countries are listed in Schedule 2 to the Order.

The power to enforce the order is exercisable by the High Court after the order has been registered.[5] Where the High Court orders forfeiture the property is disposed of in accordance with the court's directions.

Ancillary to its power to enforce a forfeiture order, the High Court has power, on the application of the government of a designated country or, where an external forfeiture order has been registered under article 10, by the CPS or HM Customs and Excise, to make a restraint order prohibiting any person from dealing with any property liable to forfeiture.[6] The procedures for applying for a restraint order and the powers available where a restraint order has been made, are similar to those available under Part VI of the Criminal Justice Act 1988.[7]

---

20 As defined in section 38(1) of the Drug Trafficking Offences Act 1986.
1   See Chapter 7 para 3.1, ie all indictable offences and the summary offences listed in Schedule 4 to the 1987 Act.
2   Not to be confused with enforcement of external confiscation orders to which a separate regime under section 96 of the Criminal Justice Act 1988 applies.
3   SI 1991/1463; the full text of the Order appears in the appendix.
4   As defined in article 2 of the Order.
5   Articles 7 and 10.
6   Articles 5 and 6.
7   See Chapter 7 para 3 et seq.

APPENDIX 1
Statutory extracts

NOTE: * * * * * denotes material which is outside the scope of this appendix.

Indictments Act 1915

(1915 c 90)

An Act to amend the Law relating to Indictments in Criminal Cases, and matters incidental or similar thereto

[23 December 1915]

3 General provisions as to indictments
(1) Every indictment shall contain, and shall be sufficient if it contains, a statement of the specific offence or offences with which the accused person is charged, together with such particulars as may be necessary for giving reasonable information as to the nature of the charge.

(2) Notwithstanding any rule of law or practice, an indictment shall, subject to the provisions of this Act, not be open to objection in respect of its form or contents if it is framed in accordance with the rules under this Act.

4 Joinder of charges in the same indictment
Subject to the provisions of the rules under this Act, charges . . . for more than one misdemeanour, . . . may be joined in the same indictment, . . .

NOTE
Words omitted repealed by the Criminal Justice Act 1948, s 83(3), Sch 10, Pt I, and the Criminal Law Act 1967, s 10(2), Sch 3, Pt III.

5 Orders for amendment of indictment, separate trial, and postponement of trial
(1) Where, before trial, or at any stage of a trial, it appears to the court that the indictment is defective, the court shall make such order for the amendment of the indictment as the court thinks necessary to meet the circumstances of the case, unless, having regard to the merits of the case, the required amendments cannot be made without injustice, . . .

(2) Where an indictment is so amended, a note of the order for amendment shall be endorsed on the indictment, and the indictment shall be treated for the purposes of the trial and for the purposes of all proceedings in connection therewith as having been found by the grand jury in the amended form.

(3) Where, before trial, or at any stage of a trial, the court is of opinion that a person accused may be prejudiced or embarrassed in his defence by reason of being charged

with more than one offence in the same indictment, or that for any other reason it is desirable to direct that the person should be tried separately for any one or more offences charged in an indictment, the court may order a separate trial of any count or counts of such indictment.

(4) Where, before trial, or at any stage of a trial, the court is of opinion that the postponement of the trial of a person accused is expedient as a consequence of the exercise of any power of the court under this Act to amend an indictment or to order a separate trial of a count, the court shall make such order as to the postponement of the trial as appears necessary.

(5) Where an order of the court is made under this section for a separate trial or for the postponement of a trial –

(a) if such an order is made during a trial the court may order that the jury are to be discharged from giving a verdict on the count or counts the trial of which is postponed or on the indictment, as the case may be; and

(b) the procedure on the separate trial of a count shall be the same in all respects as if the count had been found in a separate indictment, and the procedure on the postponed trial shall be the same in all respects (if the jury has been discharged) as if the trial had not commenced; and

(c) the court may make such order . . . as to [granting the accused person bail] and as to the enlargement of recognizances and otherwise as the court thinks fit.

(6) Any power of the court under this section shall be in addition to and not in derogation of any other power of the court for the same or similar purposes.

NOTES
Sub-s (1): words omitted repealed by the Prosecution of Offences Act 1985, s 31(6), Sch 2.
Sub-s (5): words omitted in para (c) repealed by the Prosecution of Offences Act 1985, s 31(6), Sch 2; words in square brackets in para (c) substituted by the Bail Act 1976, s 12(1), Sch 2, para 8.

Administration of Justice (Miscellaneous Provisions) Act 1933

(23 & 24 Geo 5 c 36)

An Act to abolish grand juries and amend the law as to the presentment of indictments; to provide for the summary determination of questions as to liability for death duties; to make provision for alternative procedure for the recovery of Crown debts and to enable proceedings by the Crown to be instituted in county courts in appropriate cases; to amend the procedure as to certain prerogative writs and as to trials by jury in the High Court; to amend the law as to the payment of costs by and to the Crown; to provide for the further delegation of the jurisdiction of the Master in Lunacy; and for purposes connected with the matters aforesaid.

[28 July 1933]

2 Procedure for indictment of offenders
(1) Subject to the provisions of this section, a bill of indictment charging any person with an indictable offence may be preferred by any person before a court in which the person charged may lawfully be indicted for that offence, and where a bill of indictment has been so preferred the proper officer of the court shall, if he is satisfied that the requirements of the next following subsection have been complied with, sign the bill, and it shall thereupon become an indictment and be proceeded with accordingly:

Provided that if the judge . . . of the court is satisfied that the said requirements have been complied with, he may, on the application of the prosecutor or of his own motion, direct the proper officer to sign the bill and the bill shall be signed accordingly.

(2) Subject as hereinafter provided no bill of indictment charging any person with an indictable offence shall be preferred unless either –

(a) the person charged has been committed for trial for the offence; or

[(aa) the offence is specified in a notice of transfer under section 4 of the Criminal Justice Act 1987 (serious and complex fraud); or]

[(ab) the offence is specified in a notice of transfer under section 53 of the Criminal Justice Act 1991 (violent or sexual offences against children); or]

(b) the bill is preferred [by the direction of the criminal division of the Court of Criminal Appeal] or by the direction or with the consent of a judge of the High Court . . . :

Provided that –

(i) where the person charged has been committed for trial, the bill of indictment against him may include, either in substitution for or in addition to counts charging the offence for which he was committed, any counts founded on facts or evidence disclosed in any examination or deposition taken before a justice in his presence, being counts which may lawfully be joined in the same indictment;

[(iA) in a case to which paragraph (aa) [or (ab)] above applies, the bill of indictment may include, either in substitution for or in addition to any count charging an offence specified in the notice of transfer, any counts founded on material that accompanied the copy of that notice which, in pursuance of [regulations under the relevant provision], was given to the person charged, being counts which may lawfully be joined in the same indictment;]

(ii) a charge of a previous conviction of an offence or of being a habitual criminal or a habitual drunkard may, notwithstanding that it was not included in the committal or in any such direction or consent as aforesaid, be included in any bill of indictment

[and in paragraph (iA) above "the relevant provision" means section 5(9) of the Criminal Justice Act 1987 in a case to which paragraph (aa) above applies, and paragraph 4 of Schedule 6 to the Criminal Justice Act 1991 in a case to which paragraph (ab) above applies].

(3) If a bill of indictment preferred otherwise than in accordance with the provisions of the last foregoing subsection has been signed by the proper officer of the court, the indictment shall be liable to be quashed:

Provided that –

(a) if the bill contains several counts, and the said provisions have been complied with as respects one or more of them, those counts only that were wrongly included shall be quashed under this subsection; and

(b) where a person who has been committed for trial is convicted on any indictment or any count of an indictment, that indictment or count shall not be quashed under this subsection in any proceedings on appeal, unless application was made at the trial that it should be so quashed.

NOTES

Sub-s (1): words omitted repealed by the Courts Act 1971, s 56(4), Sch II, Pt IV.

Sub-s (2): para (aa) inserted by the Criminal Justice Act 1987, s 15, Sch 2, para 1(1); para (ab) inserted by the Criminal Justice Act 1991, s 53(5), Sch 6, para 8(1); in para (b), words in square brackets inserted by the Supreme Court Act 1981, s 152(1), Sch 5, and words omitted repealed by the Prosecution of Offences Act 1985, s 31(6), Sch 2; para (iA) substituted by the Criminal Justice Act 1988, s 170(1), Sch 15, para 10, and amended by the Criminal Justice Act 1991, s 53(5), Sch 6, para 8(1).

*　*　*　*　*

Criminal Appeal Act 1968

(1968 c 19)

An Act to consolidate certain enactments relating to appeals in criminal cases to the criminal division of the Court of Appeal, and thence to the House of Lords

[8 May 1968]

PART II
APPEAL TO HOUSE OF LORDS FROM COURT OF APPEAL (CRIMINAL DIVISION)
The appeal

33 Right of appeal to House of Lords

(1) An appeal lies to the House of Lords, at the instance of the defendant or the prosecutor, from any decision of the Court of Appeal on an appeal to that court under Part I of this Act [or section 9 (preparatory hearings) of the Criminal Justice Act 1987].

(2) The appeal lies only with the leave of the Court of Appeal or the House of Lords; and leave shall not be granted unless it is certified by the Court of Appeal that a point of law of general public importance is involved in the decision and it appears to the Court of Appeal or the House of Lords (as the case may be) that the point is one which ought to be considered by that House.

[(3) Except as provided by this Part of this Act and section 13 of the Administration of Justice Act 1960 (appeal in cases of contempt of court), no appeal shall lie from any decision of the criminal division of the Court of Appeal.]

NOTES
Sub-s (1): words in square brackets inserted by the Criminal Justice Act 1987, s 15, Sch 2, para 3.
Sub-s (3): added by the Supreme Court Act 1981, s 152(1), Sch 5.

34 Application for leave to appeal

(1) An application to the Court of Appeal for leave to appeal to the House of Lords shall be made within the period of fourteen days beginning with the date of the decision of the Court; and an application to the House of Lords for leave shall be made within the period of fourteen days beginning with the date on which the application for leave is refused by the Court of Appeal.

(2) The House of Lords or the Court of Appeal may, upon application made at any time by the defendant, extend the time within which an application may be made by him to that House or the Court under subsection (1) above.

(3) An appeal to the House of Lords shall be treated as pending until any application for leave to appeal is disposed of and, if leave to appeal is granted, until the appeal is disposed of; and for purposes of this Part of this Act an application for leave to appeal shall be treated as disposed of at the expiration of the time within which it may be made, if it is not made within that time.

35 Hearing and disposal of appeal

(1) An appeal under this Part of this Act shall not be heard and determined by the House of Lords unless there are present at least three of the persons designated Lords of Appeal by section 5 of the Appellate Jurisdiction Act 1876.

(2) Any order of the House of Lords which provides for the hearing of applications for leave to appeal by a committee constituted in accordance with section 5 of the said Act of 1876 may direct that the decision of that committee shall be taken on behalf of the House.

(3) For the purpose of disposing of an appeal, the House of Lords may exercise any powers of the Court of Appeal or may remit the case to the Court.

Matters preliminary to hearing

36 Bail on appeal by defendant

The Court of Appeal may, if it seems fit, on the application of a person appealing or applying for leave to appeal to the House of Lords, [other than a person appealing or applying for leave to appeal from a decision on an appeal under section 9(11) of the Criminal Justice Act 1987 (appeals against orders or rulings at preparatory hearings),] [grant him] bail pending the determination of his appeal.

NOTE

Words in first pair of square brackets inserted by the Criminal Justice Act 1987, s 15, Sch 2, para 4, and words in second pair of square brackets substituted by the Bail Act 1976, s 12(1), Sch 2, para 43.

Theft Act 1968

(1968 c 60)

An Act to revise the law of England and Wales as to theft and similar or associated offences, and in connection therewith to make provision as to criminal proceedings by one party to a marriage against the other, and to make certain amendments extending beyond England and Wales in the Post Office Act 1953 and other enactments; and for other purposes connected therewith

[26 July 1968]

27 Evidence and procedure on charge of theft or handling stolen goods

(1) Any number of persons may be charged in one indictment, with reference to the same theft, with having at different times or at the same time handled all or any of the stolen goods, and the persons so charged may be tried together.

(2) On the trial of two or more persons indicted for jointly handling any stolen goods the jury may find any of the accused guilty if the jury are satisfied that he handled all or any of the stolen goods, whether or not he did so jointly with the other accused or any of them.

(3) Where a person is being proceeded against for handling stolen goods (but not for any offence other than handling stolen goods), then at any stage of the proceedings, if evidence has been given of his having or arranging to have in his possession the goods the subject of the charge, or of his undertaking or assisting in, or arranging to undertake or assist in, their retention, removal, disposal or realisation, the following evidence shall be admissible for the purpose of proving that he knew or believed the goods to be stolen goods: –

(a) evidence that he has had in his possession, or has undertaken or assisted in the retention, removal, disposal or realisation of, stolen goods from any theft taking place not earlier than twelve months before the offence charged; and

(b) (provided that seven days' notice in writing has been given to him of the intention to prove the conviction) evidence that he has within the five years preceding the date of the offence charged been convicted of theft or of handling stolen goods.

(4) In any proceedings for the theft of anything in the course of transmission (whether by post or otherwise), or for handling stolen goods from such a theft, a statutory

declaration made by any person that he despatched or received or failed to receive any goods or postal packet, or that any goods or postal packet when despatched or received by him were in a particular state or condition, shall be admissible as evidence of the facts stated in the declaration, subject to the following conditions: –

(a) a statutory declaration shall only be admissible where and to the extent to which oral evidence to the like effect would have been admissible in the proceedings; and

(b) a statutory declaration shall only be admissible if at least seven days before the hearing or trial a copy of it has been given to the person charged, and he has not, at least three days before the hearing or trial or within such further time as the court may in special circumstances allow, given the prosecutor written notice requiring the attendance at the hearing or trial of the person making the declaration.

(5) This section is to be construed in accordance with section 24 of this Act; and in subsection (3)(b) above the reference to handling stolen goods shall include any corresponding offence committed before the commencement of this Act.

28 Orders for restitution

[(1) Where goods have been stolen, and either a person is convicted of any offence with reference to the theft (whether or not the stealing is the gist of his offence) or a person is convicted of any other offence but such an offence as aforesaid is taken into consideration in determining his sentence, the court by or before which the offender is convicted may on the conviction [(whether or not the passing of sentence is in other respects deferred)] exercise any of the following powers –

(a) the court may order anyone having possession or control of the goods to restore them to any person entitled to recover them from him; or

(b) on the application of a person entitled to recover from the person convicted any other goods directly or indirectly representing the first-mentioned goods (as being the proceeds of any disposal or realisation of the whole or part of them or of goods so representing them), the court may order those other goods to be delivered or transferred to the applicant; or

(c) the court may order that a sum not exceeding the value of the first-mentioned goods shall be paid, out of any money of the person convicted which was taken out of his possession on his apprehension, to any person who, if those goods were in the possession of the person convicted, would be entitled to recover them from him.

(2) Where under subsection (1) above the court has power on a person's conviction to make an order against him both under paragraph (b) and under paragraph (c) with reference to the stealing of the same goods, the court may make orders under both paragraphs provided that the person in whose favour the orders are made does not thereby recover more than the value of those goods.

(3) Where under subsection (1) above the court on a person's conviction makes an order under paragraph (a) for the restoration of any goods, and it appears to the court that the person convicted has sold the goods to a person acting in good faith, or has borrowed money on the security of them from a person so acting, the court may order that there shall be paid to the purchaser or lender, out of any money of the person convicted which was taken out of his possession on his apprehension, a sum not exceeding the amount paid for the purchase by the purchaser or, as the case may be, the amount owed to the lender in respect of the loan.]

(4) The court shall not exercise the powers conferred by this section unless in the opinion of the court the relevant facts sufficiently appear from evidence given at the trial or the available documents, together with admissions made by or on behalf of any person in connection with any proposed exercise of the powers; and for this purpose "the available documents" means any written statements or admissions which were made for use, and would have been admissible, as evidence at the trial, the depositions

taken at any committal proceedings and any written statements or admissions used as evidence in those proceedings.

(5) Any order under this section shall be treated as an order for the restitution of property within the meaning of [section 30 of the Criminal Appeal Act 1968 (which relates to the effect on such orders of appeals)].

(6) References in this section to stealing are to be construed in accordance with section 24(1) and (4) of this Act.*

[(7) An order may be made under this section in respect of money owed by the Crown.]

NOTES
S 24(1) provides that "stealing" includes the offence whether committed in England or Wales or elsewhere, provided that the stealing, if not an offence under the Act, amounted to an offence where and at the time when the goods were stolen; references to stolen goods are to be construed accordingly. S 24(4) provides that stealing includes fraud and blackmail.
Sub-ss (1)–(3): substituted by the Criminal Justice Act 1972, s 64(1), Sch 5.
Sub-s (1): words in square brackets inserted by the Criminal Law Act 1977, s 65(4), Sch 12.
Sub-s (5): words in square brackets substituted by the Criminal Justice Act 1988, s 170(1), Sch 15, para 33.
Sub-s (7): added by the Criminal Justice Act 1988, s 163.

General and consequential provisions

31 Effect on civil proceedings and rights
(1) A person shall not be excused, by reason that to do so may incriminate that person or the wife or husband of that person of an offence under this Act –

(a) from answering any question put to that person in proceedings for the recovery or administration of any property, for the execution of any trust or for an account of any property or dealings with property; or
(b) from complying with any order made in any such proceedings;

but no statement or admission made by a person in answering a question put or complying with an order made as aforesaid shall, in proceedings for an offence under this Act, be admissible in evidence against that person or (unless they married after the making of the statement or admission) against the wife or husband of that person.

(2) Notwithstanding any enactment to the contrary, where property has been stolen or obtained by fraud or other wrongful means, the title to that or any other property shall not be affected by reason only of the conviction of the offender.

Criminal Justice Act 1972

(1972 c 71)

An Act to make further provision with respect to the administration of criminal justice, the criminal courts and the penal system, and to the methods of dealing with offenders (including the provision of new methods); to amend the law about qualification for jury service, the summoning of jurors and the payment of allowances in respect of jury service; to increase the penalties for certain offences and amend section 21 of the Firearms Act 1968 and section 9 of the Public Order Act 1936; and for purposes connected with those matters

[26 October 1972]

PART I
POWERS FOR DEALING WITH OFFENDERS
Restitution orders

6 Restitution orders

(1) The following provisions of this section shall have effect with respect to section 28 of the Theft Act 1968 (which enables orders for restitution and certain other orders to be made in relation to stolen property).

(2) The powers conferred by –

(a) subsection (1)(c) of the said section 28 (payment to owner of stolen goods out of money taken from the offender on his apprehension); and

(b) subsection (3) of that section (payment to purchaser of, and lender on the security of, stolen goods out of money so taken),

shall be exercisable without any application being made in that behalf or on the application of any person appearing to the court to be interested in the property concerned.

(3) The powers conferred by the said section 28 shall be exercisable not only where a person is convicted of an offence with reference to the theft of the goods in question but also where, on the conviction of a person of any other offence, the court takes an offence with reference to the theft of those goods into consideration in determining sentence.

(4) Where an order is made under the said section 28 against any person in respect of an offence taken into consideration in determining his sentence –

(a) the order shall cease to have effect if he successfully appeals against his conviction of the offence or, if more than one, all the offences, of which he was convicted in the proceedings in which the order was made;

(b) he may appeal against the order as if it were part of the sentence imposed in respect of the offence or, if more than one, any of the offences, of which he was so convicted.

(5) Any order under the said section 28 made by a magistrates' court shall be suspended –

(a) in any case until the expiration of the period for the time being prescribed by law for the giving of notice of appeal against a decision of a magistrates' court;

(b) where notice of appeal is given within the period so prescribed, until the determination of the appeal;

but this subsection shall not apply where the order is made under section 28(1)(a) or (b) and the court so directs, being of the opinion that the title to the goods to be restored or, as the case may be, delivered or transferred under the order is not in dispute.

PART III
MISCELLANEOUS PROVISIONS

46 Admissibility of written statements outside England and Wales

(1) [Section 102 of the Magistrates' Courts Act 1980 and section 9 of the Criminal Justice Act 1967 (which respectively allow written statements to be used as evidence in committal proceedings and in other criminal proceedings) and section 106 of the said Act of 1980 and section 89 of the said Act of 1967 (which punish the making of false statements which are tendered in evidence under the said section 102 or 9, as the case may be)] shall apply to written statements made in Scotland or Northern Ireland as well as to written statements made in England and Wales.

(2) [The said section 102] shall apply also to written statements made outside the United Kingdom, but, in relation to such statements, that section shall have effect with the omission of subsections (2)(b), (3A) and (7).

NOTE
Sub-ss (1), (2): words in square brackets substituted by the Magistrates' Courts Act 1980, s 154, Sch 7, para 114.

Powers of Criminal Courts Act 1973

(1973 c 62)

An Act to consolidate certain enactments relating to the powers of courts to deal with offenders and defaulters, to the treatment of offenders and to arrangements for persons on bail

[25 October 1973]

PART I

Compensation orders

35 Compensation orders against convicted persons
[(1) Subject to the provisions of this Part of this Act and to section 40 of the Magistrates' Courts Act 1980 (which imposes a monetary limit on the powers of a magistrates' court under this section), a court by or before which a person is convicted of an offence, instead of or in addition to dealing with him in any other way, may, on application or otherwise, make an order (in this Act referred to as "a compensation order") requiring him to pay compensation for any personal injury, loss or damage resulting from that offence or any other offence which is taken into consideration by the court in determining sentence [or to make payments for funeral expenses or bereavement in respect of a death resulting from any such offence, other than a death due to an accident arising out of the presence of a motor vehicle on a road; and a court shall give reasons, on passing sentence, if it does not make such an order in a case where this section empowers it to do so].

(1A) Compensation under subsection (1) above shall be of such amount as the court considers appropriate, having regard to any evidence and to any representations that are made by or on behalf of the accused or the prosecutor.]

(2) In the case of an offence under the Theft Act 1968, where the property in question is recovered, any damage to the property occurring while it was out of the owner's possession shall be treated for the purposes of subsection (1) above as having resulted from the offence, however and by whomsoever the damage was caused.

[(3) A compensation order may only be made in respect of injury, loss or damage (other than loss suffered by a person's dependants in consequence of his death) which was due to an accident arising out of the presence of a motor vehicle on a road, if –

(a) it is in respect of damage which is treated by subsection (2) above as resulting from an offence under the Theft Act 1968; or
(b) it is in respect of injury, loss or damage as respects which –

  (i) the offender is uninsured in relation to the use of the vehicle; and
  (ii) compensation is not payable under any arrangements to which the Secretary of State is a party;

and, where a compensation order is made in respect of injury, loss or damage due to such an accident, the amount to be paid may include an amount representing the whole or part of any loss of or reduction in preferential rates of insurance attributable to the accident.

(3A) A vehicle the use of which is exempted from insurance by section 144 of the Road Traffic Act 1972 is not uninsured for the purposes of subsection (3) above.

(3B) A compensation order in respect of funeral expenses may be made for the benefit of anyone who incurred the expenses.

(3C) A compensation order in respect of bereavement may only be made for the benefit of a person whose benefit a claim for damages for bereavement could be made under section 1A of the Fatal Accidents Act 1976.

(3D) The amount of compensation in respect of bereavement shall not exceed the amount for the time being specified in section 1A of the Fatal Accidents Act 1976.]

(4) *In determining whether to make a compensation order against any person, and in determining the amount to be paid by any person under such an order, the court shall have regard to his means so far as they appear or are known to the court.*

[(4A) Where the court considers –

(a) that it would be appropriate both to impose a fine and to make a compensation order; but
(b) that the offender has insufficient means to pay both an appropriate fine and appropriate compensation, the court shall give preference to compensation (though it may impose a fine as well).]

(5) . . .

NOTES
Sub-ss (1), (1A): substituted for original sub-s (1) by the Criminal Justice Act 1982, s 67; words in square brackets in sub-s (1) inserted by the Criminal Justice Act 1988, s 104.
Sub-ss (3), (3A)–(3D): substituted for original sub-s (3) by the Criminal Justice Act 1988, s 104.
Sub-s (4): prospectively substituted by the Criminal Justice Act 1988, s 170(1), Sch 15, paras 38, 40, as follows –

"(4) In determining whether to make a compensation order against any person, and in determining the amount to be paid by any person under such an order, it shall be the duty of the court –

(a) to have regard to his means so far as they appear or are known to the court; and
(b) in a case where it is proposed to make against him both a compensation order and a confiscation order under Part VI of the Criminal Justice Act 1988, also to have regard to its duty under section 72(7) of that Act (duty where the court considers that the offender's means are insufficient to satisfy both orders in full to order the payment out of sums recovered under the confiscation order of sums due under the compensation order).".

Sub-s (4A): inserted by the Criminal Justice Act 1982, s 67.
Sub-s (5): repealed by the Magistrates' Courts Act 1980, s 154, Sch 9.

[36 Enforcement and appeals

(1) A person in whose favour a compensation order is made shall not be entitled to receive the amount due to him until (disregarding any power of a court to grant leave to appeal out of time) there is no further possibility of an appeal on which the order could be varied or set aside.

(2) Rules under section 144 of the Magistrates' Courts Act 1980 may make provision regarding the way in which the magistrates' court for the time being having functions (by virtue of section 41(1) of the Administration of Justice Act 1970) in relation to the enforcement of a compensation order is to deal with money paid in satisfaction of the order where the entitlement of the person in whose favour it was made is suspended.

(3) The Court of Appeal may by order annul or vary any compensation order made by the court of trial, although the conviction is not quashed; and the order, if annulled, shall not take effect and, if varied, shall take effect as varied.

(4) Where the House of Lords restores a conviction, it may make any compensation order which the court of trial could have made.

(5) Where a compensation order has been made against any person in respect of an offence taken into consideration in determining his sentence –

(a) the order shall cease to have effect if he successfully appeals against his conviction of the offence or, if more than one, all the offences, of which he was convicted in the proceedings in which the order was made;
(b) he may appeal against the order or, if more than one, any of the offences, of which he was so convicted.]

NOTE
Substituted by the Criminal Justice Act 1988, s 105.

[37 Review of compensation orders
At any time before the person against whom a compensation order has been made has paid into court the whole of the compensation which the order requires him to pay, but at a time when (disregarding any power of a court to grant leave to appeal out of time) there is no further possibility of an appeal on which the order could be varied or set aside, the magistrates' court for the time being having functions in relation to the enforcement of the order may, on the application of the person against whom it was made, discharge the order, or reduce the amount which remains to be paid, if it appears to the court –

(a) that the injury, loss or damage in respect of which the order was made has been held in civil proceedings to be less than it was taken to be for the purposes of the order; or
(b) in the case of an order in respect of the loss of any property, that the property has been recovered by the person in whose favour the order was made; or
(c) that the means of the person against whom the order was made are insufficient to satisfy in full both the order and a confiscation order under Part VI of the Criminal Justice Act 1988 made against him in the same proceedings; or
(d) that the person against whom the order was made has suffered a substantial reduction in his means which was unexpected at the time when the compensation order was made, and that his means seem unlikely to increase for a considerable period;

but where the order was made by the Crown Court, a magistrates' court shall not exercise any power conferred by this section in a case where it is satisfied as mentioned in paragraph (c) or (d) above unless it has first obtained the consent of the Crown Court.]

NOTES
Substituted by the Criminal Justice Act 1988, s 105.

[38 Effect of compensation order on subsequent award of damages in civil proceedings
(1) This section shall have effect where a compensation order [or a service compensation order or award] has been made in favour of any person in respect of any injury, loss or damage and a claim by him in civil proceedings for damages in respect of the injury, loss or damage subsequently falls to be determined.

(2) The damages in the civil proceedings shall be assessed without regard to the order [or award]; but the plaintiff may only recover an amount equal to the aggregate of the following –

(a) any amount by which they exceed the compensation; and
(b) a sum equal to any portion of the compensation which he fails to recover,

and may not enforce the judgment, so far as it relates to a sum such as is mentioned in paragraph (b) above, without the leave of the court.]

(3) In this section a "service compensation order or award" means –

(a) an order requiring the payment of compensation under paragraph 11 of Schedule 5A to the Army Act 1955, of Schedule 5A to the Air Force Act 1955 or of Schedule 4A to the Naval Discipline Act 1957; or

(b) an award of stoppages payable by way of compensation under any of those Acts.]

NOTES
Sub-ss (1), (2): substituted by the Criminal Justice Act 1988, s 105; amended by the Army Act 1991, s 26(1), Sch 2, para 9(1)(a), (b).
Sub-s (3): added by the Army Act 1991, s 26(1), Sch 2, para 9(1)(c).

Criminal bankruptcy orders

39 Criminal bankruptcy orders against convicted persons
(1) Where a person is convicted of an offence before the Crown Court and it appears to the court that –

(a) as a result of the offence, or of that offence taken together with any other relevant offence or offences, loss or damage (not attributable to personal injury) has been suffered by one or more persons whose identity is known to the court; and

(b) the amount, or aggregate amount, of the loss or damage exceeds £15,000;

the court may, in addition to dealing with the offender in any other way (but not if it makes a compensation order against him), make a criminal bankruptcy order against him in respect of the offence or, as the case may be, that offence and the other relevant offence or offences.

(3) A criminal bankruptcy order shall specify –

(a) the amount of the loss or damage appearing to the court to have resulted from the offence or, if more than one, each of the offences;

(b) the person or persons appearing to the court to have suffered that loss or damage;

(c) the amount of that loss or damage which it appears to the court that that person, or each of those persons, has suffered; and

(d) [for the purposes of section [341(4) of the Insolvency Act 1986]] the date which appears to the court to be the earliest date on which the offence or, if more than one, the earliest of the offences, was committed.

(4) A criminal bankruptcy order may be made against two or more offenders in respect of the same loss or damage.

(5) . . .

(6) The Secretary of State may by order direct that subsection (1) above shall be amended by substituting, for the amount specified in that subsection as originally enacted or as previously amended under this subsection, such amount as may be specified in the order.

NOTES
Prospectively repealed by the Criminal Justice Act 1988, s 170(2), Sch 16, but not so as to affect any criminal bankruptcy order made before the day appointed for the repeal to come into force, and not so as to prevent the taking of any step following such an order.
Sub-s (3): in para (d), words in first (outer) pair of square brackets substituted by the Insolvency Act 1985, s 235(1), Sch 8, para 24, and words in second (inner) pair of square brackets substituted by the Insolvency Act 1986, s 439(2), Sch 14.
Sub-s (5): repealed by the Insolvency Act 1985, s 235(3), Sch 10, Pt III.

40 Appeals in the case of criminal bankruptcy orders
(1) No appeal shall lie against the making of a criminal bankruptcy order.

(2) Where a person successfully appeals to the Court of Appeal against his conviction of an offence by virtue of which such an order was made, the court shall rescind the order unless he was convicted in the same proceedings of another offence of which he remains convicted and a criminal bankruptcy order could have been made without reference to loss or damage caused by the first-mentioned offence; and where, accordingly, it does not

rescind the order it shall amend it by striking out so much of it as relates to such loss or damage.

(3) Where on appeal by a person against his conviction of an offence by virtue of which a criminal bankruptcy order was made the Court of Appeal substitutes a verdict of guilty of another offence, the court shall –

- *(a) rescind the order if a criminal bankruptcy order could not have been made against that person if he had originally been convicted of that other offence;*
- *(b) in any other case, amend the order so far as may be required in consequences of the substitution of a verdict of guilty of the other offence.*

(4) Where the Court of Appeal rescinds or amends a criminal bnakruptcy order, the rescission or amendment shall not take effect –

- *(a) in any case until the expiration of the time for applying for leave to appeal to the House of Lords against the Court of Appeal's decision on the appeal against conviction (disregarding any extension of time which may be granted under section 34 of the Criminal Appeal Act 1968);*
- *(b) if an aplication for leave to appeal is made within that time, so long as an appeal to the House of Lords is pending; and*
- *(c) if on such an appeal the conviction is restored by that House.*

(5) For the purposes of this section an appeal to the House of Lords shall be treated as pending until any application for leave to appeal is disposed of and, if leave to appeal is granted, until the appeal is disposed of; and for the purposes of this subsection an application for leave to appeal shall be treated as disposed of at the expiration of the time within which it may be made if it is not made within that time.

NOTE
Prospectively repealed by the Criminal Justice Act 1988, s 170(2), Sch 16, but not so as to affect any criminal bankruptcy order made before the day appointed for the repeal to come into force, and not so as to prevent the taking of any step following such an order.

Bail Act 1976

(1976 c 63)

An Act to make provision in relation to bail in or in connection with criminal proceedings in England and Wales, to make it an offence to agree to indemnify sureties in criminal proceedings, to make provision for legal aid limited to questions of bail in certain cases and for legal aid for persons kept in custody for inquiries or reports, to extend the powers of coroners to grant bail and for connected purposes

[15 November 1976]

Incidents of bail in criminal proceedings

3 General provisions

* * * * *

(8) Where a court has granted bail in criminal proceedings [that court or, where that court has committed a person on bail to the Crown Court for trial or to be sentenced or otherwise dealt with, that court or the Crown Court may] on application –

(a) by or on behalf of the person to whom [bail was] granted, or
(b) by the prosecutor or a constable,

vary the conditions of bail or impose conditions in respect of bail which [has been] granted unconditionally.

[(8A) Where a notice of transfer is given under section 4 of the Criminal Justice Act 1987, subsection (8) above shall have effect in relation to a person in relation to whose case the notice is given as if he had been committed on bail to the Crown Court for trial.]

*　*　*　*　*

NOTES

Sub-s (8): words in square brackets substituted by the Criminal Law Act 1977, s 65(4), Sch 12.
Sub-s (8A): inserted by the Criminal Justice Act 1987, s 15, Sch 2, para 9.

Criminal Law Act 1977

(1977 c 45)

An Act to amend the law of England and Wales with respect to criminal conspiracy; to make new provision in that law, in place of the provisions of the common law and the Statutes of Forcible Entry, for restricting the use or threat of violence for securing entry into any premises and for penalising unauthorised entry or remaining on premises in certain circumstances; otherwise to amend the criminal law, including the law with respect to the administration of criminal justice; to provide for the alteration of certain pecuniary and other limits; to amend section 9(4) of the Administration of Justice Act 1973, the Legal Aid Act 1974, the Rabies Act 1974 and the Diseases of Animals (Northern Ireland) Order 1975 and the law about juries and coroners' inquests; and for connected purposes.

[29 July 1977]

PART I
CONSPIRACY

1 The offence of conspiracy

[(1) Subject to the following provisions of this Part of this Act, if a person agrees with any other person or persons that a course of conduct shall be pursued which, if the agreement is carried out in accordance with their intentions, either –

(a) will necessarily amount to or involve the commission of any offence or offences by one or more of parties to the agreement, or
(b) would do so but for the existence of facts which render the commission of the offence or any of the offences impossible,

he is guilty of conspiracy to commit the offence or offences in question.]

[(1A) Subject to section 8 of the Computer Misuse Act 1990 (relevance of external law), if this subsection applies to an agreement, this Part of this Act has effect in relation to it as it has effect in relation to an agreement falling within subsection (1) above.

(1B) Subsection (1A) above applies to an agreement if –

(a) a party to it, or a party's agent, did anything in England and Wales in relation to it before its formation; or
(b) a party to it became a party in England and Wales (by joining it either in person or through an agent); or

(c) a party to it, or a party's agent, did or omitted anything in England and Wales in pursuance of it;

and the agreement would fall within subsection (1) above as an agreement relating to the commission of a computer misuse offence but for the fact that the offence would not be an offence triable in England and Wales if committed in accordance with the parties' intentions.]

(2) Where liability for any offence may be incurred without knowledge on the part of the person committing it of any particular fact or circumstance necessary for the commission of the offence, a person shall nevertheless not be guilty of conspiracy to commit that offence by virtue of subsection (1) above unless he and at least one other party to the agreement intend or know that that fact or circumstance shall or will exist at the time when the conduct constituting the offence is to take place.

(3) Where in pursuance of any agreement the acts in question in relation to any offence are to be done in contemplation or furtherance of a trade dispute (within the meaning of the Trade Union and Labour Relations Act 1974) that offence shall be disregarded for the purposes of subsection (1) above provided that it is a summary offence which is not punishable with imprisonment.

(4) In this Part of this Act "offence" means an offence triable in England and Wales, except that it includes murder notwithstanding that the murder in question would not be so triable if committed in accordance with the intentions of the parties to the agreement.

[(5) In the application of this Part of this Act to an agreement to which subsection (1A) above applies any reference to an offence shall be read as a reference to what would be the computer misuse offence in question but for the fact that it is not an offence triable in England and Wales.

(6) In this section "computer misuse offence" means an offence under the Computer Misuse Act 1990.]

NOTES
Sub-s (1): substituted by the Criminal Attempts Act 1981, s 5, except as to agreements entered into before 27 August 1981 (ie date of commencement of the 1981 Act) when the conspiracy continued to exist after that date.
Sub-ss (1A), (1B): inserted by the Computer Misuse Act 1990, s 7(1).
Sub-ss (5), (6): added by the Computer Misuse Act 1990, s 7(2).

2 Exemptions from liability for conspiracy
(1) A person shall not by virtue of section 1 above be guilty of conspiracy to commit any offence if he is an intended victim of that offence.

(2) A person shall not by virtue of section 1 above be guilty of conspiracy to commit any offence or offences if the only other person or persons with whom he agrees are (both initially and at all times during the currency of the agreement) persons of any one or more of the following descriptions, that is to say –

(a) his spouse;
(b) a person under the age of criminal responsibility; and
(c) an intended victim of that offence or of each of those offences.

(3) A person is under the age of criminal responsibility for the purposes of subsection (2)(b) above so long as it is conclusively presumed, by virtue of section 50 of the Children and Young Persons Act 1933, that he cannot be guilty of any offence.

3 Penalties for conspiracy
(1) A person guilty by virtue of section 1 above of conspiracy to commit any offence or offences shall be liable on conviction on indictment –

(a) in a case falling within subsection (2) or (3) below, to imprisonment for a term related in accordance with that subsection to the gravity of the offence or offences in question (referred to below in this section as the relevant offence or offences); and

(b) in any other case, to a fine.

Paragraph (b) above shall not be taken as prejudicing the application of section 30(1) of the Powers of Criminal Courts Act 1973 (general power of court to fine offender convicted on indictment) in a case falling within subsection (2) or (3) below.

(2) Where the relevant offence or any of the relevant offences is an offence of any of the following descriptions, that is to say –

(a) murder, or any other offence the sentence for which is fixed by law;

(b) an offence for which a sentence extending to imprisonment for life is provided; or

(c) an indictable offence punishable with imprisonment for which no maximum term of imprisonment is provided,

the person convicted shall be liable to imprisonment for life.

(3) Where in a case other than one to which subsection (2) above applies the relevant offence or any of the relevant offences is punishable with imprisonment, the person convicted shall be liable to imprisonment for a term not exceeding the maximum term provided for that offence or (where more than one such offence is in question) for any one of those offences (taking the longer or the longest term as the limit for the purposes of this section where the terms provided differ).

In the case of an offence triable either way the references above in this subsection to the maximum term provided for that offence are references to the maximum term so provided on conviction on indictment.

4 Restrictions on the institution of proceedings for conspiracy
(1) Subject to subsection (2) below proceedings under section 1 above for conspiracy to commit any offence or offences shall not be instituted against any person except by or with the consent of the Director of Public Prosecutions if the offence or (as the case may be) each of the offences in question is a summary offence.

(2) In relation to the institution of proceedings under section 1 above for conspiracy to commit –

(a) an offence which is subject to a prohibition by or under any enactment on the institution of proceedings otherwise than by, or on behalf or with the consent of, the Attorney General, or

(b) two or more offences of which at least one is subject to such a prohibition,

subsection (1) above shall have effect with the substitution of a reference to the Attorney General for the reference to the Director of Public Prosecutions.

(3) Any prohibition by or under any enactment on the institution of proceedings for any offence which is not a summary offence otherwise than by, or on behalf or with the consent of, the Director of Public Prosecutions or any other person shall apply also in relation to proceedings under section 1 above for conspiracy to commit that offence.

(4) Where –

(a) an offence has been committed in pursuance of any agreement; and

(b) proceedings may not be instituted for that offence because any time limit applicable to the institution of any such proceedings has expired,

proceedings under section 1 above for conspiracy to commit that offence shall not be instituted against any person on the basis of that agreement.

5 Abolitions, savings, transitional provisions, consequential amendment and repeals
(1) Subject to the following provisions of this section, the offence of conspiracy at common law is hereby abolished.

(2) Subsection (1) above shall not affect the offence of conspiracy at common law so far as relates to conspiracy to defraud, . . .

(3) Subsection (1) above shall not affect the offence of conspiracy at common law if and in so far as it may be committed by entering into an agreement to engage in conduct which –

(a) tends to corrupt public morals or outrages public decency; but
(b) would not amount to or involve the commission of an offence if carried out by a single person otherwise than in pursuance of an agreement.

(4) Subsection (1) above shall not affect –

(a) any proceedings commenced before the time when this Part of this Act comes into force;
(b) any proceedings commenced after that time against a person charged with the same conspiracy as that charged in any proceedings commenced before that time; or
(c) any proceedings commenced after that time in respect of a trespass committed before that time;

but a person convicted of conspiracy to trespass in any proceedings brought by virtue of paragraph (c) above shall not in respect of that conviction be liable to imprisonment for a term exceeding six months.

(5) Sections 1 and 2 above shall apply to things done before as well as to things done after the time when this Part of this Act comes into force, but in the application of section 3 above to a case where the agreement in question was entered into before that time –

(a) subsection (2) shall be read without the reference to murder in paragraph (a); and
(b) any murder intended under the agreement shall be treated as an offence for which a maximum term of imprisonment of ten years is provided.

(6) The rules laid down by sections 1 and 2 above shall apply for determining whether a person is guilty of an offence of conspiracy under any enactment other than section 1 above, but conduct which is an offence under any such other enactment shall not also be an offence under section 1 above.

(7) Incitement . . . to commit the offence of conspiracy (whether the conspiracy incited . . . would be an offence at common law or under section 1 above or any other enactment) shall cease to be offences.

(8) The fact that the person or persons who, so far as appears from the indictment on which any person has been convicted of conspiracy, were the only other parties to the agreement on which his conviction was based have been acquitted of conspiracy by reference to that agreement (whether after being tried with the person convicted or separately) shall not be a ground for quashing his conviction unless under all the circumstances of the case his conviction is inconsistent with the acquittal of the other person or persons in question.

(9) Any rule of law or practice inconsistent with the provisions of subsection (8) above is hereby abolished.

* * * * *

NOTES
Sub-s (2): words omitted repealed by the Criminal Justice Act 1987, s 12(2).
Sub-s (7): words omitted repealed by the Criminal Attempts Act 1981, s 10, Schedule, Pt I.

Magistrates' Courts Act 1980

(1980 c 43)

An Act to consolidate certain enactments relating to the jurisdiction of, and the practice and procedure before, magistrates' courts and the functions of justices' clerks, and to matters connected therewith, with amendments to give effect to recommendations of the Law Commission

[1 August 1980]

PART I
CRIMINAL JURISDICTION AND PROCEDURE

Committal Proceedings

7 Place of trial on indictment
A magistrates' court committing a person for trial shall specify the place at which he is to be tried, and in selecting that place shall have regard to –

   (a) the convenience of the defence, the prosecution and the witnesses,
   (b) the expediting of the trial, and
   (c) any direction given by or on behalf of the Lord Chief Justice with the concurrence of the Lord Chancellor under section 4(5) of the Courts Act 1971.

Supreme Court Act 1981

(1981 c 54)

An Act to consolidate with amendments the Supreme Court of Judicature (Consolidation) Act 1925 and other enactments relating to the Supreme Court in England and Wales and the administration of justice therein; to repeal certain obsolete or unnecessary enactments so relating; to amend Part VIII of the Mental Health Act 1959, the Courts-Martial (Appeals) Act 1968, the Arbitration Act 1979 and the law relating to county courts; and for connected purposes.

[28 July 1981]

PART III
PRACTICE AND PROCEDURE
THE CROWN COURT

Distribution of business

75 Allocation of cases according to composition of court, etc
(1) The cases or classes of cases in the Crown Court suitable for allocation respectively to a judge of the High Court and to a Circuit Judge or Recorder, and all other matters relating to the distribution of Crown Court business, shall be determined in accordance with directions given by or on behalf of the Lord Chief Justice with the concurrence of the Lord Chancellor.

(2) Subject to section 74(1), the cases or classes of cases in the Crown Court suitable for allocation to a court comprising justices of the peace (including those by way of trial

on indictment which are suitable for allocation to such a court) shall be determined in accordance with directions given by or on behalf of the Lord Chief Justice with the concurrence of the Lord Chancellor.

76 Committal for trial: alteration of place of trial
(1) Without prejudice to the provisions of this Act about the distribution of Crown Court business, the Crown Court may give directions, or further directions, altering the place of any trial on indictment, whether by varying the decision of a magistrates' court under section 7 of the Magistrates' Courts Act 1980 or [by substituting some other place for the place specified in a notice under section 4 of the Criminal Justice Act 1987 (notices of transfer from magistrates' court to Crown Court) or by varying] a previous decision of the Crown Court.

(2) Directions under section (1) may be given on behalf of the Crown Court by an officer of the court.

[(2A) Where a preparatory hearing has been ordered under section 7 of the Criminal Justice Act 1987, directions altering the place of trial may be given under subsection (1) at any time before the jury are sworn.]

(3) The defendant or the prosecutor, if dissatisfied with the place of trial as fixed by the magistrates' court, [as specified in a notice under section 4 of the Criminal Justice Act 1987, or as fixed] by the Crown Court, may apply to the Crown Court for a direction, or further direction, varying the place of trial; and the court shall take the matter into consideration and may comply with or refuse the application, or give a direction not in compliance with the application, as the court thinks fit.

(4) An application under subsection (3) shall be heard in open court by a judge of the High Court.

NOTES
Sub-s (1): words in square brackets inserted by the Criminal Justice Act 1987, s 15, Sch 2, para 10.
Sub-s (2A): inserted by the Criminal Justice Act 1987, s 15, Sch 2, para 10.
Sub-s (3): words in square brackets substituted by the Criminal Justice Act 1987, s 15, Sch 2, para 10.

77 Committal for trial: date of trial
(1) Crown Court Rules shall prescribe the minimum *and the maximum* period which may elapse between a person's committal for trial [or the giving of a notice of transfer under section 4 of the Criminal Justice Act 1987] and the beginning of the trial; and such rules may make different provision for different places of trial and for other different circumstances.

(2) The trial of a person committed by a magistrates' court –

(a) shall not begin until the prescribed minimum period has expired except with his consent and the consent of the prosecutor; *and*
(b) *shall not begin later than the expiry of the prescribed maximum period unless a judge of the Crown Court otherwise orders.*

(3) For the purposes of this section the prescribed minimum *and maximum periods* shall begin with the date of committal for trial and the trial shall be taken to begin when the defendant is arraigned.

NOTES
Sub-s (1): words in italics prospectively repealed by the Prosecution of Offences Act 1985, s 31(6), Sch 2; words in square brackets inserted by the Criminal Justice Act 1987, s 15, Sch 2, 11.
Sub-s (2): para (b) prospectively repealed by the Prosecution of Offences Act 1985, s 31(6), Sch 2.
Sub-s (3): for the words in italics, there is prospectively substituted the word "period" by the Prosecution of Offences Act 1985, s 31(5), Sch 1, Part III.

Police and Criminal Evidence Act 1984

(1984 c 60)

An Act to make further provision in relation to the powers and duties of the police, persons in police detention, criminal evidence, police discipline and complaints against the police; to provide for arrangements for obtaining the views of the community on policing and for a rank of deputy chief constable; to amend the law relating to the Police Federations and Police Forces and Police Cadets in Scotland; and for connected purposes

[31 October 1984]

PART II
POWERS OF ENTRY, SEARCH AND SEIZURE

NOTE
Pt II (ss 8–23, Sch 1): By virtue of the Criminal Justice (International Co-operation) Act 1990, s 7(1), this Part of this Act is modified so that references to serious arrestable offences in s 8 of, and Sch 1 to, this Act include any conduct which is an offence under the law of a country or territory outside the United Kingdom and would constitute a serious arrestable offence if it had occurred in any part of the United Kingdom.

Search warrants

8 Power of justice of the peace to authorise entry and search of premises
(1) If on an application made by a constable a justice of the peace is satisfied that there are reasonable grounds for believing –

(a) that a serious arrestable offence has been committed; and
(b) that there is material on premises specified in the application which is likely to be of substantial value (whether by itself or together with other material) to the investigation of the offence; and
(c) that the material is likely to be relevant evidence; and
(d) that it does not consist of or include items subject to legal privilege, excluded material or special procedure material; and
(e) that any of the conditions specified in subsection (3) below applies,

he may issue a warrant authorising a constable to enter and search the premises.

(2) A constable may seize and retain anything for which a search has been authorised under subsection (1) above.

(3) The conditions mentioned in subsection (1)(e) above are –

(a) that it is not practicable to communicate with any person entitled to grant entry to the premises;
(b) that it is practicable to communicate with a person entitled to grant entry to the premises but it is not practicable to communicate with any person entitled to grant access to the evidence;
(c) that entry to the premises will not be granted unless a warrant is produced;
(d) that the purpose of a search may be frustrated or seriously prejudiced unless a constable arriving at the premises can secure immediate entry to them.

(4) In this Act "relevant evidence", in relation to an offence, means anything that would be admissible in evidence at a trial for the offence.

(5) The power to issue a warrant conferred by this section is in addition to any such power otherwise conferred.

9 Special provisions as to access
(1) A constable may obtain access to excluded material or special procedure material for the purposes of a criminal investigation by making an application under Schedule 1 below and in accordance with that Schedule.

(2) Any Act (including a local Act) passed before this Act under which a search of premises for the purposes of a criminal investigation could be authorised by the issue of a warrant to a constable shall cease to have effect so far as it relates to the authorisation of searches –

(a) for items subject to legal privilege; or
(b) for excluded material; or
(c) for special procedure material consisting of documents or records other than documents.

10 Meaning of "items subject to legal privilege"
(1) Subject to subsection (2) below, in this Act "items subject to legal privilege" means –

(a) communications between a professional legal adviser and his client or any person representing his client made in connection with the giving of legal advice to the client;
(b) communications between a professional legal adviser and his client or any person representing his client or between such an adviser or his client or any such representative and any other person made in connection with or in contemplation of legal proceedings and for the purposes of such proceedings; and
(c) items enclosed with or referred to in such communications and made –

(i) in connection with the giving of legal advice; or
(ii) in connection with or in contemplation of legal proceedings and for the purposes of such proceedings,

when they are in the possession of a person who is entitled to possession of them.

(2) Items held with the intention of furthering a criminal purpose are not items subject to legal privilege.

11 Meaning of "excluded material"
(1) Subject to the following provisions of this section, in this Act "excluded material" means –

(a) personal records which a person has acquired or created in the course of any trade, business, profession or other occupation or for the purposes of any paid or unpaid office and which he holds in confidence;
(b) human tissue or tissue fluid which has been taken for the purposes of diagnosis or medical treatment and which a person holds in confidence;
(c) journalistic material which a person holds in confidence and which consists –

(i) of documents; or
(ii) of records other than documents.

(2) A person holds material other than journalistic material in confidence for the purposes of this section if he holds it subject –

(a) to an express or implied undertaking to hold it in confidence; or
(b) to a restriction on disclosure or an obligation of secrecy contained in any enactment, including an enactment contained in an Act passed after this Act.

(3) A person holds journalistic material in confidence for the purposes of this section if –

(a) he holds it subject to such an undertaking, restriction or obligation; and
(b) it has been continuously held (by one or more persons) subject to such an

undertaking, restriction or obligation since it was first acquired or created for the purposes of journalism.

12 Meaning of "personal records"

In this Part of this Act "personal records" means documentary and other records concerning an individual (whether living or dead) who can be identified from them and relating –

(a) to his physical or mental health;

(b) to spiritual counselling or assistance given or to be given to him; or

(c)   to counselling or assistance given or to be given to him, for the purposes of his personal welfare, by any voluntary organisation or by any individual who –

    (i)   by reason of his office or occupation has responsibilities for his personal welfare; or

    (ii) by reason of an order of a court has responsibilities for his supervision.

13 Meaning of "journalistic material"

(1) Subject to subsection (2) below, in this Act "journalistic material" means material acquired or created for the purposes of journalism.

(2) Material is only journalistic material for the purposes of this Act if it is in the possession of a person who acquired or created it for the purposes of journalism.

(3) A person who receives material from someone who intends that the recipient shall use it for the purposes of journalism is to be taken to have acquired it for those purposes.

14 Meaning of "special procedure material"

(1) In this Act "special procedure material" means –

(a) material to which subsection (2) below applies; and

(b) journalistic material, other than excluded material.

(2) Subject to the following provisions of this section, this subsection applies to material, other than items subject to legal privilege and excluded material, in the possession of a person who –

(a) acquired or created it in the course of any trade, business, profession or other occupation or for the purpose of any paid or unpaid office; and

(b) holds it subject –

    (i)   to an express or implied undertaking to hold it in confidence; or

    (ii) to a restriction or obligation such as is mentioned in section 11(2)(b) above.

(3) Where material is acquired –

(a) by an employee from his employer and in the course of his employment; or

(b) by a company from an associated company,

it is only special procedure material if it was special procedure material immediately before the acquisition.

(4) Where material is created by an employee in the course of his employment, it is only special procedure material if it would have been special procedure material had his employer created it.

(5) Where material is created by a company on behalf of an associated company, it is only special procedure material if it would have been special procedure material had the associated company created it.

(6) A company is to be treated as another's associated company for the purposes of this section if it would be so treated under section 302 of the Income and Corporation Taxes Act 1970.

15 Search warrants – safeguards

(1) This section and section 16 below have effect in relation to the issue to constables under any enactment, including an enactment contained in an Act passed after this Act, of warrants to enter and search premises; and an entry on or search of premises under a warrant is unlawful unless it complies with this section and section 16 below.

(2) Where a constable applies for any such warrant, it shall be his duty –

(a) to state –
(i) the ground on which he makes the application; and
(ii) the enactment under which the warrant would be issued;
(b) to specify the premises which it is desired to enter and search; and
(c) to identify, so far as is practicable, the articles or persons to be sought.

(3) An application for such a warrant shall be made ex parte and supported by an information in writing.

(4) The constable shall answer on oath any question that the justice of the peace or judge hearing the application asks him.

(5) A warrant shall authorise an entry on one occasion only.

(6) A warrant –

(a) shall specify –
(i) the name of the person who applies for it;
(ii) the date on which it is issued;
(iii) the enactment under which it is issued; and
(iv) the premises to be searched; and
(b) shall identify, so far as is practicable, the articles or persons to be sought.

(7) Two copies shall be made of a warrant.

(8) The copies shall be clearly certified as copies.

16 Execution of warrants

(1) A warrant to enter and search premises may be executed by any constable.

(2) Such a warrant may authorise persons to accompany any constable who is executing it.

(3) Entry and search under a warrant must be within one month from the date of its issue.

(4) Entry and search under a warrant must be at a reasonable hour unless it appears to the constable executing it that the purpose of a search may be frustrated on an entry at a reasonable hour.

(5) Where the occupier of premises which are to be entered and searched is present at the time when a constable seeks to execute a warrant to enter and search them, the constable –

(a) shall identify himself to the occupier and, if not in uniform, shall produce to him documentary evidence that he is a constable;
(b) shall produce the warrant to him; and
(c) shall supply him with a copy of it.

(6) Where –

(a) the occupier of such premises is not present at the time when a constable seeks to execute such a warrant; but
(b) some other person who appears to the constable to be in charge of the premises is present,

subsection (5) above shall have effect as if any reference to the occupier were a reference to that other person.

(7) If there is no person present who appears to the constable to be in charge of the premises, he shall leave a copy of the warrant in a prominent place on the premises.

(8) A search under a warrant may only be a search to the extent required for the purpose for which the warrant was issued.

(9) A constable executing a warrant shall make an endorsement on it stating –

(a) whether the articles or persons sought were found; and
(b) whether any articles were seized, other than articles which were sought.

(10) A warrant which –

(a) has been executed; or
(b) has not been executed within the time authorised for its execution,

shall be returned –

(i) if it was issued by a justice of the peace, to the clerk to the justices for the petty sessions area for which he acts; and
(ii) if it was issued by a judge, to the appropriate officer of the court from which he issued it.

(11) A warrant which is returned under subsection (10) above shall be retained for 12 months from its return –

(a) by the clerk to the justices, if it was returned under paragraph (i) of that subsection; and
(b) by the appropriate officer, if it was returned under paragraph (ii).

(12) If during the period for which a warrant is to be retained the occupier of the premises to which it relates asks to inspect it, he shall be allowed to do so.

17 Entry for purpose of arrest etc
(1) Subject to the following provisions of this section, and without prejudice to any other enactment, a constable may enter and search any premises for the purpose –

(a) of executing –

(i) a warrant of arrest issued in connection with or arising out of criminal proceedings; or
(ii) a warrant of commitment issued under section 76 of the Magistrates' Courts Act 1980;

(b) of arresting a person for an arrestable offence;
(c) of arresting a person for an offence under –

(i) section 1 (prohibition of uniforms in connection with political objects), . . . of the Public Order Act 1936;
(ii) any enactment contained in sections 6 to 8 or 10 of the Criminal Law Act 1977 (offences relating to entering and remaining on property);
[(iii) section 4 of the Public Order Act 1986 (fear or provocation of violence);]

(d) of recapturing a person who is unlawfully at large and whom he is pursuing; or
(e) of saving life or limb or preventing serious damage to property.

(2) Except for the purpose specified in paragraph (e) of subsection (1) above, the

powers of entry and search conferred by this section –

    (a) are only exercisable if the constable has reasonable grounds for believing that the person whom he is seeking is on the premises; and

    (b) are limited, in relation to premises consisting of two or more separate dwellings, to powers to enter and search –

        (i) any parts of the premises which the occupiers of any dwelling comprised in the premises use in common with the occupiers of any other such dwelling; and

        (ii) any such dwelling in which the constable has reasonable grounds for believing that the person whom he is seeking may be.

(3) The powers of entry and search conferred by this section are only exercisable for the purposes specified in subsection (1)(c)(ii) above by a constable in uniform.

(4) The power of search conferred by this section is only a power to search to the extent that is reasonably required for the purpose for which the power of entry is exercised.

(5) Subject to subsection (6) below, all the rules of common law under which a constable has power to enter premises without a warrant are hereby abolished.

(6) Nothing in subsection (5) above affects any power of entry to deal with or prevent a breach of the peace.

NOTE

Sub-s (1): in para (c), in sub-para (i) words omitted repealed by the Public Order Act 1986, s 40(2), (3), Sch 2, para 7, Sch 3, and sub-para (iii) added by the Public Order 1986, s 40(2), Sch 2, para 7.

18 Entry and search after arrest

(1) Subject to the following provisions of this section, a constable may enter and search any premises occupied or controlled by a person who is under arrest for an arrestable offence, if he has reasonable grounds for suspecting that there is on the premises evidence, other than items subject to legal privilege, that relates –

    (a) to that offence; or

    (b) to some other arrestable offence which is connected with or similar to that offence.

(2) A constable may seize and retain anything for which he may search under subsection (1) above.

(3) The power to search conferred by subsection (1) above is only a power to search to the extent that is reasonably required for the purpose of discovering such evidence.

(4) Subject to subsection (5) below, the powers conferred by this section may not be exercised unless an officer of the rank of inspector or above has authorised them in writing.

(5) A constable may conduct a search under subsection (1) above –

    (a) before taking the person to a police station; and

    (b) without obtaining an authorisation under subsection (4) above,

if the presence of that person at a place other than a police station is necessary for the effective investigation of the offence.

(6) If a constable conducts a search by virtue of subsection (5) above, he shall inform an officer of the rank of inspector or above that he has made the search as soon as practicable after he has made it.

(7) An officer who –

    (a) authorises a search; or

    (b) is informed of a search under subsection (6) above, shall make a record in writing –

(i)   of the grounds for the search; and

(ii) of the nature of the evidence that was sought.

(8) If the person who was in occupation or control of the premises at the time of the search is in police detention at the time the record is to be made, the officer shall make the record as part of his custody record.

Seizure etc

19 General power of seizure etc

(1) The powers conferred by subsections (2), (3) and (4) below are exercisable by a constable who is lawfully on any premises.

(2) The constable may seize anything which is on the premises if he has reasonable grounds for believing –

(a) that it has been obtained in consequence of the commission of an offence; and

(b) that it is necessary to seize it in order to prevent it being concealed, lost, damaged, altered or destroyed.

(3) The constable may seize anything which is on the premises if he has reasonable grounds for believing –

(a) that it is evidence in relation to an offence which he is investigating or any other offence; and

(b) that it is necessary to seize it in order to prevent the evidence being concealed, lost, altered or destroyed.

(4) The constable may require any information which is contained in a computer and is accessible from the premises to be produced in a form in which it can be taken away and in which it is visible and legible if he has reasonable grounds for believing –

(a) that –

(i)   it is evidence in relation to an offence which he is investigating or any other offence; or

(ii) it has been obtained in consequence of the commission of an offence; and

(b) that it is necessary to do so in order to prevent it being concealed, lost, tampered with or destroyed.

(5) The powers conferred by this section are in addition to any power otherwise conferred.

(6) No power of seizure conferred on a constable under any enactment (including an enactment contained in an Act passed after this Act) is to be taken to authorise the seizure of an item which the constable exercising the power has reasonable grounds for believing to be subject to legal privilege.

20 Extension of powers of seizure to computerised information

(1) Every power of seizure which is conferred by an enactment to which this section applies on a constable who has entered premises in the exercise of a power conferred by an enactment shall be construed as including a power to require any information contained in a computer and accessible from the premises to be produced in a form in which it can be taken away and in which it is visible and legible.

(2) This section applies –

(a) to any enactment contained in an Act passed before this Act;

(b) to sections 8 and 18 above;

(c) to paragraph 13 of Schedule 1 to this Act; and

(d) to any enactment contained in an Act passed after this Act.

21 Access and copying

(1) A constable who seizes anything in the exercise of a power conferred by any enactment, including an enactment contained in an Act passed after this Act, shall, if so requested by a person showing himself –

(a) to be the occupier of premises on which it was seized; or
(b) to have had custody or control of it immediately before the seizure,

provide that person with a record of what he seized.

(2) The officer shall provide the record within a reasonable time from the making of the request for it,

(3) Subject to subsection (8) below, if a request for permission to be granted access to anything which –

(a) has been seized by a constable; and
(b) is retained by the police for the purpose of investigating an offence,

is made to the officer in charge of the investigation by a person who had custody or control of the thing immediately before it was so seized or by someone acting on behalf of such a person, the officer shall allow the person who made the request access to it under the supervision of a constable.

(4) Subject to subsection (8) below, if a request for a photograph or copy of any such thing is made to the officer in charge of the investigation by a person who had custody or control of the thing immediately before it was so seized, or by someone acting on behalf of such a person, the officer shall –

(a) allow the person who made the request access to it under the supervision of a constable for the purpose of photographing or copying it; or
(b) photograph or copy it, or cause it to be photographed or copied.

(5) A constable may also photograph or copy, or have photographed or copied, anything which he has power to seize, without a request being made under subsection (4) above.

(6) Where anything is photographed or copied under subsection (4)(b) above, the photograph or copy shall be supplied to the person who made the request.

(7) The photograph or copy shall be so supplied within a reasonable time from the making of the request.

(8) There is no duty under this section to grant access to, or to supply a photograph or copy of, anything if the officer in charge of the investigation for the purposes of which it was seized has reasonable grounds for believing that to do so would prejudice –

(a) that investigation;
(b) the investigation of an offence other than the offence for the purposes of investigating which the thing was seized; or
(c) any criminal proceedings which may be brought as a result of –

(i) the investigation of which he is in charge; or
(ii) any such investigation as is mentioned in paragraph (b) above.

22 Retention

(1) Subject to subsection (4) below, anything which has been seized by a constable or taken away by a constable following a requirement made by virtue of section 19 or 20 above may be retained so long as is necessary in all the circumstances.

(2) Without prejudice to the generality of subsection (1) above –

(a) anything seized for the purposes of a criminal investigation may be retained, except as provided by subsection (4) below, –

(i) for use as evidence at a trial for an offence; or

    (ii) for forensic examination or for investigation in connection with an offence; and

(b) anything may be retained in order to establish its lawful owner, where there are reasonable grounds for believing that it has been obtained in consequence of the commission of an offence.

(3) Nothing seized on the ground that it may be used –

(a) to cause physical injury to any person;
(b) to damage property;
(c) to interfere with evidence; or
(d) to assist in escape from police detention or lawful custody,

may be retained when the person from whom it was seized is no longer in police detention or the custody of a court or is in the custody of a court but has been released on bail.

(4) Nothing may be retained for either of the purposes mentioned in subsection (2)(a) above if a photograph or copy would be sufficient for that purpose.

(5) Nothing in this section affects any power of a court to make an order under section 1 of the Police (Property) Act 1897.

Supplementary

23 Meaning of "premises" etc
In this Act –

    "premises" includes any place and, in particular, includes –

        (a) any vehicle, vessel, aircraft or hovercraft;
        (b) any offshore installation; and
        (c) any tent or movable structure; and

    "offshore installation" has the meaning given to it by section 1 of the Mineral Workings (Offshore Installations) Act 1971.

PART VII
DOCUMENTARY EVIDENCE IN CRIMINAL PROCEEDINGS

69 Evidence from computer records
(1) In any proceedings, a statement in a document produced by a computer shall not be admissible as evidence of any fact stated therein unless it is shown –

(a) that there are no reasonable grounds for believing that the statement is inaccurate because of improper use of the computer;
(b) that at all material times the computer was operating properly, or if not, that any respect in which it was not operating properly or was out of operation was not such as to affect the production of the document or the accuracy of its contents; and
(c) that any relevant conditions specified in rules of court under subsection (2) below are satisfied.

(2) Provision may be made by rules of court requiring that in any proceedings where it is desired to give a statement in evidence by virtue of this section such information concerning the statement as may be required by the rules shall be provided in such form and at such time as may be so required.

SCHEDULE 1
SPECIAL PROCEDURE

Section 9

NOTE
Modified as noted to Pt II (ss 8–23, Sch 1) ante.

Making of orders by circuit judge

1 If on an application made by a constable a circuit judge is satisfied that one or other of the sets of access conditions is fulfilled, he may make an order under paragraph 4 below.

2 The first set of access conditions is fulfilled if –

(a)   there are reasonable grounds for believing –

    (i)   that a serious arrestable offence has been committed;

    (ii) that there is material which consists of special procedure material or also includes special procedure material and does not also include excluded material on premises specified in the application;

    (iii) that the material is likely to be of substantial value (whether by itself or together with other material) to the investigation in connection with which the application is made; and

    (iv) that the material is likely to be relevant evidence;

(b)   other methods of obtaining the material –

    (i)   have been tried without success; or

    (ii) have not been tried because it appeared that they were bound to fail; and

(c)   it is in the public interest, having regard –

    (i)   to the benefit likely to accrue to the investigation if the material is obtained; and

    (ii) to the circumstances under which the person in possession of the material holds it,

that the material should be produced or that access to it should be given.

3 The second set of access conditions is fulfilled if –

(a)   there are reasonable grounds for believing that there is material which consists of or includes excluded material or special procedure material on premises specified in the application;

(b)   but for section 9(2) above a search of the premises for that material could have been authorised by the issue of a warrant to a constable under an enactment other than this Schedule; and

(c)   the issue of such a warrant would have been appropriate.

4 An order under this paragraph is an order that the person who appears to the circuit judge to be in possession of the material to which the application relates shall –

(a)   produce it to a constable for him to take away; or

(b)   give a constable access to it,

not later than the end of the period of seven days from the date of the order or the end of such longer period as the order may specify.

5 Where the material consists of information contained in a computer –

(a)   an order under paragraph 4(a) above shall have effect as an order to produce the material in a form in which it can be taken away and in which it is visible and legible; and

(b)   an order under paragraph 4(b) above shall have effect as an order to give a constable access to the material in a form in which it is visible and legible.

6 For the purposes of sections 21 and 22 above material produced in pursuance of an order under paragraph 4(a) above shall be treated as if it were material seized by a constable.

Notices of applications for orders

7 An application for an order under paragraph 4 above shall be made inter partes.

8 Notice of an application for such an order may be served on a person either by delivering it to him or by leaving it at his proper address or by sending it by post to him in a registered letter or by the recorded delivery service.

9 Such a notice may be served –

(a)   on a body corporate, by serving it on the body's secretary or clerk or other similar officer; and

(b)   on a partnership, by serving it on one of the partners.

10 For the purposes of this Schedule, and of section 7 of the Interpretation Act 1978 in its application to this Schedule, the proper address of a person, in the case of secretary or clerk or

other similar officer of a body corporate, shall be that of the registered or principal office of that body, in the case of a partner of a firm shall be that of the principal office of the firm, and in any other case shall be the last known address of the person to be served.

11 Where notice of an application for an order under paragraph 4 above has been served on a person, he shall not conceal, destroy, alter or dispose of the material to which the application relates except –

(a) with the leave of a judge; or
(b) with the written permission of a constable,

until –

(i)   the application is dismissed or abandoned; or
(ii) he has complied with an order under paragraph 4 above made on the application.

Issue of warrants by circuit judge

12 If on an application made by a constable a circuit judge –

(a) is satisfied –

(i)   that either set of access conditions is fulfilled; and
(ii) that any of the further conditions set out in paragraph 14 below is also fulfilled; or

(b) is satisfied –

(i)   that the second set of access conditions is fulfilled; and
(ii) that an order under paragraph 4 above relating to the material has not been complied with,

he may issue a warrant authorising a constable to enter and search the premises.

13 A constable may seize and retain anything for which a search has been authorised under paragraph 12 above.

14 The further conditions mentioned in paragraph 12(a)(ii) above are –

(a) that it is not practicable to communicate with any person entitled to grant entry to the premises to which the application relates;
(b) that it is practicable to communicate with a person entitled to grant entry to the premises but it is not practicable to communicate with any person entitled to grant access to the material;
(c) that the material contains information which –

(i)   is subject to a restriction or obligation such as is mentioned in section 11(2)(b) above; and
(ii) is likely to be disclosed in breach of it if a warrant is not issued;

(d) that service of notice of an application for an order under paragraph 4 above may seriously prejudice the investigation.

15 (1) If a person fails to comply with an order under paragraph 4 above, a circuit judge may deal with him as if he had committed a contempt of the Crown Court.

(2) Any enactment relating to contempt of the Crown Court shall have effect in relation to such a failure as if it were such a contempt.

Costs

16 The costs of any application under this Schedule and of anything done or to be done in pursuance of an order made under it shall be in the discretion of the judge.

SCHEDULE 3
PROVISIONS SUPPLEMENTARY TO SECTIONS 68 AND 69

Section 70

PART II
PROVISIONS SUPPLEMENTARY TO SECTION 69

8 In any proceedings where it is desired to give a statement in evidence in accordance with section 69 above, a certificate –

(a) identifying the document containing the statement and describing the manner in which it was produced;

(b) giving such particulars of any device involved in the production of that document as may be appropriate for the purpose of showing that the document was produced by a computer;

(c) dealing with any of the matters mentioned in subsection (1) of section 69 above; and

(d) purporting to be signed by a person occupying a responsible position in relation to the operation of the computer,

shall be evidence of anything stated in it; and for the purposes of this paragraph it shall be sufficient for a matter to be stated to the best of the knowledge and belief of the person stating it.

9 Notwithstanding paragraph 8 above, a court may require oral evidence to be given of anything of which evidence could be given by a certificate under that paragraph.

10 Any person who in a certificate tendered under paragraph 8 above in a magistrates' court, the Crown Court or the Court of Appeal makes a statement which he knows to be false or does not believe to be true shall be guilty of an offence and liable –

(a) on conviction on indictment to imprisonment for a term not exceeding two years or to a fine or to both;

(b) on summary conviction to imprisonment for a term not exceeding six months or to a fine not exceeding the statutory maximum (as defined in section 74 of the Criminal Justice Act 1982) or to both.

11 In estimating the weight, if any, to be attached to a statement regard shall be had to all the circumstances from which any inference can reasonably be drawn as to the accuracy or otherwise of the statement and, in particular –

(a) to the question whether or not the information which the information contained in the statement reproduces or is derived from was supplied to the relevant computer, or recorded for the purpose of being supplied to it, contemporaneously with the occurrence or existence of the facts dealt with in that information; and

(b) to the question whether or not any person concerned with the supply of information to that computer, or with the operation of that computer or any equipment by means of which the document containing the statement was produced by it, had any incentive to conceal or misrepresent the facts.

12 For the purposes of paragraph 11 above information shall be taken to be supplied to a computer whether it is supplied directly or (with or without human intervention) by means of any appropriate equipment.

PART III
PROVISIONS SUPPLEMENTARY TO SECTIONS 68 AND 69

13 . . .

14 For the purpose of deciding whether or not a statement is so admissible the court may draw any reasonable inference –

(a) from the circumstances in which the statement was made or otherwise came into being; or

(b) from any other circumstances, including the form and contents of the document in which the statement is contained.

15 Provision may be made by rules of court for supplementing the provisions of section 68 or 69 above or this Schedule.

NOTE
Para 13: repealed by the Criminal Justice Act 1988, s 170(2), Sch 16.

SCHEDULE 5
SERIOUS ARRESTABLE OFFENCES

Section 116

PART I
OFFENCES MENTIONED IN SECTION 116(2)(A)

1 Treason.
2. Murder.
3. Manslaughter.

4. Rape.
5. Kidnapping.
6. Incest with a girl under the age of 13.
7. Buggery with –

    (a) a boy under the age of 16; or
    (b) a person who has not consented.

8. Indecent assault which constitutes an act of gross indecency.

PART II
OFFENCES MENTIONED IN SECTION 116(2)(b)

Explosive Substances Act 1883 (c 3)

1 Section 2 (causing explosion likely to endanger life or property).

Sexual Offences Act 1956 (c 69)

2 Section 5 (intercourse with a girl under the age of 13).

Firearms Act 1968 (c 27)

3 Section 16 (possession of firearms with intent to injure).

4 Section 17(1) (use of firearms and imitation firearms to resist arrest).

5 Section 18 (carrying firearms with criminal intent).

6 . . .

Taking of Hostages Act 1982 (c 28)

7 Section 1 (hostage-taking).

Aviation Security Act 1982 (c 36)

8 Section 1 (hi-jacking).

[Criminal Justice Act 1988 (c 33)

9 Section 134 (Torture).]

[The Road Traffic Act 1988 (c 52)

10 Section 1 (causing death by [dangerous] driving).]

[Section 3A (causing death by careless driving when under the influence of drink or drugs).]

[Aviation and Maritime Security Act 1990 (c 31)]

11 Section 1 (endangering safety at aerodromes).

12 Section 9 (hijacking of ships).

13 Section 10 (seizing or exercising control of fixed platforms).]

NOTES
Para 6: repealed by the Road Traffic (Consequential Provisions) Act 1988, s 3(1), Sch 1, Pt I.
Para 9: added by the Criminal Justice Act 1988, s 170(2), Sch 15, para 102.
Para 10: entry relating to s 1 of the 1988 Act added by the Road Traffic (Consequential Provisions) Act 1988, s 4, Sch 3, para 27, and amended by the Road Traffic Act 1991, s 48, Sch 4, para 39(a); entry relating to s 3A of the 1988 Act added by s 48 of, and Sch 4, para 39(b) to, the 1991 Act.
Paras 11–13: added by the Aviation and Maritime Security Act 1990, s 53(1), Sch 3, para 8.

Companies Act 1985

(1985 c 6)

NOTE
An Act to consolidate the greater part of the Companies Act

[11 March 1985]

PART IV
INVESTIGATION OF COMPANIES AND THEIR AFFAIRS; REQUISITION OF DOCUMENTS

Appointment and functions of inspectors

431 Investigation of a company on its own application or that of its members

(1) The Secretary of State may appoint one or more competent inspectors to investigate the affairs of a company and to report on them in such manner as he may direct.

(2) The appointment may be made

(a) in the case of a company having a share capital, on the application either of not less than 200 members or of members holding not less than one tenth of the shares issued,

(b) in the case of a company not having a share capital, on the application of not less than one fifth in number of the persons on the company's register of members, and

(c) in any case, on application of the company;

(3) The application shall be supported by such evidence as the Secretary of State may require for the purpose of showing that the applicant or applicants have good reason for requiring the investigation.

(4) The Secretary of State may, before appointing inspectors, require the applicant or applicants to give security, to an amount not exceeding 5,000, or such other sum as he may by order specify, for payment of the costs of the investigation.

An order under this subsection shall be made by statutory instrument subject to annulment in pursuance of a resolution of either House of Parliament.

432 Other company investigations

(1) The Secretary of State shall appoint one or more competent inspectors to investigate the affairs of a company and report on them in such manner as he directs, if the court by order declares that its affairs ought to be so investigated.

(2) The Secretary of State may make such an appointment if it appears to him that there are circumstances suggesting –

(a) that the company's affairs are being or have been conducted with intent to defraud its creditors or the creditors of any other person, or otherwise for a fraudulent or unlawful purpose, or in a manner which is unfairly prejudicial to some part of its members, or

(b) that any actual or proposed act or omission of the company (including an act or omission on its behalf) is or would be so prejudicial, or that the company was formed for any fraudulent or unlawful purpose, or

(c) that persons concerned with the company's formation or the management of its affairs have in connection therewith been guilty of fraud, misfeasance or other misconduct towards it or towards its members, or

(d) that the company's members have not been given all the information with respect to its affairs which they might reasonably expect.

[(2A) Inspectors may be appointed under subsection (2) on terms that any report they may make is not for publication; and in such a case, the provisions of section 437(3) (availability and publication of inspectors reports) do not apply.]

(3) Subsections (1) and (2) are without prejudice to the powers of the Secretary of State under section 431; and the power conferred by subsection (2) is exercisable with respect to a body corporate notwithstanding that it is in course of being voluntarily wound up.

(4) The reference in subsection (2)(a) to a companys members includes any person who is not a member but to whom shares in the company have been transferred or transmitted by operation of law.

NOTE
Sub-s (2A): inserted by the Companies Act 1989, s 55.

433 Inspectors' powers during investigation

(1) If inspectors appointed under section 431 or 432 to investigate the affairs of a company think it necessary for the purposes of their investigation to investigate also the affairs of another body corporate which is or at any relevant time has been the companys subsidiary or holding company, or a subsidiary of its holding company or a holding company of its subsidiary, they have power to do so; and they shall report on the affairs of the other body corporate so far as they think that the results of their investigation of its affairs are relevant to the investigation of the affairs of the company first mentioned above.

(2) . . .

NOTE
Sub-s (2): repealed by the Financial Services Act 1986, ss 182, 212(3), Sch 13, para 7, Sch 17, Part I.

434 Production of documents and evidence to inspectors

(1) When inspectors are appointed under section 431 or 432, it is the duty of all officers and agents of the company, and of all officers and agents of any other body corporate whose affairs are investigated under section 433(1)

  (a) to produce to the inspectors all [documents] of or relating to the company or, as the case may be, the other body corporate which are in their custody or power,
  (b) to attend before the inspectors when required to do so, and
  (c) otherwise to give the inspectors all assistance in connection with the investigation which they are reasonably able to give.

[(2) If the inspectors consider that an officer or agent of the company or other body corporate, or any other person, is or may be in possession of information relating to a matter which they believe to be relevant to the investigation, they may require him –

  (a) to produce to them any documents in his custody or power relating to that matter,
  (b) to attend before them, and
  (c) otherwise to give them all assistance in connection with the investigation which he is reasonably able to give;

and it is that persons duty to comply with the requirement.

(3) An inspector may for the purposes of the investigation examine any person on oath, and may administer an oath accordingly.]

(4) In this section a reference to officers or to agents includes past, as well as present, officers or agents (as the case may be); and "agents", in relation to a company or other body corporate, includes its bankers and solicitors and persons employed by it as auditors, whether these persons are or are not officers of the company or other body corporate.

(5) An answer given by a person to a question put to him in exercise of powers conferred by this section (whether as it has effect in relation to an investigation under any of sections 431 to 433, or as applied by any other section in this Part) may be used in evidence against him.

[(6) In this section "documents" includes information recorded in any form; and, in relation to information recorded otherwise than in legible form, the power to require its production includes power to require the production of a copy of the information in legible form.]

NOTES
Sub-s (1): word in square brackets substituted by the Companies Act 1989, s 56(2).
Sub-ss (2), (3): substituted by the Companies Act 1989, s 56(3), (4).
Sub-s (6): added by the Companies Act 1989, s 56(5).

436 Obstruction of inspectors treated as contempt of court
[(1) If any person

(a) fails to comply with section 434(1)(a) or (c),
(b) refuses to comply with a requirement under section 434(1)(b) or (2), or
(c) refuses to answer any question put to him by the inspectors for the purposes of the investigation,

the inspectors may certify that fact in writing to the court.]

(3) The court may thereupon enquire into the case; and, after hearing any witnesses who may be produced against or on behalf of the alleged offender and after hearing any statement which may be offered in defence, the court may punish the offender in like manner as if he had been guilty of contempt of the court.

NOTE
Sub-s (1): substituted for original sub-ss (1), (2) by the Companies Act 1989, s 56(6).

437 Inspectors' reports
(1) The inspectors may, and if so directed by the Secretary of State shall, make interim reports to the Secretary of State, and on the conclusion of their investigation shall make a final report to him.
Any such report shall be written or printed, as the Secretary of State directs.

[(1A) Any persons who have been appointed under section 431 or 432 may at any time and, if the Secretary of State directs them to do so, shall inform him of any matters coming to their knowledge as a result of their investigations.]

[(1B) If it appears to the Secretary of State that matters have come to light in the course of the inspectors' investigation which suggest that a criminal offence has been committed, and those matters have been referred to the appropriate prosecuting authority, he may direct the inspectors to take no further steps in the investigation or to take only such further steps as are specified in the direction.

(1C) Where an investigation is the subject of a direction under subsection (1B), the inspectors shall make a final report to the Secretary of State only where –

(a) they were appointed under section 432(1) (appointment in pursuance of an order of the court), or
(b) the Secretary of State directs them to do so.]

(2) If the inspectors were appointed under section 432 in pursuance of an order of the court, the Secretary of State shall furnish a copy of any report of theirs to the court.

(3) In any case the Secretary of State may, if he thinks fit –

(a) forward a copy of any report made by the inspectors to the company's registered office,
(b) furnish a copy on request and on payment of the prescribed fee to –

   (i) any member of the company or other body corporate which is the subject of the report,
   (ii) any person whose conduct is referred to in the report,
   (iii) the auditors of that company or body corporate,
   (iv) the applicants for the investigation,
   (v) any other person whose financial interests appear to the Secretary of State to be affected by the matters dealt with in the report, whether as a creditor of the company or body corporate, or otherwise, and

(c) cause any such report to be printed and published.

NOTES
Sub-s (1A): inserted by the Financial Services Act 1986, s 182, Sch 13, para 7.
Sub-ss (1B), (1C): inserted by the Companies Act 1989, s 57.

438 Power to bring civil proceedings on company's behalf

(1) [If from any report made or information obtained under this Part it appears to the Secretary of State] that any civil proceedings ought in the public interest to be brought by any body corporate, he may himself bring such proceedings in the name and on behalf of the body corporate.

(2) The Secretary of State shall indemnify the body corporate against any costs or expenses incurred by it in or in connection with proceedings brought under this section.

NOTE
Sub-s (1): words in square brackets substituted by the Companies Act 1989, s 58.

439 Expenses of investigating a company's affairs

[(1) The expenses of an investigation under any of the powers conferred by this Part shall be defrayed in the first instance by the Secretary of State, but he may recover those expenses from the persons liable in accordance with this section.

There shall be treated as expenses of the investigation, in particular, such reasonable sums as the Secretary of State may determine in respect of general staff costs and overheads.]

(2) A person who is convicted on a prosecution instituted as a result of the investigation, or is ordered to pay the whole or any part of the costs of proceedings brought under section 438, may in the same proceedings be ordered to pay those expenses to such extent as may be specified in the order.

(3) A body corporate in whose name proceedings are brought under that section is liable to the amount or value of any sums or property recovered by it as a result of those proceedings; and any amount for which a body corporate is liable under this subsection is a first charge on the sums or property recovered.

(4) A body corporate dealt with by [an inspectors' report], where the inspectors were appointed otherwise than of the Secretary of States own motion, is liable except where it was the applicant for the investigation, and except so far as the Secretary of State otherwise directs.

[(5) Where inspectors were appointed –

(a) under section 431, or
(b) on an application under section 442(3),

the applicant or applicants for the investigation is or are liable to such extent (if any) as the Secretary of State may direct.]

(6) The report of inspectors appointed otherwise than of the Secretary of State's own motion may, if they think fit, and shall if the Secretary of State so directs, include a recommendation as to the directions (if any) which they think appropriate, in the light of their investigation, to be given under subsection (4) or (5) of this section.

(7) For purposes of this section, any costs or expenses incurred by the Secretary of State in or in connection with proceedings brought under section 438 (including expenses incurred under subsection (2) of it) are to be treated as expenses of the investigation giving rise to the proceedings.

(8) Any liability to repay the Secretary of State imposed by subsections (2) and (3) above is (subject to satisfaction of his right to repayment) a liability also to indemnify all persons against liability under subsections (4) and (5); and any such liability imposed by subsection (2) is (subject as mentioned above) a liability also to indemnify all persons against liability under subsection (3).

(9) A person liable under any one of those subsections is entitled to contribution from any other person liable under the same subsection, according to the amount of their respective liabilities under it.

(10) Expenses to be defrayed by the Secretary of State under this section shall, so far as not recovered under it, be paid out of money provided by Parliament.

NOTES
Sub-ss (1), (5): substituted by the Companies Act 1989, ss 59(2), (4).
Sub-s (4): words in square brackets substituted by the Companies Act 1989, s 59(3).

441 Inspectors' report to be evidence
(1) A copy of any report of inspectors appointed under [this Part], certified by the Secretary of State to be a true copy, is admissible in any legal proceedings as evidence of the opinion of the inspectors in relation to any matter contained in the report [and, in proceedings on an application under [section 8 of the Company Directors Disqualification Act 1986], as evidence of any fact stated therein].

(2) A document purporting to be such a certificate as is mentioned above shall be received in evidence and be deemed to be such a certificate, unless the contrary is proved.

NOTE
Sub-s (1): first words in square brackets substituted by the Companies Act 1989, s 61; second amendment in square brackets made by the Insolvency Act 1985, s 109, Sch 6, para 3, words in square brackets therein substituted by the Insolvency Act 1986, s 439(1), Sch 13, Part I.

Other powers of investigation available to the Secretary of State

442 Power to investigate company ownership
(1) Where it appears to the Secretary of State that there is good reason to do so, he may appoint one or more competent inspectors to investigate and report on the membership of any company, and otherwise with respect to the company, for the purpose of determining the true persons who are or have been financially interested in the success or failure (real or apparent) of the company or able to control or materially to influence its policy.

(2) The appointment of inspectors under this section may define the scope of their investigation (whether as respects the matter or the period to which it is to extend or otherwise) and in particular may limit the investigation to matters connected with particular shares or debentures.

[(3) If an application for investigation under this section with respect to particular shares or debentures of a company is made to the Secretary of State by members of the company, and the number of applicants or the amount of shares held by them is not less than that required for an application for the appointment of inspectors under section 431(2)(a) or (b), then, subject to the following provisions, the Secretary of State shall appoint inspectors to conduct the investigation applied for.

(3A) The Secretary of State shall not appoint inspectors if he is satisfied that the application is vexatious; and where inspectors are appointed their terms of appointment shall exclude any matter in so far as the Secretary of State is satisfied that it is unreasonable for it to be investigated.

(3B) The Secretary of State may, before appointing inspectors, require the applicant or applicants to give security, to an amount not exceeding 5,000, or such other sum as he may by order specify, for payment of the costs of the investigation.

An order under this subsection shall be made by statutory instrument which shall be subject to annulment in pursuance of a resolution of either House of Parliament.

(3C) If on an application under subsection (3) it appears to the Secretary of State that the powers conferred by section 444 are sufficient for the purposes of investigating the matters which inspectors would be appointed to investigate, he may instead conduct the investigation under that section.]

(4) Subject to the terms of their appointment, the inspectors powers extend to the

investigation of any circumstances suggesting the existence of an arrangement or understanding which, though not legally binding, is or was observed or likely to be observed in practice and which is relevant to the purposes of the investigation.

NOTES
Sub-ss (3), (3A)–(3C): substituted for original sub-s (3) by the Companies Act 1989, s 62.

443 Provisions applicable on investigation under s 442
(1) For purposes of an investigation under section 442, sections 433(1), 434, 436 and 437 apply with the necessary modifications of references to the affairs of the company or to those of any other body corporate, subject however to the following subsections.

(2) Those sections apply to –

(a) all persons who are or have been, or whom the inspector has reasonable cause to believe to be or have been, financially interested in the success or failure or the apparent success or failure of the company or any other body corporate whose membership is investigated with that of the company, or able to control or materially influence its policy (including persons concerned only on behalf of others), and
(b) any other person whom the inspector has reasonable cause to believe possesses information relevant to the investigation,

as they apply in relation to officers and agents of the company or the other body corporate (as the case may be).

(3) If the Secretary of State is of opinion that there is good reason for not divulging any part of a report made by virtue of section 442 and this section, he may under section 437 disclose the report with the omission of that part; and he may cause to be kept by the registrar of companies a copy of the report with that part omitted or, in the case of any other such report, a copy of the whole report.

(4) . . .

NOTE
Sub-s (4): repealed by the Companies Act 1989, s 212, Sch 24.

444 Power to obtain information as to those interested in shares, etc
(1) If it appears to the Secretary of State that there is good reason to investigate the ownership of any shares in or debentures of a company and that it is unnecessary to appoint inspectors for the purpose, he may require any person whom he has reasonable cause to believe to have or to be able to obtain any information as to the present and past interests in those shares or debentures and the names and addresses of the persons interested and of any persons who act or have acted on their behalf in relation to the shares or debentures to give any such information to the Secretary of State.

(2) For this purpose a person is deemed to have an interest in shares or debentures if he has any right to acquire or dispose of them or of any interest in them, or to vote in respect of them, or if his consent is necessary for the exercise of any of the rights of other persons interested in them, or if other persons interested in them can be required, or are accustomed, to exercise their rights in accordance with his instructions.

(3) A person who fails to give information required of him under this section, or who in giving such information makes any statement which he knows to be false in a material particular, or recklessly makes any statement which is false in a material particular, is liable to imprisonment or a fine, or both.

445 Power to impose restrictions on shares and debentures
(1) If in connection with an investigation under either section 442 or 444 it appears to the Secretary of State that there is difficulty in finding out the relevant facts about any shares (whether issued or to be issued), he may by order direct that the shares shall until further order be subject to the restrictions of Part XV of this Act.

[(1A) If the Secretary of State is satisfied that an order under subsection (1) may unfairly affect the rights of third parties in respect of shares then the Secretary of State, for the purpose of protecting such rights and subject to such terms as he thinks fit, may direct that such acts by such persons or descriptions of persons and for such purposes as may be set out in the order, shall not constitute a breach of the restrictions of Part XV of this Act.]

(2) This section, and Part XV in its application to orders under it, apply in relation to debentures as in relation to shares [save that subsection (1A) shall not so apply.].

NOTES
Sub-s (1A): added by SI 1991 No 1646, reg 5(a).
Sub-s (2): words in square brackets added by SI 1991 No 1646, reg 5(b).

446 Investigation of share dealings
(1) If it appears to the Secretary of State that there are circumstances suggesting that contraventions may have occurred, in relation to a company's shares or debentures, of section 323 or 324 (taken with Schedule 13), or of subsections (3) to (5) of section 328 (restrictions on share dealings by directors and their families; obligation of director to disclose shareholding in his own company), he may appoint one or more competent inspectors to carry out such investigations as are requisite to establish whether or not such contraventions have occurred and to report the result of their investigations to him.

(2) The appointment of inspectors under this section may limit the period to which their investigation is to extend or confine it to shares or debentures of a particular class, or both.

(3) For purposes of an investigation under this section, sections 434 [to 437] apply –

(a) with the substitution, for references to any other body corporate whose affairs are investigated under section 433(1), of a reference to any other body corporate which is, or has at any relevant time been, the company's subsidiary or holding company, or a subsidiary of its holding company, . . .

(b) . . .

(4) Sections 434 to 436 apply under the preceding subsection –

[(a) to any individual who is an authorised person within the meaning of the Financial Services Act 1986;
(b) to any individual who holds a permission granted under paragraph 23 of Schedule 1 to that Act;
(c) to any officer (whether past or present) of a body corporate which is such an authorised person or holds such a permission;
(d) to any partner (whether past or present) in a partnership which is such an authorised person or holds such a permission;
(e) to any member of the governing body or officer (in either case whether past or present) of an unincorporated association which is such an authorised person or holds such a permission],

as they apply to officers of the company or of the other body corporate.

(5)–(7) . . .

NOTES
Sub-s (3): amendment in square brackets made by the Financial Services Act 1986, s 182, Sch 13, para 8; words omitted repealed by the Companies Act 1989, s 212, Sch 24.
Sub-s (4): paras (a)–(e) substituted for original paras (a)–(c) by the Financial Services Act 1986, s 212(2), Sch 16, para 21.
Sub-s (5): repealed by the Financial Services Act 1986, ss 182, 212(3), Sch 13, para 8, Sch 17, Part I.
Sub-s (6): repealed by the Financial Services Act 1986, s 212(3), Sch 17, Part I.
Sub-s (7): repealed by the Companies Act 1989, s 212, Sch 24.

Requisition and seizure of books and papers

447 Secretary of State's power to require production of documents

(1) . . .

(2) The Secretary of State may at any time, if he thinks there is good reason to do so, give directions to [a company] requiring it, at such time and place as may be specified in the directions, to produce such [documents] as may be so specified.

(3) The Secretary of State may at any time, if he thinks there is good reason to do so, authorise an officer of his [or any other competent person], on producing (if so required) evidence of his authority, to require [a company] to produce to him (the officer [or other person]) forthwith any [documents] which [he (the officer or other person)] may specify.

(4) Where by virtue of subsection (2) or (3) the Secretary of State or an officer of his [or other person] has power to require the production of [documents] from [a company], he or the officer [or other person] has the like power to require production of those [documents] from any person who appears to him or the officer to be in possession of them; but where any such person claims a lien on [documents] produced by him, the production is without prejudice to the lien.

(5) The power under this section to require [a company] or other person to produce [documents] includes power

(a) if the [documents] are produced

(i) to take copies of them or extracts from them, and

(ii) to require that person, or any other person who is a present or past officer of, or is or was at any time employed by, [the company] in question, to provide an explanation of any of them;

(b) if the [documents] are not produced, to require the person who was required to produce them to state, to the best of his knowledge and belief, where they are.

(6) If the requirement to produce [documents] or provide an explanation or make a statement is not complied with, [the company] or other person on whom the requirement was so imposed is guilty of an offence and liable to a fine.

[Sections 732 (restriction on prosecutions), 733 (liability of individuals for corporate default) and 734 (criminal proceedings against unincorporated bodies) apply to this offence.]

(7) However, where a person is charged with an offence under subsection (6) in respect of a requirement to produce any [documents], it is a defence to prove that they were not in his possession or under his control and that it was not reasonably practicable for him to comply with the requirement.

(8) A statement made by a person in compliance with such a requirement may be used in evidence against him.

[(9) In this section "documents" includes information recorded in any form; and, in relation to information recorded otherwise than in legible form, the power to require its production includes power to require the production of a copy of it in legible form.]

NOTES

Sub-s (1): repealed by the Companies Act 1989, ss 63, 212, Sch 24.

Sub-ss (2)–(7): words in square brackets substituted or inserted by the Companies Act 1989, s 63.

Sub-s (9): added by the Companies Act 1989, s 63(7).

[448 Entry and search of premises

[(1) A justice of the peace may issue a warrant under this section if satisfied on information on oath given by or on behalf of the Secretary of State, or by a person appointed or authorised to exercise powers under this Part, that there are reasonable grounds for believing that there are on any premises documents whose production has been required under this Part and which have not been produced in compliance with the requirement.

(2) A justice of the peace may also issue a warrant under this section if satisfied on information on oath given by or on behalf of the Secretary of State, or by a person appointed or authorised to exercise powers under this Part –

(a) that there are reasonable grounds for believing that an offence has been committed for which the penalty on conviction on indictment is imprisonment for a term of not less than two years and that there are on any premises documents relating to whether the offence has been committed,

(b) that the Secretary of State, or the person so appointed or authorised, has power to require the production of the documents under this Part, and

(c) that there are reasonable grounds for believing that if production was so required the documents would not be produced but would be removed from the premises, hidden, tampered with or destroyed.

(3) A warrant under this section shall authorise a constable, together with any other person named in it and any other constables –

(a) to enter the premises specified in the information, using such force as is reasonably necessary for the purpose;

(b) to search the premises and take possession of any documents appearing to be such documents as are mentioned in subsection (1) or (2), as the case may be, or to take, in relation to any such documents, any other steps which may appear to be necessary for preserving them or preventing interference with them;

(c) to take copies of any such documents; and

(d) to require any person named in the warrant to provide an explanation of them or to state where they may be found.

(4) If in the case of a warrant under subsection (2) the justice of the peace is satisfied on information on oath that there are reasonable grounds for believing that there are also on the premises other documents relevant to the investigation, the warrant shall also authorise the actions mentioned in subsection (3) to be taken in relation to such documents.

(5) A warrant under this section shall continue in force until the end of the period of one month beginning with the day on which it is issued.

(6) Any documents of which possession is taken under this section may be retained –

(a) for a period of three months; or

(b) if within that period proceedings to which the documents are relevant are commenced against any person for any criminal offence, until the conclusion of those proceedings.

(7) Any person who intentionally obstructs the exercise of any rights conferred by a warrant issued under this section or fails without reasonable excuse to comply with any requirement imposed in accordance with subsection (3)(d) is guilty of an offence and liable to a fine.

Sections 732 (restrictions on prosecutions), 733 (liability of individuals for corporate default) and 734 (criminal proceedings against unincorporated bodies) apply to this offence.

(8) For the purposes of sections 449 and 451A (provision for security of information) documents obtained under this section shall be treated as if they had been obtained under the provision of this Part under which their production was or, as the case may be, could have been required.

(9) In the application of this section to Scotland for the references to a justice of the peace substitute references to a justice of the peace or a sheriff, and for the references to information on oath substitute references to evidence on oath.

(10) In this section "document" includes information recorded in any form.]

NOTE
Substituted by the Companies Act 1989, 64(1).

449 Provision for security of information obtained

(1) No information or document relating to a [company] which has been obtained under section 447 . . . shall, without the previous consent in writing of that [company], be published or disclosed, except to a competent authority, unless the publication or disclosure is required –

[(a) with a view to the institution of or otherwise for the purposes of criminal proceedings;]

[(ba) with a view to the institution of, or otherwise for the purposes of, any proceedings on an application under [section 6, 7 or 8 of the Company Directors Disqualification Act 1986];]

[(c) for the purposes of enabling or assisting any inspector appointed under this Part, or under section 94 or 177 of the Financial Services Act 1986, to discharge his functions;]

[(cc) for the purpose of enabling or assisting any person authorised to exercise powers under section 44 of the Insurance Companies Act 1982, section 447 of this Act, section 106 of the Financial Services Act 1986 or section 84 of the Companies Act 1989 to discharge his functions;]

[(d) for the purpose of enabling or assisting the Secretary of State or the Treasury to exercise any of their functions, under this Act, the Insider Dealing Act, *the Prevention of Fraud (Investments) Act 1958*, the Insurance Companies Act 1982, the Insolvency Act 1986, the Company Directors Disqualification Act 1986 [, the Financial Services Act 1986 or Part II, III or VII of the Companies Act 1989,]

(dd) for the purpose of enabling or assisting the Department of Economic Development for Northern Ireland to exercise any powers conferred on it by the enactments relating to companies or insolvency or for the purpose of enabling or assisting any inspector appointed by it under the enactments relating to companies to discharge his functions]

(e) . . .

[(f) for the purpose of enabling or assisting the Bank of England to discharge its functions under [the Banking Act 1987] or any other functions,

(g) for the purpose of enabling or assisting the Deposit Protection Board to discharge its functions under that Act,

(h) for any purpose mentioned in section 180(1)(b), (e), (h), [or (n)] of the Financial Services Act 1986,

[(hh) for the purpose of enabling or assisting a body established by order under section 46 of the Companies Act 1989 to discharge its functions under Part II of that Act, or of enabling or assisting a recognised supervisory or qualifying body within the meaning of that Part to discharge its functions as such;]

(i) for the purpose of enabling or assisting the Industrial Assurance Commissioner or the Industrial Assurance Commissioner for Northern Ireland to discharge his functions under the enactments relating to industrial assurance,

(j) for the purpose of enabling or assisting the Insurance Brokers Registration Council to discharge its functions under the Insurance Brokers (Registration) Act 1977,

(k) for the purpose of enabling or assisting an official receiver to discharge his functions under the enactments relating to insolvency or for the purpose of enabling or assisting a body which is for the time being a recognised professional body for the purposes of section 391 of the Insolvency Act 1986 to discharge its functions as such,

(l) with a view to the institution of, or otherwise for the purposes of, any disciplinary proceedings relating to the exercise by a solicitor, auditor, accountant, valuer or actuary of his professional duties,

[(ll) with a view to the institution of, or otherwise for the purposes of, any disciplinary proceedings relating to the discharge by a public servant of his duties;]

[(m) for the purpose of enabling or assisting an overseas regulatory authority to exercise its regulatory functions]].

[(1A) In subsection (1) –

(a) in paragraph (ll) "public servant" means an officer or servant of the Crown or of any public or other authority for the time being designated for the purposes of that paragraph by the Secretary of State by order made by statutory instrument; and

(b) in paragraph (m) "overseas regulatory authority" and "regulatory functions" have the same meaning as in section 82 of the Companies Act 1989.]

(1B) Subject to subsection (1C), subsection (1) shall not preclude publication or disclosure for the purpose of enabling or assisting any public or other authority for the time being [designated for the purposes of this subsection] by the Secretary of State by an order in a statutory instrument to discharge any functions which are specified in the order.

(1C) An order under subsection (1B) designating an authority for the purpose of that subsection may –

(a) impose conditions subject to which the publication or disclosure of any information or document is permitted by that subsection; and

(b) otherwise restrict the circumstances in which that subsection permits publication or disclosure.

(1D) Subsection (1) shall not preclude the publication or disclosure of any such information as is mentioned in section 180(5) of the Financial Services Act 1986 by any person who by virtue of that section is not precluded by section 179 of that Act from disclosing it.]

(2) A person who publishes or discloses any information or document in contravention of this section is guilty of an offence and liable to imprisonment or a fine, or both.

[Sections 732 (restriction on prosecutions), 733 (liability of individuals for corporate default) and 734 (criminal proceedings against unincorporated bodies) apply to this offence.]

[(3) For the purposes of this section each of the following is a competent authority –

(a) the Secretary of State,

(b) an inspector appointed under this Part or under section 94 or 177 of the Financial Services Act 1986,

(c) any person authorised to exercise powers under section 44 of the Insurance Companies Act 1982, section 447 of this Act, section 106 of the Financial Services Act 1986 or section 84 of the Companies Act 1989,

(d) the Department of Economic Development in Northern Ireland,

(e) the Treasury,

(f) the Bank of England,

(g) the Lord Advocate,

(h) the Director of Public Prosecutions, and the Director of Public Prosecutions for Northern Ireland,

(i) any designated agency or transferee body within the meaning of the Financial Services Act 1986, and any body administering a scheme under section 54 of or paragraph 18 of Schedule 11 to that Act (schemes for compensation of investors),

(j) the Chief Registrar of friendly societies *and the Registrar of Friendly Societies for Northern Ireland,*

(k) the Industrial Assurance Commissioner *and the Industrial Assurance Commission for Northern Ireland,*

(l) any constable,

(m) any procurator fiscal.

(3A) Any information which may by virtue of this section be disclosed to a competent authority may be disclosed to any officer or servant of the authority.]

(4) A statutory instrument containing an order under [subsection (1A)(a) or (1B)] is subject to annulment in pursuance of a resolution of either House of Parliament.]

NOTES

Sub-s (1): within the opening words, words in square brackets substituted, and words omitted repealed, by the Companies Act 1989, ss 65(1), (2), 212, Sch 24; para (a) substituted for original paras (a), (b) by the Financial Services Act 1986, s 182, Sch 13, para 9; para (ba) inserted by the Insolvency Act 1985, s 109, Sch 6, para 4, words in square brackets therein substituted by the Insolvency Act 1986, s 439(1), Sch 13, Part I; para (c) substituted, paras (cc) inserted, and para (e) repealed by the Companies Act 1989, ss 65(1), (2), 212, Sch 24; paras (d), (dd) substituted for original para (d) by the Financial Services Act 1986, s 182, Sch 13, para 9, in para (d) words in square brackets in the first place substituted by SI 1992 No 1315, art 10(1), Sch 4, para 1 and in the second place substituted by the Companies Act 1989, s 65(1), (2), in para (d) words printed in italics repealed by the Financial Services Act 1986, s 212(3), Sch 17, Pt I only insofar as is necessary to have the effect that the words cease to apply to a prospectus offering for subscription, or to any form of application for, units in a body corporate which is a recognised scheme; paras (de), (df) prospectively inserted by the Friendly Societies Act 1992, s 120(1), Sch 21, Pt I, para 7 as follows –

"(de)for the purpose of enabling or assisting the Chief Registrar of friendly societies or the Assistant Registrar of friendly societies for Scotland to discharge his functions under the enactments relating to friendly societies;

(df) for the purpose of enabling or assisting the Friendly Societies Commission to discharge its functions under the Financial Services Act 1986.";

paras (f)–(m) added by the Financial Services 1986, s 182, Sch 13, para 9; in para (f) words in square brackets substituted by the Banking Act 108(1), Sch 6, para 18; words in square brackets in para (h) substituted, para (ll) inserted, and para (m) substituted, by the Companies Act 1989, s 65(1), (2); para (hh) inserted for certain purposes, and prospectively added for remaining purposes as from a day to be appointed, by the Companies Act 1989, s 65(1), (2), for purposes see SI 1990 No 142, art 4 and SI 1991 No 878, Schedule.

Sub-s (1A): inserted by the Financial Services Act 1986, s 182, Sch 13, para 9; substituted by the Companies Act 1989, s 65(1), (3).

Sub-s (1B): inserted by the Financial Services Act 1986, s 182, Sch 13, para 9; words in square brackets substituted by the Companies Act 1989, s 65(1), (4).

Sub-ss (1C), (1D): inserted by the Financial Services Act 1986, s 182, Sch 13, para 9.

Sub-s (2): words in square brackets substituted by the Companies Act 1989, s 65(1), (5).

Sub-s (3): originally substituted with sub-s (4) for sub-s (3) as originally enacted by the Financial Services Act 1986, s 182, Sch 13, para 9; further substituted, together with sub-s (3A), by the Companies Act 1989, s 65(1), (6); words in italics in paras (j), (k) prospectively repealed, and para (jj) prospectively inserted, by the Friendly Societies Act 1992, ss 120(1), (2), Sch 21, Pt I, para 7, Sch 22, Pt I, as follows –

"(jj) the Friendly Societies Commission".

Sub-s (3A): substituted with sub-s (3) for sub-s (3) as previously in force by the Companies Act 1989, s 65(1), (6).

Sub-s (4): substituted with sub-s (3) for sub-s (3) as originally enacted by the Financial Services Act 1986, s 182, Sch 13, para 9; words in square brackets substituted by the Companies Act 1989, s 65(1), (7).

Modified by the Financial Services Act 1986 (Delegation) Order 1987, SI 1987 No 942, art 11 and the Companies Act 1989, s 88.

450 Punishment for destroying, mutilating etc company documents

(1) [An officer of a company, or of an insurance company] to which Part II of the Insurance Companies Act 1982 applies, who –

(a) destroys, mutilates or falsifies, or is privy to the destruction, mutilation or falsification of a document affecting or relating to the [company's] property or affairs, or

(b) makes, or is privy to the making of, a false entry in such a document,

is guilty of an offence, unless he proves that he had no intention to conceal the state of affairs of [the company] or to defeat the law.

(2) Such a person as above mentioned who fraudulently either parts with, alters or makes an omission in any such document or is privy to fraudulent parting with, fraudulent altering or fraudulent making of an omission in, any such document, is guilty of an offence.

(3) A person guilty of an offence under this section is liable to imprisonment or a fine, or both.

[(4) Sections 732 (restriction on prosecutions), 733 (liability of individuals for corporate default) and 734 (criminal proceedings against unincorporated bodies) apply to an offence under this section.]

[(5) In this section "document" includes information recorded in any form.]

NOTES
Sub-s (1): words in square brackets substituted by the Companies Act 1989, s 66(2).
Sub-s (4): substituted by the Companies Act 1989, s 66(3).
Sub-s (5): added by the Companies Act 1989, s 66(4).

451 Punishment for furnishing false information
A person who, in purported compliance with a requirement imposed under section 447 to provide an explanation or make a statement, provides or makes an explanation or statement which he knows to be false in a material particular or recklessly provides or makes an explanation or statement which is so false, is guilty of an offence and liable to imprisonment or a fine, or both.

[Sections 732 (restriction on prosecutions), 733 (liability of individuals for corporate default) and 734 (criminal proceedings against unincorporated bodies) apply to this offence.]

NOTE
Words in square brackets substituted by the Companies Act 1989, s 67.

[451A Disclosure of information by Secretary of State or inspector]
(1) This section applies to information obtained under sections 434 to 446.

(2) The Secretary of State may, if he thinks fit –

(a) disclose any information to which this section applies to any person to whom, or for any purpose for which, disclosure is permitted under section 449, or
(b) authorise or require an inspector appointed under this Part to disclose such information to any such person or for any such purpose.

(3) Information to which this section applies may also be disclosed by an inspector appointed under this Part to –

(a) another inspector appointed under this Part or an inspector appointed under section 94 or 1977 of the Financial Services Act 1986, or
(b) a person authorised to exercise powers under section 44 of the Insurance Companies Act 1982, section 447 of this Act, section 106 of the Financial Services Act 1986 or section 84 of the Companies Act 1989.

(4) Any information which may by virtue of subsection (3) be disclosed to any person may be disclosed to any officer or servant of that person.

(5) The Secretary of State may, if he thinks fit, disclose any information obtained under section 444 to –

(a) the company whose ownership was the subject of the investigation,
(b) any member of the company,
(c) any person whose conduct was investigated in the course of the investigation,
(d) the auditors of the company, or
(e) any person whose financial interests appear to the Secretary of State to be affected by matters covered by the investigation.]

NOTES
Inserted by the Financial Services Act 1986, s 182, Sch 13, para 10.
Substituted by the Companies Act 1989, s 68.

Supplementary

452 Privileged information

(1) Nothing in sections 431 to 446 requires the disclosure to the Secretary of State or to an inspector appointed by him –

(a) by any person of information which he would in an action in the High Court or the Court of Session be entitled to refuse to disclose on grounds of legal professional privilege except, if he is a lawyer, the name and address of his client,

(b) . . .

[(1A) Nothing in section 434, 443 or 446 requires a person (except as mentioned in subsection (1B) below) to disclose information or produce documents in respect of which he owes an obligation of confidence by virtue of carrying on the business of banking unless –

(a) the person to whom the obligation of confidence is owed is the company or other body corporate under investigation,

(b) the person to whom the obligation of confidence is owed consents to the disclosure or production, or

(c) the making of the requirement is authorised by the Secretary of State.

(1B) Subsection (1A) does not apply where the person owing the obligation of confidence is the company or other body corporate under investigation under section 431, 432 or 433.]

(2) Nothing in sections 447 to 451 compels the production by any person of a document which he would in an action in the High Court or the Court of Session be entitled to refuse to produce on grounds of legal professional privilege, or authorises the taking of possession of any such document which is in the persons possession.

(3) The Secretary of State shall not under section 447 require, or authorise an officer of his [or other person] to require, the production by a person carrying on the business of banking of a document relating to the affairs of a customer of his unless either it appears to the Secretary of State that it is necessary to do so for the purpose of investigating the affairs of the first-mentioned person, or the customer is a person on whom a requirement has been imposed under that section, or under section 44(2) to (4) of the Insurance Companies Act 1982 (provision corresponding to section 447).

NOTES
Sub-s (1): para (b) repealed by the Companies Act 1989, ss 69(2), 212, Sch 24.
Sub-ss (1A), (1B): inserted by the Companies Act 1989, s 69(3).
Sub-s (3): words in square brackets added by the Companies Act 1989, s 69(4).

453 Investigation of oversea companies

[(1) The provisions of this Part apply to bodies corporate incorporated outside Great Britain which are carrying on business in Great Britain, or have at any time carried on business there, as they apply to companies under this Act; but subject to the following exceptions, adaptations and modifications.

(1A) The following provisions do not apply to such bodies –

(a) section 431 (investigation on application of company or its members),

(b) section 438 (power to bring civil proceedings on the companys behalf),

(c) sections 442 to 445 (investigation of company ownership and power to obtain information as to those interested in shares, &c.), and

(d) section 446 (investigation of share dealings).

(1B) The other provisions of this Part apply to such bodies subject to such adaptations and modifications as may be specified by regulations made by the Secretary of State.]

(2) Regulations under this section shall be made by statutory instrument subject to annulment in pursuance of a resolution of either House of Parliament.

NOTE
Sub-ss (1), (1A), (1B): substituted for sub-s (1) as originally enacted, by the Companies Act 1989, s 70.

PART XVI
FRAUDULENT TRADING BY A COMPANY

458 Punishment for fraudulent trading
If any business of a company is carried on with intent to defraud creditors of the company or creditors of any other person, or for any fraudulent purpose, every person who was knowingly a party to the carrying on of the business in that manner is liable to imprisonment or a fine, or both.

This applies whether or not the company has been, or is in the course of being, wound up.

PART XXV
MISCELLANEOUS AND SUPPLEMENTARY PROVISIONS

721 Production and inspection of books where offence suspected
(1) The following applies if on an application made –

(a) in England and Wales, to a judge of the High Court by the Director of Public Prosecutions, the Secretary of State or a chief officer of police, or
(b) in Scotland, to one of the Lords Commissioners of Justiciary by the Lord Advocate,

there is shown to be reasonable cause to believe that any person has, while an officer of a company, committed an offence in connection with the management of the company's affairs and that evidence of the commission of the offence is to be found in any books or papers of or under the control of the company.

(2) An order may be made

(a) authorising any person named in it to inspect the books or papers in question, or any of them, for the purpose of investigating and obtaining evidence of the offence, or
(b) requiring the secretary of the company or such other officer of it as may be named in the order to produce the books or papers (or any of them) to a person named in the order at a place so named.

(3) The above applies also in relation to any books or papers of a person carrying on the business of banking so far as they relate to the company's affairs, as it applies to any books or papers of or under the control of the company, except that no such order as is referred to in subsection (2)(b) shall be made by virtue of this subsection.

(4) The decision of a judge of the High Court or of any of the Lords Commissioners of Justiciary on an application under this section is not appealable.

Company Directors Disqualification Act 1986

(1986 c 46)

An Act to consolidate certain enactments relating to the disqualification of persons from being directors of companies, and from being otherwise concerned with a company's affairs

[25 July 1986]

Preliminary

1 Disqualification orders: general
(1) In the circumstances specified below in this Act a court may, and under section 6 shall, make against a person a disqualification order, that is to say an order that he shall not, without leave of the court –

(a) be a director of a company, or

(b) be a liquidator or administrator of a company, or

(c) be a receiver or manager of a company's property, or

(d) in any way, whether directly or indirectly, be concerned or take part in the promotion, formation or management of a company,

for a specified period beginning with the date of the order.

(2) In each section of this Act which gives to a court power or, as the case may be, imposes on it the duty to make a disqualification order there is specified the maximum (and, in section 6, the minimum) period of disqualification which may or (as the case may be) must be imposed by means of the order.

(3) Where a disqualification order is made against a person who is already subject to such an order, the periods specified in those orders shall run concurrently.

(4) A disqualification order may be made on grounds which are or include matters other than criminal convictions, notwithstanding that the person in respect of whom it is to be made may be criminally liable in respect of those matters.

Disqualification for general misconduct in connection with companies

2 Disqualification on conviction of indictable offence

(1) The court may make a disqualification order against a person where he is convicted of an indictable offence (whether on indictment or summarily) in connection with the promotion, formation, management or liquidation of a company, or with the receivership or management of a company's property.

(2) "The court" for this purpose means –

(a) any court having jurisdiction to wind up the company in relation to which the offence was committed, or

(b) the court by or before which the person is convicted of the offence, or

(c) in the case of a summary conviction in England and Wales, any other magistrates' court acting for the same petty sessions area;

and for the purposes of this section the definition of "indictable offence" in Schedule 1 to the Interpretation Act 1978 applies for Scotland as it does for England and Wales.

(3) The maximum period of disqualification under this section is –

(a) where the disqualification order is made by a court of summary jurisdiction, 5 years, and

(b) in any other case, 15 years.

3 Disqualification for persistent breaches of companies legislation

(1) The court may make a disqualification order against a person where it appears to it that he has been persistently in default in relation to provisions of the companies legislation requiring any return, account or other document to be filed with, delivered or sent, or notice of any matter to be given, to the registrar of companies.

(2) On an application to the court for an order to be made under this section, the fact that a person has been persistently in default in relation to such provisions as are mentioned above may (without prejudice to its proof in any other manner) be conclusively proved by showing that in the 5 years ending with the date of the application he has been adjudged guilty (whether or not on the same occasion) of three or more defaults in relation to those provisions.

(3) A person is to be treated under subsection (2) as being adjudged guilty of a default in relation to any provision of that legislation if –

(a) he is convicted (whether on indictment or summarily) of an offence consisting in a contravention of or failure to comply with that provision (whether on his own part or on the part of any company), or

(b) a default order is made against him, that is to say an order under any of the following provisions –

    (i) [section 242(4)] of the Companies Act (order requiring delivery of company accounts),

    [(ia) section 245B of that Act (order requiring preparation of revised accounts),]

    (ii) section 713 of that Act (enforcement of company's duty to make returns),

    (iii) section 41 of the Insolvency Act (enforcement of receiver's or manager's duty to make returns), or

    (iv) section 170 of that Act (corresponding provision for liquidator in winding up),

in respect of any such contravention of or failure to comply with that provision (whether on his own part or on the part of any company).

(4) In this section "the court" means any court having jurisdiction to wind up any of the companies in relation to which the offence or other default has been or is alleged to have been committed.

(5) The maximum period of disqualification under this section is 5 years.

NOTE
Sub-s (3); words in square brackets in para (b)(i) substituted by the Companies Act 1989, s 23, Sch 10, para 35(1), (2)(a); para (ia) inserted by s 23 of, Sch 10, para 35(1), (2)(b) to, the 1989 Act.

4 Disqualification for fraud, etc, in winding up
(1) The court may make a disqualification order against a person if, in the course of the winding up of a company, it appears that he –

(a) has been guilty of an offence for which he is liable (whether he has been convicted or not) under section 458 of the Companies Act (fraudulent trading), or

(b) has otherwise been guilty, while an officer or liquidator of the company or receiver or manager of its property, of any fraud in relation to the company or of any breach of his duty as such officer, liquidator, receiver or manager.

(2) In this section "the court" means any court having jurisdiction to wind up any of the companies in relation to which the offence or other default has been or is alleged to have been committed; and "officer" includes a shadow director.

(3) The maximum period of disqualification under this section is 15 years.

5 Disqualification on summary conviction
(1) An offence counting for the purposes of this section is one of which a person is convicted (either on indictment or summarily) in consequence of a contravention of, or failure to comply with, any provision of the companies legislation requiring a return, account or other document to be filed with, delivered or sent, or notice of any matter to be given, to the registrar of companies (whether the contravention or failure is on the person's own part or on the part of any company).

(2) Where a person is convicted of a summary offence counting for those purposes, the court by which he is convicted (or, in England and Wales, any other magistrates' court acting for the same petty sessions area) may make a disqualification order against him if the circumstances specified in the next subsection are present.

(3) Those circumstances are that, during the 5 years ending with the date of the conviction, the person has had made against him, or has been convicted of, in total not less than 3 default orders and offences counting for the purposes of this section; and those offences may include that of which he is convicted as mentioned in subsection (2) and any other offence of which he is convicted on the same occasion.

(4) For the purposes of this section –

(a) the definition of "summary offence" in Schedule 1 to the Interpretation Act 1978 applies for Scotland as for England and Wales, and

(b) "default order" means the same as in section 3(3)(b).

(5) The maximum period of disqualification under this section is 5 years.

Consequences of contravention

13 Criminal penalties

(1) If a person acts in contravention of a disqualification order or of section 12(2), or is guilty of an offence under section 11, he is liable –

(a) on conviction on indictment, to imprisonment for not more than 2 years or a fine, or both; and

(b) on summary conviction, to imprisonment for not more than 6 months or a fine not exceeding the statutory maximum, or both.

15 Personal liability for company's debts where person acts while disqualified

(1) A person is personally responsible for all the relevant debts of a company if at any time –

(a) in contravention of a disqualification order or of section 11 of this Act he is involved in the management of the company, or

(b) as a person who is involved in the management of the company, he acts or is willing to act on instructions given without the leave of the court by a person whom he knows at that time to be the subject of a disqualification order or to be an undischarged bankrupt.

(2) Where a person is personally responsible under this section for the relevant debts of a company, he is jointly and severally liable in respect of those debts with the company and any other person who, whether under this section or otherwise, is so liable.

(3) For the purposes of this section the relevant debts of a company are –

(a) in relation to a person who is personally responsible under paragraph (a) of subsection (1), such debts and other liabilities of the company as are incurred at a time when that person was involved in the management of the company, and

(b) in relation to a person who is personally responsible under paragraph (b) of that subsection, such debts and other liabilities of the company as are incurred at a time when that person was acting or was willing to act on instructions given as mentioned in that paragraph.

(4) For the purposes of this section, a person is involved in the management of a company if he is a director of the company or if he is concerned, whether directly or indirectly, or takes part, in the management of the company.

(5) For the purposes of this section a person who, as a person involved in the management of a company, has at any time acted on instructions given without the leave of the court by a person whom he knew at that time to be the subject of a disqualification order or to be an undischarged bankrupt is presumed, unless the contrary is shown, to have been willing at any time thereafter to act on any instructions given by that person.

Financial Services Act 1986

(1986 c 60)

An Act to regulate the carrying on of investment business; to make related provision with respect to insurance business and business carried on by friendly societies; to make new provision with respect to the official listing of securities, offers of unlisted securities, takeover offers and insider dealing; to make provision as to the disclosure of information obtained under enactments relating to fair trading, banking companies and insurance; to make provision for securing reciprocity with other countries in respect of facilities for the provision of financial services; and for connected purposes.

[7 November 1986]

CHAPTER V
CONDUCT OF INVESTMENT BUSINESS

47 Misleading statements and practices

(1) Any person who –

(a) makes a statement, promise or forecast which he knows to be misleading, false or deceptive or dishonestly conceals any material facts; or
(b) recklessly makes (dishonestly or otherwise) a statement, promise or forecast which is misleading, false or deceptive,

is guilty of an offence if he makes the statement, promise or forecast or conceals the facts for the purpose of inducing, or is reckless as to whether it may induce, another person (whether or not the person to whom the statement, promise or forecast is made or from whom the facts are concealed) to enter or offer to enter into, or to refrain from entering or offering to enter into, an investment agreement or to exercise, or refrain from exercising, any rights conferred by an investment.

(2) Any person who does any act or engages in any c. rse of conduct which creates a false or misleading impression as to the market in or the price or value of any investments is guilty of an offence if he does so for the purpose of creating that impression and of thereby inducing another person to acquire, dispose of, subscribe for or underwrite those investments or to refrain from doing so or to exercise, or refrain from exercising, any rights conferred by those investments.

(3) In proceedings brought against any person for an offence under subsection (2) above it shall be a defence for him to prove that he reasonably believed that his act or conduct would not create an impression that was false or misleading as to the matters mentioned in that subsection.

(4) Subsection (1) above does not apply unless –

(a) the statement, promise or forecast is made in or from, or the facts are concealed in or from, the United Kingdom;
(b) the person on whom the inducement is intended to or may have effect is in the United Kingdom; or
(c) the agreement is or would be entered into or the rights are or would be exercised in the United Kingdom.

(5) Subsection (2) above does not apply unless –

(a) the act is done or the course of conduct is engaged in in the United Kingdom; or
(b) the false or misleading impression is created there.

(6) A person guilty of an offence under this section shall be liable –

(a) on conviction on indictment, to imprisonment for a term not exceeding seven years or to a fine or to both;
(b) on summary conviction, to imprisonment for a term not exceeding six months or to a fine not exceeding the statutory maximum or to both.

Supplemental

94 Investigations

(1) The Secretary of State may appoint one or more competent inspectors to investigate and report on –

(a) the affairs of, or of the manager or trustee of, any authorised unit trust scheme;
(b) the affairs of, or of the operator or trustee of, any recognised scheme so far as relating to activities carried on in the United Kingdom; or
(c) the affairs of, or of the operator or trustee of, any other collective investment scheme,

if it appears to the Secretary of State that it is in the interests of the participants to do so or that the matter is of public concern.

(2) An inspector appointed under subsection (1) above to investigate the affairs of, or of the manager, trustee or operator of, any scheme may also, if he thinks it necessary for the purposes of that investigation, investigate the affairs of, or of the manager, trustee or operator of, any other such scheme as is mentioned in that subsection whose manager, trustee or operator is the same person as the manager, trustee or operator of the first mentioned scheme.

(3) Sections 434 to 436 of the Companies Act 1985 (production of documents and evidence to inspectors), . . . ; shall apply in relation to an inspector appointed under this section as they apply to an inspector appointed under section 431 of that Act but with the modifications specified in subsection (4) below.

(4) In the provisions applied by subsection (3) above for any reference to a company . . . ; there shall be substituted a reference to the scheme under investigation by virtue of this section . . . ; and any reference to an officer . . . ; of the company shall include a reference to any director of the manager, trustee or operator of the scheme.

(5) A person shall not under this section be required to disclose any information or produce any document which he would be entitled to refuse to disclose or produce on grounds of legal professional privilege in proceedings in the High Court or on grounds of confidentiality as between client and professional legal adviser in proceedings in the Court of Session except that a lawyer may be required to furnish the name and address of his client.

(6) Where a person claims a lien on a document its production under this section shall be without prejudice to the lien.

[(7) Nothing in this section requires a person (except as mentioned in subsection (7A) below) to disclose any information or produce any document in respect of which he owes an obligation of confidence by virtue of carrying on the business of banking unless –

(a) the person to whom the obligation of confidence is owed consents to the disclosure or production, or
(b) the making of the requirement was authorised by the Secretary of State.

(7A) Subsection (7) does not apply where the person owing the obligation of confidence or the person to whom it is owed is –

(a) the manager, operator or trustee of the scheme under investigation, or
(b) a manager, operator or trustee whose own affairs are under investigation.]

(8) An inspector appointed under this section may, and if so directed by the Secretary of State shall, make interim reports to the Secretary of State and on the conclusion of his investigation shall make a final report to him.

[(8A) If it appears to the Secretary of State that matters have come to light in the course of the inspectors' investigation which suggest that a criminal offence has been committed, and those matters have been referred to the appropriate prosecuting authority, he may direct the inspectors to take no further steps in the investigation or to take only such further steps as are specified in the direction.

(8B) Where an investigation is the subject of a direction under subsection (8A), the inspectors shall make a final report to the Secretary of State only where the Secretary of State directs them to do so.]

(9) Any such report shall be written or printed as the Secretary of State may direct and the Secretary of State may, if he thinks fit –

(a) furnish a copy, on request and on payment of the prescribed fee, to the manager, trustee or operator or any participant in a scheme under investigation or any other person whose conduct is referred to in the report; and
(b) cause the report to be published.

[(10) A person who is convicted on a prosecution instituted as a result of an investigation under this section may in the same proceedings be ordered to pay the expenses of the investigation to such extent as may be specified in the order.

There shall be treated as expenses of the investigation, in particular, such reasonable sums as the Secretary of State may determine in respect of general staff costs and overheads.]

NOTES
Sub-ss (3), (4): words omitted repealed by the Companies Act 1989, s 212, Sch 24.
Sub-ss (7), (7A): substituted for the original sub-s (7) by the Companies Act 1989, s 72.
Sub-ss (8A), (8B): inserted by s 72 of the 1989 Act.
Sub-s (10): added by s 72 of the 1989 Act.

104 Power to call for information
(1) The Secretary of State may by notice in writing require a person who is authorised to carry on investment business by virtue of section 22, 24, 25 or 31 above to furnish him with such information as he may reasonably require for the exercise of his functions under this Act.

(2) The Secretary of State may by notice in writing require a recognised self-regulating organisation, recognised professional body, recognised investment exchange or recognised clearing house to furnish him with such information as he may reasonably require for the exercise of his functions under this Act.

(3) The Secretary of State may require any information which he requires under this section to be furnished within such reasonable time and verified in such manner as he may specify.

(4) Sections 60, 61 and 62 above shall have effect in relation to a contravention of a requirement imposed under subsection (1) above as they have effect in relation to a contravention of the provisions to which those sections apply.

105 Investigation powers
(1) The powers of the Secretary of State under this section shall be exercisable in any case in which it appears to him that there is good reason to do so for the purpose of investigating the affairs, or any aspect of the affairs, of any person so far as relevant to any investment business which he is or was carrying on or appears to the Secretary of State to be or to have been carrying on.

(2) Those powers shall not be exercisable for the purpose of investigating the affairs of any exempted person unless he is an appointed representative or the investigation is in respect of investment business in respect of which he is not an exempted person and shall not be exercisable for the purpose of investigating the affairs of a member of a recognised self-regulating organisation or a person certified by a recognised professional body in respect of investment business in the carrying on of which he is subject to its rules unless –

(a) that organisation or body has requested the Secretary of State to investigate those affairs; or

(b) it appears to him that the organisation or body is unable or unwilling to investigate them in a satisfactory manner.

(3) The Secretary of State may require the person whose affairs are to be investigated ("the person under investigation") or any connected person to attend before the Secretary of State at a specified time and place and answer questions or otherwise furnish information with respect to any matter relevant to the investigation.

(4) The Secretary of State may require the person under investigation or any other person to produce at a specified time and place any specified documents which appear to the Secretary of State to relate to any matter relevant to the investigation; and –

(a) if any such documents are produced, the Secretary of State may take copies or extracts from them or require the person producing them or any connected person to provide an explanation of any of them;

(b) if any such documents are not produced, the Secretary of State may require the person who was required to produce them to state, to the best of his knowledge and belief, where they are.

(5) A statement by a person in compliance with a requirement imposed by virtue of this section may be used in evidence against him.

(6) A person shall not under this section be required to disclose any information or produce any document which he would be entitled to refuse to disclose or produce on grounds of legal professional privilege in proceedings in the High Court or on grounds of confidentiality as between client and professional legal adviser in proceedings in the Court of Session except that a lawyer may be required to furnish the name and address of his client.

(7) . . .

(8) Where a person claims a lien on a document its production under this section shall be without prejudice to the lien.

(9) In this section –

"connected person", in relation to any other person means –

(a) any person who is or was that other person's partner, employee, agent, appointed representative, banker, auditor or solicitor; and

(b) where the other person is a body corporate, any person who is or was a director, secretary or controller of that body corporate or of another body corporate of which it is or was a subsidiary; and

(c) where the other person is an unincorporated association, any person who is or was a member of the governing body or an officer or controller of the association; and

(d) where the other person is an appointed representative, any person who is or was his principal; and

(e) where the other person is the person under investigation (being a body corporate), any related company of that body corporate and any person who is a connected person in relation to that company;

"documents" includes information recorded in any form and, in relation to information recorded otherwise than in legible form, [the power to require its production includes power to require the production of] a copy of the information in legible form;

"related company", in relation to a person under investigation (being a body corporate), means any other body corporate which is or at any material time was –

(a) a holding company or subsidiary of the person under investigation;

(b) a subsidiary of a holding company of that person; or

(c) a holding company of a subsidiary of that person,

and whose affairs it is in the Secretary of State's opinion necessary to investigate for the purpose of investigating the affairs of that person.

(10) Any person who without reasonable excuse fails to comply with a requirement imposed on him under this section shall be guilty of an offence and liable on summary conviction to imprisonment for a term not exceeding six months or to a fine not exceeding the fifth level on the standard scale or to both.

[(11) A person who is convicted on a prosecution instituted as a result of an investigation under this section may in the same proceedings be ordered to pay the expenses of the investigation to such extent as may be specified in the order.

There shall be treated as expenses of the investigation, in particular, such reasonable sums as the Secretary of State may determine in respect of general staff costs and overheads.]

NOTES
Sub-s (7): repealed by the Companies Act 1989, s 212, Sch 24.
Sub-s (9): words in square brackets substituted by the Companies Act 1989, s 73.
Sub-s (11): added by s 73 of the 1989 Act.

106 Exercise of investigation powers by officer etc

(1) The Secretary of State may authorise any officer of his or any other competent person to exercise on his behalf all or any of the powers conferred by section 105 above but no such authority shall be granted except for the purpose of investigating the affairs, or any aspects of the affairs, of a person specified in the authority.

(2) No person shall be bound to comply with any requirement imposed by a person exercising powers by virtue of an authority granted under this section unless he has, if required to do so, produced evidence of his authority.

[(2A) A person shall not by virtue of an authority under this section be required to disclose any information or produce any documents in respect of which he owes an obligation of confidence by virtue of carrying on the business of banking unless –

(a) he is the person under investigation or a related company,
(b) the person to whom the obligation of confidence is owed is the person under investigation or a related company,
(c) the person to whom the obligation of confidence is owed consents to the disclosure or production, or
(d) the imposing on him of a requirement with respect to such information or documents has been specifically authorised by the Secretary of State.

In this subsection "documents", "person under investigation" and "related company" have the same meaning as in section 105.]

(3) Where the Secretary of State authorises a person other than one of his officers to exercise any powers by virtue of this section that person shall make a report to the Secretary of State in such manner as he may require on the exercise of those powers and the results of exercising them.

NOTE
Sub-s (2A): inserted by the Companies Act 1985, s 73(1), (5).

177 Investigations into insider dealing

(1) If it appears to the Secretary of State that there are circumstances suggesting that there may have been a contravention of section 1, 2, 4, or 5 of the Company Securities (Insider Dealing) Act 1985, he may appoint one or more competent inspectors to carry out such investigations as are requisite to establish whether or not any such contravention has occurred and to report the results of their investigations to him.

(2) The appointment under this section of an inspector may limit the period during which he is to continue his investigation or confine it to particular matters.

[(2A) At any time during the investigation the Secretary of State may vary the appointment by limiting or extending the period during which the inspector is to continue his investigation or by confining the investigation to particular matters.]

(3) If the inspectors consider that any person is or may be able to give information concerning any such contravention they may require that person –

(a) to produce to them any documents in his possession or under his control relating to the company in relation to whose securities the contravention is suspected to have occurred or to its securities;

(b) to attend before them; and
(c) otherwise to give them all assistance in connection with the investigation which he is reasonably able to give;

and it shall be the duty of that person to comply with that requirement.

(4) An inspector may examine on oath any person who he considers is or may be able to give information concerning any such contravention, and may administer an oath accordingly.

(5) The inspectors shall make such interim reports to the Secretary of State as they think fit or he may direct and on the conclusion of the investigation they shall make a final report to him.

[(5A) If the Secretary of State thinks fit, he may direct the inspector to take no further steps in the investigation or to take only such further steps as are specified in the direction; and where an investigation is the subject of such a direction, the inspectors shall make a final report to the Secretary of State only where the Secretary of State directs them to do so.]

(6) A statement made by a person in compliance with a requirement imposed by virtue of this section may be used in evidence against him.

(7) A person shall not under this section be required to disclose any information or produce any document which he would be entitled to refuse to disclose or produce on grounds of legal professional privilege in proceedings in the High Court or on grounds of confidentiality as between client and professional legal adviser in proceedings in the Court of Session.

[(8) A person shall not under this section be required to disclose any information or produce any document in respect of which he owes an obligation of confidence by virtue of carrying on the business of banking unless –

(a) the person to whom the obligation of confidence is owed consents to the disclosure or production, or
(b) the making of the requirement was authorised by the Secretary of State.]

(9) Where a person claims a lien on a document its production under this section shall be without prejudice to his lien.

(10) In this section "document" includes information recorded in any form; and in relation to information recorded otherwise than in legible form [the power to require its production includes power to require the production of] a copy of the information in legible form.

[(11) A person who is convicted on a prosecution instituted as a result of an investigation under this section may in the same proceedings be ordered to pay the expenses of the investigation to such extent as may be specified in the order.
There shall be treated as expenses of the investigation, in particular, such reasonable sums as the Secretary of State may determine in respect of general staff costs and overheads.]

NOTES
Sub-s (2A): inserted by the Companies Act 1989, s 74.
Sub-s (5A): inserted by the Companies Act 1989, s 74.
Sub-s (8): substituted by s 74 of the 1989 Act.
Sub-s (10): words in square brackets substituted by s 74 of the 1989 Act.
Sub-s (11): added by s 74 of the 1989 Act.

178 Penalties for failure to co-operate with s 177 investigations
(1) If any person –

(a) refuses to comply with any request under subsection (3) of section 177 above; or
(b) refuses to answer any question put to him by the inspectors appointed under that

section with respect to any matter relevant for establishing whether or not any suspected contravention has occurred.

the inspectors may certify that fact in writing to the court and the court may inquire into the case.

(2) If, after hearing any witness who may be produced against or on behalf of the alleged offender and any statement which may be offered in defence, the court is satisfied that he did without reasonable excuse refuse to comply with such a request or answer any such question, the court may –

(a) punish him in like manner as if he had been guilty of contempt of the court; or
(b) direct that the Secretary of State may exercise his powers under this section in respect of him;

and the court may give a direction under paragraph (b) above notwithstanding that the offender is not within the jurisdiction of the court if the court is satisfied that he was notified of his right to appear before the court and of the powers available under this section.

(3) Where the court gives a direction under subsection (2)(b) above in respect of an authorised person the Secretary of State may serve a notice on him –

(a) cancelling any authorisation of his to carry on investment business after the expiry of a specified period after the service of the notice;
(b) disqualifying him from becoming authorised to carry on investment business after the expiry of a specified period;
(c) restricting any authorisation of his in respect of investment business during a specified period to the performance of contracts entered into before the notice comes into force;
(d) prohibiting him from entering into transactions of a specified kind or entering into them except in specified circumstances or to a specified extent;
(e) prohibiting him from soliciting business from persons of a specified kind or otherwise than from such persons; or
(f) prohibiting him from carrying on business in a specified manner or otherwise than in a specified manner.

(4) The period mentioned in paragraphs (a) and (c) of subsection (3) above shall be such period as appears to the Secretary of State reasonable to enable the person on whom the notice is served to complete the performance of any contracts entered into before the notice comes into force and to terminate such of them as are of a continuing nature.

(5) Where the court gives a direction under subsection (2)(b) above in the case of an unauthorised person the Secretary of State may direct that any authorised person who knowingly transacts investment business of a specified kind, or in specified circumstances or to a specified extent, with or on behalf of that unauthorised person shall be treated as having contravened rules made under Chapter V of Part I of this Act or, in the case of a person who is an authorised person by virtue of his membership of a recognised self-regulating organisation or certification by a recognised professional body, the rules of that organisation or body.

(6) A person shall not be treated for the purposes of subsection (2) above as having a reasonable excuse for refusing to comply with a request or answer a question in a case where the contravention or suspected contravention being investigated relates to dealing by him on the instructions or for the account of another person, by reason that at the time of the refusal –

(a) he did not know the identity of that other person; or
(b) he was subject to the law of a country or territory outside the United Kingdom which prohibited him from disclosing information relating to the dealing without the consent of that other person, if he might have obtained that consent or obtained exemption from that law.

(7) A notice served on a person under subsection (3) above may be revoked at any time by the Secretary of State by serving a revocation notice on him; and the Secretary of State shall revoke such a notice if it appears to him that he has agreed to comply with the relevant request or answer the relevant question.

(8) The revocation of such a notice as is mentioned in subsection (3)(a) above shall not have the effect of reviving the authorisation cancelled by the notice except where the person would (apart from the notice) at the time of the revocation be an authorised person by virtue of his membership of a recognised self-regulating organisation or certification by a recognised professional body; but nothing in this subsection shall be construed as preventing any person who has been subject to such a notice from again becoming authorised after the revocation of the notice.

(9) If it appears to the Secretary of State –

(a) that a person on whom he serves a notice under subsection (3) above is an authorised person by virtue of an authorisation granted by a designated agency or by virtue of membership of a recognised self-regulating organisation or certification by a recognised professional body; or
(b) that a person on whom he serves a revocation notice under subsection (7) above was such an authorised person at the time that the notice which is being revoked was served,

he shall serve a copy of the notice on that agency, organisation or body.

(10) The functions to which section 114 above applies shall include the functions of the Secretary of State under this section but any transfer of those functions shall be subject to a reservation that they are to be exercisable by him concurrently with the designated agency and so as to be exercisable by the agency subject to such conditions or restrictions as the [Treasury] may from time to time impose.

NOTE
Sub-s (10): word in square brackets substituted by the Transfer of Functions (Financial Services) Order 1992, SI 1992 No 1315, art 10(1), Sch 4, para 3.

PART VIII
RESTRICTIONS ON DISCLOSURE OF INFORMATION

179 Restrictions on disclosure of information
(1) Subject to section 180 below, information which is restricted information for the purposes of this section and relates to the business or other affairs of any person shall not be disclosed by a person mentioned in subsection (3) below ("the primary recipient") or any person obtaining the information directly or indirectly from him without the consent of the person from whom the primary recipient obtained the information and if different, the person to whom it relates.

(2) Subject to subsection (4) below, information is restricted information for the purposes of this section if it was obtained by the primary recipient for the purposes of, or in the discharge of his functions under, this Act or any rules or regulations made under this Act (whether or not by virtue of any requirement to supply it made under those provisions).

(3) The persons mentioned in subsection (1) above are –

(a) the Secretary of State;
[(aa) the Treasury;]
(b) any designated agency, transferee body or body administering a scheme under section 54 above;
(c) the Director General of Fair Trading;
(d) the Chief Registrar of friendly societies;
(e) the Registrar of Friendly Societies for Northern Ireland;
(f) the Bank of England;

(g) any member of the Tribunal;

(h) any person appointed or authorised to exercise any powers under section 94, 106 or 177 above; . . . ;

(i) any officer or servant of any such person [as is mentioned in paragraphs (a) to (h) above];

[(j) any constable or other person named in a warrant issued under this Act].

(4) Information shall not be treated as restricted information for the purposes of this section if it has been made available to the public by virtue of being disclosed in any circumstances in which or for any purpose for which disclosure is not precluded by this section.

(5) Subject to section 180 below, information obtained by the competent authority in the exercise of its functions under Part IV of this Act or received by it pursuant to a Community obligation from any authority exercising corresponding functions in another member State shall not be disclosed without the consent of the person from whom the competent authority obtained the information and, if different, the person to whom it relates.

(6) Any person who contravenes this section shall be guilty of an offence and liable –

(a) on conviction on indictment, to imprisonment for a term not exceeding two years or to a fine or to both;

(b) on summary conviction, to imprisonment for a term not exceeding three months or to a fine not exceeding the statutory maximum or to both.

NOTES
Sub-s (3): para (aa) inserted by the Transfer of Functions (Financial Services) Order 1992, SI 1992 No 1315, art 10(1), Sch 4, para 4; para (e) prospectively substituted by the Friendly Societies Act 1992, s 98(a), Sch 18, Pt I, para 4, as follows –
"(e) the Friendly Societies Commission";
paras (h), (i) amended, and para (j) added, by the Companies Act 1989, s 75(1).

180 Exceptions from restrictions on disclosure
(1) Section 179 above shall not preclude the disclosure of information –

(a) with a view to the institution of or otherwise for the purposes of criminal proceedings;

(b) with a view to the institution of or otherwise for the purposes of any civil proceedings arising under or by virtue of this Act or proceedings before the Tribunal;

[(bb) for the purpose of enabling or assisting the Treasury to exercise any of their powers under this Act or under Part III or VII of the Companies Act 1989;]

(c) for the purpose of enabling or assisting the Secretary of State to exercise any powers conferred on him by this Act or by the enactments relating to companies, insurance companies or insolvency [or by Part II, III or VII of the Companies Act 1989] or for the purpose of enabling or assisting any inspector appointed by him under the enactments relating to companies to discharge his functions;

(d) for the purpose of enabling or assisting the Department of Economic Development for Northern Ireland to exercise any powers conferred on it by the enactments relating to companies or insolvency or for the purpose of enabling or assisting any inspector appointed by it under the enactments relating to companies to discharge his functions;

[(e) for the purpose –

(i) of enabling or assisting a designated agency to discharge its functions under this Act or Part VII of the Companies Act 1989,

(ii) of enabling or assisting a transferee body or the competent authority to discharge its functions under this Act, or

(iii) of enabling or assisting the body administering a scheme under section 54 above to discharge its functions under the scheme;]

(f) for the purpose of enabling or assisting the Bank of England to discharge its functions under [the Banking Act 1987] or any other functions;

(g) for the purpose of enabling or assisting the Deposit Protection Board to discharge its functions under that Act;

(h) for the purpose of enabling or assisting the Chief Registrar of friendly societies or the Registrar of Friendly Societies for Northern Ireland to discharge his functions under this Act or under the enactments relating to friendly societies or building societies;

[(hh) for the purpose of enabling or assisting a body established by order under section 46 of the Companies Act 1989 to discharge its functions under Part II of that Act, or of enabling or assisting a recognised supervisory or qualifying body within the meaning of that Part to discharge its functions as such;]

(i) for the purpose of enabling or assisting the Industrial Assurance Commissioner or the Industrial Assurance Commissioner for Northern Ireland to discharge his functions under the enactments relating to industrial assurance;

(j) for the purpose of enabling or assisting the Insurance Brokers Registration Council to discharge its functions under the Insurance Brokers (Registration) Act 1977;

(k) for the purpose of enabling or assisting an official receiver to discharge his functions under the enactments relating to insolvency or for the purpose of enabling or assisting a body which is for the time being a recognised professional body for the purposes of section 391 of the Insolvency Act 1986 to discharge its functions as such;

(l) for the purpose of enabling or assisting the Building Societies Commission to discharge its functions under the Building Societies Act 1986;

(m) for the purpose of enabling or assisting the Director General of Fair Trading to discharge his functions under this Act;

(n) for the purpose of enabling or assisting a recognised self-regulating organisation, recognised investment exchange, recognised professional body, or recognised clearing house to discharge its functions as such;

(o) with a view to the institution of, or otherwise for the purposes of, any disciplinary proceedings relating to the exercise by a solicitor, auditor, accountant, valuer or actuary of his professional duties;

[(oo) with a view to the institution of, or otherwise for the purposes of, any disciplinary proceedings relating to the discharge by a public servant of his duties;]

(p) for the purpose of enabling or assisting any person appointed or authorised to exercise any powers under [section 44 of the Insurance Companies Act 1982, section 447 of the Companies Act 1985,] section 94, 106 or 177 above [or section 84 of the Companies Act 1989] to discharge his functions;

(q) for the purpose of enabling or assisting an auditor of an authorised person or a person approved under section 108 above to discharge his functions;

[(qq) for the purpose of enabling or assisting an overseas regulatory authority to exercise its regulatory functions;]

(r) if the information is or has been available to the public from other sources;

(s) in a summary or collection of information framed in such a way as not to enable the identity of any person to whom the information relates to be ascertained; or

(t) in pursuance of any Community obligation.

[(1A) In subsection (1) –

(a) in paragraph (oo) "public servant" means an officer or servant of the Crown or of any public or other authority for the time being designated for the purposes of that paragraph by order of the Secretary of State; and

(b) in paragraph (qq) "overseas regulatory authority" and "regulatory functions" have the same meaning as in section 82 of the Companies Act 1989.]

(2) Section 179 above shall not preclude the disclosure of information to the Secretary of State or to the Treasury if the disclosure is made in the interests of investors or in the public interest.

(3) Subject to subsection (4) below, section 179 above shall not preclude the disclosure of information for the purpose of enabling or assisting any public or other authority for the time being [designated for the purposes of this subsection] by an order made by the Secretary of State to discharge any functions which are specified in the order.

(4) An order under subsection (3) above designating an authority for the purposes of that subsection may –

(a) impose conditions subject to which the disclosure of information is permitted by that subsection; and
(b) otherwise restrict the circumstances in which that subsection permits disclosure.

(5) Section 179 above shall not preclude the disclosure –

(a) of any information contained in an unpublished report of the Tribunal which has been made available to any person under this Act, by the person to whom it was made available or by any person obtaining the information directly or indirectly from him;
(b) of any information contained in any notice or copy of a notice served under this Act, notice the contents of which has not been given to the public, by the person on whom it was served or any person obtaining the information directly or indirectly from him;
(c) of any information contained in the register kept under section 102 above by virtue of subsection (1)(e) of that section, by a person who has inspected the register under section 103(2) or (3) above or any person obtaining the information directly or indirectly from him.

(6) . . . ;

(7) Section 179 above shall not preclude the disclosure of information by the Director General of Fair Trading or any officer or servant of his or any person obtaining the information directly or indirectly from the Director or any such officer or servant if the information was obtained by the Director or any such officer or servant for the purposes of or in the discharge of his functions under this Act (whether or not he was the primary recipient of the information within the meaning of section 179 above) and the disclosure is made –

(a) for the purpose of enabling or assisting the Director, the Secretary of State or any other Minister, the Monopolies and Mergers Commission or any Northern Ireland department to discharge any function conferred on him or them by the Fair Trading Act 1973 (other than Part II or III of that Act), the Restrictive Trade Practices Act 1976 or the Competition Act 1980; or
(b) for the purposes of any civil proceedings under any of those provisions;

and information shall not be treated as restricted information for the purposes of section 179 above if it has been made available to the public by virtue of this subsection.

(8) The Secretary of State may by order modify the application of any provision of this section so as –

(a) to prevent the disclosure by virtue of that provision; or
(b) to restrict the extent to which disclosure is permitted by virtue of that provision,

of information received by a person specified in the order pursuant to a Community obligation from a person exercising functions in relation to a collective investment scheme who is also so specified.

(9) An order under [subsection (1A)(a), (3) or (8)] above shall be subject to annulment in pursuance of a resolution of either House of Parliament.

NOTES
Sub-s (1): para (bb) inserted by the Transfer of Functions (Financial Services) Order 1992, SI 1992 No 1315, art 10(1), Sch 4, para 5; para (c) amended, and para (e) substituted, by the Companies Act

1989, s 75; para (f) amended by the Banking Act 1987, s 108(1), Sch 6, para 27(3); para (h) prospectively substituted by the Friendly Socieities Act 1992, s 98(a), Sch 18, Pt I, para 5, as follows –
    "(h) for the purpose of enabling or assisting the Friendly Societies Commission to discharge its functions under this Act, the enactments relating to friendly societies or the enactments relating to industrial assurance";

paras (hh), (oo) inserted by the Companies Act 1989, s 75; para (p) amended, and para (qq) inserted by the Companies Act 1989, s 75.
Sub-s (1A): inserted by the Companies Act 1989, s 75.
Sub-s (3): amended by s 75 of the 1989 Act.
Sub-s (6): repealed by ss 75, 212 of, and Sch 24 to, the 1989 Act.
Sub-s (9): amended by s 75 of the 1989 Act.

Criminal Justice Act 1987

(1987 c 38)

An Act to make further provision for the investigation of and trials for fraud; and for connected purposes

[15 May 1987]

BE IT ENACTED by the Queen's most Excellent Majesty, by and with the advice and consent of the Lords Spiritual and Temporal, and Commons, in this present Parliament assembled, and by the authority of the same, as follows: –

PART I
FRAUD

Serious Fraud Office

1 The Serious Fraud Office
(1) A Serious Fraud Office shall be constituted for England and Wales and Northern Ireland.

(2) The Attorney General shall appoint a person to be the Director of the Serious Fraud Office (referred to in this Part of this Act as "the Director"), and he shall discharge his functions under the superintendence of the Attorney General.

(3) The Director may investigate any suspected offence which appears to him on reasonable grounds to involve serious or complex fraud.

(4) The Director may, if he thinks fit, conduct any such investigation in conjunction either with the police or with any other person who is, in the opinion of the Director, a proper person to be concerned in it.

(5) The Director may –

(a) institute and have the conduct of any criminal proceedings which appear to him to relate to such fraud; and
(b) take over the conduct of any such proceedings at any stage.

(6) The Director shall discharge such other functions in relation to fraud as may from time to time be assigned to him by the Attorney General.

(7) The Director may designate for the purposes of subsection (5) above any member of the Serious Fraud Office who is –

(a) a barrister in England and Wales or Northern Ireland;
(b) a solicitor of the Supreme Court; or
(c) a solicitor of the Supreme Court of Judicature of Northern Ireland.

(8) Any member so designated shall, without prejudice to any functions which may have been assigned to him in his capacity as a member of that Office, have all the powers of the Director as to the institution and conduct of proceedings but shall exercise those powers under the direction of the Director.

(9) Any member so designated who is a barrister in England and Wales or a solicitor of the Supreme Court shall have, in any court, the rights of audience enjoyed by solicitors holding practising certificates and shall have such additional rights of audience in the Crown Court in England and Wales as may be given by virtue of subsection (11) below.

(10) The reference in subsection (9) above to rights of audience enjoyed in any court by solicitors includes a reference to rights enjoyed in the Crown Court by virtue of any direction given by the Lord Chancellor under section 83 of the Supreme Court Act 1981.

(11) For the purposes of giving members so designated who are barristers in England and Wales or solicitors of the Supreme Court additional rights of audience in the Crown Court in England and Wales, the Lord Chancellor may give any such direction as respects such members as he could give under the said section 83.

(12) Any member so designated who is a barrister in Northern Ireland or a solicitor of the Supreme Court of Judicature of Northern Ireland shall have –

(a) in any court the rights of audience enjoyed by solicitors of the Supreme Court of Judicature of Northern Ireland and, in the Crown Court in Northern Ireland, such additional rights of audience as may be given by virtue of subsection (14) below; and

(b) in the Crown Court in Northern Ireland, the rights of audience enjoyed by barristers employed by the Director of Public Prosecutions for Northern Ireland.

(13) Subject to subsection (14) below, the reference in subsection (12)(a) above to rights of audience enjoyed by solicitors of the Supreme Court of Judicature of Northern Ireland is a reference to such rights enjoyed in the Crown Court in Northern Ireland as restricted by any direction given by the Lord Chief Justice of Northern Ireland under section 50 of the Judicature (Northern Ireland) Act 1978.

(14) For the purpose of giving any member so designated who is a barrister in Northern Ireland or a solicitor of the Supreme Court of Judicature of Northern Ireland additional rights of audience in the Crown Court in Northern Ireland, the Lord Chief Justice of Northern Ireland may direct that any direction given by him under the said section 50 shall not apply to such members.

(15) Schedule 1 to this Act shall have effect.

(16) For the purposes of this section (including that Schedule) references to the conduct of any proceedings include references to the proceedings being discontinued and to the taking of any steps (including the bringing of appeals and making of representations in respect of applications for bail) which may be taken in relation to them.

(17) In the application of this section (including that Schedule) to Northern Ireland references to the Attorney General are to be construed as references to him in his capacity as Attorney General for Northern Ireland.

2 Director's investigation powers

(1) The powers of the Director under this section shall be exercisable, but only for the purposes of an investigation under section 1 above, [or, on a request made by the Attorney General of the Isle of Man, Jersey or Guernsey, under legislation corresponding to that section and having effect in the Island whose Attorney General makes the request,] in any case in which it appears to him that there is good reason to do so for the purpose of investigating the affairs, or any aspect of the affairs, of any person.

(2) The Director may by notice in writing require the person whose affairs are to be investigated ("the person under investigation") or any other person whom he has reason to believe has relevant information to [answer questions or otherwise furnish information with respect to any matter relevant to the investigation at a specified place and either at a specified time or forthwith].

(3) The Director may by notice in writing require the person under investigation or any other person to produce at [such place as may be specified in the notice and either forthwith or at such time as may be so specified] any specified documents which appear to the Director to relate to any matter relevant to the investigation or any documents of a specified [description] which appear to him so to relate; and –

(a) if any such documents are produced, the Director may –

    (i)   take copies or extracts from them;
    (ii) require the person producing them to provide an explanation of any of them;

(b) if any such documents are not produced, the Director may require the person who was required to produce them to state, to the best of his knowledge and belief, where they are.

(4) Where, on information on oath laid by a member of the Serious Fraud Office, a justice of the peace is satisfied, in relation to any documents, that there are reasonable grounds for believing –

(a) that –

    (i)   a person has failed to comply with an obligation under this section to produce them;
    (ii) it is not practicable to serve a notice under subsection (3) above in relation to them; or
    (iii) the service of such a notice in relation to them might seriously prejudice the investigation; and

(b) that they are on premises specified in the information,

he may issue such a warrant as is mentioned in subsection (5) below.

(5) The warrant referred to above is a warrant authorising any constable –

(a) to enter (using such force as is reasonably necessary for the purpose) and search the premises, and
(b) to take possession of any documents appearing to be documents of the description specified in the information or to take in relation to any documents so appearing any other steps which may appear to be necessary for preserving them and preventing interference with them.

(6) Unless it is not practicable in the circumstances, a constable executing a warrant issued under subsection (4) above shall be accompanied by an appropriate person.

(7) In subsection (6) above "appropriate person" means –

(a) a member of the Serious Fraud Office; or
(b) some person who is not a member of that Office but whom the Director has authorised to accompany the constable.

(8) A statement by a person in response to a requirement imposed by virtue of this section may only be used in evidence against him –

(a) on a prosecution for an offence under subsection (14) below; or
(b) on a prosecution for some other offence where in giving evidence he makes a statement inconsistent with it.

(9) A person shall not under this section be required to disclose any information or produce any document which he would be entitled to refuse to disclose or produce on

grounds of legal professional privilege in proceedings in the High Court, except that a lawyer may be required to furnish the name and address of his client.

(10) A person shall not under this section be required to disclose information or produce a document in respect of which he owes an obligation of confidence by virtue of carrying on any banking business unless –

(a) the person to whom the obligation of confidence is owned consents to the disclosure or production; or
(b) the Director has authorised the making of the requirement or, if it is impracticable for him to act personally, a member of the Serious Fraud Office designated by him for the purposes of this subsection has done so.

(11) Without prejudice to the power of the Director to assign functions to members of the Serious Fraud Office, the Director may authorise any competent investigator (other than a constable) who is not a member of that Office to exercise on his behalf all or any of the powers conferred by this section, but no such authority shall be granted except for the purpose of investigating the affairs, or any aspect of the affairs, of a person specified in the authority.

(12) No person shall be bound to comply with any requirement imposed by a person exercising powers by virtue of any authority granted under subsection (11) above unless he has, if required to do so, produced evidence of his authority.

(13) Any person who without reasonable excuse fails to comply with a requirement imposed on him under this section shall be guilty of an offence and liable on summary conviction to imprisonment for a term not exceeding six months or to a fine not exceeding level 5 on the standard scale or to both.

(14) A person who, in purported compliance with a requirement under this section –

(a) makes a statement which he knows to be false or misleading in a material particular; or
(b) recklessly makes a statement which is false or misleading in a material particular,

shall be guilty of an offence.

(15) A person guilty of an offence under subsection (14) above shall –

(a) on conviction on indictment, be liable to imprisonment for a term not exceeding two years or to a fine or to both; and
(b) on summary conviction, be liable to imprisonment for a term not exceeding six months or to a fine not exceeding the statutory maximum, or to both.

(16) Where any person –

(a) knows or suspects that an investigation by the police or the Serious Fraud Office into serious or complex fraud is being or is likely to be carried out; and
(b) falsifies, conceals, destroys or otherwise disposes of, or causes or permits the falsification, concealment, destruction or disposal of documents which he knows or suspects are or would be relevant to such an investigation,

he shall be guilty of an offence unless he proves that he had no intention of concealing the facts disclosed by the documents from persons carrying out such an investigation.

(17) A person guilty of an offence under subsection (16) above shall –

(a) on conviction on indictment, be liable to imprisonment for a term not exceeding 7 years or to a fine or to both; and
(b) on summary conviction, be liable to imprisonment for a term not exceeding 6 months or to a fine not exceeding the statutory maximum or to both.

(18) In this section, "documents" includes information recorded in any form and, in relation to information recorded otherwise than in legible form, references to its production include references to producing a copy of the information in legible form.

(19) In the application of this section to Scotland, the reference to a justice of the peace is to be construed as a reference to the sheriff; and in the application of this section to Northern Ireland, subsection (4) above shall have effect as if for the references to information there were substituted references to a complaint.

NOTES
Sub-s (1): amended by the Criminal Justice Act 1988, s 143.
Sub-ss (2), (3): amended by the Criminal Justice Act 1988, s 170(1), Sch 15, paras 112, 113.
This section extends to Scotland and is extended to Guernsey and Jersey as modified by SI 1989 No 674, art 2, and SI 1989 No 675, art 2.

3 Disclosure of information

(1) Where any information subject to an obligation of secrecy under the Taxes Management Act 1970 has been disclosed by the Commissioners of Inland Revenue or an officer of those Commissioners to any member of the Serious Fraud Office for the purposes of any prosecution of an offence relating to inland revenue, that information may be disclosed by any member of the Serious Fraud Office –

(a) for the purposes of any prosecution of which that Office has the conduct;
(b) to any member of the Crown Prosecution Service for the purposes of any prosecution of an offence relating to inland revenue; and
(c) to the Director of Public Prosecutions for Northern Ireland for the purposes of any prosecution of an offence relating to inland revenue,

but not otherwise.

(2) Where the Serious Fraud Office has the conduct of any prosecution of an offence which does not relate to inland revenue, the court may not prevent the prosecution from relying on any evidence under section 78 of the Police and Criminal Evidence Act 1984 (discretion to exclude unfair evidence) by reason only of the fact that the information concerned was disclosed by the Commisioners of Inland Revenue or an officer of those Commissioners for the purposes of any prosecution of an offence relating to inland revenue.

(3) Where any information is subject to an obligation of secrecy imposed by or under any enactment other than an enactment contained in the Taxes Management Act 1970, the obligation shall not have effect to prohibit the disclosure of that information to any person in his capacity as a member of the Serious Fraud Office but any information disclosed by virtue of this subsection may only be disclosed by a member of the Serious Fraud Office for the purposes of any prosecution in England and Wales, Northern Ireland or elsewhere and may only be discosed by such a member if he is designated by the Director for the purposes of this subsection.

(4) Without prejudice to his power to enter into agreements apart from this subsection, the Director may enter into a written agreement for the supply of information to or by him subject, in either case, to an obligation not to disclose the information concerned otherwise than for a specified purpose.

(5) Subject to subsections (1) and (3) above and to any provision of an agreement for the supply of information which restricts the disclosure of the information supplied, information obtained by any person in his capacity as a member of the Serious Fraud Office may be disclosed by any member of that Office designated by the Director for the purposes of this subsection –

(a) to any government department or Northern Ireland department or other authority or body discharging its functions on behalf of the Crown (including the Crown in right of Her Majesty's Government in Northern Ireland);
(b) to any competent authority;
(c) for the purposes of any prosecution in England and Wales, Northern Ireland or elsewhere; and

(d) for the purposes of assisting any public or other authority for the time being designated for the purposes of this paragraph by an order made by the Secretary to discharge any functions which are specified in the order.

(6) The following are competent authorities for the purposes of subsection (5) above –

(a) an inspector appointed under Part XIV of the Companies Act 1985 or Part XV of the Companies (Northern Ireland) Order 1986;
(b) an Official Receiver;
(c) the Accountant in Bankruptcy;
[(d) the official receiver for Northern Ireland;]
(e) a person appointed to carry out an investigation under section 55 of the Building Societies Act 1986.
(f) a body administering a compensation scheme under section 54 of the Financial Services Act 1986;
(g) an inspector appointed under section 94 of that Act;
(h) a person exercising powers by virtue of section 106 of that Act;
(i) an inspector appointed under section 177 of that Act or any corresponding enactment having effect in Northern Ireland;
[(j) a person appointed by the Bank of England under section 41 of the Banking Act 1987 to carry out an investigation and make a report;]
(k) a person exercising powers by virtue of section 44(2) of the Insurance Companies Act 1982;
(l) any body having supervisory, regulatory or disciplinary functions in relation to any profession or any area of commercial activity; and
(m) any person or body having, under the law of any country or territory outside the United Kingdom, functions corresponding to any of the functions of any person or body mentioned in any of the foregoing paragraphs.

(7) An order under subsection (5)(d) above may impose conditions subject to which, and otherwise restrict the circumstances in which, information may be disclosed under that paragraph.

NOTE
Sub-s (6): para (d) substituted by SI 1989 No 2405 (NI 19), art 381(2), Sch 9, Part II, para 57; para (j) substituted by the Criminal Justice Act 1988, s 170(1), Sch 15, para 111.

Transfer of cases to Crown Court

4 Notices of transfer and designated authorities
(1) If –

(a) a person has been charged with an indictable offence; and
(b) in the opinion of an authority designated by subsection (2) below or of one of such an authority's officers acting on the authority's behalf the evidence of the offence charged –

(i) would be sufficient for the person charged to be committed for trial; and
(ii) reveals a case of fraud of such seriousness and complexity that it is appropriate that the management of the case should without delay be taken over by the Crown Court; and

(c) before the magistrates' court in whose jurisdiction the offence has been charged begins to inquire into the case as examining justices the authority or one of the authority's officers acting on the authority's behalf gives the court a notice (in this Act referred to as a "notice of transfer") certifying that opinion,

the functions of the magistrates' court shall cease in relation to the case, except as provided by section 5(3) [, (7A)] and (8) below and by [section 20(4) of the Legal Aid Act 1988].

(2) The authorities mentioned in subsection (1) above (in this Act referred to as "designated authorities") are –

(a) the Director of Public Prosecutions;
(b) the Director of the Serious Fraud Office;
(c) the Commissioners of Inland Revenue;
(d) the Commissioners of Customs and Excise; and
(e) the Secretary of State.

(3) A designated authority's decision to give notice of transfer shall not be subject to appeal or liable to be questioned in any court.

NOTES
Sub-s (1): first amendment in square brackets made by the Criminal Justice Act 1988, s 144(1), (2); second words in square brackets substituted by the Legal Aid Act 1988, s 45(1), (3), Sch 5, para 22.

5 Notices of transfer – procedure
(1) A notice of transfer shall specify the proposed place of trial and in selecting that place the designated authority shall have regard to the considerations to which section 7 of the Magistrates' Courts Act 1980 requires a magistrates' court committing a person for trial to have regard when selecting the place at which he is to be tried.

(2) A notice of transfer shall specify the charge or charges to which it relates and include or be accompanied by such additional matter as regulations under subsection (9) below may require.

(3) If a magistrates' court has remanded a person to whom a notice of transfer relates in custody, it shall have power, subject to section 4 of the Bail Act 1976 and regulations under section 22 of the Prosecution of Offences Act 1985 –

(a) to order that he shall be safely kept in custody until delivered in due course of law; or
(b) to release him on bail in accordance with the Bail Act 1976, that is to say, by directing him to appear before the Crown Court for trial;

and where his release on bail is conditional on his providing one or more surety or sureties and, in accordance with section 8(3) of the Bail Act 1976, the court fixes the amount in which the surety is to be bound with a view to his entering into his recognizance subsequently in accordance with subsections (4) and (5) or (6) of that section, the court shall in the meantime make an order such as is mentioned in paragraph (a) of this subsection.

(4) If the conditions specified in subsection (5) below are satisfied, a court may exercise the powers conferred by subsection (3) above [in relation to a person charged without his] being brought before it in any case in which by virtue of section 128(3A) of the Magistrates' Courts Act 1980 it would have power further to remand him on an adjournment such as is mentioned in that subsection.

(5) The conditions mentioned in subsection (4) above are –

(a) that the person [in question] has given his written consent to the powers conferred by subsection (3) above being exercised without his being brought before the court; and
(b) that the court is satisfied that, when he gave his consent, he knew that the notice of transfer had been issued.

(6) Where notice of transfer is given after [a person to whom it relates] has been remanded on bail to appear before [a magistrates' court] on an appointed day, the requirement that he shall so appear shall cease on the giving of the notice, unless the notice states that it is to continue.

(7) Where the requirement that a person [to whom the notice of transfer relates] shall appear before [a magistrates' court] ceases by virtue of subsection (6) above, it shall be

his duty to appear before the Crown Court at the place specified by the notice of transfer as the proposed place of trial or at any place substituted for it by a direction under section 76 of the Supreme Court Act 1981.

[(7A) If the notice states that the requirement is to continue, when a person to whom the notice relates appears before the magistrates' court, the court shall have –

(a) the powers and duty conferred on a magistrates' court by subsection (3) above, but subject as there provided; and

(b) power to enlarge, in the surety's absence, a recognizance conditioned in accordance with section 128(4)(a) of the Magistrates' Courts Act 1980 so that the surety is bound to secure that the person charged appears also before the Crown Court.]

(8) For the purposes of the Criminal Procedure (Attendance of Witnesses) Act 1965 –

(a) any magistrates' court for the petty sessions area for which the court from which a case was transferred sits shall be treated as examining magistrates; and

(b) a person [indicated in the notice of transfer as a proposed witness] shall be treated as a person who has been examined by the court.

(9) The Attorney General –

(a) shall by regulations make provision requiring the giving of a copy of a notice of transfer, together with a statement of the evidence on which any charge to which it relates is based –

(i) to [any person to whom the notice of transfer relates]; and

(ii) to the Crown Court sitting at the [place specified by the notice of transfer as the] proposed place of trial; and

(b) may by regulations make such further provision in relation to notices of transfer, including provision as to the duties of a designated authority in relation to such notices, as appears to him to be appropriate.

(10) The power to make regulations conferred by subsection (9) above shall be exercisable by statutory instrument subject to annulment in pursuance of a resolution of either House of Parliament.

(11) Any such regulations may make different provision with respect to different cases or classes of case.

NOTES
Sub-ss (4)–(7), (8), (9): words in square brackets substituted or added by the Criminal Justice Act 1988, s 144(1), (3).
Sub-s (7A): added by the Criminal Justice Act 1988, s 144(1), (4).

6 [Applications for dismissal]
[(1) Where notice of transfer has been given, any person to whom the notice relates, at any time before he is arraigned (and whether or not an indictment has been preferred against him), may apply orally or in writing to the Crown Court sitting at the place specified by the notice of transfer as the proposed place of trial for the charge, or any of the charges, in the case to be dismissed; and the judge shall dismiss a charge (and accordingly quash a count relating to it in any indictment preferred against the applicant) if it appears to him that the evidence against the applicant would not be sufficient for a jury properly to convict him.

(2) No oral application may be made under subsection (1) above unless the applicant has given the Crown Court sitting at the place specified by the notice of transfer as the proposed place of trial written notice of his intention to make the application.

(3) Oral evidence may be given on such an application only with the leave of the judge or by his order, and the judge shall give leave or make an order only if it appears to him,

having regard to any matters stated in the application for leave, that the interests of justice require him to do so.

(4) If the judge gives leave permitting, or makes an order requiring, a person to give oral evidence, but he does not do so, the judge may disregard any document indicating the evidence that he might have given.

(5) Dismissal of the charge, or all the charges, against the applicant shall have the same effect as a refusal by examining magistrates to commit for trial, except that no further proceedings may be brought on a dismissed charge except by means of the preferment of a voluntary bill of indictment.

(6) Crown Court Rules may make provision for the purposes of this section and, without prejudice to the generality of this subsection –

(a) as to the time or stage in the proceedings at which anything required to be done is to be done (unless the court grants leave to do it at some other time or stage);
(b) as to the contents and form of notices or other documents;
(c) as to the manner in which evidence is to be submitted; and
(d) as to persons to be served with notices or other material.]

NOTE
Substituted by the Criminal Justice Act 1988, s 144(1), (5).

Preparatory hearings

7 Power to order preparatory hearing
(1) Where it appears to a judge of the Crown Court that the evidence on an indictment reveals a case of fraud of such seriousness and complexity that substantial benefits are likely to accrue from a hearing (in this Act referred to as a "preparatory hearing") before the jury are sworn, for the purpose of –

(a) identifying issues which are likely to be material to the verdict of the jury;
(b) assisting their comprehension of any such issues;
(c) expediting the proceedings before the jury; or
(d) assisting the judge's management of the trial,

he may order that such a hearing shall be held.

(2) A judge may make an order under subsection (1) above on the application either of the prosecution or of the person indicted or, if the indictment charges a number of persons, any of them, or of his own motion.

(3) If a judge orders a preparatory hearing, he may also order the prosecution to prepare and serve any documents that appear to him to be relevant and whose service could be ordered at the preparatory hearing by virtue of this Part of this Act or Crown Court Rules.

(4) Where –

(a) a judge has made an order under subsection (3) above; and
(b) the prosecution have complied with it,

the judge may order the person indicted or, if the indictment charges a number of persons, any of them to prepare and serve any documents that appear to him to be relevant and whose service could be so ordered at the preparatory hearing.

(5) An order under this section may specify the time within which it is to be complied with, but Crown Court Rules may make provision as to the minimum or maximum time that may be specified for compliance.

8 Commencement of trial and arraignment
(1) If a judge orders a preparatory hearing, the trial shall begin with that hearing.

(2) Arraignment shall accordingly take place at the start of the preparatory hearing.

9 The preparatory hearing
(1) At the preparatory hearing the judge may exercise any of the powers specified in this section.

(2) The judge may adjourn a preparatory hearing from time to time.

(3) He may determine –

(a) ...
(b) any question as to the admissibility of evidence; and
(c) any other question of law relating to the case.

(4) He may order the prosecution –

(a) to supply the court and the defendant or, if there is more than one, each of them with a statement (a "case statement") of the following –

    (i) the principal facts of the prosecution case;
    (ii) the witnesses who will speak to those facts;
    (iii) any exhibits relevant to those facts;
    (iv) any proposition of law on which the prosecution proposes to rely; and
    (v) the consequences in relation to any of the counts in the indictment that appear to the prosecution to flow from the matters stated in pursuance of sub-paragraphs (i) to (iv) above;

(b) to prepare their evidence and other explanatory material in such a form as appears to him to be likely to aid comprehension by the jury and to supply it in that form to the court and to the defendant or, if there is more than one, to each of them;
(c) to give the court and the defendant or, if there is more than one, each of them notice of documents the truth of the contents of which ought in the prosecution's view to be admitted and of any other matters which in their view ought to be agreed;
(d) to make any amendments of any case statement supplied in pursuance of an order under paragraph (a) above that appear to the court to be appropriate, having regard to objections made by the defendant or, if there is more than one, by any of them.

(5) Where –

(a) a judge has ordered the prosecution to supply a case statement; and
(b) the prosecution have complied with the order,

he may order the defendant or, if there is more than one, each of them –

    (i) to give the court and the prosecution a statement in writing setting out in general terms the nature of his defence and indicating the principal matters on which he takes issue with the prosecution;
    (ii) to give the court and the prosecution notice of any objections that he has to the case statement;
    (iii) to inform the court and the prosecution of any point of law (including a point as to the admissibility of evidence) which he wishes to take, and any authority on which he intends to rely for that purpose;
    (iv) to give the court and the prosecution a notice stating the extent to which he agrees with the prosecution as to documents and other matters to which a notice under subsection (4)(c) above relates and the reason for any disagreement.

(6) Crown Court Rules may provide that except to the extent that disclosure is required –

(a) by section 11 of the Criminal Justice Act 1967 (alibi); or
(b) by rules under section 81 of the Police and Criminal Evidence Act 1984 (expert evidence),

a summary required by virtue of subsection (5) above need not disclose who will give evidence.

(7) A judge making an order under subsection (5) above shall warn the defendant or, if there is more than one, all of them of the possible consequence under section 10(1) below of not complying with it.

(8) If it appears to a judge that reasons given in pursuance of subsection (5)(iv) above are inadequate, he shall so inform the person giving them, and may require him to give further or better reasons.

(9) An order under this section may specify the time within which any specified requirement contained in it is to be complied with, but Crown Court Rules may make provision as to the minimum or maximum time that may be specified for compliance.

(10) An order or ruling made at or for the purposes of a preparatory hearing shall have effect during the trial, unless it appears to the judge, on application made to him during the trial, that the interests of justice require him to vary or discharge it.

(11) An appeal shall lie to the Court of Appeal from any order or ruling of a judge under subsection (3)(b) or (c) above, but only with the leave of the judge or of the Court of Appeal.

(12) Subject to rules of court made under section 53(1) of the Supreme Court Act 1981 (power by rules to distribute business of Court of Appeal between its civil and criminal divisions), the jurisdiction of the Court of Appeal under subsection (11) above shall be exercised by the criminal division of the court; and the reference in that subsection to the Court of Appeal shall be construed as a reference to that division.

(13) The judge may continue a preparatory hearing notwithstanding that leave to appeal has been granted under subsection (11) above, but no jury shall be sworn until after the appeal has been determined or abandoned.

(14) On the termination of the hearing of an appeal, the Court of Appeal may confirm, reverse or vary the decision appealed against.

NOTE
Sub-s (3): para (a) repealed by the Criminal Justice Act 1988, s 170(2), Sch 16.

10 Provisions relating to later stages of trial
(1) Where there has been a preparatory hearing, any party may depart from the case which he disclosed at the hearing but, in the event of such a departure or of failure to comply with a requirement imposed at the hearing, the judge or, with the leave of the judge, any other party may make such comment as appears to him to be appropriate and the jury may draw such inference as appears proper.

(2) In deciding whether to give leave the judge shall have regard in all cases –

(a) to the extent of any departure from a case indicated at the preparatory hearing; and
(b) to whether there was any justification for it.

(3) Except as provided by this section no part –

(a) of a statement supplied under section 9(5) above; or
(b) of any other information relating to the case for the defendant or, if there is more than one, the case for any of them, which was given at the preparatory hearing,

may be disclosed at a stage in the trial after the jury have been sworn without the consent of the person who supplied or gave it.

Reporting restrictions

11 Restrictions on reporting applications for dismissal and preparatory hearings

(1) Except as provided by this section, it shall not be lawful to publish in Great Britain a written report, or to [include a relevant programme for reception] in Great Britain [a report of proceedings to which this section applies which contains] any matter other than that permitted by this section.

[(1A) This section applies –

(a) to an application under section 6(1) above; and
(b) to a preparatory hearing and any appeal or application for leave to appeal relating to such a hearing.]

[(2) An order that subsection (1) above shall not apply to reports –

(a) of an application under section 6(1) above;
(b) of a preparatory hearing;
(c) of an appeal to the Court of Appeal under section 9(11) above; or
(d) of an application for leave to appeal under that subsection,

may be made –

(i) in a case falling within paragraph (a), (b) or (d) above, by the judge dealing with the matter; and
(ii) in a case falling within paragraph (c) above, by the Court of Appeal.]

(3) Where in the case of two or more accused one of them objects to the making of an order under subsection (2) above, the court shall make the order if, and only if, it is satisfied, after hearing the representations of the accused, that it is in the interests of justice to do so.

(4) An order under subsection (2) above shall not apply to reports of proceedings under subsection (3) above, but any decisions of the court to make or not to make such an order may be contained in reports published [or included in a relevant programme] before the time authorised by subsection (5) below.

(5) It shall not be unlawful under this section to publish, [or include in a relevant programme] a report of an application under section 6(1) above containing any matter other than that permitted by subsection (8) below where the application is succesful.

(6) Where –

(a) two or more persons were jointly charged; and
(b) applications under section 6(1) above are made by more than one of them,

subsection (5) above shall have effect as if for the words "the application is" there were substituted the words "all the applications are".

(7) It shall not be unlawful under this section to publish [or include in a relevant programme] a report of an unsuccessful application or a preparatory hearing at the conclusion of the trial of the person charged, or of the last of the persons charged to be tried.

(8) The following matters may be contained in a report published [or included in a relevant programme] without an order under subsection (2) above before the time authorised by subsections (5) and (6) above, that is to say –

(a) the identity of the court and the name of the judge;
(b) the names, ages, home addresses and occupations of the accused and witnesses;
(c) any relevant business information;
(d) the offence or offences, or a summary of them, with which the accused is or are charged;
(e) the names of counsel and solicitors . . . in the proceedings;

(f) where the proceedings are adjourned, the date and place to which they are adjourned;

(g) any arrangements as to bail;

(h) whether legal aid was granted to the accused or any of the accused.

(9) The following is relevant business information for the purposes of subsection (8) above –

(a) any address used by the accused for carrying on a business on his own account;

(b) the name of any business which he was carrying on on his own account at any relevant time;

(c) the name of any firm in which he was a partner at any relevant time or by which he was engaged at any such time;

(d) the address of any such firm;

(e) the name of any company of which he was a director at any relevant time or by which he was otherwise engaged at any such time;

(f) the address of the registered or principal office of any such company; and

(g) any working address of the accused in his capacity as a person engaged by any such company.

[(9A) In subsection (9) above "engaged" means engaged under a contract of service or a contract for services.]

(10) The addresses that may be published or [included in a relevant programme] under subsection (8) above are addresses –

(a) at any relevant time; and

(b) at the time of their publication [or inclusion in a relevant programme].

(11) . . .

(12) If a report is published [or included in a relevant programme] in contravention of this section, the following persons, that is to say –

(a) in the case of a publication of a written report as part of a newspaper or periodical, any proprietor, editor or publisher of the newspaper or periodical;

(b) in the case of a publication of a written report otherwise than as part of a newspaper or periodical, the person who publishes it;

[(c) in the case of the inclusion of a report in a relevant programme, any body corporate which is engaged in providing the service in which the programme is included and any person having functions in relation to the programme corresponding to those of an editor of a newspaper,]

shall be liable on summary conviction to a fine not exceeding level 5 on the standard scale.

(13) Proceedings for an offence under this section shall not, in England and Wales, be instituted otherwise than by or with the consent of the Attorney General.

(14) Subsection (1) above shall be in addition to, and not in derogation from, the provisions of any other enactment with respect to the publication of reports of court proceedings.

(15) In this section –

    . . .

    . . .

"publish", in relation to a report, means publish the report, either by itself or as part of a newspaper or periodical, for distribution to the public.

["relevant programme" means a programme included in a programme service (within the meaning of the Broadcasting Act 1990).]

["relevant time" means a time when events giving rise to the charges to which the proceedings relate occurred.]

NOTES

Sub-s (1): first words in square brackets substituted by the Broadcasting Act 1990, s 203(1), Sch 20, para 47; second words in square brackets substituted by the Criminal Justice Act 1988, s 170(1), Sch 15, paras 112, 114.

Sub-ss (1A), (9A): added by the Criminal Justice Act 1988, s 170(1), Sch 15, paras 112, 114.

Sub-s (2): substituted by the Criminal Justice Act 1988, s 170(1), Sch 15, paras 112, 114.

Sub-ss (4), (5), (7), (10), (12): words in square brackets substituted by the Broadcasting Act 1990, s 203(1), Sch 20, para 47.

Sub-s (8): words in square brackets substituted by the Broadcasting Act 1990, s 203(1), Sch 20, para 47; words omitted from para (e) repealed by Criminal Justice Act 1988, s 170(2), Sch 16.

Sub-s (11): repealed by the Criminal Justice Act 1988, s 170(2), Sch 16.

Sub-s (15): definitions omitted repealed, and definition "relevant programme" added, by the Broadcasting Act 1990, s 203(1), (3), Sch 20, para 47, Sch 21; definition "relevant time" added by the Criminal Justice Act 1988, s 170(1), Sch 15, paras 112, 114.

Conspiracy to defraud

12 Charges of and penalty for conspiracy to defraud

(1) If –

(a) a person agrees with any other person or persons that a course of conduct shall be pursued; and

(b) that course of conduct will necessarily amount to or involve the commission of any offence or offences by one or more of the parties to the agreement if the agreement is carried out in accordance with their intentions,

the fact that it will do so shall not preclude a charge of conspiracy to defraud being brought against any of them in respect of the agreement.

(2) . . .

(3) A person guilty of conspiracy to defraud is liable on conviction on indictment to imprisonment for a term not exceeding 10 years or a fine or both.

NOTE

Sub-s (2): amends the Criminal Law Act 1977, s 5(2).

PART III

GENERAL AND SUPPLEMENTARY

13 Northern Ireland

(1) An Order in Council under paragraph 1(1)(b) of Schedule 1 to the Northern Ireland Act 1974 (legislation for Northern Ireland in the interim period) which contains a statement that it [is made only for purposes corresponding to those of] any provision of this Act to which this section applies –

(a) shall not be subject to paragraph 1(4) and (5) of that Schedule (affirmative resolution of both Houses of Parliament); but

(b) shall be subject to annulment in pursuance of a resolution of either House.

(2) The provisions of this Act to which this section applies are sections 4 to 12.

NOTE

Sub-s (1): amended by the Criminal Justice Act 1988, s 170(1), Sch 15, paras 112, 115.

14 Financial provision

There shall be paid out of money provided by Parliament –

(a) any expenses incurred under this Act by a Minister of the Crown; and

(b) any increase attributable to the provisions of this Act in the sums payable out of such money under any other Act.

15 Minor and consequential amendments

The enactments mentioned in Schedule 2 to this Act shall have effect with the amendments there specified (being minor amendments and amendments consequential on the foregoing provisions of this Act).

16 Commencement

(1) Subject to subsection (3) below, this Act shall come into force on such day as the Secretary of State may by order made by statutory instrument appoint; and different days may be appointed in pursuance of this subsection for different provisions or different purposes of the same provision.

(2) An order under subsection (1) above may make such transitional provision as appears to the Secretary of State to be necessary or expedient in connection with any provision thereby brought into force.

(3) The following provisions shall come into force on the day this Act is passed –

section 13;

this section;

sections 17 and 18.

17 Extent

(1) Subject to the following provisions of this section, this Act extends to England and Wales only.

(2) The following provisions extend also to Scotland –

section 2;

section 11;

section 16;

this section; and

section 18.

(3) The following provisions extend also to Northern Ireland –

section 1 (including Schedule 1) and sections 2 and 3;

section 16;

this section; and

section 18.

(4) Section 13 above extends to Northern Ireland only.

(5) The extent of any amendment of an enactment in Schedule 2 to this Act is the same as that of the enactment amended.

(6) Her Majesty may by Order in Council direct that section 2 above shall extend, subject to such modifications as may be specified in the Order, to any of the Channel Islands.

(7) In subsection (6) above "modifications" includes additions, omissions and amendments.

18 Citation

This Act may be cited as the Criminal Justice Act 1987.

SCHEDULE 1
THE SERIOUS FRAUD OFFICE

Section 1

General

1 There shall be paid to the Director of the Serious Fraud Office such remuneration as the Attorney General may, with the approval of the Treasury, determine.

2 The Director shall appoint such staff for the Serious Fraud Office as, with the approval of the Treasury as to numbers, remuneration and other terms and conditions of service, he considers necessary for the discharge of his functions.

3 (1) As soon as practicable after 4th April in any year the Director shall make to the Attorney General a report on the discharge of his functions during the year ending with that date.

(2) The Attorney General shall lay before Parliament a copy of every report received by him under sub-paragraph (1) above and shall cause every such report to be published.

Procedure

4 (1) Where any enactment (whenever passed) prohibits the taking of any step –

(a) except by the Director of Public Prosecutions or except by him or another; or
(b) without the consent of the Director of Public Prosecutions or without his consent or the consent of another,

it shall not prohibit the taking of any such step by the Director of the Serious Fraud Office.

(2) In this paragraph references to the Director of Public Prosecutions include references to the Director of Public Prosecutions for Northern Ireland.

5 (1) Where the Director has the conduct of any criminal proceedings in England and Wales, the Director of Public Prosecutions shall not in relation to those proceedings be subject to any duty by virtue of section 3(2) of the Prosecution of Offences Act 1985.

(2) Where the Director has the conduct of any criminal proceedings in Northern Ireland, the Director of Public Prosecutions for Northern Ireland shall not in relation to those proceedings be required to exercise any function under Article 5 of the Prosecution of Offences (Northern Ireland) Order 1972.

6 (1) Where the Director or any member of the Serious Fraud Office designated for the purposes of section 1[(5)] above, ("designated official") gives notice to any justice of the peace that he has instituted, or is conducting, any criminal proceedings in England and Wales, the justice shall –

(a) at the prescribed time and in the prescribed manner; or
(b) in a particular case, at the time and in the manner directed by the Attorney General;

send him every recognizance, information, certificate, deposition, document and thing connected with those proceedings which the justice is required by law to deliver to the appropriate officer of the Crown Court.

(2) Where the Director or any designated official gives notice that he has instituted, or is conducting, any criminal proceedings in Northern Ireland –

(a) to a resident magistrate or a justice of the peace in Northern Ireland;
(b) to a clerk of petty sessions in Northern Ireland,

the person to whom the notice is given shall –

(i) at the prescribed time and in the prescribed manner; or
(ii) in a particular case, at the time and in the manner directed by the Attorney General,

send him every recognizance, complaint, certificate, deposition, document and thing connected with those proceedings which that person is required by law to deliver to the appropriate officer of the Crown Court.

(3) The Attorney General may make regulations for the purpose of supplementing this paragraph; and in this paragraph "prescribed" means prescribed by the regulations.

(4) The Director or, as the case may be, designated official shall –

(a) subject to the regulations, cause anything which is sent to him under this paragraph to be delivered to the appropriate officer of the Crown Court; and
(b) be under the same obligation (on the same payment) to deliver to an applicant copies of anything so sent as that officer.

7 (1) The Attorney General may make regulations requiring the chief officer of any police force to which the regulations are expressed to apply to give to the Director information with respect to every offence of a kind prescribed by the regulations which is alleged to have been committed in his area and in respect of which it appears to him that there is a prima facie case for proceedings.

(2) The regulations may also require every such chief officer to give to the Director such information as the Director may require with respect to such cases or classes of case as he may from time to time specify.

8 (1) The Attorney General may, with the approval of the Treasury, by regulations make such provision as he considers appropriate in relation to –

(a) the fees of counsel briefed to appear on behalf of the Serious Fraud Office in any criminal proceedings; and
(b) the costs and expenses of witnesses attending to give evidence at the instance of the Serious Fraud Office and, subject to sub-paragraph (2) below, [of] any other person who in the opinion of that Office necessarily attends for the purpose of the case otherwise than to give evidence.

(2) The power conferred on the Attorney General by sub-paragraph (1)(b) above only relates to the costs and expenses of an interpreter if he is required because of the lack of English of a person attending to give evidence at the instance of the Serious Fraud Office.

(3) The regulations may, in particular –

(a) prescribe scales or rates of fees, costs or expenses; and
(b) specify conditions for the payment of fees, costs or expenses.

(4) Regulations made under sub-paragraph (1)(b) above may provide that scales or rates of costs and expenses shall be determined by the Attorney General with the consent of the Treasury.

[(5) In sub-paragraph (1)(b) above "attends" means attends at the court or elsewhere.]

9 (1) Any power to make regulations under this Schedule shall be exercisable by statutory instrument subject to annulment in pursuance of a resolution of either House of Parliament.

(2) Any such regulations may make different provision with respect to different cases or classes of case.

NOTES
Para 6: sub-para (1) amended by the Criminal Justice Act 1988, s 170(1), Sch 15, paras 112, 116. Para 8: sub-para (1)(b) amended, and sub-para (5) added, by the Criminal Justice Act 1988, s 166(5).

SCHEDULE 2
MINOR AND CONSEQUENTIAL AMENDMENTS

Section 15

. . .

NOTES
This Schedule amends the Administration of Justice (Miscellaneous Provisions) Act 1933, s 2, the Criminal Justice Act 1967, s 11(8), the Criminal Appeal Act 1968, ss 33(1), 36, 38, the Prosecution of Offences (Northern Ireland) Order 1972 (SI 1972 No 538), art 5(3), the Bail Act 1976, s 3, the Supreme Court Act 1981, ss 76, 77(1), 81(1), and the Prosecution of Offences Act 1985, ss 3(2), 16, 18(2).
Paras 7, 8: repealed by the Legal Aid Act 1988, s 45(2), (3), Sch 6.
Repealed in part by the Criminal Justice Act 1988, s 170(2), Sch 16.

Criminal Justice (Scotland) Act 1987

(1987 c 41)

An Act to make provision for Scotland as regards the recovery of the proceeds of drug trafficking; to make further provision as regards criminal justice in Scotland; and for connected purposes

[15 May 1987]

PART II
MISCELLANEOUS

Investigation of serious or complex fraud

51 Lord Advocate's direction

(1) Where it appears to the Lord Advocate –

(a) that a suspected offence may involve serious or complex fraud; and
(b) that, for the purpose of investigating the affairs or any aspect of the affairs of any person, there is good reason to do so,

he may give a direction under this section.

(2) Where a direction is given under this section, sections 52 to 54 of this Act shall apply as regards the investigation of the offence; and any person (other than a constable) nominated by the Lord Advocate either generally or in respect of a particular case (in those sections referred to as "a nominated officer") shall be entitled to exercise the powers and functions conferred by those sections.

(3) A direction under this section shall be signed by the Lord Advocate.

52 Powers of investigation

(1) A nominated officer may by notice in writing require the person whose affairs are to be investigated ("the person under investigation") or any other person who he has reason to believe has relevant information to [answer questions or otherwise furnish information with respect to any matter relevant to the investigation at a specified place and either at a specified time or forthwith].

(2) A nominated officer may by notice in writing require the person under investigation or any other person to produce at [such place as may be specified in the notice and either forthwith or at such time as may be so specified] any specified documents which appear to a nominated officer to relate to any matter relevant to the investigation or any documents of a specified [description] which appear to him so to relate; and –

(a) if any such documents are produced, a nominated officer may –

(i) take copies or extracts from them;
(ii) require the person producing them to provide an explanation of any of them;

(b) if any such documents are not produced, a nominated officer may require the person who was required to produce them to state, to the best of his knowledge and belief, where they are.

(3) Where, on a petition presented by the procurator fiscal, the sheriff is satisfied, in relation to any documents, that there are reasonable grounds for believing –

(a) that –

(i) a person has failed to comply with an obligation under this section to produce them;
(ii) it is not practicable to serve a notice under subsection (2) above in relation to them; or

(iii) the service of such a notice in relation to them might seriously prejudice the investigation; and

(b) that they are on premises specified in the petition,

he may issue such a warrant as is mentioned in subsection (4) below.

(4) The warrant referred to in subsection (3) above is a warrant authorising a constable together with any other persons named in the warrant –

(a) to enter (using such force as is reasonably necessary for the purpose) and search the premises; and

(b) to take possession of any documents appearing to be documents of the description specified in the petition or to take in relation to any documents so appearing any other steps which may appear to be necessary for preserving them and preventing interference with them.

(5) A statement by a person in response to a requirement imposed by virtue of this section may only be used in evidence against him –

[(a)] in a prosecution for an offence under section 2 of the False Oaths (Scotland) Act 1933 [; or

(b) in a prosecution for some other offence where in giving evidence he makes a statement inconsistent with it].

(6) A person shall not under this section be required to disclose any information or produce any document which is an item subject to legal privilege within the meaning of section 40 of this Act; except that a lawyer may be required to furnish the name and address of his client.

(7) No person shall be bound to comply with any requirement imposed by a person exercising power by virtue of a nomination under section 51(2) of this Act unless he has, if required to do so, produced evidence of his authority.

(8) In this section –

"documents" includes information recorded in any form and, in relation to information recorded otherwise than in legible form, references to its production include references to producing a copy of the information in legible form; and

"premises" has the same meaning as in section 40 of this Act.

(9) This section and sections 51 and 53 of this Act shall apply to England and Wales and Northern Ireland; and for the purposes of such application any reference –

(a) to the sheriff shall be construed as a reference to a justice of the peace; and

(b) to a petition presented by the procurator fiscal shall be construed –

(i) in England and Wales as a reference to an information laid by a nominated officer;

(ii) in Northern Ireland as a reference to a complaint laid by a nominated officer.

NOTE
Sub-ss (1), (2), (5): words in square brackets substituted or added by the Criminal Justice Act 1988, s 170(1), Sch 15, para 117.

53 Offences in relation to investigations under section 52

(1) Where any person –

(a) knows or suspects that an investigation under section 52 of this Act is being carried out or is likely to be carried out; and

(b) falsifies, conceals, destroys or otherwise disposes of, or causes or permits the falsification, concealment, destruction or disposal of documents which he knows or suspects or has reasonable grounds to suspect are or would be relevant to such an investigation,

he shall be guilty of an offence.

(2) In proceedings against a person for an offence under subsection (1) above, it shall be a defence to prove –

(a) that he did not know or suspect that by acting as he did he was likely to prejudice the investigation; or
(b) that he had lawful authority or reasonable excuse for acting as he did.

(3) A person guilty of an offence under subsection (1) above shall be liable –

(a) on conviction on indictment, to imprisonment for a term not exceeding seven years or to a fine or to both; and
(b) on summary conviction, to imprisonment for a term not exceeding six months or to a fine not exceeding the statutory maximum or to both. .

(4) Any person who fails to comply with a requirement imposed on him under the said section 52 shall be guilty of an offence and liable on summary conviction to imprisonment for a term not exceeding six months or to a fine not exceeding level 5 on the standard scale or to both.

(5) In proceedings against a person for an offence under subsection (4) above, it shall be a defence to prove that he had a reasonable excuse for acting as he did.

Criminal Justice Act 1988

(1988 c 33)

An Act to make fresh provision for extradition; to amend the rules of evidence in criminal proceedings; to provide for the reference by the Attorney General of certain questions relating to sentencing to the Court of Appeal; to amend the law with regard to the jurisdiction and powers of criminal courts, the collection, enforcement and remission of fines imposed by coroners, juries, supervision orders, the detention of children and young persons, probation and the probation service, criminal appeals, anonymity in cases of rape and similar cases, orders under sections 4 and 11 of the Contempt of Court Act 1981 relating to trials on indictment, orders restricting the access of the public to the whole or any part of a trial on indictment or to any proceedings ancillary to such a trial and orders restricting the publication of any report of the whole or any part of a trial on indictment or any such ancillary proceedings, the alteration of names of petty sessions areas, officers of inner London magistrates' courts and the costs and expenses of prosecution witnesses and certain other persons; to make fresh provision for the payment of compensation by the Criminal Injuries Compensation Board; to make provision for the payment of compensation for a miscarriage of justice which has resulted in a wrongful conviction; to create an offence of torture and an offence of having an article with a blade or point in a public place; to create further offences relating to weapons; to create a summary offence of possession of an indecent photograph of a child; to amend the Police and Criminal Evidence Act 1984 in relation to searches, computer data about fingerprints and bail for persons in customs detention; to make provision in relation to the taking of body samples by the police in Northern Ireland; to amend the Bail Act 1976; to give a justice of the peace power to authorise entry and search of premises for offensive weapons; to provide for the enforcement of the Video Recordings Act 1984 by officers of a weights and measures authority and in Northern Ireland by officers of the Department of Economic Development; to extend to the purchase of easements and other rights over land the power to purchase land conferred on the Secretary of State by section 36 of the Prison Act 1952; and for connected purposes.

[29 July 1988]

PART II
DOCUMENTARY EVIDENCE IN CRIMINAL PROCEEDINGS

23 First-hand hearsay

(1) Subject –

   (a) to subsection (4) below;

   (b) to paragraph 1A of Schedule 2 to the Criminal Appeal Act 1968 (evidence given orally at original trial to be given orally at retrial); and

   (c) to section 69 of the Police and Criminal Evidence Act 1984 (evidence from computer records),

a statement made by a person in a document shall be admissible in criminal proceedings as evidence of any fact of which direct oral evidence by him would be admissible if –

   (i) the requirements of one of the paragraphs of subsection (2) below are satisfied; or

   (ii) the requirements of subsection (3) below are satisfied.

(2) The requirements mentioned in subsection (1)(i) above are –

   (a) that the person who made the statement is dead or by reason of his bodily or mental condition unfit to attend as a witness;

   (b) that –

      (i) the person who made the statement is outside the United Kingdom; and

      (ii) it is not reasonably practicable to secure his attendance; or

   (c) that all reasonable steps have been taken to find the person who made the statement, but that he cannot be found.

(3) The requirements mentioned in subsection (1)(ii) above are –

   (a) that the statement was made to a police officer or some other person charged with the duty of investigating offences or charging offenders; and

   (b) that the person who made it does not give oral evidence through fear or because he is kept out of the way.

(4) Subsection (1) above does not render admissible a confession made by an accused person that would not be admissible under section 76 of the Police and Criminal Evidence Act 1984.

24 Business etc documents

(1) Subject –

   (a) to subsections (3) and (4) below;

   (b) to paragraph 1A of Schedule 2 to the Criminal Appeal Act 1968; and

   (c) to section 69 of the Police and Criminal Evidence Act 1984,

a statement in a document shall be admissible in criminal proceedings as evidence of any fact of which direct oral evidence would be admissible, if the following conditions are satisfied –

   (i) the document was created or received by a person in the course of a trade, business, profession or other occupation, or as the holder of a paid or unpaid office; and

   (ii) the information contained in the document was supplied by a person (whether or not the maker of the statement) who had, or may reasonably be supposed to have had, personal knowledge of the matters dealt with.

(2) Subsection (1) above applies whether the information contained in the document was supplied directly or indirectly but, if it was supplied indirectly, only if each person through whom it was supplied received it –

(a) in the course of a trade, business, profession or other occupation; or
(b) as the holder of a paid or unpaid office.

(3) Subsection (1) above does not render admissible a confession made by an accused person that would not be admissible under section 76 of the Police and Criminal Evidence Act 1984.

(4) A statement prepared otherwise than in accordance with [section 3 of the Criminal Justice (International Co-operation) Act 1990] or an order under paragraph 6 of Schedule 13 to this Act or under section 30 or 31 below for the purposes –

(a) of pending or contemplated criminal proceedings; or
(b) of a criminal investigation,

shall not be admissible by virtue of subsection (1) above unless –

(i) the requirements of one of the paragraphs of subsection (2) of section 23 above are satisfied; or
(ii) the requirements of subsection (3) of that section are satisfied; or
(iii) the person who made the statement cannot reasonably be expected (having regard to the time which has elapsed since he made the statement and to all the circumstances) to have any recollection of the matters dealt with in the statement.

NOTE
Sub-s (4): words in square brackets substituted by the Criminal Justice (International Co-operation) Act 1990, s 31(1), Sch 4, para 6(2).

25 Principles to be followed by court
(1) If, having regard to all the circumstances –

(a) the Crown Court –

(i) on a trial on indictment;
(ii) on an appeal from a magistrates' court; or
(iii) on the hearing of an application under section 6 of the Criminal Justice Act 1987 (applications for dismissal of charges of fraud transferred from magistrates' court to Crown Court); or

(b) the criminal division of the Court of Appeal; or
(c) a magistrates' court on a trial of an information,

is of the opinion that in the interests of justice a statement which is admissible by virtue of section 23 or 24 above nevertheless ought not to be admitted, it may direct that the statement shall not be admitted.

(2) Without prejudice to the generality of subsection (1) above, it shall be the duty of the court to have regard –

(a) to the nature and source of the document containing the statement and to whether or not, having regard to its nature and source and to any other circumstances that appear to the court to be relevant, it is likely that the document is authentic;
(b) to the extent to which the statement appears to supply evidence which would otherwise not be readily available;
(c) to the relevance of the evidence that it appears to supply to any issue which is likely to have to be determined in the proceedings; and
(d) to any risk, having regard in particular to whether it is likely to be possible to controvert the statement if the person making it does not attend to give oral

evidence in the proceedings, that its admission or exclusion will result in unfairness to the accused or, if there is more than one, to any of them.

NOTE
Modified by Sch 13 to this Act.

26 Statements in documents that appear to have been prepared for purposes of criminal proceedings or investigations

Where a statement which is admissible in criminal proceedings by virtue of section 23 or 24 above appears to the court to have been prepared, otherwise than in accordance with [section 3 of the Criminal Justice (International Co-operation) Act 1990] or an order under paragraph 6 of Schedule 13 to this Act or under section 30 or 31 below, for the purposes –

(a) of pending or contemplated criminal proceedings; or
(b) of a criminal investigation,

the statement shall not be given in evidence in any criminal proceedings without the leave of the court, and the court shall not give leave unless it is of the opinion that the statement ought to be admitted in the interests of justice; and in considering whether its admission would be in the interests of justice, it shall be the duty of the court to have regard –

(i) to the contents of the statement;
(ii) to any risk, having regard in particular to whether it is likely to be possible to controvert the statement if the person making it does not attend to give oral evidence in the proceedings, that its admission or exclusion will result in unfairness to the accused or, if there is more than one, to any of them; and
(iii) to any other circumstances that appear to the court to be relevant.

NOTE
Words in square brackets substituted by the Criminal Justice (International Co-operation) Act 1990, s 31(1), Sch 4, para 6(2).

27 Proof of statements contained in documents

Where a statement contained in a document is admissible as evidence in criminal proceedings, it may be proved –

(a) by the production of that document; or
(b) (whether or not that document is still in existence) by the production of a copy of that document, or of the material part of it,

authenticated in such manner as the court may approve; and it is immaterial for the purposes of this subsection how many removes there are between a copy and the original.

28 Documentary evidence – supplementary

(1) Nothing in this Part of this Act shall prejudice –

(a) the admissibility of a statement not made by a person while giving oral evidence in court which is admissible otherwise than by virtue of this Part of this Act; or
(b) any power of a court to exclude at its discretion a statement admissible by virtue of this Part of this Act.

(2) Schedule 2 to this Act shall have effect for the purpose of supplementing this Part of this Act.

PART III
OTHER PROVISIONS ABOUT EVIDENCE IN CRIMINAL PROCEEDINGS

30 Expert reports

(1) An expert report shall be admissible as evidence in criminal proceedings, whether or not the person making it attends to give oral evidence in those proceedings.

(2) If it is proposed that the person making the report shall not give oral evidence, the report shall only be admissible with the leave of the court.

(3) For the purpose of determining whether to give leave the court shall have regard –

(a) to the contents of the report;
(b) to the reasons why it is proposed that the person making the report shall not give oral evidence;
(c) to any risk, having regard in particular to whether it is likely to be possible to controvert statements in the report if the person making it does not attend to give oral evidence in the proceedings, that its admission or exclusion will result in unfairness to the accused or, if there is more than one, to any of them; and
(d) to any other circumstances that appear to the court to be relevant.

(4) An expert report, when admitted, shall be evidence of any fact or opinion of which the person making it could have given oral evidence.

(5) In this section "expert report" means a written report by a person dealing wholly or mainly with matters on which he is (or would if living be) qualified to give expert evidence.

31 Form of evidence and glossaries

For the purpose of helping members of juries to understand complicated issues of fact or technical terms Crown Court Rules may make provision –

(a) as to the furnishing of evidence in any form, notwithstanding the existence of admissible material from which the evidence to be given in that form would be derived; and
(b) as to the furnishing of glossaries for such purposes as may be specified;

in any case where the court gives leave for, or requires, evidence or a glossary to be so furnished.

PART VI
CONFISCATION OF THE PROCEEDS OF AN OFFENCE

71 Confiscation orders

(1) The Crown Court and a magistrates' court shall each have power, in addition to dealing with an offender in any other way, to make an order under this section requiring him to pay such sum as the court thinks fit.

(2) The Crown Court may make such an order against an offender where –

(a) he is found guilty of any offence to which this Part of this Act applies; and
(b) it is satisfied –

(i) that he has benefited from that offence or from that offence taken together with some other offence of which he is convicted in the same proceedings, or which the court takes into consideration in determining his sentence, and which is not a drug trafficking offence; and
(ii) that his benefit is at least the minimum amount.

(3) A magistrates' court may make such an order against an offender where –

(a) he is convicted of an offence listed in Schedule 4 to this Act; and
(b) it is satisfied –

(i) that he has benefited from that offence or from that offence taken together with some other offence listed in that Schedule of which he is convicted in the same proceedings, or which the court takes into consideration in determining his sentence; and
(ii) that his benefit is at least the minimum amount.

(4) For the purposes of this Part of this Act a person benefits from an offence if he obtains property as a result of or in connection with its commission and his benefit is the value of the property so obtained.

(5) Where a person derives a pecuniary advantage as a result of or in connection with the commission of an offence, he is to be treated for the purposes of this Part of this Act as if he had obtained as a result of or in connection with the commission of the offence a sum of money equal to the value of the pecniary advantage.

(6) The sum which an order made by a court under this section requires an offender to pay must be at least the minimum amount, but must not exceed –

(a) the benefit in respect of which it is made; or
(b) the amount appearing to the court to be the amount that might be realised at the time the order is made,

whichever is the less.

(7) For the purposes of this Part of this Act the minimum amount is 10,000 or such other amount as the Secretary of State may specify by order made by statutory instrument.

(8) A statutory instrument containing an order made by the Secretary of State under this section shall be subject to annulment in pursuance of a resolution of either House of Parliament.

(9) In this Part of this Act –

(a) an order made by a court under this section is referred to as a "confiscation order";
(b) "drug trafficking offence" has the same meaning as in the Drug Trafficking Offences Act 1986;
(c) references to an offence to which this Part of this Act applies are references to any offence which –

 (i) is listed in Schedule 4 to this Act; or
 (ii) if not so listed, is an indictable offence, other than a drug trafficking offence [or an offence under Part III of the Prevention of Terrorism (Temporary Provisions) Act 1989]; and

(d) a person against whom proceedings have been instituted for an offence to which this Part of this Act applies is referred to (whether or not he has been convicted) as "the defendant".

NOTE
Sub-s (9): words in square brackets inserted by the Prevention of Terrorism (Temporary Provisions) Act 1989, s 25(1), Sch 8, para 10(1), (2).

72 Making of confiscation orders

(1) A court shall not make a confiscation order unless the prosecutor has given written notice to the court to the effect that it appears to him that, were the court to consider that it ought to make such an order, it would be able to make an order requiring the offender to pay at least the minimum amount.

(2) If the prosecutor gives the court such a notice, the court shall determine whether it ought to make a confiscation order.

(3) When considering whether to make a confiscation order the court may take into account any information that has been placed before it showing that a victim of an offence to which the proceedings relate has instituted, or intends to institute, civil proceedings against the defendant in respect of loss, injury or damage sustained in connection with the offence.

(4) If the court determines that it ought to make such an order, the court shall, before sentencing or otherwise dealing with the offender in respect of the offence or, as the case

may be, any of the offences concerned, determine the amount to be recovered in his case by virtue of this section and make a confiscation order for that amount specifying the offence or offences.

(5) Where a court makes a confiscation order against a defendant in any proceedings, it shall be its duty, in respect of any offence of which he is convicted in those proceedings, to take account of the order before –

(a) imposing any fine on him;
(b) making any order involving any payment by him, other than an order under section 35 of the Powers of Criminal Courts Act 1973 (compensation orders); or
(c) making any order under –

    (i) section 27 of the Misuse of Drugs Act 1971 (forfeiture orders); or
    (ii) section 43 of the Powers of Criminal Courts Act 1973 (deprivation orders),

but subject to that shall leave the order out of account in determining the appropriate sentence or other manner of dealing with him.

(6) No enactment restricting the power of a court dealing with an offender in a particular way from dealing with him also in any other way shall by reason only of the making of a confiscation order restrict the court from dealing with an offender in any way it considers appropriate in respect of an offence to which this Part of this Act applies.

(7) Where –

(a) a court makes both a confiscation order and an order for the payment of compensation under section 35 of the Powers of Criminal Courts Act 1973 against the same person in the same proceedings; and
(b) it appears to the court that he will not have sufficient means to satisfy both the orders in full,

it shall direct that so much of the compensation as will not in its opinion be recoverable because of the insufficiency of his means shall be paid out of any sums recovered under the confiscation order.

73 Statements, etc relevant to making confiscation orders

(1) Where –

(a) a defendant has been convicted of an offence to which this Part of this Act applies and the prosecutor tenders to the court a statement as to any matters relevant –

    (i) to determining whether the defendant has benefited from the offence or from any other offence to which this Part of this Act applies of which he is convicted in the same proceedings or which is taken into consideration in determining his sentence; or
    (ii) to an assessment of the value of the defendant's benefit from the offence or any other offence to which this Part of this Act applies of which he is so convicted or which is so taken into consideration; and

(b) the defendant accepts to any extent any allegation in the statement;

the court may, for the purposes of so determining or making such an assessment, treat his acceptance as conclusive of the matters to which it relates.

(2) Where –

(a) a statement is tendered under subsection (1)(a) above, and
(b) the court is satisfied that a copy of that statement has been served on the defendant,

the court may require the defendant to indicate to what extent he accepts each allegation in the statement and, so far as he does not accept any such allegation, to indicate any matters he proposes to rely on.

(3) If the defendant fails in any respect to comply with a requirement under subsection (2) above, he may be treated for the purposes of this section as accepting every allegation in the statement apart from –

(a) any allegation in respect of which he has complied with the requirement; and
(b) any allegation that he has benefited from an offence or that any property was obtained by him as a result of or in connection with the commission of an offence.

(4) Where –

(a) there is tendered to the court by the defendant a statement as to any matters relevant to determining the amount that might be realised at the time the confiscation order is made; and
(b) the prosecutor accepts to any extent any allegation in the statement;

the court may, for the purposes of that determination, treat the acceptance by the prosecutor as conclusive of the matters to which it relates.

(5) An allegation may be accepted or a matter indicated for the purposes of this section either –

(a) orally before the court; or
(b) in writing in accordance with rules of court.

(6) If the court is satisfied as to any matter relevant for determining the amount that might be realised at the time the confiscation order is made (whether by an acceptance under this section or otherwise), the court may issue a certificate giving the court's opinion as to the matters concerned and shall do so if satisfied that the amount that might be realised at the time the confiscation order is made is less than the amount the court assesses to be the value of the defendant's benefit from the offence or, if more than one, all the offences in respect of which the order may be made.

74 Definition of principal terms used
(1) In this Part of this Act, "realisable property" means, subject to subsection (2) below –

(a) any property held by the defendant; and
(b) any property held by a person to whom the defendant has directly or indirectly made a gift caught by this Part of this Act.

(2) Property is not realisable property if –

(a) an order under section 43 of the Powers of Criminal Courts Act 1973 (deprivation orders);
(b) an order under section 27 of the Misuse of Drugs Act 1971 (forfeiture orders); . . .
(c) an order under section 223 or 436 of the Criminal Procedure (Scotland) Act 1975 (forfeiture of property) [or
(d) an order under section 13(2), (3) or (4) of the Prevention of Terrorism (Temporary Provisions) Act 1989 (forfeiture orders),]

is in force in respect of the property.

(3) For the purposes of this Part of this Act the amount that might be realised at the time a confiscation order is made is –

(a) the total of the values at that time of all the realisable property held by the defendant, less
(b) where there are obligations having priority at that time, the total amounts payable in pursuance of such obligations,

together with the total of the values at that time of all gifts caught by this Part of this Act.

(4) Subject to the following provisions of this section, for the purposes of this Part of this Act the value of property (other than cash) in relation to any person holding the property –

(a) where any other person holds an interest in the property, is –

    (i) the market value of the first-mentioned person's beneficial interest in the property, less

    (ii) the amount required to discharge any incumbrance (other than a charging order) on that interest; and

(b) in any other case, is its market value.

(5) References in this Part of this Act to the value at any time (referred to in subsection (6) below as "the material time") of any property obtained by a person as a result of or in connection with the commission of an offence are references to –

(a) the value of the property to him when he obtained it adjusted to take account of subsequent changes in the value of money; or

(b) where subsection (6) below applies, the value there mentioned,

whichever is the greater.

(6) If at the material time he holds –

(a) the property which he obtained (not being cash); or

(b) property which, in whole or in part, directly or indirectly represents in his hands the property which he obtained,

the value referred to in subsection (5)(b) above is the value to him at the material time of the property mentioned in paragraph (a) above or, as the case may be, of the property mentioned in paragraph (b) above, so far as it so represents the property which he obtained, but disregarding any charging order.

(7) Subject to subsection (12) below, references in this Part of this Act to the value at any time (referred to in subsection (8) below as "the material time") of a gift caught by this Part of this Act are references to –

(a) the value of the gift to the recipient when he received it adjusted to take account of subsequent changes in the value of money; or

(b) where subsection (8) below applies, the value there mentioned,

whichever is the greater.

(8) Subject to subsection (12) below, if at the material time he holds –

(a) the property which he received (not being cash); or

(b) property which, in whole or in part, directly or indirectly represents in his hands the property which he received;

the value referred to in subsection (7) above is the value to him at the material time of the property mentioned in paragraph (a) above or, as the case may be, of the property mentioned in paragraph (b) above so far as it so represents the property which he received, but disregarding any charging order.

(9) For the purposes of subsection (3) above, an obligation has priority at any time if it is an obligation of the defendant to –

(a) pay an amount due in respect of a fine, or other order of a court, imposed or made on conviction of an offence, where the fine was imposed or order made before the confiscation order; or

(b) pay any sum which would be included among the preferential debts (within the meaning given by section 386 of the Insolvency Act 1986) in the defendant's bankruptcy commencing on the date of the confiscation order or winding up under an order of the court made on that date.

(10) A gift (including a gift made before the commencement of this Part of this Act) is caught by this Part of this Act if –

(a) it was made by the defendant at any time after the commission of the offence or, if more than one, the earliest of the offences to which the proceedings for the time being relate; and

(b) the court considers it appropriate in all the circumstances to take the gift into account.

(11) The reference in subsection (10) above to an offence to which the proceedings for the time being relate includes, where the proceedings have resulted in the conviction of the defendant, a reference to any offence which the court takes into consideration when determining his sentence.

(12) For the purposes of this Part of this Act –

(a) the circumstances in which the defendant is to be treated as making a gift include those where he transfers property to another person directly or indirectly for a consideration the value of which is significantly less than the value of the consideration provided by the defendant; and

(b) in those circumstances, the preceding provisions of this section shall apply as if the defendant had made a gift of such share in the property as bears to the whole property the same proportion as the difference between the values referred to in paragraph (a) above bears to the value of the consideration provided by the defendant.

NOTE
Sub-s (2): word omitted repealed, and sub-para (d) added by the Prevention of Terrorism (Temporary Provisions) Act 1989, s 25(1), Sch 8, para 10(1), (3).

Enforcement, etc of confiscation orders

75 Application of procedure for enforcing fines
(1) Where the Crown Court orders the defendant to pay an amount under this Part of this Act, sections 31(1) to (3C) and 32(1) and (2) of the Powers of Criminal Courts Act 1973 (powers of Crown Court in relation to fines and enforcement of Crown Court fines) shall have effect as if that amount were a fine imposed on him by the Crown Court.

(2) Where a magistrates' court orders the defendant to pay an amount under this Part of this Act, that amount shall be treated as a fine for the purposes of section 31(3) of the Magistrates' Courts Act 1980 (general limit on the power of a magistrates' court to impose imprisonment not to apply in the case of imprisonment in default).

(3) Where –

(a) a warrant of commitment is issued for a default in payment of an amount ordered to be paid under this Part of this Act in respect of an offence; and

(b) at the time the warrant is issued, the defendant is liable to serve a term of custody in respect of the offence;

the term of imprisonment or of detention under section 9 of the Criminal Justice Act 1982 (detention of persons aged 17 to 20 for default) to be served in default of payment of the amount shall not begin to run until after the term mentioned in paragraph (b) above.

(4) The reference in subsection (3) above to the term of custody which the defendant is liable to serve in respect of the offence is a reference to the term of imprisonment or detention in a young offender institution which he is liable to serve in respect of the offence; and for the purposes of this subsection –

(a) consecutive terms and terms which are wholly or partly concurrent shall be treated as a single term; and

(b) there shall be disregarded –

    (i) any sentence suspended under section 22(1) of the Powers of Criminal Courts Act 1973 which has not taken effect at the time the warrant is issued;

    (ii) in the case of a sentence of imprisonment passed with an order under section 47(1) of the Criminal Law Act 1977, any part of the sentence which the defendant has not at that time been required to serve in prison; and

    (iii) any term of imprisonment or detention fixed under section 31(2) of the Powers of Criminal Courts Act 1973 for which a warrant of commitment has not been issued at that time.

(5) In the application of Part III of the Magistrates' Courts Act 1980 to amounts payable under confiscation orders –

(a) such an amount is not a sum adjudged to be paid by a conviction for the purposes of section 81 (enforcement of fines imposed on young offenders) or a fine for the purposes of section 85 (remission of fines); and

(b) in section 87 (enforcement by High Court or county court), subsection (3) shall be omitted.

(6) This section applies in relation to confiscation orders made by the criminal division of the Court of Appeal, or by the House of Lords on appeal from that division, as it applies in relation to confiscation orders made by the Crown Court, and the reference in subsection (1) above to the Crown Court shall be construed accordingly.

76 Cases in which restraint orders and charging orders may be made

(1) The powers conferred on the High Court by sections 77(1) and 78(1) below are exercisable where –

(a) proceedings have been instituted in England and Wales against the defendant for an offence to which this Part of this Act applies;

(b) the proceedings have not been concluded; and

(c) either a confiscation order has been made or it appears to the court that there are reasonable grounds for thinking that a confiscation order may be made in them.

(2) Those powers are also exercisable where –

(a) the court is satisfied that, whether by the laying of an information or otherwise, a person is to be charged with an offence to which this Part of this Act applies; and

(b) it appears to the court that a confiscation order may be made in proceedings for the offence.

(3) For the purposes of sections 77, 78 and 92 below at any time when those powers are exercisable before proceedings have been instituted –

(a) references in this Part of this Act to the defendant shall be construed as references to the person referred to in subsection (2)(a) above;

(b) references in this Part of this Act to the prosecutor shall be construed as references to the person who the High Court is satisfied is to have the conduct of the proposed proceedings; and

(c) references in this Part of this Act to realisable property shall be construed as if, immediately before that time, proceedings had been instituted against the person referred to in subsection (2)(a) above for an offence to which this Part of this Act applies.

(4) Where the court has made an order under section 77(1) or 78(1) below by virtue of subsection (2) above, the court shall discharge the order if proceedings in respect of the offence are not instituted (whether by the laying of an information or otherwise) within such time as the court considers reasonable.

77 Restraint orders

(1) The High Court may by order (referred to in this Part of this Act as a "restraint order") prohibit any person from dealing with any realisable property, subject to such conditions and exceptions as may be specified in the order.

(2) Without prejudice to the generality of subsection (1) above, a restraint order may make such provision as the court thinks fit for living expenses and legal expenses.

(3) A restraint order may apply –

(a) to all realisable property held by a specified person, whether the property is described in the order or not; and
(b) to realisable property held by a specified person, being property transferred to him after the making of the order.

(4) This section shall not have effect in relation to any property for the time being subject to a charge under section 78 below.

(5) A restraint order –

(a) may be made only on an application by the prosecutor;
(b) may be made on an ex parte application to a judge in chambers; and
(c) shall provide for notice to be given to persons affected by the order.

(6) A restraint order –

(a) may be discharged or varied in relation to any property; and
(b) shall be discharged when proceedings for the offence are concluded.

(7) An application for the discharge or variation of a restraint order may be made by any person affected by it.

(8) Where the High Curt has made a restraint order, the court may at any time appoint a receiver –

(a) to take possession of any realisable property, and
(b) in accordance with the court's directions, to manage or otherwise deal with any property in respect of which he is appointed,

subject to such exceptions and conditions as may be specified by the court; and may require any person having possession of property in respect of which a receiver is appointed under this section to give possession of it to the receiver.

(9) For the purposes of this section, dealing with property held by any person includes (without prejudice to the generality of the expression) –

(a) where a debt is owed to that person, making a payment to any person in reduction of the amount of the debt; and
(b) removing the property from Great Britain.

(10) Where the High Court has made a restraint order, a constable may for the purpose of preventing any realisable property being removed from Great Britain, seize the property.

(11) Property seized under subsection (10) above shall be dealt with in accordance with the court's directions.

(12) The Land Charges Act 1972 and the Land Registration Act 1925 shall apply –

(a) in relation to restraint orders, as they apply in relation to orders affecting land made by the court for the purpose of enforcing judgments or recognisances; and
(b) in relation to applications for restraint orders, as they apply in relation to other pending land actions.

(13) The prosecutor shall be treated for the purposes of section 57 of the Land Registration Act 1925 (inhibitions) as a person interested in relation to any registered

land to which a restraint order or an application for such an order relates.

78 Charging orders in respect of land, securities, etc

(1) The High Court may make a charging order on realisable property for securing the payment to the Crown –

(a) where a confiscation order has not been made, of an amount equal to the value from time to time of the property charged; and

(b) in any other case, of an amount not exceeding the amount payable under the confiscation order.

(2) For the purposes of this Part of this Act, a charging order is an order made under this section imposing on any such realisable property as may be specified in the order a charge for securing the payment of money to the Crown.

(3) A charging order –

(a) may be made only on an application by the prosecutor;

(b) may be made on an ex parte application to a judge in chambers;

(c) shall provide for notice to be given to persons affected by the order; and

(d) may be made subject to such conditions as the court thinks fit and, without prejudice to the generality of this paragraph, such conditions as it thinks fit as to the time when the charge is to become effective.

(4) Subject to subsection (6) below, a charge may be imposed by a charging order only on –

(a) any interest in realisable property, being an interest held beneficially by the defendant or by a person to whom the defendant has directly or indirectly made a gift caught by this Part of this Act –

(i) in any asset of a kind mentioned in subsection (5) below; or

(ii) under any trust; or

(b) any interest in realisable property held by a person as trustee of a trust if the interest is in such an asset or is an interest under another trust and a charge may by virtue of paragraph (a) above be imposed by a charging order on the whole beneficial interest under the first-mentioned trust.

(5) The assets referred to in subsection (4) above are –

(a) land in England and Wales; or

(b) securities of any of the following kinds –

(i) government stock;

(ii) stock of any body (other than a building society) incorporated within England and Wales;

(iii) stock of any body incorporated outside England and Wales or of any country or territory outside the United Kingdom, being stock registered in a register kept at any place within England and Wales;

(iv) units of any unit trust in respect of which a register of the unit holders is kept at any place within England and Wales.

(6) In any case where a charge is imposed by a charging order on any interest in an asset of a kind mentioned in subsection (5)(b) above, the court may provide for the charge to extend to any interest or dividend payable in respect of the asset.

(7) The court may make an order discharging or varying the charging order and shall make an order discharging the charging order if the proceedings for the offence are concluded or the amount payment of which is secured by the charge is paid into court.

(8) An application for the discharge or variation of a charging order may be made by any person affected by it.

79 Charging orders: supplementary provisions

(1) The Land Charges Act 1972 and the Land Registration Act 1925 shall apply in relation to charging orders as they apply in relation to orders or writs issued or made for the purpose of enforcing judgments.

(2) Where a charging order has been registered under section 6 of the Land Charges Act 1972, subsection (4) of that section (effect of non-registration of writs and orders registrable under that section) shall not apply to an order appointing a receiver made in pursuance of the charging order.

(3) Subject to any provision made under section 80 below or by rules of court, a charge imposed by a charging order shall have the like effect and shall be enforceable in the same courts and in the same manner as an equitable charge created by the person holding the beneficial interest or, as the case may be, the trustees by writing under their hand.

(4) Where a charging order has been protected by an entry registered under the Land Charges Act 1972 or the Land Registration Act 1925, an order under section 78(7) above discharging the charging order may direct that the entry be cancelled.

(5) The Secretary of State may by order made by statutory instrument subject to annulment in pursuance of a resolution of either House of Parliament amend section 78 above by adding to or removing from the kinds of asset for the time being referred to there any asset of a kind which in his opinion ought to be so added or removed.

(6) In this section and section 78 above, "building society", "dividend", "government stock", "stock" and "unit trust" have the same meanings as in the Charging Orders Act 1979.

80 Realisation of property

(1) Where –

(a) a confiscation order is made;
(b) the order is not subject to appeal; and
(c) the proceedings in which it was made have not been concluded,

the High Court may, on an application by the prosecutor, exercise the powers conferred by subsections (2) to (6) below.

(2) The court may appoint a receiver in respect of realisable property.

(3) The court may empower a receiver appointed under subsection (2) above, under section 77 above or in pursuance of a charging order –

(a) to enforce any charge imposed under section 78 above on realisable property or on interest or dividends payable in respect of such property; and
(b) in relation to any realisable property other than property for the time being subject to a charge under section 78 above, to take possession of the property subject to such conditions or exceptions as may be specified by the court.

(4) The court may order any person having possession of realisable property to give possession of it to any such receiver.

(5) The court may empower any such receiver to realise any realisable property in such manner as the court may direct.

(6) The court may order any person holding an interest in realisable property to make such payment to the receiver in respect of any beneficial interest held by the defendant or, as the case may be, the recipient of a gift caught by this Part of this Act as the court may direct and the court may, on the payment being made, by order transfer, grant or extinguish any interest in the property.

(7) Subsections (4) to (6) above do not apply to property for the time being subject to a charge under section 78 above.

(8) The court shall not in respect of any property exercise the powers conferred by subsections (3)(a), (5) or (6) above unless a reasonable opportunity has been given for persons holding any interest in the property to make representations to the court.

81 Application of proceeds of realisation and other sums
(1) Subject to subsection (2) below, the following sums in the hands of a receiver appointed under this Part of this Act or in pursuance of a charging order, that is –

  (a) the proceeds of the enforcement of any charge imposed under section 78 above;
  (b) the proceeds of the realisation, other than by the enforcement of such a charge, of any property under section 77 or 80 above; and
  (c) any other sums, being property held by the defendant;

shall first be applied in payment of such expenses incurred by a person acting as an insolvency practitioner as are payable under section 87(2) below and then shall, after such payments (if any) as the High Court may direct have been made out of those sums, be applied on the defendant's behalf towards the satisfaction of the confiscation order.

(2) If, after the amount payable under the confiscation order has been fully paid, any such sums remain in the hands of such a receiver, the receiver shall distribute them –

  (a) among such of those who held property which has been realised under this Part of this Act, and
  (b) in such proportions,

as the High Court may direct after giving a reasonable opportunity for such persons to make representations to the court.

(3) The receipt of any sum by a justices' clerk on account of an amount payable under a confiscation order shall reduce the amount so payable, but the justices' clerk shall apply the money received for the purposes specified in this section and in the order so specified.

(4) The justices' clerk shall first pay any expenses incurred by a person acting as an insolvency practitioner and payable under section 87(2) below but not already paid under subsection (1) above.

(5) If the money was paid to the justices' clerk by a receiver appointed under this Part of this Act or in pursuance of a charging order, the justices' clerk shall next pay the receiver's remuneration and expenses.

(6) After making –

  (a) any payment required by subsection (4) above; and
  (b) in a case to which subsection (5) above applies, any payment required by that subsection,

the justices' clerk shall reimburse any amount paid under section 88(2) below.

(7) The justices' clerk shall finally pay any compensation directed to be paid out of any sums recovered under the confiscation order under section 72(7) above.

(8) Any balance in the hands of the justices' clerk after he has made all payments required by the foregoing provisions of this section shall be treated for the purposes of section 61 of the Justices of the Peace Act 1979 (application of fines, etc.) as if it were a fine imposed by a magistrates' court.

(9) Where under subsection (3) above a sum falls to be applied in payment both of compensation and of other outgoings –

  (a) the person entitled to the compensation shall be liable to pay to the Secretary of State such an amount as bears to the remuneration or expenses the same proportion as the amount payable in accordance with the direction under section 72(7) above bears to the total amount payable under the confiscation order;
  (b) the justices' clerk shall deduct from the amount falling to be applied in payment

of the compensation an amount equal to the amount of any liability arising by virtue of paragraph (a) above;

(c) notwithstanding the deduction under paragraph (b) above, the person entitled to the compensation shall be treated as having received the whole amount which falls to be applied in payment of it; and

(d) the amount deducted shall be treated for the purposes of section 61 of the Justices of the Peace Act 1979 as if it were a fine imposed by a magistrates' court.

(10) In this section, "justices' clerk" has the same meaning as in the Justices of the Peace Act 1979.

82 Exercise of powers by High Court or receiver

(1) This section applies to the powers conferred on the High Court by sections 77 to 81 above or on the Court of Session by sections 90 to 92 below, or on a receiver appointed under this Part of this Act or in pursuance of a charging order.

(2) Subject to the following provisions of this section, the powers shall be exercised with a view to making available for satisfying the confiscation order or, as the case may be, any confiscation order that may be made in the defendant's case the value for the time being of realisable property held by any person by the realisation of such property.

(3) In the case of realisable property held by a person to whom the defendant has directly or indirectly made a gift caught by this Part of this Act the powers shall be exercised with a view to realising no more than the value for the time being of the gift.

(4) The powers shall be exercised with a view to allowing any person other than the defendant or the recipient of any such gift to retain or recover the value of any property held by him.

(5) An order may be made or other action taken in respect of a debt owed by the Crown.

(6) In exercising those powers, no account shall be taken of any obligations of the defendant or of the recipient of any such gift which conflict with the obligation to satisfy the confiscation order.

83 Variation of confiscation orders

(1) If, on an application by the defendant in respect of a confiscation order, the High Court is satisfied that the realisable property is inadequate for the payment of any amount remaining to be recovered under the order the court shall issue a certificate to that effect, giving the court's reasons.

(2) For the purposes of subsection (1) above –

(a) in the case of realisable property held by a person who has been adjudged bankrupt or whose estate has been sequestrated the court shall take into account the extent to which any property held by him may be distributed among creditors; and

(b) the court may disregard any inadequacy in the realisable property which appears to the court to be attributable wholly or partly to anything done by the defendant for the purpose of preserving any property held by a person to whom the defendant had directly or indirectly made a gift caught by this Part of this Act from any risk of realisation under this Part of this Act.

(3) Where a certificate has been issued under subsection (1) above, the defendant may apply –

(a) where the confiscation order was made by the Crown Court, to that court; and

(b) where the confiscation order was made by a magistrates' court, to a magistrates' court for the same area, for the amount to be recovered under the order to be reduced.

(4) The Crown Court shall, on an application under subsection (3) above –

(a) substitute for the amount to be recovered under the order such lesser amount as the court thinks just in all the circumstances of the case; and
(b) substitute for the term of imprisonment or of detention fixed under subsection (2) of section 31 of the Powers of Criminal Courts Act 1973 in respect of the amount to be recovered under the order a shorter term determined in accordance with that section in respect of the lesser amount.

(5) A magistrates' court shall, on an application under subsection (3) above, substitute for the amount to be recovered under the order such lesser amount as the court thinks just in all the circumstances of the case.

84 Bankruptcy of defendant etc

(1) Where a person who holds realisable property is adjudged bankrupt –

(a) property for the time being subject to a restraint order made before the order adjudging him bankrupt, and
(b) any proceeds of property realised by virtue of section 77(8) or 80(5) or (6) above for the time being in the hands of a receiver appointed under section 77 or 80 above,

is excluded from the bankrupt's estate for the purposes of Part IX of the Insolvency Act 1986.

(2) Where a person has been adjudged bankrupt, the powers conferred on the High Court by sections 77 to 81 above or on a receiver so appointed or on the Court of Session by sections 90 to 92 below shall not be exercised in relation to –

(a) property for the time being comprised in the bankrupt's estate for the purposes of that Part of that Act;
(b) property in respect of which his trustee in bankruptcy may (without leave of court) serve a notice under section 307 [308 or 308A] of that Act (after-acquired property and tools, clothes, etc. exceeding value of reasonable replacement [and certain tenancies]); and
(c) property which is to be applied for the benefit of creditors of the bankrupt by virtue of a condition imposed under section 280(2)(c) of that Act.

(3) Nothing in that Act shall be taken as restricting, or enabling the restriction of, the exercise of those powers.

(4) Subsection (2) above does not affect the enforcement of a charging order –

(a) made before the order adjudging the person bankrupt; or
(b) on property which was subject to a restraint order when the order adjudging him bankrupt was made.

(5) Where, in the case of a debtor, an interim receiver stands appointed under section 286 of that Act and any property of the debtor is subject to a restraint order, the powers conferred on the receiver by virtue of that Act do not apply to property for the time being subject to the restraint order.

(6) Where a person is adjudged bankrupt and has directly or indirectly made a gift caught by this Part of this Act –

(a) no order shall be made under section 339 or 423 of that Act (avoidance of certain transactions) in respect of the making of the gift at any time when proceedings for an offence to which this Part of this Act applies have been instituted against him and have not been concluded or when property of the person to whom the gift was made is subject to a restraint order or charging order; and
(b) any order made under either of those sections after the conclusion of the

proceedings shall take into account any realisation under this Part of this Act of property held by the person to whom the gift was made.

(7) In any case in which a petition in bankruptcy was presented, or a receiving order or adjudication in bankruptcy was made, before 29th December 1986 (the date on which the Insolvency Act 1986 came into force), this section shall have effect with the following modifications –

(a) for references to the bankrupt's estate for the purposes of Part IX of that Act there shall be substituted references to the property of the bankrupt for the purposes of the Bankruptcy Act 1914;
(b) for references to the Act of 1986 and sections 280(2)(c), 286, 339 and 423 of that Act there shall be respectively substituted references to the Act of 1914 and to sections 26(2), 8, 27 and 42 of that Act;
(c) the references in subsection (5) to an interim receiver appointed as there mentioned include, where a receiving order has been made, a reference to the receiver constituted by virtue of section 7 of the Act of 1914; and
(d) subsection (2)(b) shall be omitted.

NOTE
Sub-s (2): words in square brackets substituted or inserted by the Housing Act 1988, s 140(1), Sch 17, Pt I, para 83.

85 Sequestration in Scotland of defendant etc
(1) Where the estate of a person who holds realisable property is sequestrated –

(a) property for the time being subject to a restraint order made before the award of sequestration, and
(b) any proceeds of property realised by virtue of section 77(8) or 80(5) or (6) above for the time being in the hands of a receiver appointed under section 77 or 80 above,

is excluded from the debtor's estate for the purposes of the Bankruptcy (Scotland) Act 1985.

(2) Where an award of sequestration has been made, the powers conferred on the High Court by sections 77 to 81 above or on a receiver so appointed or on the Court of Session by sections 90 to 92 below shall not be exercised in relation to –

(a) property comprised in the whole estate of the debtor within the meaning of section 31(8) of that Act, and
(b) any income of the debtor which has been ordered, under subsection (2) of section 32 of that Act, to be paid to the permanent trustee or any estate which, [under subsection (10) of section 31 of that Act or subsection (6) of the said section 32 of that Act], vests in the permanent trustee

and it shall not be competent to submit a claim in relation to the confiscation order to the permanent trustee in accordance with section 48 of that Act.

(3) Nothing in that Act shall be taken as restricting, or enabling the restriction of, the exercise of those powers.

(4) Subsection (2) above does not affect the enforcement of a charging order –

(a) made before the award of sequestration; or
(b) on property which was subject to a restraint order when the award of sequestration was made.

(5) Where, during the period before sequestration is awarded, an interim trustee stands appointed under the proviso to section 13(1) of that Act and any property in the debtor's estate is subject to a restraint order, the powers conferred on the trustee by virtue of that Act do not apply to property for the time being subject to the restraint order.

(6) Where the estate of a person is sequestrated and he has directly or indirectly made a gift caught by this Part of this Act –

(a) no decree shall be granted under section 34 or 36 of that Act (gratuitous alienations and unfair preferences) in respect of the making of the gift at any time when proceedings for an offence to which this Part of this Act applies have been instituted against him and have not been concluded or when property of the person to whom the gift was made is subject to a restraint order or charging order, and

(b) any decree made under either of those sections after the conclusion of the proceedings shall take into account any realisation under this Act of property held by the person to whom the gift was made.

(7) In any case in which, notwithstanding the coming into force of the Bankruptcy (Scotland) Act 1985, the Bankruptcy (Scotland) Act 1913 applies to a sequestration, subsection (2) above shall have effect as if for paragraphs (a) and (b) thereof there were substituted the following paragraphs –

"(a) property comprised in the whole property of the debtor which vests in the trustee under section 97 of the Bankruptcy (Scotland) Act 1913,

(b) any income of the bankrupt which has been ordered under subsection (2) of section 98 of that Act to be paid to the trustee of any estate which, under subsection (1) of that section, vests in the trustee,";

and subsection (3) above shall have effect as if for the reference therein to the Act of 1985 there were substituted a reference to the Act of 1913.

NOTE
Sub-s (2): words in square brackets substituted by the Housing Act 1988, s 140(1), Sch 17, Pt I, para 84.

86 Winding up of company holding realisable property

(1) Where realisable property is held by a company and an order for the winding up of the company has been made or a resolution has been passed by the company for the voluntary winding up, the functions of the liquidator (or any provisional liquidator) shall not be exercisable in relation to –

(a) property for the time being subject to a restraint order made before the relevant time, and

(b) any proceeds of property realised by virtue of section 77(8) or 80(5) or (6) above for the time being in the hands of a receiver appointed under section 77 or 80 above.

(2) Where, in the case of a company, such an order has been made or such a resolution has been passed, the powers conferred on the High Court by sections 77 to 80 above or on a receiver so appointed or on the Court of Session by sections 90 to 92 below shall not be exercised in relation to any realisable property held by the company in relation to which the functions of the liquidator are exercisable –

(a) so as to inhibit him from exercising those functions for the purpose of distributing any property held by the company to the company's creditors; or

(b) so as to prevent the payment out of any property of expenses (including the remuneration of the liquidator or any provisional liquidator) properly incurred in the winding up in respect of the property.

(3) Nothing in the Insolvency Act 1986 shall be taken as restricting, or enabling the restriction of, the exercise of those powers.

(4) Subsection (2) above does not affect the enforcement of a charging order made before the relevant time or on property which was subject to a restraint order at the relevant time.

(5) For the purposes of the application of Parts IV and V of the Insolvency Act 1986 (winding up of registered companies and winding up of unregistered companies) to a company which the Court of Session has jurisdiction to wind up, a person is not a creditor in so far as any sum due to him by the company is due in respect of a confiscation order.

(6) In this section –

"company" means any company which may be wound up under the Insolvency Act 1986; and

"the relevant time" means –

(a) where no order for the winding up of the company has been made, the time of the passing of the resolution for voluntary winding up;

(b) where such an order has been made and, before the presentation of the petition for the winding up of the company by the court, such a resolution had been passed by the company, the time of the passing of the resolution; and

(c) in any other case where such an order has been made, the time of the making of the order.

(7) In any case in which a winding up of a company commenced or is treated as having commenced before 29th December 1986, this section shall have effect with the substitution for references to the Insolvency Act 1986 of references to the Companies Act 1985.

87 Insolvency officers dealing with property subject to restraint order
(1) Without prejudice to the generality of any enactment contained in the Insolvency Act 1986 or in any other Act, where –

(a) any person acting as an insolvency practitioner seizes or disposes of any property in relation to which his functions are not exercisable because it is for the time being subject to a restraint order; and

(b) at the time of the seizure or disposal he believes, and has reasonable grounds for believing, that he is entitled (whether in pursuance of an order of the court or otherwise) to seize or dispose of that property,

he shall not be liable to any person in respect of any loss or damage resulting from the seizure or disposal except in so far as the loss or damage is caused by his negligence in so acting; and a person so acting shall have a lien on the property, or the proceeds of its sale, for such of his expenses as were incurred in connection with the liquidation, bankruptcy or other proceedings in relation to which the seizure or disposal purported to take place and for so much of his remuneration as may reasonably be assigned for his acting in connection with those proceedings.

(2) Any person who, acting as an insolvency practitioner, incurs expenses –

(a) in respect of such property as is mentioned in paragraph (a) of subsection (1) above and in so doing does not know and has no reasonable grounds to believe that the property is for the time being subject to a restraint order; or

(b) other than in respect of such property as is so mentioned, being expenses which, but for the effect of a restraint order, might have been met by taking possession of and realising the property,

shall be entitled (whether or not he has seized or disposed of that property so as to have a lien under that subsection) to payment of those expenses under section 81(1) or (4) above.

(3) In this Part of this Act the expression "acting as an insolvency practitioner" shall be construed in accordance with section 388 (interpretation) of the said Act of 1986 except that for the purposes of such construction the reference in subsection (2)(a) of that section to a permanent or interim trustee in a sequestration shall be taken to include

a reference to a trustee in sequestration and subsection (5) of that section (which provides that nothing in the section is to apply to anything done by the official receiver) shall be disregarded; and the expression shall also comprehend the official receiver acting as receiver or manager of the property.

88 Receivers: supplementary provisions

(1) Where a receiver appointed under this Part of this Act or in pursuance of a charging order takes any action –

(a) in relation to property which is not realisable property, being action which he would be entitled to take if it were such property;

(b) believing, and having reasonable grounds for believing, that he is entitled to take that action in relation to that property,

he shall not be liable to any person in respect of any loss or damage resulting from his action except in so far as the loss or damage is caused by his negligence.

(2) Any amount due in respect of the remuneration and expenses of a receiver so appointed shall, if no sum is available to be applied in payment of it under section 81(5) above, be paid by the prosecutor or, in a case where proceedings for an offence to which this Part of this Act applies are not instituted, by the person on whose application the receiver was appointed.

89 Compensation

(1) If proceedings are instituted against a person for an offence or offences to which this Part of this Act applies and either –

(a) the proceedings do not result in his conviction for any such offence, or

(b) where he is convicted of one or more such offences –

(i) the conviction or convictions concerned are quashed, or

(ii) he is pardoned by Her Majesty in respect of the conviction or convictions concerned,

the High Court may, on an application by a person who held property which was realisable property, order compensation to be paid to the applicant if, having regard to all the circumstances, it considers it appropriate to make such an order.

(2) The High Court shall not order compensation to be paid in any case unless the court is satisfied –

(a) that there has been some serious default on the part of a person concerned in the investigation or prosecution of the offence concerned, being a person mentioned in subsection (5) below; and

(b) that the applicant has suffered loss in consequence of anything done in relation to the property by or in pursuance of an order under this Part of this Act.

(3) The Court shall not order compensation to be paid in any case where it appears to the Court that the proceedings would have been instituted or continued even if the serious default had not occurred.

(4) The amount of compensation to be paid under this section shall be such as the High Court thinks just in all the circumstances of the case.

(5) Compensation payable under this section shall be paid –

(a) where the person in default was or was acting as a member of a police force, out of the police fund out of which the expenses of that police force are met;

(b) where the person in default was a member of the Crown Prosecution Service or acting on behalf of the service, by the Director of Public Prosecutions;

(c) where the person in default was a member of the Serious Fraud Office, by the Director of that Office;

(d) where the person in default was an officer within the meaning of the Customs and Excise Management Act 1979, by the Commissioners of Customs and Excise; and

(e) where the person in default was an officer of the Commissioners of Inland Revenue, by those Commissioners.

Enforcement in Scotland

90 Recognition and enforcement of orders in Scotland

(1) An order to which this section applies shall, subject to this section and section 91 below, have effect in the law of Scotland but shall be enforced in Scotland only in accordance with this section and that section.

(2) A receiver's functions under or for the purpose of section 77, 80 or 81 above shall, subject to this section and section 91 below, have effect in the law of Scotland.

(3) If an order to which this section applies is registered under this section –

(a) the Court of Session shall have, in relation to its enforcement, the same power;

(b) proceedings for or with respect to its enforcement may be taken; and

(c) proceedings for or with respect to any contravention of such an order (whether before or after such registration) may be taken,

as if the order had originally been made in that Court.

(4) Nothing in this section enables any provision of an order which empowers a receiver to do anything in Scotland under section 80(3)(a) above to have effect in the law of Scotland.

(5) The orders to which this section applies are orders of the High Court –

(a) made under section 77, 78 or 81 above;

(b) relating to the exercise by that Court of its powers under those sections; or

(c) relating to receivers in the performance of their functions under any of them,

but not including an order in proceedings for enforcement of any such order.

(6) References in this section to an order under section 77 above include references to a discharge under section 76(4) above of such an order.

(7) In this section and in sections 91 and 93 below, "order" means any order, direction or judgment by whatever name called.

(8) Nothing in any order of the High Court under section 80(6) above prejudices any enactment or rule of law in respect of the recording of deeds relating to heritable property in Scotland or the registration of interests in such property.

91 Supplementary

(1) The Court of Session shall, on application made to it in accordance with rules of court for registration of an order to which section 90 above applies, direct that the order shall, in accordance with such rules, be registered in that Court.

(2) Subsections (1) and (3) of that section and subsection (1) above are subject to any provision made by rules of court –

(a) as to the manner in which and conditions subject to which orders to which that section applies are to be enforced in Scotland;

(b) for the sisting of proceedings for enforcement of such an order;

(c) for the modification or cancellation of the registration of such an order if the order is modified or revoked or ceases to have effect.

(3) This section and that section are without prejudice to any enactment or rule of law as to the effect of notice or the want of it in relation to orders of the High Court.

(4) The Court of Session shall have the like power to make an order under section 1 of

the Administration of Justice (Scotland) Act 1972 (extended power to order inspection of documents, etc.) in relation to proceedings brought or likely to be brought under this Part of this Act in the High Court as if those proceedings had been brought or were likely to be brought in the Court of Session.

(5) The Court of Session may, additionally, for the purpose of –

(a) assisting the achievement in Scotland of the purposes of orders to which section 90 above applies,
(b) assisting receivers performing functions thereunder or for the purposes of section 77, 80 or 81 above,

make such orders and do otherwise as seems to it appropriate.

92 Inhibition and arrestment of property in Scotland

(1) On the application of the prosecutor, the Court of Session may, in respect of –

(a) heritable realisable property in Scotland affected by a restraint order registered under section 90 above (whether such property generally or particular such property) grant warrant for inhibition against any person with an interest in that property;
(b) moveable realisable property so affected (whether such property generally or particular such property) grant warrant for arrestment if the property would be arrestable were the person entitled to it a debtor;

and, subject to the provisions of this section, the warrant –

(i) shall have effect as if granted on the dependence of an action for debt at the instance of the prosecutor against the person and may be executed, recalled, loosed or restricted accordingly;
(ii) where granted under subsection (1)(a) above, shall have the effect of letters of inhibition and shall forthwith be registered by the prosecutor in the register of inhibitions and adjudications.

(2) Section 155 of the Titles to Land Consolidation (Scotland) Act 1868 (effective date of inhibition) shall apply in relation to an inhibition for which warrant has been granted under subsection (1)(a) above as that section applies to an inhibition by separate letters or contained in a summons.

(3) In the application of section 158 of the said Act of 1868 (recall of inhibition) to such inhibition as is mentioned in subsection (2) above, references in that section to a particular Lord Ordinary shall be construed as references to any Lord Ordinary.

(4) Any power of the Court of Session to recall, loose or restrict inhibitions or arrestments shall, in relation to an inhibition or arrestment proceeding upon a warrant under this section and without prejudice to any other consideration lawfully applying to the exercise of the power, be exercised with a view to achieving the purposes specified in section 80 above.

(5) That an inhibition or arrestment has been executed under subsection (1) above in respect of property shall not prejudice the exercise of a receiver's powers under or for the purposes of section 77, 80 or 81 above in respect of that property.

(6) No inhibition or arrestment executed under subsection (1) above shall have effect once, or in so far as, the restraint order affecting the property in respect of which the warrant for such inhibition or arrestment has been granted has ceased to have effect in respect of that property; and the prosecutor shall –

(a) apply for the recall, or as the case may be restriction, of the inhibition or arrestment accordingly; and
(b) ensure that recall, or restriction, of an inhibition on such application is reflected in the register of inhibitions and adjudications.

93 Proof in Scotland of High Court Orders
A document purporting to be a copy of an order under or for the purposes of this Part of this Act by the High Court and to be certified as such by a proper officer of that Court shall, in Scotland, be sufficient evidence of the order.

Enforcement of external orders

94 Enforcement of Northern Ireland Orders
(1) Her Majesty may by Order in Council provide that for the purposes of sections 76 to 89 above, this Part of this Act shall have effect as if –

- (a) references to confiscation orders included a reference to orders made by courts in Northern Ireland which appear to Her Majesty to correspond to confiscation orders;
- (b) references to proceedings in England and Wales or to the institution or conclusion in England and Wales of proceedings included a reference to proceedings in Northern Ireland or to the institution or conclusion in Northern Ireland of proceedings, as the case may be; and
- (c) the references to the laying of an information in section 76(2) and (4) above included references to making a complaint under Article 20 of the Magistrates' Courts (Northern Ireland) Order 1981.

(2) An Order in Council under this section may provide for those sections to have effect in relation to anything done or to be done in Northern Ireland subject to such further modifications as may be specified in the Order.

(3) An Order in Council under this section may contain such incidental, consequential and transitional provisions as Her Majesty considers expedient.

(4) An Order in Council under this section shall not be made unless a draft of the Order has been laid before Parliament and approved by resolution of each House of Parliament.

95 Enforcement of Northern Ireland order in Scotland
(1) Her Majesty may by Order in Council provide that for the purposes of any part of the law of Northern Ireland which appears to Her Majesty to correspond to this Part of this Act sections 90 to 93 above shall have effect as they have effect for the purposes of this Part subject to such modifications as may be specified in the Order.

(2) An Order in Council under this section may contain such incidental, consequential and transitional provisions as Her Majesty considers expedient.

(3) An Order in Council under this section shall not be made unless a draft of the Order has been laid before Parliament and approved by resolution of each House of Parliament.

96 Enforcement of other external orders
(1) Her Majesty may by Order in Council –

- (a) direct in relation to a country or territory outside the United Kingdom designated by the Order ("a designated country") that, subject to such modifications as may be specified, this Part of this Act shall apply to external confiscation orders and to proceedings which have been or are to be instituted in the designated country and may result in an external confiscation order being made there;
- (b) make –
  - (i) such provision in connection with the taking of action in the designated country with a view to satisfying a confiscation order;
  - (ii) such provision as to evidence or proof of any matter for the purposes of this section and section 97 below; and

(iii) such incidental, consequential and transitional provision,

as appears to Her Majesty to be expedient; and

(c) without prejudice to the generality of this subsection, direct that in such circumstances as may be specified proceeds which arise out of action taken in the designated country with a view to satisfying a confiscation order shall be treated as reducing the amount payable under the order to such extent as may be specified.

(2) In this Part of this Act –

"external confiscation order" means an order made by a court in a designated country for the purpose –

(a) of recovering –

(i) property obtained as a result of or in connection with conduct corresponding to an offence to which this Part of this Act applies; or
(ii) the value of property so obtained; or

(b) of depriving a person of a pecuniary advantage so obtained; and

"modifications" includes additions, alterations and omissions.

(3) An Order in Council under this section may make different provision for different cases or classes of case.

(4) The power to make an Order in Council under this section includes power to modify this Part of this Act in such a way as to confer power on a person to exercise a discretion.

(5) An Order in Council under this section shall not be made unless a draft of the order has been laid before Parliament and approved by resolution of each House of Parliament.

97 Registration of external confiscation orders

(1) On an application made by or on behalf of the government of a designated country, the High Court may register an external confiscation order made there if –

(a) it is satisfied that at the time of registration the order is in force and not subject to appeal;
(b) it is satisfied, where the person against whom the order is made did not appear in the proceedings, that he received notice of the proceedings in sufficient time to enable him to defend them; and
(c) it is of the opinion that enforcing the order in England and Wales would not be contrary to the interests of justice.

(2) In subsection (1) above "appeal" includes –

(a) any proceedings by way of discharging or setting aside a judgment; and
(b) an application for a new trial or a stay of execution.

(3) The High Court shall cancel the registration of an external confiscation order if it appears to the court that the order has been satisfied by payment of the amount due under it or by the person against whom it was made serving imprisonment in default of payment or by any other means.

Miscellaneous and supplemental

98 Disclosure of information subject to contractual restriction upon disclosure

(1) Where a person discloses to a constable –

(a) a suspicion or belief that any property –

(i) has been obtained as a result of or in connection with the commission or an offence to which this Part of this Act applies; or

(ii) derives from property so obtained; or

(b) any matter on which such a suspicion or belief is based,

the disclosure shall not be treated as a breach of any restriction upon the disclosure of information imposed by contract.

(2) . . .

NOTE
Sub-s (2): repealed by the Police Officers (Central Service) Act 1989, s 3, Schedule.

99 Authorisation of delay in notifying arrest etc
(1) The Police and Criminal Evidence Act 1984 shall be amended as follows.

(2), (3) . . .

(4) Without prejudice to section 20(2) of the Interpretation Act 1978, the Police and Criminal Evidence Act 1984 (Application to Customs and Excise) Order 1985 shall apply to sections 56 and 58 of the Police and Criminal Evidence Act 1984 as those sections have effect by virtue of this section.

NOTE
Sub-ss (2), (3): amend the Police and Criminal Evidence Act 1984, ss 56(5A), 58(8A).

100 Power to inspect Land Register, etc
(1) The Chief Land Registrar (in this section referred to as "the registrar") shall, on an application under subsection (2) or (4) below made in relation to a person specified in the application or to property so specified, provide the applicant with any information kept by the registrar under the Land Registration Act 1925 which relates to the person or property so specified.

(2) An application may be made by –

(a) any police officer not below the rank of superintendent;
(b) any Crown Prosecutor; or
(c) any member of the Serious Fraud Office designated for the purposes of section 1 of the Criminal Justice Act 1987; or
(d) any person commissioned by the Commissioners of Customs and Excise not below the rank of senior executive officer; or
(e) any person authorised in that behalf by the Commissioners of Inland Revenue not below the rank of senior executive officer;

and on an application under this subsection an appropriate certificate shall be given to the registrar.

(3) In subsection (2) above "appropriate certificate" means a certificate –

(a) that a person specified in the certificate has committed or that there are reasonable grounds for suspecting that a person so specified has committed an offence to which this Part of this Act applies; and
(b) that there are reasonable grounds for suspecting that there is information kept by the registrar which is likely to be of substantial value (whether by itself or together with other information) to an investigation into whether the person so specified has benefited from the commission of the offence or in facilitating the recovery of the value of the property obtained by that person from or in connection with the offence.

(4) An application may be made by a receiver appointed under this Part of this Act and on an application under this subsection there shall be given to the registrar –

(a) a document certified by the proper officer of the court to be a true copy of the order appointing the receiver; and

(b) a certificate that there are reasonable grounds for suspecting that there is information kept by the registrar which is likely to facilitate the exercise of the powers conferred on the receiver in respect of the person or property specified in the application.

(5) The reference in subsection (1) above to the provision of information is a reference to its provision in documentary form.

(6) The references to senior executive officers in subsection (2) above include references to equivalent departmental grades.

(7) This section shall cease to have effect on the day appointed under section 3(2) of the Land Registration Act 1988 for the coming into force of that Act.

101 Abolition of power to make criminal bankruptcy order
(1) The power to make a criminal bankruptcy order which section 39 of the Powers of Criminal Courts Act 1973 confers on the Crown Court is abolished.

(2) Nothing in subsection (1) above –

(a) shall affect any criminal bankruptcy order made before this section comes into force; or
(b) shall prevent the taking of any step following such an order.

102 Part VI – Interpretation
(1) In this Part of this Act –

"constable" includes a person commissioned by the Commissioners of Customs and Excise;

"interest", in relation to property, includes right;

"property" includes money and all other property, real or personal, heritable or moveable, including things in action and other intangible or incorporeal property.

(2) The expressions listed in the left-hand column below are respectively defined or (as the case may be) fall to be construed in accordance with the provisions of this Act listed in the right-hand column in relation to those expressions.

Expression	*Relevant provision*
Benefited from an offence	Section 71(4)
Charging order	Section 78(2)
Confiscation order	Section 71(9)(a)
Dealing with property	Section 77(9)
Defendant	Section 71(9)(d)
Gift caught by this Part of this Act	Section 74(10)
Making a gift	Section 74(12)
Offence to which this Part of this Act applies	Section 71(9)(c)
Realisable property	Section 74(1)
Restraint order	Section 77(1)
Value of gift	Section 74(7) and (8)
Value of property	Section 74(4) to (6)

(3) This Part of this Act applies to property wherever situated.

(4) References in this Part of this Act to offences include a reference to offences committed before the commencement of this Part of this Act; but nothing in this Part of this Act confers any power on any court in connection with proceedings against a person for an offence instituted before the commencement of this Part of this Act.

(5) References in this Part of this Act to property obtained, or to a pecuniary advantage derived, in connection with the commission of an offence include a reference to property obtained or to a pecuniary advantage derived, both in that connection and in some other connection.

(6) The following provisions shall have effect for the interpretation of this Part of this Act.

(7) Property is held by any person if he holds any interest in it.

(8) References to property held by a person include a reference to property vested in his trustee in bankruptcy, permanent or interim trustee within the meaning of the Bankruptcy (Scotland) Act 1985 or liquidator.

(9) References to an interest held by a person beneficially in property include a reference to an interest which would be held by him beneficially if the property were not so vested.

(10) Property is transferred by one person to another if the first person transfers or grants to the other any interest in the property.

(11) Proceedings for an offence are instituted –

(a) when a justice of the peace issues a summons or warrant under section 1 of the Magistrates' Courts Act 1980 in respect of that offence;

(b) when a person is charged with the offence after being taken into custody without a warrant;

(c) when a bill of indictment is preferred under section 2 of the Administration of Justice (Miscellaneous Provisions) Act 1933 in a case falling within paragraph (b) of subsection (2) of that section;

and where the application of this subsection would result in there being more than one time for the institution of proceedings, they shall be taken to have been instituted at the earliest of those times.

(12) Proceedings are concluded –

(a) when (disregarding any power of a court to grant leave to appeal out of time) there is no further possibility of a confiscation order being made in the proceedings;

(b) on the satisfaction of a confiscation order made in the proceedings (whether by payment of the amount due under the order or by the defendant serving imprisonment in default).

(13) An order is subject to appeal until (disregarding any power of a court to grant leave to appeal out of time) there is no further possibility of an appeal on which the order could be varied or set aside.

103 Amendments of Drug Trafficking Offences Act 1986 and Criminal Justice (Scotland) Act 1987

(1) The amendments of the Drug Trafficking Offences Act 1986 specified in Part I of Schedule 5 to this Act (which make certain provisions of that Act correspond to provisions of this Part of this Act) shall have effect.

(2) The amendments of the Criminal Justice (Scotland) Act 1987 specified in Part II of that Schedule shall also have effect.

SCHEDULE 2
DOCUMENTARY EVIDENCE – SUPPLEMENTARY

Section 28

1 Where a statement is admitted as evidence in criminal proceedings by virtue of Part II of this Act –

(a) any evidence which, if the person making the statement had been called as a witness, would have been admissible as relevant to his credibility as a witness shall be admissible for that purpose in those proceedings;

(b) evidence may, with the leave of the court, be given of any matter which, if that person had been called as a witness, could have been put to him in cross-examination as relevant to his credibility as a witness but of which evidence could not have been adduced by the cross-examining party; and

(c) evidence tending to prove that that person, whether before or after making the statement, made (whether orally or not) some other statement which is inconsistent with it shall be admissible for the purpose of showing that he has contradicted himself.

2 A statement which is given in evidence by virtue of Part II of this Act shall not be capable of corroborating evidence given by the person making it.

3 In estimating the weight, if any, to be attached to such a statement regard shall be had to all the circumstances from which any inference can reasonably be drawn as to its accuracy or otherwise.

4 Without prejudice to the generality of any enactment conferring power to make them –

(a) Crown Court Rules;

(b) Criminal Appeal Rules; and

(c) rules under section 144 of the Magistrates' Courts Act 1980,

may make such provision as appears to the authority making any of them to be necessary or expedient for the purposes of Part II of this Act.

5 Expressions used in Part II of this Act and in Part I of the Civil Evidence Act 1968 are to be construed in Part II of this Act in accordance with section 10 of that Act.

6 In Part II of this Act "confession" has the meaning assigned to it by section 82 of the Police and Criminal Evidence Act 1984.

SCHEDULE 4
CONFISCATION ORDERS

Section 71

PART I
OFFENCES IN RESPECT OF WHICH MAGISTRATES' COURTS MAY
MAKE CONFISCATION ORDERS

Enactment	Description of offence
LONDON GOVERNMENT ACT 1963 (c. 33) Schedule 12 – paragraph 10(1) and (2), in relation only to an offence to which sub-paragraph (3A) of paragraph 10 applies.	Offences relating to the use of places in Greater London for public dancing or music or other public entertainment of the like kind.
PRIVATE PLACES OF ENTERTAINMENT (LICENSING) ACT 1967 (c. 19) Section 4(1) Section 4(2), in relation only to an offence referred to in sub-section(3A) (b) of section 4.	Offences relating to the use of places for dancing, music or other entertainment of the like kind which is not a public entertainment but is provided for private gain.

Enactment	Description of offence
LOCAL GOVERNMENT (MISCELLANEOUS PROVISIONS) ACT 1982 (c. 30) Schedule 1 – paragraph 12(1) and(2), in relation only to an offence to which sub-paragraph (2B) of paragraph 12 applies.	Offences relating to the use of places outside Greater London for public dancing or music or other public entertainment of the like kind (not being in the open air) or for public musical entertainment held wholly or mainly in the open air on private land.
Schedule 3 – paragraphs 20 and 21.	Offences relating to sex establishments.
VIDEO RECORDINGS ACT 1984 (c. 39) Section 9 Section 10	Supplying video recording of unclassified work. Possession of video recording of unclassified work for the purpose of supply.
CINEMAS ACT 1985 (c. 13) Section 10(1)(a)	Use of unlicensed premises for exhibition which requires alicence.

NOTES
Substituted by SI 1990 No 1570, art 3.

PART II
ORDERS VARYING LIST OF OFFENCES

1 The Secretary of State may by order made by statutory instrument amend Part I of this Schedule by removing any offence from or adding any offence to the offences listed in it.

2 A statutory instrument containing an order under paragraph 1 above shall be subject to annulment in pursuance of a resolution of either House of Parliament.

Companies Act 1989

(1989 c 40)

An Act to amend the law relating to company accounts; to make new provision with respect to the persons eligible for appointment as company auditors; to amend the Companies Act 1985 and certain other enactments with respect to investigations and powers to obtain information and to confer new powers exercisable to assist overseas regulatory authorities; to make new provision with respect to the registration of company charges and otherwise to amend the law relating to companies; to amend the Fair Trading Act 1973; to enable provision to be made for the payment of fees in connection with the exercise by the Secretary of State, the Director General of Fair Trading and the Monopolies and Mergers Commission of their functions under Part V of that Act; to make provision for safeguarding the operation of certain financial markets; to amend the Financial Services Act 1986; to enable provision to be made for the recording and transfer of title to securities without a written instrument; to amend the Company Directors Disqualification Act 1986, the Company Securities (Insider Dealing) Act 1985, the Policyholders Protection Act 1975 and the law relating to building societies; and for connected purposes

[16 November 1989]

PART III
INVESTIGATIONS AND POWERS TO OBTAIN INFORMATION
Powers exercisable to assist overseas regulatory authorities

82 Request for assistance by overseas regulatory authority

(1) The powers conferred by section 83 are exercisable by the Secretary of State for the purpose of assisting an overseas regulatory authority which has requested his assistance in connection with inquiries being carried out by it or on its behalf.

(2) An "overseas regulatory authority" means an authority which in a country or territory outside the United Kingdom exercises –

(a) any function corresponding to –

    (i) a function under the Financial Services Act 1986 of a designated agency, transferee body or competent authority (within the meaning of that Act),

    (ii) a function of the Secretary of State under the Insurance Companies Act 1982, the Companies Act 1985 or the Financial Services Act 1986, or

    (iii) a function of the Bank of England under the Banking Act 1987, or

(b) any function in connection with the investigation of, or the enforcement of rules (whether or not having the force of law) relating to, conduct of the kind prohibited by the Company Securities (Insider Dealing) Act 1985, or

(c) any function prescribed for the purposes of this subsection by order of the Secretary of State, being a function which in the opinion of the Secretary of State relates to companies or financial services.

An order under paragraph (c) shall be made by statutory instrument which shall be subject to annulment in pursuance of a resolution of either House of Parliament.

(3) The Secretary of State shall not exercise the powers conferred by section 83 unless he is satisfied that the assistance requested by the overseas regulatory authority is for the purposes of its regulatory functions.

An authority's "regulatory functions" means any functions falling within subsection (2) and any other functions relating to companies or financial services.

(4) In deciding whether to exercise those powers the Secretary of State may take into account, in particular –

(a) whether corresponding assistance would be given in that country or territory to an authority exercising regulatory functions in the United Kingdom;

(b) whether the inquiries relate to the possible breach of a law, or other requirement, which has no close parallel in the United Kingdom or involves the assertion of a jurisdiction not recognised by the United Kingdom;

(c) the seriousness of the matter to which the inquiries relate, the importance to the inquiries of the information sought in the United Kingdom and whether the assistance could be obtained by other means;

(d) whether it is otherwise appropriate in the public interest to give the assistance sought.

(5) Before deciding whether to exercise those powers in a case where the overseas regulatory authority is a banking supervisor, the Secretary of State shall consult the Bank of England.

A "banking supervisor" means an overseas regulatory authority with respect to which the Bank of England has notified the Secretary of State, for the purposes of this subsection, that it exercises functions corresponding to those of the Bank under the Banking Act 1987.

(6) The Secretary of State may decline to exercise those powers unless the overseas regulatory authority undertakes to make such contribution towards the costs of their exercise as the Secretary of State considers appropriate.

(7) References in this section to financial services include, in particular, investment business, insurance and banking.

83 Power to require information, documents or other assistance

(1) The following powers may be exercised in accordance with section 82, if the Secretary of State considers there is good reason for their exercise.

(2) The Secretary of State may require any person –

(a) to attend before him at a specified time and place and answer questions or otherwise furnish information with respect to any matter relevant to the inquiries,

(b) to produce at a specified time and place any specified documents which appear to the Secretary of State to relate to any matter relevant to the inquiries, and

(c) otherwise to give him such assistance in connection with the inquiries as he is reasonably able to give.

(3) The Secretary of State may examine a person on oath and may administer an oath accordingly.

(4) Where documents are produced the Secretary of State may take copies or extracts from them.

(5) A person shall not under this section be required to disclose information or produce a document which he would be entitled to refuse to disclose or produce on grounds of legal professional privilege in proceedings in the High Court or on grounds of confidentiality as between client and professional legal adviser in proceedings in the Court of Session, except that a lawyer may be required to furnish the name and address of his client.

(6) A statement by a person in compliance with a requirement imposed under this section may be used in evidence against him.

(7) Where a person claims a lien on a document, its production under this section is without prejudice to his lien.

(8) In this section "documents" includes information recorded in any form; and, in relation to information recorded otherwise than in legible form, the power to require its production includes power to require the production of a copy of it in legible form.

84 Exercise of powers by officer, &c

(1) The Secretary of State may authorise an officer of his or any other competent person to exercise on his behalf all or any of the powers conferred by section 83.

(2) No such authority shall be granted except for the purpose of investigating –

(a) the affairs, or any aspects of the affairs, of a person specified in the authority, or

(b) a subject-matter so specified,

being a person who, or subject-matter which, is the subject of the inquiries being carried out by or on behalf of the overseas regulatory authority.

(3) No person shall be bound to comply with a requirement imposed by a person exercising powers by virtue of an authority granted under this section unless he has, if required, produced evidence of his authority.

(4) A person shall not by virtue of an authority under this section be required to disclose any information or produce any documents in respect of which he owes an obligation of confidence by virtue of carrying on the business of banking unless –

(a) the imposing on him of a requirement with respect to such information or documents has been specifically authorised by the Secretary of State, or

(b) the person to whom the obligation of confidence is owed consents to the disclosure or production.

In this subsection "documents" has the same meaning as in section 83.

(5) Where the Secretary of State authorises a person other than one of his officers to exercise any powers by virtue of this section, that person shall make a report to the Secretary of State in such manner as he may require on the exercise of those powers and the results of exercising them.

85 Penalty for failure to comply with requirement, &c

(1) A person who without reasonable excuse fails to comply with a requirement imposed on him under section 83 commits an offence and is liable on summary conviction to imprisonment for a term not exceeding six months or to a fine not exceeding level 5 on the standard scale, or both.

(2) A person who in purported compliance with any such requirement furnishes information which he knows to be false or misleading in a material particular, or recklessly furnishes information which is false or misleading in a material particular, commits an offence and is liable –

(a) on conviction on indictment, to imprisonment for a term not exceeding two years or to a fine, or both;

(b) on summary conviction, to imprisonment for a term not exceeding six months or to a fine not exceeding the statutory maximum, or both.

86 Restrictions on disclosure of information

(1) This section applies to information relating to the business or other affairs of a person which –

(a) is supplied by an overseas regulatory authority in connection with a request for assistance, or

(b) is obtained by virtue of the powers conferred by section 83, whether or not any requirement to supply it is made under that section.

(2) Except as permitted by section 87 below, such information shall not be disclosed for any purpose –

(a) by the primary recipient, or

(b) by any person obtaining the information directly or indirectly from him,

without the consent of the person from whom the primary recipient obtained the information and, if different, the person to whom it relates.

(3) The "primary recipient" means, as the case may be –

(a) the Secretary of State,

(b) any person authorised under section 84 to exercise powers on his behalf, and

(c) any officer or servant of any such person.

(4) Information shall not be treated as information to which this section applies if it has been made available to the public by virtue of being disclosed in any circumstances in which, or for any purpose for which, disclosure is not precluded by this section.

(5) A person who contravenes this section commits an offence and is liable –

(a) on conviction on indictment, to imprisonment for a term not exceeding two years or to a fine, or both;

(b) on summary conviction, to imprisonment for a term not exceeding three months or to a fine not exceeding the statutory maximum, or both.

87 Exceptions from restrictions on disclosure

(1) Information to which section 86 applies may be disclosed –

(a) to any person with a view to the institution of, or otherwise for the purposes of, relevant proceedings,

(b) for the purpose of enabling or assisting a relevant authority to discharge any relevant function (including functions in relation to proceedings),

(c) to the Treasury, if the disclosure is made in the interests of investors or in the public interest,

(d) if the information is or has been available to the public from other sources,

(e) in a summary or collection of information framed in such a way as not to enable the identity of any person to whom the information relates to be ascertained, or

(f) in pursuance of any Community obligation.

(2) The relevant proceedings referred to in subsection (1)(a) are –

(a) any criminal proceedings,

(b) civil proceedings arising under or by virtue of the Financial Services Act 1986 and proceedings before the Financial Services Tribunal, and

(c) disciplinary proceedings relating to –

(i) the exercise by a solicitor, auditor, accountant, valuer or actuary of his professional duties, or

(ii) the discharge by a public servant of his duties.

(3) In subsection (2)(c)(ii) "public servant" means an officer or servant of the Crown or of any public or other authority for the time being designated for the purposes of that provision by order of the Secretary of State.

(4) The relevant authorities referred to in subsection (1)(b), and the relevant functions in relation to each such authority, are as follows –

Authority	*Functions*
The Secretary of State.	Functions under the enactments relating to companies, insurance companies or insolvency, or under the Financial Services Act 1986 or Part II, this Part or Part VII of this Act.
[The Treasury	Functions under the Financial Services Act 1986 or under this Part or Part VII of this Act.]
An inspector appointed under Part XIV of the Companies Act 1985 or section 94 or 177 of the Financial Services Act 1986.	Functions under that Part or that section.
A person authorised to exercise powers under section 44 of the Insurance Companies Act 1982, section 447 of the Companies Act 1985, section 106 of the Financial Services Act 1986 or section 84 of this Act.	Functions under that section.
An overseas regulatory authority.	Its regulatory functions (within the meaning of section 82 of this Act).
The Department of Economic Development in Northern Ireland or a person appointed or authorised by that Department.	Functions conferred on it or him by the enactments relating to companies or insolvency.
A designated agency within the meaning of the Financial Services Act 1986.	Functions under that Act or Part VII of this Act.
A transferee body or the competent authority within the meaning of the Financial Services Act 1986.	Functions under that Act.
The body administering a scheme under section 54 of the Financial Services Act 1986.	Functions under the scheme.

Authority	*Functions*
A recognised self-regulating organisation, recognised professional body, recognised investment exchange, recognised clearing house or recognised self-regulating organisation for friendly societies (within the meaning of the Financial Services Act 1986).	Functions in its capacity as an organisation, body, exchange or clearing house recognised under that Act.
The Chief Registrar of friendly societies, the *Registrar of Friendly Societies for Northern Ireland* andthe Assistant Registrar of Friendly Societies for Scotland.	Functions under *the Financial Services Act 1986* or the enactments relating to friendly societies orbuilding societies.
The Bank of England.	Functions under the Banking Act 1987 and any other functions.
The Deposit Protection Board.	Functions under the Banking Act 1987.
A body established by order under section 46 of this Act.	Functions under Part II of this Act.
A recognised supervisory or qualifying body within the meaning of Part II of this Act.	Functions as such a body.
The Industrial Assurance Commissioner and the Industrial Assurance Commissioner for Northern Ireland.	Functions under the enactments relating to industrial assurance.
The Insurance Brokers Registration Council.	Functions under the Insurance Brokers (Registration) Act 1977.
The Official Receiver or, in Northern Ireland, the Official Assignee for company liquidations or for bankruptcy.	Functions under the enactments relating to insolvency.
A recognised professional body (within the meaning of section 391 of the Insolvency Act 1986).	Functions in its capacity as such a body under the Insolvency Act 1986.
The Building Societies Commission.	Functions under the Building Societies Act 1986.
The Director General of Fair Trading.	Functions under the Financial Services Act 1986.

(5) The Secretary of State may by order amend the Table in subsection (4) so as to –

(a) add any public or other authority to the Table and specify the relevant functions of that authority,

(b) remove any authority from the Table, or

(c) add functions to, or remove functions from, those which are relevant functions in relation to an authority specified in the Table;

and the order may impose conditions subject to which, or otherwise restrict the circumstances in which, disclosure is permitted.

(6) An order under this section shall be made by statutory instrument which shall be subject to annulment in pursuance of a resolution of either House of Parliament.

NOTES

Sub-s (4) – Table: entry relating to the Treasury inserted by the Transfer of Functions (Financial Services) Order 1992, SI 1992 No 1315, art 10(1), Sch 4, para 12; in entry relating to friendly societies, words in italics prospectively repealed by the Friendly Societies Act 1992, s 120(2), Sch 22,

Pt I; after that entry, there is prospectively inserted the following entry by s 120(1) of, and Sch 21, para 11 to, the 1992 Act –

"The Friendly Societies Commission   Functions under the enactments relating to friendly societies or under the Financial Services Act 1986.".

88 Exercise of powers in relation to Northern Ireland

(1) The following provisions apply where it appears to the Secretary of State that a request for assistance by an overseas regulatory authority may involve the powers conferred by section 83 being exercised in Northern Ireland in relation to matters which are transferred matters within the meaning of the Northern Ireland Constitution Act 1973.

(2) The Secretary of State shall before deciding whether to accede to the request consult the Department of Economic Development in Northern Ireland, and if he decides to accede to the request and it appears to him –

(a) that the powers should be exercised in Northern Ireland, and
(b) that the purposes for which they should be so exercised relate wholly or primarily to transferred matters,

he shall by instrument in writing authorise the Department to exercise in Northern Ireland his powers under section 83.

(3) The following provisions have effect in relation to the exercise of powers by virtue of such an authority with the substitution for references to the Secretary of State of references to the Department of Economic Development in Northern Ireland –

(a) section 84 (exercise of powers by officer, &c),
(b) section 449 of the Companies Act 1985, section 53 or 54 of the Building Societies Act 1986, sections 179 and 180 of the Financial Services Act 1986, section 84 of the Banking Act 1987 and sections 86 and 87 above (restrictions on disclosure of information), and
(c) section 89 (authority for institution of criminal proceedings);

and references to the Secretary of State in other enactments which proceed by reference to those provisions shall be construed accordingly as being or including references to the Department.

(4) The Secretary of State may after consultation with the Department of Economic Development in Northern Ireland revoke an authority given to the Department under this section.

(5) In that case nothing in the provisions referred to in subsection (3)(b) shall apply so as to prevent the Department from giving the Secretary of State any information obtained by virtue of the authority; and (without prejudice to their application in relation to disclosure by the Department) those provisions shall apply to the disclosure of such information by the Secretary of State as if it had been obtained by him in the first place.

(6) Nothing in this section affects the exercise by the Secretary of State of any powers in Northern Ireland –

(a) in a case where at the time of acceding to the request it did not appear to him that the circumstances were such as to require him to authorise the Department of Economic Development in Northern Ireland to exercise those powers, or
(b) after the revocation by him of any such authority;

and no objection shall be taken to anything done by or in relation to the Secretary of State or the Department on the ground that it should have been done by or in relation to the other.

89 Prosecutions

Proceedings for an offence under section 85 or 86 shall not be instituted –

(a) in England and Wales, except by or with the consent of the Secretary of State or the Director of Public Prosecutions;

(b) in Northern Ireland, except by or with the consent of the Secretary of State or the Director of Public Prosecutions for Northern Ireland.

90 Offences by bodies corporate, partnerships and unincorporated associations

(1) Where an offence under section 85 or 86 committed by a body corporate is proved to have been committed with the consent or connivance of, or to be attributable to any neglect on the part of, a director, manager, secretary or other similar officer of the body, or a person purporting to act in any such capacity, he as well as the body corporate is guilty of the offence and liable to be proceeded against and punished accordingly.

(2) Where the affairs of a body corporate are managed by its members, subsection (1) applies in relation to the acts and defaults of a member in connection with his functions of management as to a director of a body corporate.

(3) Where an offence under section 85 or 86 committed by a partnership is proved to have been committed with the consent or connivance of, or to be attributable to any neglect on the part of, a partner, he as well as the partnership is guilty of the offence and liable to be proceeded against and punished accordingly.

(4) Where an offence under section 85 or 86 committed by an unincorporated association (other than a partnership) is proved to have been committed with the consent or connivance of, or to be attributable to any neglect on the part of, any officer of the association or any member of its governing body, he as well as the association is guilty of the offence and liable to be proceeded against and punished accordingly.

91 Jurisdiction and procedure in respect of offences

(1) Summary proceedings for an offence under section 85 may, without prejudice to any jurisdiction exercisable apart from this section, be taken against a body corporate or unincorporated association at any place at which it has a place of business and against an individual at any place where he is for the time being.

(2) Proceedings for an offence alleged to have been committed under section 85 or 86 by an unincorporated association shall be brought in the name of the association (and not in that of any of its members), and for the purposes of any such proceedings any rules of court relating to the service of documents apply as in relation to a body corporate.

(3) Section 33 of the Criminal Justice Act 1925 and Schedule 3 to the Magistrates' Courts Act 1980 (procedure on charge of offence against a corporation) apply in a case in which an unincorporated association is charged in England and Wales with an offence under section 85 or 86 as they apply in the case of a corporation.

(4) In relation to proceedings on indictment in Scotland for an offence alleged to have been committed under section 85 or 86 by an unincorporated association, section 74 of the Criminal Procedure (Scotland) Act 1975 (proceedings on indictment against bodies corporate) applies as if the association were a body corporate.

(5) Section 18 of the Criminal Justice Act (Northern Ireland) 1945 and Schedule 4 to the Magistrates' Courts (Northern Ireland) Order 1981 (procedure on charge of offence against a corporation) apply in a case in which an unincorporated association is charged in Northern Ireland with an offence under section 85 or 86 as they apply in the case of a corporation.

(6) A fine imposed on an unincorporated association on its conviction of such an offence shall be paid out of the funds of the association.

Criminal Justice (International Co-operation) Act 1990

(1990 c 5)

An Act to enable the United Kingdom to co-operate with other countries in criminal proceedings and investigations; to enable the United Kingdom to join with other countries in implementing the Vienna Convention against Illicit Traffic in Narcotic Drugs and Psychotropic Substances; and to provide for the seizure, detention and forfeiture of drug trafficking money imported or exported in cash

[5 April 1990]

PART I
CRIMINAL PROCEEDINGS AND INVESTIGATIONS
Mutual service of process

1 Service of overseas process in United Kingdom
(1) This section has effect where the Secretary of State receives from the government of, or other authority in, a country or territory outside the United Kingdom –

  (a) a summons or other process requiring a person to appear as defendant or attend as a witness in criminal proceedings in that country or territory; or
  (b) a document issued by a court exercising criminal jurisdiction in that country or territory and recording a decision of the court made in the exercise of that jurisdiction,

together with a request for it to be served on a person in the United Kingdom.

(2) The Secretary of State or, where the person to be served is in Scotland, the Lord Advocate may cause the process or document to be served by post or, if the request is for personal service, direct the chief officer of police for the area in which that person appears to be to cause it to be personally served on him.

(3) Service by virtue of this section of any such process as is mentioned in subsection (1)(a) above shall not impose any obligation under the law of any part of the United Kingdom to comply with it.

(4) Any such process served by virtue of this section shall be accompanied by a notice –

  (a) stating the effect of subsection (3) above;
  (b) indicating that the person on whom it is served may wish to seek advice as to the possible consequences of his failing to comply with the process under the law of the country or territory where it was issued; and
  (c) indicating that under that law he may not, as a witness, be accorded the same rights and privileges as would be accorded to him in criminal proceedings in the United Kingdom.

(5) Where a chief officer of police is directed under this section to cause any process or document to be served he shall after it has been served forthwith inform the Secretary of State or, as the case may be, the Lord Advocate when and how it was served and (if possible) furnish him with a receipt signed by the person on whom it was served; and if the chief officer has been unable to cause the process or document to be served he shall forthwith inform the Secretary of State or, as the case may be, the Lord Advocate of that fact and of the reason.

(6) In the application of this section to Northern Ireland for references to a chief officer of police there shall be substituted references to the Chief Constable of the Royal Ulster Constabulary.

2 Service of United Kingdom process overseas
(1) Process of the following descriptions, that is to say –

  (a) a summons requiring a person charged with an offence to appear before a court in the United Kingdom; and

(b) a summons or order requiring a person to attend before a court in the United Kingdom for the purpose of giving evidence in criminal proceedings,

may be issued or made notwithstanding that the person in question is outside the United Kingdom and may be served outside the United Kingdom in accordance with arrangements made by the Secretary of State.

(2) In relation to Scotland subsection (1) above applies to any document which may competently be served on any accused person or on any person who may give evidence in criminal proceedings.

(3) Service of any process outside the United Kingdom by virtue of this section shall not impose any obligation under the law of any part of the United Kingdom to comply with it and accordingly failure to do so shall not constitute contempt of any court or be a ground for issuing a warrant to secure the attendance of the person in question or, in Scotland, for imposing any penalty.

(4) Subsection (3) above is without prejudice to the service of any process (with the usual consequences for non-compliance) on the person in question if subsequently effected in the United Kingdom.

Mutual provision of evidence

3 Overseas evidence for use in United Kingdom
(1) Where on an application made in accordance with subsection (2) below it appears to a justice of the peace or a judge or, in Scotland, to a sheriff or a judge –

(a) that an offence has been committed or that there are reasonable grounds for suspecting that an offence has been committed; and
(b) that proceedings in respect of the offence have been instituted or that the offence is being investigated,

he may issue a letter ("a letter of request") requesting assistance in obtaining outside the United Kingdom such evidence as is specified in the letter for use in the proceedings or investigation.

(2) An application under subsection (1) above may be made by a prosecuting authority or, if proceedings have been instituted, by the person charged in those proceedings.

(3) A prosecuting authority which is for the time being designated for the purposes of this section by an order made by the Secretary of State by statutory instrument may itself issue a letter of request if –

(a) it is satisfied as to the matters mentioned in subsection (1)(a) above; and
(b) the offence in question is being investigated or the authority has instituted proceedings in respect of it.

(4) Subject to subsection (5) below, a letter of request shall be sent to the Secretary of State for transmission either –

(a) to a court or tribunal specified in the letter and exercising jurisdiction in the place where the evidence is to be obtained; or
(b) to any authority recognised by the government of the country or territory in question as the appropriate authority for receiving requests for assistance of the kind to which this section applies.

(5) In cases of urgency a letter of request may be sent direct to such a court or tribunal as is mentioned in subsection (4)(a) above.

(6) In this section "evidence" includes documents and other articles.

(7) Evidence obtained by virtue of a letter of request shall not without the consent of such an authority as is mentioned in subsection (4)(b) above be used for any purpose other than that specified in the letter; and when any document or other article obtained pursuant to a letter of request is no longer required for that purpose (or for any other

purpose for which such consent has been obtained), it shall be returned to such an authority unless that authority indicates that the document or article need not be returned.

(8) In exercising the discretion conferred by section 25 of the Criminal Justice Act 1988 (exclusion of evidence otherwise admissible) in relation to a statement contained in evidence taken pursuant to a letter of request the court shall have regard –

- (a) to whether it was possible to challenge the statement by questioning the person who made it; and
- (b) if proceedings have been instituted, to whether the local law allowed the parties to the proceedings to be legally represented when the evidence was being taken.

(9) In Scotland evidence obtained by virtue of a letter of request shall, without being sworn to by witnesses, be received in evidence in so far as that can be done without unfairness to either party.

(10) In the application of this section to Northern Ireland for the reference in subsection (1) to a justice of the peace there shall be substituted a reference to a resident magistrate and for the reference in subsection (8) to section 25 of the Criminal Justice Act 1988 there shall be substituted a reference to Article 5 of the Criminal Justice (Evidence, Etc.) (Northern Ireland) Order 1988.

4 United Kingdom evidence for use overseas
(1) This section has effect where the Secretary of State receives –

- (a) from a court or tribunal exercising criminal jurisdiction in a country or territory outside the United Kingdom or a prosecuting authority in such a country or territory; or
- (b) from any other authority in such a country or territory which appears to him to have the function of making requests of the kind to which this section applies,

a request for assistance in obtaining evidence in the United Kingdom in connection with criminal proceedings that have been instituted, or a criminal investigation that is being carried on, in that country or territory.

(2) If the Secretary of State or, if the evidence is to be obtained in Scotland, the Lord Advocate is satisfied –

- (a) that an offence under the law of the country or territory in question has been committed or that there are reasonable grounds for suspecting that such an offence has been committed; and
- (b) that proceedings in respect of that offence have been instituted in that country or territory or that an investigation into that offence is being carried on there,

he may, if he thinks fit, by a notice in writing nominate a court in England, Wales or Northern Ireland or, as the case may be, Scotland to receive such of the evidence to which the request relates as may appear to the court to be appropriate for the purposes of giving effect to the request.

(3) Where it appears to the Secretary of State or, as the case may be, the Lord Advocate that the request relates to a fiscal offence in respect of which proceedings have not yet been instituted he shall not exercise his powers under subsection (2) above unless –

- (a) the request is from a country or territory which is a member of the Commonwealth or is made pursuant to a treaty to which the United Kingdom is a party; or
- (b) he is satisfied that the conduct constituting the offence would constitute an offence of the same or a similar nature if it had occurred in the United Kingdom.

(4) For the purpose of satisfying himself as to the matters mentioned in subsection (2)(a) and (b) above the Secretary of State or, as the case may be, the Lord Advocate shall regard as conclusive a certificate issued by such authority in the country or territory in question as appears to him to be appropriate.

(5) In this section "evidence" includes documents and other articles.

(6) Schedule 1 to this Act shall have effect with respect to the proceedings before a nominated court in pursuance of a notice under subsection (2) above.

5 Transfer of United Kingdom prisoner to give evidence or assist investigation overseas
(1) The Secretary of State may, if he thinks fit, issue a warrant providing for any person ("a prisoner") serving a sentence in a prison or other institution to which the Prison Act 1952 or the Prisons (Scotland) Act 1989 applies to be transferred to a country or territory outside the United Kingdom for the purpose –

(a) of giving evidence in criminal proceedings there; or
(b) of being identified in, or otherwise by his presence assisting, such proceedings or the investigation of an offence.

(2) No warrant shall be issued under this section in respect of any prisoner unless he has consented to being transferred as mentioned in subsection (1) above and that consent may be given either –

(a) by the prisoner himself; or
(b) in circumstances in which it appears to the Secretary of State inappropriate, by reason of the prisoner's physical or mental condition or his youth, for him to act for himself, by a person appearing to the Secretary of State to be an appropriate person to act on his behalf;

but a consent once given shall not be capable of being withdrawn after the issue of the warrant.

(3) The effect of a warrrant under this section shall be to authorise –

(a) the taking of the prisoner to a place in the United Kingdom and his delivery at a place of departure from the United Kingdom into the custody of a person representing the appropriate authority of the country or territory to which the prisoner is to be transferred; and
(b) the bringing of the prisoner back to the United Kingdom and his transfer in custody to the place where he is liable to be detained under the sentence to which he is subject.

(4) Where a warrant has been issued in respect of a prisoner under this section he shall be deemed to be in legal custody at any time when, being in the United Kingdom or on board a British ship, British aircraft or British hovercraft, he is being taken under the warrant to or from any place or being kept in custody under the warrant.

(5) A person authorised by or for the purposes of the warrant to take the prisoner to or from any place or to keep him in custody shall have all the powers, authority, protection and privileges –

(a) of a constable in the part of the United Kingdom in which that person is for the time being; or
(b) if he is outside the United Kingdom, of a constable in the part of the United Kingdom to or from which the prisoner is to be taken under the warrant.

(6) If the prisoner escapes or is unlawfully at large, he may be arrested without warrant by a constable and taken to any place to which he may be taken under the warrant issued under this section.

(7) In subsection (4) above –

"British aircraft" means a British-controlled aircraft within the meaning of section 92 of the Civil Aviation Act 1982 (application of criminal law to aircraft) or one of Her Majesty's aircraft;

"British hovercraft" means a British-controlled hovercraft within the meaning of that section as applied in relation to hovercraft by virtue of provisions made under the Hovercraft Act 1968 or one of Her Majesty's hovercraft;

> "British ship" means a British ship for the purposes of the Merchant Shipping Acts 1894 to 1988 or one of Her Majesty's ships;

and in this subsection references to Her Majesty's aircraft, hovercraft or ships are references to aircraft, hovercraft or, as the case may be, ships belonging to or exclusively employed in the service of Her Majesty in right of the Government of the United Kingdom.

(8) In subsection (6) above "constable", in relation to any part of the United Kingdom, means any person who is a constable in that or any other part of the United Kingdom or any person who, at the place in question has, under any enactment including subsection (5) above, the powers of a constable in that or any other part of the United Kingdom.

(9) This section applies to a person in custody awaiting trial or sentence and a person committed to prison for default in paying a fine as it applies to a prisoner and the reference in subsection (3)(b) above to a sentence shall be construed accordingly.

(10) In the application of this section to Northern Ireland for the reference in subsection (1) to the Prison Act 1952 there shall be substituted a reference to the Prison Act (Northern Ireland) 1953.

6 Transfer of overseas prisoner to give evidence or assist investigation in the United Kingdom
(1) This section has effect where –

(a) a witness order has been made or a witness summons or citation issued in criminal proceedings in the United Kingdom in respect of a person ("a prisoner") who is detained in custody in a country or territory outside the United Kingdom by virtue of a sentence or order of a court or tribunal exercising criminal jurisdiction in that country or territory; or
(b) it appears to the Secretary of State that it is desirable for a prisoner to be identified in, or otherwise by his presence to assist, such proceedings or the investigation in the United Kingdom of an offence.

(2) If the Secretary of State is satisfied that the appropriate authority in the country or territory where the prisoner is detained will make arrangements for him to come to the United Kingdom to give evidence pursuant to the witness order, witness summons or citation or, as the case may be, for the purpose mentioned in subsection (1)(b) above, he may issue a warrant under this section.

(3) No warrant shall be issued under this section in respect of any prisoner unless he has consented to being brought to the United Kingdom to give evidence as aforesaid or, as the case may be, for the purpose mentioned in subsection (1)(b) above but a consent once given shall not be capable of being withdrawn after the issue of the warrant.

(4) The effect of the warrant shall be to authorise –

(a) the bringing of the prisoner to the United Kingdom;
(b) the taking of the prisoner to, and his detention in custody at, such place or places in the United Kingdom as are specified in the warrant; and
(c) the returning of the prisoner to the country or territory from which he has come.

(5) Subsections (4) to (8) of section 5 above shall have effect in relation to a warrant issued under this section as they have effect in relation to a warrant issued under that section.

(6) A person shall not be subject to the Immigration Act 1971 in respect of his entry into or presence in the United Kingdom in pursuance of a warrant under this section but if the warrant ceases to have effect while he is still in the United Kingdom –

(a) he shall be treated for the purposes of that Act as if he has then illegally entered the United Kingdom; and
(b) the provisions of Schedule 2 to that Act shall have effect accordingly except that

paragraph 20(1) (liability of carrier for expenses of custody etc. of illegal entrant) shall not have effect in relation to directions for his removal given by virtue of this subsection.

(7) This section applies to a person detained in custody in a country or territory outside the United Kingdom in consequence of having been transferred there –

(a) from the United Kingdom under the Repatriation of Prisoners Act 1984; or

(b) under any similar provision or arrangement from any other country or territory,

as it applies to a person detained as mentioned in subsection (1) above.

Additional co-operation powers

7 Search etc for material relevant to overseas investigation

(1) Part II of the Police and Criminal Evidence Act 1984 (powers of entry, search and seizure) shall have effect as if references to serious arrestable offences in section 8 of and Schedule 1 to that Act included any conduct which is an offence under the law of a country or territory outside the United Kingdom and would constitute a serious arrestable offence if it had occurred in any part of the United Kingdom.

(2) If, on an application made by a constable, a justice of the peace is satisfied –

(a) that criminal proceedings have been instituted against a person in a country or territory outside the United Kingdom or that a person has been arrested in the course of a criminal investigation carried on there;

(b) that the conduct constituting the offence which is the subject of the proceedings or investigation would constitute an arrestable offence within the meaning of the said Act of 1984 if it had occurred in any part of the United Kingdom; and

(c) that there are reasonable grounds for suspecting that there is on premises in the United Kingdom occupied or controlled by that person evidence relating to the offence other than items subject to legal privilege within the meaning of that Act,

he may issue a warrant authorising a constable to enter and search those premises and to seize any such evidence found there.

(3) The power to search conferred by subsection (2) above is only a power to search to the extent that is reasonably required for the purpose of discovering such evidence as is there mentioned.

(4) No application for a warrant or order shall be made by virtue of subsection (1) or (2) above except in pursuance of a direction given by the Secretary of State in response to a request received –

(a) from a court or tribunal exercising criminal jurisdiction in the overseas country or territory in question or a prosecuting authority in that country or territory; or

(b) from any other authority in that country or territory which appears to him to have the function of making requests for the purposes of this section;

and any evidence seized by a constable by virtue of this section shall be furnished by him to the Secretary of State for transmission to that court, tribunal or authority.

(5) If in order to comply with the request it is necessary for any such evidence to be accompanied by any certificate, affidavit or other verifying document the constable shall also furnish for transmission such document of that nature as may be specified in the direction given by the Secretary of State.

(6) Where the evidence consists of a document the original or a copy shall be transmitted, and where it consists of any other article the article itself or a description, photograph or other representation of it shall be transmitted, as may be necessary in order to comply with the request.

(7) The Treasury may by order direct that any powers which by virtue of this section are exercisable by a constable shall also be exercisable by, or by any person acting under

the direction of, an officer commissioned by the Commissioners of Customs and Excise under section 6(3) of the Customs and Excise Management Act 1979; and the Secretary of State may by order direct that any of those powers shall also be exercisable by a person of any other description specified in the order.

(8) An order under subsection (7) above shall be made by statutory instrument subject to annulment in pursuance of a resolution of either House of Parliament.

(9) In the application of this section to Northern Ireland for references to the Police and Criminal Evidence Act 1984, to Part II and section 8 of and to Schedule 1 to that Act there shall be substituted references to the Police and Criminal Evidence (Northern Ireland) Order 1989, to Part III and Article 10 of and to Schedule 1 to that Order.

8 Search etc for material relevant to overseas investigation: Scotland

(1) If, on an application made by the procurator fiscal, it appears to the sheriff –

(a) that there are reasonable grounds for believing that an offence under the law of a country or territory outside the United Kingdom has been committed; and
(b) that the conduct constituting that offence would constitute an offence punishable by imprisonment if it had occurred in Scotland,

the sheriff shall have the like power to grant warrant authorising entry, search and seizure by any constable as he would have at common law in respect of any offence punishable at common law in Scotland.

(2) No application for a warrant shall be made by virtue of subsection (1) above except in pursuance of a direction given by the Lord Advocate in response to a request received by the Secretary of State –

(a) from a court or tribunal exercising criminal jurisdiction in the overseas country or territory in question or a prosecuting authority in that country or territory; or
(b) from any other authority in that country or territory which appears to him to have the function of making requests for the purpose of this section,

and any evidence seized by the constable by virtue of this section shall be furnished by him to the Lord Advocate for transmission to that court, tribunal or authority.

(3) If in order to comply with the request it is necessary for any such evidence to be accompanied by any certificate, affidavit or other verifying document the constable shall also furnish for transmission such document of that nature as may be specified in the direction given by the Lord Advocate.

(4) Where the evidence consists of a document the original or a copy shall be transmitted, and where it consists of any other article the article itself or a description, photograph or other representation of it shall be transmitted, as may be necessary in order to comply with the request.

(5) The Treasury may by order direct that any powers to enter, search or seize granted by virtue of subsection (1) above which may be exercised by a constable shall also be exercisable by, or by any person acting under the direction of, an officer commissioned by the Commissioners of Customs and Excise under section 6(3) of the Customs and Excise Management Act 1979; and the Secretary of State may by order direct that any of those powers shall also be exercisable by a person of any other description specified in the order.

(6) An order under subsection (5) above shall be made by statutory instrument subject to annulment in pursuance of a resolution of either House of Parliament.

9 Enforcement of overseas forfeiture orders

(1) Her Majesty may by Order in Council provide for the enforcement in the United Kingdom of any order which –

(a) is made by a court in a country or territory outside the United Kingdom designated for the purposes of this section by the Order in Council; and

(b) is for the forfeiture and destruction, or the forfeiture and other disposal, of anything in respect of which an offence to which this section applies has been committed or which was used in connection with the commission of such an offence.

(2) Without prejudice to the generality of subsection (1) above an Order in Council under this section may provide for the registration by a court in the United Kingdom of any order as a condition of its enforcement and prescribe requirements to be satisfied before an order can be registered.

(3) An Order in Council under this section may include such supplementary and incidental provisions as appear to Her Majesty to be necessary or expedient and may apply for the purposes of the Order (with such modifications as appear to Her Majesty to be appropriate) any provisions relating to confiscation or forfeiture orders under any other enactment.

(4) An Order in Council under this section may make different provision for different cases.

(5) No Order in Council shall be made under this section unless a draft of it has been laid before and approved by a resolution of each House of Parliament.

(6) This section applies to any offence which corresponds to or is similar to an offence under the Misuse of Drugs Act 1971, a drug trafficking offence as defined in section 38(1) of the Drug Trafficking Offences Act 1986, an offence to which section 1 of the Criminal Justice (Scotland) Act 1987 relates or an offence to which Part VI of the Criminal Justice Act 1988 applies.

Supplementary

10 Rules of court
(1) Provision may be made by rules of court for any purpose for which it appears to the authority having power to make the rules that it is necessary or expedient that provision should be made in connection with any of the provisions of this Part of this Act.

(2) Rules made for the purposes of Schedule 1 to this Act may, in particular, make provision with respect to the persons entitled to appear or take part in the proceedings to which that Schedule applies and for excluding the public from any such proceedings.

(3) An Order in Council under section 9 above may authorise the making of rules of court for any purpose specified in the Order.

(4) Rules of court made under this section by the High Court in Scotland shall be made by Act of Adjournal.

(5) This section is without prejudice to the generality of any existing power to make rules.

11 Application to courts-martial etc
(1) Section 2 above applies also to a summons requiring a person charged with a civil offence to appear before a service court (whether or not in the United Kingdom) or to attend before such a court for the purpose of giving evidence in proceedings for such an offence; and a warrant may be issued under section 6 above where –

(a) such a summons has been issued in respect of a prisoner within the meaning of that section; or
(b) it appears to the Secretary of State that it is desirable for such a prisoner to be identified in, or otherwise by his presence to assist, such proceedings or the investigation of such an offence.

(2) Section 5 above applies also to a person serving a sentence of detention imposed by a service court or detained in custody awaiting trial by such a court.

(3) In this section "a civil offence" has the same meaning as in the Army Act 1955, the Air Force Act 1955 and the Naval Discipline Act 1957 and "service court" means a court-martial constituted under any of those Acts or a Standing Civilian Court.

SCHEDULE 1
UNITED KINGDOM EVIDENCE FOR USE OVERSEAS:
PROCEEDINGS OF NOMINATED COURT

Section 4(6)

Securing attendance of witnesses

1 The court shall have the like powers for securing the attendance of a witness for the purpose of the proceedings as it has for the purpose of other proceedings before the court.

2 In Scotland the court shall have power to issue a warrant to officers of law to cite witnesses for the purpose of the proceedings and section 320 of the Criminal Procedure (Scotland) Act 1975 shall apply in relation to such a witness.

Power to administer oaths

3 The court may in the proceedings take evidence on oath.

Privilege of witnesses

4 (1) A person shall not be compelled to give in the proceedings any evidence which he could not be compelled to give –

 (a) in criminal proceedings in the part of the United Kingdom in which the nominated court exercises jurisdiction; or
 (b) subject to sub-paragraph (2) below, in criminal proceedings in the country or territory from which the request for the evidence has come.

(2) Sub-paragraph (1)(b) above shall not apply unless the claim of the person questioned to be exempt from giving the evidence is conceded by the court, tribunal or authority which made the request.

(3) Where such a claim made by any person is not conceded as aforesaid he may (subject to the other provisions of this paragraph) be required to give the evidence to which the claim relates but the evidence shall not be transmitted to the court, tribunal or authority which requested it if a court in the country or territory in question, on the matter being referred to it, upholds the claim.

(4) Without prejudice to sub-paragraph (1) above a person shall not be compelled under this Schedule to give any evidence if his doing so would be prejudicial to the security of the United Kingdom; and a certificate signed by or on behalf of the Secretary of State or, where the court is in Scotland, by or on behalf of the Lord Advocate to the effect that it would be so prejudicial for that person to do so shall be conclusive evidence of that fact.

(5) Without prejudice to sub-paragraph (1) above a person shall not be compelled under this Schedule to give any evidence in his capacity as an officer or servant of the Crown.

(6) In this paragraph references to giving evidence include references to answering any question and to producing any document or other article and the reference in sub-paragraph (3) above to the transmission of evidence given by a person shall be construed accordingly.

Transmission of evidence

5 (1) The evidence received by the court shall be furnished to the Secretary of State or, in Scotland, the Lord Advocate for transmission to the court, tribunal or authority that made the request.

(2) If in order to comply with the request it is necessary for the evidence to be accompanied by any certificate, affidavit or other verifying document, the court shall also furnish for transmission such document of that nature as may be specified in the notice nominating the court.

(3) Where the evidence consists of a document the original or a copy shall be transmitted, and where it consists of any other article the article itself or a description, photograph or other representation of it shall be transmitted, as may be necessary in order to comply with the request.

Supplementary

6 For the avoidance of doubt it is hereby declared that the Bankers Books' Evidence Act 1879 applies to the proceedings as it applies to other proceedings before the court.

7 No order for costs shall be made in the proceedings.

Statutory instruments

SI 1988 No 1691

Criminal Justice Act 1987 (Notice of Transfer) Regulations 1988

1 Citation and commencement
These Regulations may be cited as the Criminal Justice Act 1987 (Notice of Transfer) Regulations 1988 and shall come into force on 31st October 1988.

2 Interpretation
In these Regulations –

"designated authority" means an authority designated by section 4(2) of the Criminal Justice Act 1987; and

"notice of transfer" means a notice given under section 4(1) of that Act.

3 Notice of transfer
A notice of transfer given by or on behalf of a designated authority shall be in Form 1 in the Schedule to these Regulations, or in a form to the like effect.

4 Notice to defendant
Where a notice of transfer is given by or on behalf of designated authority, a copy of the notice shall be given by or on behalf of the authority to any person to whom the notice of transfer relates (or, if he is acting by a solicitor, to his solicitor) together with –

(a) a notice in Form 2 in the Schedule to these Regulations, or in a form to the like effect; and
(b) a statement of the evidence on which any charge to which the notice of transfer relates is based.

5 Notice to Crown Court
Where a notice of transfer is given by or on behalf of a designated authority, a copy of the notice shall be given by or on behalf of the authority to the appropriate officer of the Crown Court sitting at the place specified by the notice of transfer as the proposed place of trial together with –

(a) a copy of the notice referred to in paragraph (a) of regulation 4 above and copies of the material enclosed with that notice; and
(b) the statement referred to in paragraph (b) of that regulation.

6 Notice to prison governor etc
Where a notice of transfer is given by or on behalf of a designated authority, a copy of the notice shall be given by or on behalf of the authority to any person who has custody of any person to whom the notice of transfer relates together with a copy of the notice referred to in paragraph (a) of regulation 4 above.

SCHEDULE

FORM 1

CRIMINAL JUSTICE ACT 1987

THE QUEEN

v

NOTICE OF TRANSFER OF CASE TO THE CROWN COURT

To the Clerk to the Justices   Magistrates' Court

1 I am [an officer of]
[acting on behalf of him/them].

2   has/have been charged with the indictable offence/offences specified in the Schedule of Charges attached to this Form.

3 The Magistrates' Court in whose jurisdiction the offence/offences has/have been charged has not begun to enquire into the case as examining justices.

4 I certify that in my opinion the evidence of the offence/offences charged –

(a) would be sufficient for   to be committed for trial, and
(b) reveals a case of fraud of such seriousness and complexity that it is appropriate that the management of the case should without delay be taken over by the Crown Court.

5 Accordingly, the functions of the Magistrates' Court cease in relation to the case, except as provided by section 5(3), (7A) and (8) of the Criminal Justice Act 1987 and by section 28(7A) of the Legal Aid Act 1974.

6 The proposed place of trial is the Crown Court sitting at [Where this notice relates to more than one person, paragraph 7 below is to be completed in respect of each person to whom it relates.]

7   was on the   day of   19   remanded in custody to appear at   Magistrates' Court on the   day of   19   . Notice has been given to him requesting him to indicate whether he consents to the Court exercising its powers under section 5(3) of the Criminal Justice Act 1987 without his being brought before the Court.

or

7   was on the   day of   19   remanded on bail to appear at   Magistrates' Court on the   day of   19   . [Notice has been given to him that this requirement has now ceased but that it is his duty to appear before the Crown Court sitting at   , or at such other place as shall be notified to him, on a date to be notified to him.] [Notice has been given to him that this requirement continues.]

8 I propose to invite the Magistrates' Court to make an order under section 1 of the Criminal Procedure (Attendance of Witnesses) Act 1965 in respect of each of the witnesses listed in the Schedule of Proposed Witnesses attached to this Form.

Dated this   day of   19   .

Name
Title

SCHEDULE OF CHARGES
SCHEDULE OF PROPOSED WITNESSES

FORM 2

CRIMINAL JUSTICE ACT 1987

THE QUEEN

v

NOTICE TO PERSON TO WHOM A NOTICE OF TRANSFER RELATES

To   of

1 Under section 4 of the Criminal Justice Act 1987 I have given to   Magistrates' Court a notice of transfer in relation to the charges specified in the notice, a copy of which is

attached. Accordingly, the case is transferred to the Crown Court. The proposed place of trial is the Crown Court sitting at

2 The Crown Court may give directions altering the place of trial. If you are dissatisfied with the proposed place of trial stated in the notice of transfer, or the place of trial as substituted by a direction of the Crown Court, you may apply to the Crown Court to vary the place of trial.

3 On the   day of   19   Magistrates' Court remanded you in custody to appear on the   day of   19   . [The Court later granted you bail subject to certain conditions which you failed to meet, and accordingly you have remained in custody to appear on that day.] Under section 5(3) of the Criminal Justice Act 1987 the Magistrates' Court has power –

(a) to order that you shall be safely kept in custody until delivered in due course of law, or
(b) to release you on bail in accordance with the Bail Act 1976, that is to say, by directing you to appear before the Crown Court for trial.

The Magistrates' Court may exercise those powers without your being brought before the Court if –

(a) you have given your written consent, and
(b) the Court is satisfied that, when you gave your consent, you knew that the notice of transfer had been issued.

You may give your consent by signing the attached form of consent and passing it to the prison governor for him to send it to the Magistrates' Court by the   day of   19   (the date of your next appearance).

or

3 On the   day of   19   Magistrates' Court remanded you on bail to appear on the day of   19   . That requirement has ceased and in accordance with section 5(7) of the Criminal Justice Act 198? it is your duty to appear before the Crown Court sitting at   , or at such other place as may be notified to you, on a date to be notified to you.

or

3 On the   day of   19   Magistrates' Court remanded you on bail to appear on the   day of   19   . You are required to so appear notwithstanding the giving of the notice of transfer.

4 The bill of indictment against you may include, either in substitution for or in addition to any count charging an offence specified in the notice of transfer, any counts founded on evidence set out in the material that accompanies this notice, being counts which may lawfully be joined in the same indictment.

5 I enclose a list of witnesses –

(a) indicating those whom the Crown proposes to call to give oral evidence at your trial (and in whose case the Magistrates' Court will be invited to make a witness order under section 1(1) of the Criminal Procedure (Attendance of Witnesses) Act 1965); and
(b) indicating those whose attendance at your trial the Crown considers unnecessary on the ground that their evidence is unlikely to be required or unlikely to be disputed (and in whose case the Magistrates' Court will be invited to make a conditional witness order under section 1(2) of that Act),

together with in each case copies of the statements or other documents outlining the evidence of those witnesses.

6 I also enclose a list of the exhibits in your case together with copies of those exhibits which are in documentary form.

7 At any time before you are arraigned at the Crown Court you may apply orally or in writing to the Crown Court for the charge/any of the charges to be dismissed on the ground that the evidence which has been disclosed is not sufficient for a jury properly to convict you of it. If you wish to apply for the charge/any of the charges to be dismissed, you should make a written application not later than 28 days after the day on which the notice of transfer was given or give notice within the same period of your intention to do so orally, in accordance with the requirements of the Criminal Justice Act 1987 (Dismissal of Transferred Charges) Rules 1988. These periods may be extended on application to the Crown Court.

8 At your trial you may not be permitted to adduce evidence of an alibi unless you give notice of

particulars of the alibi in accordance with section 11 of the Criminal Justice Act 1967. Such notice should be given to me within 7 days of the giving of the notice of transfer.

Dated this   day of   19   .

Name

Title

FORM 3

CRIMINAL JUSTICE ACT 1987

THE QUEEN

v

CONSENT FORM FOR PERSON REMANDED IN CUSTODY

To the Clerk to the Justices   Magistrates' Court

I have received a copy of notice of transfer issued under section 4 of the Criminal Justice Act 1987 relating to my case.

I hereby consent to the   Magistrates' Court exercising its powers under section 5(3) of that Act without may being brought before it. (Those powers are described in paragraph 3 of the notice issued to me entitled "Notice to Person to whom a Notice of Transfer relates".)

Dated this   day of   19   .

Signed

SI 1988 No 1695

Criminal Justice Act 1987 (Dismissal of Transferred Charges) Rules 1988

1 Citation, commencement and interpretation

(1) These Rules may be cited as the Criminal Justice Act 1987 (Dismissal of Transferred Charges) Rules 1988 and shall come into force on 31st October 1988.

(2) In these Rules, "the Act" means the Criminal Justice Act 1987.

2 Oral applications for dismissal

(1) Where notice of transfer has been given by the prosecution under section 4 of the Act and a person to whom it relates proposes to apply orally under section 6(1) thereof for any charge in the case to be dismissed, he shall give notice in writing in Form 5301 of his intention to the appropriate officer of the Crown Court at the place specified by the notice of transfer as the proposed place of trial.

(2) A notice of intention to make such an application shall be given not later than 28 days after the day on which notice of transfer was given, and a copy thereof shall be given at the same time to the authority by or on behalf of whom notice of transfer was given and to any other person to whom the notice of transfer relates.

(3) The time for giving notice may be extended, either before or after it expires, by the Crown Court, on an application made in accordance with paragraph (4) below.

(4) An application for an extension of time for giving notice shall be made in writing in Form 5301 specifying the grounds of the application and shall be sent to the

appropriate officer of the Crown Court; and a copy thereof shall be given at the same time to the authority by or on behalf of whom notice of transfer was given and to any other person to whom the notice of transfer relates.

(5) The appropriate officer of the Crown Court shall give notice in Form 5303 of the judge's decision on an application under paragraph (3) above –

(a) to the applicant;
(b) to the authority by or on behalf of whom notice of transfer was given; and
(c) to any other person to whom the notice of transfer relates.

(6) A notice of intention to make an application under section 6(1) of the Act shall be accompanied by a copy of any material on which the applicant relies and shall –

(a) specify the charge or charges to which it relates; and
(b) state whether the leave of the judge is sought under section 6(3) of the Act to adduce oral evidence on the application, indicating what witnesses it is proposed to call at the hearing.

(7) Where leave is sought from the judge for oral evidence to be given on an application, notice of his decision, indicating what witnesses are to be called if leave is granted, shall be given by the appropriate officer of the Crown Court in Form 5303 to the authority by or on behalf of whom the notice of transfer was given and to any other party to whom notice of transfer relates.

(8) Where an application for dismissal under section 6(1) of that Act is to be made orally, the appropriate officer of the Crown Court shall list the application for hearing before a judge of the Crown Court.

3 Written applications for dimissal

(1) A written application for dismissal under section 6(1) of the Act shall be made in Form 5301.

(2) The application shall be sent to the appropriate officer of the Crown Court and shall be accompanied by a copy of any statement or other document, and identify any article, on which the applicant relies.

(3) A copy of the application and of any accompanying documents shall be given at the same time to the authority by or on behalf of whom notice of transfer was given and to any other person to whom the notice of transfer relates.

(4) A written application for dismissal shall be made not later than 28 days after the day on which notice of transfer was given unless the time for making the application is extended, either before or after it expires, by the Crown Court; and paragraphs (4) and (5) of rule 2 above shall apply for the purposes of this paragraph as if references therein to giving notice of intention to make an oral application were references to making a written application under this rule.

4 Prosecution reply

(1) Not later than seven days from the date of service of notice of intention to apply orally for the dismissal of any charge contained in a notice of transfer, the authority by or on behalf of whom notice of transfer was given may apply to the Crown Court for leave under section 6(3) of the Act to adduce oral evidence at the hearing of the application, indicating what witnesses it is proposed to call.

(2) Not later than seven days from the date of receiving a copy of an application for dismissal under rule 3(2) above, the authority by or on behalf of whom notice of transfer was given may apply to the Crown Court for an oral hearing of the application.

(3) An application under paragraph (1) or (2) above shall be made in writing in Form 5302 to the appropriate officer of the Crown Court specifying the grounds of the

application and, in the case of an application under paragraph (2) above, stating whether the leave of the judge is sought under section 6(3) of the Act to adduce oral evidence and, if so, indicating what witnesses it is proposed to call.

(4) Notice of the judge's determination upon an application under paragraph (1) or (2) above, indicating what witnesses (if any) are to be called shall be served in Form 5303 by the appropriate officer of the Crown Court on the authority making the application and on any other party to whom the notice of transfer relates.

(5) Where, having received the material specified in rule 2(6) or, as the case may be, rule 3(2) above, the authority by or on behalf of whom notice of transfer was given proposes to adduce in reply thereto any written comments or any further evidence, the authority shall serve any such comments, copies of the statements or other documents outlining the evidence of any proposed witnesses and copies of any further documents on the appropriate officer of the Crown Court not later than fourteen days from the date of receiving the said material, and shall at the same time serve copies thereof on all parties to whom the notice of transfer relates.

(6) The time for –

(a) making an application under paragraph (1) or (2) above; or
(b) serving any material on the appropriate officer of the Crown Court under paragraph (5) above,

may be extended, either before or after it expires, by the Crown Court, on an application made in accordance with paragraph (7) below.

(7) An application for an extension of time under paragraph (6) above shall be made in writing in Form 5302 and shall be served on the appropriate officer of the Crown Court; and a copy thereof shall be served at the same time on to the applicant for dismissal and on any other person to whom the notice of transfer relates.

5 Determination of applications for dismissal – procedural matters

(1) A judge may grant leave for a witness to give oral evidence on an application for dismissal notwithstanding that notice of intention to call the witness has not been given in accordance with the foregoing provisions of these Rules.

(2) Where an application for dismissal is determined otherwise than at an oral hearing, the appropriate officer of the Crown Court shall as soon as practicable, send to all the parties to the case a notice, in Form 5304, of the outcome of the application.

6 Service of documents

(1) Any notice or other document which is required by these Rules to be given to any person may be served personally on that person or sent to him by post at his usual or last known residence or place of business in England and Wales or, in the case of a company, at the company's registered office in England or Wales.

(2) If the person to be served is acting by a solicitor, the notice or other document may be served by delivering it, or sending it by post, to the solicitor's address for service.

7 Forms

(1) Any reference in these Rules to a form is a reference to a form set out in the Schedule to these Rules.

(2) The forms set out in the Schedule to these Rules or forms substantially to the like effect may be used with such variations as the circumstances may require.

SCHEDULE FORMS

**Application for dismissal of transferred charge(s)
under s.6 Criminal Justice Act 1987**

This form may be used to give notice of intention to apply orally, or to apply in writing, for dismissal of transferred charge(s), for application to call witnesses or for an extension of time within which to apply. Applications for dismissal must be received by the Court named in the notice of transfer, within 28 days of the date on that notice.

A copy of this form and of any statements or documentary evidence on which the applicant relies must be served at the same time on the authority by, or on behalf of whom, the notice of transfer was given and on any other person to whom the notice of transfer relates.

Case Details

Enter the name of the Court shown on the Notice of Transfer, the case no., and the date of the Notice

The Crown Court at　　　　　　　Crown Court Case Number

Date of notice of transfer

Designated Authority

State name and address of the applicant to whom this application relates. (If in custody give address where detained.)

Applicant Surname
　　　Forenames
　　　Address

　　　　　　　　　　Date of birth

Application

Tick box as appropriate

☐ Notice of intention to apply *orally* for dismissal s.6(2) CJA 1987

☐ Application to call witnesses in support of application for dismissal s.6(3) CJA 1987

☐ Application for extension of time within which to give notice of intention to make an oral application.

☐ *Written* application for dismissal

☐ Application for extension of time within which to make a written application.

If applying for an extension only you will need to submit a complete form in due course.

Charges

Specify all charges and indicate those to which this application applies

(If applying only for an extension, you do not need to complete this section)

Form 5301 Application for dismissal of transferred charge(s) or for extension of time

Grounds for applying

(a) Application for dismissal: The evidence which has been disclosed would not be sufficient for a jury to properly convict.

(b) Application for extension of time:

If applying for an extension, state the grounds

For oral applications, indicate which witnesses you propose to call, if leave is given. For oral and written applications identify any material on which you rely

Witnesses and material on which you rely (copies of all documents must be attached)

Signature of applicant	Details of any person signing on behalf of applicant
	Name
Date	Solicitor/Counsel* Address
	Reference

**Application by prosecution for oral hearing
of defence application for dismissal**

This form may be used by the prosecution to apply for:

- an oral hearing of a defence application for dismissal;
- an application for leave to call witnesses; or
- an extension of time within which to apply for a) an oral hearing or b) to submit documents.

An application by the prosecution for an oral hearing, or for an extension of time within which to apply for an oral hearing, must be made within 7 days of receipt of notice of the defence application for dismissal. Written comments or material must be submitted to the appropriate officer of the court within 14 days of the date of receipt of the defence application. A copy of this form must be given to the applicant for dismissal and to any other person to whom the application to dismiss relates.

Case Details

Enter the name of the Court shown on the notice of transfer, the case no., and the date of receipt of the defence application

The Crown Court at   Crown Court
                                Case Number:

Date of receipt of copy of defence application:

State the name(s) and address(es) of the defendant(s) to whom this application relates. If in custody, give address where detained.

Defendant(s)* Surname
         Forename(s)
            Address

                                Date of birth:

Application

State the name, address and reference

Designated authority: Ref:

Tick as appropriate

☐ Application for an oral hearing

☐ Application for leave to call witnesses under s.6(3) CJA 1987

☐ Application for extension of time within which to apply for oral hearing

☐ Application for extension of time within which to submit documents

---

Charges

Specify all charges and indicate those to which the application for dismissal applies and those on which the prosecution intend to respond

---

Grounds for applying

State the grounds on which the application is being made

Witnesses

Indicate which witnesses you propose to call, if leave is given

---

Signature   **Date**

Form 5302 Application by Prosecution for oral hearing or for extension of time

In the Crown Court at
**Notification of Court's Determination on Applications
under s.6 CJA 1987**   Case Number

This form shall be used for notifying all parties of the court's determination of the
following applications:
- by the prosecution for oral hearing of a defence application for dismissal;
- by the defence or prosecution for leave to call witnesses;
- by the defence or prosecution for an extension of time within which to lodge an
  application for oral hearing; or
- by the prosecution for extension of time within which to submit material to the
  court.

Case Details

Defendant(s)   Surname:
            Forename(s):
                Address:
            (if in custody give
        address where detained)   Date of birth:

Charges (indicate those to which the application applies)

Nature of Application

☐   Application by prosecution for oral hearing of application for dismissal of
    transferred charge(s) s.6(1)CJA 1987

☐   Defence*/Prosecution* application for leave to call witnesses s.6(3)CJA 1987

☐   Defence*/Prosecution* application for extension of time within which to
    lodge an application for oral hearing

☐   Prosecution application for extension of time within which to submit written
    comments or other material to the court.

*delete as appropriate

Form 5303 Notice of Court Decision on application for oral hearing etc., or extension of time Page 1 of 2

Court's Decision

(Specify court's decision on each application considered. Where an application is
refused the reasons for refusal should be stated.)

Signed   Date
(an Officer of the Court)

In the Crown Court at

**Notification of the Court's determination
of a written application for dismissal of transferred charge(s)
under s.6(1) Criminal Justice Act 1987**

Case Number

Case Details

Defendant(s)   Surname:
          Forename(s):
          Address:
    (if in custody give
  address where detained)   Date of birth:

Charges *(Those on which dismissal was sought to be separately identified)**

Court's Decision

(Specify court's decision. Where an application is refused the reasons for refusal should be stated. Include details of any bail variations, and counts substituted, added or quashed).

Signed   Date
(an Officer of the Court)

Form 5304 Notification of Judge's determination of application for dismissal

SI 1988 No 1699

Criminal Justice Act 1987
(Preparatory Hearings) Rules 1988

1 Citation and interpretation

(1) These Rules may be cited as the Criminal Justice Act 1987 (Preparatory Hearings) Rules 1988.

(2) In these Rules "the Act" means the Criminal Justice Act 1987.

2 Commencement

These Rules shall come into force on 31st October 1988 and shall apply in relation to any case where –

   (a) the case is committed for trial on or after that date; or

   (b) a notice of transfer in respect of the case is given under section 4 of the Act on or after that date; or

   (c) consent is given by a judge of the High Court on or after that date to the preferment of a bill of indictment in respect of the case.

3 Form of application for a preparatory hearing

(1) An application in pursuance of section 7(2) of the Act shall be made in writing in Form 5305 to the appropriate officer of the Crown Court at the place specified by the notice of transfer as the proposed place of trial and shall include a concise statement of the grounds, having regard to the matters specified in subsection (1) of that section, for the making of the application.

(2) The person making the application shall at the same time serve a copy thereof on the other party or, if there is more than one, each of the other parties in the case.

4 Time for making application

(1) An application for a preparatory hearing shall be made not later than 28 days after the day on which the case was committed for trial or, as the case may be, a notice of transfer or consent to the preferral of a bill of indictment was given in relation to the case.

(2) Where an application for dismissal of a charge has not been granted an application for a preparatory hearing in relation to that charge shall be made not later than seven days after the day on which the application for its dismissal was determined.

(3) The time for making an application for a preparatory hearing may be extended, either before or after it expires, on an application made in accordance with paragraph (4) below.

(4) An application for an extension of time under paragraph (3) above shall be made in writing in Form 5305, specifying the grounds of the application and served on the appropriate officer of the Crown Court, and a copy thereof shall be served on the other party or if there is more than one, each of the other parties in the case.

(5) The appropriate officer of the Crown Court shall give notice of the judge's decision on an application under paragraph (3) above to the applicant and to the other party or, if there is more than one, each of the other parties in the case.

5 Notification of order for preparatory hearing

Notice of an order for a preparatory hearing shall be given in Form 5306 and shall be served by the appropriate officer of the Crown Court on each person indicted and on the prosecution.

6 Disclosure of prosecution case
Where an order is made under section 7(3) or 9(4) of the Act for the prosecution to prepare and serve any documents, the order shall identify the documents to be served and require the prosecution to serve a copy of each such document on each person indicted; and the appropriate officer of the Crown Court shall serve a copy of the order on each person indicted and on the prosecution.

7 Defence disclosure
(1) Where an order is made under section 7(4) or 9(5) of the Act the appropriate officer of the Crown Court shall serve a copy of the order in Form 5307 on each party to whom the order applies and on the prosecution.

(2) Except to the extent that disclosure is required –

(a) by section 11 of the Criminal Justice Act 1967 (alibi); or
(b) by rules under section 81 of the Police and Criminal Evidence Act 1984 (expert evidence),

a statement required by virtue of an order under the said section 7(4) or 9(5)(i) or (iv) need not disclose who will give evidence; and the order shall include a statement to that effect.

(3) The order shall include a warning that if any party departs from the case which he disclosed at the preparatory hearing, or fails to comply with a requirement imposed at the hearing –

(a) the judge or, with the leave of the judge, any other party may make such comment as appears to him appropriate and the jury may draw such inference as appears proper; and
(b) where the court is satisfied that any such departure or failure on the part of a defendant constitutes an unnecessary or improper act or omission on his part, and that another party to the proceedings has incurred costs as a result thereof, the court may make an order as to the payment of those costs by the defendant under section 19 of the Prosecution of Offences Act 1985.

8 Orders at or for purposes of preparatory hearings – supplementary
(1) Where a judge makes an order at or for the purposes of a preparatory hearing, the order shall so far as is practicable set out the matters required to be done thereunder by reference to the relevant provisions of section 9(4) or, as the case may be, (5) of the Act.

(2) Without prejudice to any other requirements which may be imposed on a party under Part I of the Act, it shall be the duty of a party where a judge has made an order for a preparatory hearing to inform the court of any significant matter which might affect the proper and convenient trial of the case.

9 Service of documents
(1) Any notice or other document which is required by these Rules to be given to any person may be served personally on that person or sent to him by post at his usual or last known residence or place of business in England or Wales or, in the case of a company, at the company's registered office in England and Wales.

(2) If the person to be served is acting by a solicitor, the notice or other document may be served by delivering it, or sending it by post, to the solicitor's address for service.

10 Forms
(1) Any reference in these Rules to a form is a reference to a form set out in the Schedule to these Rules.

(2) The form set out in the Schedule to these Rules or forms substantially to the like effect may be used with such variations as the circumstances may require.

SCHEDULE FORMS

Rule 10

Application for Preparatory Hearing
under s.7(1) Criminal Justice Act 1987
or for extension of time within which to apply

An application for a preparatory hearing, or for an extension of time, must be made within 28 days after the day on which the case was committed for trial, or a notice of transfer or consent to the preferral of a bill of indictment was given or within 7 days of rejection of an application for dismissal.

A copy of this form must be given at the same time to the other party or parties in this case.

Case Details

Enter the name of the Court shown on the notice of transfer, and the case no

The Crown Court at

Crown Court
Case Number:

Date of   notice of transfer*
           committal for trial*

*delete as appropriate

           consent to preferral of bill of indictment*
           rejection of application for dismissal*

State the name(s) of the defendant(s) to whom this application relates (if in custody give address where detained)

Defendant(s)   Surname:
                Forename(s):
                Address

                                Date of birth:

Application

Tick as appropriate   ☐   Defence   ☐   Prosecution/Designated Authority

                       ☐   Application for a preparatory hearing s.7(1)CJA 1987

                       ☐   Application for extension of time within which to apply for a preparatory hearing

Charges

Specify all charges

Grounds for applying

State the grounds on which the application is being made

Signature   Details of any person applying on behalf of applicant
of applicant   Name

Solicitor/Counsel   Address
Date   Reference

Form 5305 Application for preparatory hearing or for extension of time

In the Crown Court at
**Notification of the Court's Determination
of an Application and/or Order for
a Preparatory Hearing under s.7 CJA 1987**

Crown Court Case Number

Case Details

Defendant(s)   Surname:
              Forename(s):
(indicate to whom application relates)

Date of birth:

Charges
(specify all charges)

Determination of Application

☐ Granted   ☐ Refused   ☐ Ordered by Judge

Reasons for refusal:

Date and time of hearing (if known):

Identify each document to be prepared and served on each party by the
prosecution under s.7(3)CJA 1987, and any time limit.

Signed   Date
(an Officer of the Court)

In the Crown Court at
**Order for Defence Disclosure prior to Preparatory Hearing
under s.7(4) or at Preparatory Hearing
under s.9(5) Criminal Justice Act 1987**   Crown Court Case Number

Case Details

Defendant (where there is more than one, a separate form to be completed for each)
Surname:
Forename(s):   Date of birth:

Charges (specify all charges)

Requirements

Date by which any of these specified requirements is to be complied with:

Note: A summary required by virtue of s.9(5)(i) CJA 1987 need not disclose who
will give evidence except to the extent that disclosure is required by s.11
CJA 1967 (alibi) or rules under s.81 Police & Criminal Evidence Act 1984
(expert witness)

Warning

*If any party departs from the case which he disclosed at the preparatory hearing, or
fails to comply with a requirement imposed at the hearing*

*(a) the judge or, with the leave of the judge, any other party may make such
comment as appears to him appropriate and the jury may draw such inference as
appears proper; and*

*(b) where the court is satisfied that any such departure or failure on the part of the
defendant constitutes an unnecessary or improper act or omission on his part,
and that another party to the proceedings has incurred costs as a result thereof,
the court may make an order as to payment of those costs by the defendant
under s.19 of the Prosecution of Offences Act 1985.*

Signed   Date
(an Officer of the Court)

Form 5307 Order for defence disclosure prior to or at preparatory hearing.

SI 1988 No 1700

Criminal Justice Act 1987
(Preparatory Hearings) (Interlocutory Appeals) Rules 1988

1 Citation and commencement

These Rules may be cited as the Criminal Justice Act 1987 (Preparatory Hearings) (Interlocutory Appeals) Rules 1988 and shall come into force on 31st October 1988.

2 Interpretation

(1) In these Rules, unless the context otherwise requires –

"the Act of 1968" means the Criminal Appeal Act 1968 and

"the Act of 1987" means the Criminal Justice Act 1987;

"appellant" means an appellant under section 9(11) of the Act of 1987 including a person who has given notice of application for leave to appeal;

"judge of the court" means a judge of the High Court or the Court of Appeal;

"the principal Rules" means the Criminal Appeal Rules 1968;

"registrar" means the registrar of criminal appeals of the Court of Appeal; and

"respondent" means a party in whose favour is made the order or ruling, or part thereof, appealed against by the appellant.

(2) In reckoning any period of time for the purposes of these Rules, where, apart from this paragraph, the period in question, being a period of 7 days or less, would include a Saturday, Sunday or bank holiday, Christmas Day or Good Friday, that day shall be excluded.

In this paragraph "bank holiday" means a day which is, or is to be observed as, a bank holiday, or a holiday, under the Banking and Financial Dealings Act 1971, in England and Wales.

(3) Any reference in these Rules to a rule is a reference to a rule contained in these Rules.

3 Notice of appeal

(1) An application to the judge of the Crown Court for leave to appeal under section 9(11) of the Act of 1987 shall be made orally within two days of the making of the order or ruling to which it relates.

(2) Unless the application is made on the occasion of the order or ruling to which it relates, the appellant shall serve notice in writing thereof, specifying the grounds of the application, on the appropriate officer of the Crown Court and on all parties to the hearing directly affected by the order or ruling in question.

(3) The appellant shall within seven days from the said order or ruling serve notice of appeal therefrom or, as the case may be, of an application to the Court of Appeal for leave to appeal on –

(a) the registrar;

(b) the appropriate officer of the Crown Court; and

(c) all parties to the preparatory hearing directly affected by the said order or ruling.

(4) The time for giving notice under paragraph (3) above may be extended, before or after it expires, by the Court of Appeal.

(5) A notice of appeal or of an application for leave to appeal shall be in Form 1A(1).

(6) If notice in writing of an application for leave to appeal was, under paragraph (2) above, served on the Crown Court, a copy thereof shall accompany the notice of appeal or, as the case may be, of an application for leave to appeal required under paragraph (3) above to be served on the registrar.

(7) Notice of appeal or of an application for leave to appeal may be given either in respect of the whole or any part of the order to which it relates and shall –

(a) specify any question of law in respect of which the appeal is brought and, where appropriate, such facts of the case as are necessary for its proper consideration;

(b) summarise the arguments intended to be put to the Court of Appeal; and

(c) specify any authorities intended to be cited.

(8) Where the judge of the Crown Court has given leave to appeal the notice of appeal shall state that fact and specify the grounds on which leave is given.

(9) Notice of appeal or of an application for leave to appeal shall be accompanied by any documents or other things (or copies thereof) necessary for the proper determination of the appeal or application.

4 Respondent's notice

(1) Upon receiving notice of appeal or of an application for leave to appeal, the respondent if he desires to oppose the appeal, shall, within seven days of receipt of the notice, serve a notice in Form 1A(2) on the registrar, –

(a) stating the date on which the appellant's notice was received by the respondent;

(b) summarising his response to the arguments of the appellant; and

(c) specifying the authorities which he intends to cite,

and shall at the same time serve a copy thereof on the appellant and any other party to the proceedings directly affected by the order or ruling and on the appropriate officer of the Crown Court.

(2) The time for giving notice under this rule may be extended, either before or after it expires, by the Court of Appeal.

5 Persons in custody

(1) A person in custody shall be entitled to be present on the hearing of an appeal, or an application for leave to appeal, under section 9(11) of the Act, to which he is a party.

(2) Except as provided by paragraph (1) above, a person in custody shall not be entitled to be present on the hearing of an appeal, or an application for leave to appeal, under the said section 9(11), except –

(a) on an application to the Crown Court for leave to appeal, with the leave of the judge; or

(b) on an appeal, or an application to the Court of Appeal for leave to appeal, with the leave of the Court.

(3) An application for leave to be present under paragraph (2) above may be made –

(a) by serving notice in Form 1A(3) on the registrar; or

(b) orally to the judge or the Court.

6 Supply of documentary and other exhibits

Rule 8 of the principal Rules (supply of documentary and other exhibits) shall apply in relation to an appellant and a respondent under section 9(11) of the Act of 1987 as it applies in relation to an appellant and a respondent under Part I of the Act of 1968.

7 Abandonment of proceedings

Rule 10 of the principal Rules (abandonment of proceedings) shall apply for the purposes of an appeal or an application for leave to appeal by an appellant under section 9(11) of the Act of 1987 as it applies to an appeal or application for leave under Part I of the Act of 1968, except that –

(a) notice thereof shall be served on the registrar in Form IA(4); and

(b) the requirement under paragraph (3) of the said rule 10 for the registrar to send a copy of a notice of abandonment of proceedings to the Secretary of State shall be omitted.

8 Powers exercisable by single judge

(1) The following powers may be exercised by a judge of the court in the same manner as they may be exercised by the court and subject to the same provisions, namely –

(a) to give leave to appeal under section 9(11) of the Act of 1987;

(b) to extend, under rule 3, the time within which notice of appeal or of an application for leave to appeal must be given;

(c) to extend the time within which a notice under rule 4 of opposition to an appeal or application for leave to appeal must be given by the respondent; and

(d) to give leave, in pursuance of rule 5, for a person in custody to be present at any proceedings.

(2) A judge of the court shall, for the purpose of exercising any of the powers specified above, sit in such place as he appoints, and may sit otherwise than in open court.

9 Determination by full court

(1) Where a judge of the court has refused an application on the part of an applicant to exercise in his favour any of the powers referred to in rule 8, the applicant may have the application determined by the court by serving a notice in Form 1A(5) on the registrar within 7 days, or such longer period as a judge of the court may fix, from the date on which notice of the refusal was served on him by the registrar.

(2) The notice shall be signed by, or on behalf of, the applicant.

(3) If the notice is not signed by the applicant and the applicant is in custody, the registrar shall, as soon as practicable after receiving the notice, send a copy of it to the applicant.

(4) If such a notice is not served on the registrar within the said 7 days or such longer period as a judge of the court may fix, the application shall be treated as having been refused by the court.

10 Notice of determination of court

(1) The registrar shall, as soon as practicable, serve notice of any determination by the Court of Appeal or by any judge of the court under rule 8 on –

(a) the applicant; and

(b) any other party to the appeal; and

(c) any person given leave under rule 5(2) to be present at the hearing of the appeal.

(2) The registrar shall, as soon as practicable, serve notice on the appropriate officer of the Crown Court at the place of trial of the order of the Court of Appeal disposing of an appeal or application for leave to appeal.

11 Service of documents

(1) Subject to paragraph (2) below, rule 21 of the principal Rules (service of documents) shall apply for the purposes of an appeal or an application for leave to appeal under section 9(11) of the Act of 1987 as it applies for the purposes of Part I of the Act of 1968.

(2) Where any document is required under any of these Rules to be served on any party to the proceedings, service may be effected by serving it on his solicitor if he has one.

12 The registrar

(1) The registrar may require the Crown Court at the place of trial to furnish the Court of Appeal with any assistance or information which it may require for the purpose of exercising its jurisdiction.

(2) Subject to paragraphs (3) and (4) below the registrar shall give as long notice in advance as reasonably possible of the date of hearing of any appeal or application –

(a) to the appellant; and

(b) to the respondent and any other party directly affected by the order or ruling to which the appeal or application under section 9(11) of the Act of 1987 relates.

(3) Paragraph (2) above shall not apply to proceedings before a judge of the court under rule 8.

(4) Where a party to whom notice is required to be given by this rule is at the material time in custody, notice shall instead be given to the person having custody of him.

13 Forms

(1) Any reference in these Rules to a form, unless the context otherwise requires, is a reference to a form set out in the Schedule to these Rules.

(2) The forms set out in the Schedule to these Rules or forms substantially to the like effect may be used with such variations as the circumstances may require.

SCHEDULE FORMS

Rule 13

The Court of Appeal Criminal Division

Form **IA(1)**

**NOTICE and GROUNDS of appeal or application for leave to appeal
s.9(11) Criminal Justice Act 1987   CAO No.   /   /
(Preparatory Hearing)**

Please read the notes for guidance overleaf
Write in BLACK INK and USE BLOCK CAPITALS

The Appellant

Prison Index No

give full name   Surname _____

If in custody give   Forename _____
Prison Index No.
and address where   Address _____
detained

Post code _____ Date of Birth _____

Preparatory Hearing   at _____Crown Court

Name of Judge _____

Dates of hearing _____ Indictment Number_____

Ruling/Order in respect of which appeal or application for leave to appeal is made:

Application to the Crown Court *(Please tick as appropriate)*

State whether there was an application to the   No ☐ Yes ☐
Judge of the Crown Court for leave to appeal

If yes, was the application granted No ☐ Yes ☐

Ancillary Applications   *SEE NOTES 6 & 9*

The appellant is applying for: *Please tick as appropriate*

☐ Extension of time in which to give notice of appeal or application for leave to appeal (give
   reasons below)

☐ Legal aid

☐ Leave to be present at the application for leave to appeal

If you require an extension of time in which to give notice of appeal state reasons:

Notes for guidance on the completion of form IA(1)

1   Appeal lies to the Court of Appeal Criminal Division from an order or ruling of a judge at a preparatory hearing under s.9(3)(b) or (c) of the Criminal Justice Act 1987 with the leave of that judge or of the Court of Appeal. This form should be served on the Registrar of Criminal Appeals within 7 days from the making of the order or ruling. An application to the judge of the Crown Court for leave to appeal may be made orally within 2 days of the making of the order or ruling. Where such an application for leave has been made to the judge of the Crown Court, that fact must be stated in the notice.

2   This notice will be treated as a notice of appeal where leave to appeal is not required.

3   A copy of this notice, including these notes for guidance, must be served on the appropriate officer of the Crown Court and on all parties to the preparatory hearing who are directly affected by the order or ruling within 7 days of making the order.

4   In reckoning the period of time for notice of appeal etc., if the period includes Saturday, Sunday, Bank Holiday, Christmas Day or Good Friday, that day is excluded.

5   This notice must be accompanied by any documents or other items (or copies thereof) necessary for the proper determination of the appeal or application. If reasons were given for the order or ruling, Counsel's note thereof should be included in the documents and where the note has been approved by the judge in the Crown Court, that fact should be endorsed upon the copy provided to the Registrar.

6   Legal aid may be granted for the purposes of an application for leave to appeal or an appeal by the Crown Court or the Court of Appeal – s.28(8A) of the Legal Aid Act 1974. If legal aid has been granted by the Crown Court, the appellant should so inform the Registrar.

7   Grounds of appeal settled by counsel must be signed by counsel.

8   A party in whose favour the order or ruling was made – the respondent – wishing to oppose the apeal must within 7 days of receipt of his copy of this notice serve on the Registrar, with copies to the appellant and all parties directly affected by the order or ruling, a notice stating the date on which the appellant's notice was received, summarising his response to the arguments of the appellant and specifying the authorities he intends to cite.

9   An accused person in custody who is not a party to the appeal may apply for leave to be present at the proceedings in the Court of Appeal using form 1A(3).

Grounds of appeal *(see note 7)*

1 Specify the question of law in respect of which the appeal is brought (and where appropriate, such facts of the case as are necessary for the proper consideration of the question of law).

2 Summarise the arguments that you intend to put to the Court of Appeal, (specifying any authorities to be cited).

Signature

Details of any person signing on behalf of the appellant:

Signature of appellant

Name _____

Solicitor/Counsel*   *Delete as appropriate

Address _____

_____

Date _____   _____

Solicitor's Ref. _____

For Prison Use

This notice was handed to me by the appellant today.

Signed _____

Prison Officer

Date _____

Appellant's Index No. _____

For Criminal Appeal Office Use

Received (date) _____

Acknowledged (date) _____

The Court of Appeal Criminal Division

NOTICE and GROUNDS of opposition to appeal
s.9(11) Criminal Justice Act 1987   **CAO No.**   /   /
(Preparatory Hearing)

Write in BLACK INK and USE BLOCK CAPITALS

The Respondent   Prison Index No

give full name   Surname _____

If in custody give   Forenames _____
Prison Index No.
and address where   Address _____
detained
                          Post code _____ Date of birth _____

Preparatory Hearing   at _____Crown Court

                          Name of Judge _____

                          Dates of hearing _____ Indictment Number_____

          Date on which appellant's notice of appeal was received_____

The Respondent is applying for *Please tick as appropriate*

☐ Extension of time in which to give notice of opposition to appeal (give reasons below) reasons below)

☐ Legal aid

☐ Leave to be present at the application for leave to appeal

If you require an extension of time in which to give notice of opposition to appeal state reasons:

Grounds Summarise the arguments you intend to put to the Court of Appeal, specifying any authorities to be cited

Signature

Details of any person signing on behalf of the respondent:

Signature of respondent

Name _____
Solicitor/Counsel*   *Delete as appropriate

_____

Address _____

_____

Date _____

_____

Solicitor's Ref. _____

For Prison Use
This notice was handed to me by the respondent today.

Signed _____
                    Prison Officer
Date _____

Respondent's Index No. _____

For Criminal Appeal Office Use

Received (date) _____

Acknowledged (date) _____

The Court of Appeal Criminal Division

NOTICE of application for leave to be present at hearing of appeal or application for leave to appeal s.9(11) Criminal Justice Act 1987   CAO No.   /   /

Write in BLACK INK and USE BLOCK CAPITALS

The Applicant

Prison Index No

give full name   Surname ——————————————

If in custody give Prison Index No. and address where detained

Forenames ——————————————————

Address ————————————————————

Post code ———————— Date of birth ——————

Preparatory Hearing   at ————————————————Crown Court

Dates of hearing ——————————Indictment Number ——————

Date on which appellant's notice of appeal was received——————

The applicant applies for leave to be present
State the grounds for your application:

Signature

Signature of applicant

——————————————

Date ——————————————

Details of any person signing on behalf of the applicant:

Name ——————————————
Solicitor/Counsel*   *Delete as appropriate

Address ——————————————

——————————————

Solicitor's Ref. ——————————————

For Prison Use
This notice was handed to me by the applicant today.

Signed ——————————————
                              Prison Officer
Date ——————————

Applicant's Index No. ——————————

For Criminal Appeal Office Use

Received (date) ——————————

Acknowledged (date) ——————————

The Court of Appeal Criminal Division

NOTICE of Abandonment of Proceedings
s.9(11) Criminal Justice Act 1987   CAO No.   /   /

Write in BLACK INK and USE BLOCK CAPITALS

The Appellant

Prison Index No

give full name   Surname ——————

*If in custody give
Prison Index No.
and address where
detained*

Forenames ———————————————————

Address ———————————————————

Post code ——————— Date of birth ———————

Preparatory Hearing   at ———————————Crown Court

Name of Judge ————————————————

Dates of hearing ——————— Indictment Number ————

I abandon proceedings in the Court of Appeal

Details of any person signing on behalf
of the appellant:

Signature of appellant

Name ————————————
Solicitor/Counsel*   *Delete as appropriate

———————————————

Address ————————————

————————————

Date ———————————

Post Code ————————

Solicitor's Ref. ————————

For Criminal Appeal Office Use

Received (date) ———————————

Acknowledged (date) ———————————

Copies to: ——————— Crown Court

The Governor ———————————

The Court of Appeal Criminal Division

Determination by single judge
s.9(11) Criminal Justice Act 1987   CAO No.   /   /

Write in BLACK INK and USE BLOCK CAPITALS

The Appellant

Prison Index No

Give full name   Surname _____

Forenames _____

Address where _____
detained
_____

Post code _____ Date of birth _____

Address if not _____
detained
_____

Post Code _____

ORDER by the Hon. Mr. Justice

Applications considered

☐ a. Extension of time   ☐ c. Legal aid

☐ b. Leave to appeal against order/ruling   ☐ d. Leave to be present

---

Decision
(if legal aid is granted please indicate the number of Counsel and whether Solicitors are included)

Note: If an application has been refused see overleaf

Observations to the Appellant *(if leave is refused)*

I have considered the papers in your case and your grounds of appeal

Signed _____ Dated _____

1. Date 1A(5) sent to the appellant

    (a) This form was sent by the Registrar

        on (date) _____

    (b) If the appellant is in custody.
        This form was handed to the appellant

        today (date) _____

        (Signed) _____
                                 (Prison Officer)

2. If an application is refused

        Applications refused by a Judge may be renewed for consideration by the full court, or may be abandoned (using Form 1A(4)).

3. Renewal notice to the Registrar. The following applications are renewed.

        Signed _____ (Appellant)

        Dated _____

4. Notes

1   Appellants must use section 3 of this part of the form for the renewal of applications.
2   An application not renewed in time will be treated as if refused by the full court, which will not extend the time unless the circumstances are wholly exceptional. The time limits are as follows:
        • If the appellant is not in custody, the form must be returned to the Registrar (Criminal Appeal Office) to reach him within 7 days of the date shown at 1(a).
        • If the appellant is in custody the form must be handed in to the Prison Authority (or other person having custody) within 7 days of the date shown at 1(b).
3   If you wish to obtain advice you should do so within the time allowed. The Court cannot give advice.
4   The appellant will receive two copies of Form 1A(5) and should retain one.

For Prison Use
This form was handed to me by the appellant today.

Signed _____
                     Prison Officer
Date _____

Appellant's Index No. _____

For Criminal Appeal Office Use

Received (date) _____

Acknowledged (date) _____

SI 1988 No 1701

Magistrates' Courts (Notices of Transfer) Rules 1988

1 Citation and Commencement
These Rules may be cited as the Magistrates' Courts (Notices of Transfer) Rules 1988 and shall come into force on 31st October 1988.

2 Interpretation
In these Rules –

"the Act" means the Criminal Justice Act 1987;

"designated authority" means an authority referred to in section 4(2) of the Act;

"notice of transfer" means a notice referred to in section 4(1)(c) of the Act.

3 Transfer on bail
(1) Where a person in respect of whom notice of transfer has been given is granted bail under section 5(3) or (7A) of the Act by the magistrates' court to which notice of transfer was given, the clerk of the court shall give notice thereof in writing to the governor of the prison or remand centre to which the said person would have been committed by that court if he had been committed in custody for trial.

(2) Where notice of transfer is given in respect of a corporation the clerk of the court to which notice of transfer was given shall give notice thereof to the governor of the prison to which would be committed a male over 21 committed by that court in custody for trial.

4 Notice where person removed to hospital
Where a transfer direction has been given by the Secretary of State under section 47 or 48 of the Mental Health Act 1983 in respect of a person remanded in custody by a magistrates' court and, before the direction ceases to have effect, notice of transfer is given in respect of that person, the clerk of the court to which notice of transfer was given shall give notice thereof in writing –

(a) to the governor of the prison to which that person would have been committed by that court if he had been committed in custody for trial; and
(b) to the managers of the hospital where he is detained.

5 Variation of arrangements for bail
(1) A person who intends to make an application to a magistrates' court under section 3(8) of the Bail Act 1976 as that subsection has effect under section 3(8A) of that Act shall give notice thereof in writing to the clerk of the court to which the application is to be made, and to the designated authority or the defendant, as the case may be, and to any sureties concerned.

(2) Where, on an application referred to in paragraph (1) above, a magistrates' court varies or imposes any conditions of bail the clerk of the court shall send to the appropriate officer of the Crown Court a copy of the record made in pursuance of section 5 of the Bail Act 1976 relating to such variation or imposition of conditions.

6 Making of witness orders where person charged is not required to appear
Where by virtue of section 5(6) of the Act, a person charged is no longer required to appear before a magistrates' court to which notice of transfer in respect of him has been given, that court shall fix a date on which it will exercise its functions under section 5(8) of the Act and shall cause notice thereof to be given to the said person and to the designated authority concerned.

7 Documents etc to be sent to Crown Court
As soon as practicable after a magistrates' court to which notice of transfer has been given has discharged the functions reserved to it under section 4(1) of the Act, the clerk

of the magistrates' court shall send to the appropriate officer of the Crown Court –

 (a) a list of the names, addresses and occupations of the witnesses in respect of whom witness orders have been made;

 (b) a copy of the record made in pursuance of section 5 of the Bail Act 1976 relating to the grant or withholding of bail in respect of the accused;

 (c) any recognizance entered into by any person as surety for the accused together with a statement of any enlargement thereof;

 (d) a copy of any legal aid order previously made in the case;

 (e) a copy of any contribution order previously made in the case under section 7 of the Legal Aid Act 1982;

 (f) a copy of any legal aid application previously made in the case which has been refused;

 (g) any statement of means already submitted.

8 Forms

The forms set out in the Schedule to these Rules or forms to the like effect may be used in connection with proceedings in a magistrates' court to which a notice of transfer has been given.

SCHEDULE

Rule 8

FORM 1

Warrant of commitment: transfer to Crown Court for trial (Bail Act 1976, ss. 3, 4; Criminal Justice Act 1987, s. 5; MC Rules 1981, rr. 94, 95, 97; MC (Notices of Transfer) Rules 1988, r. 8).

.... Magistrates' Court (Code)

Date: ....

Accused: .... Age: .... years

Address: ....

....

Alleged offence: (particulars and statute)

The proceedings against the accused in respect of the above offence have been transferred to the Crown Court at

Direction: [You, [the constables of .... Police Force] [AB], are hereby required to convey the accused to .... [prison] [remand centre] and there deliver the accused to the Governor thereof, together with this warrant; and you the Governor, to receive into your custody and, unless the accused is released on bail in the meantime, to keep the accused until the accused is delivered in due course of law.]

 [You, the Governor of .... [prison] [remand centre] are hereby required to keep the accused in your custody and, unless the accused is released on bail in the meantime, to keep the accused until the accused is delivered in due course of law.]

*Bail: After complying with the condition(s) specified in Schedule I hereto, the accused shall be released on bail subject to the condition(s) specified in Schedule II hereto, and with a duty to surrender to the custody of the Crown Court at the time and place for the time being appointed by that court.

Justice of the Peace
[or By order of the Court
Clerk of the Court]

SCHEDULE 1

Conditions to be complied with before release on bail

To provide .... suret[y][ies] in the sum of £................. [each] to secure the accused's surrender to custody at the time and place appointed.

†

SCHEDULE II

Conditions to be complied with after release on bail

†

---

* Delete if bail is not granted.

† Insert condition(s) as appropriate (including in Schedule I directions under MC Rules 1981, and 98 in respect of any pre-release conditions).

FORM 2

Notice to governor of prison of persons bailed to appear before Crown Court after notice of transfer (Criminal Justice Act 1987, s. 5(3), (7A), MC (Notices of Transfer) Rules 1988, r. 3).

.... Magistrates' Court (Code)

Notice of transfer given on ....

Persons bailed on .... to appear before the

Crown Court at ....

Name and Age	Brief description of offence
....	....
....	....
....	....
....	....

Justices' Clerk

To the Governor HM Prison/Remand Centre ....

FORM 3

Notice on transfer of proceedings in respect of a person subject to transfer direction under section 47 or 48 of the Mental Health Act 1983 (MC (Notices of Transfer) Rules 1988, r. 4).

.... Magistrates' Court (Code)

Date: ....

To the Governor: [prison] ....

Address: ....

....

To the Managers: [hospital] ....

Address: ....

....

Notice: The proceedings in respect of the accused named below, who is subject to a transfer direction under section 47 or 48 of the Mental Health Act 1983 and is detained at the above hospital, have been transferred to the Crown Court at ....and it was today ordered that he be safely kept in custody until delivered in due course of law.

Accused: .... Age: .... years

Address: ....

....

Alleged offence: (short particulars and statute)

Clerk of the Court

FORM 4

Witness order (CP(A of W) Act 1965, ss 1(1))
MC Rules 1981, r 8; MC (Notices of Transfer) Rules 1988, r. 8).

.... Magistrates' Court (Code)

Date: ....

To: ....
(Witness)

Address: ....

....

Order: That * [if notice is later given to you to that effect] you attend and give evidence at the trial of .... at the Crown Court at ....].

† [You are no longer required to attend at ....Magistrates' Court on .... in accordance with the summons dated ....].

Justice of the Peace.
[By order of the Court
Justices' Clerk]

NOTE.—Failure to comply with this order may render you liable to imprisonment for 3 months or a fine. You will be notified of the date and time at which you are to attend by the appropriate officer of the Crown Court, to whom any enquiry should be addressed.

---

* Delete unless the order is a conditional order.
† Delete unless a summons has been issued under s. 97 MC Act 1980.

FORM 5

Record of decision to vary conditions of bail or impose conditions on bail granted unconditionally (criminal cases) (Bail Act 1976, s.5; MC Rules 1981, rr. 66, 90; MC (Notices of Transfer) Rules 1988, r. 5).

.... Magistrates' Court (Code)

Date: ....

Accused: ....

Date of birth: ....

Alleged offence[s]; (short particulars and statute)

The accused having been granted bail by the above magistrates' court on ....
(date) and being under a duty under section 5(7) of the Criminal Justice Act 1987
to appear before the Crown Court at .... at a time to be notified

[and the said bail being subject to conditions].

Application having been made by .... under section
3(8) of the Bail Act 1976 for [variation] [imposition] of bail conditions.

Decision: The condition(s) to be complied with by the accused in respect of the said bail shall now be as specified in Schedule I and II hereto.

*Reasons: The conditions of bail were [varied] [imposed] for the following reason(s):

Signature ....
Justice of the Peace.

[Clerk of the Court
present during these proceedings]

SCHEDULE 1

Conditions to be complied with before release on bail

To provide .... suret[y][ies] in the sum of £................ [each] to secure the defendant's surrender to custody at the time and place appointed.

†

SCHEDULE II

Conditions to be complied with after release on bail

†

---

* Delete if section 4 of the Bail Act 1976 does not apply.
† Insert condition(s) as appropriate (including in Schedule I directions under MC Rules 1981, r. 85 in respect of any pre-release conditions).

SI 1982 No 1109
Crown Court Rules 1982

PART V
MISCELLANEOUS

25AA Statements etc relevant to making confiscation orders under the Criminal Justice Act 1988

[(1) Where a defendant has been convicted of an offence to which Part VI of the Criminal Justice Act 1988 applies and the prosecutor or the defendant proposes to tender to the Crown Court any statement or other document under section 73 of that Act (statements, etc. relevant to making confiscation orders) he shall serve it within such time as the court may require on the appropriate officer of the Crown Court, and at the same time serve a copy thereof on the defendant or the prosecutor, as the case may be.

(2) Any statement tendered to the Crown Court by the prosecutor or the defendant under section 73 of the said Act of 1988 shall include the following particulars, namely –

(a) the name of the defendant and the indictment number;
(b) the name of the person by whom the statement is tendered and, if different, the name of the person by whom it is made;
(c) the date on which and the place where the conviction for the offence occurred;
(d) the facts relied on in support of any allegation or matter indicated.]

30 Service of summons or order outside the United Kingdom

[Where a witness summons or order is issued or made by the Crown Court in accordance with section 2(1) of the Criminal Justice (International Co-operation) Act 1990 for service outside the United Kingdom it shall be sent forthwith by the appropriate officer of the Crown Court to the Secretary of State with a view to its being served there in accordance with arrangements made by the Secretary of State.]

31 Application for letters of request

[(1) Notice of an application under section 3(1) of the Criminal Justice (International Co-operation) Act 1990 (overseas evidence for use in the United Kingdom) shall be given to the appropriate officer of the Crown Court and shall –

(a) be made in writing, save that the court may in exceptional circumstances dispense with the need for notice;
(b) state the particulars of the offence which it is alleged has been committed or the grounds upon which it is suspected that an offence has been committed;
(c) state whether proceedings in respect of the offence have been instituted or the offence is being investigated;
(d) include particulars of the assistance requested in the form of a draft letter of request.

(2) The application may be heard ex parte.

(3) When hearing the application the court may, if it thinks it necessary in the interests of justice, direct that the public be excluded from the court.

(4) The powers conferred on the Crown Court by paragraph (3) above shall be in addition and without prejudice to any other powers of the court to hear proceedings in camera.

(5) Where in a case of urgency the Crown Court sends a letter of request direct to any court or tribunal in accordance with section 3(5) of the Criminal Justice (International Co-operation) Act 1990, the appropriate officer of the Crown Court shall forthwith notify the Secretary of State of this and send with the notification a copy of the letter of request.]

32 Proceedings before a nominated court

[(1) Where the Crown Court receives evidence in proceedings before a nominated court in pursuance of a notice under section 4(2) of the Criminal Justice (International Co-operation) Act 1990 the court may, if it thinks it necessary in the interests of justice, direct that the public be excluded from the court.

(2) The powers conferred on the Crown Court by paragraph (1) above shall be in addition and without prejudice to any other powers of the court to hear proceedings in camera.

(3) Where the Crown Court receives evidence in proceedings mentioned in paragraph (1) above the appropriate officer of the Crown Court shall make a record of –

(a) which persons with an interest in the proceedings were present;
(b) which of the said persons were represented and by whom;
(c) whether any of the said persons were denied the opportunity of cross-examining a witness as to any part of his testimony and the reasons for any such denial.

(4) When so requested by the Secretary of State, the appropriate officer of the Crown Court shall send to him a copy of the record as mentioned in paragraph (3) above.]

33 Application for increase in term of imprisonment in default of payment – drug trafficking

[(1) The following provisions of this rule shall have effect for the purposes of applications under subsection (2) of section 15 of the Criminal Justice (International Co-operation) Act 1990 (which provides for interest on sums unpaid under confiscation orders in drug trafficking cases).

(2) Notice of application under subsection (2) of the said section 15 to increase the term of imprisonment or detention fixed in default of payment of a confiscation order by a person ("the defendant") shall be made by the prosecutor in writing to the appropriate officer of the Crown Court.

(3) A notice under paragraph (2) above shall –

(a) state the name and address of the defendant;
(b) specify the grounds for the application;
(c) give details of the enforcement measures taken, if any; and
(d) include a copy of the confiscation order.

(4) On receiving a notice under paragraph (2) above, the appropriate officer of the Crown Court shall –

(a) forthwith send to the defendant and the magistrates' court required to enforce payment of the confiscation order under section 32(1) of the Powers of Criminal Courts Act 1973, a copy of the said notice; and
(b) notify in writing the applicant and the defendant of the date, time and place appointed for the hearing of the application.

(5) Where the Crown Court makes an order pursuant to an application mentioned in paragraph (1) above, the appropriate officer of the Crown Court shall send forthwith a copy of the order –

(a) to the applicant;
(b) to the defendant;
(c) where the defendant is at the time of the making of the order in custody, to the person having custody of him; and
(d) to the magistrates' court mentioned in paragraph (4)(a) above.]

SI 1985 No 1800

Police and Criminal Evidence Act 1984 (Application to Customs and Excise) Order 1985

1 This Order may be cited as the Police and Criminal Evidence Act 1984 (Application to Customs and Excise) Order 1985 and shall come into operation on 1st January 1986.

2 (1) In this Order, unless the context otherwise requires –

"the Act" means the Police and Criminal Evidence Act 1984;

"assigned matter" has the meaning given to it by section 1 of the Customs and Excise Management Act 1979;

"the customs and excise Acts" has the meaning given to it by section 1 of the Customs and Excise Management Act 1979;

"customs office" means a place for the time being occupied by Her Majesty's Customs and Excise;

"officer" means a person commissioned by the Commissioners of Customs and Excise under section 6(3) of the Customs and Excise Management Act 1979.

(2) A person is in customs detention for the purpose of this Order if –

(a) he has been taken to a customs office after being arrested for an offence; or
(b) he is arrested at a customs office after attending voluntarily at the office or accompanying an officer to it,

and is detained there or is detained elsewhere in the charge of an officer, and nothing shall prevent a detained person from being transferred between customs detention and police detention.

3 (1) Subject to the modifications in paragraphs (2) and (3) of this article, in articles 4 to 11 below and in Schedule 2 to this Order, the provisions of the Act contained in Schedule 1 to this Order which relate to investigations of offences conducted by police officers or to persons detained by the police shall apply to investigations conducted by officers of Customs and Excise of offences which relate to assigned matters, and to persons detained by such officers.

(2) The Act shall have effect as if the words and phrases in Column 1 of Part 1 of Schedule 2 to this Order were replaced by the substitute words and phrases in Column 2 of that Part.

(3) Where in the Act any act or thing is to be done by a constable of a specified rank, that act or thing shall be done by an officer of at least the grade specified in Column 2 of Part 2 of Schedule 2 to this Order, and the Act shall be interpreted as if the substituted grade were specified in the Act.

4 Nothing in the application of the Act to Customs and Excise shall be construed as conferring upon an officer any power –

(a) to charge a person with any offence;
(b) to release a person on bail;
(c) to detain a person for an offence after he has been charged with that offence.

5 (1) Where in the Act a constable is given power to seize and retain any thing found upon a lawful search of person or premises, an officer shall have the same power notwithstanding that the thing found is not evidence of an offence in relation to an assigned matter.

(2) Nothing in the application of the Act to Customs and Excise shall be construed to prevent any thing lawfully seized by a person under any enactment from being accepted and retained by an officer.

(3) Section 21 of the Act (access and copying) shall not apply to any thing seized as liable to forfeiture under the customs and excise Acts.

6 In its application by virtue of article 3 above the Act shall have effect as if the following section were inserted after section 14 –

"14A. Material in the possession of a person who acquired or created it in the course of any trade, business, profession or other occupation or for the purpose of any paid or unpaid office and which relates to an assigned matter, as defined in section 1 of the Customs and Excise Management Act 1979, is neither excluded material nor special procedure material for the purposes of any enactment such as is mentioned in section 9(2) above.".

7 Section 18(1) of the Act shall be modified as follows: –

"18.–(1) Subject to the following provisions of this section, an officer of Customs and Excise may enter and search any premises occupied or controlled by a person who is under arrest for any arrestable offence which relates to an assigned matter, as defined in section 1 of the Customs and Excise Management Act 1979, if he has reasonable grounds for suspecting that there is on the premises evidence, other than items subject to legal privilege, that relates –

(a) to that offence; or
(b) to some other arrestable offence which is connected with or similar to that offence.".

8 (1) The Commissioners of Customs and Excise shall keep on an annual basis the written records mentioned in subsection (1) of section 50 of the Act.

(2) The Annual Report of the Commissioners of Her Majesty's Customs and Excise shall contain information about the matters mentioned in subsection (1) of section 50 of the Act in respect of the period to which it relates.

9 (1) Section 55 of the Act shall have effect as if it related only to things such as are mentioned in subsection (1)(a) of that section.

(2) The Annual Report of the Commissioners of Her Majesty's Customs and Excise shall contain the information mentioned in subsection (15) of section 55 of the Act about searches made under that section.

10 Section 77(3) of the Act shall be modified to the extent that the definition of "independent person" shall, in addition to the persons mentioned therein, also include

an officer or any other person acting under the authority of the Commissioners of Customs and Excise.

11 Where any provision of the Act as applied to Customs and Excise –

(a) confers a power on an officer, and
(b) does not provide that the power may only be exercised with the consent of some person other than an officer,

the officer may use reasonable force, if necessary, in the exercise of the power.

SCHEDULE 1

PROVISIONS OF THE ACT APPLIED TO CUSTOMS AND EXCISE

Article 3

Section 8

Section 9 and Schedule 1
Section 15
Section 16
Section 17(1)(b), (2), (4)
Section 18 subject to the modification in article 7 hereof
Section 19
Section 20
Section 21 subject to the modifications in article 5 hereof
Section 22(1) to (4)
Section 28
Section 29
Section 30(1) to (4)(a) and (5) to (11)
Section 31
Section 32(1) to (9) subject to the modifications in article 5 hereof
Section 34(1) to (5)
Section 35
Section 36
Section 37
Section 39
Section 40
Section 41
Section 42
Section 43
Section 44
Section 50 subject to the modification in article 8 hereof
Section 51(d)
Section 52
Section 54
Section 55 subject to the modifications in articles 5 and 9 hereof
Section 56(1) to (9)
Section 57(1) to (9)
Section 58(1) to (11)
Section 62
Section 63
Section 64(1) to (6)
[Section 107]

NOTES

Amended by SI 1987 No 439, art 3.

SCHEDULE 2

Article 3

PART I

Substitution of equivalent words and phrases in the Act

Where in the Act a word or phrase specified in Column 1 below is used, in the application of the Act to Customs and Excise, there shall be substituted the equivalent word or phrase in Column 2 below —

Column 1	Column 2
WORDS AND PHRASES USED IN THE ACT	SUBSTITUTED WORDS AND PHRASES
area	collection
chief officer	collector
constable	officer
designated police station	designated customs office
officer of a force maintained by	
a police authority	officer
	collection
police area	
police detention (except in section 118 and in section 39(1)(a) the second time the words occur)	customs detention
police force	HM Commissioners of Customs and Excise
police officer	officer
police station	customs office
rank	grade
station	customs office
the police	HM Customs and Excise

NOTES
Applied by the Drug Trafficking Offences Act 1986, s 32(4).
The Act: Police and Criminal Evidence Act 1984.

PART II

Equivalent grades of officers.

Where in the Act an act or thing is to be done by a constable of the rank specified in Column 1 below, that same act or thing shall, in the application of the Act to Customs and Excise, be done by an officer of at least the grade specified in Column 2 below –

Column 1	Column 2
RANK OF CONSTABLE	GRADE OF OFFICER
sergeant	executive officer
inspector	higher executive officer
chief inspector	higher executive officer
superintendent	senior executive officer
chief superintendent	grade 7

NOTES
Words in square brackets added by SI 1987 No 439, art 4.
Applied by the Drug Trafficking Offences Act 1986, s 32(4).
The Act: Police and Criminal Evidence Act 1984.

SI 1991 No 1074

Magistrates' Courts (Criminal Justice (International Co-operation)) Rules 1991

1 Citation and commencement
These Rules may be cited as the Magistrates' Courts (Criminal Justice (International Co-operation)) Rules 1991 and shall come into force on 10th June 1991.

2 Interpretation
In these Rules "the Act" means the Criminal Justice (International Co-operation) Act 1990.

3 Service of summons or order outside the United Kingdom
Where a summons is issued or order is made by a magistrates' court in accordance with section 2(1) of the Act for service outside the United Kingdom it shall be sent by the justices' clerk to the Secretary of State with a view to its being served there in accordance with arrangements made by the Secretary of State.

4 Proof of service of summons outside the United Kingdom
(1) The service on any person of a summons issued under section 2(1) of the Act may be proved in any legal proceedings by a certificate given by or on behalf of the Secretary of State.

(2) A statement in any such certificate as is mentioned in paragraph (1) above:

(a) that a summons has been served;
(b) of the manner in which service was effected;
(c) of the date upon which a summons was served,

shall be admissible as evidence of any facts so stated.

5 Notice of application for letters of request
Notice of an application under section 3(1) (overseas evidence for use in the United Kingdom) of the Act shall be given to the justices' clerk of a magistrates' court and shall –

(a) be made in writing, save that the court may in exceptional circumstances dispense with the need for notice;
(b) state the particulars of the offence which it is alleged has been committed or the grounds upon which it is suspected that an offence has been committed;
(c) state whether proceedings in respect of the offence have been instituted or the offence is being investigated; and
(d) include particulars of the assistance requested in the form of a draft letter of request.

6 Hearing of application for letters of request
(1) An application under section 3(1) of the Act –

(a) shall be heard in a petty-sessional court-house;
(b) may be heard ex parte.

(2) When hearing an application under section 3(1) of the Act the court may, if it thinks it necessary in the interests of justice, direct that the public be excluded from the court.

(3) The powers conferred on a magistrates' court by the preceding paragraph shall be in addition and without prejudice to any other powers of the court to hear proceedings in camera.

7 Letters of request in urgent cases
Where in a case of urgency a magistrates' court sends a letter of request direct to any court or tribunal in accordance with section 3(5) of the Act, the justices' clerk shall

forthwith notify the Secretary of State of this and send with the notification a copy of the letter of request.

8 Proceedings before a nominated court

(1) In proceedings before a nominated court pursuant to a notice under section 4(2) of the Act the court may, if it thinks it necessary in the interests of justice, direct that the public be excluded from the court.

(2) The powers conferred on a magistrates' court by the preceding paragraph shall be in addition and without prejudice to any other powers of the court to hear proceedings in camera.

9 Court register of proceedings before a nominated court

(1) Where a magistrates' court receives evidence in proceedings pursuant to a notice under section 4(2) of the Act, the justices' clerk shall note in the register –

(a) particulars of the proceedings;
(b) without prejudice to the generality of (a) above –

    (i)   which persons with an interest in the proceedings were present;
    (ii) which of the said persons were represented and by whom;
    (iii) whether any of the said persons were denied the opportunity of cross-examining a witness as to any part of his testimony.

(2) Such part of the register as relates to proceedings mentioned in paragraph (1) above shall be kept in a separate book.

(3) Save as authorised by the Secretary of State, or with the leave of the court, such part of the register as relates to proceedings mentioned in paragraph (1) above shall not be open to inspection by any person.

(4) When so requested by the Secretary of State, the justices' clerk shall send to him a copy of an extract of the register as it relates to any proceedings mentioned in paragraph (1) above.

SI 1971 No 2084

Indictments (Procedure) Rules 1971

2 In these Rules –

"the appropriate officer" means such officer as may be designated for the purpose in question by arrangements made by or on behalf of the Lord Chancellor;

"the Act" means the Administration of Justice (Miscellaneous Provisions) Act 1933;

"committal proceedings" means proceedings before a magistrates' court acting as examining justices;

"depositions" means depositions taken before justices under the Magistrates' Courts Act 1952 or under the Children and Young Persons Act 1933 and includes written statements tendered in evidence under section 2 of the Criminal Justice Act 1967, any document exhibited to such depositions or statements and the statement of the accused:

Provided that any requirement of these Rules that an application should be accompanied by a copy of any depositions, shall as respects documents exhibited to those depositions, be satisfied if a copy of such parts only of the exhibits as are, in the opinion of the applicant, material, accompanies the application, and the application contains an express statement to that effect.

4 Subject as hereinafter provided, a bill of indictment shall be preferred before the Crown Court by delivering the bill to the appropriate officer of the Crown Court:

Provided that where with the assent of the prosecutor the bill is prepared by, or under the supervision of, the appropriate officer it shall not be necessary for the bill to be delivered to the appropriate officer but as soon as it has been settled to his satisfaction it shall be deemed to have been duly preferred.

5 [(1) Subject to the provisions of this rule, a bill of indictment shall be preferred –

(a) where a defendant has been committed for trial, within a period of 28 days commencing with the date of committal, or

(b) where a notice of transfer has been given under section 4 of the Criminal Justice Act 1987, within a period of 28 days commencing with the date on which notice is given.

[(c) Where a notice of transfer has been served under section 53 of the Criminal Justice Act 1991 (notices of transfer in certain cases involving children), within a period of 28 days commencing with the date on which notice is served.]]

(2) The period referred to in paragraph (1) may, on the application of the person preferring the bill of indictment or otherwise, be extended by a judge of the Crown Court before or after it has expired; and any period so extended may be further extended in like manner.

(3) Notwithstanding paragraph (2), the first extension of the period may be granted by the appropriate officer of the Crown Court provided that the period of the extension does not exceed 28 days; but if the appropriate officer is of the opinion that the first extension of the period should not be granted, he shall refer the application to a judge of the Crown Court who shall determine the application himself.

(4) An application under paragraph (2) shall –

(a) be in writing unless a judge of the Crown Court otherwise directs; and

(b) include a statement of the reasons why an extension of the period referred to in paragraph (1) is necessary.

(5) Where an application under paragraph (2) is made after the expiry of the period referred to in paragraph (1) or, as the case may be, the expiry of that period as extended under paragraph (2), the application shall in addition include a statement of the reasons why the application was not made before the expiry of the period or, as the case may be, the extended period.]

NOTES
Rule 5 substituted by SI 1983 No 284.
Para (1) was further substituted by SI 1988 No 1738, reg 2 and para (1)(c) was inserted by SI 1992 No 2197.

6 An application under section 2(2)(b) of the Act for consent to the preferment of a bill of indictment may be made to a judge of the High Court.

SI 1991 No 2873

Criminal Justice Act 1988 (Designated Countries and Territories) Order 1991

1 Title, commencement and extent

(1) This Order may be cited as the Criminal Justice Act 1988 (Designated Countries and Territories) Order 1991 and shall come into force on the tenth day after the day on which it is made.

(2) This Order extends to England and Wales only.

2 Interpretation

In this Order –

"the Act" means the Criminal Justice Act 1988;

"country" means a country or territory;

"designated country" means a country or territory designated under article 3(1) below;

"appropriate authority of a designated country" means an authority specified opposite that country in Schedule 1 to this Order;

"a court of a designated country" includes a court of any state or territory of a designated country.

3 Designation of and application of the Act to countries and territories

(1) Each of the countries specified in Schedule 1 to this Order is hereby designated for the purposes of sections 96 and 97 of the Act.

(2) In relation to a designated country, Part VI of the Act shall apply, subject to the modifications specified in Schedule 2 to this Order, to external confiscation orders and to proceedings which have been or are to be instituted in the designated country and may result in an external confiscation order being made there, and, accordingly, in relation to such orders and such proceedings, Part VI of the Act and Schedule 4 thereto shall have effect as set out in Schedule 3 to this Order.

4 Proof of orders and judgment of court of a designated country

(1) For the purposes of sections 96 and 97 of the Act, and of the other provisions of the Act as applied under article 3(2) above –

(a) any order made or judgment given by a court of a designated country purporting to bear the seal of that court or to be signed by any person in his capacity as a judge, magistrate or officer of the court, shall be deemed without further proof to have been duly sealed or, as the case may be, to have been signed by that person; and

(b) a document, duly authenticated, which purports to be a copy of any order made or judgment given by a court of a designated country shall be deemed without further proof to be a true copy.

(2) A document purporting to be a copy of any order made or judgment given by a court of a designated country is duly authenticated for the purpose of paragraph (1)(b) above if it purports to be certified by any person in his capacity as a judge, magistrate or officer of the court in question or by or on behalf of the appropriate authority of the designated country.

5 Evidence in relation to proceedings and orders in a designated country

(1) For the purposes of sections 96 and 97 of the Act, and of the other provisions of the Act as applied under article 3(2) above, a certificate purporting to be issued by or on behalf of the appropriate authority of a designated country stating –

(a) that proceedings have been instituted and have not been concluded, or that proceedings are to be instituted, there;

(b) that an external confiscation order is in force and is not subject to appeal;

(c) that all or a certain amount of the sum payable under an external confiscation order remains unpaid in the designated country, or that other property recoverable under an external confiscation order remains unrecovered there;

(d) that any person has been notified of any proceedings in accordance with the law of the designated country; or

(e) that an order (however described) made by a court of the designated country has the purpose

(i) of recovering property obtained as a result of or in connection with conduct to which Part VI of the Act applies or the value of property so obtained; or

    (ii) of depriving a person of a pecuniary advantage so obtained,

shall, in any proceedings in the High Court, be admissible as evidence of the facts so stated.

(2) In any such proceedings a statement contained in a document, duly authenticated, which purports to have been received in evidence or to be a copy of a document so received, or to set out or summarise evidence given in proceedings in a court of a designated country, shall be admissible as evidence of any fact stated therein.

(3) A document is duly authenticated for the purposes of paragraph (2) above if it purports to be certified by any person in his capacity as judge, magistrate or officer of the court of the designated country, or by or on behalf of the appropriate authority of the designated country, to have been received in evidence or to be a copy of a document so received, or, as the case may be, to be the original document containing or summarising the evidence or a true copy of that document.

(4) Nothing in this article shall prejudice the admission of any evidence, whether contained in any document or otherwise, which is admissible apart from this article.

6 Representation of government of a designated country

A request for assistance sent to the Secretary of State by the appropriate authority of a designated country shall, unless the contrary is shown, be deemed to constitute the authority of the government of that country for the Crown Prosecution Service or the Commissioners of Customs and Excise to act on its behalf in any proceedings in the High Court under section 97 of the Act or any other provision of the Act as applied by article 3(2) above.

7 Satisfaction of confiscation order in a designated country

(1) Where –

    (a) a confiscation order has been made under section 71 of the Act; and

    (b) a request has been sent by the Secretary of State to the appropriate authority of a designated country for assistance in enforcing that order; and

    (c) in execution of that request property is recovered in that country,

the amount payable under the confiscation order shall be treated as reduced by the value of the property so recovered.

(2) For the purposes of this article, and without prejudice to the admissibility of any evidence which may be admissible apart from this paragraph, a certificate purporting to be issued by or on behalf of the appropriate authority of a designated country stating that property has been recovered there in execution of a request by the Secretary of State, stating the value of the property so recovered and the date on which it was recovered shall, in any proceedings in a court in England and Wales, be admissible as evidence of the facts so stated.

8 Currency conversion

(1) Where the value of property recovered as described in article 7(1) above is expressed in a currency other than that of the United Kingdom, the extent to which the amount payable under the confiscation order is to be reduced under that paragraph shall be calculated on the basis of the exchange rate prevailing on the date on which the property was recovered in the designated country concerned.

(2) Where an amount of money payable or remaining to be paid under an external confiscation order registered in the High Court under section 97 of the Act is expressed in a currency other than that of the United Kingdom, for the purpose of any action taken in relation to that order under the Act as applied under article 3(2) above the amount shall be converted into the currency of the United Kingdom on the basis of the exchange rate prevailing on the date of registration of the order.

(3) For the purposes of this article a written certificate purporting to be signed by any

person acting in his capacity as an officer of any bank in the United Kingdom and stating the exchange rate prevailing on a specified date shall be admissible as evidence of the facts so stated.

SCHEDULE 1

DESIGNATED COUNTRIES

Article 3(1)

Designated country	Appropriate authority
Italy	the Ministry of Justice
Nigeria	the Attorney General of the Federation of the Republic of Nigeria
Sweden	the Ministry of Foreign Affairs

SCHEDULE 2

MODIFICATIONS OF PART VI OF THE CRIMINAL JUSTICE ACT 1988

Article 3(2)

1 For section 71 there shall be substituted the following section:

"External confiscation orders

71 (1) An order made by a court in a designated country for the purpose –

(a) of recovering –

    (i) property obtained as a result of or in connection with conduct to which this Part of this Act applies; or
    (ii) the value of property so obtained; or

(b) of depriving a person of a pecuniary advantage so obtained,

is referred to in this Part of this Act as an "external confiscation order", and "a designated country" means a country or territory designated under article 3(1) of the Criminal Justice Act 1988 (Designated Countries and Territories) Order 1991.

(2) Section 97 below shall have effect with respect to the registration of external confiscation orders.

(3) In subsection (1) above the reference to an order includes any order, decree, direction or judgment, or any part thereof, however described.

(4) Where a person derives a pecuniary advantage as a result of or in connection with conduct to which this Part of this Act applies, he is to be treated for the purposes of this Part of this Act as if he had obtained as a result of or in connection with the conduct a sum of money equal to the value of the pecuniary advantage.".

2 Sections 72 and 73 shall be omitted.

3 For section 74 there shall be substituted the following section:

"74 Definition of principal terms used
(1) In this Part of this Act –

(a) "drug trafficking offence" has the same meaning as in the Drug Trafficking Offences Act 1986;
(b) references to conduct to which this Part of this Act applies are references to conduct corresponding to any offence which –

    (i) is listed in Schedule 4 to this Act; or
    (ii) if not listed, is an indictable offence, other than a drug trafficking offence or an offence under Part III of the Prevention of Terrorism (Temporary Provisions) Act 1989; and

(c) a person against whom an external confiscation order has been made, or a person against whom proceedings which may result in an external confiscation order being made have been, or are to be, instituted in a court of a designated country, is referred to as "the defendant".

(2) In this Part of this Act, "realisable property" means, subject to subsection (3) below –

(a) in relation to an external confiscation order in respect of specified property, the property which is specified in the order; and

(b) in any other case –

    (i) any property held by the defendant; and

    (ii) any property held by a person to whom the defendant has directly or indirectly made a gift caught by this Part of this Act.

(3) Property is not realisable property if –

(a) an order under section 43 of the Powers of Criminal Courts Act 1973 (deprivation orders);

(b) an order under section 27 of the Misuse of Drugs Act 1971 (forfeiture orders);

(c) an order under section 223 or 436 of the Criminal Procedure (Scotland) Act 1975 (forfeiture of property);

(d) an order under section 13(2), (3) or (4) of the Prevention of Terrorism (Temporary Provisions) Act 1989 (forfeiture orders); or

(e) an order under section 71 above,

is in force in respect of the property.

(4) For the purposes of subsection (3)(e) above, modifications effected by paragraph 1 of Schedule 2 to the Criminal Justice Act 1988 (Designated Countries and Territories) Order 1991 shall be disregarded.

(5) Subject to the following provisions of this section, for the purposes of this Part of this Act the value of property (other than cash) in relation to any person holding the property –

(a) where any other person holds an interest in the property, is

    (i) the market value of the first-mentioned person's beneficial interest in the property, less

    (ii) the amount required to discharge any incumbrance (other than a charging order) on that interest; and

(b) in any other case, is its market value.

(6) References in this Part of this Act to the value at any time (referred to in subsection (7) below as "the material time") of any property obtained by a person as a result of or in connection with conduct are references to –

(a) the value of the property to him when he obtained it adjusted to take account of subsequent changes in the value of money; or

(b) where subsection (7) below applies, the value there mentioned,

whichever is the greater.

(7) If at the material time he holds –

(a) the property which he obtained (not being cash); or

(b) property which, in whole or in part, directly or indirectly represents in his hands the property which he obtained,

the value referred to in subsection (6)(b) above is the value to him at the material time of the property mentioned in paragraph (a) above or, as the case may be, of the property mentioned in paragraph (b) above, so far as it so represents the property which he obtained, but disregarding any charging order.

(8) Subject to subsection (11) below, references in this Part of this Act to the value at any time (referred to in subsection (9) below as "the material time") of a gift caught by this Part of this Act are references to –

(a) the value of the gift to the recipient when he received it adjusted to take account of subsequent changes in the value of money; or

(b) where subsection (9) below applies, the value there mentioned,

whichever is the greater.

(9) Subject to subsection (11) below, if at the material time he holds –

(a) the property which he received (not being cash); or

(b) property which, in whole or in part, directly or indirectly represents in his hands the property which he received;

the value referred to in subsection (8) above is the value to him at the material time of the property mentioned in paragraph (a) above or, as the case may be, of the property mentioned in paragraph (b) above so far as it so represents the property which he received, but disregarding any charging order.

(10) A gift (including a gift made before the commencement of the Criminal Justice Act 1988 (Designated Countries and Territories) Order 1991) is caught by this Part of this Act if –

(a) it was made by the defendant at any time after the conduct to which the external confiscation order relates; and
(b) the court considers it appropriate in all the circumstances to take the gift into account.

(11) For the purposes of this Part of this Act –

(a) the circumstances in which the defendant is to be treated as making a gift include those where he transfers property to another person directly or indirectly for a consideration the value of which is significantly less than the value of the consideration provided by the defendant; and
(b) in those circumstances, the preceding provisions of this section shall apply as if the defendant had made a gift of such share in the property as bears to the whole property the same proportion as the difference between the values referred to in paragraph (a) above bears to the value of the consideration provided by the defendant.".

4 Section 75 shall be omitted.

5 In section 76 –

(a) for subsection (1)(a) there shall be substituted:

"(a) proceedings have been instituted against the defendant in a designated country,";

(b) for subsection (1)(c) there shall be substituted:

"(c) either an external confiscation order has been made in the proceedings or it appears to the High Court that there are reasonable grounds for thinking that such an order may be made in them.";

(c) for subsection (2) there shall be substituted:

"(2) Those powers are also exercisable where it appears to the High Court that proceedings are to be instituted against the defendant in a designated country and that there are reasonable grounds for thinking that an external confiscation order may be made in them.";

(d) subsection (3) shall be omitted; and
(e) in subsection (4), for the words from "proceedings" to "otherwise)", there shall be substituted the words "the proposed proceedings are not instituted".

6 In section 77 –

(a) for subsection (3)(a) and (b) there shall be substituted:

"(a) where an application under subsection (5) below relates to an external confiscation order made in respect of specified property, to property which is specified in that order; and
(b) in any other case –

   (i) to all realisable property held by a specified person, whether the property is described in the restraint order or not; and
   (ii) to realisable property held by a specified person, being property transferred to him after the making of the restraint order.";

(b) in paragraph (a) of subsection (5) for the words "the prosecutor" there shall be substituted the words "or on behalf of the government of a designated country or, in a case where an external confiscation order has been registered under section 97 below, by a receiver appointed under section 80 below, a Crown Prosecutor or a person authorised in that behalf by the Commissioners of Customs and Excise", and for paragraph (c) of that subsection there shall be substituted the following paragraph:

"(c) notwithstanding anything in Order 11 of the Rules of the Supreme Court may provide for service on, or the provision of notice to, persons affected by the order in such manner as the High Court may direct.";

(c) for subsection (6)(b) there shall be substituted:

"(b) shall be discharged when the proceedings in relation to which the order was made are concluded.";

(d) in subsections (9)(b) and (10) for the words "Great Britain" there shall be substituted the words "England and Wales"; and

(e) in subsection (13), for the words "The prosecutor" there shall be substituted the words "A person applying for a restraint order under subsection (5)(a) above".

7 In section 78 –

(a) for subsection (1)(a) and (b) there shall be substituted the following:

"(a) where a fixed amount is payable under an external confiscation order, of an amount not exceeding the amount so payable; and

(b) in any other case, of an amount equal to the value from time to time of the property charged.";

(b) in subsection (3)(a) for the words "the prosecutor" there shall be substituted the words "or on behalf of the government of a designated country or, in a case where an external confiscation order has been registered under section 97 below, by a receiver appointed under section 80 below, a Crown Prosecutor or a person authorised in that behalf by the Commissioners of Customs and Excise", and for paragraph (c) of that subsection there shall be substituted the following paragraph:

"(c) notwithstanding anything in Order 11 of the Rules of the Supreme Court shall provide for service on, or the provision of notice to, persons affected by the order in such manner as the High Court may direct;"; and

(c) in subsection (7) for the words "for the offence" there shall be substituted the words "against the defendant in the designated country".

8 In section 79, subsection (5) shall be omitted.

9 After section 79 there shall be inserted the following section:

"Applications for restraint and charging orders

79A Notwithstanding anything in rule 3(2) of Order 115 of the Rules of the Supreme Court 1965, an application under section 77(5) or 78(3) above shall be supported by an affidavit which shall –

(a) state, where applicable, the grounds for thinking that an external confiscation order may be made in the proceedings instituted or to be instituted in the designated country concerned;

(b) to the best of the deponent's ability, give particulars of the realisable property in respect of which the order is sought and specify the person or persons holding such property;

(c) in a case to which section 76(2) above applies, indicate when it is intended that proceedings should be instituted in the designated country concerned,

and the affidavit may, unless the court otherwise directs, contain statements of information or belief with the sources and grounds thereof.".

10 In section 80, for subsection (1) there shall be substituted the following two subsections:

"(1) Where an external confiscation order has been registered in the High Court under section 97 below, the High Court may, on the application of a Crown Prosecutor or a person authorised in that behalf by the Commissioners of Customs and Excise, exercise the powers conferred by subsections (1A) to (6) below.

(1A) In respect of any sum of money payable under the external confiscation order the court may make a garnishee order as if the sum were due to the Crown in pursuance of a judgment or order of the High Court, but any such order shall direct that the sum payable be paid to the High Court.".

11 In section 81 –

(a) in subsection (1), for the words from "sums", in the last place where it occurs, to the end of the subsection, there shall be substituted the words "be paid to the High Court and applied for the purposes specified in subsections (4) to (6) below and in the order so specified.";

(b) in subsection (2), for the words "If, after the amount payable under the confiscation order", there shall be substituted the words "Where a fixed amount is payable under the external confiscation order and, after that amount";

(c)   subsection (3) shall be omitted;

(d)   in subsection (4), for the words "The justices' clerk shall first", there shall be substituted the words "Any sums paid to the High Court under subsection (1) above or under an order made under section 80(1A) above or otherwise in satisfaction of an external confiscation order shall be first applied to";

(e)   for subsection (5) there shall be substituted the following subsection –

"(5) If the money was paid to the High Court by a receiver appointed under section 77 or 80 above or in pursuance of a charging order the receiver's remuneration and expenses shall next be paid.";

(f)   in subsection (6), for the words "After making" there shall be substituted the words "After there has been made", and for the words "the justices' clerk shall reimburse any amount paid under section 88(2) below" there shall be substituted the words "any amount paid under section 88(2) below shall be reimbursed.";

(g)   subsection (7) shall be omitted;

(h)   for subsection (8) there shall be substituted the following subsection –

"(8) Any sums remaining after all the payments required to be made under the foregoing provisions of this section have been made shall be paid into the Consolidated Fund."; and

(i)   subsections (9) and (10) shall be omitted.

12 In section 82 –

(a)   in subsection (1) the words "or on the Court of Session by sections 90 to 92 below," shall be omitted;

(b)   in subsection (2), for the words from "making available" to the end of the subsection there shall be substituted the words "recovering property which is liable to be recovered under an external confiscation order registered in the High Court under section 97 below or, as the case may be, with a view to making available for recovery property which may become liable to be recovered under any external confiscation order which may be made in the defendant's case."; and

(c)   in subsection (6), after the word "the" in the fourth place where it occurs, there shall be inserted the word "external".

13 Section 83 shall be omitted.

14 In section 84 –

(a)   in subsection (2) the words "or on the Court of Session by sections 90 to 92 below" shall be omitted;

(b)   in subsection (6)(a), the words "proceedings for an offence to which this Part of this Act applies have been instituted against him and have not been concluded or when" shall be omitted;

(c)   in subsection (6)(b), for the words "conclusion of the proceedings" there shall be substituted the words "discharge of the restraint or charging order"; and

(d)   for subsection (7) there shall be substituted the following subsection:

"(7) In any case in which a petition in bankruptcy was presented, or a receiving order or an adjudication in bankruptcy was made, before 29th December 1986 (the date on which the Insolvency Act 1986 came into force), subsection (2) shall have effect as if –

(a)   for the reference to the bankrupt's estate for the purposes of Part IX of the Insolvency Act 1986 there were substituted a reference to the property of the bankrupt for the purposes of the Bankruptcy Act 1914;

(b)   for the reference to section 280(2)(c) of the Act of 1986 there were substituted a reference to section 26(2) of that Act; and

(c)   subsection (2)(b) were omitted.".

15 For section 85 there shall be substituted the following section:

"85 (1) Where an award of sequestration has been made under the Bankruptcy (Scotland) Act 1985 by the Court of Session, in relation to a person who holds realisable property, the powers conferred on the High Court by sections 77 to 81 above or on a receiver so appointed shall not be exercised in relation to –

(a)   property comprised in the whole estate of the debtor within the meaning of section 31(8) of that Act, and

(b) any income of the debtor which has been ordered, under subsection (2) of section 32 of that Act, to be paid to the permanent trustee or any estate which, under subsection (10) of section 31 of that Act, or subsection (6) of the said section 32, vests in the permanent trustee.

(2) Subsection (1) above does not affect the enforcement of a charging order –

(a) made before the award of sequestration; or
(b) on property which was subject to a restraint order when the award of sequestration was made.

(3) In any case in which, notwithstanding the coming into force of the Bankruptcy (Scotland) Act 1985, the Bankruptcy (Scotland) Act 1913 applies to a sequestration, subsection (1) above shall have effect as if for paragraphs (a) and (b) thereof there were substituted the following paragraphs –

"(a) property comprised in the whole property of the debtor which vests in the trustee under section 97 of the Bankruptcy (Scotland) Act 1913,
(b) any income of the bankrupt which has been ordered under subsection (2) of section 98 of that Act to be paid to the trustee of any estate which, under subsection (1) of that section, vests in the trustee.".".

16 In section 86 –

(a) in subsection (2) the words "or in the Court of Session by sections 90 to 92 below" shall be omitted; and
(b) subsection (5) shall be omitted.

17 In subsection (3) of section 87 the words from "except that" to "trustee in sequestration" shall be omitted.

18 In subsection (2) of section 88, the words "by the prosecutor or, in a case where proceedings for an offence to which this Part of this Act applies are not instituted," shall be omitted.

19 Sections 89 to 96 shall be omitted.

20 Sections 98 to 101 shall be omitted.

21 In section 102 –

(a) for the list of expressions and relevant provisions in subsection (2) there shall be substituted –

Expression	Relevant provision
Charging order	Section 78(2)
External Confiscation Order	Section 71(1)
Dealing with property	Section 77(9)
Defendant	Section 74(1)(c)
Gift caught by this Part of this Act	Section 74(10)
Making a gift	Section 74(11)
Conduct to which this Part of this Act applies	Section 74(1)(b)
Realisable property	Section 74(2)
Restraint order	Section 77(1)
Value of gift	Section 74(8) and (9)
Value of property	Section 74(5) to (7)

(b) subsection (4) shall be omitted;
(c) at the end of subsection (5) the fullstop shall be omitted and there shall be added the words ", and whether received before or after the commencement of the Criminal Justice Act 1988 (Designated Countries and Territories) Order 1991.";
(d) for subsection (11), there shall be substituted the following:

"(11) Proceedings are instituted in a designated country when –

(a) under the law of the designated country concerned one of the steps specified in relation to that country in the right-hand column of the Appendix to this section has been taken there in respect of alleged conduct by the defendant to which this Part of this Act applies; or
(b) an application has been made to a court in a designated country for an external confiscation order,

and where the application of this subsection would result in there being more than one time for the institution of proceedings, they shall be taken to have been instituted at the earliest of those times."; and

(e) for subsection (12), there shall be substituted the following:

"(12) Proceedings are concluded –

(a) when (disregarding any power of a court to grant leave to appeal out of time) there is no further possibility of an external confiscation order being made in the proceedings;
(b) on the satisfaction of an external confiscation order made in the proceedings (whether by the recovery of all property liable to be recovered, or the payment of any amount due, or otherwise).": and

(f) at the end, the following Appendix shall be added –

"APPENDIX
INSTITUTION OF PROCEEDINGS

Section 102(11))

Designated country	Point at which proceedings are instituted
Italy	(a) when a person is notified, in accordance with article 369 of the Italian Code of Criminal Procedure, that a prosecution against him is in process; (b) when a proposal for the application of a preventative measure is laid before a court.
Sweden	when a public prosecutor has established that there are reasonable grounds to suspect that a person has committed an offence and accordingly the prosecutor is obliged under the Code of Judicial Procedure to notify the person of the suspicion."

22 Section 103 shall be omitted.

23 In Schedule 4 –

(a) in Part I the entries relating to the London Government Act 1963 and the Local Government (Miscellaneous Provisions) Act 1982 shall be omitted; and
(b) Part II shall be omitted.

SCHEDULE 3
PART VI OF THE CRIMINAL JUSTICE ACT 1988 AS MODIFIED

Article 3(2)

External confiscation orders

71 (1) An order made by a court in a designated country for the purpose –

(a) of recovering –

(i)   property obtained as a result of or in connection with conduct to which this Part of this Act applies; or
(ii) the value of property so obtained; or

(b) of depriving a person of a pecuniary advantage so obtained,

is referred to in this Part of this Act as an "external confiscation order", and "a designated country" means a country or territory designated under article 3(1) of the Criminal Justice Act 1988 (Designated Countries and Territories) Order 1991.

(2) Section 97 below shall have effect with regard to the registration of external confiscation orders.

(3) In subsection (1) above the reference to an order includes any order, decree, direction or judgment, or any part thereof, however described.

(4) Where a person derives a pecuniary advantage as a result of or in connection with conduct to which this Part of this Act applies, he is to be treated for the purposes of this Part of this Act as if he had obtained as a result of or in connection with the conduct a sum of money equal to the value of the pecuniary advantage.

Definition of principal terms used

74 (1) In this Part of this Act –

(a) "drug trafficking offence" has the same meaning as in the Drug Trafficking Offences Act 1986;
(b) references to conduct to which this Part of this Act applies are references to conduct corresponding to any offence which –

  (i) is listed in Schedule 4 to this Act; or
  (ii) if not listed, is an indictable offence, other than a drug trafficking offence or an offence under Part III of the Prevention of Terrorism (Temporary Provisions) Act 1989; and

(c) a person against whom an external confiscation order has been made, or a person against whom proceedings which may result in an external confiscation order being made have been, or are to be, instituted in a court of a designated country, is referred to as "the defendant".

(2) In this Part of this Act, "realisable property" means, subject to subsection (3) below –

(a) in relation to an external confiscation order in respect of specified property, the property which is specified in the order; and
(b) in any other case –

  (i) any property held by the defendant; and
  (ii) any property held by a person to whom the defendant has directly or indirectly made a gift caught by this Part of this Act.

(3) Property is not realisable property if –

(a) an order under section 43 of the Powers of Criminal Courts Act 1973 (deprivation orders);
(b) an order under section 27 of the Misuse of Drugs Act 1971 (forfeiture orders);
(c) an order under section 223 or 436 of the Criminal Procedure (Scotland) Act 1975 (forfeiture of property);
(d) an order under section 13(2), (3) or (4) of the Prevention of Terrorism (Temporary Provisions) Act 1989 (forfeiture orders); or
(e) an order under section 71 above,

is in force in respect of the property.

(4) For the purposes of subsection (3)(e) above, modifications effected by paragraph 1 of Schedule 2 to the Criminal Justice Act 1988 (Designated Countries and Territories) Order 1991 shall be disregarded.

(5) Subject to the following provisions of this section, for the purposes of this Part of this Act the value of property (other than cash) in relation to any person holding the property –

(a) where any other person holds an interest in the property, is –

  (i) the market value of the first-mentioned person's beneficial interest in the property, less
  (ii) the amount required to discharge any incumbrance (other than a charging order) on that interest; and

(b) in any other case, is its market value.

(6) References in this Part of this Act to the value at any time (referred to in subsection (7) below as "the material time") of any property obtained by a person as a result of or in connection with conduct are references to –

(a) the value of the property to him when he obtained it adjusted to take account of subsequent changes in the value of money; or

(b) where subsection (7) below applies, the value there mentioned,

whichever is the greater.

(7) If at the material time he holds –

(a) the property which he obtained (not being cash); or

(b) property which, in whole or in part, directly or indirectly represents in his hands the property which he obtained,

the value referred to in subsection (6)(b) above is the value to him at the material time of the property mentioned in paragraph (a) above or, as the case may be, of the property mentioned in paragraph (b) above, so far as it so represents the property which he obtained, but disregarding any charging order.

(8) Subject to subsection (11) below, references in this Part of this Act to the value at any time (referred to in subsection (9) below as "the material time") of a gift caught by this Part of this Act are references to –

(a) the value of the gift to the recipient when he received it adjusted to take account of subsequent changes in the value of money; or

(b) where subsection (9) below applies, the value there mentioned,

whichever is the greater.

(9) Subject to subsection (11) below, if at the material time he holds –

(a) the property which he received (not being cash); or

(b) property which, in whole or in part, directly or indirectly represents in his hands the property which he received;

the value referred to in subsection (8) above is the value to him at the material time of the property mentioned in paragraph (a) above or, as the case may be, of the property mentioned in paragraph (b) above so far as it so represents the property which he received, but disregarding any charging order.

(10) A gift (including a gift made before the commencement of the Criminal Justice Act 1988 (Designated Countries and Territories) Order 1991) is caught by this Part of this Act if –

(a) it was made by the defendant at any time after the conduct to which the external confiscation order relates; and

(b) the court considers it appropriate in all the circumstances to take the gift into account.

(11) For the purposes of this Part of the Act –

(a) the circumstances in which the defendant is to be treated as making a gift include those where he transfers property to another person directly or indirectly for a consideration the value of which is significantly less than the value of the consideration provided by the defendant; and

(b) in those circumstances, the preceding provisions of this section shall apply as if the defendant had made a gift of such share in the property as bears to the whole property the same proportion as the difference between the values referred to in paragraph (a) above bears to the value of the consideration provided by the defendant.

Cases in which restraint orders and charging orders may be made

76 (1) The powers conferred on the High Court by sections 77(1) and 78(1) below are exercisable where –

(a) proceedings have been instituted against the defendant in a designated country;

(b) the proceedings have not been concluded; and

(c) either an external confiscation order has been made in the proceedings or it appears to the High Court that there are reasonable grounds for thinking that such an order may be made in them.

(2) Those powers are also exercisable where it appears to the High Court that proceedings are to be instituted against the defendant in a designated country and that there are reasonable grounds for thinking that an external confiscation order may be made in them.

(4) Where the court has made an order under section 77(1) or 78(1) below by virtue of subsection (2) above, the court shall discharge the order if the proposed proceedings are not instituted within such time as the court considers reasonable.

Restraint Orders

77 (1) The High Court may by order (referred to in this Part of this Act as a "restraint order") prohibit any person from dealing with any realisable property, subject to such conditions and exceptions as may be specified in the order.

(2) Without prejudice to the generality of subsection (1) above, a restraint order may make such provision as the court thinks fit for living expenses and legal expenses.

(3) A restraint order may apply –

(a) where an application under subsection (5) below relates to an external confiscation order made in respect of specified property, to property which is specified in that order; and

(b) in any other case –

   (i)   to all realisable property held by a specified person, whether the property is described in the restraint order or not; and
   (ii) to realisable property held by a specified person, being property transferred to him after the making of the restraint order.

(4) This section shall not have effect in relation to any property for the time being subject to a charge under section 78 below.

(5) A restraint order –

(a) may be made only on an application by or on behalf of the government of a designated country or, in a case where an external confiscation order has been registered under section 97 below, by a receiver appointed under section 80 below, a Crown Prosecutor or a person authorised in that behalf by the Commissioners of Customs and Excise;

(b) may be made on an ex parte application to a judge in chambers; and

(c) notwithstanding anything in Order 11 of the Rules of the Supreme Court may provide for service on, or the provision of notice to, persons affected by the order in such manner as the High Court may direct.

(6) a restraint order –

(a) may be discharged or varied in relation to any property; and

(b) shall be discharged when the proceedings in relation to which the order was made are concluded.

(7) An application for the discharge or variation of a restraint order may be made by any person affected by it.

(8) Where the High Court has made a restraint order, the court may at any time appoint a receiver –

(a) to take possession of any realisable property, and

(b) in accordance with the court's directions, to manage or otherwise deal with any property in respect of which he is appointed,

subject to such exceptions and conditions as may be specified by the court; and may require any person having possession of property in respect of which a receiver is appointed under this section to give possession of it to the receiver.

(9) For the purposes of this section, dealing with property held by any person includes (without prejudice to the generality of the expression) –

(a) where a debt is owed to that person, making a payment to any person in reduction of the amount of the debt; and

(b) removing the property from England and Wales.

(10) Where the High Court has made a restraint order, a constable may for the purpose of preventing any realisable property being removed from England and Wales, seize the property.

(11) Property seized under subsection (10) above shall be dealt with in accordance with the court's directions.

(12) The Land Charges Act 1972 and the Land Registration Act 1925 shall apply –

(a)   in relation to restraint orders, as they apply in relation to orders affecting land made by the court for the purpose of enforcing judgments or recognisances; and

(b)   in relation to applications for restraint orders, as they apply in relation to other pending land actions.

(13) A person applying for a restraint order under subsection (5)(a) above shall be treated for the purposes of section 57 of the Land Registration Act 1925 (inhibitions) as a person interested in relation to any registered land to which a restraint order or an application for such an order relates.

Charging orders in respect of land, securities, etc.

78 (1) The High Court may make a charging order on realisable property for securing the payment to the Crown –

(a)   where a fixed amount is payable under an external confiscation order, of an amount not exceeding the amount so payable; and

(b)   in any other case, of an amount equal to the value from time to time of the property charged.

(2) For the purposes of this Part of this Act, a charging order is an order made under this section imposing on any such realisable property as may be specified in the order a charge for securing the payment of money to the Crown.

(3) A charging order –

(a)   may be made only on an application by or on behalf of the government of a designated country or, in a case where an external confiscation order has been registered under section 97 below, by a receiver appointed under section 80 below, a Crown Prosecutor or a person authorised in that behalf by the Commissioners of Customs and Excise;

(b)   may be made on an ex parte application to a judge in chambers;

(c)   notwithstanding anything in Order 11 of the Rules of the Supreme Court shall provide for service on, or the provision of notice to, persons affected by the order in such manner as the High Court may direct; and

(d)   may be made subject to such conditions as the court thinks fit and, without prejudice to the generality of this paragraph, such conditions as it thinks fit as to the time when the charge is to become effective.

(4) Subject to subsection (6) below, a charge may be imposed by a charging order only on –

(a)   any interest in realisable property, being an interest held beneficially by the defendant or by a person to whom the defendant has directly or indirectly made a gift caught by this Part of this Act

(i) in any asset of a kind mentioned in subsection (5) below; or
(ii) under any trust; or

(b)   any interest in realisable property held by a person as trustee of a trust if the interest is in such an asset or is an interest under another trust and a charge may by virtue of paragraph (a) above be imposed by a charging order on the whole beneficial interest under the first-mentioned trust.

(5) The assets referred to in subsection (4) above are –

(a)   land in England and Wales; or
(b)   securities of any of the following kinds

(i)   government stock;
(ii) stock of any body (other than a building society) incorporated within England and Wales;
(iii) stock of any body incorporated outside England and Wales or of any country or territory outside the United Kingdom, being stock registered in a register kept at any place within England and Wales;
(iv) units of any unit trust in respect of which a register of the unit holders is kept at any place within England and Wales.

(6) In any case where a charge is imposed by a charging order on any interest in an asset of a kind mentioned in subsection (5)(b) above, the court may provide for the charge to extend to any interest or dividend payable in respect of the asset.

(7) The court may make an order discharging or varying the charging order and shall make an order discharging the charging order if the proceedings against the defendant in the designated country are concluded or the amount payment of which is secured by the charge is paid into court.

(8) An application for the discharge or variation of a charging order may be made by any person affected by it.

Charging orders: supplementary provisions

79 (1) The Land Charges Act 1972 and the Land Registration Act 1925 shall apply in relation to charging orders as they apply in relation to orders or writs issued or made for the purpose of enforcing judgments.

(2) Where a charging order has been registered under section 6 of the Land Charges Act 1972, subsection (4) of that section (effect of non-registration of writs and orders registrable under that section) shall not apply to an order appointing a receiver made in pursuance of the charging order.

(3) Subject to any provision made under section 80 below or by rules of court, a charge imposed by a charging order shall have the like effect and shall be enforceable in the same courts and in the same manner as an equitable charge created by the person holding the beneficial interest or, as the case may be, the trustees by writing under their hand.

(4) Where a charging order has been protected by an entry registered under the Land Charges Act 1972 or the Land Registration Act 1925, an order under section 78(7) above discharging the charging order may direct that the entry be cancelled.

(5) In this section and section 78 above, "building society", "dividend", "government stock", "stock" and "unit trust" have the same meanings as in the Charging Orders Act 1979.

Applications for restraint and charging orders

79A Notwithstanding anything in rule 3(2) of Order 115 of the Rules of the Supreme Court 1965, an application under section 77(5) or 78(3) above shall be supported by an affidavit which shall –

(a) state, where applicable, the grounds for thinking that an external confiscation order may be made in the proceedings instituted or to be instituted in the designated country concerned;
(b) to the best of the deponent's ability, give particulars of the realisable property in respect of which the order is sought and specify the person or persons holding such property;
(c) in a case to which section 76(2) above applies, indicate when it is intended that proceedings should be instituted in the designated country concerned,

and the affidavit may, unless the court otherwise directs, contain statements of information or belief with the sources and grounds thereof.

Realisation of property

80 (1) Where an external confiscation order has been registered in the High Court under section 97 below, the High Court may, on the application of a Crown Prosecutor or a person authorised in that behalf by the Commissioners of Customs and Excise, exercise the powers conferred by subsections (1A) to (6) below.

(1A) In respect of any sum of money payable under the external confiscation order the court may make a garnishee order as if the sum were due to the Crown in pursuance of a judgment or order of the High Court, but any such order shall direct that the sum payable be paid to the High Court.

(2) The court may appoint a receiver in respect of realisable property.

(3) The court may empower a receiver appointed under subsection (2) above, under section 77 above or in pursuance of a charging order –

(a) to enforce any charge imposed under section 78 above on realisable property or on interest or dividends payable in respect of such property; and
(b) in relation to any realisable property other than property for the time being subject to a charge under section 78 above, to take possession of the property subject to such conditions or exceptions as may be specified by the court.

(4) The court may order any person having possession of realisable property to give possession of it to any such receiver.

(5) The court may empower any such receiver to realise any realisable property in such manner as the court may direct.

(6) The court may order any person holding an interest in realisable property to make such payment to the receiver in respect of any beneficial interest held by the defendant or, as the case may be, the recipient of a gift caught by this Part of this Act as the court may direct and the court may, on the payment being made, by order transfer, grant or extinguish any interest in the property.

(7) Subsections (4) and (6) above do not apply to property for the time being subject to a charge under section 78 above.

(8) The court shall not in respect of any property exercise the powers conferred by subsection (3)(a), (5) or (6) above unless a reasonable opportunity has been given for persons holding any interest in the property to make representations to the court.

Application of proceeds of realisation and other sums

81 (1) Subject to subsection (2) below, the following sums in the hands of a receiver appointed under this Part of this Act or in pursuance of a charging order, that is –

(a) the proceeds of the enforcement of any charge imposed under section 78 above;
(b) the proceeds of the realisation, other than by the enforcement of such a charge, of any property under section 77 or 80 above; and
(c) any other sums, being property held by the defendant,

shall first be applied in payment of such expenses incurred by a person acting as an insolvency practitioner as are payable under section 87(2) below and then shall, after such payments (if any) as the High Court may direct have been made out of those sums, be paid to the High Court and applied for the purposes specified in subsections (4) to (6) below and in the order so specified.

(2) Where a fixed amount is payable under the external confiscation order and, after that amount has been fully paid, any such sums remain in the hands of such a receiver, the receiver shall distribute them –

(a) among such of those who held property which has been realised under this Part of this Act, and
(b) in such proportions,

as the High Court may direct after giving a reasonable opportunity for such persons to make representations to the court.

(4) Any sums paid to the High Court under subsection (1) above or under an order made under section 80(1A) above or otherwise in satisfaction of an external confiscation order shall be first applied to pay any expenses incurred by a person acting as an insolvency practitioner and payable under section 87(2) below but not already paid under subsection (1) above.

(5) If the money was paid to the High Court by a receiver appointed under section 77 or 80 above or in pursuance of a charging order the receiver's remuneration and expenses shall next be paid.

(6) After there has been made –

(a) any payment required by subsection (4) above; and
(b) in a case to which subsection (5) above applies, any payment required by that subsection,

any amount paid under section 88(2) below shall be reimbursed.

(8) Any sums remaining after all the payments required to be made under the foregoing provisions of this section have been made shall be paid into the Consolidated Fund.

Exercise of powers by High Court or receiver

82 (1) This section applies to the powers conferred on the High Court by sections 77 to 81 above or on a receiver appointed under this Part of this Act or in pursuance of a charging order.

(2) Subject to the following provisions of this section, the powers shall be exercised with a view to recovering property which is liable to be recovered under an external confiscation order registered in the High Court under section 97 below or, as the case may be, with a view to making available for recovery property which may become liable to be recovered under any external confiscation order which may be made in the defendant's case.

(3) In the case of realisable property held by a person to whom the defendant has directly or indirectly made a gift caught by this Part of this Act the powers shall be exercised with a view to realising no more than the value for the time being of the gift.

(4) The powers shall be exercised with a view to allowing any person other than the defendant or the recipient of any such gift to retain or recover the value of any property held by him.

(5) An order may be made or other action taken in respect of a debt owed by the Crown.

(6) In exercising those powers, no account shall be taken of any obligations of the defendant or of the recipient of any such gift which conflict with the obligation to satisfy the external confiscation order.

Bankruptcy of defendant etc.

84 (1) Where a person who holds realisable property is adjudged bankrupt –

(a) property for the time being subject to a restraint order made before the order adjudging him bankrupt, and
(b) any proceeds of property realised by virtue of section 77(8) or 80(5) or (6) above for the time being in the hands of a receiver appointed under section 77 or 80 above,

is excluded from the bankrupt's estate for the purposes of Part IX of the Insolvency Act 1986.

(2) Where a person has been adjudged bankrupt, the powers conferred on the High Court by sections 77 to 81 above or on a receiver so appointed shall not be exercised in relation to –

(a) property for the time being comprised in the bankrupt's estate for the purposes of that Part of that Act;
(b) property in respect of which his trustee in bankruptcy may (without leave of court) serve a notice under section 307 or 308 or 308A of that Act (after-acquired property and tools, clothes, etc. exceeding value of reasonable replacement and certain tenancies); and
(c) property which is to be applied for the benefit of creditors of the bankrupt by virtue of a condition imposed under section 280(2)(c) of that Act.

(3) Nothing in that Act shall be taken as restricting, or enabling the restriction of, the exercise of those powers.

(4) Subsection (2) above does not affect the enforcement of a charging order –

(a) made before the order adjudging the person bankrupt; or
(b) on property which was subject to a restraint order when the order adjudging him bankrupt was made.

(5) Where, in the case of a debtor, an interim receiver stands appointed under section 286 of that Act and any property of the debtor is subject to a restraint order, the powers conferred on the receiver by virtue of that Act do not apply to property for the time being subject to the restraint order.

(6) Where a person is adjudged bankrupt and has directly or indirectly made a gift caught by this Part of this Act –

(a) no order shall be made under section 339 or 423 of that Act (avoidance of certain transactions) in respect of the making of the gift at any time when property of the person to whom the gift was made is subject to a restraint order or charging order; and
(b) any order made under either of those sections after the discharge of the restraint or charging order shall take into account any realisation under this Part of this Act of property held by the person to whom the gift was made.

(7) In any case in which a petition in bankruptcy was presented, or a receiving order or an adjudication in bankruptcy was made, before 29th December 1986 (the date on which the Insolvency Act 1986 came into force), subsection (2) above shall have effect as if –

(a) for the reference to the bankrupt's estate for the purposes of Part IX of the Insolvency Act 1986 there were substituted a reference to the property of the bankrupt for the purposes of the Bankruptcy Act 1914;
(b) for the reference to section 280(2)(c) of the Act of 1986 there were substituted a reference to section 26(2) of that Act; and
(c) subsection (2)(b) were omitted.

Sequestration in Scotland of defendant etc.

85 (1) Where an award of sequestration has been made under the Bankruptcy (Scotland) Act 1985 by the Court of Session, in relation to a person who holds realisable property, the powers conferred

on the High Court by sections 77 to 81 above or on a receiver so appointed shall not be exercised in relation to –

    (a) property comprised in the whole estate of the debtor within the meaning of section 31(8) of that Act, and

    (b) any income of the debtor which has been ordered, under subsection (2) of section 32 of that Act, to be paid to the permanent trustee or any estate which, under subsection (10) of section 31 of that Act or subsection (6) of the said section 32, vests in the permanent trustee.

(2) Subsection (1) above does not affect the enforcement of a charging order –

    (a) made before the award of sequestration; or

    (b) on property which was subject to a restraint order when the award of sequestration was made.

(3) In any case in which, notwithstanding the coming into force of the Bankruptcy (Scotland) Act 1985, the Bankruptcy (Scotland) Act 1913 applies to a sequestration, subsection (1) above shall have effect as if for paragraphs (a) and (b) thereof there were substituted the following paragraphs –

    "(a) property comprised in the whole property of the debtor which vests in the trustee under section 97 of the Bankruptcy (Scotland) Act 1913,

    (b) any income of the bankrupt which has been ordered under subsection (2) of section 98 of that Act to be paid to the trustee of any estate which, under subsection (1) of that section, vests in the trustee.".

Winding up of company holding realisable property

86 (1) Where realisable property is held by a company and an order for the winding up of the company has been made or a resolution has been passed by the company for the voluntary winding up, the functions of the liquidator (or any provisional liquidator) shall not be exercisable in relation to –

    (a) property for the time being subject to a restraint order made before the relevant time, and

    (b) any proceeds of property realised by virtue of section 77(8) or 80(5) or (6) above for the time being in the hands of a receiver appointed under section 77 or 80 above.

(2) Where, in the case of a company, such an order has been made or such a resolution has been passed, the powers conferred on the High Court by sections 77 to 80 above or on a receiver so appointed shall not be exercised in relation to any realisable property held by the company in relation to which the functions of the liquidator are exercisable –

    (a) so as to inhibit him from exercising those functions for the purpose of distributing any property held by the company to the company's creditors; or

    (b) so as to prevent the payment out of any property of expenses (including the remuneration of the liquidator or any provisional liquidator) properly incurred in the winding up in respect of the property.

(3) Nothing in the Insolvency Act 1986 shall be taken as restricting, or enabling the restriction of, the exercise of those powers.

(4) Subsection (2) above does not affect the enforcement of a charging order made before the relevant time or on property which was subject to a restraint order at the relevant time.

(6) In this section –

       "company" means any company which may be wound up under the Insolvency Act 1986; and

       "the relevant time" means –

    (a) where no order for the winding up of the company has been made, the time of the passing of the resolution for voluntary winding up;

    (b) where such an order has been made and, before the presentation of the petition for the winding up of the company by the court, such a resolution had been passed by the company, the time of the passing of the resolution; and

    (c) in any other case where such an order has been made, the time of the making of the order.

(7) In any case in which a winding up of a company commenced or is treated as having commenced before 29th December 1986, this section shall have effect with the substitution for

references to the Insolvency Act 1986 of references to the Companies Act 1985.

Insolvency officers dealing with property subject to restraint order

87 (1) Without prejudice to the generality of any enactment contained in the Insolvency Act 1986 or in any other Act, where –

(a) any person acting as an insolvency practitioner seizes or disposes of any property in relation to which his functions are not exercisable because it is for the time being subject to a restraint order; and

(b) at the time of the seizure or disposal he believes, and has reasonable grounds for believing, that he is entitled (whether in pursuance of an order of the court or otherwise) to seize or dispose of that property,

he shall not be liable to any person in respect of any loss or damage resulting from the seizure or disposal except in so far as the loss or damage is caused by his negligence in so acting; and a person so acting shall have a lien on the property, or the proceeds of its sale, for such of his expenses as were incurred in connection with the liquidation, bankruptcy or other proceedings in relation to which the seizure or disposal purported to take place and for so much of his remuneration as may reasonably be assigned for his acting in connection with those proceedings.

(2) Any person who, acting as an insolvency practitioner, incurs expenses –

(a) in respect of such property as is mentioned in paragraph (a) of subsection (1) above and in so doing does not know and has no reasonable grounds to believe that the property is for the time being subject to a restraint order; or

(b) other than in respect of such property as is so mentioned, being expenses which, but for the effect of a restraint order, might have been met by taking possession of and realising the property,

shall be entitled (whether or not he has seized or disposed of that property so as to have a lien under that subsection) to payment of those expenses under section 81(1) or (4) above.

(3) In this Part of this Act the expression "acting as an insolvency practitioner" shall be construed in accordance with section 388 (interpretation) of the said Act of 1986 and subsection (5) of that section (which provides that nothing in the section is to apply to anything done by the official receiver) shall be disregarded; and the expression shall also comprehend the official receiver acting as receiver or manager of the property.

Receivers: Supplementary provisions

88 (1) Where a receiver appointed under this Part of this Act or in pursuance of a charging order takes any action –

(a) in relation to property which is not realisable property, being action which he would be entitled to take if it were such property;

(b) believing, and having reasonable grounds for believing, that he is entitled to take that action in relation to that property,

he shall not be liable to any person in respect of any loss or damage resulting from his action except in so far as the loss or damage is caused by his negligence.

(2) Any amount due in respect of the remuneration and expenses of a receiver so appointed shall, if no sum is available to be applied in payment of it under section 81(5) above, be paid by the person on whose application the receiver was appointed.

Registration of external confiscation orders

97 (1) On an application made by or on behalf of the government of a designated country, the High Court may register an external confiscation order made there if –

(a) it is satisfied that at the time of registration the order is in force and not subject to appeal;

(b) it is satisfied, where the person against whom the order is made did not appear in the proceedings, that he received notice of the proceedings in sufficient time to enable him to defend them; and

(c) it is of the opinion that enforcing the order in England and Wales would not be contrary to the interests of justice.

(2) In subsection (1) above "appeal" includes –

(a) any proceedings by way of discharging or setting aside a judgment; and

(b) an application for a new trial or a stay of execution.

(3) The High Court shall cancel the registration of an external confiscation order if it appears to the court that the order has been satisfied by payment of the amount due under it or by the person against whom it was made serving imprisonment in default of payment or by any other means.

Part VI – Interpretation

102 (1) In this Part of this Act

"constable" includes a person commissioned by the Commissioners of Customs and Excise;

"interest", in relation to property, includes right;

"property" includes money and all other property, real or personal, heritable or moveable, including things in action and other intangible or incorporeal property.

(2) The expressions listed in the left-hand column below are respectively defined or (as the case may be) fall to be construed in accordance with the provisions of this Act listed in the right-hand column in relation to those expressions.

EXPRESSION	RELEVANT PROVISION
Charging order	Section 78(2)
External Confiscation Order	Section 71(1)
Dealing with property	Section 77(9)
Defendant	Section 74(1)(c)
Gift caught by this Part of this Act	Section 74(10)
Making a gift	Section 74(11)
Conduct to which this Part of this Act applies	Section 74(1)(b)
Realisable property	Section 74(2)
Restraint order	Section 77(1)
Value of gift	Section 74(8) and (9)
Value of property	Section 74(5) to (7)

(3) This Part of this Act applies to property wherever situated.

(5) References in this Part of this Act to property obtained, or to a pecuniary advantage derived, in connection with the commission of an offence include a reference to property obtained, or to a pecuniary advantage derived, both in that connection and in some other connection, and whether received before or after the commencement of the Criminal Justice Act 1988 (Designated Countries and Territories) Order 1991.

(6) The following provisions shall have effect for the interpretation of this Part of this Act.

(7) Property is held by any person if he holds any interest in it.

(8) References to property held by a person include a reference to property vested in his trustee in bankruptcy, permanent or interim trustee within the meaning of the Bankruptcy (Scotland) Act 1985 or liquidator.

(9) References to an interest held by a person beneficially in property include a reference to an interest which would be held by him beneficially if the property were not so vested.

(10) Property is transferred by one person to another if the first person transfers or grants to the other any interest in the property.

(11) Proceedings are instituted in a designated country when –

(a) under the law of the designated country concerned one of the steps specified in relation to that country in the right-hand column of the Appendix hereto has been taken there in respect of alleged conduct by the defendant to which this Part of this Act applies; or

(b) an application has been made to a court in a designated country for an external confiscation order, and where the application of this subsection would result in there being more than one time for the institution of proceedings, they shall be taken to have been instituted at the earliest of those times.

(12) Proceedings are concluded –

(a) when (disregarding any power of a court to grant leave to appeal out of time) there is no further possibility of an external confiscation order being made in the proceedings;

(b) on the satisfaction of an external confiscation order made in the proceedings (whether by the recovery of all property liable to be recovered, or the payment of any amount due, or otherwise).

(13) An order is subject to appeal until (disregarding any power of a court to grant leave to appeal out of time) there is no further possibility of an appeal on which the order could be varied or set aside.

APPENDIX
INSTITUTION OF PROCEEDINGS

Section 102(11)

Designated country	Point at which proceedings are instituted
Italy	(a) when a person is notified, in accordance with article 369 of the Italian Code of Criminal Procedure, that a prosecution against him is in process;
	(b) when a proposal for the application of a preventative measure is laid before a court
Sweden	when a public prosecutor has established that there are reasonable grounds to suspect that a person has committed an offence and accordingly the prosecutor is obliged under the Code of Judicial Procedure to notify the person of the suspicion.

SCHEDULE 4
TO THE CRIMINAL JUSTICE ACT 1988 AS MODIFIED

Section 74

CORRESPONDING CONDUCT–SUMMARY OFFENCES

Enactment	Description of offence
PRIVATE PLACES OF ENTERTAINMENT (LICENSING) ACT 1967 (c. 19)	
Section 4(1)	Offences relating to the use of places for dancing, music or other entertainment of the like kind which is not a public entertainment but provided for private gain.
Section 4(2), in relation only to an offence referred to in subsection (3A)(b) of section 4.	
VIDEO RECORDINGS ACT 1984 (c.39)	
Section 9	Supplying video recording of unclassified work.
Section 10	Possession of video recording of unclassified work for the purpose of supply.
CINEMAS ACT 1985 (c.13)	
Section 10(1)(a)	Use of unlicensed premises for exhibition which requires a licence.

SI 1965 No 1776

Rules of the Supreme Court (Revision) 1965

ORDER 115

CONFISCATION AND FORFEITURE IN CONNECTION WITH CRIMINAL CHARGES

[PART 1. DRUG TRAFFICKING OFFENCES ACT] [AND CRIMINAL JUSTICE (INTERNATIONAL CO-OPERATION) ACT 1990]

NOTES

Order 115 added by SI 1986 No 2289, r 17. Title of Order substituted by SI 1991 No 1884, r 21. Part 1 heading amended by SI 1989 No 386, r 4 and SI 1991 No 1884, r 22.

1 Interpretation

(1) In this Part of this Order, "the Act" means the Drug Trafficking Offences Act 1986 and a section referred to by number means the section so numbered in the Act.

(2) Expressions used in this Part of this Order which are used in the Act have the same meanings in this Part of this Order as in the Act.

NOTES

Substituted by SI 1989 No 386, r 4.

2 Assignment of proceedings

[Subject to rule 12,] The jurisdiction of the High Court under the Act shall be exercised by a judge of the Chancery Division or of the Queen's Bench Division in chambers.

NOTES

Amended by SI 1988 No 298, r 23.

3 Application for restraint order or charging order

(1) An application for a restraint order under section 8 or for a charging order under section 9 (to either of which may be joined an application for the appointment of a receiver) may be made by the prosecutor ex parte by originating motion.

(2) An application under paragraph (1) shall be supported by an affidavit, which shall:

(a) state the grounds for believing that the defendant has benefited from drug trafficking;

(b) state, as the case may be, either that proceedings have been instituted against the defendant for a drug trafficking offence (giving particulars of the offence) and that they have not been concluded or [that, whether by the laying of an information or otherwise, a person is to be charged with such an offence];

(c) to the best of the deponent's ability, give full particulars of the realisable property in respect of which the order is sought and specify the person or persons holding such property;

(d) where proceedings have not been instituted, verify that the prosecutor is to have the conduct of the proposed proceedings;

(e) where proceedings have not been instituted, indicate when it is intended that they should be instituted.

(3) An originating motion under paragraph (1) shall be entitled in the matter of the defendant, naming him, and in the matter of the Act, and all subsequent documents in the matter shall be so entitled.

(4) Unless the Court otherwise directs, an affidavit under paragraph (2) may contain statements of information or belief with the sources and grounds thereof.

NOTES
Para (2): words in square brackets substituted by SI 1989 No 386, r 5.

4 Restraint order and charging order

(1) A restraint order may be made subject to conditions and exceptions, including but not limited to conditions relating to the indemnifying of third parties against expenses incurred in complying with the order, and exceptions relating to living expenses and legal expenses of the defendant, but the [prosecutor] shall not be required to give an undertaking to abide by any order as to damages sustained by the defendant as a result of the restraint order.

(2) Unless the Court otherwise directs, a restraint order made ex parte shall have effect until a day which shall be fixed for the hearing inter partes of the application and a charging order shall be an order to show cause, imposing the charge until such day.

(3) Where a restraint order is made the prosecutor shall serve copies of the order and of the affidavit in support on the defendant and on all other named persons restrained by the order and shall notify all other persons or bodies affected by the order of its terms.

(4) Where a charging order is made the prosecutor shall [. . .] serve copies of the order and of the affidavit in support on the defendant and, where the property to which the order relates is held by another person, on that person and shall serve a copy of the order on such of the persons or bodies specified in Order 50, rule 2(1)(b) to (d) as shall be appropriate.

NOTES
Para (1): word in square brackets substituted by SI 1989 No 1307, r 5.
Para (4): words omitted revoked by SI 1990 No 492, r 5.

5 Discharge or variation of order

(1) Any person or body on whom a restraint order or a charging order is served or who is notified of such an order may apply by summons to discharge or vary the order.

(2) The summons and any affidavit in support shall be lodged with the court and served on the prosecutor and, where he is not the applicant, on the defendant, not less than two clear days before the date fixed for the hearing of the summons.

(3) Upon the court being notified that proceedings for the offences have been concluded or that the amount payment of which is secured by a charging order has been paid into court, any restraint order or charging order, as the case may be, shall be discharged.

6 Further application by prosecutor

(1) Where a restraint order or a charging order has been made the prosecutor may apply by summons or, where the case is one of urgency, ex parte: –

(a) to discharge or vary such order, or
(b) for a restraint order or a charging order in respect of other realisable property, or
(c) for the appointment of a receiver.

(2) An application under paragraph (1) shall be supported by an affidavit which, where the application is for a restraint order or a charging order, shall to the best of the deponent's ability give full particulars of the realisable property in respect of which the order is sought and specify the person or persons holding such property.

(3) The summons and affidavit in support shall be lodged with the court and served on the defendant and, where one has been appointed in the matter, on the receiver, not less than two clear days before the date fixed for the hearing of the summons.

(4) Rule 4(3) and (4) shall apply to the service of restraint orders and charging orders respectively made under this rule on persons other than the defendant.

7 Realisation of property

(1) An application by the prosecutor under section 11 shall, where there have been proceedings against the defendant in the High Court, be made by summons and shall otherwise be made by originating motion.

(2) The summons or originating motion, as the case may be, shall be served with the evidence in support not less than 7 days before the date fixed for the hearing of the summons on: –

(a) the defendant,
(b) any person holding any interest in the realisable property to which the application relates, and
(c) the receiver, where one has been appointed in the matter.

(3) The application shall be supported by an affidavit, which shall, to the best of the deponent's ability, give full particulars of the realisable property to which it relates and specify the person or persons holding such property, and a copy of the confiscation order, of any certificate issued by the Crown Court under section 4(2) and of any charging order made in the matter shall be exhibited to such affidavit.

(4) The court may, on an application under section 11, exercise the power conferred by section 12(1) to direct the making of payments by the receiver.

8 Receivers

(1) Subject to the provisions of this rule, the provisions of Order 30, rules 2 to 8 shall apply where a receiver is appointed in pursuance of a charging order or under section 8 or 11.

(2) Where the receiver proposed to be appointed has been appointed receiver in other proceedings under the Act, it shall not be necessary for an affidavit of fitness to be sworn or for the receiver to give security, unless the Court otherwise orders.

(3) Where a receiver has fully paid the amount payable under the confiscation order and any sums remain in his hands, he shall apply by summons for directions as to the distribution of such sums.

(4) A summons under paragraph (3) shall be served with any evidence in support not less than 7 days before the date fixed for the hearing of the summons on: –

(a) the defendant, and
(b) any other person who held property realised by the receiver.

9 Certificate of inadequacy

(1) The defendant may apply by summons for a certificate under section 14(1).

(2) A summons under paragraph (1) shall be served with any supporting evidence not less than 7 days before the date fixed for the hearing of the summons on the prosecutor and on the receiver, where one has been appointed in the matter.

10 Compensation

An application for an order under section 19 shall be made by summons, which shall be served, with any supporting evidence, on the person alleged to be in default and on the relevant authority under section 19(4) not less than 7 days before the date fixed for the hearing of the summons.

11 Disclosure of information

[(1) An application by the prosecutor under section 30 shall be made by summons, which shall state the nature of the order sought and whether material sought to be disclosed is to be disclosed to a receiver appointed under section 8 or 11 or in pursuance of a charging order or to a person mentioned in section 30(8).

(2) The summons and affidavit in support shall be served on the authorised Government Department in accordance with Order 77, rule 4 not less than 7 days before the date fixed for the hearing of the summons.

(3) The affidavit in support of an application under paragraph (1) shall state the grounds for believing that the conditions in section 30(4) and, if appropriate, section 30(7) are fulfilled.

12 Exercise of powers under sections 24A and [26A]
The powers conferred on the High Court by sections 24A and [26A] may be exercised by a judge in chambers and a master of the Queen's Bench Division.

NOTES
Rules 12-21 added by SI 1988 No 298, r 24.
Figure in square brackets added by SI 1989 No 386, r 6.

13 Application for registration
An application for registration of an order specified in an Order in Council made under section 24A or of an external confiscation order under section [26A(1)] may be made ex parte.

NOTES
Rules 12-21 added by SI 1988 No 298, r 24.
Figure in square brackets substituted by SI 1989 No 386, r 7.

14 Evidence in support of application under section 24A
An application for registration of an order specified in an Order in Council made under section 24A must be supported by an affidavit –

(i) exhibiting the order or a certified copy thereof, and
(ii) stating, to the best of the deponent's knowledge, particulars of what property the person against whom the order was made holds in England and Wales, giving the source of the deponent's knowledge.

NOTES
Rules 12-21 added by SI 1988 No 298, r 24.

15 Evidence in support of application under section [26A(1)]
[(1)] An application for registration of an external confiscation order must be supported by an affidavit –

(a) exhibiting the order or a verified or otherwise duly authenticated copy thereof and, where the order is not in the English language, a translation thereof into English certified by a notary public or authenticated by affidavit, and
(b) stating –

   (i) that the order is in force and is not subject to appeal,
   (ii) where the person against whom the order was made did not appear in the proceedings, that he received notice thereof in sufficient time to enable him to defend them,
   (iii) in the case of money, either that at the date of the application the sum payable under the order has not been paid or the amount which remains unpaid, as may be appropriate, or, in the case of other property, the property which has not been recovered, and
   (iv) to the best of the deponent's knowledge, particulars of what property the person against whom the order was made holds in England and Wales, giving the source of the deponent's knowledge.

[(2) Unless the Court otherwise directs, an affidavit for the purposes of this rule may contain statements of information or belief with the sources and grounds thereof].

NOTES
Rules 12-21 added by SI 1988 No 298, r 24.
Para (1): numbered as such by SI 1991 No 1884, r 23.
Para (2): added by SI 1991 No 1884, r 23.

16 Register of orders
(1) There shall be kept in the Central Office under the direction of [the Master of the Crown Office] a register of the orders registered under the Act.

(2) There shall be included in such register particulars of any variation or setting aside of a registration, [and of any execution issued on a registered order.

NOTES
Rules 12-21 added by SI 1988 No 298, r 24.
Para (1): words in square brackets substituted by SI 1991 No 1884, r 24.
Para (2): words in square brackets substituted by SI 1989 No 1307, r 6.

17 Notice of registration
(1) Notice of the registration of an order must be served on the person against whom it was obtained by delivering it to him personally or by sending it to him at his usual or last known address or place of business or in such other manner as the Court may direct.

(2) Service of such a notice out of the jurisdiction is permissible without leave, and Order 11, rules 5, 6 and 8 shall apply in relation to such a notice as they apply in relation to a writ.

(3) [. . .]

NOTES
Rules 12-21 added by SI 1988 No 298, r 24.
Para (3): revoked by SI 1991 No 1884, r 25.

18 Application to vary or set aside registration
An application by the person against whom an order was made to vary or set aside the registration of an order must be made to a judge by summons supported by affidavit.

NOTES
Rules 12-21 added by SI 1988 No 298, r 24.

19 Enforcement of order
(1) [. . .]

(2) If an application is made under rule 18, an order shall not be enforced until after such application is determined.]

NOTES
Rules 12-21 added by SI 1988 No 298, r 24.
Para (1): revoked by SI 1991 No 1884, r 25.

20 Variation, satisfaction and discharge of registered order
Upon the court being notified by the applicant for registration that an order which has been registered has been varied, satisfied or discharged, particulars of the variation, satisfaction or discharge, as the case may be, shall be entered in the register.

NOTES
Rules 12-21 added by SI 1988 No 298, r 24.

21 Rules to have effect subject to Orders in Council
Rules 12 to 20 shall have effect subject to the provisions of the Order in Council made under section 24A or, as the case may be, of the Order in Council made under section 26.

NOTES
Rules 12-21 added by SI 1988 No 298, r 24.

21A Criminal Justice (International Co-operation) Act 1990: external forfeiture orders
The provisions of this Part of this Order shall, with such modifications as are necessary and subject to the provisions of any Order in Council made under section 9 of the Criminal Justice (International Co-operation) Act 1990, apply to proceedings for the registration and enforcement of external forfeiture orders as they apply to such proceedings in relation to external confiscation orders.

For the purposes of this rule, an external forfeiture order is an order made by a court in a country or territory outside the United Kingdom which is enforceable in the United Kingdom by virtue of any such Order in Council.

NOTES
Rule added by SI 1991 No 1884, r 26.

PART II. PART VI OF THE CRIMINAL JUSTICE ACT 1988

22 Interpretation
(1) In this Part of this Order, "the 1988 Act" means the Criminal Justice Act 1988 and a section referred to by number means the section so numbered in that Act.

(2) Expressions which are used in this Part of this Order which are used in the 1988 Act have the same meanings in this Part of this Order as in the 1988 Act.

NOTES
Rules 22, 23 added by SI 1989 No 386, r 8.

23 Application of Part I of Order 115
Part I of Order 115 (except rule 11) shall apply for the purposes of proceedings under Part VI of the 1988 Act with the necessary modifications and, in particular, –

- (a) references to drug trafficking offences and to drug trafficking shall be construed as references to offences to which Part VI of the 1988 Act applies and to committing such an offence;
- (b) references to the Drug Trafficking Offences Act 1986 shall be construed as references to the 1988 Act and references to sections 4(2), 8, 9, 11, 12(1), 14(1), 19, 19(4), 26 and 26A of the 1986 Act shall be construed as references to sections 73(6), 77, 78, 80, 81(1), 83(1), 89, 89(5), 96 and 97 of the 1988 Act respectively;
- (c) rule 3(2) shall have effect as if the following sub-paragraphs were substituted for sub-paragraphs (a) and (b) –

"(a) state, as the case may be, either that proceedings have been instituted against the defendant for an offence to which Part VI of the 1988 Act applies (giving particulars of the offence) and that they have not been concluded or that, whether by the laying of an information or otherwise, a person is to be charged with such an offence;
- (b) state, as the case may be, either that a confiscation order has been made or the grounds for believing that such an order may be made;" and

- (d) rule 7(3) shall have effect as if the words "certificate issued by a magistrates' court or the Crown Court" were substituted for the words "certificate issued by the Crown Court".

NOTES
Rules 22, 23 added by SI 1989 No 386, r 8.

24 Interpretation
In this Part of this Order –

- (a) "the Act" means the Prevention of Terrorism (Temporary Provisions) Act 1989;
- (b) "Schedule 4" means Schedule 4 to the Act; and
- (c) expressions used have the same meanings as they have in Part III of, and Schedule 4 to, the Act.

NOTES
Rules 24-36 added by SI 1989 No 1307, r 7.

25 Assignment of proceedings
(1) Subject to paragraph (2), the jurisdiction of the High Court under the Act shall be exercised by a judge of the Queen's Bench Division or of the Chancery Division in chambers.

(2) The jurisdiction conferred on the High Court by paragraph 9 of Schedule 4 may also be exercised by a master of the Queen's Bench Division.

NOTES
Rules 24-36 added by SI 1989 No 1307, r 7.

26 Application for restraint order
(1) An application for a restraint order under paragraphs 3 and 4 of Schedule 4 may be made by the prosecutor ex parte by originating motion.

(2) An application under paragraph (1) shall be supported by an affidavit, which shall:

(a) state, as the case may be, either that proceedings have been instituted against a person for an offence under Part III of the Act and that they have not been concluded or that, whether by the laying of an information or otherwise, a person is to be charged with such an offence; and, in either case, give particulars of the offence;

(b) state, as the case may be, that a forfeiture order has been made in the proceedings or the grounds for believing that such an order may be made;

(c) to the best of the deponent's ability, give full particulars of the property in respect of which the order is sought and specify the person or persons holding such property and any other persons having an interest in it;

(d) where proceedings have not been instituted, verify that the prosecutor is to have the conduct of the proposed proceedings;

(e) where proceedings have not been instituted, indicate when it is intended that they should be instituted.

(3) An originating motion under paragraph (1) shall be entitled in the matter of the defendant, naming him, and in the matter of the Act, and all subsequent documents in the matter shall be so entitled.

(4) Unless the Court otherwise directs, an affidavit under paragraph (2) may contain statements of information or belief with the sources and grounds thereof.

NOTES
Rules 24-36 added by SI 1989 No 1307, r 7.

27 Restraint Order
(1) A restraint order may be made subject to conditions and exceptions, including but not limited to conditions relating to the indemnifying of third parties against expenses incurred in complying with the order, and exceptions relating to living expenses and legal expenses of the defendant, but the prosecutor shall not be required to give an undertaking to abide by any order as to damages sustained by the defendant as a result of the restraint order.

(2) Unless the Court otherwise directs, a restraint order made ex parte shall have effect until a day which shall be fixed for the hearing inter partes of the application.

(3) Where a restraint order is made the prosecutor shall serve copies of the order and of the affidavit in support on the defendant and on all other persons affected by the order.

NOTES
Rules 24-36 added by SI 1989 No 1307, r 7.

28 Discharge or variation of order

(1) Subject to paragraph (2), an application to discharge or vary a restraint order shall be made by summons.

(2) Where the case is one of urgency, an application under this rule by the prosecutor may be made ex parte.

(3) The application and any affidavit in support shall be lodged with the court and, where the application is made by summons, shall be served on the following persons (other than the applicant) –

(a) the prosecutor;
(b) the defendant; and
(c) all other persons restrained or otherwise affected by the order;

not less than two clear days before the date fixed for the hearing of the summons.

(4) Where a restraint order has been made and has not been discharged, the prosecutor shall notify the court when proceedings for the offence have been concluded, and the court shall thereupon discharge the restraint order.

(5) Where an order is made discharging or varying a restraint order, the applicant shall serve copies of the order of discharge or variation on all persons restrained by the earlier order and shall notify all other persons affected of the terms of the order of discharge or variation.

NOTES
Rules 24-36 added by SI 1989 No 1307, r 7.

29 Compensation
An application for an order under paragraph 7 of Schedule 4 shall be made by summons, which shall be served, with any supporting evidence, on the person alleged to be in default and on the relevant authority under paragraph 7(5) not less than 7 days before the date fixed for the hearing of the summons.

NOTES
Rules 24-36 added by SI 1989 No 1307, r 7.

30 Application for registration
An application for registration of a Scottish order, a Northern Ireland order or an Islands order may be made ex parte.

NOTES
Rules 24-36 added by SI 1989 No 1307, r 7.

31 Evidence in support of application
[(1)] An application for registration of any such order as is mentioned in rule 30 must be supported by an affidavit –

(a) exhibiting the order or a certified copy thereof, and
(b) which shall, to the best of the deponent's ability, give particulars of such property in respect of which the order was made as is in England and Wales, and specify the person or persons holding such property.

[(2) Unless the Court otherwise directs, an affidavit for the purposes of this rule may contain statements of information or belief with the sources and grounds thereof].

NOTES
Rules 24-36 added by SI 1989 No 1307, r 7.
Para (1): numbered as such by SI 1991 No 1884, r 23.
Para (2): added by SI 1991 No 1884, r 23.

32 Register of orders
(1) There shall be kept in the Central Office under the direction of [the Master of the Crown Office] a register of the orders registered under the Act.

(2) There shall be included in such register particulars of any variation or setting aside of a registration, and of any execution issued on a registered order.

NOTES
Rules 24-36 added by SI 1989 No 1307, r 7.
Para (1): words in square brackets substituted by SI 1991 No 1884, r 24.

33 Notice of registration
(1) Notice of the registration of an order must be served on the person or persons holding the property referred to in rule 31(1)(b) and any other persons appearing to have an interest in that property.

(2) Service of such a notice out of the jurisdiction is permissible without leave, and Order 11, rules 5, 6 and 8 shall apply in relation to such a notice as they apply in relation to a writ.

(3) [. . .]

NOTES
Rules 24-36 added by SI 1989 No 1307, r 7.
Para (3): revoked by SI 1991 No 1884, r 25.

34 Application to vary or set aside registration
An application to vary or set aside the registration of an order must be made to a judge by summons supported by affidavit.
This rule does not apply to a variation or cancellation under rule 36.

NOTES
Rules 24-36 added by SI 1989 No 1307, r 7.

35 Enforcement of order
(1) [. . .]

(2) If an application is made under rule 34, an order shall not be enforced until after such application is determined.

(3) This rule does not apply to the taking of steps under paragraph 5 or 6 of Schedule 4, as applied by paragraph 9(6) of that Schedule.

NOTES
Rules 24-36 added by SI 1989 No 1307, r 7.
Para (1): revoked by SI 1991 No 1884, r 25.

36 Variation and cancellation of registration
If effect has been given (whether in England and Wales or elsewhere) to a Scottish, Northern Ireland or Islands order, or if the order has been varied or discharged by the court by which it was made, the applicant for registration shall inform the court and –

  (a) if such effect has been given in respect of all the money or other property to which the order applies, or if the order has been discharged by the court by which it was made, registration of the order shall be cancelled;
  (b) if such effect has been given in respect of only part of the money or other property, or if the order has been varied by the court by which it was made, registration of the order shall be varied accordingly.

NOTES
Rules 24-36 added by SI 1989 No 1307, r 7.

Practice directions

PRACTICE DIRECTION (CROWN COURT: FRAUD TRIALS) (NO 20)

Crown Court – Practice – Distribution of business – Crown Court centres dealing with serious and complex fraud trials – Supreme Court Act 1981 (c 54), s 75(1) – Criminal Justice Act 1987 (c 38), s 5(1)

1. With the concurrence of the Lord Chancellor and pursuant to section 75(1) of the Supreme Court Act 1981 I make with effect from 2 October 1990 the following direction with regard to the place of trial for cases of serious and complex fraud transferred to the Crown Court under the Criminal Justice Act 1987.

2. The proposed place of trial specified in the notice of transfer under section 5(1) of the Criminal Justice Act 1987 shall be one of the following Crown Court Centres:

Circuit	Centres
Midland and Oxford	Birmingham
	Leicester
	Nottingham
	Oxford
	Stafford
	Wolverhampton
North Eastern	Leeds
	Newcastle
	Sheffield
	Teesside
Northern	Liverpool
South Eastern	Aylesbury
	Central Criminal Court
	Chelmsford
	Guildford
	Isleworth
	Knightsbridge
	Maidstone
	Middlesex Guildhall
	Norwich
	Snaresbrook
	Southwark
	Wood Green

Circuit	*Centres*
Wales and Chester	Cardiff
	Mold
	Swansea
Western	Bristol
	Exeter
	Portsmouth
	Southampton
	Winchester

3. *Practice Direction (Crown Court: Fraud Trials)* [1988] 1 WLR 1161 made on 22 September 1988 is hereby revoked.

LORD LANE CJ
2 October 1990

PRACTICE NOTE

COURT OF APPEAL, CRIMINAL DIVISION
LORD LAND CJ, KENNEDY AND JUDGE JJ
11 DECEMBER 1990

Criminal law – Bill of indictment – Preferment – Application for grant of voluntary bill – Application to High Court judge – Procedure – Documents etc to accompany application – Written submissions on behalf of defendant – Administration of Justice (Miscellaneous Provisions) Act 1933, s 2(2)(b) – Indictments (Procedure) Rules 1971.

Lord Lane CJ gave the following direction at the sitting of the court in relation to applications under s 2(2)(b) of the Administration of Justice (Miscellaneous Provisions) Act 1933 for the direction or consent of a judge of the High Court to the preferment of a bill of indictment, commonly known as applications for the grant of voluntary bills.

1. The usual means of bringing a defendant to trial on indictment is by committal for trial in the magistrates' court. A voluntary bill should only be granted where good reason to depart from the normal procedure is clearly shown and only where the interests of justice, rather than considerations of administrative convenience, require it.

2. Application must not only comply with each paragraph of the Indictment (Procedure) Rules 1971, SI 1971/1253, but must also be accompanied by (a) a copy of any charges on which the defendant has been committed for trial, (b) a copy of any charges on which his committal for trial was refused by the magistrates' court, (c) a copy of any existing indictment which has been preferred in consequence of his committal, (d) a summary of the evidence or other document which (i) identifies the pages in the accompanying statements and exhibits where the essential evidence said to support that count is to be found, and (e) marginal markings of the relevant passages on the pages of the statement and exhibits identified under sub-para (d)(ii).

3. Paragraph 2 should be complied with in relation to each defendant named in the indictment for which leave is sought, whether or not it is proposed to prefer any new count against him.

4. In exceptional circumstances, the judge may invite written submissions on behalf of any defendant affected if, in his judgment, the interest of justice so require.

5. This practice direction will take effect on 1 January 1991.

NP Metcalfe Esq
Barrister

PRACTICE DIRECTION
(CRIME; CONSPIRACY)

1977 May 9   Lord Widgery CJ, Park and Watkins JJ

*Crime – Indictment – Joinder of charges – Conspiracy and
substantive counts – Justification or election necessary*

Lord Widgery CJ, at the sitting of the court, published the following practice direction made after consultation with the judges of the Queen's Bench Division:

1. In any case where an indictment contains substantive counts and a related conspiracy count, the judge should require the prosecution to justify the joinder, or, failing justification, to elect whether to proceed on the substantive or on the conspiracy counts.

2. A joinder is justified for this purpose if the judge considers that the interests of justice demand it.

LNW

N. CENTRAL CRIMINAL COURT: PRACTICE RULES

The following Practice Rules have been in operation since November 21, 1977 and have, in effect, been adopted at most, if not all, Crown Court centres.

A practice direction, or pre-trial review, is to be distinguished from a preparatory hearing held in a case of serious fraud pursuant to sections 7, 8 and 9 of the *Criminal Justice Act* 1987 . . . : *Re Gunarwardena and others* (1990) 91 Cr App R 55, CA . . .

Practice Rules, November 21, 1977

1. Any case may be listed for practice directions within these Rules upon an application in writing made to the Court by solicitors acting for any party, or by any unrepresented party, provided that the court is satisfied that the case is fit for such practice directions. If no party makes application the Court may list the case for such practice directions of its own volition.

2. The Court shall determine the time and place of the hearing.

3. At least 14 days' notice of hearing shall be given, unless the parties agree to shorter notice, and that notice shall not be given on a date earlier that 14 days after the preferment of a bill of indictment.

4. (a) Hearings for practice directions under Rule 5 may be dealt with in Chambers before any Judge of the Court.
    (b) A represented Defendant shall be present at hearings in Chambers

unless he elects not to attend.

(c) Hearings for directions and orders under Rule 6 and the making of orders under Rule 7 shall be held and made in open Court by the Judge allocated to try the case.

(d) All Defendants shall be present in Court at hearings under Rule 4(c) except with the leave of the Court.

(e) Hearings under Rule 4(a) and (c) shall be attended by Counsel briefed to conduct the case on trial or in special circumstances Counsel specifically instructed to deal with the matters arising under Rules 5 and 6.

5. At a hearing under Rule 4(a) Counsel will be expected to be able to inform the Court,

(a) of the pleas to be tendered on trial;

(b) of the prosecution witnesses required at trial as shown on the committal documents and any notices of further evidence then delivered and of the availability of such witnesses;

(c) of any additional witnesses who may be called by the prosecution and the evidence that they are expected to give; if the statements of these witnesses are not then available for service a summary of the evidence that they are expected to give shall be supplied in writing;

(d) of facts which can be and are admitted and which can be reduced to writing in accordance with section 10(2)(b) of the *Criminal Justice Act 1967*, within such time as may be agreed at the hearing and of the witnesses whose attendance will not be required at trial;

(e) of the probable length of the trial;

(f) of exhibits and schedules which are and can be admitted;

(g) of issues, if any, then envisaged as to the mental or medical condition of any Defendant or witness;

(h) of any point of law which may arise on trial, any question as to the admissibility of evidence which then appears on the face of the papers and of any authority on which either party intends to rely as far as can be possibly envisaged at that stage;

(i) of the names and addresses of witnesses from whom statements have been taken by the prosecution but who are not going to be called and, in appropriate cases, disclosure of the contents of those statements;

(j) of any alibi not then disclosed in conformity with the *Criminal Justice Act* 1967;

(k) of the order and pagination of the papers to be used by the prosecution at the trial and of the order in which the witnesses for the prosecution will be called;

(l) of any other significant matter which might affect the proper and convenient trial of the case.

6. At a hearing under Rule 4(c) in open Court, the Judge who is to try the case may hear and rule upon any application by any party relating to the severance of any count or any Defendant and to amend or provide further and better particulars of any count in the indictment. The Judge may order particulars relating to any Count to be delivered within such time as he may direct.

7. The Judge may make such order or orders as lie within his powers as appear to him to be necessary to secure the proper and efficient trial of the case.

8. Subject to the provisions of sections 9 and 10 of the *Criminal Justice Act* 1967, admissions made under Rule 5 may be used at the trial.

Index